The New York Times

**WILL SHORTZ PRESENTS
A YEAR OF CROSSWORDS**

The New York Times

WILL SHORTZ PRESENTS
A YEAR OF CROSSWORDS
365 Puzzles to Keep You Sharp

Edited by Will Shortz

ST. MARTIN'S GRIFFIN ❧ NEW YORK

ACROSS

1 Initials for 56-Across
5 Beginning on
9 Scottish landowner
14 Grand ___ (annual race)
15 Scruff
16 Take in or let out
17 Serving on a jury, e.g.
19 Mean-spirited
20 Elvis's "Blue ___ Shoes"
21 Look up to
22 Channel with "Anderson Cooper 360°"
25 Bride's attendant
27 Get a closer look, as with a camera
29 Molten tar, e.g.
30 Not an accidental fire
31 Saintly glow
33 Some NCO's
37 Sudden military action
38 Enrollee at 56-Across
39 Magazine fig.
40 Armenia and Azerbaijan, once: Abbr.
41 Fashionable Christian
42 Jug band instrument
43 Noah's boat
44 Clean, as a floor
45 Rural area
51 Unlock, in verse
52 Sanctuary
53 Father and victim of Oedipus
55 Play lightly, as a guitar
56 School whose motto consists of the last words of 17-, 25- and 45-Across

60 Pan-fry
61 Commedia dell'___
62 Aviated
63 "A Doll's House" playwright
64 River of Flanders
65 Sax type

DOWN

1 It's scanned at checkout: Abbr.
2 ___ Lanka
3 1,004, in old Rome
4 W.W. II foe, with "the"
5 Like llamas and Incas
6 Riyadh resident
7 Made a choice
8 Tina of "30 Rock"
9 Cry from a crow's nest
10 1836 battle site
11 "___ the bag"

12 Fashionable again
13 Alternative to a clothesline
18 Curry ingredient
21 "The game is ___": Sherlock Holmes
22 Ivan, Nicholas and Peter
23 Author Ephron and others
24 Military denial
26 Leering sort
28 Hip '60s types
31 Poem with exactly 17 syllables
32 Hoopla
33 "Shoo!"
34 Thingamajig
35 Army unit
36 Rifle attachment
38 Electronic storage device
42 Excite

43 Keenness of mind
44 Blogger, for one
45 Low-voiced singers
46 Take ___ at (try)
47 "Hannah Montana" star Miley
48 1971 Jane Fonda/Donald Sutherland film
49 Padres and Pirates, informally
50 First small bite
54 Divan
56 Modus operandi
57 Under the weather
58 Equipment in badminton and fishing
59 Start of D.C.'s ZIP codes or area code

by Gary J. Whitehead

ACROSS

1 Signs of life
7 Part of U.S.M.A.: Abbr.
11 Wood used for wine barrels
14 Like some accidents or garages
15 Miss from Marseille: Abbr.
16 ___ de France
17 Comment about comic actor Martin when standing next to a peewee?
19 Fireplace wood
20 "Tony n' ___ Wedding" (Off Broadway hit starting in 1988)
21 Military force
22 They outrank kings
23 Knife wound
24 Campus area
25 Something found in a Parliament
26 Comment about actor Jack, racially speaking?
31 Nimbleness
34 Architect I. M. ___
35 "For example . . ."
36 Place for a marquee
37 Still green
39 "___ Poetica"
40 Anger
42 Like ironed pants, often
43 Comment about well-dressed pop singer James?
46 ___ Peacock (Clue character)
47 Irritating sort
48 ___ Cass Elliot
52 Former drink marketed as "zomething different"
54 Letters
55 When doubled, band with the 1984 #1 hit "The Reflex"

56 Wash. neighbor
57 Comment about impressionist Rich when playing a packed house?
59 Anthem contraction
60 Baldwin or Guinness
61 Green, purple or red food
62 Vote to kill a bill
63 Sieve, essentially
64 Nothing to write home about?

DOWN

1 Adds to a blog
2 Still standing, as a target
3 Hotelier Helmsley
4 The record score in this game is 1,049 points
5 Vittles
6 Holy Hindu's title

7 Acela operator
8 Seafood-based party food
9 Friend
10 N.J. neighbor
11 Emergency of 1973 or 1979
12 Lotion ingredient
13 Fraternity party staples
18 Impertinent
22 "That hit the spot!"
24 Local staffer for Al Jazeera, e.g.
25 Hair braider, e.g.
27 Puts a cap on
28 Painter who had a point to make?
29 It's on a roll
30 Looked over
31 Hail ___
32 Lady in waiting?
33 "Wrapping up . . ."

38 50 Cent genre
41 Settings for mansions
42 Relax, slangily, with "out"
44 Org. defending the Second Amendment
45 On/off ___
49 Shaded recess
50 Home of L. L. Bean
51 Unsettled feeling
52 Jewish homeland
53 Glimmering
54 About 4% of a marathon
55 Have supper
57 Escape
58 Canon camera

by David Liben-Nowell

ACROSS

1 Sped
6 Bit of smoke
10 Biblical wise men
14 Remove, as pencil marks
15 P.G.A.'s Isao
16 Burden
17 Laundry that's often food-stained
19 Animal balancing a beachball on its nose
20 French friend
21 Fix, as a bathroom floor
22 Pinnacle
23 With 57-Across, game that includes the starts of 17-, 29-, 48- and 64-Across
25 Catch some Z's
26 Assist
27 Twisty highway curves
29 How much you really earned
33 ___ Percé (Indian tribe)
35 Sting or Prince
36 ___-tac-toe
39 Ballot marks
41 Org. with the Wizards and Warriors
42 Hurricane's center
43 Ones in disbelief?
46 Hosp. scan
48 Hoosier university
50 Computer acronym
54 Grain in Cheerios
55 Pepsi-___
57 See 23-Across
58 Word before speed or after time
60 Ones said to be "trustworthy, loyal, helpful, friendly . . ."
62 ___ Guevara
63 x or y line on a graph
64 Lakeshore rental, perhaps
66 Surrender
67 Tribe allied with the Missouri, once
68 Garlicky sauce
69 Lyric poems
70 Truckloads
71 French Impressionist Claude

DOWN

1 Record again
2 "The Man in the Iron Mask" role for Jeremy Irons
3 Airplane sections
4 Course for some immigrants: Abbr.
5 Bucks and does
6 Serve, as at a restaurant
7 Air purifier, of sorts
8 Common Halloween costume
9 Tree with needles
10 Artworks made of many pieces
11 Brief story that might open a speech
12 Where America's Day Begins
13 ___ of Man
18 Trailblazed
24 Patton or Petraeus: Abbr.
26 Turkey's capital
28 One who puts women down
30 Warhead weapon, for short
31 Month of the Kentucky Derby and Indianapolis 500
32 Before, to a poet
34 Gusto
36 Key above Caps Lock
37 "Give ___ whirl!"
38 Salt, e.g.
40 Disconnected, musically
44 Passes, as time
45 Used as a platform
47 AOL, for one
49 Escapes
51 Butterfly protector
52 Get some air
53 "Aha!"
56 The "A" in NATO: Abbr.
58 City midway between Austin and Dallas
59 Chopped down
60 Good name for a Dalmatian
61 Line in an A-line
65 Book that might be subtitled "A Life"

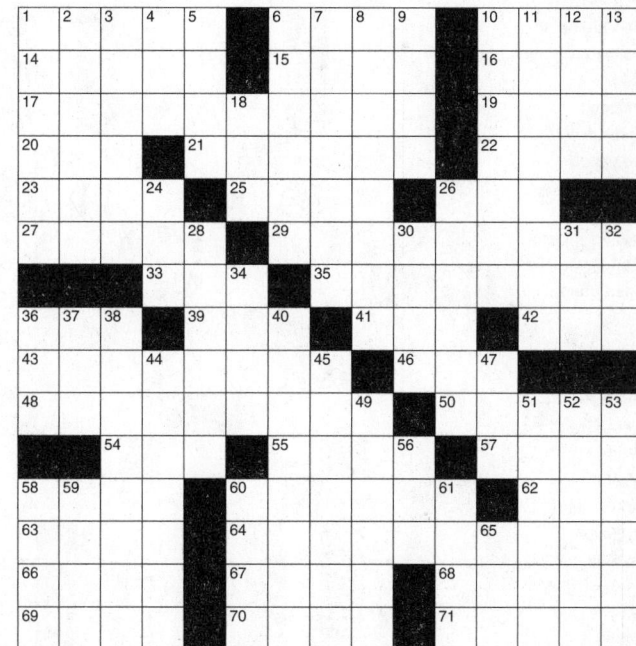

by Alex Vratsanos

ACROSS

1 Places to retire
5 This's partner
9 Ancient marketplace
14 Cosmonaut Gagarin
15 Move like molasses
16 He once placed a "long-distance call" to Aldrin and Armstrong
17 Stroller to Soho
18 Like the White Rabbit
19 "Have a bite!"
20 Indie studio's offering, maybe
23 Place getting a lot of buzz?
24 Whisk wielder
25 Go (for)
28 Hankering
29 Company in a 2011 merger with the Huffington Post
31 Drink named after a Scottish hero
33 Unusually chromatic performance ensemble
36 Director Kazan
39 "___ Rosenkavalier"
40 It may be upped
41 Mostly idled
46 Valentino rival
47 Crime scene evidence
48 Engage in pugilism
51 Prefix with conservative
52 Comedy Central's "___.0"
55 By the deadline
57 Thick alternative to a blanket
60 "Three Coins in the Fountain" fountain
62 McFlurry flavor
63 Movie format for a big date?
64 "Peer Gynt" writer
65 Country with a hammer-and-sickle flag, for short
66 Colt's mother
67 Petrol measure
68 Orioles, Eagles or Cardinals
69 Resorts

DOWN

1 Incidental activity
2 The Continent
3 Entice
4 Swahili for "lion"
5 "Shoulda listened to me!"
6 Romance novelist Tami
7 Early Mexican
8 Enforcement provisions
9 Like some lens coatings
10 "The ___ With the Dragon Tattoo"
11 Military intelligence, e.g., according to George Carlin
12 Louis XIV, par exemple
13 Grasshopper's partner in an old fable
21 Caspian Sea feeder
22 Decorative plant
26 Sulk
27 Enter with a keyboard
30 Mother of Castor and Pollux
32 Country music's Paisley
33 The Crimson Tide, familiarly
34 Mal de ___
35 Longtime Yankee third baseman, informally
36 Israel's Abba
37 Bit of fishing gear
38 Far from prudish
42 Tangle up
43 The Belmonts' frontman, in 1950s music
44 Military outfit
45 Modern running companion?
48 Computer graphics option
49 Mark who was the 1998 P.G.A. Player of the Year
50 Persian king in 2006's "300"
53 Pack member
54 Contender in the Belmont
56 Decorates, as a Christmas tree
58 More than
59 Maricopa County city
60 Up to, in adspeak
61 Stat for 35-Down

by Doug Peterson and Angela Olson Halsted

ACROSS

1 Big bother
7 Folk singer Guthrie
11 Month of the Indianapolis 500
14 Bona fide
15 Attack on the fridge, say
16 Future embryos
17 Easily offended
19 Whole lot
20 Hits on the noggin
21 Signals silently
22 Policy expert
23 Greedy type
24 Little trickster
26 Playful swimmer
28 Inclined to mince words
32 ___ Pet (sprouting figurine)
35 Filmdom's "Norma ___"
36 Old ___ (U.S. flag)
37 Scavenge (for)
38 One with a negative outlook on life
41 French female friend
42 Dairy spokescow
44 Air passenger protection org.
45 If ___ be
46 Lacking courage
50 Tooth problem
51 Yahoo! alternative
52 Respectful Turkish title
55 Peter Pan pursuer
57 Trifling
59 Got it wrong
61 ___ Mahal
62 Cowardly
64 Long, long ___
65 Sheltered at sea
66 Force out of office
67 Protective wear in a highchair
68 Nonvegetarian sandwiches, informally
69 Caused some winter havoc, maybe

DOWN

1 Emerge from an egg
2 Sound heard before "Gesundheit!"
3 Police trap
4 Shipwrecked
5 Timmy's TV dog
6 Fraternal lodge member
7 River through Florence
8 Haphazard
9 Is dishonest with
10 Unusual
11 Accommodations for a family on the go?
12 River beside the Royal Shakespeare Theatre
13 Pull sharply
18 Like a fair ball as opposed to a foul ball
22 Marshy habitat
25 Painter Chagall
27 Pull sharply
28 Show for the early-to-bed crowd
29 Busybody
30 Southernmost of the Great Lakes
31 Not naturally colored
32 Food processor?
33 Luau dance
34 Employee-abetted crime
39 Zionist's homeland
40 "Elder" or "Younger" Roman statesman
43 And so forth, for short
47 Champion figure skater Dorothy
48 Place for a lace
49 7's retail partner?
52 Valentine piercer
53 Birds in a gaggle
54 Did sums
55 Attack with a dagger
56 Biblical gift bearers
58 Deli loaves
60 Property after a default, for short
62 Chem class component
63 Passport and driver's license, in brief

by Lynn Lempel

ACROSS

1 Limo-riding sorts
5 Noncom naval personnel
9 Puppeteer Lewis
14 Adept
15 Russia's ___ Mountains
16 Bird that flies with its neck retracted
17 "Dallas," e.g.
19 Keep an ___
20 Directs rush-hour traffic?
22 Green-lights
23 "Aladdin" prince
24 Prefix with metric
25 Posts abusive comments about a team supporter?
31 New Jersey hockey squad
34 "Angela's Ashes" follow-up
35 Hubbub
36 Like days when you forget to take an umbrella, all too often?
37 Woodrow Wilson is the only U.S. president to have one
38 Betty ___ ("Grease" role)
40 Duke's athletic grp.
41 Source of lots of living-room arm-waving
42 Astronaut Collins
43 Blend an illegal street drug?
47 Stephen of "V for Vendetta"
48 G.I.'s entertainment provider
49 Gardner of "The Night of the Iguana"
52 Ask "Is this really diet soda?," for instance?
57 Hearing-related
58 Beachwear
59 Summation signifier, in math
60 "Stormy Weather" singer Horne
61 Like a total solar eclipse
62 They're often taken in rehab
63 Part of Y.M.C.A.: Abbr.
64 Rightmost column in an addition

DOWN

1 Explorer ___ da Gama
2 Old Apple
3 Schedules
4 Mo. of Mexican Independence Day
5 Cathedral toppers
6 Event before the main event
7 Scull propellers
8 Airplane wing component
9 "You've got to be kidding!"
10 Jimi Hendrix's first single
11 Base times height, for a rectangle
12 No ___ at the 13-Down
13 See 12-Down
18 By mouth
21 Web site visits
25 Feature of many a 1950s car
26 Work ___
27 Grauman of Grauman's Chinese Theater
28 Discombobulate
29 Woodworking tool
30 Lunchtime, often
31 Inconclusive outcome
32 Every one
33 Part of Caesar's boast
37 Crusty dish
38 Some cameras
39 Kind
41 "Come again?"
42 George who founded Kodak
44 Roadie's tote
45 Magnetic induction units
46 Confrontations
49 Beelike
50 "À ___ santé!"
51 Cathedral areas
52 Throw in the towel
53 Desire
54 Cuba, por ejemplo
55 Is in the red
56 Coin with a map on its back
57 Animal present at Jesus' birth, in tradition

by Kelsey Boes

ACROSS

1 Betty of comics
5 Manufacture
9 ___ liberales (studies at universidades)
14 Car whose logo has four rings
15 Forearm bone
16 Parasite
17 Che Guevara or Lady Gaga
18 Desserts akin to cobblers
19 Allan-___ (Robin Hood compadre)
20 1990s runnings of the Bulls?
23 Practice boxing
24 General tendency
25 Manufacture
27 Kids' vehicles on tracks
30 Loud, as a crowd
31 Manual's intended reader
32 Excellent, in dated slang
33 ___-la-la
36 Word after ginger or brown
37 Homemade music compilation . . . or a hint to the circled letters
40 Charged particle
41 Implement you might wring
42 "You have no ___!"
43 Leftover part
44 Sandwiches that may have sour cream and salsa
46 Wakens
49 Queen who financed Columbus, to the Spanish
51 Crazy as ___
52 Bawls
53 Some gymwear
58 Cutting-edge technology?

60 Aide: Abbr.
61 "Hold your horses!"
62 Honor ___ thieves
63 Harness for oxen
64 Where sailors go
65 After-dinner candies
66 Bridge
67 Ball material for a cat

DOWN

1 Worms and such, to a fisherman
2 "That hurt!"
3 Stench
4 Application to improve a batter's grip
5 Bert or Ernie
6 Martians and Venusians
7 Work, as dough
8 Direction after Near, Middle or Far
9 Chicken ___ king

10 One end of the Suez Canal
11 Groups battling big government
12 Brilliance
13 ___ Khan ("The Jungle Book" tiger)
21 Mess up
22 Leftover part
26 Memorization
27 U.S. territory in W.W. II fighting
28 Norway's capital
29 Watch
30 "Eureka!"
32 School open house organizer: Abbr.
34 Kennedy matriarch
35 Tidbits for aardvarks
37 Runners in lab mazes
38 Winners of some televised singing competitions

39 Deletes, with "out"
43 Escape
45 Not present
46 "Sarah Palin's ___" of 2010–11 TV
47 No-good
48 Alley-___
49 Ayatollah's faith
50 "Me too!"
51 "The Fox and the Grapes" storyteller
54 House ___ and Means Committee
55 Cape Canaveral org.
56 Level
57 Kyle and Kenny's friend on "South Park"
59 Some N.F.L. linemen

by Joseph Samulak

ACROSS

1 Opportunity to hit
6 Disco ___ of "The Simpsons"
9 Pool divisions
14 Top-quality
15 Coop resident
16 Nonsensical
17 3.14159
20 "Send help!"
21 Spanish muralist José María ___
22 Danny of "Do the Right Thing"
23 Jazz aficionado
24 Talk trash about
25 72, at Pebble Beach
26 −273.15°C
31 Military aviators, collectively
32 Sail through
33 "Born Free" lioness
36 Island of the Minotaur
37 Phone letters for 6
38 Muddies
39 Former N.F.L. great Junior ___
40 Laze, with "out"
41 Source of fine rugs
42 299,792,458 meters/second
45 Frost's "The ___-Repeated Dream"
47 Amendment that repealed Prohibition
48 ___ Cruces, N.M.
49 Manufacturer's payback
51 Lectern's locale
52 Creature with elbowed antennae
55 6.022×10^{23}
58 October Revolution leader
59 Ararat lander
60 Kids' song refrain
61 Spiner of "Star Trek: T.N.G."
62 Home heating option
63 Dawdle

DOWN

1 iPhone programs
2 The Stooges, e.g.
3 Pollster's worry
4 Part of a public address system
5 It's first on the leaderboard
6 There's one in "puzzle"
7 It's dangerous to do while driving
8 Prefix with dimensional
9 Be a go-between
10 Minimum poker loss
11 Manicurist's supply
12 ___ Gay
13 Sir, abroad
18 King's domain
19 Polenta grain
24 Retro art style
26 Suffix for the wealthy
27 Sternum
28 Partner of "took notice"
29 "Dancing With the Stars" dance
30 Corporate shuffle, for short
31 Window units, briefly
34 Knife incision
35 Cool ___ cucumber
37 Health plan prefix
38 Released again on CD, say
40 In a pique
41 Nothing fancy
43 Not extinct
44 Chemistry lab vessels
45 Power Flosser brand
46 Flu symptom
50 Not "fer"
51 Explorer of kiddie TV
52 Genesis brother
53 Moonmate of Buzz
54 "Iliad" locale
56 Use for an old T-shirt
57 Farrow of "Rosemary's Baby"

by Tom Baring

ACROSS

1 President who won the 2009 Nobel Peace Prize
6 Signs of boredom
11 Waitress at Mel's Diner
14 Blossom part
15 Fill with joy
16 Hawaiian garland
17 20th Century Fox picture?
19 ___ and yang
20 Rug, so to speak
21 Movie, informally
23 Prospers
26 Basketball venues
27 "60 Minutes" pundit Andy
28 Type who's always causing trouble
30 Diarist Nin
31 Playwright Edward who wrote "The Zoo Story"
32 "If only ___ listened . . ."
35 French seas
36 Universal picture?
37 Western tie
38 Next-to-last Greek letter
39 Library book stamp
40 Crooner Mel
41 Hangmen's tools
43 Drink after a shot
44 Dannon product
46 White House family after the Fords
47 Prefix with task or grain
48 Less well off
50 CBS forensic drama
51 Columbia picture?
56 From ___ Z
57 Speechify
58 Less than 90°, as an angle
59 Info entered on an I.R.S. form
60 Cowell formerly of "American Idol"
61 "Heavy" music genre

DOWN

1 Photo ___ (occasions for 1-Across)
2 Honey maker
3 One day ___ time
4 Bond likes these "shaken, not stirred"
5 Recesses
6 Sounds from pounds
7 "I cannot tell ___"
8 Worker's pay
9 Extreme degree
10 Release
11 TriStar picture?
12 Classic German camera
13 Sounds from sties
18 Nephew of Donald Duck
22 Chicken drumstick
23 Vagabond
24 Sharpens
25 MGM picture?
26 "Zip-___-Doo-Dah"
28 Things moving in lava lamps
29 "Dear" advice columnist
31 On the safe side, at sea
33 Big name in glue
34 They aren't just talkers
36 Sudden wind
37 Regatta
39 Chips with a Cool Ranch flavor
40 Early morning hour
42 Publicly gay
43 Low-___ diet
44 Places to swim or play b-ball
45 Gives the boot to
46 Songwriter Leonard
48 British baby buggy
49 Twice tetra-
52 ". . . ___ quit!"
53 Same old same old
54 Airport posting: Abbr.
55 Family member: Abbr.

by Paul Johnson

ACROSS

1 Grumpy expression
6 Dollop
10 Do a traditional Monday chore
14 Anthem's opener
15 Capitol ___
16 Winemaking province of Italy
17 Warning about a chubby guy in some skimpy swimwear?
20 Chief Theban deity
21 Many a four-wheel drive transport, for short
22 Religion, to the masses, per Marx
23 Condo, e.g.
25 "Wheel of Fortune" action
26 No-good, awful frozen waffle?
33 Have a life
34 First word of the Lord's Prayer
35 They may have "II" or "III" after their names
36 "A Woman Speaks" writer Anaïs
37 Villages
39 Lead pumper, in old slang
40 Meditation on a mat
42 She-sheep
43 Fern's seed
45 Icy winter greeting?
49 "___ for the poor"
50 Ruhr road
51 Former Polish capital
54 Part of H.R.H.
55 Right-hand person
59 Result of cleaning up some building toys?
62 Sign on a shop's door
63 One may be leading or supporting

64 Arctic, for one
65 Gen ___ (boomers' kids)
66 Custodian's ringful
67 Alternative to purchase

DOWN

1 Couch
2 Bosom buddy
3 Capital near Lillehammer
4 Squirrels' stash
5 Fleur-de-___
6 Area in need of urban renewal
7 Actor Schreiber
8 Like Mother Hubbard
9 Filmed bits that don't make it on the air
10 Lanai ladies
11 Researching whales, say

12 "A.S.A.P.!"
13 Camouflage
18 Au ___
19 ". . . hear ___ drop"
24 W.S.J. rival
25 Bedazzle
26 Patron saint of France
27 Zeus bound him to an eternally revolving wheel
28 Fab Four name
29 Dry (off)
30 Nikolai who wrote "Diary of a Madman"
31 Bump on a tree
32 Bone: Prefix
37 Collaboration
38 Temple University team
41 Rouses

43 "Quiet!"
44 Sinners may do it
46 E-journal
47 Everglades birds
48 Cartoonist Thomas
51 Kentucky's Fort ___
52 Hitchcock classic seemingly filmed in one continuous take
53 DiMag, e.g., for his entire career
54 "Monty Python and the ___ Grail"
56 Notion
57 "___ you're told!"
58 Cousin of -ette or -trix
60 Bathwater temperature tester
61 "You've got mail" co.

by Andrea Carla Michaels and Johanna Fenimore

ACROSS

1 Edible frog parts
5 Fuzzy image
9 Pesto herb
14 Burn soother
15 Life of Riley
16 "Biography" network, once
17 Place of refuge, redundantly
19 Pandemonium
20 Trample
21 Nerdy sort
23 "Treasure Island" monogram
24 Not 'neath
25 Wire service inits.
27 No ___ for wear
29 Icy expanse, redundantly
33 Effect of the moon's gravity
36 Chop off
37 2006 title film character who says "Pamela! I no find you attractive anymore! . . . Not!"
38 Theater award
39 '50s Ford flop
42 Anise-flavored liqueur
43 ___ Gras
45 Bullring "Bravo!"
46 Feds who nabbed Capone
47 Synopsis, redundantly
51 Response to a bad pun
52 Valedictorian's rank
53 Play-___ (kid's stuff)
56 Submachine gun
58 Dig like a pig
60 Eight-armed creatures
62 1924 Edna Ferber novel
64 Where snowbirds head, redundantly
66 Chicken: Sp.

67 Utah city
68 Where the Himalayas are
69 Extract metals from by heating
70 Marquis de ___
71 Ding on a car door, e.g.

DOWN

1 Cowgirl's rope
2 Fill with joy
3 Errand runner
4 Leak slowly
5 Thinny-thin person
6 W.C.
7 Like a car with 20,000 miles on its odometer
8 Celebrity
9 Massage for a person who's prone

10 Sound while receiving a 9-Down
11 Military percussion instrument
12 Much-loved celebrity
13 Minus
18 Length of many a TV drama
22 Decay
26 Polo Ralph Lauren competitor
28 Having one's nose in the air
29 Holder of birdseed
30 ___ salts
31 Bulldoze
32 Lots and lots
33 Dead center?
34 Letter-shaped structural support
35 Lighter-than-air aircraft
40 "Tickle Me" doll

41 1972 Bill Withers hit whose title precedes "when you're not strong"
44 Excuse for a lapse
48 ___ Paulo, Brazil
49 Start of a Spanish count
50 LP's and CD's: Abbr.
53 Extinguish
54 Choose to participate
55 Pair of cymbals operated by a pedal
56 Mail letters
57 Take off like a rocket
59 When tripled, a W.W. II movie
61 "The Wind in the Willows" hopper
63 Under the weather
65 Say "I do"

by Ellen Leuschner

ACROSS

1 With 1-Down, "Jeopardy!" feature
6 Chat room "Yikes!"
9 House haunter
14 Nostalgic tune
15 In favor of
16 Happen again
17 "___ Gold" (Fonda film)
18 You, on the Riviera
19 ___ nous
20 Cousin of a yarmulke
22 Remove snow from, e.g., as a car
24 Julia Roberts ex ___ Lovett
25 One often depicted on a Wheaties box
27 "To be," to Brutus
28 Go-ahead signal
32 Soup's partner
34 Parting word
35 In favor of
38 Palin parodist Tina
39 Backwoods mother
41 Driver's license datum
42 Old Apple messaging software
44 Intermediate, in law
46 Holiday bloom
49 Broccoli ___
53 Beat by a wide margin
54 One-___ (old ball game)
55 One with a 1.0 G.P.A.
58 Rat (on)
60 Rocker Turner's autobiography
61 Old telecom giant
63 Stairstep part
64 Possum player
65 Unagi, at a sushi bar
66 Nut with a cupule
67 Pat down

68 Word that can follow the first part or precede the second part of 22-, 28-, 46- or 55-Across
69 Minister's home

DOWN

1 See 1-Across
2 Bowling lanes
3 Things to live up to
4 People with mortgages, e.g.
5 "___ know" ("O.K., O.K.")
6 Frequently, in verse
7 Freeloaded
8 Distinctive part of a car's front
9 Central Park concert site
10 Paul who played Laszlo
11 Prefix with -genarian
12 ___ music (Beach Boys genre)
13 Not kosher
21 Feature of old quarters
23 Bard's nightfall
26 Breakfast-in-bed item
29 M.R.E. eaters
30 When doubled, a giggle
31 Guy's prom rental
33 At night
35 Jack Horner's treat
36 "His Master's Voice" co.
37 Sounds of surprise
39 Sporty Spice's other nickname
40 Up to now

43 Brings into harmony
44 Herbal beverage
45 Risqué reading
47 ___ v. Wade
48 Suddenly thrusted, as with a sword
50 Follows, as advice
51 Farm machines
52 Endless, in verse
55 "What's the ___?"
56 Milky Way unit
57 Polynesian carving
59 Ancient Syria
62 English cathedral town

by Bill Thompson

ACROSS

1 Promgoers' car
5 Clark of "Gone With the Wind"
10 Exam for future docs
14 The "A" of U.A.E.
15 Ryan of "Love Story"
16 Cincinnati's place
17 Legendary 1920s–'30s Harlem nightspot
19 Hospital units
20 Make certain
21 Extracts (from)
23 Attack from above
26 English cathedral town
27 Dark purple
30 Caesar of 1950s TV
31 Birthplace of Muhammad
34 Lawyers' org.
35 Croat or Serb
37 Old Turkish pooh-bahs
38 Neither's partner
39 Popular Massachusetts vacation area
41 Concert stage item
42 One who talks, talks, talks
44 ___ d'Ivoire
45 Envision
46 What dark clouds may portend
47 Show hosts, for short
48 Long, long time
49 Puppy's bite
50 Kind of plane or projection
53 Modus operandi of a toilet plunger
56 Inuit
60 Et ___ (and others)
61 Pioneering French designer with her own fragrance
64 Bugs in "A Bug's Life"
65 Singsong syllables
66 "That's a ___ off my mind!"
67 Evan or Birch of Indiana politics
68 ___ in the right direction
69 B&B's

DOWN

1 Negligee material
2 Fe, to scientists
3 Cushions for tumblers
4 Slow to catch on
5 Dead duck
6 Org. led by Mandela, once
7 ___ Paese cheese
8 Sang the praises of
9 German river to the North Sea
10 Items hanging in cribs
11 Comic actor who shares a name with a Washington suburb
12 Secretary, e.g.
13 Fling
18 Table scrap
22 Like the film "Arthur" in 2011
24 "And make it snappy!"
25 Small amount of blood serum . . . or a title for this puzzle
27 Feelings of hunger
28 W.W. II ship sinker
29 Capital of Nevada
32 Traditional Hitchcock appearance in a Hitchcock film
33 Colorado town or tree
35 Shrimp dish
36 Fall behind
37 One calling the kettle black
40 Price
43 Like the Union Jack
47 Homes that may have circular drives
48 Soluble salt mixture
51 Summary
52 Baseball bat wood
53 Swedish auto
54 Wrist/elbow connector
55 Eight: Prefix
57 Closing ___ (surrounding)
58 Like a bully
59 Cutlass or Super 88 of bygone autodom
62 Mouse hunter
63 Bullfight cheer

by Kevin Donovan

14 EASY

ACROSS

1 Port-au-Prince native
8 Tarzan and others
14 One who's not sure what's up?
16 Associate
17 Guinevere to Lancelot?
19 Greek god with a bow and arrow
20 Competed in a marathon
21 Cleanser with the old slogan "Nothing can hold a can to . . ."
22 News org.
24 Like some restrictions
26 Shopper for woolen goods?
31 Flip again, as a coin
32 "Whatever happened to . . . ?" subjects
38 Give out
39 Peanut butter container
40 Blast from the past
41 Sci-fi blockbuster of 2009
43 Afghans, e.g.
44 Ewing, DeBusschere and Frazier?
46 Noisy fight
51 ___ Palmas
52 One way to go when playing poker
53 Pride
55 End-of-week cry
59 Universal tie?
63 Not-so-big big bird
64 Power to influence people or things
65 Abandon
66 Out, but not about

DOWN

1 Fit
2 Food thickener
3 Chinese leader?
4 Mr. Potato Head and G.I. Joe
5 Prefix with -meric or -metric
6 Arm of the Justice Dept.
7 Kind of acid
8 Couples retreat?
9 Pound parts
10 Writer T. S.
11 Molten rock
12 Old anesthetic
13 Meshlike
15 When said three times, a dance
18 Win over
22 16th seed's bracket win, e.g.
23 Greek letters
25 Org. whose Web site has a "Where's My Refund?" section
26 One of the angels on "Charlie's Angels"
27 Cozy home
28 "___ girl!"
29 See the sights
30 Uniform shade
33 Petty officers, informally
34 Director Kazan
35 Dutch cheese
36 Cost in dollars of the world's first TV ad in 1941
37 Congressional period: Abbr.
39 Bruce who won the 1976 Olympic decathlon
42 ___ Pictures (old studio)
43 Rap sheet abbr.
45 Garlic units
46 Gathered (in)
47 They parallel radii
48 Thick-soled shoes
49 Sir or madam
50 Figure out (from)
54 Many a drain cleaner nowadays
55 Banks of daytime TV
56 Farm animal with horns
57 "Bus Stop" playwright
58 Graze (on)
60 Giant Mel
61 Holiday prelude
62 Bloodshot

by Mark Feldman

ACROSS

1 Parts of molecules
6 Schools for cadets: Abbr.
11 Tip of a Tiparillo, e.g.
14 Funnywoman O'Donnell
15 Flower from Holland
16 Enemy
17 Whiskey sour garnish
19 Robert Browning's "___ Lippo Lippi"
20 Horse-drawn vehicle often mentioned in Sherlock Holmes stories
21 Artist's studio
23 "___ no evil . . ."
24 Pet food brand
26 Raggedy Ann, e.g.
27 Gibson garnish
31 Take out for ___ (test-drive)
34 Old U.S. gas brand with a tiger symbol
35 Quiet ___ mouse
36 Mayo or cream cheese
38 Journalist, e.g.
41 Heavyweight champ after Liston
42 Resistance units
46 Kind of board at a nail salon
47 Martini garnish
51 U.S.S. Enterprise counselor
52 Musical work
53 Sound at a kennel
56 Conductor Bernstein
58 Shower cap?
61 ___ and outs
62 Bloody Mary garnish
64 Prez before J.F.K.
65 Accustom
66 Actor Sal
67 C.I.A. forerunner
68 Wanderer
69 Opposite of deletes, in typesetting

DOWN

1 Nickname of a Yankee with a $275 million contract
2 Bulls in bullfights
3 Missouri river or tribe
4 Popular Christmas dessert
5 ___ Genesis (old video game console)
6 Being risked
7 ___-de-sac (dead-end street)
8 Noms de plume
9 Webster's, e.g.: Abbr.
10 Big name in small swimwear
11 Station that's part of a TV network
12 Sour grapes type
13 ". . . ___ no evil . . ."
18 Attorney General Holder
22 Actor Chaney
25 Org. with the New York Red Bulls and Los Angeles Galaxy
28 Once ___ lifetime
29 ___ Jones Industrials
30 Not any
31 P.D.Q.
32 Hair woe
33 Flowers on a proverbial path
37 .
39 Title for Mike Huckabee: Abbr.
40 "That wasn't an empty threat!"
43 Gangster
44 Swab, as a floor
45 Couldn't shpeak shtraight [hic]?
48 Long time
49 B vitamin
50 "___, old chap!"
54 German river whose valley is known for wine
55 Side of a diamond
56 Adriatic resort near Venice
57 Nevada city near Lake Tahoe
59 Beliefs
60 Bout enders, for short
63 ___ of Good Feelings

by Nina Rulon-Miller

ACROSS

1. Doorframe part
5. ___ Vecchio (Florence landmark)
10. Can't-miss event
14. Bridge maven Sharif
15. What some sprays eliminate
16. Bouillabaisse, e.g.
17. [White]
19. PBS science series
20. Put down some chips
22. Tool for a confident solver
23. Sound engineer's control
26. [Yellow]
28. Without a time limit, as a contract
31. Bring together
32. DVR button
33. No-calorie drink
37. [Green]
39. Richards of the Stones
40. [Red]
44. Jan Brady player on "The Brady Bunch"
47. Emissions watchdog, for short
48. Long look
51. Just barely
53. [Blue]
57. Professional with an apron
58. Table scrap
59. Texas flag feature
62. Water
64. [Orange]
68. Troubadour's instrument
69. Patronize, as a restaurant
70. Rock's Better Than ___
71. Professor Marvel in "The Wizard of Oz," e.g.
72. Dungeon hardware
73. In need of recharging

DOWN

1. "___ Boys" (Louisa May Alcott book)
2. Hearing aid?
3. West of Hollywood
4. German port on the Weser
5. President after Tyler
6. Jim Davis cartoon dog
7. One without a permanent address
8. Cleveland Indians nickname, with "the"
9. Cosmetician Lauder
10. Yahoo! competitor
11. Perfect place
12. Most common dice rolls
13. Jew's-harp sounds
18. Had the guts
21. Like much folk music: Abbr.
23. Links alert
24. Very top
25. Tenth: Prefix
27. Present time, briefly
29. "Swoosh" company
30. How a quarterback may throw a ball
34. Up to, in ads
35. Ballgame souvenir
36. "Good golly!"
38. U. of Maryland player
41. Furniture hardwood
42. Early Ron Howard role
43. Henry VIII's sixth, Catherine ___
45. Bit of bridal attire
46. Kid-lit elephant
48. Lighthouse locales
49. Rotational force
50. Sharp as a tack
52. Listened, old-style
54. Marisa of "My Cousin Vinny"
55. Close to, in poetry
56. Slowly, on a score
60. Bird in a bevy
61. Preschoolers
63. ___ Lingus
65. Suffix with moral or popular
66. Gun lobby org.
67. Roam (about)

by Michael Black

ACROSS

1 French-speaking nation in the Americas
6 Network with an eye logo
9 ___ colada
13 *Eloquent
16 "Crazy" bird
17 *British novelist who wrote "London Fields"
18 Liter or meter
19 Crafty
20 *College near Philadelphia
22 Mets' ballpark until 2008
24 Symbol on Superman's chest
25 *Having both Republican and Democratic support
30 Degree after an M.A., perhaps
33 "___ do" ("Not possible")
34 Hot cocoa container, maybe
35 Japanese "yes"
36 Unfinished project . . . or, literally, what the answers to the eight starred clues contain?
41 Where a bear hibernates
42 Go kaput
43 See 40-Down
44 Kerfuffle
45 *National discount store chain
48 Dove's sound
50 Whacked-out mental state
51 *Container next to a bowl of cereal
56 The last "W" in WWW
59 Morales of "NYPD Blue"
60 *Like some checks and vendors
63 "Or ___!" (threat)

64 *Gradually separated
65 Pictures inked on the body, in slang
66 Lawn base
67 Wigwam relative

DOWN

1 Easter roasts
2 Asia's shrinking ___ Sea
3 Humble response to a compliment
4 Palindromic bird
5 Here in 1-Across
6 Scratch, as a cat might a sofa
7 Crimson Tide school, for short
8 Start to wake up
9 Prunes, originally
10 Where the Northern Lights occur
11 Dark film genre
12 ___ meridiem (morning: Lat.)
14 Al who won four Indy 500s
15 D.C. winter hrs.
21 Rooster's mate
22 Train for a boxing match
23 Baseball's Hammerin' ___
25 Bent at a curtain call
26 Antiestablishment figure
27 Urge
28 Spanish "south"
29 In the past
31 Hurry
32 What everyone brings to a potluck dinner
33 Nothing
37 Words before "You may kiss the bride"
38 Nothing

39 Saxophonist Stan
40 With 43-Across, yttrium or scandium
45 ___ Martens (shoes)
46 Loved to pieces
47 Corp. creativity department
49 Dust Bowl migrants
51 Encounter
52 Jamaica, por ejemplo
53 Place to enter a PIN
54 Letters after pis
55 Record for later viewing, in a way
56 Shawl, e.g.
57 French "to be"
58 Tiny part of a computer's memory
61 Congratulate nonverbally
62 King Kong, e.g.

by Joel Fagliano

ACROSS

1. "Ars gratia artis" studio
4. Had a hunch
8. Attack via plane, in a way
14. Fair-hiring letters
15. Toast topper
16. Manny of 1970s–'80s baseball
17. Performer with a self-titled HBO special in 2006
19. Fire & Ice cosmetics company
20. Tabriz native
21. Yalie
23. Part of E.U.: Abbr.
24. Green machines?
25. Performer with a self-titled ABC series in 1996
29. Bottom of a crankcase
31. "Senses Working Overtime" band
32. Suffix with elephant
33. Main line
35. Perform as one
37. Performer with a self-titled Comedy Central series from 2003 to 2006
41. Fundamental belief
42. Lend ___ (help)
43. In the manner of
44. The Beatles' "___ Loser"
47. Like Dickens's Dodger
50. Performer with a self-titled PBS series from 1977 to 1982
53. Fit to serve
55. Many a federal holiday: Abbr.
56. Perfection, in some sports
57. Big name in pest control
58. Subject of scientific mapping
60. "Captain Marvel" publisher . . . and a hint to 17-, 25-, 37- and 50-Across

63. Recipient of coal for Christmas
64. The whole kit and caboodle
65. Scot's refusal
66. Equilibrium
67. City tricked with a wooden horse
68. Alternative to cable

DOWN

1. Newspaper, television, etc.
2. Customize for, as an audience
3. "My friend," in Marseille
4. Centers of attention
5. "Don't Bring Me Down" band, informally
6. 1-Across's roarer
7. Straphanger's buy, once
8. Inflexible about rules
9. Uno + due
10. Styx, for one
11. Like soil in a delta
12. City on the Arno
13. Ages and ages
18. Place in shackles
22. Flexible about rules
25. Ste. Jeanne ___
26. Literary collection: Abbr.
27. One way to tell where someone is from
28. As of now
30. Word before license or justice
34. Energizer letters
36. What one might return to after a slump
37. Bologna or salami
38. Crushing snake
39. Excellent, in slang
40. Thespian's aim
41. Tiny bit

45. Buccaneer's buddies
46. N.Y.C.'s Park or Lex
48. Mean-spirited
49. Some German cameras
51. Turners on tuners
52. Conclude by
54. Photographer Adams
57. Like mud between one's toes, say
58. "Pygmalion" monogram
59. Facetious "Who, me?"
61. Pigskin snapper: Abbr.
62. Whisper sweet nothings

by Albert R. Picallo

ACROSS

1 With 69-Across where to find the ends of 17-, 22-, 32-, 43-, 54- and 61-Across
5 Organization for the supersmart
10 ___-in-the-blank
14 Most eligible for military service
15 State in NE India
16 Not working
17 Q-tip, e.g.
19 Hall-of-Famer Musial
20 Whole ___ and caboodle
21 Tetley product
22 It points to the minutes
24 Terse four-star review
27 Danish toy blocks
28 Prefix with plunk or plop
29 French notions
32 Presidential candidate's #2
36 Letter after chi
39 The Bard of ___ (Shakespeare)
40 Lifeless
41 Arkin of Hollywood
42 Part of the head that moves when you talk
43 Excellent, slangily
45 Snapshot
46 007 creator Fleming
47 Reproductive part of a fungus
50 Tire-changing group at a Nascar race
54 Sticky stuff on a baseball bat
57 Middling grade
58 ___ Newton (Nabisco treat)
60 W.W. II foe, with "the"
61 Condiment that's O.K. for observant Jews
64 Hysterically funny sort
65 Letter-shaped construction piece
66 Folkie Guthrie
67 Casino game with numbers
68 Slender amphibians
69 See 1-Across

DOWN

1 Sell at a pawnshop
2 How French fries are fried
3 Become friendly with
4 Dr. Seuss's "The Cat in the ___"
5 Like a lion or horse
6 Piece of French writing
7 Australian state whose capital is Sydney: Abbr.
8 Volvo rival
9 Prefix with dextrous
10 Uses a rod and reel
11 Item on a dog collar
12 Grassy plain of the Southwest
13 Gives for a time
18 Onetime "S.N.L." regular Cheri
23 Great happiness
25 ___ diagram (logic tool)
26 1994 Jean-Claude Van Damme sci-fi film
30 Unlit
31 Suffix with Rock
32 British rule in colonial India
33 The Cavaliers of the A.C.C.
34 Actor Robert De ___
35 Pesky insect
36 Airline ticket cost
37 Holder of a squid's 38-Down
38 It's held in a squid's 37-Down
41 Slightly open
43 Guitarist Atkins
44 Kitchen gadget for processing potatoes
45 Magician's cry
47 Start of a fire
48 Mischievous fairy
49 Weekly satirical paper, with "The"
51 Instant-messaging program for Macs
52 Swarms (with)
53 Cather who wrote "O Pioneers!"
55 Similar (to)
56 Judge's attire
59 Old Pontiac muscle cars
62 Make clothes
63 Carrier to Oslo

by Ian Livengood

ACROSS

1 One of the Pleiades
5 Q.: When is a door not a door? A.: When it's ___
9 Pickpocket, e.g.
14 ID in a library vol.
15 Dunce cap shape
16 Three-wheeled Asian cab
17 "Peanuts" figure . . . or some fabulous fall soup?
20 "For rent"
21 Figure in academia
22 Nein : German :: ___ : Russian
23 Subway turners
25 Much-derided 1980s—'90s car
27 Calif. setting for "Stand and Deliver"
30 Words to swear by
34 Off-road wheels, for short
36 Rhyme scheme for Frost's "Stopping by Woods on a Snowy Evening"
38 Onion-flavored roll
39 Early 1970s dance . . . or some smelly soup?
43 Kenyan tribesman
44 Suffix with opal
45 Key to get out of a jam?
46 At a chop shop, perhaps
48 Tennis's Graf
51 Exam for an aspiring Esq.
53 Ray of "GoodFellas"
56 Ways to the Web: Abbr.
59 It may be put on a pedestal
62 Gloomy, in verse
63 Nickname for snowboarder Shaun White . . . or some airborne soup?
66 Paddled craft
67 Canceled
68 Old camera settings, for short
69 Many-headed challenge for Hercules
70 Like flicks seen without special glasses
71 Instrument played with a plectrum

DOWN

1 Baseball gloves
2 "Give it ___!" ("Try!")
3 "Yes, if you ask me"
4 German chancellor Merkel
5 Score 100% on
6 "The Grapes of Wrath" family name
7 The "a" in a.m.
8 Compensate for loss
9 Channel for old films
10 Like a swinging pendulum, say
11 "Eww! Gross!"
12 "Night" author Wiesel
13 Helvetica, e.g.
18 Hwys.
19 "One" on a penny
24 Lee of Marvel Comics
26 Mongolian desert
28 Okeechobee, e.g.
29 Chasm
31 "Calm down!"
32 Shouts at a fútbol game
33 Harmony
34 $20 dispensers
35 "What's ___?"
37 No. at a brokerage
40 Becomes smitten by
41 Sometimes-illegal turns, in slang
42 Dog command
47 The Midshipmen
49 Relative of Rex
50 Not casual
52 Corrupt
54 One of a Turkic people
55 Got out of bed
56 Allergic reaction
57 One-horse carriage
58 Be in limbo
60 Author C. P. ___
61 Frozen waffle brand
64 Grazing ground
65 Thomas Mann's "Der ___ in Venedig"

by Tony Orbach

ACROSS

1 Ice cream utensil
6 Sea creature that moves sideways
10 "But wait! There's more . . ."
14 Cuban "line" dance
15 Lasso
16 Italian "bye"
17 Crowd sounds
18 Baldwin of "30 Rock"
19 Bullets
20 Buffalo wings or bruschetta, e.g.
23 Kid's "shooter" projectile
24 Formula ___ racing
25 Overly
26 Kanye West's genre
28 "E" on a baseball scoreboard
30 Sylvania product
31 Rightmost number on a grandfather clock
32 Dish under a teacup
34 High point
35 Pittsburgh Pirates hero of the 1960 World Series
39 Perry with the 1956 #1 hit "Hot Diggity"
40 Winners' opposites
41 Auto additive brand
42 Hole-punching tools
44 Swung and missed
48 Equal: Prefix
49 W. Hemisphere alliance
50 Allow
51 "___ Baba and the 40 Thieves"
52 Music source on many an old fairground
56 Western writer Grey
57 Heading into overtime
58 Source of amber

59 ___-European languages
60 Prefix with potent or present
61 Ridiculous
62 "No bid"
63 Noble gas
64 Weasel family member

DOWN

1 Predicament
2 "The Last of the Mohicans" author
3 Commensurate (with)
4 Shrek, for one
5 Rustic
6 Hula hoops in the 1950s, e.g.
7 Part to play
8 Camera openings
9 "Take a chill pill!"
10 Military sch.
11 Verse often beginning "There once was a . . ."
12 "Spider-Man" series director
13 Tic-tac-toe victory
21 All together
22 Burgle
27 Baked dessert
29 Norway's capital
30 Jeff who founded Amazon.com
33 Gives teams a short break
34 Professional org.
35 Neighbor of South Africa
36 Seizes, as a car
37 Direct elsewhere
38 Handel's "Messiah," e.g.
39 CBS forensic series

42 Time Warner spinoff of '09
43 Serve attentively
45 Pesters
46 Jerry's ex on "Seinfeld"
47 Supper
50 Ushered
53 Old-fashioned Speed Wagons
54 Greek philosopher known for paradoxes
55 Landlord's due
56 Nothing . . . or a hint to what's hidden in 20-, 35- and 52-Across

by Stanley Newman

ACROSS

1 Cut down, as a photo
5 Big Apple?
9 Like many bathroom floors
14 Poland's Walesa
15 It gets hammered
16 Rub out
17 Brainstorm
18 Be rewarded for a pious life, as the devout believe
20 Abyss
22 Shipping container
23 Stereotypical sitcom greeting
26 Hypotheticals
29 U.F.O. crew
30 Roman "I"
31 Sirius ___ (satellite broadcaster)
33 Former Japanese capital
35 "The Flintstones" pet
36 Castle on the Thames
41 Doll call
42 Spanish finger food
43 A girl was from there in a 1964 hit song
47 His big day is in June
48 Rx watchdog
51 Finger count
52 Pet store purchase
55 Big, big, big
56 Aired again
57 Invisible writing on a computer screen . . . or a component of 18-, 23-, 36- and 52-Across?
62 All's counterpart
63 "Doe, ___ . . ."
64 Les États-___
65 Puts on
66 Chinese restaurant request

67 Force unit
68 Apt rhyme of "aahs"

DOWN

1 Overused expression
2 In very high demand
3 "___ Eleven"
4 Developmental period
5 Suffix with seem or teem
6 Chinese chairman
7 Gee follower
8 Laundry brand
9 Be on the brink of toppling
10 "Dies ___"
11 Restroom, informally
12 WNW's opposite
13 Room for trophies, maybe
19 Soccer great Mia

21 "Balderdash!"
24 Inventor Sikorsky
25 Mr. ___, Japanese sleuth
26 Peculiar: Prefix
27 Neighbor of a Swede
28 ___ Canals
32 Tacks on
33 Skater Michelle
34 Frequently, to a bard
36 Mending aid
37 Muscat's land
38 Disney dog
39 Memorable 1995 hurricane with a gem of a name?
40 Low point
41 Cambridge univ.
44 Anita of "La Dolce Vita"
45 Appearance

46 Available for breeding
48 Farcical 1960s sitcom with the Indian character Roaring Chicken
49 Troi on "Star Trek: T.N.G."
50 "Gunsmoke" star James
53 Minuscule
54 Minds, as a fire
55 Laudatory poems
57 Solo of "Star Wars"
58 Vow at an altar
59 Those people, in Brooklyn
60 Mark, as a ballot
61 Syllable after 6-Down

by David Steinberg

ACROSS

1 Handkerchief stuffed in the mouth, e.g.
4 "The 59th Street Bridge Song (___ Groovy)" (1967 hit)
10 Start for a plant
14 Hwy.
15 Provide with the latest info
16 Friend in war
17 Giant Mel
18 Anti-abortion position
20 Cry to a horse that's the opposite of "Giddyup!"
22 Allow
23 Place to get a facial
24 Abandoned, in a way
27 Incorporate, as a picture in a blog
31 Kermit, e.g.
32 Ice cream flavor that's a synonym for "boring"
34 Up and about
36 Announced
38 Landon who lost to F.D.R. in 1936
39 Not shown in theaters
43 Suffix with plug
44 Not feral
45 2000 comedy "Me, Myself & ___"
46 Place to play foosball or Ping-Pong
49 Wall Street pessimist
50 Arcade coin
51 Satisfactory
56 Josh
58 Meadow
59 Concerning
60 Having no illusions or pretensions
65 Singer ___ King Cole
66 Little of this and that
67 Fiat
68 Big Australian bird
69 Move text around
70 Mrs. with a famous cow
71 Lo-___ screen

DOWN

1 Canine threat
2 "Casey ___ Bat"
3 Go astray
4 Wearing this is a PETA peeve
5 Afterword
6 Barely beaten
7 Christine of "Chicago Hope"
8 Hairy TV cousin
9 Fishermen cast them
10 Deli meat
11 Football's Manning
12 Rice Krispies' Snap, Crackle or Pop
13 Change from brunette to blonde, say
19 "___ sesame"
21 Heart parts
25 Doughnuts, topologically speaking
26 What you might R.S.V.P. to via a computer
28 1982 Harrison Ford sci-fi film
29 Funny DeGeneres
30 Actor Willem
33 Hubbub.
34 Of ___ (somewhat)
35 Canonized fifth-century pope
36 SeaWorld whale
37 Green machine?
40 Sporty Pontiac of years past
41 Competes (for)
42 Tehran native
47 Tie again, as a necktie
48 "I'm working ___"
49 Yachtsman, e.g.
52 Come in second
53 ___ cotta
54 Box on a bowling scoresheet
55 Baby-to-be
57 Dumb ox
60 Mother of a fawn
61 Superannuated
62 Nintendo console with a remote
63 Snaky fish
64 "You there!"

by Milo Beckman

ACROSS

1 Handled, as a matter
6 Sleepaway, e.g.
10 Wood strip
14 "Er . . . um . . ."
15 Instrument heard in Sonny & Cher's "I Got You Babe"
16 Currency that replaced the drachma
17 "Spitting" snake
18 Roller coaster, e.g.
19 Rigging support
20 Bolt
23 Cousin of Muhammad
25 Sharer of an exclamation point on a keyboard
26 Locale of the Île de la Cité
27 Bolt
32 Tatum of "Paper Moon"
33 The "she" in the lyric "She walked up to me and she asked me to dance"
34 Window part
35 Unlikely to hug, say
37 Frozen dessert franchise
41 Part of the Old World
42 Wipe the slate clean
43 Bolt
47 Marble, for one
49 What "-" may mean: Abbr.
50 511, to Caesar
51 Bolt
56 Wrist/elbow connector
57 Every family has one
58 Energy
61 Toy sometimes pulled with a rope
62 Leer
63 It's a blessing
64 Half of a famous split personality
65 Unite under fire?
66 Smarts

DOWN

1 Word to an attack dog
2 ___, amas, amat . . .
3 They have homes that many people visit
4 Protective covering
5 Hot, scoring-wise
6 Pupil coverer
7 Somewhat
8 Number in statistics
9 ___ review
10 Renter
11 Foreign domestic
12 Choo-choo
13 See 24-Down
21 Like Brahms's Symphony No. 3
22 Jimmy Carter's alma mater: Abbr.
23 Famous ___ cookies
24 With 13-Down, "Stormy Weather" singer

28 Sound from a weary person sinking into a hot tub
29 ___-Kettering Institute
30 Also
31 Figure in Santa's workshop
35 Result of a fire
36 On fire
37 Play about Capote
38 1972 #1 hit for Sammy Davis Jr., with "The"
39 Vitamin whose name sounds like a bingo call
40 Mountain sighting
41 Writer James
42 Drinks that are often ladled
43 Given for a time
44 Attack, as across a boundary

45 "Absolutely!"
46 Born as
47 Snow when it's around 32°F
48 British boob tube
52 Store
53 Persuade
54 Big maker of 59-Down
55 Folk tales and such
59 Office staples, for short
60 ___-haw

by Michael Farabaugh

ACROSS

1 You can stick them in your ear
6 "Planet of the ___"
10 Soft, thick lump
14 Sum
15 Leap
16 Learning by memorization
17 Bolivian capital
18 Mideast leader: Var.
19 The "a" in a.m.
20 Legendary San Francisco music/comedy club where Lenny Bruce and Woody Allen have performed
23 To the ___ degree
24 Extremity
25 Got rid of some tobacco juices, say
28 Ali Baba's magic words
35 Counterpart of hers
36 Puppeteer Lewis
37 High-end watchmaker
38 Bonus
40 Quarry, e.g.
41 Amalgamate
42 Poet/playwright Jones
43 ___ self-defense
45 Tavern
46 Bad place to live when the river rises
48 Deposit around a river's mouth
49 Road surfacing material
50 Cartoon frame
52 Everything . . . or what might cover an everything 62-Across?
60 The "A" in U.A.W.
61 Group of birds
62 Item whose varieties include the endings of 20-, 28- and 46-Across

64 Deborah of "The King and I"
65 50–50
66 Online-only publication
67 Sized up visually
68 45 or 78
69 Results of bumps to a bumper

DOWN

1 Ice cream amts.
2 Brazenly promote
3 "The Seven Year ___"
4 Mother or father
5 Caught some Z's
6 Not fully shut
7 The heart, essentially
8 Actor Jannings who won the first Best Actor Oscar
9 Wild shopping sessions
10 Junior's junior
11 Actress Anderson
12 "Beetle Bailey" bulldog
13 "___ there, done that"
21 "This isn't looking good"
22 Minimal lead in baseball
25 Bookcase part
26 Dot on a computer screen
27 Houston baseballer
29 Vatican-related
30 "Fear of Fifty" writer Jong
31 Capone henchman
32 What a murder suspect needs
33 Zinc or zirconium
34 Apply, as pressure
36 Got ready for a tongue depressor, say

39 The Greek "khalix" (pebble) for the English "calculus," e.g.
44 Ruler part
47 Examined deeply
48 Schlock
51 Fix deeply and tightly
52 Seize
53 ___ Lewis and the News
54 To live, to Lévy
55 ___ Strauss jeans
56 After-work times, in classifieds
57 Harmony
58 Opposed to, in dialect
59 Check for a landlady
63 "___ Misérables"

by Andrea Carla Michaels and Michael Blake

ACROSS

1 Hungry mouth
4 Person assisting a worship service
10 Jockey's whip
14 Lincoln, the Rail-Splitter
15 Place for a bookcase
16 Auto company whose name is Latin for "listen"
17 Title of respect
18 Longtime New York theater critic
20 Emphatic follow-up to yes or no
22 Corporate dept. that may include labs
23 Actor in 1960s TV's "77 Sunset Strip"
26 Nary a soul
29 Tropical citrus fruit
30 Fleischmann's product
32 Wilson of "Midnight in Paris"
33 Spanish king
34 Popular card game since 1954
37 Speck
38 Org. issuing many refunds
39 TV/film/stage actor once married to actress Meredith Baxter
45 Informer
48 International furniture retailer
49 Facility
50 Madame Chanel
51 Italian city famous for its cheese
53 Big dog
56 Yankee great Roger
58 Came ashore
59 Prime cooking spot
63 ___ de mer
64 "___ She Sweet"
65 "That's it for me"
66 Get along in years
67 Memo
68 Conflict waged between navies
69 ___ diem

DOWN

1 Rubber man?
2 Cut
3 In an odd manner
4 ___ Davenport, long-running "Doonesbury" character
5 Aunt ___ of "Oklahoma!"
6 Start of the third century
7 "Mazel ___!"
8 Be in charge of
9 Singer McEntire
10 Nowadays they usually have power locks and windows
11 Decrepit
12 Pindar creation
13 Fraternity letters
19 The Atlantic's Cape ___
21 Baseball stat
24 ___ pros. (court record abbr.)
25 Building extension
27 Born, in Brittany
28 Naval officer below lieut.
31 Annual theater award
34 Quaintly stylish
35 Barry Manilow's "Could ___ Magic"
36 Suffix with contradict
37 Old Mitsubishi model
39 Fondue feature
40 Alias
41 First U.S. state to abolish slavery
42 "It seems evident that . . ."
43 Alphabet trio
44 Beak
45 Motorist's guide
46 Farmland spread
47 Real young 'un
50 Piers Morgan's channel
52 Realm of beauty
54 Justice Kagan
55 Less done, as steak
57 Long-legged wader
59 Ceiling addition
60 ___ de la Plata
61 Nutritional allotment, for short
62 At once

by Bernice Gordon

ACROSS

1 Necklace fasteners
7 "Entourage" cable channel
10 Talks like this in "Star Wars" films he does
14 Cut the mustard
15 Dada artist Jean
16 Landed
17 Property with a mansion
18 "Fat chance, laddie"
19 Griffin who created "Wheel of Fortune"
20 Charleston is its capital
23 "All seats have been sold" sign
24 First part of a ski jump
25 Longest river in Deutschland
29 ___, Crackle and Pop
31 Trumpet's saliva-draining key
33 Skirt's edge
35 ___ Paulo, Brazil
36 Perry Mason's field
37 Kitchen cleanup cloth
41 Samuel Langhorne ___
44 Simile's center
45 Author Asquith of children's books
47 511, in old Rome
48 Not a unanimous ruling
52 Role in "Young Frankenstein"
55 "Laughing" animal
56 Biblical word with "thou"
58 Deposit, as an egg
60 Swedish liquor with memorable ads
63 Melt
66 Qty.
67 Jack the ___
68 Elvis's "___ Las Vegas"
69 Doctor's charge
70 Log-in info
71 Fix, as a cat
72 Finish
73 Eagle's grabbers

DOWN

1 Masticates
2 Focused-beam emitters
3 Takes steps in response to
4 32-card game
5 Venomous snake
6 Oktoberfest vessel
7 Abrupt finishes to phone conversations
8 Genius
9 Ready for business
10 Japanese motorcycle maker
11 Bullfight cheer
12 North, east, west or south: Abbr.
13 Off-road transport, briefly
21 Four Monopoly properties: Abbr.
22 Chicago columnist Kupcinet
26 Fashion magazine founded in France
27 ___ the Terrible
28 What literally comes from the north, east, west and south?
30 "Feels great!"
32 Informed
34 Sportscaster Albert
37 Bit of Morse code
38 Look-for-it children's game
39 Common event the day after Thanksgiving
40 Favorable sign
42 Permit for leaving a country
43 Russian fighter jet
46 Stiffly phrased
49 Sort of
50 Indenting key
51 College Web site suffix
53 One who knows the ropes
54 Earn tons of, as dough
57 Walk proudly
59 Distance units on a football field
61 Not threatened
62 German car
63 Appliances hidden in seven answers in this puzzle
64 It's rotated when doing the twist
65 Palindromic girl

by Patrick Merrell

ACROSS

1 It gets patted on the bottom
5 Tableland
9 Lead-in to boy or girl
13 Surveyor's calculation
14 Raring to go
15 Gershwin and Glass
16 Ticket usable on more than one trip
18 Basketball hoops
19 Gerund's finish
20 When repeated, cry to a vampire
21 ___ accompli
22 They make a king laugh
26 Available if needed
28 One who's supposed to be available if needed
29 End-of-list abbr.
31 Diamond cover
32 Life, in short
33 Neck cover
35 Smells bad
38 Mel who batted left and threw right
39 Become oblivious to one's surroundings
41 Completely untrained
42 Home of Arizona State University
44 Stir up, as a fire
45 Suffix with brigand
46 "___ well"
48 Alternative to .com or .org
49 Bean type
50 Like maps, iguanas and rock walls
52 Bad-mouth
54 Counterparts of dits
55 Cut with a sweeping motion
57 Greek H
58 Theater sign

59 Fast marching pace . . . or a hint to 16- and 39-Across and 10- and 24-Down
64 Dairy Queen purchase
65 Shortstop Smith who won 13 consecutive Gold Glove Awards
66 Cajole
67 Lollapalooza
68 "Butt out," briefly
69 Novelist Victor

DOWN

1 Bit of body art, for short
2 Train schedule abbr.
3 Meadow
4 Dentist's target
5 Apple on a table
6 "My word!"
7 Prefix with comic
8 Raring to go
9 Expedia calculation
10 Interval in which something is tested
11 Indian tongue
12 Helper: Abbr.
14 Artist born in 30-Down
17 WSW's opposite
22 Frilly neckwear
23 Type of type
24 Las Vegas staple
25 Nixon aide Maurice
27 ___ blanche
30 Minotaur's home
33 Former Cleveland Orchestra conductor George
34 General ___, former maker of Jell-O and Sanka
36 Rapper West

37 Promise
40 Luau instrument
43 Wall cover
47 Rarely
49 Grab
50 Anglo-___
51 Lollapalooza
53 Noshed
54 Art ___
56 "The Godfather" author
60 Drool catcher
61 Debtor's letters
62 O or Cosmo
63 Prefix with skeleton

by Susan Gelfand

ACROSS

1 One of the "hands" in the command "shake hands"
4 Result of a burst dike
9 "O.K., O.K. . . . tell me!"
14 "So that's it!"
15 Caffè ___
16 Healing plants
17 Unused parts of a cell phone plan
20 Youngster
21 Encircle
22 Stun, as with a police gun
23 British lockup
26 Wander
28 Formal meal at a table
33 "One more time!"
35 Hops kiln
36 Lab eggs
37 X-rated flick
38 Arid
39 What a soldier wears that has a serial no.
41 Any port ___ storm
42 Letters before omegas
44 Hammerin' Hank and others
45 Question that's a classic pickup line
48 Instrument for a Muse
49 La ___ Tar Pits
50 Mountain lion
53 Chemical suffixes
55 Three Wise Men
59 Death row inmate's hope
63 Finnish bath
64 Big name in printers
65 See 57-Down
66 Person who uses the "five-finger discount"
67 Medicinal amounts
68 Juice suffix

DOWN

1 Segment
2 "___, matey!"
3 Send to base on balls
4 Pop music's ___ & Eddie
5 Restroom, informally
6 Verdi opera
7 Other: Sp.
8 Actress Rebecca
9 Novelist Fleming
10 Substance in wheat flour
11 Minuscule amount
12 Flying geese formations
13 To be, in old Rome
18 American ___ (veterans' group)
19 Apple devices with earbuds
24 Wither
25 "___ to a Nightingale"
27 Impair the quality of
28 "Git!"
29 Less favorable
30 Off
31 2007 film "___ Almighty"
32 ___-to-riches
33 Heroic tale
34 It's prohibited
38 Exigency
40 Had visions during sleep
43 Letter flourish
44 Where Nigeria is: Abbr.
46 Comic Boosler
47 Keep thinking about, with "on"
50 Whispered attention-getter
51 Salt Lake City's state
52 Hawaiian island
54 Int'l fair
56 Verdi opera
57 With 65-Across, comment that might be heard after the start of 17-, 28-, 45- or 59-Across
58 Playwright William
60 Clumsy sort
61 Iowa college
62 Young ___ (kids)

by Keith Talon

ACROSS

1 Nile bird
5 A ditz hasn't one
9 __ Downs
14 "High Hopes" lyricist
16 Slightest amount
17 Guilty plea, say
18 Lilylike garden plant
19 It might make the nose wrinkle
20 Singer with the #1 R&B hit "I Feel for You"
22 Suffix with ox- or sulf-
23 "Paper Moon" father and daughter
24 Biscotti flavor
26 Like Batman, the Lone Ranger, etc.
29 Hagen of stage and screen
30 Japan's "way of the gods" religion
32 Eurasian duck
36 Pre-K child
37 Scam . . . or an apt title for this puzzle?
39 Useless tic-tac-toe line
40 Certain blood type, for short
42 Economist Friedman
43 Suffix with no-good
44 __ Pieces
46 Aides: Abbr.
48 Dead Sea Scrolls ascetic
51 Grafton's "__ for Outlaw"
52 He was Sonny to Marlon Brando's Vito
56 Chilly
58 54-Down by Verdi
59 Allowed to wander, as a chicken
61 Handle the fixin's for a party, say
62 Boxer who almost upset Joe Louis in 1941
63 "I'm done!"

64 Jonas who developed a polio vaccine
65 Formerly, once

DOWN

1 "A miss __ good . . ."
2 Sport with a birdie
3 Having no delay
4 Says "Cheese!"
5 Hypo meas.
6 Nonclerical
7 "Looks like I goofed"
8 City of central Sicily
9 Gaseous hydrocarbon
10 Sneakers brand sported by Abdul-Jabbar
11 The younger Obama girl
12 Of base 8
13 Intends
15 Fashion monogram

21 Indiana University campus site
24 Grand Theft __
25 Upper-left key
26 Cooper cars
27 Protractor measure
28 Field goal percentages and such
31 Class for cooking, sewing, etc.
33 Priest's honorific
34 Illuminated notices above theater doors
35 Stir-fry vessels
38 Bambi's aunt
41 Welcomer at Walmart, e.g.
45 Make certain
47 Give comfort to
48 Give the heave-ho
49 Politico Palin
50 Strike down

53 Place for B-2s and B-52s: Abbr.
54 Operatic highlight
55 Dudley Do-Right's heartthrob
56 Mission conclusion?
57 Car ding
60 Yellowstone beast

by Patrick McIntyre

ACROSS

1 Common interjection on 27-/44-Across
5 Corn, wheat or soybeans
9 Mobile downloadables
13 Ark builder
14 Amours
16 Underground part of a plant
17 Where plank-walkers end up on 27-/44-Across
20 Often-purple flowers
21 500 sheets
22 Big bird Down Under
23 "It's the ___ I can do"
25 "Hold it!," on 27-/44-Across
27 With 44-Across, annual celebration on 9/19
31 That woman
32 Yours, in Tours
33 Never, in Nuremberg
34 Gog and ___ (enemies of God, in Revelation)
36 Deep-toned woodwind
38 Bird in a "tuxedo"
40 Malevolent spirit
41 Cushion
42 Actress Swenson of "Benson"
43 Asian electronics giant
44 See 27-Across
46 Treasure on 27-/44-Across
48 Sometimes-sprained joint
49 Pretend
50 Watch sound
52 Playmate of Tinky Winky, Dipsy and Po
57 "I don't believe it!," on 27-/44-Across

60 "___ la Douce"
61 Ultimate authority
62 "The Art of Fugue" composer
63 Onetime competitor of Nair
64 Glowing gas
65 Hello, on 27-/44-Across

DOWN

1 "I've fallen . . . ___ can't get up!"
2 Surf sound
3 Sitar player Shankar
4 John ___-Davies of the "Lord of the Rings" trilogy
5 Get near to
6 Harry Potter's best friend
7 Be a foreman of

8 Onetime money in Spain
9 Curve
10 Do some investigating
11 Sonnets and haikus
12 Peacock's walk
15 1970s radical org.
18 Set, as mousse
19 Resident of Nebraska's largest city
24 Related (to)
26 ___ burger (meatless dish)
27 Key on the far left of a keyboard
28 Not much
29 Take immediate steps
30 Destiny
34 Award hung on a chain or ribbon
35 Prefix with byte
37 Immature egg cell

38 The "P" of PRNDL
39 Aye's opposite
41 Ocular inflammation also known as conjunctivitis
44 Dot-chomping character in a classic arcade game
45 What there's no "I" in
46 Place to wash up
47 Autumn hue
51 1040 org.
53 "Mamma Mia" group
54 Jacob's first wife
55 California-based oil giant
56 Like a used barbecue pit
58 Winery container
59 General on a Chinese menu

by Julian Lim

ACROSS

1 PC hearts
5 Capital ENE of Fiji
9 "Star Wars" director George
14 Mont Blanc, par exemple
15 Table salt, chemically
16 Chip away
17 Way to reduce spending
19 Broadcaster
20 Coach Parseghian
21 URL ending
22 ___ instant
23 Pre-sporting-event songs
29 Baldwin of "30 Rock"
30 Genesis mariner
31 Deli side
32 Fabergé collectible
35 River to the Caspian
37 Author Levin
38 President Taft's foreign policy
43 N.Y.C.'s Park or Lex
44 Union collections
45 "Alice" spinoff
46 Nimble-fingered
48 Long skirt
50 Malone of "Into the Wild"
54 Areas targeted for economic revitalization
58 Part of Miss Muffet's meal
59 Kitchen gadget brand
60 "Mighty ___ a Rose"
61 Director Kurosawa
63 Some vacation expenses . . . or a hint to the starts of 17-, 23-, 38- and 54-Across
66 Echolocation acronym
67 Kind of sax
68 Play opener
69 Speaks silently
70 One pitied by Mr. T
71 McJob doer

DOWN

1 Poolside enclosure
2 Mice or men
3 "This just in . . ." announcement
4 Line part: Abbr.
5 Composer Bruckner
6 Game with four "ghosts"
7 Post-O.R. stop
8 PC key near the space bar
9 Was biased
10 Heep and others
11 First wife of Julius Caesar
12 Suffix with block or cannon
13 Sun. speech
18 Prefix with friendly
22 Divided 50–50
24 Reykjavik's land: Abbr.
25 15th-century French king nicknamed "the Prudent"
26 Seniors' org.
27 Painter Chagall
28 Have influence on
33 Wander, with "about"
34 In a mood to complain
36 Follower of a chat room joke
38 Miami-___ County
39 Place for a roast
40 More than liberal
41 Very expensive
42 Voodoo charm
47 Persian Gulf capital
49 Sees through, in a way
51 Intertwine
52 On the verge of
53 Invites to enter one's home
55 Brings up
56 Heap kudos on
57 Suffix meaning "animals"
61 Balaam's beast
62 Fish in backyard pools
63 U.K. fliers
64 "Xanadu" rock grp.
65 Salary ceiling

by Daniel Raymon

ACROSS

1 Little argument
5 Result of a mosquito bite
9 /
14 Gas company famous for its toy trucks
15 Classic soda brand
16 Acknowledge as true, as a crime
17 Operatic solo
18 Signal, as a cab
19 Common mirage image
20 Some McDonald's burgers
23 Four-baggers: Abbr.
24 View
25 Look up to
29 It might make you go "Achoo!"
31 January 1 for the Rose Bowl, e.g.
35 Good, in Guatemala
36 Wild pig
37 ___ exhaust
38 Part of a 2005 Harry Potter title
41 "That's ___ haven't heard"
42 Paris airport
43 Be a cast member of
44 Double-___ (oboe, e.g.)
45 Bus. opposite
46 Party south of the border
47 Years on end
49 Partners for mas
50 1987 Stanley Kubrick classic
59 Lightning-fast Bolt
60 Actor Morales
61 ___ avis
62 Tooth: Prefix
63 For fear that
64 French friends
65 Heavy carts
66 Tibetan priest
67 Word that can follow the start of 20-, 38- or 50-Across

DOWN

1 N.B.A. nickname until 2011
2 Llama land
3 It's north of the Indian Ocean
4 Former Russian royal
5 "Yoo-hoo" response
6 They may stream down the cheeks
7 Chocolate-___
8 Hawaiian port
9 English biscuit served with tea
10 Items for gamblers who cheat
11 Area that may have stained-glass windows
12 Use a teaspoon in tea, e.g.
13 "Bonanza" brother
21 Pulsate painfully
22 Improperly seize
25 Despise
26 One of the Allman Brothers
27 Brawl
28 Cheating on a spouse
29 April 1 victims
30 ___ Gaga
32 Female relations
33 Not said explicitly
34 1941 chart-topper "Maria ___"
36 Drill a hole
39 Michaels of "S.N.L."
40 Mrs. Gorbachev
46 Tex-Mex wrap
48 Old Dodges
49 Ecto- or proto- ending
50 Elmer with a double-barreled shotgun
51 Manipulator
52 Actress Turner
53 Explain to
54 On an ocean voyage
55 Creature that sidles
56 ___ Sutra
57 Attorney General Holder
58 Work to do

by David Gray

ACROSS

1 Medicine holder
5 Walk ungracefully
11 Nick, say
14 Rights advocacy grp.
15 This point forward
16 Bon ___
17 *Area in front of a coop
19 Grand Canyon part
20 Cornfield call
21 Sea eagle
22 Some Saturns
23 *Modern school memento
28 Beatle lover
29 More clever
30 Wee, informally
31 Baseball's Blue Moon
33 O.R. figures
34 One working with checks and balances, for short
35 *Braided floor covering
37 *More than enough
41 "___ the season"
42 Play about Capote
43 Bosnian, e.g.
44 Larklike bird
47 Ore-Ida parent company
49 Language suffix
50 *Elemental parts of human nature
53 Posh
54 Letter from Homer?
55 ___ v. Wade
56 Former White House press secretary Fleischer
57 *Discover to be fibbing
62 Bee follower
63 Opposed (to)
64 Hobbling, say
65 Actors Burns and Wynn
66 Guardian Angels' toppers
67 Event with booths

DOWN

1 Hoover or Oreck, for short
2 German "I"
3 Noted 1964 convert to Islam
4 Susan of soaps
5 Character in a Beatles song
6 Wine: Prefix
7 They may be hard to find at a tearjerker
8 More loved
9 "___ Doone"
10 Knock off
11 Strand
12 Some acids
13 Composer ___-Korsakov
18 Kit ___ (chocolate bars)
22 Metal supports in skyscrapers
23 Opportunity, metaphorically
24 ___-European
25 Sticky stuff
26 When repeated, a noted panda
27 Takeback, briefly
32 Break from responsibilities, informally
34 Sovereign lands . . . or what are hidden in the answers to the six starred clues
36 "Lovely" Beatles girl
37 Baseball Hall-of-Famer Speaker
38 Actor Baldwin
39 Creator of the G.O.P. elephant
40 The "Y" in Y.S.L.
42 Like a small farm, perhaps
44 France's Élysée, for one
45 Hardened
46 Fairies
47 One getting lots of doubles and home runs, say
48 The Jewish people
51 It might be taken by a sailor
52 Author Zora ___ Hurston
57 Request inside (or outside?) a wine bar
58 Pres. when NATO was formed
59 Loosey-goosey
60 Mischief-maker
61 Fair-hiring inits.

by Peter A. Collins

ACROSS

1 Teenage Mutant ___ Turtles
6 Perfect school grade
11 Bar bill
14 Spring zodiac sign
15 Promote
16 When a plane is due in, for short
17 Wins a dispute
19 Some "General Hospital" roles, in brief
20 Sci-fi vehicle
21 Cry between "ready" and "go"
22 I.R.S. experts
23 Microscope part
26 Pompous pronoun
29 Clean air org.
30 Recent: Prefix
31 Pretty good
32 YouTube upload
34 Andy Warhol genre
37 "It's a mystery to me"
42 Two-front, as a Coast Guard rescue
43 Practical application
44 Italian shrimp dish
47 Blaster's buy
49 Call ___ day
50 Sob stories
53 Off-road bikes, for short
54 Cameo shape
55 Numeral at the top of grandfather clocks
56 Yonder yacht
58 "___ Misérables"
59 In romantic pursuit
64 Annoy
65 Draw forth
66 43rd president's nickname
67 Crime lab evidence
68 Satisfy, as a mortgage
69 Shuts tightly

DOWN

1 Remind too often
2 Wrath
3 Trivial complaint
4 Subject of Handel's "Messiah"
5 Beginning on
6 16th president's nickname
7 Rap artist's entourage
8 Less lofty
9 National paper
10 Home for hogs
11 Place of worship
12 When many duels were held
13 Long-eared hound
18 Make mention of
22 Bit of desert flora
23 ___ Strauss jeans
24 Grand-scale
25 Zilch
27 Optimistic feelings
28 Umpire's yell
30 Vacation resort policy, perhaps
33 Tooth covering
35 Soccer spectator's shout
36 Student of Socrates
38 Compound containing O_3
39 Hang around (for)
40 "House Hunters" cable channel
41 Thumbs-up votes
44 Unemotional
45 Where to find stalactites and stalagmites
46 Fairbanks's home
48 "M*A*S*H" soft drink
51 Equip
52 So-called "white magic"
53 Put up a fuss
57 Discontinues
59 The "p" in m.p.h.
60 "Just a cotton-pickin' minute!"
61 Bout-sanctioning org.
62 Olive ___ (Popeye's sweetie)
63 W. Hemisphere alliance

by Stanley Newman

ACROSS

1 Band with the 22×
  platinum album "Back
  in Black"
5 Second-in-command
  to Captain Kirk
10 State south of
  Manitoba: Abbr.
14 Mythological hammer
  thrower
15 Bejeweled headgear
16 River to the Seine
17 Make gentle
18 Innocent ___ proven
  guilty
19 TV show for which Bill
  Cosby won
  three Emmys
20 Squelches early
23 Immigrant's course:
  Abbr.
24 Donkey
25 Ones dealing in
  futures?
29 Like the sound of
  a teakettle
32 Move so as to
  hear better, say
33 Took care of,
  as a bill
34 Got the wrinkles out
38 Mai ___
39 Capital of Latvia
40 Queen, en Español
41 Edible seaweed
42 Raptorial seabird
43 Syrup sources
44 Pseudonym of the
  artist Romain de
  Tirtoff
45 Likes a whole lot
47 Caveat ___
49 Stanley who
  co-directed "Singin'
  in the Rain"
50 Bit of song and dance,
  e.g.
53 "Ain't ___ shame?"
54 51-Down's talent . . .
  or what the circled
  squares represent?

59 Puzzle with a start
  and a finish
62 Scent
63 Once again
64 Smart ___
65 Drainage system
66 Michael of "Arrested
  Development"
67 Half-and-half carton,
  often
68 Name of eight
  English kings
69 Water whirled

DOWN

1 Envelope abbr.
2 Spiced Indian tea
3 Pricey bubbly
4 Lover of Troilus in a
  Shakespeare play
5 Gobsmack
6 Vessel of 1492
7 "#@*!" and such

8 Breaks down, in
  a way
9 Former "Meet the
  Press" host Marvin
10 "Beats me!"
11 Insult, slangily
12 Nile reptile
13 Critical
21 "___ be back!"
22 Like many items
  listed on eBay
26 Put on a show
27 Theater district
28 One taking potshots
29 Butter or mayo
30 Weave, shag or
  braids
31 Turkish "dollars"
32 Tenancy document
35 What people think
  of you, for short
36 Word with baby, bath
  or banana

37 Uptown dir. in N.Y.C.
41 Stayed with the leader
43 Computer list
46 Turn down, as a
  manuscript
48 Russian fighter jet
50 Say "O.K."
51 Circus performer
52 Official with a
  stopwatch
55 Deep cut
56 ___ a one
57 Anyone who can
  speak Klingon, e.g.
58 Go to and fro
59 "The Amazing Race"
  necessity
60 "Prince ___"
  ("Aladdin" song)
61 Buddhist state

by Dan Feyer

ACROSS

1 Scratch
4 Cries out loud
8 Football team with a blue horseshoe on its helmet
13 ___-Wan Kenobi
14 Annoying computer message
16 Nail a test
17 Stogie holder
19 Letter after eta
20 Kitchen range
21 Florida city on the Gulf
23 Singer Horne
25 "___ the Explorer" (Nickelodeon show)
26 NBC skit show since '75
27 What a TV host often reads from
30 Type
32 "The buck stops here" pres.
33 Place to hang a jacket
39 Words in an analogy
41 Thurman of Hollywood
42 Pet lovers' org.
43 Sign of alien life, some say
47 Chihuahua's bark
48 Tiny amount
49 Army do
52 HBO alternative
55 Fishing sticks
58 "I cannot tell ___"
59 Fessed up
62 Follow
65 Japanese port
66 The French Open is the only Grand Slam tournament played on this
68 "On the ___ hand . . ."
69 Completely dead, as an engine
70 "Here ___ Again" (1987 Whitesnake hit)
71 Razz
72 Projects for beavers
73 Card below a jack

DOWN

1 Footwear that may be worn with PJs
2 Somewhat
3 Verdi opera
4 Venus's sister with a tennis racket
5 "The Lord of the Rings" creature
6 Bric-a-___
7 "'Tis a pity"
8 Bit of razzing
9 Cinco + tres
10 Lecherous looks
11 Mythical giant
12 Play for time
15 Seized vehicle
18 With: Fr.
22 Clapton of rock
24 Path of a fly ball
27 Trendy
28 The Beatles' "Back in the ___"
29 Gloomy
31 Dramatic boxing results, briefly
34 "Mad Men" network
35 Soft powder
36 Astronaut's attire
37 Off-white shade
38 President whose father co-founded Yale's Skull and Bones
40 Choose (to)
44 Auto maintenance
45 One who's worshiped
46 ___ of Good Feelings
50 Chooses for office
51 Excessive lover of the grape
52 Get a move on
53 Waste maker, in a proverb
54 Midwest city whose name is a poker variety
56 All 52 cards
57 Leafy course
60 Just manages, with "out"
61 California's ___ Valley
63 Longing
64 School on the Thames
67 "Dee-lish!"

by Ian C. Livengood

ACROSS

1 Convenience for working travelers
7 The latest
11 Tire holder
14 Dog that merits "Good boy!"
15 Score all over
16 Hoppy brew
17 Tumblers
19 Coal holder
20 Perry of "Beverly Hills 90210"
21 Flu symptom
22 Execs' degs.
23 /, to a bowler
25 Beethoven's Third
27 Frank's wife before Mia
30 N.F.L. ball carriers
31 Result of pushing too hard?
32 Tumblers
37 PC whizzes
38 Miler Sebastian
39 Crinkly sole material
41 Tumblers
44 "Would ___ to you?"
45 Bailed-out insurance co.
46 Scores for 30-Across
47 Money spent
49 Stomach problem
51 Mice, to owls
52 Marie with two Nobels
54 "Woe is me!"
58 First of three X's or O's
59 Tumblers
61 "Dig in!"
62 ___ of Man
63 Garlicky shrimp dish
64 Nonfielding A.L. players
65 Rare airline offering, nowadays
66 Repeated

DOWN

1 Lounge around
2 "___ Ben Adhem"
3 Hunt-and-___ (typing method)
4 Little squirts
5 U.K. wordsmith's ref.
6 Quick-to-erect homes
7 Born yesterday, so to speak
8 "Behold," to Caesar
9 Cabbie's query
10 The "S" in CBS: Abbr.
11 Old-fashioned pregnancy check
12 Hipbone-related
13 Good problem solvers, as a group
18 Big name in Italian fashion
22 Wisdom teeth, e.g.
24 Otto von Bismarck's realm
26 Protective part of a trunk
27 Play a role
28 Penthouse perk
29 Ones making plans
33 Unfriendly, as a greeting
34 Playfully shy
35 King's trappings
36 Went flat-out
40 Problem for lispers
42 Jingly pocket item
43 Requirement to hunt or drive
47 Made a choice
48 Dickens's ___ Heep
49 "Family Matters" dweeb
50 Big Indian
53 The Bruins' sch.
55 Long wheels
56 Mont Blanc, par exemple
57 Lost traction
59 Huck's raftmate
60 700, to Caesar

by Ed Sessa

ACROSS

1 Fateful day for Caesar
5 All-night dance party
9 Laboratory maze runners
13 Scrabble draw
14 Completely confused
16 The "E" in Q.E.D.
17 Stratford-upon-___
18 Manicurists treat them
19 Sluggish from sedatives
20 Catch Groucho while fishing?
22 Blues player's instrument?
24 18-wheeler
25 Chaotic battles
26 French farewell
28 Falafel holders
29 Cereal that doesn't really taste like anything?
31 Period of duty
35 1930s—'40s prez
36 Beyond repair
38 Expected to arrive
39 Islamic decree
42 Wildcat that can't sit still?
45 Dances to Hawaiian music
47 Astronaut Armstrong and others
48 Burning emergency signals
50 New ___ (35-Across's program)
51 Levy paid by white-collar workers?
52 Formal wear for one's belly?
56 Cupid, to the Greeks
57 What an electric meter indicates
59 Corn bread
60 "99 Luftballons" singer
61 Fabric that's glossy on one side
62 Feudin' with, say
63 June 6, 1944
64 Left the scene
65 Numbers to be crunched

DOWN

1 Type used for emphasis: Abbr.
2 Hard-to-please celeb
3 North Carolina university
4 Submits, as a manuscript
5 Rampaged
6 Creator of the game Missile Command
7 Engine type pioneered by the Buick Special
8 Snakelike fish
9 Most sunburned
10 Got out of bed
11 Spanish finger food
12 River of Hades
15 Plus column entry
21 Easily cowed
23 "Regrettably . . ."
25 Scramble
26 Alan who played Hawkeye
27 Object thrown in a pub
28 17th-century diarist Samuel
29 Teen girl's close chum, for short
30 Laugh track sounds
32 Pastoral poem
33 Convent residents
34 Common cowboy nickname
37 Slumlord's building
40 "How about it?"
41 Otherworldly glow
43 500 sheets of paper
44 Large leaf on which a frog may repose
46 Upscale marquee owned by Toyota
48 Dismissed from "The Apprentice"
49 Helmsley known as the Queen of Mean
50 Began eating
51 Look after, as a bar
52 London art gallery
53 "Animal House" party costume
54 Peck, pint or pound
55 Leather-wearing TV princess
58 Lumberjack's tool

by Patrick Berry

ACROSS

1 ___ the Hutt ("Return of the Jedi" villain)
6 Stuff to wear
10 Not of the clergy
14 Take a weapon from
15 Flu symptom
16 "The King and I" governess
17 Starch: a cross between ___?
20 "___ the season . . ."
21 Oscar winner for "Moonstruck"
22 Swinger who loves Jane
23 Underwire garment
24 Pre-euro Italian currency
25 Pimple: a cross between ___?
31 Sad poem
32 Pinnacle
33 Call at first base, maybe
36 Messenger ___
37 What Visine is dispensed in
38 Sunbeam
39 Apple Store offerings
41 Concerning
42 "Love Lockdown" singer West
44 Hisses: a cross between ___?
47 Word before "Boy," "Love" and "Come Back" in titles to #1 songs
48 Construction project in Genesis
49 Classic Chevy model
52 Leatherworking tools
54 No. on a college transcript
57 Beetles: a cross between ___?
60 Isaac's eldest
61 Rural road sign
62 Like helium
63 Deck hands
64 Cashless transaction
65 Seen-it-all feeling

DOWN

1 Merely
2 Not a fan of
3 Sounds in "Old MacDonald Had a Farm"
4 Reaction to a cold snap
5 "Take a hike!"
6 "Let's Get It On" singer
7 Petri dish gel
8 Choose flight instead of fight
9 Parents set them for kids
10 Prizes in early Olympics
11 1998 animated film loosely based on "Brave New World"
12 Machu Picchu resident
13 "Come Fly With Me" lyricist Sammy
18 Title that's a homophone of 13-Down
19 Instrument on Ireland's coat of arms
23 Panhandle
24 Walked with one foot asleep, say
25 Salon treatment
26 Forearm bone
27 Get through to
28 Charles ___, hero of "A Tale of Two Cities"
29 Contempt
30 Makes at work
34 Dunaway of "Chinatown"
35 They may be lazy or wandering
37 Breaks up
40 Outbacks and Foresters
42 Alley seen on TV
43 Pump
45 Festive occasion
46 Malevolent Hindu goddess
49 "That doesn't surprise me!"
50 Mountain with a flat top
51 Distinctively shaped fruit
52 On the ocean
53 Les Nessman's station in a 1978–82 sitcom
54 Isolated valley
55 Home of former U.N. Secretary General Javier Pérez de Cuéllar
56 Italian wine region
58 Mountain ___
59 Spike TV, once

by Patrick Berry

ACROSS

1 Elba or Capri
5 Pleasant, weatherwise
10 Measure of sugar: Abbr.
14 Reduction of sugar intake, e.g.
15 Trojan War epic
16 Pro ___ (proportionately)
17 Where sad trash collectors get together?
19 Savings options for the golden yrs.
20 Stadium area
21 Cow sound
22 Mends, as socks
23 The "P" of PT boat
25 Put to good effect
27 Rock's ___ Rose
28 Where future motorists get together?
31 Architect I. M. ___
32 Fencer's sword
33 End of a student's e-mail address
34 Living off the land?
36 Smidgen
38 Org. for a Big Apple cop
42 Sir ___ McKellen
45 Snap up
48 Rousing cry at a ring
49 Where elderly picnickers get together?
53 Hair spiffer-upper
54 Holey brewing gadget
55 Spa treatment that might include two cucumber slices
57 Group of eight
58 Cries of surprise
61 Arrests
62 Soul singer Redding
63 Where stranded canoeists get together?

66 Lacking company
67 "I feel the same"
68 Gentleman's partner
69 Basic work units
70 Colorado skiing town
71 Yankee superslugger, to fans

DOWN

1 Coup leader ___ Amin
2 Extra costs of smoking and drinking
3 "Just forget about this"
4 Once-popular anesthetic
5 Offer on eBay
6 Grad
7 Chauffeur-driven auto
8 Plan, as an itinerary
9 Fabric amts.

10 Preliminary test
11 Hispanic neighborhood
12 One of four for "The Star-Spangled Banner"
13 Got a D or better
18 Wash away, as soil
22 Conked out
23 Elderly Smurf
24 Cut (off)
26 French tea
29 Spider's creation
30 Whinny
35 Sites for military flights
37 Prefix with athlete
39 Boo Boo's buddy in Jellystone Park
40 "Go right ahead"
41 Texas computer giant started in a dorm room

43 Not much
44 Stanley Cup org.
46 Furry extraterrestrial in a 1980s sitcom
47 Mel with "1,000 voices"
49 Actor Peter of "Becket"
50 Course taken by a plane or missile
51 Dining
52 Gets hitched in haste
56 Former French president Nicolas Sarkozy's wife
59 URL starter
60 Pump or loafer
63 "Kill Bill" co-star Thurman
64 Seemingly forever
65 Elizabethan dramatist Thomas

by Lynn Lempel

ACROSS

1 Nurses at the bar
5 "Pipe down!"
9 Derive logically
14 Bad child's stocking filler
15 Indiana/Kentucky border river
16 Sound from a stable
17 Kendrick of "Up in the Air"
18 ___ contendere
19 North Dakota city
20 Time in the title of a 1965 Wilson Pickett hit
23 Skedaddles
24 Trial fig.
25 Doo-woppers ___ Na Na
28 TV oilman-turned-private eye
33 Doll's cry
37 Aussie bounder
38 Friars Club event
39 Multiple-dwelling buildings
43 Chop finely
44 Light bulb inventor's inits.
45 Light carriage
46 Droopy-eared dog
50 Small bill
51 ___-wolf
52 Perform better than
57 Question that follows "O Brother" in film . . . and a hint to this puzzle's theme
61 Grotto isle of Italy
64 Grotto color at 61-Across
65 Java servers
66 Say "#%@!"
67 Calls upon
68 20–0 baseball score, say
69 Ill-suited
70 "___ we forget . . ."
71 Keeps after taxes

DOWN

1 Con jobs
2 Greek column style
3 Bamboo-munching critter
4 Way of looking at things
5 ___ Kong
6 "We're in trouble!"
7 Delta deposit
8 Commotion
9 Yet to happen, at law
10 In the vicinity
11 Douglas ___
12 Cadbury confection
13 Letter before sigma
21 Suffix in poli sci
22 Ear-related prefix
25 Squirrel away
26 Minor prophet of the Old Testament
27 Prone to fidgeting
29 Prepare for combat
30 Tip of a boot
31 Scout's rider of early TV
32 ___-chef (kitchen's number two)
33 Cuban musical form
34 Bee-related
35 Parson's home
36 Circle segments
40 Vacation souvenir wear
41 Letter after sigma
42 Old biddy
47 Everyday article
48 Like some teas
49 Part of a pointillist painting
53 Driver's one-eighty
54 Severe pang
55 Glazed or powdered item
56 Gives the boot
57 Cylindrical sandwich
58 Threat-ending word
59 Razor-billed birds
60 Take five
61 CBS drama with DNA testing
62 Bristle on barley
63 Split ___

by C. W. Stewart

ACROSS

1 "Now!," in a memo
5 Prefix with morphosis
9 Knight's protection
14 Colorado skiing mecca
15 Man from Oman, e.g.
16 Jeweler's magnifying tool
17 Simultaneously
19 Beatnik's "Gotcha"
20 "Damn!," e.g.
21 Minnesota's capital
22 Like many itchy mutts
26 Oscar : film :: ___ : TV
27 "Get ___ here!" ("Scram!")
28 Get guns again
30 Yellow, as a banana
31 Art of "The Honeymooners"
34 Star pitcher
37 Likely reaction to fried ants
38 Creature who might disagree with the saying at the ends of 17-, 22-, 48- and 56-Across
39 Opposite of mult.
40 "O Sole ___"
41 Perjury and piracy, for two
42 Vena ___ (passage to the heart)
43 Author Ephron and others
45 Not liquid or gaseous
46 Honey makers
48 Be deliberative
52 Moral standards
54 Bar mitzvah scroll
55 "Now!," in Nicaragua
56 Not wanting to be shot?
60 Send, as payment
61 Paradigm of happiness

62 Final Four org.
63 Gown
64 ___ Ranger
65 Airhead

DOWN

1 Actress Gardner
2 "I've got a mule, and her name is ___"
3 Be under the weather
4 Throw a bone to
5 Indigenous New Zealanders
6 Young's partner in accounting
7 "Be silent," musically
8 Honest ___ (presidential moniker)
9 Came down to earth
10 TV's "___ Room"

11 "It's hard to be humble when you're as great as I am" speaker
12 Drug from poppies
13 Answer
18 Oom-pah-pah instrument
21 Derisive looks
22 Discussion site
23 One of the Mario Brothers
24 Classic 1982 movie line spoken with an outstretched finger
25 Bert's pal on "Sesame Street"
29 Affirmative vote
31 Gem units
32 Like the witness in "Witness"
33 Meas. of engine speed

35 Honda model with a palindromic name
36 Circumvent
38 Passé TV hookup
42 Ranch worker
44 Egyptian god of the underworld
45 Proxima Centauri, for one
46 Feature of Dumbledore or Merlin
47 Old-time anesthetic
49 Author Calvino
50 "___ is an island . . ."
51 Krispy ___ doughnuts
53 Meowers
56 250, in old Rome
57 Chem., for one
58 Fedora or fez
59 Big name in Bosox history

by Jeff Chen

ACROSS

1 Course in the biology dept.
5 Prize won by Obama and Carter
10 Pickle containers
14 Rogen of "Knocked Up"
15 Strong adhesive
16 Black cloud or black cat, to some
17 Do-it-yourselfer's activity
19 Spanish sparkling wine
20 Came next
21 Compares (to)
23 With 51-Across, nitpick . . . or a hint to 17-, 37- and 60-Across
25 Affirmatives
26 Turns down
29 Last word of "For He's a Jolly Good Fellow"
31 Altogether it's worth the most bonus troops in Risk
32 Giraffe's cousin
34 Snowmobile part
37 New York singing group that last performed in 2007
41 It's "the word"
42 Ability
43 Digital camera mode
44 Reminder of an old wound
45 Tot's enclosure
48 Suffix with Kafka or Zola
51 See 23-Across
52 Come together
55 Preparing to drive, with "up"
59 Half-pint
60 Forum cheer
62 Govt. meat-stamping org.
63 What "O" stands for in the magazine business
64 Knock for a loop
65 Son of John and Yoko
66 "GoodFellas" Oscar winner Joe
67 Gulp from a flask

DOWN

1 ___ Stadium (Big Apple tennis locale)
2 Vegas gas
3 Dinero dispensers
4 Bar habitué's order, maybe
5 Replaceable part of a phonograph
6 Antonym: Abbr.
7 Blowhard's claim
8 Interstate sign
9 Vega's constellation
10 Big name in underwear
11 Pile up
12 Show with skits
13 Alternatives to buttons
18 Contract negotiators, for short
22 Critic of the selfless
24 Weathercaster's pressure line
26 Chicago mayor Emanuel
27 Jacob's twin
28 Unwilling to budge
29 Place for a facial
30 Short albums, for short
33 "___-Tiki"
34 With 57-Down, memorable "Seinfeld" character, with "the"
35 Charlie Brown toy that's often "eaten" by a tree
36 Steel component
38 Show host
39 ___ culpa
40 TV's Clampetts, e.g.
44 Mideast bigwig
46 Nutlike Chinese fruit
47 Two-dimensional measure
48 Hosiery shades
49 Drunk
50 Post-lecture session, informally
51 Ones named in a will
53 Woodworking or metalworking class
54 Superman costume part
56 "Vidi," translated
57 See 34-Down
58 Pitcher Maddux with four Cy Young Awards
61 Fond du ___, Wis.

by Kristian House

ACROSS

1 Healthful retreats
5 Suitcases
9 Minor quarrel
13 Result of four balls, in baseball
14 Ear-related
15 Nothin'
16 "A Death in the Family" author
17 1964 Beatles hit
19 Part of school that includes push-ups and situps
21 Hive dweller
22 Alternative rock genre
23 Showman associated with the quote "There's a sucker born every minute"
28 Religious observance
30 Illustrator Edward
31 WSW's opposite
32 Determined to do
33 Ski lift
34 Somewhat
35 Family groups
36 Gangster's gun
37 "Et tu, ___?"
38 Is bedridden, say
39 Sumptuous
40 More fit
41 Hawaiian souvenir
42 Any of the Seven Dwarfs, by profession
43 Constricting snakes
44 Chinese restaurant chain
46 "___ the ramparts . . ."
47 Superannuated
48 Acidity or alkalinity
52 Rating of "Avatar"
57 Neat
58 Hawaiian island
59 Expenditures
60 Consumer
61 Collector's ___
62 Seven things for a sailor
63 Stable locks?

DOWN

1 Exchange
2 Call on an intercom, as a doctor
3 Baldwin who has hosted "S.N.L." more times than anyone else
4 Some Halloween costumes
5 Kiss
6 "Exodus" hero
7 Rodeo female
8 Drool
9 Expression that includes a lip curl
10 Salary
11 Brouhaha
12 Sigma's follower
14 Lhasa ___ (dog)
18 Calf's meat
20 Prayer enders
23 U.S. mail holders
24 Merchant
25 Part of a galaxy
26 Brings together
27 Something that's fed along a street
28 What the Red Cross provides
29 *Like this clue*
30 Like tennis rackets and harps
32 Where dandruff accumulates
34 Place where trees are studied
37 Tower of ___
39 Retired hockey great Eric
42 West African land
45 Dull
46 Cry of panic
48 Things to hang hats on
49 MasterCard competitor
50 Place of bliss
51 Bard's instrument
52 Hawaiian dish
53 Gangster's gun
54 Article seen in many places
55 Election day: Abbr.
56 Pilot's approximation, for short

by David Steinberg

ACROSS

1 "Mamma Mia" singers
5 Sheath of connective tissue
11 Buddy, for short
14 Object of pity for Mr. T
15 Parthenon goddess
16 Sock-in-the-gut reaction
17 1960 Jerry Lewis fairy tale spoof
19 UV ray-blocking stat
20 Once known as
21 Stephen of "Still Crazy"
22 Suit to ___
23 Reality show featuring Whitney Houston and her then-husband
28 Help pull off a crime
29 $5 bills, slangily
30 Radius neighbors
31 Judge's wear
32 Poppycock
33 "Ciao for now!"
34 NBC show with skits, in brief
35 Part of a bray
36 Mrs. Gorbachev
37 Eurasian range
39 M.D. concerned with tonsils
40 Backyard pond fish
43 Great Chicago Fire scapegoat Mrs. ___
45 "Just as I suspected!"
46 "Hor." neighbor, on old TVs
47 Second offer, as on eBay
48 Flair
49 Poems of praise
50 Healthy delivery, perhaps
53 Some QB turnovers: Abbr.
54 Rap's Dr. ___
55 Norma ___ (Sally Field role)

56 Up to, in ads
57 Bowl over
62 Suffix with ethyl
63 Got back, as hair by a Rogaine user
64 Nephew of Abel
65 ___ Bingle (Crosby)
66 Think creatively
67 Invitation letters

DOWN

1 N.Y. Jets' org.
2 Avril Lavigne's "Sk8er ___"
3 Rhett and Scarlett's child
4 Firm, as pasta
5 A way off
6 Antismuggling org.
7 Cold dessert
8 People profiled in People
9 Furniture decoration

10 Small battery
11 Dish often served with franks
12 Suspended ore conveyor, e.g.
13 Side with the ball
18 Brain wave monitor, briefly
22 Van Gogh's "Sunflowers" setting
23 Granola servings
24 Black, in poetry
25 With no room to spare
26 High-pitched double-reeds
27 Salesman's exhortation
33 Daiquiri fruit
35 Corporate head?
36 Post-op program
38 Claude of "Casablanca"

41 Cookie with creme in the middle
42 ___-bitsy
43 Traveled like Sputnik
44 Like Simba or Nala
45 "Solve for x" subject
46 First spacecraft to reach Uranus and Neptune
48 Cause to see red
51 Sat
52 Comment during a cold snap
57 Popular party day: Abbr.
58 Vegas action
59 Meadow mother
60 Part of U.S.S.R.: Abbr.
61 Recipe amt.

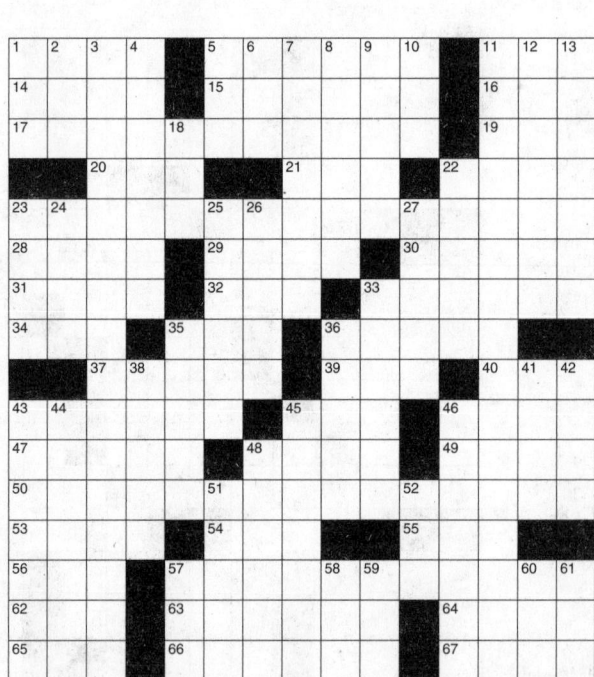

by Scott Atkinson

ACROSS

1 Sailing
5 "Remember the ___!" (Texan's cry)
10 "___ and Circumstance"
14 Mideast royal name
15 "She loves me, she loves me not . . ." flower part
16 Memento of an old wound
17 Acquire sudden riches
19 Capture
20 Boxing venue
21 Alter, as the Constitution
23 Slowing, in music: Abbr.
24 Talk, talk and talk some more
25 Groove
27 Tincture of ___
29 Help out a panhandler
33 Suffix with ethyl
34 Make peeved
35 Central street name
36 Big stingers
39 Cheer for a toreador
40 Bridge positions
41 Capital of Samoa
42 Charged particle
43 Greyhound, e.g.
44 What multiple winners of a lottery must do
50 Equipment next to swings and seesaws
51 Popeye's Olive ___
52 ___ out a living
53 Old nuclear regulatory org.
54 Bigwig
57 Florida key, e.g.
59 Portable product for music lovers
61 Absolutely amazed
63 Queue
64 Black-and-white cookies
65 Classic name for a French poodle
66 Observes
67 Busybody
68 One-spot cards

DOWN

1 Tests, as ore
2 Minor despot
3 "I've got it!"
4 Deuce follower, in tennis
5 Human's hairy cousin
6 Smooth, in music
7 Proton's place
8 Y chromosome carrier
9 Satan
10 Winter clock setting in L.A.
11 Flutelike instruments
12 Achieving success
13 Fifth and sixth graders, typically
18 Actresses Allen and Black
22 Cry from Homer Simpson
26 Apply
28 Table linen fabric
30 Made good on, as a loan
31 "Winnie-the-Pooh" writer
32 Before, poetically
36 Christmas drinks
37 Symbol of Americanism
38 Polymeric compound in breast implants
39 "How exciting!"
40 The Father of Geometry
42 Birth announcement for babies with blue caps
43 Chesapeake ___
45 X
46 Odds and ends for sale
47 Relating to the lower part of the upper body
48 Michael of "Caddyshack"
49 Popular computer game with geometric shapes
55 Make yawn
56 Actor Wilson
58 Davenport
60 ___ Moines, Iowa
62 That: Sp.

by Mark Feldman

ACROSS

1 Elia ___, "East of Eden" director
6 ___ Romana
9 100
14 Bayer anti-inflammatory
15 Ginger ___
16 Sports car extras
17 Like a boxer before a fight
18 *Former 'N Sync member
20 ___ de France
21 Olivia's love in "Twelfth Night"
22 Ice cream specification
24 Stuck
28 S-shaped molding
29 It might be examined with a loupe
31 Macaroni's form
32 Li'l ___ (comics guy)
34 Pennsylvania port
35 ___ gin fizz
36 Limit, as a salary
37 *Bygone Hollywood star known for tough-guy roles
40 Where many Apr. checks are sent
41 L.A. gangster
43 Malarial fever
44 Spout forth
46 Assume
47 Vietnam War's ___ offensive
48 Follower of Don or San
49 "MADtv" bit
51 English novelist Nick who wrote "About a Boy"
53 Not wake until noon, say
56 Group that rushes
58 What the answers to the four starred clues are?
61 Chariot race locale
62 ___ spades
63 Size between sm. and lg.
64 ___ list
65 Do the devil's work?
66 Will Smith title role
67 They follow quarters

DOWN

1 Child's racing vehicle
2 Cold
3 *Explorer of the Rockies
4 C-rated
5 Flanders of "The Simpsons"
6 More ghostlike
7 "Sadly . . ."
8 TV heroine in a leather skirt
9 Dined at home
10 Small craft of W.W. II
11 Mauna ___
12 Increases
13 Frying-butter sound
19 "The Charge of the Light Brigade" war zone
21 Country music's David Allan ___
23 ___ Cruz (name on old Mexican maps)
25 *Classical guitarist with four Grammys
26 Stop in midstream
27 Ed in Reagan's cabinet
29 Tile-setter's bucketful
30 Land west of England
32 Bank holdings: Abbr.
33 Sharon's predecessor as Israeli P.M.
34 Helpful kind of piece for a jigsaw puzzle doer
38 Barber's supply
39 "___ Song" (Elton John hit)
42 Lab supply source?
45 Roamed without restriction
48 Lil ___ (rapper who popularized crunk)
50 Like some chins
51 Official language of India
52 One-named New Age musician
54 Mrs. 55-Down on "The Avengers"
55 See 54-Down
57 Itar-___ news agency
58 Budget add-ons
59 "Rocks"
60 Religious sch.
61 Commercials

by Gareth Bain

ACROSS

1 With 10- and 65-Across, 1971 hit by the Who
7 Bit of acne, slangily
10 See 1-Across
14 Slowly, on a musical score
15 Pitching whiz
16 Hollywood's Howard and Perlman
17 Haters
18 Teachers' org.
19 "Take ___ from me!"
20 SAT org.
21 Pennsylvania ___ (White House locale: Abbr.)
23 Older woman's plaything, in slang
25 ___ palm
27 Turns at high speed
28 1967 hit by Van Morrison
32 Broadcast again
33 Peaks for yodelers
34 Where London is: Abbr.
37 Ridiculous
38 Guy's date
39 Sleep problem
41 Boatload
42 Funnywoman Rudner
43 Stratum
44 1970 hit by Sugarloaf
48 Floor cover that doesn't reach the walls
50 Greek H's
51 Who said "The joke's on you, Riddler!"
52 ___ diavolo (spicy sauce)
53 Legal profession
56 Snobs put them on
57 "I would say . . . ," text messages
59 Chicago university
62 Old dagger
63 ___-Mex
64 Part of the conspiracy
65 See 1-Across
66 Cathedral town near Cambridge
67 Where to find the songs in this grid . . . or an appropriate title for this puzzle?

DOWN

1 Jesus in the manger, e.g.
2 Change, as text
3 Crones
4 "Can ___ now?"
5 Annual coll. hoops contest
6 Medicine amount
7 Western writer Grey
8 Winter sculpture medium
9 Packets from Twinings of London, e.g.
10 Donkey, often
11 Actress married to Kurt Weill
12 The "U" of U.S.S.R.
13 TV sports awards
22 Taking a long trip at sea
24 ". . . ___ quit!"
25 Pond swimmer
26 One of two wives of Henry VIII
27 Phonograph successor
28 London native, informally
29 Gambling mecca
30 Part of a Florida orchard
31 Delight
35 Scholarship basis
36 Indiana city on Lake Michigan
39 "M*A*S*H" star
40 Buddies
42 What the Beatles never did
45 One of 11 Egyptian pharaohs
46 Historical stretch
47 Latin list ender
48 Humiliate
49 Puddle-producing
52 Clever
53 Capital of West Germany
54 "I cannot tell ___"
55 "Darn!"
58 Funnyman Brooks
60 Province next to Que.
61 Whom Uncle Sam wants

by Peter A. Collins

50 EASY

ACROSS

1 Some jazz
4 Opposite of alta
8 Involuntary jerks
14 Singer with a negative-sounding name
15 Bunches
16 Been-there-done-that
17 Shout upon reaching a destination
19 Fix
20 Foot of verse
21 Salon sound
23 Give a hand
24 Vote in
26 "Wouldn't that be nice"
30 Exact look-alike
32 Backs up another time, as computer data
33 Kind of duty or center
35 Basketball's Alcindor
36 Line to Penn Sta.
37 Sandwich shop staple, in brief
38 Intro to many an adage
41 "Don't gimme no ___!"
42 Fayetteville campus, briefly
44 Suffix with brom-
45 "Duck, duck" follower
47 Taking potshots (at)
49 "The King and I" actress
50 1998 Spike Lee joint
52 When doubled, displaying affection, informally
56 Trojan's sch.
57 South African money
59 "Can't help ya!"
60 Popular daytime talk show, once
63 "Well, look who's back!"
65 Powered
66 Follow
67 Election Day no.
68 Size up
69 Baby naming, e.g.
70 "___, though I walk . . ."

DOWN

1 David who sang "Let's Dance"
2 Either "Paper Moon" co-star
3 French apple
4 Scolding word to a dog
5 Drinks for Chaucer's Miller
6 Add one's voice to others
7 Dusty room, often
8 Frat. counterpart
9 Files a complaint, say
10 Four- or five-star officer
11 Wicked women
12 Foaming at the mouth
13 Pig's place
18 "Dancing With the Stars" airer
22 Whittles (down)
25 Knucklehead
27 Like Enya's music
28 Where eagles dare?
29 Sticker inits.
31 Ancient Chinese divination book
33 Exact look-alike
34 "Just my luck"
35 Caustic substance
37 Outback
39 "J. ___," 2011 film
40 Part of N.Y.S.E.
43 One of 12 in the New Testament
46 Circular gasket
48 Yens
49 Obi-Wan ___
51 One called "hizzoner"
53 Covered with suds
54 Flavor enhancer
55 Dirt spreader
58 Piece played by a pair
60 Painter's deg.
61 Switz. neighbor
62 Side jobs for actors
64 Agreement with the captain

by Victor Fleming

ACROSS

1 Move like water
5 Apple computer
9 Attacked, as a challenge
14 "What ___ do to deserve this?"
15 ___ Lee cakes
16 Fatter than fat
17 "Famous" cookie name
18 Put ___ act
19 Piece of microfilm
20 Notorious 1920s–'30s bank robber
23 Sticky stuff
24 Terse note from the boss
25 Walk clumsily
29 Prepared to give a "Jeopardy!" response
33 America Ferrera's Emmy-winning role
36 Brain surgeon's prefix
37 Big Band ___ (1930s–'40s)
38 Almost straight up and down, as a cliff
40 Fugitive's flight
41 Big rigs
44 Hardly a beauty queen
47 Naval workers
49 ___ fizz (cocktail)
50 Fast train to New York City
53 The Beatles "___ Loves You"
54 1940s–'50s wrestler with golden locks
60 Shun
61 Much-kicked body part
62 Middle of the eye
64 Attend homecoming, say
65 Bell sound
66 Crime solver Wolfe of fiction
67 Lhasa apso or Labrador
68 Sophomore or junior
69 Dancer Verdon

DOWN

1 Rx watchdog org.
2 Like Dali's watches
3 Fragrance
4 Smart aleck
5 Springfield's minor-league team on "The Simpsons"
6 Lots of
7 Bedouins, e.g.
8 Birchbark boat
9 Dustin of "Rain Man"
10 Kansas town on the Chisholm Trail
11 Art ___
12 Like fireplace grates
13 Nettled, with "off"
21 ___ of the Unknowns
22 "Aw, quit ___ bellyachin'!"
25 Twenty questions attempt
26 Shake on it
27 Andes animal
28 URL starter
30 Solzhenitsyn's "The ___ Archipelago"
31 Tehran native
32 All-female group's policy
34 Business card abbr.
35 Approving votes
39 Light-colored beer or the glass it comes in
42 John Lennon song with the refrain "You may say I'm a dreamer . . ."
43 Left the Union
45 N.Y.C. area near the Village
46 Making catcalls
48 Recent: Prefix
51 Hot-blooded
52 ". . . old woman who lived in ___"
54 Apparel
55 Above
56 Don Juan type
57 Actress Lollobrigida
58 Got longer, like Pinocchio's nose
59 The Emerald Isle
63 Charlie Sheen, to Martin

by Andrea Carla Michaels

ACROSS

1 LPs and 45s
6 Cools, as drinks
10 Traffic components
14 With 5-Down, where "Quiet!" is often yelled
15 "Not guilty," e.g.
16 Eye part
17 Like some stickers
20 Spicy cuisine
21 Sweetie
22 Make fun of
23 Enemy of Spider-Man
27 Identify in a Facebook photo
29 Source of stress for a coll. senior
30 Where shingles go
31 Mea ___
33 Pants part
34 Cutlass or Delta 88
38 Navigation aid for Hansel and Gretel
42 Tale
43 Thumbs-up vote
44 Card game of Spanish origin
45 Almanac contents
47 Not Rep. or Ind.
49 Wood in archery bows
50 Degrees of separation in a Hollywood parlor game
53 Building made of bricks
55 Branch
56 Branch
59 1976 ABBA song . . . or a hint to the starts of 17-, 23-, 38- and 50-Across
63 Prime draft status
64 Possesses
65 Probably will, after "is"
66 Deborah of "The King and I"
67 Bygone Tunisian V.I.P.'s
68 "Get clean" program

DOWN

1 "O mighty Caesar! ___ thou lie so low?": Shak.
2 Move slowly
3 One finishing a marathon in eight hours, say
4 Leader of a meeting
5 See 14-Across
6 "There's an app for that" device
7 Trolley sound
8 Day's end, to a poet
9 Downcast
10 Writing with wedges and such
11 Birdlike
12 Ones dressed in stripes, for short
13 Secure
18 Often-impersonated diva
19 Normandy battle site
24 "Gosh almighty!"
25 Utah city
26 Crash and burn
27 Franchise offering "soft serve" and "hand scooped"
28 Subtle glow
32 Chinese zoo attraction
33 Color
35 Feature of the ancient palace of Minos at Knossos
36 Urgent
37 Large amount
39 Ancient Roman censor
40 Actress Meg
41 Tut's resting place
46 ___-deucy (backgammon variety)
47 Compulsion by threat
48 TV award
50 Screwup
51 Mrs. Doubtfire, e.g.
52 Run to Las Vegas, perhaps
53 Crazedly
54 Finished
57 Self-referential, in modern lingo
58 Like many restaurants without a liquor lic.
60 Like some '60s fashion
61 Run a tab
62 Disfigure

by Aimee Lucido

ACROSS

1 Triangular sail
4 Mrs. Eisenhower
9 Shopping centers
14 Shipping magnate Onassis
15 Change, as the Constitution
16 Get a move on
17 Candy that comes in a dispenser
18 "Ramblin' Rose" singer, 1962
20 "___ of robins in her hair"
22 Founder of the Persian Empire
23 Earnings after expenses
27 Song word repeated after "Que"
30 Features of Venice
31 Counter, as an argument
32 Designer Schiaparelli
35 Night school subj.
36 Ultimate thing
37 Beatles hairdo
38 Knuckleheads
40 Shepherd's locale
41 Kind of gown or shower
43 Response to a doctor's request, perhaps
44 Barristers' degs.
45 Sea eagles
46 Galoot
48 Unable to hear
49 "Fuhgeddaboudit!"
53 Material for a doctor's glove
55 Pago Pago whereabouts
56 Christmastime productions
61 Commercials
62 Philosopher who wrote the "Republic"
63 Girl's name meaning "loved"

64 Maiden name preceder
65 Move in a greenhouse, say
66 Midnight visits to the refrigerator
67 "You've got mail" co.

DOWN

1 Land of the Rising Sun
2 "Goodnight, ___" (#1 hit of 1950)
3 "Carmen" composer
4 "Om," e.g.
5 Doctors' org.
6 Encountered
7 Squid's defense
8 Despots' decrees
9 Roman Cath. title
10 Charged with a crime
11 It's up for grabs on a court
12 Online "ha-ha"
13 Sault ___ Marie
19 Albany is its capital: Abbr.
21 Pet adoption agcy.
24 TV newsman Roger
25 Quick
26 Sarcastic "Go ahead, keep talking"
28 Governed
29 Rand McNally product
31 E.R. personnel
32 Surround firmly
33 Peter of "Casablanca"
34 Mock rock band in a 1984 film
36 One of filmdom's Coen brothers
38 "Illmatic" rapper
39 "Othello" villain
42 In reality
44 Mother of Castor and Pollux

46 Part of a freight train
47 Get-out-of-class slips
49 Teachers' union, in brief
50 Big kitchen appliance maker
51 Cowboys' jamboree
52 Artist's stand
54 Gait between walk and canter
56 "All Things Considered" airer
57 Suffix with glob
58 Sportage maker
59 U.K. record label
60 Crimson

by Kenneth J. Berniker

ACROSS

1 1862 battle site
7 'Fros, e.g.
10 The "A" in SEATO
14 Fruit named after a town in Turkey
15 Menace in "Raiders of the Lost Ark"
16 Holders of some dry bouquets
17 Valuable discoveries
18 Be healthy, like a type of meal?
20 Disappear, like a moving vehicle?
21 Who said "You are alone now. Last man. You are lone ranger"
22 Burn on the outside
24 Obtrusively bright, like a needlefish?
28 "Gödel, Escher, ___" (Douglas Hofstadter book)
31 Raunchy
34 Familiar femme
35 "The Star-Spangled Banner" land
36 Magna ___
37 Colorado resort
38 Cosmonaut's destination, once
39 Love, like a popular singer?
41 Annapolis inits.
42 Actress Sarah of "Parenthood"
44 Steal
45 Hwy.
46 Golden ___
47 Most common blood designation
48 Phobia
49 Touch up, like a candidate for office?
51 ___ al-Fayed (friend of Diana)
53 Wyatt and Virgil of the Wild West
56 Hurt, like a groan-inducing joke?

60 Wave menacingly, like a red-hot iron?
63 Elevator pioneer Otis
64 ___ May, surrogate mother for Spider-Man
65 Golfer's concern
66 Bacon amount
67 Citi Field team
68 What the "turn on" part refers to in "Tune in, turn on, drop out"
69 Plan

DOWN

1 Onetime "S.N.L."-type show
2 ___-kiri
3 "The Heat ___"
4 Extravagant, like a W.C.?
5 Fat
6 Rosh ___

7 Nutty
8 Christiania, today
9 Soft and absorbent
10 Northern and southern lights
11 ___ Lankan
12 Maze accesses
13 Cigar tip
19 Actress Hagen
23 Make more refined
25 Adulterated
26 Sleep en la tarde
27 Marilu of "Taxi"
28 Unjustified accusation
29 Italian cheese
30 California town where Clint Eastwood was mayor
32 Unclothe
33 Followed
36 Includes in an e-mailing
37 "Feels so good!"

40 Aids for dog-walkers
43 Points in the right direction
47 Excitation
48 Do away with, like a 1950s car feature?
50 Down
52 Fond ___, Wis.
54 Pitchfork-shaped letters
55 Molt
57 "___ Dead?" (Mark Twain play)
58 A son of Noah
59 Big-eared hopper
60 Kapow!
61 Regret
62 Cupboard crawler

by Steven E. Atwood

ACROSS

1 High praise
6 Light bulb unit
10 Ring up
14 Piano practice piece
15 Geographical datum
16 Woodwind able to provide an orchestra's tuning note
17 *One who's an empty threat
19 Journal on YouTube, maybe
20 Not just any
21 "I concur!"
22 Onionlike soup ingredients
23 Luxurious
24 "Dona ___ and Her Two Husbands"
26 *Willie Mays, positionally
31 High: Fr.
33 Sp. lady
34 Turn suddenly
35 Amend
37 Hosp. parts . . . or what the answers to the six starred clues each have twice
39 Dutch painter Jan
40 Grew disenchanted
42 Visitors from beyond
44 Lip-puckering
45 *What a waiter might be holding when he says "Say when"
48 Swear
49 Lecher's look
50 Sky-blue
53 Former Houston footballer
55 Heavenly body
58 Music genre for Joan Baez
59 *Lawn-Boy or Toro product
61 Actress Hathaway of "The Princess Diaries"
62 Actor/songwriter Novello

63 Basketball venue
64 Caboose
65 Sharpies, e.g.
66 Gives for a while

DOWN

1 Retained
2 Home of the Sundance Film Festival
3 Bamboozle
4 Poem for the praiseworthy
5 Sunday morning address
6 "Don't go anywhere . . . I'll be back"
7 Jason's ship, in myth
8 Start 18 holes
9 Paving goo
10 *Enclosure with a manuscript or résumé
11 Up to the task
12 "Behold!"
13 Important parts of dancers
18 Exams
22 Major theater chain
23 *Spider-Man's alter ego
25 Fleur-de-___
26 Prankster
27 Not so well-done
28 Gloomy, in verse
29 Last word in the Lord's Prayer, before "Amen"
30 The ___ Is Too Damn High Party
31 Gate hardware
32 Skin soother
36 Christopher of "Superman"
38 Ben and Jerry
41 Rap's Dr. ___

43 Curling of the lip
46 Settled routine
47 Akin to skin?
50 Come from ___
51 The "Z" of DMZ
52 Bone paralleling the radius
54 "Victory is mine!"
55 Wilson of "Wedding Crashers"
56 Tear up
57 They give women a lift
59 Backup singer for Gladys Knight
60 Miner's pay dirt

by Gary Cee

ACROSS

1 Doctrine
6 "___ of the D'Urbervilles"
10 Bit of hair standing up
14 Targeted, with "in on"
15 Fe, on the periodic table
16 Burn soother
17 Nimble
18 Entangle
19 Fort ___ (gold repository)
20 "Go!"
23 Doctor's charge
24 Glimpsed
25 Big name in copiers
26 "Look how perfectly I performed!"
27 Vigorous
31 Aviated
34 Web address, for short
36 Wood for black piano keys, once
37 V.I.P.'s transport
38 Separate . . . or a hint to this puzzle's theme
41 Razor brand
42 Billy the Kid, for Henry McCarty
44 Bygone Russian space station
45 "Fargo" director
46 Messed up, as a message
49 Eat like a bird
51 Anglo-Saxon writing symbol
52 No. starting with an area code
53 Firms: Abbr.
56 Sherlock Holmes phrase, when on a case
60 Horse's halter?

61 Temperate
62 ___ ball soup
63 Big rabbit features
64 Salinger heroine
65 Animal that plays along streams
66 Shade of color
67 More's opposite
68 All set

DOWN

1 Grain husks
2 Scalawag
3 Author Zola
4 Farmer's place, in a children's ditty
5 Black Sea port
6 Dance in "The Rocky Horror Picture Show"
7 Cleveland's lake
8 Vile
9 Underhanded

10 Surprised and flustered
11 Bone that parallels the radius
12 Groceries
13 Moniker for a Lone Star cowboy
21 Italian city where "The Taming of the Shrew" is set
22 Sharpen, as a knife
26 Going in side-by-side pairs
28 Mr. ___, John P. Marquand detective
29 About, on a memo
30 Greenish blue
31 Old Glory, for one
32 Reader's Digest co-founder Wallace

33 Arab ruler
35 Take it on the ___ (flee)
39 Dangerous ocean currents
40 Oak and teak
43 Hit hard, as a baseball
47 Tooth cover
48 Death
50 Hullabaloo
53 Terra ___ (tile material)
54 Seeped
55 Tale
56 Southeast Asian cuisine
57 Tooter
58 Classic street liners
59 Destiny
60 Drenched

by Jill Denny and Jeff Chen

ACROSS

1 Voice above tenor
5 Cross : Christianity :: ___ : Judaism
9 Interior design
14 Cries from Homer Simpson
15 Very very
16 Going brand?
17 Number between eins and drei
18 Neeson of "Clash of the Titans"
19 Track-and-field events
20 *"Ocean's Eleven" actor
23 Follower of spy or web
24 Any Beatles song, now
25 *Tweaks
28 Enters Facebook, maybe
30 Annoys incessantly
31 Female flock member
32 N.B.A. nickname
36 Film units
37 *Small sci-fi vehicle
40 Rapper's crew
43 Director Apatow
44 Obstruction for salmon
47 Culmination of a Casey Kasem countdown
49 Book size
52 *"Get Smart" device
56 Toothpaste with "green sparkles"
57 Falsity
58 *Blastoff spot
60 Uses sleight of hand on
62 Head of Québec
63 French girlfriend
65 Aerodynamic
66 Tied, as a score
67 "Boy Meets World" boy
68 Late

69 Organize alphabetically, say
70 Chips in the pot

DOWN

1 Carpenter's curved cutter
2 Uncalled-for insult, say
3 U2 guitarist
4 Brother and husband of Isis
5 Arias, usually
6 Robin Hood or Jesse James
7 "Same here"
8 Director Polanski
9 Obama, e.g.: Abbr.
10 Performed, as one's duties
11 Purify
12 Quaker breakfast offering
13 Prescriptions, for short
21 Keanu Reeves's role in "The Matrix"
22 Middling grade
24 Chilean cheer
26 Poi source
27 Aves.
29 Foreign policy grp.
33 Pilgrimage to Mecca
34 Kwik-E-Mart clerk
35 Proof ending
37 Well-regarded
38 Fall through the cracks?
39 A.S.A.P.
40 A TD is worth six: Abbr.
41 "So beauuutiful!"
42 Unwanted plot giveaway
44 "Yeah, like that'll ever happen"
45 Groveled
46 Blondie, to Alexander and Cookie
48 Rangers' org.
50 "That's awful"
51 Fleecy fiber
53 Hall's musical partner
54 ___ Laredo, Mexico
55 Go in
59 50 ___ ("Candy Shop" rapper)
60 Winter clock setting in Nev.
61 Heavens
64 Storm center . . . or, phonetically, letter that can precede the ends of the answers to the five starred clues to spell popular electronic products

by José Chardiet

ACROSS

1 Point that marks the beginning of a change
5 Rainbows, basically
9 Blunder
14 Palo ___, Calif.
15 Jacket
16 Affliction said to be caused by worry
17 One of 12 for the Alcoholics Anonymous program
18 Robust
19 More courteous
20 Special offer at an airline Web site
23 Japanese electronics brand
24 Scottish castle for British royals
29 Special offer at a supermarket
32 "___ your age!"
35 Scuba tankful
36 Midwest tribe
37 Depressed
38 Place for phys ed
39 "The Murders in the Rue Morgue" writer
41 Depressed
42 Way too weighty
44 Arrow shooter
45 Attempt
46 Special offer at a diner
50 Element with the symbol Ta
51 Rotini or rigatoni
56 Special offer at a car dealership
59 One of three people walking into a bar, in many a joke
63 Fox's "American ___"
64 Sir Geraint's wife, in Arthurian legend
65 François's farewell
66 Mission control org.
67 Prince Charles's sister

68 ___ pole (Indian emblem)
69 Campbell who sang "Rhinestone Cowboy"
70 Corrosive alkalis

DOWN

1 Groups on "Saturday Night Live"
2 The "U" of UHF
3 Writer Gertrude
4 Opium flower
5 Yearn (for)
6 What buffalo do in "Home on the Range"
7 .45, e.g., for a firearm
8 Upright, inscribed stone tablets
9 TV western that ran for 20 seasons
10 Muhammad ___, opponent of 53-Down

11 TV monitor?
12 Lawyer's charge
13 Blunder
21 Bit of real estate
22 Santa's helper
25 ". . . ___ quit!"
26 Henhouse perch
27 Egypt's Sadat
28 Like many old water pipes
30 What a farmer bales
31 Edge
32 Skyward
33 Snake that a snake charmer charms
34 Sixth-grader, usually
38 Flower also known as a cranesbill
39 Campaign pro
40 "Wise" bird
43 Put in rollers
44 Having two methods

47 "Shine a Little Love" rock grp.
48 Really angry
49 Passer of secret documents
52 "What ___!" (possible response to 20-, 29-, 46- and 56-Across)
53 ___ Liston, opponent of 10-Down
54 Bale binder
55 Much of Chile
57 Sniffer
58 Verve
59 Double-crosser
60 Hubbub
61 Chomped (on)
62 Busy one?

by Freddie Cheng

EASY 59

ACROSS

1 Tiny scissor cut
5 Sphere
10 Annoyance at a barbecue
14 Lug
15 "I'm outta here!"
16 Aachen article
17 Nice through and through . . . or not
20 Mother, in Milan
21 Pin's place
22 Charlemagne's dominion: Abbr.
23 Like some stares
25 Levy on cigarettes and booze
27 Really digs . . . or not
33 Woman who raised Cain
34 58 minutes past the hour
35 Hogwash
38 Portland, Ore., college from which Steve Jobs dropped out
40 Uses a dagger
42 33-Across's partner
43 Invite to the penthouse, say
45 Some Iroquois
47 2008 Super Bowl M.V.P. Manning
48 Most wretched . . . or not
51 One of academia's Seven Sisters
53 Many a 16-year-old Southern belle
54 Bridge expert Culbertson
55 Maryland athletes, for short
59 Shepherded, in a way
63 Speaks with brutal honesty . . . or not
66 Rock's Mötley ___
67 Club that doesn't beat much

68 "L'___ c'est moi": Louis XIV
69 Terse order to a chauffeur
70 Evaluate
71 Title girl in a 1922 hit

DOWN

1 Flower stalk
2 Exploding star
3 Couple on a gossip page
4 Learner's ___
5 Priestly attire
6 Train transportation
7 Singer James
8 Kind of tide
9 "Gunsmoke" star James
10 ___-Xer
11 Certain vigilante
12 End of ___
13 Bygone communication
18 America's Cup entry
19 "Can I give you ___?"
24 Some evergreens
26 Writer Ephron
27 Juno's counterpart
28 Connecticut and Virginia, in Monopoly: Abbr.
29 Defect
30 Monopoly purchase
31 Japanese seaport
32 Book of the Apocrypha
36 Buddies
37 Give off
39 Nicknames
41 Bit of watermelon waste
44 11th-grade exams, for short

46 Ingemar Johansson or Ingrid Bergman
49 Tater Tots maker
50 Funnyman Conan
51 Climbing legume
52 Old Oldsmobile
56 Itinerary parts: Abbr.
57 Bonus
58 "The Bicycle Thief" director Vittorio De ___
60 Bus driver on "The Simpsons"
61 Lab container
62 "Cómo ___?"
64 Stan who co-created Spider-Man
65 Lock opener

by Peter A. Collins

ACROSS

1 Aids for treasure hunters
5 Babble on
10 "Ali ___ and the 40 Thieves"
14 "The Time Machine" people
15 Environmentalist in a Dr. Seuss story
16 Muscat's country
17 "Yes, go on"
19 William ___, Hopalong Cassidy player
20 Spotted cat
21 Supers oversee them: Abbr.
23 Dove's sound
24 1969 Stevie Wonder hit
27 Harvard color
29 T on a test
30 Wedding dress material
31 Sony rival
33 Famed '50s flop
37 Eggs in labs
38 Former host of TV's "Last Comic Standing"
41 The way, in philosophy
42 "You'll love the way we fly" airline
44 Con's opposite
45 Suffix with Oktober
46 On ___ with (equal to)
49 Salad greens
51 Big name in paint
55 Meadow
56 Dark shade of blue
57 Go over again with a blue pencil
60 Eye part
62 Location in a Donizetti opera
64 Scrabble piece
65 Actress Graff
66 Florence's river
67 Lemon peel

68 These: Sp.
69 Without ice, as a drink

DOWN

1 "Take ___ your leader"
2 Baldwin of "30 Rock"
3 Tending to cause an argument
4 Words before "And here I thought . . ."
5 Great deal
6 CD-___
7 Clamoring
8 La Brea attraction
9 University attended by J. K. Rowling
10 ___ for apples
11 BP partner

12 Louisiana waterway
13 Compound conjunction
18 Comfy footwear, for short
22 Like some Kraut
25 Suffix with depend
26 Club ___
27 Dummkopf
28 Four-star review
32 Electric guitar need
34 Longshoreman
35 Simplicity
36 Auction groups
38 Where Mount Fuji is
39 Utah city
40 Toast recipients
43 ___ Mahal
45 What many a young boy wants to grow up to be

47 Charlotte ___, capital of the U.S. Virgin Islands
48 Coke and Pepsi, e.g.
50 No idle person
51 Fast-moving attack
52 Hair-raising
53 Tough as ___
54 Citi Field player, for short
58 New Rochelle campus
59 Horse's gait
61 Card game based on matching groups of three
63 Letters after L

by David Blake

ACROSS

1 Like the air in a cigar bar
6 In heaps
11 Medallioned vehicle
14 Soup server's implement
15 Dins from dens
16 Ill temper
17 Davy Jones's locker
19 Hoops org.
20 Irksome type
21 Look forward to
22 Foot problem, perhaps
23 Motel extra
25 Playful puppies, at times
27 S'more ingredient
32 Frisk, with "down"
33 "Gone With the Wind" plantation
34 Loonlike bird
37 VW or BMW
39 "Hold the rocks," at a bar
42 ___ mater
43 "All ___ is metaphor, and all metaphor is poetry": G. K. Chesterton
45 Shaker contents
47 Pop music's ___ Lobos
48 Site of London's Great Exhibition of 1851
52 Yucky, in baby talk
54 Cap-and-crown org.?
55 Shore washer
56 Rich soil deposit
59 Repairs some tears
63 Big fuss
64 Veneration of a cult image
66 Turkey piece
67 ___ Street, Perry Mason's secretary
68 Name associated with the starts of 17-, 27-, 48- and 64-Across

69 Sterile hosp. areas
70 "As You Like It" forest
71 Food for birds

DOWN

1 Barely edible fare
2 Knight's club
3 Keatsian works
4 Coffee ___ (social gathering)
5 Cash in Kyoto
6 Ship's front
7 Least bit
8 Monterrey miss, e.g.
9 Rated X
10 Mil. award
11 Rags-to-riches heroine
12 Shady area
13 Grizzlies, e.g.
18 Dynamic Duo member
22 Setting for a Marx Brothers farce
24 Cheerios grain
26 UPS delivery: Abbr.
27 Transcript nos.
28 Brother of Fidel
29 Responders to "Sic 'em!"
30 ___-Magnon
31 Mrs. Gorbachev
35 Coll. football star, e.g.
36 Life of Riley
38 One way to eat ham
40 Low-___ (for dieters)
41 City across the Rio Grande from Ciudad Juárez
44 Cheat, in 43-Across

46 Little bit
49 Electrician's alloy
50 Ineligible for kiddie prices, say
51 Old TV canine
52 Author Calvino
53 Fall drink
57 Magazine title that's a pronoun
58 Trumpeting bird
60 "Pride and Prejudice" actress Jennifer
61 Like jokers, sometimes
62 1974 Gould/ Sutherland spoof
64 Mrs. McKinley
65 N.F.L. ball carriers

by Ed Sessa

ACROSS

1 Musical pace
6 Tractor maker John
11 Do (up), as a fly
14 Bird-related
15 Opposite of exit
16 ___ Today (newspaper)
17 County ENE of San Francisco
19 Was ahead
20 ___ & Tina Turner Revue
21 Greek H's
22 Debate topics
24 Hall-of-Famer Williams
25 End of many URL's
26 ___ Easton Ellis, author of "American Psycho"
27 What a programmer writes
32 They get an eyeful
35 Take to court
36 Nutritionists' nos.
37 Hit with a hammer
38 "No ___!" ("Uncle!," in Spanish)
39 Evenings in Paris
40 Coup d'___
41 Lowest-priced gas grade: Abbr.
42 Japanese religion
43 Monica player on "Friends"
46 Language in Lahore
47 Broadcast
48 China's Three Gorges project
51 Alternative to a Quarter Pounder
54 Photographed
55 "Yes, madame"
56 Palindromic girl's name
57 Winter afflictions
60 Observer of Yom Kippur
61 Eating pork, to an observant 60-Across

62 Dark, as a room
63 Pose a question
64 Does' companions
65 Irascible

DOWN

1 Implied
2 Draw forth
3 Extracted ore
4 Butter serving
5 Publicly known
6 Leave suddenly
7 Grandson of Adam
8 Org. that produces college entrance exams
9 Pensioner
10 Blackboard accessory
11 Native of eastern South Africa
12 "Oh, right"
13 Goalie protectors
18 Elementary units

23 Largest of the Virgin Islands
26 A/C measures
27 Vitamin brand promoted as "Complete from A to Zinc"
28 Custom
29 Chief Norse god
30 Missile that might be tipped with curare
31 Old U.S. gas brand
32 Source of some of the oil for 31-Down
33 Attend
34 Hawaiian feast
38 It might start with "Starters"
39 Clever travel suggestion
41 British soldier in the American Revolution

42 Offspring
44 Political pamphlets
45 Brutes in "Gulliver's Travels"
48 Ken and Barbie
49 Cheating bookkeeper's fear
50 "Play ___ for Me"
51 Lower California, for short
52 Burl who won an Oscar for "The Big Country"
53 Get an eyeful
54 Pollution that may sting the eyes
58 Deg. from Wharton
59 Last number in a countdown

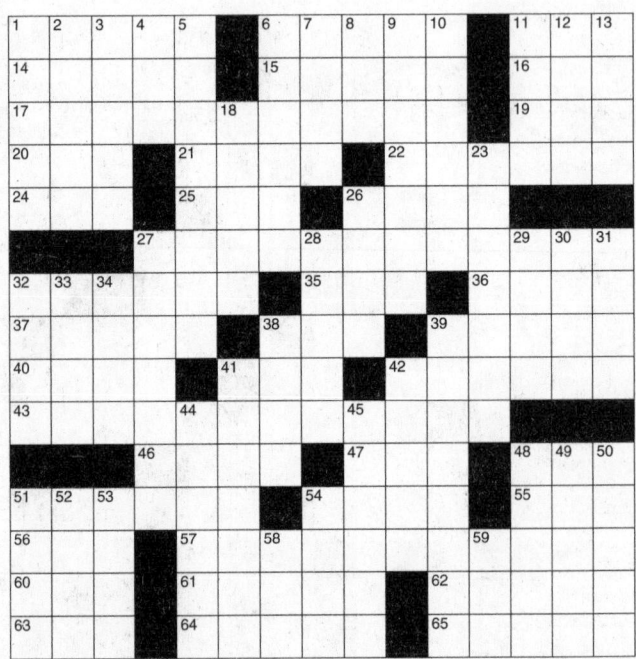

by Janet R. Bender

ACROSS

1 Pet welfare org.
5 Nobel Peace Prize city
9 This puzzle has 78
14 Georgetown athlete
15 Stack-serving chain, for short
16 Slowly, on a score
17 The whole __
19 Pindar, notably
20 Had a bug
21 Mementos of a caning
23 Autodom's Beetle is one, slangily
25 The whole __
30 Double curve
31 Nail-biting margin of victory
34 William Jennings Bryan, for one
35 Regain consciousness suddenly
37 React to a crowing rooster, say
38 The whole __
42 Twosome
43 Raptor's grippers
44 Lover in a Shakespeare title
47 Cabinet position: Abbr.
48 B'way success sign
51 The whole __
53 Ran through, as a credit card
55 Expels forcefully
58 Battery terminal
59 Subtly suggest
63 The whole __
65 Shampoo brand
66 Rock music's Rush, for one
67 Revivalists, informally
68 Potter's potions professor
69 What the sun does at dusk
70 This, in Toledo

DOWN

1 Bundle, as wheat
2 Track bettors play them
3 Presoak, wash and rinse
4 Sounded content
5 Salad bar bowlful
6 Clarinetist Artie
7 Prospector's strike
8 Gems from Australia
9 Ninth-inning hurler, often
10 Took charge
11 Prefix with -form
12 U.F.O. crew
13 Sighter of pink elephants
18 "Beats me!"
22 Even if, briefly
24 Vehicle on a trailer, perhaps
26 St. __ (Caribbean hot spot)
27 Suffix with problem
28 Munch on chips, say
29 College sr.'s test
32 Rotisserie rod
33 Lab burners of old
35 Biblical sin city
36 Gawk at
38 Align
39 "Hell __ no fury . . ."
40 Around-the-house footwear, for short
41 Nonetheless
42 "__ Boot"
45 Get cozy
46 Talk, talk, talk
48 Future ferns
49 Mark of a rifle's laser sight
50 "The Battleship Potemkin" port
52 Most Monopoly income
54 Totally absurd
56 Electrician's hookup
57 Foul mood
59 Modern navigation tool, for short
60 Directional suffix
61 __ Party movement
62 Tour de France peak
64 Aurora's counterpart

by Mike Torch

ACROSS

1 Sleeping, say
5 Got up
10 Sleep
14 Sitarist Shankar
15 Squiggle over an "n"
16 ___ podrida (spicy stew)
17 Tempo?
20 Gait faster than a trot
21 Bumbling
22 Fannie ___
25 Marc who sang "Walking in Memphis"
26 Marry
27 Cry when a judge enters a courtroom
29 Swindle
30 "60 Minutes" network
33 "The Kiss" sculptor
34 Bush adviser Rove
36 Simba's love in "The Lion King"
37 Ka-ching?
40 "Listen!"
41 Fishing poles
42 Sheeplike
43 Idiot
44 Perch
45 DNA units
47 ___ Alamos, N.M.
48 "Sesame Street" character with a unibrow
49 Inexact fig.
50 Long, drawn-out stories
53 Like the arms of a starfish
55 Spectrum?
60 Top-notch
61 Cancel
62 Look out a window, say
63 What top seeds often get at the starts of tournaments
64 Moisten while cooking
65 Alluring

DOWN

1 Linkletter who hosted TV's "House Party"
2 "___! Humbug!"
3 She raised Cain
4 Kind of brake
5 Shorthand takers
6 Marry
7 Ancient
8 Skunk's defense
9 Dict. offering
10 Quarterfinals or semifinals
11 Something ___ (a lulu)
12 Err
13 Saying "I'm not sure that dress looks perfect on you," e.g.
18 "Scarface" star Al
19 Bearing
22 Mrs. George Washington
23 Hawaiian greetings
24 Tribal advisers, typically
26 Gobble (down)
28 Hazard
29 Put X's over
30 Tooth next to a premolar
31 Mixes
32 "Thou ___" (Jesus' response to Pilate)
35 Total (up)
36 Bright star
38 Leon who wrote "Exodus"
39 Human
44 Mediocre
46 Play (with)
47 Spikes, as a drink
48 Buildings with lofts
50 Knife
51 Greeting to a matey
52 DNA element
53 Author Jaffe
54 They're kissable
56 "Chocolate" dog
57 "___ whiz!"
58 Put a spell on
59 Hear, as a case

by Diane Baker van Hoff

ACROSS

1 Pressure meas.
4 One who's devilishly devoted?
9 Opening in the Navy?
14 Orange Monopoly avenue
16 Yves Saint Laurent fragrance
17 They're up
19 Ready to serve
20 ___ Park (Coney Island destination)
21 Kind of basis in accounting
25 Gullibility
30 Asian holiday
31 Some Wall Street Journal charts
33 Topic for Madame de Pompadour and Louis XV
34 "Begone!"
35 They're waiting to be persuaded
41 Beta dog's view
42 ___ 180 (about-faces)
43 Western entrances
47 Shooter's choice, briefly
50 "Sweet" bloomer
51 Chocolate-coated marshmallow sandwich
53 Working hard
55 "Star Trek: T.N.G." counselor Deanna
56 Category for 17-, 31-, 35- and 43-Across
63 Proverbial prevention portion
64 Not in its original form, as an article
65 Argentine money
66 Herbert Hoover, by birth
67 Ernie on a green

DOWN

1 Small craft with launching tubes
2 Occasion when everyone holds hands, maybe
3 Raid target
4 Short mo.
5 "This ___ test"
6 Subj. for some foreigners
7 1994 Jodie Foster title role
8 Attack, as false science
9 Gas
10 Well-put
11 Dead heat
12 Dog that should be on a leash
13 ___ Beagle
15 Practically touching
18 Take ___ (snooze)
22 "Semper Fi" grp.
23 Yours, to Yves
24 Turned up
26 Windows XP successor
27 "___ homo"
28 Symbol of wistfulness
29 Forecasting figs.
32 Words to live by
33 Houston skaters
35 ___ Minor
36 NPR host Conan
37 Tony-winning Tyne
38 Awful end
39 ___ Beach, Fla.
40 Italian bone
44 Some Oklahomans
45 "Phooey!"
46 Composer Shostakovich
47 Preternatural creature
48 Cousin of Lancelot
49 1910–36 for George V, and 1936–52 for George VI
52 Abbr. on a food package
54 Dutch film director van Gogh
56 Shirt or blouse
57 Photoshop adjustment
58 Connected crowd
59 Sgt., e.g.
60 "So cute!"
61 Refrain syllable
62 Idolatry, for one

by Paula Gamache

ACROSS

1 Something to scratch
5 "Hannah Montana" star Miley
10 Height: Prefix
14 Roman tyrant
15 Small egg
16 ___ the line (obeyed)
17 Applaud
18 Taxi's ticker
19 Any volume of the Oxford English Dictionary
20 Accept an inevitable hardship
23 Source of after-hours $$$
25 Giants great Mel
26 Clarinet, oboe and saxophone
27 Ham it up
32 Swap
33 Sardine containers
34 Boozehounds
35 Poet Pound and others
37 Emcee's spot
41 Succulent houseplant
42 Comedy, sci-fi or romance
43 Fall for a flimflam
48 Site of many Chicago touchdowns
49 The other woman
50 Suffix like -like
51 Understand what's happening
56 "How could ___?"
57 Film vault collection
58 Burden
61 ___ Reader (alternative magazine)
62 Davy Crockett died defending it, with "the"
63 Fully red, as a raspberry
64 Peat source
65 Alternative to a convertible
66 Furrow, as the brow

DOWN

1 Abbr. at the end of a company's name
2 ___ Aviv
3 Stuffed sole stuffing
4 Indian doll maker
5 "The Iceman ___"
6 Actress Mimieux of "The Time Machine"
7 Babe with a bat
8 Beekeeper in a 1997 film
9 Many a Bosnian
10 Churchill's predecessor and successor
11 Hoosegow
12 Cure
13 Clifford ___, "Awake and Sing!" dramatist
21 Carry
22 Vases
23 Is a cast member
24 "Comin' ___ the Rye"
28 Vocabulary: Abbr.
29 Toss (about)
30 "Alias" org.
31 Warrant officer's superior: Abbr.
35 Building wing
36 Dr. Seuss' "If I Ran the ___"
37 Society girl, for short
38 "Delta of Venus" author
39 What the white of an eye surrounds
40 Actor Rogen of "Knocked Up"
41 Pub quaffs
42 Richard of "Chicago"
43 Japanese for "the way of the gods"
44 Conestogas, e.g.
45 Craggy mountain ridges
46 "___ & Louise," 1991 film
47 Jim who created Kermit the Frog
48 Hatred
52 Chorus syllables
53 The "T" in TV
54 President
55 Cry made while cracking a whip, maybe
59 Wire service inits.
60 "Quiet on the ___!"

by David Poole

ACROSS

1 Kind of balloon
5 Total
10 Laundry unit
14 Not ___ many words
15 ___ Granada (old Spanish colony in the Americas)
16 Org. for Annika Sorenstam
17 Oyster ___
18 Cooler, to a hip-hopper
19 Broccoli centers?
20 Goal of 39-Across
23 Whitman or Whittier
24 Gives a leg up
27 Swipe at the store
29 Bucks and rams
32 Extreme
33 ___ & the Blowfish
35 Part of a jug band
37 Lockup
38 Objective
39 Activity associated with the word ladder formed by 1-, 10-, 70- and 72-Across
42 What a swish shot swishes
43 Ton
45 Mary ___ of cosmetics
46 Battlefield shout
48 Grand ___ National Park
50 ___-ray Discs
52 Glasgow negations
53 Decorates
55 Tirade
57 39-Across, for one
63 Latin lover's word?
65 "Shut up!"
66 Ski-___ (snowmobiles)
67 "Not a chance"
68 Ryan of "The Beverly Hillbillies"
69 Subdivision map
70 Incite
71 Sniggled
72 Olympic prize

DOWN

1 Tilt
2 ___'acte
3 Between ports
4 Rehearsed perfectly
5 Manga-like art form
6 Lake Superior port
7 Shoulder muscle, briefly
8 Sclera neighbor
9 Second section
10 Rapper born James Todd Smith
11 Batting position
12 AARP membership concern
13 "___ Kapital"
21 Braga of Hollywood
22 Letters from a short person?
25 Judges and juries
26 Dirty
27 Dirty
28 Dice roller's exclamation
30 ___ alcohol
31 Litigate
33 "___ luego"
34 Lodge member
36 Audi alternative
40 Trucker's place
41 Greek New Age musician
44 Wool variety
47 Like most of the Harry Potter films
49 Havana-to-Miami dir.
51 Bearlike
54 "The World of ___ Wong"
56 Wasn't passive
58 Ominous
59 Audi alternative
60 Part of a plea
61 Mine find
62 Abbr. on a city limit sign
63 Oscar-winning director Lee
64 Jersey greeting?

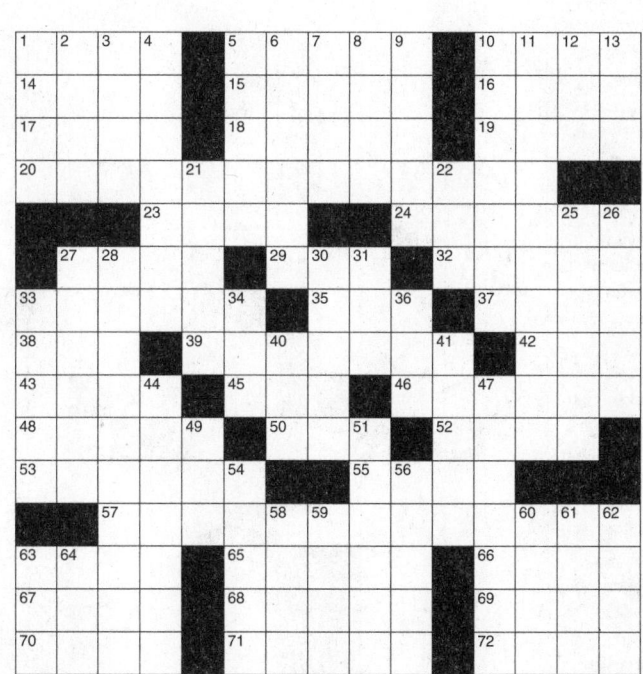

by Peter A. Collins

ACROSS

1 Letter after beta
6 Go 80 m.p.h., say
11 Place to get a mud bath
14 Stevie Wonder's "My Cherie ___"
15 Uncle's special little girl
16 Sunbathe
17 Unpredictable sort
19 No longer chic
20 Italian wine province
21 Back of a boat
22 Kelly Clarkson and Fantasia
24 End-of-the-week office dress policy, maybe
28 Have high hopes
31 Drooping, as a rabbit's ears
32 Yucatán Indian
33 Audition tape
35 Cousin of an ostrich
38 Permanently sever ties
42 Paris's ___ de la Cité
43 Austrian peaks
44 Laugh-a-minute folks
45 Appetizer, entree or dessert
47 President of Egypt before Sadat
48 Franciscan order member
53 Ooze
54 "Alley ___"
55 Greek love god
59 "___ Abner"
60 What each of the characters named at the ends of 17-, 24-, 38- and 48-Across is
64 ___ Vegas
65 French place of learning
66 Anne Frank's hideout
67 "Go, bullfighter!"

68 "Give it ___!" ("Quit harping!")
69 Like an untended garden

DOWN

1 Grand party
2 "Famous" cookie guy
3 No longer worth debating
4 One in a jam?
5 "What ___ the chances?"
6 Awful mistake
7 Ship of Columbus
8 Early night, to a poet
9 Environmental prefix
10 Robert of "Meet the Parents"
11 Got up
12 ___ Abdul, former judge of 22-Across
13 Having the jitters
18 24 cans of beer, e.g.
23 Word after skinny or salsa
25 Pisa's river
26 Baby sheep
27 Bloom: Sp.
28 Both: Prefix
29 Author Bellow
30 "And our love become a funeral ___" (lyric from the Doors' "Light My Fire")
33 Indian metropolis
34 Telepath's "gift," in brief
35 Divas have sensitive ones
36 Apportion, with "out"
37 Lenin's land, for short
39 Ogden who wrote "Candy / Is dandy / But liquor / Is quicker"
40 Tehran is its capital
41 Quaint computer insert
45 Firecracker that fizzles
46 Drink served with a mint leaf
47 "Ain't gonna happen"
48 Pablo Casals's instrument
49 Like some symmetry
50 Throb
51 Christmas carols
52 Sacred choral work
56 Baptism or bar mitzvah
57 Roman author of "Metamorphoses"
58 Cabinet head: Abbr.
61 RCA product
62 Buck's mate
63 Crow's call

by Andrea Carla Michaels and Jennifer Nutt

ACROSS

1 Some Strauss compositions
7 Lip
11 Thanksgiving side dish
14 Defensive statement
15 "That hurt!"
16 It's a cinch, in Sapporo
17 Weapon for Clyde Barrow
20 Japanese luxury auto
21 Specter
22 1959 top 10 hit for Ricky Nelson
25 Funeral stand
26 Zero
27 Loafers, e.g.
32 Landed property
34 Politico Paul
35 "In principio ___ Verbum" (words from John 1:1)
36 Van Gogh's "Bedroom in ___"
37 "Help!" . . . and a hint to 17-, 27-, 42- and 53-Across
38 Give a noncommittal answer
39 Small cave, poetically
40 Beanie Babies, once
41 "How fa-a-ancy!"
42 Tired routine, colloquially
45 Weapon for Iraqi insurgents: Abbr.
46 Conservationist on the California commemorative quarter
47 Pours, as wine
49 Electrify
52 Chart again
53 1966 album that concludes with "I Am a Rock"
58 Stores for 1-Down
59 Footnote abbr.
60 South American camelids
61 Turndowns
62 They make the highlights in highlights
63 Igloo dweller

DOWN

1 Dogfaces
2 Org. on a toothpaste box
3 Melancholy
4 7'1" 1993 N.B.A. Rookie of the Year
5 Some iTunes downloads
6 With resolve
7 Cushioned seat
8 Neighbor of Ger.
9 Bicycle maker since 1895
10 Coasts
11 ___ Bear
12 Touch
13 Ho Chi ___ City
18 Independent, in Ingolstadt
19 North Carolina athlete
22 Like a street urchin, typically
23 ___ del Fuego
24 Zig and zag, in skiing
25 They might follow bad calls
28 Urges on
29 Establish by decree
30 Hatchling in an aerie
31 Places
33 1976 hit that begins "Someone's knockin' at the door"
37 Iraq's ___ City
38 Noises from a county fair contest
40 Passes quickly
41 Distance between posts on a highway, maybe
43 Surpassed
44 Some works for heroes
48 Vertically, to a sailor
49 "Baseball Tonight" airer
50 Letters in love letters
51 Ornery sort
52 Country mail rtes.
54 Confit d'___ (potted goose)
55 It indicates a void in some govt. records
56 Ending with spy or sky
57 That: Sp.

by Michael Sharp

ACROSS

1 Some ski lifts
6 "___ pronounce you man and wife"
10 Basic idea
14 Funnywoman Silverman
15 Actress Ward
16 Regarding
17 By any means necessary
20 Reggae relative
21 Seized property, informally
22 Company that introduced Quik in 1948
23 ___ facto
24 Mom's partner
25 ___ Lingus
26 Work that offers no chance for advancement
30 Approximately
31 "Twelfth Night" duke
32 Atlantic or Pacific
34 Lake on the California/Nevada border
35 Four Monopoly assets: Abbr.
36 Argentine tots
40 Hotshot
42 Burr and Copland
43 Letters after chis
46 Line showing the relationship between an interest rate and maturity date
48 Carpet
49 Uncertainties
50 "And while ___ the subject . . ."
51 Pacific weather phenomenon
53 ___ Bator
54 Place for giraffes and hippos
57 Instruction to someone who's on fire
60 "Gone With the Wind" plantation
61 22-Across flavor, for short
62 Was sick
63 Like a line, in brief
64 Ages and ages
65 Catches

DOWN

1 General ___ chicken
2 Certificate of deposit offerer
3 Region
4 Uncooked
5 It puts a point on a pencil
6 Crustacean with seven pairs of legs
7 Emperor who "fiddled"
8 Suffix with pay
9 Starstruck sort, maybe
10 Gangsters' guns
11 1987 flop starring Warren Beatty and Dustin Hoffman
12 Inscribed pillars
13 Bullfighter
18 Like some questions
19 Brit. word reference
23 Everyday expressions
24 Hospital V.I.P.'s
26 Speck
27 Paleozoic, e.g.
28 Cigarette residue
29 Author ___ Luis Borges
30 Narrow margin in a baseball game
33 Snakes that can put you in a tight spot?
35 Muckraker Jacob
37 Neither here ___ there
38 Letter holder: Abbr.
39 NNW's reverse
41 Coercively
42 Madison Avenue pro
43 Part of a magician's mumbo-jumbo
44 Islamic sovereign
45 Pay no mind to
47 Purple flowers
49 Not Dem. or Rep.
52 Apple debut of 2010
53 Atop
54 Author Émile
55 Cassini who designed for Jackie
56 Discontinued G.M. car
58 "Well, what have we here?!"
59 ___ Tin Tin

by Oliver Hill

ACROSS

1 Dealer in hot goods
6 Siestas
10 "No need to wake me!"
14 Huge, poetically
15 Tons
16 Destination of many 1960s–'70s airplane hijackings
17 "Ooh-la-la!"
18 "___ funny!"
19 Genghis ___
20 Title for a South American mensch?
23 "Hair" extra
26 Bro's sibling
27 "Gone With the Wind" studio
28 Flight board abbr.
29 Perfectly
32 Tiredness
34 Result of heating a certain fruit too long?
37 Tempo
38 Bunny's move
39 "Gotcha"
42 Informal headwear that can't be shared?
47 Nancy in Congress
49 Biblical figure whose name means "hairy" in Hebrew
50 Easily smashable tennis shot
51 German "Oh!"
52 ID on I.R.S. forms
54 Sinks
56 Secretive singer Baez?
60 Plot division
61 Composer Stravinsky
62 Transparent
66 What a Katze catches
67 No longer wild
68 Skirt
69 Rifles and such
70 Meat-and-potatoes dish
71 Program for getting clean, briefly

DOWN

1 Aladdin's hat
2 Musician Brian
3 When repeated, a phrase of reproof
4 Make wavy
5 Some academic retirees
6 Peaceful race in "Avatar"
7 Waugh who wrote "Island in the Sun"
8 A facial may open them
9 Hellish
10 Gross
11 Self-proclaimed "astronaut of boxing"
12 Congo tributary
13 Southernmost country in Central America
21 Really bright, as colors
22 John McCain's alma mater: Abbr.
23 Door fastener
24 "My Friend ___" of 1950s TV
25 "A Whiter Shade of Pale" group
30 Ottoman V.I.P.
31 Cut above the flank
33 Sir Geraint's faithful wife
35 Casino game with a caller
36 Police dept. alerts
40 Get ___ the ground floor
41 Runs off at the mouth
43 Old U.S. gas brand
44 Final movie of Marilyn Monroe and Clark Gable, with "The"
45 Rhyme scheme for Frost's "Stopping by Woods on a Snowy Evening"
46 Carefully worded
47 Word before bottom or party
48 Prius, e.g.
53 Harass
55 Wound soother
57 "The Untouchables" character
58 "I, Claudius" setting
59 Sport with shells
63 "___, Pray, Love" (2006 Elizabeth Gilbert best seller)
64 Hubbub
65 Tyrannosaurus ___

by Caleb Madison and J.A.S.A. Crossword Class

ACROSS

1 Sleepwear, informally
4 Law enforcement org. featured in "Bullitt"
8 Like a requiem
14 ___ de Janeiro
15 Tennis's Nastase
16 Former vice president Dan
17 Where Claudius is during Hamlet's "To be, or not to be" soliloquy
19 Defeat, as an incumbent
20 More than a gentle tap
21 Inexpensive pen
22 Actress Vardalos of "My Big Fat Greek Wedding"
23 Bouquet
25 Any time now
28 Biblical verb ending
29 12th grader
30 Rams' madams?
31 One who goes a-courting
33 Three-time Masters winner Sam
35 Extra plateful
40 Stick out like ___ thumb
41 Early computer that weighed 30 tons
43 Old Turkish leaders
46 Matchbox racer
49 Tiny bite
50 Position for Babe Ruth
52 Normandy battle site
53 1960s world chess champion Mikhail ___
54 Tennis legend Laver
55 Make a grand speech
57 More nonsensical
59 Things a clock has . . . or, literally, what 17-, 25-, 35- and 50-Across are

62 Creek
63 Les États-___
64 ___ gratias (thanks be to God: Lat.)
65 Feared African fly
66 This, in Tijuana
67 Bird that gives a hoot

DOWN

1 ___ or con
2 Skippy alternative
3 Form of tap dance
4 In ___ (as found)
5 Served on fire, as cherries jubilee
6 Sty
7 Ruby or Sandra of film
8 Acorn lover
9 ¹⁄₁₆ pound
10 Some grad school degrees
11 "See ya later"
12 Actress/director May
13 Changes the price of, as at the supermarket
18 Reluctant to meet people, say
21 Frontiersman Daniel
23 Sunday seat
24 Plains tribe
26 Kind of lens with a wide angle
27 Saw to a seat at church, say
29 Sellout signs
32 Online money
34 Copycat
36 "No thank you"
37 R2-D2, for one
38 Video game maker that owns the Seattle Mariners
39 Collins on the Op-Ed page
42 "___ Sharkey" of 1970s TV
43 Warhol or Wyeth
44 San Francisco nine
45 Blazing
47 Performers with big red noses
48 Dexterous
51 Club finance officer: Abbr.
52 Depot: Abbr.
56 "I see," facetiously
58 Butterfly catcher
59 U.S. Election Day, e.g.: Abbr.
60 Morning moisture
61 Note above fa

by Richard Chisholm

ACROSS

1 Nosh
5 O.T. book that never mentions God: Abbr.
9 Jack who could eat no fat
14 Certain charge card, informally
15 Aria, typically
16 Ragú rival
17 Tiffany creation
18 Ones ranking below cpls.
19 Conger catcher
20 Bit of derring-do
22 Here and now
24 Alpha's opposite
26 "Swan Lake" swan
27 Put the tape back to the start
30 French actor Alain
32 Cremona craftsman
33 Pastoral poem
34 Big mouth, slangily
38 "__ Pinafore"
39 Writing on an envelope
42 Photo blowup: Abbr.
43 When doubled, a food fish
45 Oboe or clarinet
46 Less than 90°
48 Big tournaments for university teams, informally
50 Fled to wed
51 Nickelodeon's parent company
54 Anglo-__
56 Aromatic sticks
58 Home entertainment centerpiece
62 Producer of sweat and tears, but not blood
63 "Go ahead!"
65 Done
66 Painting surface
67 Auto on the autobahn
68 In the cellar
69 Web-footed mammal
70 Catchall abbreviation
71 "What __?"

DOWN

1 Unit of cotton
2 Supersized movie screen format
3 Short-term worker, for short
4 Take advantage of
5 Spotted
6 Start of either syllable in "ginger"
7 An attentive doc gives it to a patient
8 Doctor's place: Abbr.
9 Swimwear brand
10 Show, in a show-and-tell
11 Lease to a new tenant
12 15-percenter
13 Rich cake
21 __ vincit amor
23 Status symbol car, familiarly
25 Prepare to drive, as a golf ball
27 Obama adviser Emanuel
28 Austen novel
29 Get the grime off
31 Gave the once-over
33 Invention starter
35 Sign on for another tour
36 A chip or two to start with
37 Said "Not guilty!," e.g.
40 Small amounts
41 Permanent provider
44 Make boiling mad
47 Say "There, there" to, say
49 Flier with a 10-foot wingspan
50 Wonderfully foreign
51 "The Road" star Mortensen
52 Fjord, e.g.
53 "With __ of thousands!" (movie ad boast)
55 They turn litmus paper red
57 Cheese with a red coat
59 Ellipsoid
60 Minus
61 Art Deco artist
64 Non's opposite

by Paula Gamache and Ed Stein

ACROSS

1 Limerick or sonnet
5 "Shut yo' mouth!"
9 Sales talk
14 Jai __
15 Solo for Pavarotti
16 Commie
17 Use of a corporate jet, say
18 Pepper grinder
19 Heavenly harp player
20 Green Berets
23 Pest attracted to light
24 Volcanic spew
25 Words before serious, ready or listening
28 Fill all the way
30 The Peacock Network
33 Frenzied state
35 Mrs. Dithers in "Blondie"
36 Brings up
37 "Everybody Hurts" band
38 Revolutionary War hero John Paul __
39 Las Vegas figures
40 Out-of-studio TV broadcast
42 Opposite of NNW
43 First, second, third or home
44 Nuclear experiments, for short
45 __ Lanka
46 __ monster
47 Popular date time . . . or a phrase that can precede the starts of 20-, 33- and 40-Across
53 Chinese province where Mao was born
54 Spain's longest river
55 Hoity-toity manners
57 Bandleader Shaw
58 Jesús of the 1960s Giants
59 It's just a thought
60 "Project Runway" host Klum
61 Take a breather
62 Requirement

DOWN

1 Soft food for babies
2 Cheers at a fútbol match
3 Dodge City lawman Wyatt
4 Portrayer of Austin Powers, "international man of mystery"
5 Chew the scenery
6 Dickens's __ Heep
7 Spot for a pot
8 Two quarters
9 Few and far between
10 Tiny bit of salt
11 William who wrote "The Dark at the Top of the Stairs"
12 Manages, with "out"
13 Twitter titter
21 Operator of the largest brewery facility in the world
22 "Ye gods!," for one
25 Hairstyles of Sly and the Family Stone
26 Swamp plants
27 Escape, as arrest
28 Jobs in Silicon Valley
29 Pinnacle
30 Forbidden acts
31 QB Favre
32 Assignments for Sam Spade
34 Colored part of the eye
35 "Say what?"
38 Martial arts champion-turned-film star
40 Lion's home
41 Certain game cancellation
43 Pacific sultanate
45 Unflashy
46 Pita sandwiches
47 "My pleasure!"
48 Prefix with knock
49 "__ Abby"
50 Up to the task
51 Enroll in a witness protection program, say
52 Apple or maple
53 "When pigs fly!"
56 Down in the dumps

by Randall J. Hartman

ACROSS

1 Think about
7 Rock's Steely ___
10 Pentagon V.I.P.'s: Abbr.
14 Kind of reasoning, after "a"
15 Ginger ___
16 Help in wrongdoing
17 Entertainment you might have a hand in?
19 "Encore!"
20 Meat slice on the highest shelf?
22 Class with crayons
25 Scotland's Firth of ___
26 Trail user
27 Advertising sheet blowing in the wind?
32 Like presses ready for printing
33 It has feet in a line
34 Droop
37 Sir Anthony formerly of 10 Downing Street
38 Made thinner
40 Carry on
41 Oui's opposite
42 ___ Cooper (car)
43 English county
44 Curly lock tints?
47 Grove components
50 Big ___
51 Buttonless shirt
52 Dribble from an icicle?
57 Series finale, in brief
58 Nor'easters, often
62 Ocean motion
63 Be under par
64 Keyless
65 Broke ground?
66 QB pickups: Abbr.
67 ___ public

DOWN

1 Very, very soft, in music
2 Okla. school
3 Quick drink
4 L-___ (Parkinson's treatment)
5 Put up
6 Mass, e.g.
7 Author Roald
8 Lily of Africa
9 Colorful amphibian
10 Chess ploy
11 Something to read on a Kindle
12 Chutzpah
13 Manage the helm
18 Eye sore
21 Sound before "Your fly is open"
22 "The X-Files" subject
23 Sonata movement
24 Coin at an arcade
28 When doubled, a breath freshener
29 When to celebrate Earth Day
30 Axis, once
31 Was ahead
34 Nicholas or Patrick
35 Share an opinion
36 Fliers in V's
38 Wrestler's goal
39 Director Lee
40 Question of identity
42 Hit's opposite
43 Feature of a fugue
44 Staggered
45 Big game hunter?
46 Resident of Oklahoma's second-largest city
47 Canines, e.g.
48 Two to one or three to one
49 Skirt
53 Heavy cart
54 A.T.F. agents' activity
55 Removes a squeak from
56 Driver's nonverbal "hello"
59 Cellular stuff
60 "Striving to better, oft we ___ what's well": Shak.
61 Like a fox

by MaryEllen Uthlaut

ACROSS

1 Homes for hens
6 Scrapes (out)
10 Sarcastic exclamation
14 Sneeze sound
15 Converse
16 Pixar's "Finding ___," 2003
17 "I'll be through in a minute"
19 Recipe direction
20 See 38-Across
21 Game show group
22 Ending for a female Smurf
23 Puts into law
25 Settle, as a debt
27 Owls' cries
30 Girl who plays football, perhaps
33 Response to "Are too!"
36 ___ salts
38 With 20-Across, just for fun
39 Part of a shoelace tie
40 Word that can precede the starts of 17- and 62-Across and 11- and 35-Down
41 Boat loading area
42 Fliers of U.F.O.'s
43 Barton of the Red Cross
44 Erases, as a computer's memory
45 Mount Everest guide
47 Big name in printers
49 "Pride and Prejudice" beau
51 Like Papa Bear's porridge, to Goldilocks
55 Expo
57 Australian animal that munches on eucalyptus leaves
60 Like Lindbergh's famous flight
61 "___ and Let Die" (Paul McCartney hit)

62 Husband of a trophy wife, maybe
64 ___ of March
65 Creme-filled cookie
66 ___ March, Saul Bellow protagonist
67 Future's opposite
68 Gen ___ (thirtysomethings)
69 Poodle or dachshund, e.g.

DOWN

1 Monthly TV bill
2 Separator of continents
3 Margaret Mitchell's Scarlett
4 Serving in Homer Simpson's favorite dinner
5 Boar's mate
6 "At Last" singer James

7 Madeline of "Blazing Saddles"
8 Wabbit's "wival"
9 What a paleontologist reconstructs
10 Pants length measurement
11 Flapper of old toondom
12 Give off
13 Ripped
18 ___ facto
24 Wee one
26 Small dog, in brief
28 Trillion: Prefix
29 Mold's origin
31 First word in many a fairy tale
32 Is a chatterbox
33 Pub draughts
34 One drawn to a flame
35 Loses altitude fast
37 Trade

40 Scandalous 1919 Chicago baseball team
41 Triceratops, e.g.
43 Lifeguard's skill, for short
44 Try to win the hand of
46 Most uncommon
48 Symbol on a flag
50 "___ the One That I Want" ("Grease" song)
52 ___-podge
53 Classics station song
54 Played (with)
55 Freak (out)
56 Opera set in ancient Egypt
58 Follower of new or golden
59 Neighbor of Cambodia
63 Pat gently, as with makeup

by Aimee Lucido

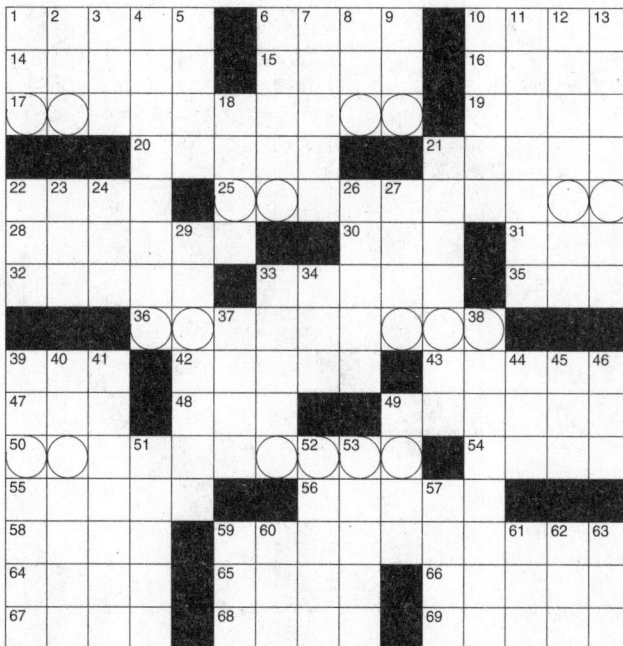

ACROSS

1 Standing
6 Features of Sophocles plays
10 Peeve, with "off"
14 Rolls for dinner
15 Major constellation?
16 Something an undercover agent might wear
17 In consecutive order
19 Knowing, as a secret
20 Big news on the sports page
21 Bean on the screen
22 Cracker brand
25 Just barely legit
28 Gets used (to)
30 Consideration for when to arrive at the airport: Abbr.
31 But: Lat.
32 It's read from right to left
33 Senseless
35 Give it a go
36 What a slow person may need
39 Nada
42 Word written on the Saudi flag
43 "Dig in!"
47 Summer cooler
48 Place for a ring
49 Astronomer Halley
50 Slip-up
54 Sound accompanying a cloud of smoke
55 It's flashed by an officer
56 Musical set in Buenos Aires
58 Epps of "House"
59 Fragile articles . . . or a hint to the things named by the circled letters
64 Cloud ___
65 Endure
66 Arafat's birthplace
67 Stats for a QB

68 You, to a Quaker
69 Went "tap tap tap" on a keyboard

DOWN

1 What makes a pin spin?
2 Regret
3 Abbr. after a lawyer's name
4 Cheekiness
5 Auditorium balcony, e.g.
6 One-up
7 More arid
8 That, to Tomás
9 "I've got a mule, her name is ___"
10 Pirouette
11 "No, you go, really"
12 Bing Crosby, e.g.
13 Anthony of the Supreme Court

18 Busts
21 Chose from a menu
22 It's smelled when something's fishy
23 Response to "Who wants ice cream?!"
24 Driveway surface
26 ___ by chocolate (calorie-heavy dessert)
27 Explosive Sicilian?
29 "Masterpiece ___"
33 Less active
34 Source of intelligence: Abbr.
37 Sunburn soother
38 Team that has a tankful of rays in the back of its ballpark
39 It's driven over the ice between periods

40 The "King" in "The Last King of Scotland"
41 Locket, often
44 Excessively
45 Game featuring 108 cards
46 Alternative to a print version: Abbr.
49 Christine's lover in "The Phantom of the Opera"
51 Shrek and Fiona, in "Shrek"
52 Witherspoon of "Legally Blonde"
53 Egg-shaped
57 Ambassador's asset
59 Alternative to a Philly cheesesteak
60 Cheerleader's cheer
61 Cup's edge
62 Before, in verse
63 Garden shop offering

by Eshan Mitra

ACROSS

1 Plunge
5 More dishonorable
10 "What ___!" ("That was fun!")
14 "I loved, loved, loved that!" review
15 Capital of Ghana
16 Fitzgerald who sang "A-Tisket A-Tasket"
17 "Designing Women" actress is intelligent?
19 Bridle part
20 "Excuse me . . ."
21 Husband-to-be
23 Little pooches
27 Person producing Bordeaux or Beaujolais
28 What a gofer is sent on
29 Takes little steps
30 Jumped
31 Willy with a chocolate factory
32 The Windy City, for short
35 Viva ___
36 Does some mending
37 Pleased
38 Suffix with Siam
39 Daring
40 Roger who played 007
41 Batter's position
43 It might produce a snore in Sonora
44 Capital of Suffolk, England
46 Hold
47 Saying "Please" and "How do you do?," say
48 Tense
49 Chief Norse god
50 "Blondie" cartoonist is not old?
56 Chop up
57 Anouk of le cinéma
58 Mongols' home
59 Fifth Avenue landmark
60 Lords and ladies
61 Retained

DOWN

1 Nickname of a 6'7" former basketball great
2 "Norma ___"
3 Eggs
4 Cross or Parker
5 Clobbered
6 Topmost points
7 Many an e-mail "click here" offer
8 Go astray
9 Squealers
10 Infuse with carbon dioxide
11 "Fatal Attraction" actress is nearby?
12 Girl who went through a looking glass
13 Less addled
18 Superdome player
22 Machu Picchu resident
23 Look (into)
24 Cookies in a box lunch
25 "White Rabbit" singer is smooth?
26 Open the mouth wide
27 "My cousin" in a 1992 film
29 Man with a code
31 Keep an eye on
33 Mates for does
34 Notions
36 Corner sitter's headwear
37 "Anything ___"
39 Trot or canter
40 Like eyes when you're getting nostalgic, maybe
42 Twists and turns, as a tendril
43 Drunkards
44 Products for music downloads
45 Speakers' places
46 Nervous person in a hospital waiting room, perhaps
48 Use a stop clock on
51 Hurry
52 "Mighty" fine home for a squirrel?
53 "What's the ___?"
54 Tuck's partner
55 Gangster's gun

by Bernice Gordon

ACROSS

1 "The Hobbit" hero
6 College V.I.P.'s
11 Drs.' org.
14 ___ flu
15 Mother ___
16 Defeat by just a tad
17 Entree on many a Chinese menu
20 Pioneering anti-AIDS drug
21 Blackener of Santa's boots
22 Oscar winner Jannings
23 "No shirt, no shoes, no service," e.g.
25 Cramped alternative to a basement
29 Clear the board
31 "I could ___ horse!"
32 Signs to heed
34 Rotting
38 Pastor, for short
39 Pets . . . or what the starts of 17-, 25-, 50- and 61-Across are all kinds of
42 It can be cast
43 Tabriz residents
45 "Goodnight" girl of old song
47 Greek peak
48 Amber is a fossilized one
50 Old New Yorkers, e.g.
54 Lots
57 Prefix with cultural
58 Intl. group with many generals
60 Big milestone for a young co.
61 Basic hotel banquet entree
66 Still
67 Anticipate
68 River that drains more than 20% of France
69 Date
70 Labor's partner
71 Attack

DOWN

1 King of the elephants in a children's book series
2 Trooper on the highway
3 "The Loco-Motion" singer, 1962
4 Dracula's altered form
5 Telephone numbers without letters
6 Prior to
7 Island south of Sicily
8 Suffix with direct
9 Small change: Abbr.
10 It may precede "Don't let anyone hear!"
11 Inner self
12 Make like
13 Beatles record label
18 Fabled fliers
19 Settle a debt with
24 Directional suffix
26 Sports Illustrated span
27 Feature of many a bodice
28 Equilibrium
30 Franciscans' home
32 ". . . ___ quit!"
33 Debussy's "La ___"
34 Affairs
35 Facial recognition aid
36 Diarist Anaïs
37 "___ whiz!"
40 News agency that was the first to report on Sputnik
41 Genetic materials
44 Mobile phone giant
46 Small inlet
48 Shows shock, e.g.
49 Book after Neh.
50 ___ breath
51 Concur
52 Where Minos reigned
53 Out of shape
55 Word with grand or soap
56 Largish musical group
59 Many works at the Met
62 Patsy
63 Eero Saarinen designed its J.F.K. terminal
64 Viking ship need
65 Runner Sebastian

by Adam G. Perl

ACROSS

1 Name repeated in the lyric "Whatever ___ wants, ___ gets"
5 Teeter-totter
11 ___ Moines
14 Apple computer
15 Hitting of a golf ball
16 Nothing's opposite
17 Shows petulant anger
19 "Fee, ___, foe, fum"
20 Cheri formerly of "S.N.L."
21 Exam for H.S. seniors
22 Seep
23 Gets lucky
27 Hot tar, e.g.
29 "Here ___ comes, Miss America"
30 Heir, but not an heiress
31 ___ mater
33 "Lucky Jim" author Kingsley
36 Painter Picasso
40 Doesn't stonewall, say
43 Pro ___ (perfunctory)
44 Tiny time unit: Abbr.
45 Like an omelet
46 Toronto's prov.
48 ___ Pérignon
50 Lone Star State nickname
51 Reacts slightly
57 Run amok
58 Cheer for a matador
59 "Ave ___." (Latin prayer)
62 Fourth of July celebration inits.
63 Shows affection unexpectedly
66 They, in Marseille
67 Eight English kings
68 Fitzgerald known as the First Lady of Song
69 Volleyball court divider
70 How china may be sold
71 Possible response to a grabby boyfriend

DOWN

1 Quick weight loss option, informally
2 Leave out
3 Recent arrival
4 Ghana's capital
5 Opposite of NNW
6 Co. that oversees the 21-Across
7 Rub out
8 Couches
9 Dogs whose tails curl up the back
10 Rainy
11 Actor Willem
12 Doolittle of "Pygmalion"
13 Streamlined
18 Chart-toppers
22 Highly decorative
24 Addams who created "The Addams Family"
25 Muscular fellow
26 Knocks on the noggin
27 Large iron hook
28 Medley
32 Not quite
34 100 is average for them
35 Soft leather
37 Cause of goose bumps, perhaps
38 Pricey seating section
39 Gem with colored bands
41 Carvey who used to say "Well, isn't that special?"
42 Environmental sci.
47 Govt. securities
49 Papa's partner
51 Boston N.H.L.'er
52 Window or middle alternative
53 Raise a glass to
54 Justice Kagan
55 Senior, junior and sophomore
56 Rice wines
60 Cuba, por ejemplo
61 "Rush!," on an order
63 ___ Na Na
64 Soapmaker's need
65 Fast jet, for short

by Janice M. Putney

ACROSS

1 Cornfield sounds
5 Scarf material
9 Any member of the genus Homo
14 "___ happens . . ."
15 Black
16 In ___ (not yet born)
17 Prevalent
18 Having two or three kids in a family, nowadays
19 What to "Come see the softer side of," in a slogan
20 Two charts?
23 ___ v. Wade
24 Nav. rank
25 Severely affected
27 Dr. Seuss title
32 Gloom's partner
33 Shipment to a smeltery
34 Audited a class, say
36 Winter highway department needs
39 See 43-Across
41 Like some stock
43 With 39-Across, kind of engine
44 Massage
46 Retro photo tone
48 New Orleans-to-Detroit dir.
49 Some airport data: Abbr.
51 Drained
53 Danced at Rio's Carnival, maybe
56 Homer Simpson's Indian friend
57 Mideast grp.
58 Edit?
64 Sharp
66 Recipe step starter
67 Approve

68 Implement for an apple
69 Israel's Golda
70 "Lonesome" tree
71 Lets (up)
72 Basic subj. for a surgeon
73 Goals

DOWN

1 Fault-find
2 Large part of a world atlas
3 Coffee shop convenience for a laptop
4 Not mono
5 Bird spec
6 ___ about (approximately)
7 Gumbo staple
8 ___ node

9 Point on a line?
10 Suffix with suburban
11 A bushel of Boscs?
12 Boo-boo
13 Gave medicine
21 Raggedy ___ (dolls)
22 Concealed
26 Full or half nelson
27 What a debtor might be in
28 Algerian port
29 French father's affairs?
30 Western tribe
31 Spoke (up)
35 Back of the neck
37 Ebb
38 Toboggan, e.g.
40 Cutting remark
42 Shred
45 Fabric dealers, to Brits

47 Coleridge's sacred river
50 Large quantity
52 One side of "the pond"
53 Gap
54 Foil-making giant
55 Comedy alternative
59 Fall place
60 1998 Sarah McLachlan song
61 Related
62 Hourglass fill
63 Prominent features of a "Cats" poster
65 Plumbing fitting

by Mike Torch

ACROSS

1 Frame job
6 Taste
11 Somme summer
14 Love to pieces
15 Clara Barton, e.g.
16 Rank above maj.
17 Michelle Obama and Laura Bush
19 Singer Yoko
20 Sicilian spewer
21 On a grand scale
22 Somersault
23 Highway troopers
26 Of greatest age
29 Poi source
30 The Beach Boys' "___ John B"
31 Drinker's next-day woe
35 Submarine sandwich
36 Early synthesizers
38 Great review
39 Eave
41 Tendon
42 Cubes in a casino
43 E-mail predecessor
45 Oppressive regime
49 ___ Canal, waterway through Schenectady
50 "___ la Douce"
51 Lane of the Daily Planet
55 Beachgoer's shade
56 Tenet of chivalry
59 Had something
60 Assists at a heist
61 Cosmetician Lauder
62 Plural of "la" and "le"
63 West Pointer
64 Unexpected win

DOWN

1 Opposite of "out" in baseball
2 Tighten the writin'?
3 Ripped
4 ___ Major
5 Hamster, for one
6 Speak sharply to
7 Bad news for a taxpayer
8 Sticker
9 Sugar suffix
10 Hi-___ monitor
11 Food-poisoning bacteria
12 Gin's partner
13 Run off to a judge in Vegas, say
18 Allows
22 Put the pedal to the metal
23 Mo. when fall starts
24 Lousy reviews
25 URL ending that's not "com" or "gov"
26 Mt. McKinley's is 20,320 ft.
27 Oral history
28 Like a dire situation
30 HBO rival
31 Animal in a sty
32 It shows which way the wind blows
33 At any time
34 FF's opposite
36 Spray used on rioters
37 Completely biased
40 Drunk's outburst
41 Jeanne d'Arc, e.g.: Abbr.
43 Least plausible, as an excuse
44 Hellenic H's
45 Daisy part
46 Pontificate
47 Actors speak them
48 Hackneyed
51 Daffy Duck has one
52 Table scraps
53 "Now you're making sense"
54 Proofreader's "reinstate" mark
56 Fond du ___, Wis.
57 Atty.'s org.
58 Fire: Fr.

by Adam G. Perl

ACROSS

1 Andean land
5 Race for hot rods
9 Open, as a pill bottle
14 Photoshop option
15 Actress Skye
16 Indira Gandhi's family name
17 *Bid adieu, informally
19 Live
20 Family beginnings
21 Boise-to-Phoenix dir.
23 Thanksgiving invitee, commonly: Abbr.
24 Is on the hunt
26 *Failure by a narrow margin
28 Captain's record
29 Gorilla famously taught to use sign language
31 "Brain" of a computer, briefly
32 Topographic map notation: Abbr.
34 Lavish affection (on)
36 Beasts of burden
40 *Like Oprah Winfrey and Michael Jordan
43 Villa ___
44 Take ___ of (sample)
45 Where a pear's seeds are
46 Spot for a shot
48 Not a major haircut
50 Flamenco cry
51 *It's often ordered à la mode
55 Meddle (with)
57 'Do that one would rarely wear a hat with
58 Online portal since Windows 95 was launched
59 Book of divine guidance
60 Argot
62 Singer of the lyric formed by the ends of the answers to the four starred clues

66 Building wing, e.g.
67 French brainchild
68 It may be off the wall
69 Irritable
70 Fruity drinks
71 Card game popular in Germany

DOWN

1 Mac alternatives
2 Never-ratified women-related measure, for short
3 King of the Cowboys
4 Violinist's stroke
5 Coca-Cola Zero, e.g.
6 Rips off
7 "___ better?"
8 Fliers in V's
9 Like a good golf score
10 Novel
11 Dear, in 12-Down
12 Van Gogh locale
13 Attracts
18 Fatty part of an egg
22 ___ fly (certain baseball hit, for short)
24 Answer, in court
25 Husband of Pocahontas
26 Characteristic of bland food and bad dressers
27 Swing or rock
30 Coffee cultivated on Mauna Loa
33 Life-or-death
35 Mideast noble
37 Cleavage-revealing dress feature
38 Hall-of-Famer Combs who played with Gehrig and Ruth

39 Malfoy's look, in the Harry Potter books
41 The Changing of the Guard, e.g.
42 Abstracts
47 Brit. legislators
49 Painter Chagall
51 Chopin's "Polonaise in ___ Major, Op. 53"
52 Group of lions
53 Places for ornamental fish
54 Neighbor of Bhutan
56 No enrollees at Smith College
59 Joint for a beggar?
61 Caught
63 Bizarre
64 "I caught you!"
65 Word after waste and want

by Paula Gamache

ACROSS

1 Close with a bang
5 Crimson Tide, to fans
9 Loss's opposite
13 Aria da ___
14 Establishment with hair dryers
15 Hip about
16 Muscat is its capital
17 Warning
18 Slightly open, as a door
19 Shifting piece of the earth's crust
22 Exist naturally
23 ___ Royal Highness
24 Cut (off), as with a sweeping motion
27 Supped
28 ___Vista (search engine)
31 Dwell
33 Extraterrestrial's transportation
35 Lotion ingredient
38 Psychology 101 topic
39 Sail holder
40 Quadrennial soccer championship
45 Traveled with Huck Finn, e.g.
46 Those, in Tijuana
47 ___-town (Cubbies' home)
50 Surgeons' workplaces, for short
51 Sponsors' spots
53 Showy cock's object of affection
55 Los Angeles Philharmonic summer venue
59 Dud
61 The Hunter constellation
62 Merle Haggard's "___ From Muskogee"
63 "I bet you won't go bungee jumping," e.g.
64 Give 10% to one's church
65 A/C opening
66 Gave the boot
67 Impudence
68 Energy output units

DOWN

1 Nova ___, Canada
2 Bemoan
3 Cochise or Geronimo
4 Del ___ Foods
5 Storied isle near Java
6 Actor Baldwin
7 Undergo transformation, as one image into another
8 Stag's pride
9 Billy or nanny
10 Oscar winner Huston
11 Make ___ habit
12 Neither's partner
14 In a rational way
20 ___ vaccine
21 General location
25 Poems of praise
26 Bouncy
29 Stadium level
30 Viewpoint
32 Drainage pit
33 Impressive act
34 Dwellers on Mount Olympus
35 Hardly a close-cut hairdo
36 Fabricator
37 Not on land, as an oil rig
41 Prosperity
42 Stock in nonstandard quantities
43 Gangster known as Scarface
44 Exploited
47 Snug necklace
48 Felling
49 Small bays
52 Neighbor of Israel
54 Over
56 ___ page (newspaper part)
57 Jokesters
58 Sounds of amazement
59 Prescription safety org.
60 Too permissive

by Robert Fisher

Note: The answers to the 12 starred clues have something in common. What is it?

ACROSS

1 *Reno and 38-Across, for two
7 Maze runner
13 All piled up
15 *Procter & Gamble deodorizer
16 *Sweet Italian wine
17 *Fitting
18 Indy initials
19 Mauna ___
20 Cheater's utterance
24 Cavalry blade
26 Band with the 2008 song "Electric Feel"
30 "It's all coming back to me now"
32 Parental palindrome
33 *The second "M" of MGM
34 *Roundabout, for one
36 ___ Nevada
37 Downed
38 See 1-Across
40 Bailed-out co. in 2009 news
41 Latter-day Saint
43 *Actress Lewis of "Natural Born Killers"
45 *Hanna-Barbera's ___ Doggie
46 Stewart of "The Daily Show"
47 Knight's need
48 Dead river?
49 Mongoose's foe
51 Small vortex
52 Stop start?
53 Lode deposit
55 *Cosmetics chain whose name comes from the Greek for "beauty"
59 *Nadya Suleman, mother of 14, familiarly
64 *Nays
65 Productive

66 Hannibal of "The Silence of the Lambs"
67 *Remove nails from

DOWN

1 Halpert of "The Office"
2 Santa ___
3 Not wide: Abbr.
4 Canadian query closers
5 Oolong and others
6 Puts (away), as for safekeeping
7 Outcast
8 Start of a spell
9 Dude
10 Workout unit
11 ___ dye
12 Parisian possessive
14 Nickname of the dictator who said "I know the Haitian people because I am the Haitian people"
15 Like some U.F.O. sightings
20 Sleepers
21 Game in which only one team scores
22 Working well together
23 Private eye
25 Heist of a sort
26 Fannie ___
27 Did the watusi, e.g.
28 Deserved
29 "Coriolanus" or "Richard III"
31 Missouri city, informally
33 Some skirts
35 Actor Holm
36 G string?

39 Car option that slides open
42 Mingle
44 Summer on the Seine
46 Pop's ___ Brothers
49 Apple implement
50 Rainbowlike
52 Part of a melody
54 Raison d'___
55 "___ Digital Shorts"
56 Want ad abbr.
57 Common pipe material, briefly
58 Trendy
60 Like some stocks, for short
61 1,000 G's
62 Suffix with pay or plug
63 Cat call

by Jose Chardiet

ACROSS

1 Officials behind batters
5 Scarlett who says "I'll never be hungry again"
10 Dame Hess at a piano
14 What to call a king
15 Caution light's color
16 Chick's chirp
17 Preowned
18 Where Jodie lives?
20 Survey a second time
22 ___ de Cologne
23 To the ___ (fully)
24 With 53-Across, where Victoria lives?
28 Say "Boo!" to, say
30 Ernie on the links
31 Moonshine device
32 Dirty dishes often collect in them
33 Hair colorers
35 Weekly TV show with guest hosts, for short
36 Broadcast
37 Where Donna lives?
41 A clown might get it in the face
42 Jr.'s son
43 Heady brews
46 Current conductors
49 Rachel Maddow's network
51 Singleton
52 Nonreactive, chemically
53 See 24-Across
55 Co. with a lot of connections?
56 Inexact no.
58 Multigenerational stories
59 Where Sally lives?

64 Starchy tropical root
65 Not working
66 Camel caravan's stop
67 "You too?" à la Caesar
68 Trial run
69 Scents
70 Well-kept

DOWN

1 Seized, as the throne
2 Scroogelike
3 Debaters' basic assumptions
4 Many a family car
5 Clodhopper
6 Payer of some hosp. bills
7 "Washboard" muscles
8 Give a new version of, as a story
9 Square footage

10 Dashboard abbr.
11 Royal attendant in a Gilbert and Sullivan operetta
12 Comment
13 Uppermost points
19 Moscow's land
21 Dell or Toshiba products, for short
25 "Who's there?" response
26 "Knotty" wood
27 Cry from a bailiff when a judge walks in
29 Around, in a date
34 "Fantastic!"
36 Cover story
38 Covered with a fine spray
39 Bowlers' targets
40 Stretch

44 Former Web reference from Microsoft
45 Ushers to the exit
46 Nintendo product for the gym-averse, maybe
47 Not outdoors
48 Disgusts
49 Wild-riding squire of "The Wind in the Willows"
50 Savings acct. alternatives
54 Consumed
57 "Scram!"
60 Permit
61 Troops' support grp.
62 Walter Raleigh or Walter Scott
63 Twisty road curve

by Lynn Lempel

ACROSS

1 Mynah bird, e.g.
6 Has to
10 Send by FedEx or UPS
14 Mrs. Perón
15 Worker welfare grp.
16 Noted tower site
17 Seventh day, in the Bible?
19 Westernmost Aleutian
20 "I'll have another"
21 "Tired blood" tonic
23 Cheesy sandwich
25 Having all one's marbles
26 Truth stretcher
30 Go hog wild
32 P, in Greece
35 One way to think or read
36 Homo vis-à-vis humans
37 Homo sapiens
38 "The Wizard of Oz" coward
39 What a roof is usually built on
40 Dagger
41 Bit of Web video gear
42 Small earrings
43 A sheriff may round one up
44 Horatian creation
45 Hunter's garb, for short
46 Like a mud puddle
47 Cheer (for)
49 Vintners' valley
51 Cash-back deals
54 Condiment at Nathan's
59 Touch on
60 $10 bill enclosed in a Valentine card?
62 "Jeepers!"
63 Pioneering D.J. Freed
64 Home, sweet home
65 Picnic intruders
66 Join with a blowtorch
67 Religious council

DOWN

1 Note from the boss
2 "Terrible" czar
3 What a D.J. speaks into
4 Tabloids twosome
5 Ricocheted, as a cue ball
6 Tasty mushroom
7 Be hooked on
8 Thick carpet
9 Brings on a date
10 Onetime colonial power in the Philippines
11 One-third of a strikeout?
12 "That's all there ___ it!"
13 Left-handed Beatle
18 Term of address used by Uncle Remus
22 Slum vermin
24 Trample underfoot
26 Edie of "The Sopranos"
27 Homeric epic
28 Statue of a post-W.W. II baby?
29 Sloppy joe holder
31 Bed-and-breakfasts
33 Unduly severe
34 Like a good singer
36 Wearing a long face
39 Result of a governor's signing
40 "Inka Dinka ___"
42 Loch Lomond local
43 Blood bank supplies
46 Cowboy boot feature
48 Solemn vows
50 Make changes in
51 Sitar music
52 Black, to bards
53 Dover ___
55 Man-shaped mug
56 In a bit, in poems
57 Give a makeover
58 Did some batiking
61 Kilmer of film

by Fred Piscop

ACROSS

1 Healing ointment
5 Partner
9 David who sang "Space Oddity"
14 1-Across ingredient
15 Enthusiastic
16 Like some on-the-spot wireless networks
17 *Toy that's thrown
19 Point of no return?
20 What an E may stand for
21 Deck wood
23 China's ___ Zedong
24 Like a clear night sky
26 Tic
28 1492, 1776, 2001, etc.
30 Seek divine help from
33 Indent key
36 Back of the neck
38 Silents star Normand
39 Has an exciting opening number, say . . . or what the answer to each starred clue does?
43 Knight's attire
44 Actor Jared
45 Fig. on a vitamin bottle
46 Possible result of an animal bite
48 Door fastener
51 Jimmy of the Daily Planet
53 Bizarre
57 Angsty music genre
59 Look searchingly
61 "Certainly, madame!"
62 Domino's offering
64 *Situation set to explode
66 "Pirates of the Caribbean" locales
67 In the thick of
68 One who ran away with the spoon, in a nursery rhyme
69 Directors Ethan and Joel
70 Slothful
71 Kiln for hops

DOWN

1 Toyland visitors
2 Overhead
3 Bath sponge
4 Dali's "The Persistence of ___"
5 Invaders in an H. G. Wells story
6 Gardner of film
7 Windshield glare reducer
8 A hexagon has six of them
9 Comeuppance for evil actions, supposedly
10 Laudatory poem
11 *Guitar accessory that adds vibrato
12 Itsy-bitsy bit
13 Canyon sound effect
18 Gardner of mystery
22 Download for an iPhone
25 Fish with a net
27 Sad-sounding car company?
29 Sales pitch
31 Be inclined (to)
32 ___ Korbut, 1972 Soviet gymnastics star
33 Old Russian autocrat
34 Gillette razor
35 *Hoodwink
37 Singers James and Jones
40 Agitate
41 Ignore a property owner's signs, perhaps
42 Warm bedtime beverage
47 Visualize
49 Rock's Mötley ___
50 Bob or beehive
52 Country with Sherpas
54 Finnish cell phone giant
55 "___ who?!"
56 Number in an octet
57 "Ben-Hur," for one
58 Soup with sushi
60 Italia's capital
63 Buddhist sect
65 Brainiac

by Jonah Kagan

ACROSS

1 With 17-Across, event of 10/30/10
6 & 10 Sobriquet for Bill O'Reilly used by 39-Across
14 Duck, as a question
15 Real comedian
16 Tolstoy's Karenina
17 See 1-Across
20 Knights
21 White House fiscal grp.
22 Deals in a fantasy league
23 Fashionably old
25 Reuniongoer
27 Buffoon
28 Gambler's best friend?
33 Wizards' and Celtics' org.
36 Winner when heads loses
38 πr^2, for a circle
39 Organizer of the 54-/65-Across
41 Organizer of the 1-/17-Across
44 Uffizi display
45 Tempest
47 Troubadour's song
48 Object of loathing
51 Envoy's bldg.
53 "Shake ___!"
54 With 65-Across, event of 10/30/10
57 Song part
61 Duo
63 Breakfast place that's often open 24 hrs.
65 See 54-Across
68 "Caro nome," e.g.
69 Cook in a way, as tuna or beef tenderloin
70 Rehem, say
71 Not straight
72 Award won for 39- and 41-Across's programs
73 "The Fountainhead" hero

DOWN

1 "Darn it!"
2 To have, to Henri
3 Peter of "Casablanca"
4 Deceives
5 They are 3 ft. long
6 Annual coronation site
7 Complete miss in basketball
8 "The Tell-Tale Heart" writer
9 Offered for breeding
10 Eric who played the Hulk in 2003
11 An OK city
12 Throw in a few chips, say
13 Tampa Bay team
18 How a practical joke or a subway train may be taken
19 "Be All You Can Be" group
24 2.5%/year interest, e.g.
26 Rodeo rope
29 Supreme Court's sphere
30 ___ Mountains, Europe/Asia separator
31 Michael of "Scott Pilgrim vs. the World"
32 1918 song girl whose name was sung with a stutter
33 Final Four inits.
34 Brought into the world
35 Utah ski resort
37 Informal reply to "Who's there?"
40 Wager
42 2 or 3 on the Richter scale, maybe
43 Jane Austen meddler
46 Wrestling duo
49 Smog, e.g.
50 Go by, as time
52 S.O.S alternative
55 Tony-winning Rivera
56 Act like an overly protective parent
57 Pierce
58 Ripped
59 Comparable (to)
60 Tidy
62 Cautious
64 Employee discount, e.g.
66 Opposite of masc.
67 Swiss river

by Chris Handman

ACROSS

1 Not reacting to pain, say
6 Playboy centerfold, e.g.
11 Col. Sanders's restaurant
14 Go round and round
15 Tennis champ Agassi
16 ". . . ___ he drove out of sight"
17 Aid for a person with a limp
19 Yang's counterpart
20 Sound from a mouse
21 Blue Ribbon beer brewer
23 Brussels ___
26 Arabian V.I.P.'s
27 River past Westminster Palace
28 Party handouts
30 "That's ___!" ("Not true!")
31 Cosmetician Adrien
32 Machine tooth
35 ___ Alamos, N.M.
36 Drug from Colombia
38 "Long ___ and far away . . ."
39 Virgil's 61
40 Long-armed ape, for short
41 Late West Virginia senator Robert
42 W.W. II admiral Chester
44 Island where many a 40-Across lives
46 Disheveled
48 Most boneheaded
49 One out of prison
50 Mick Jagger and bandmates, informally
52 ___ carte
53 1941 Orson Welles classic
58 Architect I. M. ___

59 French word before cuisine or couture
60 Respected tribe member
61 ID on an I.R.S. form
62 ___ a positive note
63 Actress Winona

DOWN

1 Opposite NNE
2 Old "Up, up and away" carrier
3 Texaco's business
4 Irritating
5 In-group
6 Senate gofers
7 Early Peruvian
8 Fargo's home: Abbr.
9 Keats's "Ode on a Grecian ___"
10 Hotel room door feature
11 Nixon's Florida home
12 Pat down, as for weapons
13 Number after a decimal in a price
18 Items in a Planters can
22 ___ Lingus
23 Play for time
24 Showy flowers
25 Creating a ruckus
26 Stereotypical Swedish man's name
28 Writer Kafka
29 Fat as ___
31 Nervous as ___
33 Fairy tale monsters
34 Whom Vladimir and Estragon were waiting for, in a Beckett play
36 War chief Black Horse's tribe
37 Copier input: Abbr.

41 In a quick and lively manner
43 Judge in the O. J. Simpson trial
44 Common shape for a dog biscuit
45 First game of the season
46 Harvests
47 Connections for car wheels
48 Egg carton count
50 Poker variety
51 Latin jazz great Puente
54 Author Fleming or McEwan
55 Put two and two together
56 Jacqueline Kennedy ___ Bouvier
57 Blunder

by Holden Baker

ACROSS

1 Toy gun shot
4 Machine that was often cloned
9 Molecular matter
13 "Don't Bring Me Down" band, for short
14 It may be "golden" in mathematics
15 Kind of shark
16 Where a cowpuncher may work
18 Sweat spot
19 School attended by James Bond . . . and Ian Fleming
20 Big bears
22 Drink made with vodka, coffee liqueur and cream
26 Equipment for Olympian Lindsey Vonn
27 Aunts, in Arles
30 "Exodus" hero
33 Grades in the mid-70s
35 "Arrivederci"
36 "Sorry if that rude word offended you"
40 Double-reed woodwind
41 Prefix with -morphism
42 "What a pleasant surprise!"
43 Letter-writing prisoner, perhaps
46 Quatre + un
48 Play whence the phrase "the most unkindest cut of all"
53 Group for young people coping with parental substance abuse
55 "Othello" villain
56 Green fruit
57 What the last words in 16-, 22-, 36- and 48-Across are
61 ___ fixe
62 "Fiddler on the Roof" milkman
63 Game cube
64 Signs of approval
65 Pictures that may be difficult to focus on
66 Word repeated in a classic "When Harry Met Sally . . ." scene

DOWN

1 Moisten, as grass
2 Animator Don
3 "Same here"
4 Like the verb "to be": Abbr.
5 Sheep's cry
6 Everest, e.g.: Abbr.
7 Selects
8 Any regular on "The View," e.g.
9 Atmosphere, as at a restaurant
10 Quentin who directed "Inglourious Basterds"
11 "I get it already!"
12 Does some lawn work
17 Sinusitis docs
21 1/7 of a Spanish week
23 Kitchen utensil brand name
24 Nothing, in Paris
25 1972 #2 hit for Bill Withers
28 Individually
29 Greenwich Village neighbor
30 Individually
31 "Streamers" playwright David
32 Exhibiting fierce determination
34 Matches, as two tapes
37 Sheriffs' sidekicks
38 Bank guarantor, for short
39 "Five Women" author Jaffe
44 Word that can follow pale, brown or cask
45 Told fibs
47 British monarch beginning in '52
49 Overseas diplomat in N.Y.C., say
50 Little Orphan Annie's dog
51 Texas A&M athlete
52 Rock's Guns N' ___
53 Like, with "to"
54 Beach resort at the entrance to the Lagoon of Venice
58 Model Herzigova
59 Six-Day War land: Abbr.
60 Word with the longest entry in the O.E.D.

by Brendan Emmett Quigley

ACROSS

1 Path of a Hail Mary pass
4 "Remember the ___!" (cry of 1836)
9 Wranglers, e.g.
14 ___ de Janeiro
15 Pine exudation
16 Baby hooter
17 The Braves, on scoreboards
18 "Carpe diem"
20 Officer's identification
22 Family car
23 Imitate
24 Poverty
26 Burst of wind
28 Quickly satisfy one's hunger
34 "___ the land of the free . . ."
35 Spike, as the punch
36 Birth-related
38 Large number
40 Harvests
43 Owner of the bed that was too soft in "Goldilocks and the Three Bears"
44 Takes on, as workers
46 Diploma feature
48 Hosp. employee
49 Rough-and-tumble outdoor kids' game
53 London art gallery
54 Secular
55 Where you might get into hot water?
58 Passover feast
61 Motored
64 Commonplace utterance . . . or a description of 18-, 28- and 49-Across?
67 Half a dozen
68 Shake hands (on)
69 Schindler of "Schindler's List"
70 Touch on the shoulder, say

71 Breakfast, lunch and dinner
72 First-time drivers, often
73 ___-mo

DOWN

1 The "A" in U.A.E.
2 Hayworth of "Cover Girl"
3 Late 1940s to about 1990
4 Weapons depot
5 Actor ___ J. Cobb
6 Sale tag words
7 1987 Masters winner Larry
8 Fidgety
9 First impeached U.S. president
10 Mother in a flock
11 Alan of "Crimes and Misdemeanors"
12 Certain tide
13 Eye problem
19 Fully stretched
21 Talk and talk and talk
25 Ski lift
27 Squad
28 Exclamation before "darn it!"
29 Excavated item, maybe
30 What most of hail is
31 Razz
32 Regardless of the results
33 Busch Gardens locale
37 Singer k. d. ___
39 Openly grieved
41 Caress
42 Comic Mort
45 Squirrels away

47 Captains and commanders
50 Lone Star State sch.
51 Extremely popular
52 Tree with cones
55 Offer that's too good to be true, often
56 Beep, as a doctor
57 Gillette brand
59 Gaelic tongue
60 ___ over the coals
62 Medicine bottle
63 World's fair
65 Animation frame
66 ___ Bernardino Mountains

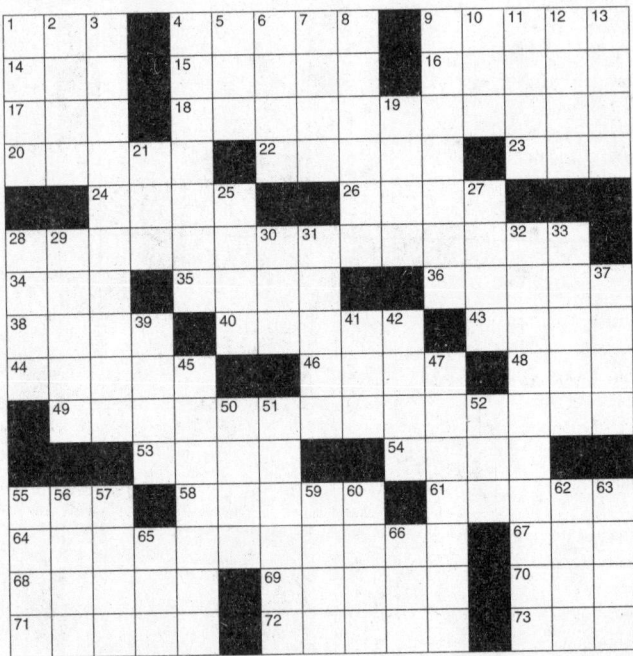

by John Dunn

ACROSS

1 Like a cool cat
4 Not the brightest bulb on the tree
8 U. of Maryland team
13 "___ seeing things?"
14 "Hollyoaks" actress ___ Atkinson
15 Bozo
16 Fuel for some trucks
18 Eating only certain things
19 With 55-Across, source of this puzzle's quote (which starts in box #38)
21 Rick's "Casablanca" love
22 Word after public or private
23 Shopping mecca
26 Danish astronomer Brahe
29 Scott in an 1857 Supreme Court case
33 Chest: Prefix
35 Touch down
37 Manning of the gridiron
38 "Au contraire!"
39 "In what way?"
40 Cast out
42 Where cranberries grow
43 In stitches
45 Calls during curtain calls
46 Wooden shoe's sound
48 How nonreading musicians play
50 Lean (on)
51 Yevtushenko's "Babi ___"
53 Abound (with)
55 See 19-Across
62 Jewish holiday in Adar
63 Insect known for conducting raids
64 "Inferno" writer

65 Wind indicators
66 Calendar unit
67 Powerful chess piece
68 Added stipulations
69 Leave slack-jawed

DOWN

1 Muslim's pilgrimage
2 Mideast leader
3 Place to fish from
4 Does some business with
5 "Don't worry about me"
6 Year the Department of Homeland Security was created
7 Visibly terrified
8 Slightly drunk
9 Trimmed to fit, say
10 Filthy ___
11 Pig's container, in a saying

12 Pig's container
14 Earth sci.
17 Some beach house supports
20 Gas in lights
23 "Morning Joe" TV channel
24 "You're such ___" (teen put-down)
25 "Unhand me!"
27 Any "Jurassic Park" dinosaur
28 "Yee-___!"
30 Chaucer pilgrim
31 It shines in España
32 Like a space cadet
34 Santa syllables
36 ___ Spiegel (German magazine)
39 Numbered rte.
41 Big name in GPS devices
44 River of Aragón

45 Zephyrs
47 It glitters but isn't gold
49 Within easy reach
52 Madison Avenue workers
54 Cupid, to the Greeks
55 Party with poi
56 Author Sarah ___ Jewett
57 Broad bean
58 Certain Fed
59 "Nothin'"
60 Be a busy beaver
61 Eye woe
62 A.S.A.P.

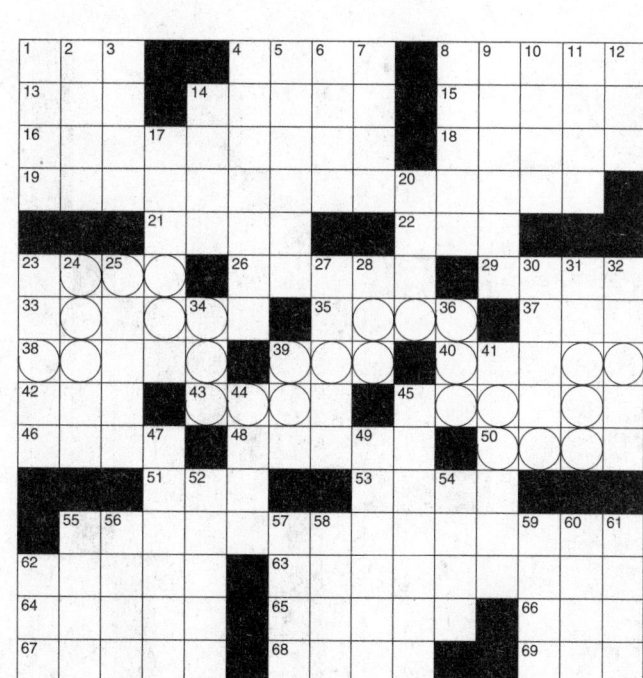

by Daniel A. Finan

ACROSS

1 Dog's bark
7 Nincompoop
10 Regarding, on a memo
14 ___ and 3-Down
15 "Xanadu" grp.
16 Refrigerate
17 Italian cheese that's often grated
18 Fishing pole
19 Greek god with a bow and arrow
20 Editors' marks meaning "put back in"
21 Commercial lead-in for Rooter
22 ___ and 10-Down
23 Latin "to be"
24 Disputed region between Pakistan and India
26 Office transcribers
28 Stylish again
32 Pooh's friend in "Winnie-the-Pooh"
35 Staircase aid
36 Flew high
37 Bottoms of crankcases
39 Not natural
40 Smitten
41 What may have the makings of a hero?
42 Calls from Rocky
43 Foot gear for an N.H.L.'er
44 Unfasten
46 Having a fright
48 Competent
52 ___ and 38-Down
55 Christian in fashion
56 Cloudless
57 Chorister's voice
58 Frequent, in verse
59 City north of San Francisco
60 Gin flavoring
61 Hwy.
62 ___ and 49-Down
63 Easter roasts
64 Road curve
65 Tenant

DOWN

1 Lower in rank
2 Becomes inoperable, maybe, as an old machine
3 14-Across and ___
4 Playing marbles
5 Govt. rules
6 To's opposite
7 Spray type
8 Lazy people
9 Gomorrah's sister city
10 22-Across and ___
11 Romance writer Roberts
12 Corner piece in chess
13 Besides
21 Indian princesses
24 "The Family Circus" cartoonist Bil
25 Funny in a twisted way
27 Commit a basketball infraction
29 Buffet meal carrier
30 Edit menu command
31 Tributes in verse
32 Louis XIV et Louis XVI
33 Sty sound
34 Earthen pot
36 Dieter's meal, maybe
38 52-Across and ___
39 Poetic rhythm
41 Lowers in rank
44 Snow buildups
45 Mideast confections
47 Idolize
49 62-Across and ___
50 Hanukkah treat
51 Irregularly edged
52 Hit TV show set in Korea
53 Jazz great Fitzgerald
54 Elemental unit
56 Part of an apple
59 Gridiron grp.

by Emily L. Lilly

ACROSS

1 Surmise
6 Say "Oh, that was nothing," say
11 "I ___ you one!"
14 Awaken
15 "M," "W." or "Z"
16 Small dog, for short
17 Picture in one's head
19 Barnyard male
20 Gucci of fashion
21 Face-to-face test
22 Seven-times-a-week newspaper
24 Shaving woes
26 New Orleans sandwiches, informally
27 "Do you have any jacks?" response, maybe
30 Bedding material
31 Basketballer nicknamed the Big Aristotle
32 Washer cycle
34 Nittany Lions' sch.
37 Regained one's winning status . . . or a hint to this puzzle's circled letters
41 "The buck stops here" prez
42 Speech setting
43 First, second and reverse
44 Suitcase attachment, for short
47 Justice Stephen of the Supreme Court
48 $100,000/year, e.g.
50 Rice dish
52 A-number-one
53 Flintstones' pet
54 It takes a while to tell
58 Carpenter's curved tool
59 Seabed
62 32-Down's woodlands mate
63 Carpenter's smoothing tool
64 Al ___ (like some noodles)
65 Goof
66 Madrid man
67 Faint with ecstasy

DOWN

1 "Joy of Cooking" author Rombauer
2 Holiday number
3 Supply with money
4 Native of the land known by natives as Eesti
5 Stephen of "V for Vendetta"
6 Smug look
7 Postaccident conditions
8 Indianapolis 500 track, e.g.
9 Biblical fruit
10 Use for sustenance
11 Football ploy
12 Like a sheep
13 TV awards
18 ___ Lomond
23 Grandpa on "The Simpsons"
25 Emerald ___
26 Pub order
27 One dressed in black, maybe
28 Cross to bear
29 Garden enrichment
30 Propaganda, often
32 62-Across's woodlands mate
33 Honor society letter
35 Desertlike
36 "Back in the ___"
38 Time of reckoning
39 Indian tourist city
40 Hearty entree that may be cooked in a Dutch oven
45 Beaver's work
46 Scout units
47 Gooey mass
48 Diamond alternative
49 Zeal
50 Elton John's instrument
51 Word before self or strength
53 College V.I.P.
55 "___ extra cost!"
56 Head for
57 "You said it, brother!"
60 The Indians or Browns, on a scoreboard
61 Some E.R. cases

by Ian Livengood

ACROSS

1 Wrestling surfaces
5 Small plateaus
10 Gets on in years
14 Pioneering razor with a pivoting head
15 Bright-eyed and bushy-tailed
16 Tedious way to learn
17 Actor Penn with two 23-Across
18 Big name in Scotch
19 Bart Simpson's brainy sister
20 Meal money in Manitoba?
23 Academy Awards
24 Show that launched Eddie Murphy and Chevy Chase, for short
25 Gangster's gun
28 Golf peg
29 Quick bite
32 Persistent, irritating critic
34 Meal money in California?
36 Unconscious state
39 Cenozoic or Mesozoic
40 Scots Gaelic
41 Meal money in Tuscany?
46 Comic's asset
47 Feudal worker
48 Tanning lotion letters
51 Spanish "that"
52 Actor Cage, familiarly
54 Daytona 500 acronym
56 Meal money in Massachusetts?
60 Was sorry about
62 The Ram
63 Benevolent and Protective Order group
64 Not much
65 Boardinghouse window sign
66 Baldwin of "30 Rock"
67 Not his
68 New Mexico county whose seat is Alamogordo
69 Actress Sedgwick of "The Closer"

DOWN

1 Georgia's bulldog or Princeton's tiger
2 "Relax, soldier!"
3 Hypnotized state
4 Yemen's capital
5 President after Jefferson
6 Home of Zeno
7 Stitched
8 Most Yemenis
9 Eerie
10 Folkie Guthrie
11 On the path to great success
12 U.F.O.'s crew
13 Word repeated in the lyric "From ___ to shining ___"
21 Villain in the title of a James Bond book
22 Ali, before he was Ali
26 Part of baseball's postseason: Abbr.
27 Rug rat
30 British W.W. II gun
31 Parsley, sage, rosemary and thyme
33 Played records at a party, say
34 Where Timbuktu is
35 Opposite of well done
36 Quote from, as a legal case
37 Elevator pioneer Elisha
38 Who owned the too-soft bed that Goldilocks tried
42 Quaint roadside stops
43 Energetically, in music
44 Che Guevara's given name
45 ". . . to buy ___ pig"
48 Mulder's partner on "The X-Files"
49 Green Bay athlete
50 Sprite alternative
53 French painter of "Le Pont de Mantes"
55 The "turf" part of "surf and turf"
57 2:1 or 3:1
58 River near the Great Pyramids
59 Wanton look
60 "Go, team!"
61 Sport-___ (vehicle)

by David Poole

ACROSS

1 Native encountered by Pizarro
5 Shakespeare, with "the"
9 D sharp equivalent
14 "Silent Night" or "Away in a Manger"
15 "By Jove!"
16 Novelist ___ Carol Oates
17 *What "S.R.O." indicates
19 Capital of more than 15 states
20 Arthritis preceder
21 Indy quick-change artists
23 Broadway singer/actress Verdon
26 Part of N.B.
27 *The Magi, e.g.
31 Pal
35 Kanga's little one
36 O'Brien's late-night predecessor and successor
37 Like wet paint
39 Helpers: Abbr.
41 "That hurts!" cries
43 "It's ___ of the times"
44 Kind of league
46 Like about half of a team's games
48 Mauna ___
49 ___ doble (Spanish dance)
50 *Sound from a palace bathroom?
53 What lines with stars at the end indicate in comics
55 Boyfriend
56 "Agreed!"
60 Stilted response to "Who's there?"
64 ___ City, S.D.
65 What the answer to each starred clue is
68 Wield, as influence
69 The "A" in A-Rod

70 Alike: Fr.
71 Response to a schoolyard denial
72 Make a fuss at a public meeting, maybe
73 Use a lasso on

DOWN

1 Skinny
2 Entre ___ (confidentially)
3 Boston cager, briefly
4 Claim
5 Prefix with hazard
6 Tempe sch.
7 Blacksmith's tool
8 Hiding the gray, say
9 VCR button
10 *Group with the 1951 hit "Tell Me Why," with "the"
11 Orpheus' instrument

12 Have ___ (lose it)
13 Thomas Hardy heroine
18 "Do you have a better idea?"
22 Flip
24 Barely make, with "out"
25 Madre's boy
27 "The Sound of Music" family name
28 One of 12 Minor Prophets of the Hebrew Bible
29 Alternatives to reds and whites
30 "Don't even think about it!"
32 Japanese verse form
33 Yens
34 Talking bird
38 Upscale London district

40 *Makeup of a double date
42 Mop
45 Shallowest of the Great Lakes
47 Sam Adams product
51 At the same level (with)
52 Writer of "The 95 Theses"
54 Supplement
56 Steamed
57 What planes do after landing
58 Whipped along
59 Role for 23-Across in "Damn Yankees"
61 Shakespearean schemer
62 [Just like that!]
63 Like some threats
66 Novelist Kesey
67 Bus. card datum

by Richard Chisholm

ACROSS

1 "___ hands are the devil's tools"
5 "Nonsense!"
9 Webster of Webster's dictionary
13 Do library study
14 Convention center event, for short
15 Romance or sci-fi
16 Priestly robes
17 ___ year (period of 366 days)
18 Pitchers
19 Wildflower from which the cultivated carrot originated
22 "When ___ See You Again" (1974 #2 hit)
23 AOL or MSN: Abbr.
24 Former C.I.A. chief Porter ___
26 Enzyme suffix
27 Something that is ultimately ruinous
31 Cincinnati baseball team
33 Homer Simpson exclamation
34 Nervous
35 & 37 Hair accessory . . . or a literal hint to 19-, 27-, 47- and 56-Across
39 ___ point (very center)
42 Kind of sauce
43 Bank no.
47 Orange item set out by a highway crew
51 "Bali ___" ("South Pacific" song)
52 It may hit a bull's-eye
53 Nearly worthless amount
54 Region
56 Very best
60 Toboggans
61 "Drat!"
62 Taj Mahal city

63 11 ___ and spices (KFC secret ingredients)
64 German river where American and Soviet forces met in 1945
65 Bridle strap
66 "___ can you see . . . ?"
67 Marsh plant
68 German three

DOWN

1 It started in 2003 with the bombing of Baghdad
2 Comic actor Dom
3 Tagged for identification
4 1950s Ford flop
5 Lugosi of horror films
6 Plow team
7 "Cómo está usted?" language
8 [Keeping fingers crossed]
9 Incoming administration's to-do list
10 Minimal paint job
11 Nabs
12 "___ Just Not That Into You" (2009 film)
15 Hair goop
20 Suffix with refuse
21 Letters on a Coppertone bottle
25 "Once bitten, twice ___"
28 Boise's home: Abbr.
29 Lawn base
30 Aykroyd of the Blues Brothers
32 Handed a raw deal from

36 Santa helper
37 Hiss accompanier
38 Literary Rand
39 Bouquets-to-order co.
40 Magic 8 Balls, e.g.
41 Classic Porsche model
42 Fight that's less than a brawl
44 San Diego footballer
45 Some diet drinks have one
46 Kettledrums
48 Doctrine
49 Author James Fenimore
50 Before, poetically
55 Modern greeting form
57 Long-eared equine
58 Toothpaste holder
59 Hurried
60 "___ 'nuff"

by Elizabeth A. Long

ACROSS

1 Farm newborn
5 Yankees' "$275 million man," informally
9 Test proctor's command
14 Like dental surgery
15 "Good one!"
16 Blow the socks off
17 ___ mater
18 The "Y" in Y.S.L.
19 Helicopter part
20 Is ranked #1
23 Bizarre
24 Climate-change protocol city
25 Wee bit
27 Disney dwarf with glasses
30 Sign on a construction site fence
35 Lavatory door sign
37 Part of a school year: Abbr.
38 Carrots' plate-mates
39 Brief visit along the way
42 Declines to participate
44 ___ Sutra
45 Play from which the word "robot" comes
47 Civic maker
48 Dry cleaner's fluid
52 Suffix with slogan
53 Bummed out
54 Congested area, sometimes
56 Drinking binge
59 Megabucks
64 Rig out
66 Fodder holder
67 Part of an apple or the earth
68 Socially polished
69 Source of indigo dye
70 Solemnly swear
71 Whip-cracker
72 Outside of a watermelon
73 Glasgow gal

DOWN

1 Ulster, for one
2 Folkie who sang of Alice
3 Magic item of folklore
4 Toper's back-pocket item
5 "Moving on then . . ."
6 Construction fasteners
7 Forest felines
8 Arnaz of "I Love Lucy"
9 Toper's expense
10 Weezer's music genre
11 Cat in una casa
12 Shirt brand
13 Dweeby sort
21 Like a universal donor's blood
22 Tread heavily
26 Toper, slangily
27 PC storage units
28 Coming up
29 Andrew of New York politics
31 Prefix with con or classical
32 Sierra ___
33 Honor, on a diploma
34 Astronomical red giant
36 Tiffs
40 Corleone who broke Michael's heart
41 "Fee fi fo ___"
43 Rhythmic humming sound
46 "William Tell" composer
49 Ice-T or Ice Cube
50 Isaac Stern's instrument
51 Wrap around
55 L.A.'s area, for short
56 "Surely you ___"
57 Light blue
58 Island "where America's day begins"
60 Pre-1917 autocrat
61 Suddenly bright star
62 Amor's Greek counterpart
63 Trees yielding archery bow wood
65 "___ Got a Secret"

by Kristian House

ACROSS

1 Native Louisianan
6 Sass
9 Future's opposite
13 Make a grand speech
14 Physician's org.
15 Pinnacles
17 Appreciated
18 In good order
20 Adam and Eve's first home
21 Watch intently
22 Actor Stephen of "Michael Collins"
23 Annie Oakley, for one
26 Bandleader Shaw and others
29 Mate for 60-Down
30 Combat stress syndrome
35 Watch chains
38 Disney frame
39 Last installment of "The Godfather"
41 Cultural support org.
42 "Stop right there!"
44 Pull a bed prank on
46 Cow sound
48 Funnywoman Boosler
49 Wool gatherer
55 Thanksgiving side dish
56 Rosebush hazards
57 Make woozy
61 Bootblack's service
63 "The Taming of the ___"
64 Ankle bones
65 Title for Galahad
66 "___ bleu!"
67 Viewed
68 Tetley product
69 Set of cultural values

DOWN

1 Porter who wrote "Night and Day"
2 Saharan
3 Gyllenhaal of "Love & Other Drugs"
4 Knife, fork or spoon
5 Rorem who composed the opera "Our Town"
6 Modern surgical tool
7 Zoot-suiter's "Got it!"
8 Noah's ark groupings
9 Congregation leader
10 German exclamation
11 Wagers from those in the know
12 Shelter made of buffalo skin, maybe
16 Blacken, as a steak
19 Oom-___
21 Succeed in appearing to be
24 Lend a hand
25 Buffoon
26 Yiddish writer Sholem
27 Perlman of "Cheers"
28 "Go on . . ."
31 Prince's title: Abbr.
32 Plains Indian
33 Round fig.
34 Writers of bad checks
36 Has-___
37 Overfill
40 ___ of Wight
43 One on the Statue of Liberty is almost three feet long
45 Construction worker
47 Chooses to participate
49 The "S" in CBS: Abbr.
50 Laughs
51 Library admonition
52 Lift
53 W.W. II correspondent Pyle
54 "It's the end of ___"
58 St. Louis's Gateway ___
59 0
60 Mates for a 29-Across
62 Language suffix
63 Opposite of NNW

by Richard Chisholm

ACROSS

1 Neighbor of Kuwait
5 Sugar source
10 Ice Follies venue
14 Half of Mork's sign-off
15 Volunteer's cry
16 Arabian Peninsula sultanate
17 Governor in Austin?
19 Area that may have stained-glass windows
20 Come together
21 Card player's boo-boo
23 All the world's one, to the Bard
25 Unwelcome result of a shopping spree?
27 Chow down
28 Give kudos
30 "Black gold"
31 Sluggers' stats
33 Life stories, for short
35 Nut jobs
39 Bit of Sunday TV scheduling . . . or a hint to 17-, 25-, 50- and 59-Across
42 Aid in finding sunken ships
43 Part of a wedding cake
44 Jackson or Winslet
45 Sock hop locale
47 Galifianakis of "The Hangover"
49 Actress Farrow
50 Airport baggage handler?
54 Like half of a pair of dentures
56 Do the work of a florist or an orchestrator
57 "S O S," e.g.
58 Belly laugh
59 Sheep's accuser?
64 Cut and paste, say
65 Pungent-smelling
66 Lowdown
67 Say isn't so
68 Presidents Tyler and Taylor, for two
69 Plastic brick brand

DOWN

1 Abbr. at the end of a co. name
2 Cheerleader's cry
3 Walt Disney's specialty
4 "The Caine Mutiny" captain
5 Oven user's aid
6 Leave dumbstruck
7 Snapshots, for short
8 Cousin of an alpaca
9 Weather-affecting current
10 Place for a "Bridge Out" sign
11 Rock and Roll Hall of Fame architect
12 Like Fran Drescher's voice
13 Mournful peal
18 Have a hunch
22 Bit of equipment for a circus clown
23 Feudal drudges
24 Verboten
25 Burden of the conscience-stricken
26 Put on a pedestal
29 Attorney's org.
32 Event that may include blue films
34 Dirty campaign tactic
36 Bubbly drink
37 Protruding navel
38 Gaff, to a fisherman
40 Orator William Jennings ___
41 Rainbow shape
46 Dr. Phil's last name
48 Hip-shaking dance
50 Actor Leto of "American Psycho"
51 Chip away at
52 Choo-choo
53 Stacy who played Mike Hammer
55 Danger
57 Degs. for many profs
60 CAT scan alternative
61 A smoker might bum one
62 Trio after D
63 Kanga's baby

by Andrea Carla Michaels and Kent Clayton

ACROSS

1 Boeing 747s, e.g.
5 Out of bed for the day
10 Rand McNally product
13 Resting on
14 Part of the eye
15 In bed all day, maybe
16 Profits
18 Hornets' and Nuggets' org.
19 Industrial city of Germany
20 Winter precipitation
22 Gulf war missiles
25 Town dump, e.g.
28 Othello's supposed rival for Desdemona's affection
30 "Beep beep" maker
31 Commotion
32 Teacher, after exams
35 "Quickly!," on an order
39 The, grammatically
42 Musial of the Cardinals
43 Egyptian god of the underworld
44 Last in a sequence: Abbr.
45 ___ of Man
47 Actress Reynolds of "The Unsinkable Molly Brown"
49 Dodge City lawman
54 The "T" in TWA
55 German Hermann
56 Use the pink end of a pencil
58 Antlered animal
59 Emmy-winning nature series narrated by David Attenborough
65 Ginger ___
66 Grapefruit-like fruit
67 ___ as shootin'
68 Wrecker's job
69 Kick out of school
70 Shed thing hidden in 16-, 25-, 39-, 49- and 59-Across

DOWN

1 Feb. preceder
2 Summer in France
3 Tyke
4 Goes 80, say
5 Extend a subscription
6 Turner's 1986 rock autobiography
7 ___ City (Las Vegas)
8 London's locale: Abbr.
9 Former Egyptian leader with a lake named after him
10 Many a West Virginia worker
11 "The Zoo Story" playwright Edward
12 Oro y ___ (Montana's motto)
14 B&O and Short Line: Abbr.
17 Give, as homework
21 Island west of Maui
22 A lot
23 Citadel student
24 Stars and Stripes land, for short
26 Remove wool from
27 Hot
29 Baltimore baseballer
33 Bewildered
34 "Agnus ___"
36 Swim with the fishes, say
37 Bold poker bet
38 "For ___ sake!"
40 The J. and K. in J. K. Rowling: Abbr.
41 African fly pest
46 Vast treeless plain
48 Suckling site
49 Bread choice that's not white or rye
50 Mello ___ (soft drink)
51 Off-kilter
52 Actress Zellweger
53 Suave or VO5 competitor
57 From ___ Z
60 Bagel topper
61 What a guitar may be hooked up to
62 Regret
63 Gay singing syllable
64 Billy Joel's "Tell ___ About It"

by Patrick Blindauer

ACROSS

1 End of a fable
6 Place to pray
9 Game with knights
14 Hitch on the run
15 "To a . . ." poem
16 8½"×14" paper size
17 Monica with two U.S. Open wins
18 Without reluctance
20 Make a legislative speech, e.g.
22 Ear doctor
23 Vote in favor
26 Go ballistic
30 Greedy person's cry before and after "all"
31 Get clean, as in rehab
32 No longer active: Abbr.
34 Catchall category
37 Popular cameras
39 Shade of green
40 Rapper's entourage
44 Choir voice
45 Be stir-crazy
49 "___ Ramsey" (1970s western)
50 "Pay to ___" (check words)
51 Where one might 20-, 26- and 45-Across?
57 Summer woe
60 ___ Jean (Marilyn, originally)
61 How the euphoric walk
62 They, in Tours
63 Bothered incessantly
64 Summer who sang "Love to Love You Baby"
65 Police dept. title
66 Performed superbly

DOWN

1 Go well together
2 Dairy case bar
3 See 11-Down
4 Mimicked
5 Anne Rice vampire
6 Propelled
7 Imposing building
8 Sturdily built
9 Advertising award
10 English king crowned in 1100
11 With 3-Down, Chinese restaurant offering
12 Mineo of film
13 On the ___ (furtively)
19 Hand moisturizer, e.g.
21 "Come again?"
24 Sign up
25 Ballplayers' representatives
26 Like state-of-the-art gadgetry
27 Get a lungful
28 Bit of gym attire
29 61, in old Rome
30 Swabbie's handful
33 General on Chinese menus
35 33⅓, for an LP
36 Tearful one
38 Penn of "Harold & Kumar" films
41 Olympian's no-no
42 Put in chains
43 Most weird
46 Strands during the winter, perhaps
47 Director Craven
48 Fight venues
52 More, in adspeak
53 "Letting Go" novelist Philip
54 Layered cookie
55 Neighbor of Yemen
56 9-Across ending
57 Cover with turf
58 Half of dos
59 A Bobbsey twin

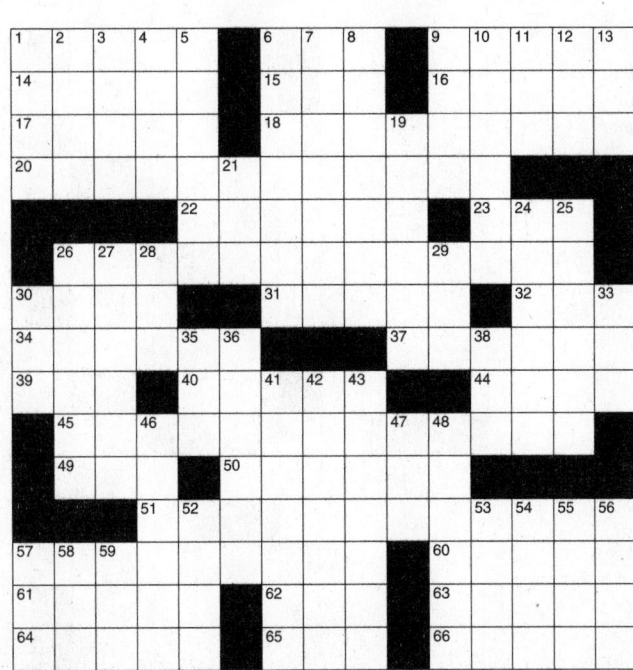

by Mark Feldman

ACROSS

1 Jump
5 1960s–'70s R&B singer Marilyn
10 Observe the Sabbath
14 Norway's capital
15 Thin as ___
16 "Beetle Bailey" bulldog
17 Game played with strings looped over the fingers
19 Spicy Asian cuisine
20 Shaking a leg
21 Feather pen
22 Self-description of someone who's surprised
25 Farmer-turned-conman in a 1960s sitcom
28 Not much
29 Designer Geoffrey
30 Oklahoma city named for the daughter of its first 4-Down
31 Many miles off
35 Docs' org.
36 Long time
40 Hole in one
41 Song for one
43 Electrocute, in slang
44 Former name for Congo
46 Big hauler
48 Called balls and strikes
50 Taro
54 Bosc and Bartlett
55 Move to another job, say
59 Smarting
60 What a greedy person may grab
62 The "O" in CD-ROM
63 Disney mermaid
64 Prayer starter
65 Meal on a military base
66 Ashen, as a complexion
67 Blows away

DOWN

1 ___ Ness monster
2 Biblical twin who sold his birthright
3 Cockpit readings: Abbr.
4 One who "always rings twice," in an old movie
5 Jarhead
6 Ill-tempered
7 Bum, as a cigarette
8 OPEC supply
9 Cheer for a toreador
10 Capitol feature
11 Body of values
12 Suddenly stop, as an engine
13 French fabric
18 Like Dolly the sheep
21 Sine ___ non
23 When said three times, "and so on"
24 Fawn's father
25 Many corp. hirees
26 San ___, Italian resort on the Mediterranean
27 "Physician, ___ thyself"
30 Nile snake
32 Place to buy cotton candy
33 Farming unit
34 Wetlands plant
37 Princess in L. Frank Baum books
38 Loss's opposite
39 Modern toll-paying convenience
42 Fish-eating birds
45 Event for stunt pilots
47 Quizzical utterances
48 Early computer forum
49 Pathetically small
50 ___ salts
51 Africa's Sierra ___
52 Some English nobles
53 Un + deux
56 Othello's betrayer
57 "Oh, ___ up!"
58 Nancy Drew's beau and others
60 Napkin's place
61 Savings for one's later years, for short

by Donna Hoke

ACROSS

1 Do a double-take, e.g.
6 Made a choice
11 Composition of Jack Haley's Oz character
14 God, to Muslims
15 Gaucho's plain
16 "Six Feet Under" network
17 F.A.A. supervisors?
19 Belief suffix
20 Start of a countdown
21 Jerome who composed "Ol' Man River"
22 Dolts
24 Object to online commentary?
27 Cosine's reciprocal
30 "Waiting for Lefty" playwright
31 It's walked on pirate ships
32 ". . . ___ saw Elba"
34 Awaiting scheduling, initially
37 Holiday smokes?
41 Broadcast
42 Strong desires
43 Tickle
44 Want badly, with "for"
47 Least amiable
48 Cleaned up after a spill?
52 Tilter's weapon
53 ___-Tass news agency
54 Martinique, par exemple
57 Heavenly body
58 Defamation in the Garden of Eden?
62 Fertility clinic cells
63 Potter's potions professor
64 Playing pieces in Rummikub
65 Nat Geo, for one
66 Snap course
67 Wield, as power

DOWN

1 Totally absorbed
2 Vogue competitor
3 Shepard in space
4 Pink-slip
5 "Lola" band
6 Start of grace, maybe
7 Fallback strategy
8 Subject of a cigarette rating
9 Shut down
10 Prescription measure
11 "You're right"
12 "The Wild Duck" playwright Henrik
13 Chinese restaurant request
18 Out of alignment
23 Bilko or Friday: Abbr.
24 Gershwin's "The ___ Love"
25 Windblown soil
26 Keatsian or Pindaric
27 Pet advocacy org.
28 Grades K—12
29 Allotment of one, usually, for an airline passenger
32 Make improvements to
33 Turned chicken
35 One calling the shots
36 "I'd hate to break up ___"
38 One of four on a Rolls
39 Cut jaggedly
40 Mideast potentate: Var.
45 Catchall abbr.
46 Free from anxiety
47 Font option: Abbr.
48 Burst into flower
49 Maggot or grub
50 Hardly macho
51 Totally lost
54 Pink-slip
55 Lecher's look
56 Once, old-style
59 Paternity suit evidence
60 Smallish batteries
61 Give a thumbs-down

by Alan Arbesfeld

ACROSS

1 Half of the Dynamic Duo
7 33⅓, e.g., for a record: Abbr.
10 Envision
13 Stir up
14 Prefix with space
15 Word after sales or income
16 Second-stringer
18 One thing ___ time
19 Window framework
20 Milan opera house La ___
21 Rapper ___ Wayne
22 Compensation in bills and coins
25 Put a cork in
29 Mao ___-tung
30 "Great taste . . . less filling!" sloganeer
34 Still red, as a steak
38 Loosened, as a 57-Down
39 Before, poetically
40 Eskimo boat
41 Miss ___ USA
42 1986 Keanu Reeves film
44 Tip of a boot
46 Gets rigid
47 Car in the Playmates' 1958 hit "Beep Beep"
53 Suffix with rational or civil
54 Someone who gives you the willies
55 Opened one's eyes in the morning
59 Place
60 Classic TV intro . . . or a hint to the starts of 16-, 22-, 30-, 42- and 47-Across
63 Not con
64 "What's ___ for me?"
65 Magazine manager
66 Hankering
67 Banned insecticide, for short
68 Take down a peg or two

DOWN

1 Nickname for Barbara
2 Environs
3 A lot
4 A lot
5 ___ Wednesday
6 Just off the assembly line
7 Chart again
8 Church dignitary
9 Some eels
10 Like week-old bread
11 Dine at home
12 Glorify
14 Design feature over many a gate
17 Stupidhead
22 Prompted
23 Easter mo., often
24 Fish-tailed males
25 Porn
26 Fork prong
27 Merrie ___ England
28 Base of a column
31 Hawaiian garland
32 Newspaper columnist Kupcinet
33 Golf peg
35 Assists
36 Fulminate
37 Barely manages, with "out"
40 Consumer
42 Ram into from behind
43 ___ 1 (Me.-to-Fla. highway)
45 Flower often used in a 31-Down
47 A bit cold
48 Sky-blue
49 Place atop
50 Kind of badge for a Boy Scout
51 Reddish-purple bit in a salad
52 Records turning at 33⅓ 7-Across
55 Capricious desire
56 "Hold ___ your hat!"
57 Shoelace problem
58 Brontë's "Jane ___"
61 ___ Bartlet, president on, "The West Wing"
62 Poem of praise

by C. W. Stewart

ACROSS

1 Bookcase unit
6 Drill instructor's rank, often: Abbr.
9 Animal trap
14 Tool with a bubble
15 Poet who created the Ushers
16 Color variations
17 Fight card venue
18 Have payables
19 Comment to the audience
20 Distance runner's skirt?
23 Catches some rays
24 Beats it
28 Chicken, so to speak
32 Season after printemps
33 Compete
34 Military sandwich?
37 "Candid Camera" request
39 Bottom-of-letter abbr.
40 Clear wrap
42 Battle of Normandy city
43 Emitted a contented sigh
45 Outstanding crowd scene actor?
47 Sch. in Troy, N.Y.
48 Sussex suffix
50 Most robust
51 Plaything with a fulcrum
53 Defense in a snow fight
55 Valuable truck?
61 Company behind the game Battlezone
64 Hurler's asset
65 Applied 3-in-One to
66 Netflix rental
67 Juno or NetZero, for short
68 Serving a purpose
69 Antler sporters
70 Utmost in degree
71 Dry runs

DOWN

1 Verbal assault
2 Zeus' wife
3 Partner of anon
4 "Havana" actress Olin
5 Render pancake-shaped
6 Dish's runaway partner, in rhyme
7 Graduation attire
8 Abound (with)
9 Batting positions
10 Boot camp reply
11 Young Skywalker's nickname
12 "Curse you, ___ Baron!"
13 U-turn from WNW
21 Where the Styx flows
22 Believer's suffix
25 Take to the sky
26 Four-lap runners, often
27 Witnessed in the area of
28 Slings mud at
29 Cocktail hour nibble
30 Jughead's buddy
31 Stir up
32 Abba of Israel
35 Not risky
36 Mentalist Geller
38 1140, in old Rome
41 India's longest-serving P.M.
44 Works of Pepys and others
46 Visits a diner
49 Neighbor of Nor.
52 Bit of parsley
53 Leading the pack
54 Get-up-and-go
56 Genesis brother
57 Webmaster's creation
58 Yale students
59 Disappear à la Frosty
60 Fateful day for Caesar
61 Pro-___ (some tourneys)
62 Huggies wearer
63 Gardner of "Mogambo"

by Robert A. Doll

ACROSS

1 Tiddlywinks or tag
5 Leftover cloth bit
10 Moon-landing vehicles, for short
14 The Bard of ___ (Shakespeare)
15 Michelangelo masterpiece
16 "Peter Pan" pirate
17 Reaction of a sore loser
19 Boxer Oscar ___ Hoya
20 Bosom buddy
21 ___-hour traffic
23 Lung protector
24 Food from heaven
25 Head honcho
27 Shelley's "___ to the West Wind"
28 Cartoonish baby cry
30 Gives in (to)
31 Scotch and ___
33 Rioter's haul
36 Triumphant cries
37 Be productive . . . or what the answers at 17-, 25-, 53- and 63-Across do?
40 Hate
43 Highlands denials
44 Sounds of amazement
48 Country music's Tritt
50 Mattress problem
52 "Just kidding!"
53 They protect car buyers
56 City NW of Orlando
58 Reactions to adorable babies
59 Accessory that might say "Miss Universe"
60 "The ___ Bunch" of 1970s TV
61 AARP part: Abbr.
63 Select the best and leave the rest
66 Earl ___ tea
67 Seoul's home

68 Melville work set in Tahiti
69 Brontë's Jane
70 Boiling indication
71 Puts in stitches

DOWN

1 Windbag's output
2 Guacamole need
3 Lamented the loss of
4 Energy company that filed for bankruptcy in 2001
5 Energetic for one's age
6 Org. in "The Bourne Identity"
7 Copy, for short
8 Enjoyed immensely
9 Elapse
10 '60s hallucinogen
11 Valuable green stone

12 Bill & ___ Gates Foundation
13 "Chilean" fish
18 Munch on like a mouse
22 Jean-Bertrand Aristide's country
24 May and June: Abbr.
25 Locust tree feature
26 "That's swell!"
29 Lobster ___ Newburg
32 From the beginning, in Latin
34 Arthur Miller's "Death ___ Salesman"
35 Lock of hair
38 Brockovich and Moran
39 It's between Can. and Mex.
40 On the loose

41 Anheuser-Busch, for one
42 Pet with cheek pouches
45 Words after stop or turn
46 "My heavens!"
47 RR stop
49 Pants that are dressier than jeans
51 Graphically violent
54 ___ in the dark
55 Question of location
57 Mafia bosses
60 Stoker who created Dracula
62 It may have made a blonde blonde
64 Stephen of "The Crying Game"
65 Bout enders, briefly

by Paula Gamache

ACROSS

1 Pooh-pooh, with "at"
6 Way up a ski slope
10 School zone warning
14 TV signal component
15 Beatles meter maid
16 Topper for Charles de Gaulle
17 *Antishoplifting force
20 Roll-call call
21 D.C.'s Pennsylvania, e.g.
22 Antiseptic element
23 Early James Bond foe
25 With 46-Across, be angry . . . or what you can do inside the answers to the six starred clues
26 *Marching band percussion
30 Lower chamber of Russia's parliament
34 In a cautious way
35 Excuse maker's word
36 X ___ xylophone
37 Satan's doings
38 State of confusion
39 Verge
40 Word with a handshake
41 Shell game spheroid
42 Hold tight
43 Some annexes
44 *Rims
46 See 25-Across
47 Prospector's strike
48 Financially solvent
52 E-mail attachment, for short
53 MasterCard alternative
57 *Textbooks for instructors
60 Nagging desire
61 In a snit
62 Subject of much Mideast praise
63 Pigskin supports
64 Manly man
65 Missouri Indian

DOWN

1 Window part
2 Just adorable
3 ___-Eaters (shoe inserts)
4 *School evacuation exercises
5 A McCoy, to a Hatfield
6 "Key Largo" Oscar winner Claire ___
7 Orthodontist's concern
8 Wolfed down
9 Most risqué
10 Losing streak
11 Jeans maker ___ Strauss
12 Ready for business
13 Like an oracle
18 Foppish dresser
19 Tip of a wingtip
24 Reunion group: Abbr.
25 Full of oneself
26 Nobel or Celsius
27 Orange feature
28 Popular typeface
29 W.W. II sea menace
30 *Evel and Robbie Knievel, for two
31 Taking habitually
32 Cut into tiny bits
33 Hippies' crosses
38 Hatfield/McCoy affair
39 Ran in the wash
41 Anne Bradstreet, for one
42 Spring bloomers
45 Said "bos'n" for "boatswain," e.g.
46 When repeated, gung-ho
48 Engaged in a 38-Down
49 Big bash
50 Add a kick to
51 Phil who sang "Draft Dodger Rag"
52 Chile's northern neighbor
54 Seat of Allen County, Kan.
55 Hang-up
56 1975 Wimbledon winner
58 Pure baloney
59 "___ Te Ching"

by C. W. Stewart

110 EASY

ACROSS

1 Go back and forth in deciding
6 Traffic tie-ups
10 Hit hard
14 Common cause of food poisoning
15 Qatari ruler
16 Melville novel
17 Alaska boondoggle in 2008 campaign news
20 Eliot's "Adam ___"
21 Roman 552
22 Put a spell on
23 Relative of an ostrich
25 Part of a mushroom
27 Place to get gas
33 Minds
34 Tue. follower
35 Having ___ of fun
37 Yukon S.U.V. maker
38 Very hot and dry
42 Uno + due
43 Reach across
45 '60s–'70s service site
46 Molecule parts
48 Full-size Fords
52 Quaker pronoun
53 Where Obama was born
54 Texas A&M player
57 Summit
59 Degrees for corp. execs
63 Gets ready to crash
66 Cotton unit
67 State north of Ill.
68 MetLife competitor
69 Still sleeping
70 Suffix with major
71 Bygone anesthetic

DOWN

1 Jack who played Sgt. Friday
2 Plot unit
3 Null and ___
4 Getting on in years
5 Semi-tractor trailer
6 Trans-Atlantic air traveler's woe
7 Mine, in Marseille
8 Reverend
9 Sellout sign
10 Western part of the Czech Republic
11 "Don't leave home without it" card
12 Achy
13 Cleared weeds, say
18 Genesis garden
19 Hone
24 Snake's sound
26 "Didn't I do great?!"
27 Clouds (up)
28 1980s hardware that used Microsoft Basic
29 Old Renault
30 Beturbaned seer
31 10th-century Holy Roman emperor
32 ___ Jean Baker (Marilyn Monroe)
36 Eliot of "The Untouchables"
39 "The Diary of ___ Frank"
40 Lose one's temper
41 Sodium hydroxide, to a chemist
44 Observed
47 Dizzy Gillespie's instrument
49 Cry on a roller coaster
50 Force
51 Vehicle with a medallion
54 "Dancing Queen" group
55 Snatch
56 Near-hurricane-force wind
58 Part of P.O. or P.S.
60 The Wife of ___ (Chaucer character)
61 Teen affliction
62 One of seven in the Big Dipper
64 Stockholm's land: Abbr.
65 Fannie ___

by Ron and Nancy Byron

ACROSS

1 Ear part
5 Date with an M.D.
9 Restaurant chain whose logo features a western hat
14 Gumbo vegetable
15 Carson predecessor
16 Long-legged fisher
17 Germy dessert, to a five-year-old?
19 "Hello, Don Ho!"
20 Part of S.W.A.K.
21 Greek god of war
23 "Are you ___ out?"
24 Bird known for making baskets
26 Best Supporting Actor for "Cocoon"
28 Not many
30 Grub consumed around the dinner table?
33 Sasha and Malia's father
35 Prayer's end
36 No-brainer in school
37 Meditation syllables
38 It might be fixed or frozen
43 Picket line crosser
45 October blooms
46 One who's daft about archaeology?
51 Cornstarch brand
52 Sound before a blessing
53 Pitcher Satchel
55 Peter the Great, for one
56 [Oh, my stars!]
59 Twenty : English :: ___ : Italian
62 No longer sick
64 X, to a pirate?
66 "___ having fun yet?"
67 Hard-core followers, in politics
68 "Garfield" canine
69 Good name for a lingerie salesman?
70 Zenith
71 Prefix with phone

DOWN

1 "Livin' la Vida ___"
2 "Enough already!"
3 Young chickens suitable for dinner
4 Erodes
5 Monkey's uncle?
6 Mango alternative
7 Ark unit
8 Genealogy chart
9 Cry of discovery
10 Help from a bullpen
11 Rodeo horse
12 Start of a pirate's chant
13 Caught in a trap
18 Mideast land since 1948: Abbr.
22 "Dollar days" event
25 ___ Bridge, connecting Manhattan, Queens and the Bronx
27 Mocking birds?
28 Prez on a penny
29 Air safety grp.
31 "West Side Story" shout during "The Dance at the Gym"
32 Sends an OMG or LOL, say
34 Tokyo-based synthesizer maker
37 Big galoot
39 Parent in the wings, perhaps
40 Play to the balcony?
41 Bit of energy
42 General on Chinese menus
44 Drano target
45 One of the eight states bordering Tenn.
46 Influential moneybags
47 "And I'm the queen of England"
48 Yellow
49 Cunning
50 Stand against
54 It climbs the walls
57 Pop group whose name is coincidentally a rhyme scheme
58 Ivory, e.g.
60 Math subj. with many functions
61 Big furniture retailer
63 Susan of "L.A. Law"
65 Many a cowpoke's handle

by Patrick Blindauer and Rebecca Young

ACROSS

1 Not striped, as a billiard ball
6 Apple or quince
10 With 18-Across, the Tour de France, for one
14 Diagonal line, on a bowling score sheet
15 Carrier to Tel Aviv
16 Applications
17 Extend, as a subscription
18 See 10-Across
19 Profound
20 Game show catchphrase #1
23 When a plane or train is due, for short
24 Come out of a coma
25 Buenos Aires's country: Abbr.
28 Golf course pitfall
31 Medieval martial art
35 Ford auto, briefly
37 Game show catchphrase #2
39 Corporate raider Carl
41 Sign before Virgo
42 Neighbor of a petal
43 Game show catchphrase #3
46 Repetitive learning technique
47 Prisoner
48 H.S. junior's hurdle
50 Thoroughfares: Abbr.
51 Save, in a way, as some shows
53 However, briefly
55 Game show catchphrase #4
61 Moccasin decoration
62 Salvador who painted "The Persistence of Memory"
63 Halloweenish
65 Ricelike pasta
66 Analogous (to)
67 Les ___-Unis
68 Comic book heroes originally called the Merry Mutants
69 Identify
70 Krispy Kreme offering

DOWN

1 Belarus or Ukraine, once: Abbr.
2 Org. with many Mideast members
3 Turner who was known as the Sweater Girl
4 Actress Cara
5 Early New York governor Clinton
6 Lima's locale
7 Oil of ___
8 Noisy bird
9 Raise
10 Big Super Bowl advertiser, traditionally
11 "So that's it!"
12 Nautical bottom
13 Clairvoyant's claim
21 Taverns
22 Green-lights
25 Firenze friends
26 What a drone airplane may do, for short
27 Former Texas senator Phil
29 "___ Lang Syne"
30 Before surgery
32 Cosa Nostra leaders
33 Hilton rival
34 Man and Wight
36 Two-timed
38 Things two-timers break
40 "Reward" for poor service
44 Reno resident, e.g.
45 Western mil. alliance
49 Kind of movie glasses
52 Japanese port
54 Shelley's "___ the West Wind"
55 Four years, for a U.S. president
56 Fog or smog
57 Slight, as chances
58 Merlot, for one
59 Charter member of 2-Down
60 In ___ (as originally located)
61 Practice pugilism
64 Superlative suffix

by Adam Cohen

ACROSS

1 #1 position
5 According to
10 I.R.S. figures: Abbr.
14 Coal cart
15 Handed (out)
16 First Indian tribe met by Lewis and Clark
17 Bird watcher's accessory
19 The Crimson Tide, familiarly
20 Week-___-glance calendar
21 What a coach driver holds
22 2, for one
23 Trace of color
25 Tide or Cheer
28 Beetles sacred to ancient Egyptians
30 Language suffix
31 Prefix with content
32 "___ recall . . ."
33 One of five in "Julius Caesar"
34 ___ d'Ivoire (African land)
35 Essential part necessary for fulfilling a goal . . . or what 17-, 25-, 48- and 57-Across all have?
39 Droids
40 Flee
41 ___ de Cologne
42 Winter hrs. in Bermuda
43 Peace, in Peru
44 Compresses, informally
48 Symbol of life
51 Ones in a gaggle
52 "So long"
53 Demolish
55 Young fellow
56 Certain iPod or skirt
57 Cheesy Mexican snack
60 Knievel on a motorcycle
61 Smarty
62 Working without ___
63 Actor Beatty and others
64 Wuss
65 What a jack-of-all-trades is master of, supposedly

DOWN

1 Baseball statistics
2 "Everyone's a ___"
3 Procrastinator's response
4 Rock music subcategory
5 Together, on musical scores
6 Sphere and cube
7 Smoothing tool
8 Suffix with election
9 Things with shoulders: Abbr.
10 Edna Ferber novel
11 Young starlet's promoter, maybe
12 Propose for election
13 Where Starbucks was founded
18 Ironing line
22 Rap's Dr. ___
24 There are about 28.35 of these in an ounce
26 Georgia ___
27 High regard
29 Place for a petri dish
33 Sign at a convenience store
34 Save the Whales, for one
35 Plummet
36 Got
37 Disconcert
38 Measured
39 "Who Let the Dogs Out" group
43 Score components: Abbr.
44 Equilibrium
45 "Absolutely not!"
46 ___ Institute, California retreat center for alternative education
47 Tranquilize
49 Stirs
50 Neighborhoods
54 Wacky
57 Ones making handoffs, for short
58 Geller with supposed psychic powers
59 McEwan or McKellen

by Zoe Wheeler

ACROSS

1 Placed on a wall, as a picture
5 "It is ___ told by an idiot . . .": Macbeth
10 Went in haste
14 Butterlike spread
15 [See grid]
16 High-protein food often found in vegetarian cuisine
17 Lollapalooza
18 Make up for, as sins
19 Duos
20 The "P" in P.T.A.
22 Wrigley Field or Camden Yards
24 Facts and figures
26 Envision
27 "The racer's edge"
30 Boulder's home: Abbr.
32 Took for a trial run
37 In the poorest of taste, as a novel
40 Nozzle connector
41 Exactly what's expected
44 Sir ___ Guinness
45 Device that measures gas properties
46 Ankle-related
49 Classical opera redone by Elton John
50 180° from NNW
51 ___ cit. (in the place cited)
53 "Deadly" septet
55 Geometric curve
60 Cinco de Mayo party
64 "Washingtons"
65 "Thank you, Henri"
67 Tex's sidekick
68 Luau instruments, for short
69 [See grid]
70 Having length and width only, briefly
71 Vessel in "Cast Away"
72 Creation that's almost human
73 Concorde fleet

DOWN

1 Hula ___
2 Radius's neighbor
3 ___-do-well
4 Like an unfortunate torero
5 Slaughterhouse
6 Onesie wearer
7 Lots
8 Singer Horne and actress Olin
9 Shoelace hole
10 Internet address opener
11 Early state in presidential campaigns
12 Get an ___ effort
13 Dawn's opposite
21 Cheese-covered chip
23 Stan of Marvel Comics
25 Prince Valiant's wife
27 March 17 honoree, for short
28 Syllables in a gay refrain
29 Gadget for someone on K.P. duty
31 Milo of "Ulysses"
33 Elisabeth of "Leaving Las Vegas"
34 Legal wrongs
35 Mountain road features
36 Plow manufacturer
38 Certain NCOs
39 Actresses Garr and Hatcher
42 Systematized, as laws
43 Resident on the tip of the Arabian Peninsula
47 Tirana's land: Abbr.
48 Appeared on the horizon
52 Easy to understand
54 Back-to-school mos.
55 Preside over the tea ceremony
56 Paul who wrote "My Way"
57 Snorkeling site
58 Kind of prof. or D.A.
59 Ship in search of the Golden Fleece
61 Old sayings
62 Harness race gait
63 Comments further
66 151, in old Rome

by Holden Baker

ACROSS

1 This plus that
5 Breath freshener
9 In the style of: Suffix
14 First razor with a pivoting head
15 Child of invention?
16 Boast of
17 *Mark the transition from an old year to the new, maybe
19 Restaurant owner in an Arlo Guthrie song
20 Mercenary in the American Revolution
21 ___ Hawkins Day
23 "Enough already!"
24 Like a post-fender-bender fender
27 Common paper size: Abbr.
28 Concept in Confucianism
30 ___ extra cost
31 Burping in public, e.g.
34 Place for a hot pie to cool
35 Billboard
36 Roth ___
37 *Measure with strides
40 Fellows
41 Backgammon pair
43 Pub projectile
44 An Astaire
46 Questions
47 Stat for Babe Ruth: Abbr.
48 Uno + due
49 "Come on!"
51 Neighbor of Macedonia and Montenegro
54 Get in touch with
56 Slob's opposite
58 Factory
60 *New neighbors event
62 Italian bowling game
63 "___ and the Real Girl" (2007 film)
64 Irritate
65 Some are practical
66 Chichi
67 Interval on a scale

DOWN

1 "Brandenburg Concertos" composer
2 Oklahoma Indians
3 Object of Teddy Roosevelt's "busting"
4 Millennium Falcon pilot in "Star Wars"
5 Where trapeze artists meet
6 Runaway bride's response?
7 Partner of improved
8 What bronzers simulate
9 Circumvent
10 California's ___ Valley, known as "America's salad bowl"
11 *Period of contemplation
12 Dad's bro
13 Summer in Montréal
18 First-rate
22 Name widely avoided in Germany
25 Georgia of "The Mary Tyler Moore Show"
26 "Death Be Not Proud" poet
28 Wedding cake layers
29 Oodles and oodles
31 ___ basin
32 Pop up
33 *Reverse a position
34 Permanent reminder
38 Like single-purpose committees
39 Jill's portrayer on "Charlie's Angels"
42 Heart and soul
45 Ones who owe
48 Itty-bitty
50 Entrances to exclusive communities
51 "Hägar the Horrible" dog
52 Arctic native
53 Airplane seating request
55 "Hi, José!"
57 Hang on to . . . or a word that can precede either half of the answer to each starred clue
58 Common sandwich for a brown-bagger
59 W.C.
61 3, 4 or 5, usually, for a golf hole

by Paula Gamache

ACROSS

1 Harold of "Ghostbusters"
6 "Stainless" metal
11 Krazy ___
14 "Alas and ___"
15 "You gotta be kidding me!"
16 Misery
17 They're choosy about what they chew
19 Quaint lodging
20 12 months from now
21 Dressed in lab attire
23 Morning droplets
24 Use a Singer machine
26 ___ vera
27 Mach 1 breaker
29 "Ben-___"
31 Siberian city
34 Certain Indonesian
37 Sensational 1990s–2000s talk show host
39 Walled city near Madrid
40 Blown-up photo: Abbr.
41 Many-___ (large, as an estate)
42 Popular online reference
44 Couples (with)
45 Drink at a sushi bar
46 AOL alternative
47 Round about the belly
48 Concerning, on a memo
50 Miracle-___ (garden care brand)
52 G.I. grub
55 Speaker's stand
58 Say "Holy cow!" or "Hot dog!"
61 ___ of Good Feelings, 1817–25
62 Walt Disney creation
64 Tire fill
65 Sell online
66 Nash who wrote "I don't mind eels / Except as meals"
67 "On ___ Majesty's Secret Service"
68 Small baked desserts
69 Interminably

DOWN

1 Swift
2 1950s Dior dress style
3 Bird important in Mayan symbology
4 Very unpleasant
5 ___ terrier
6 Trap
7 Tyke
8 Providers of sheep's milk
9 Politician's add-on
10 Disinfectant brand
11 Store on TV that sells KrustyO's cereal
12 Super-duper
13 Care for, with "to"
18 Sunup direction
22 Beat Generation persona
25 Annoying complaining
27 Noteworthy
28 Lose it
30 The Bruins of the N.C.A.A.
32 ___-Ball (arcade game)
33 Some colorful sneakers
34 Highest-grossing film before "Star Wars"
35 Adidas alternative
36 "It Must Be Him" singer, 1967
37 Ruby and scarlet
38 "___ Rock" (Simon & Garfunkel hit)
43 Retired, as a female professor
47 Cunning
49 Convened anew, as the Senate
51 Projector items
52 Bea Arthur role
53 No longer in bed
54 Alter, as text
55 Sister of Rachel
56 Upstate New York's ___ Canal
57 Raleigh's home: Abbr.
59 "Get the lead out!"
60 The Olympic rings, e.g.
63 Collection of items for a modelist

by Scott Atkinson

ACROSS

1 Brainy Simpson
5 Try, as a case
9 In pieces
14 A Grimm beginning?
15 Lui : him :: ___ : her
16 First unelected president
17 Suffix with dino-
18 Fabrications
19 Faintest residue
20 Outcome of many a boxing match . . . or 38- and 36-Down
23 Sniggler
24 St. Louis Blues org.
25 One in the hand?
28 Pig's home
29 Corn units
33 Venerate
35 It's sometimes good to get back to them
37 Wood-shaping tool
38 Interstates . . . or 60-Down and 65-Across
43 "Yikes!"
44 Three-ingredient treats
45 Well-thought-out
48 "___, you noblest English . . . !": "Henry V"
49 ___ favor
52 Something to roll over, briefly
53 Brit. reference
55 Weeper of mythology
57 Crushed by sorrow . . . or 5-Across and 63-Down
62 Greek porticos
64 Skateboard trickster's track
65 Partner of means
66 Nail-biting
67 Modern storage units, briefly
68 "Aha!"
69 Early Icelandic literary works
70 U.S. Open's ___ Stadium
71 Drag racing org.

DOWN

1 The second number in a record
2 Peevish
3 Mulder's "X-Files" partner
4 Cliffside nest
5 Didn't give away
6 Author Wiesel
7 A Baldwin brother
8 Sticky stuff
9 Fifth-century emperor remembered as the epitome of cruelty
10 Expert in match play, for short?
11 "The West Wing" actor who played Arnold Vinick
12 Camcorder button abbr.
13 Uno + due
21 Tire pattern
22 Theater admonition
26 Snug as a bug in a rug
27 Flock females
30 Enzyme suffix
31 Clears (of)
32 Ordinary schlub
34 Statutes
35 Wait
36 Priory of ___ (group in "The Da Vinci Code")
38 Tenth: Prefix
39 Noted lab assistant
40 Tramp
41 Miracle-___
42 Temporary tattoo dye
46 Hangmen's tools
47 Shatner's "___War"
49 Soapmaking stuff
50 One following directions
51 Exodus locale
54 Skin: Suffix
56 Golfer Hale ___
58 Tabula ___
59 Scottish rejections
60 Daily temperature stat
61 Otherwise
62 Fr. holy woman
63 Slugger Williams

by Alex Fay

ACROSS

1 Harvard and Wharton degs.
5 ___ Millions (multistate lottery)
9 *With 68-Across, lingerie model's asset
13 Continental coin
14 Starting on
15 Prefix with iliac
16 *It may end up in a chop shop
18 Outerwear for an operagoer
19 On the job
20 Equipment in craps
22 Caustic drain opener
23 It means nothing
25 Own up to one's sins
27 *What you drop uncooked spaghetti or a tea bag into
32 Accepted, as a proposal
33 Gives in
37 Old Navy libation
38 Word describing the answer to each of the starred clues
40 Drink through a straw
41 Assembly of 100
44 Caviar or frogs' legs
47 *Bloody Mary seasoner
49 Mount ___, California observatory site
52 Where the Blues Brothers got their start, familiarly
53 Him: Fr.
54 Affirmative votes
56 "But what to do?!"
61 Popular pain reliever
63 *Supplier of electricity to subway trains
65 Sister's daughter
66 Scouting outing
67 Shaving mishap
68 See 9-Across
69 Imitates
70 Change for a five

DOWN

1 Mini-plateau
2 Thing in an ashtray
3 Lined up, after "in"
4 All alone
5 ". . . one giant leap for ___": Neil Armstrong
6 PC bailout key
7 Egg on
8 Sahara's place
9 Gal in an old song standard
10 Élève's school
11 Dentistry photos
12 Joins, as oxen
15 Start of an act
17 Bert's Muppet buddy
21 Mass-market fragrance maker
24 Width's opposite: Abbr.
26 Citrus soft drink introduced in the 1960s
27 Diamond bases
28 Grimm figure
29 Cast-___ stomach
30 Smooth, in music
31 "Whose ___ these are I think I know": Frost
34 Hawaiian wingding
35 800, to Caesar
36 Kind of terrier
39 Private eyes, for short
42 Husk-wrapped Mexican dish
43 Online auction house
45 Capital of England, to Parisians
46 Stranded in the middle of the ocean, say
48 Franklin known as the Queen of Soul
49 Alternative strategy if things don't work out
50 The "A" in A/V
51 Existed
55 Frigate or freighter
57 River through Florence
58 Cause for a game delay
59 Cursor movers
60 Fraternal group
62 Slippery, as winter sidewalks
64 Prez after Give 'em Hell Harry

by Paula Gamache

ACROSS

1 Warm-up for the college-bound
5 Vena ___ (blood line to the heart)
9 Victory overcoming 100-to-1 odds, e.g.
14 Prefix with sphere
15 Horatian verses
16 ___ del Rey, Calif.
17 Shi'ite leader
18 Lead-in to tiller
19 Put a duty on
20 Chocolate candy from Portugal?
23 Gist
24 Missing link, possibly
28 Milne hopper
29 "___ grip!"
31 "Don't Bring Me Down" grp.
32 African nomad who hasn't had a thing to drink?
36 Rep. rival
37 Mississippi senator Cochran
38 Generous ___ fault
39 Small amount
40 Tummy muscles
41 Lively Indian dance?
45 ___ polloi
46 "High Hopes" lyricist Sammy
47 Pizza ___
48 French schools
50 Fill and then some
54 Drum that's under all the others?
57 No. 2 in the statehouse
60 See 61-Across
61 Molecular 60-Across
62 How a bride and groom leave the altar, metaphorically
63 60-Across of computer memory
64 "Treasure Island," for one

65 Lecher
66 Required element in many figure skating competitions
67 Lead-in to while

DOWN

1 Lover: Suffix
2 They're followed by the finals
3 Heap up
4 Filled with trees
5 Pipe material for Frosty the Snowman
6 Acrobat software maker
7 Presidential "no"
8 "___ of the Sun" (Jack London novel)
9 Feeling well
10 Vehicle that taxis
11 Instrument for Kenny G
12 Part of a storm or a potato
13 Small amount
21 ___ about (approximately)
22 Diminish
25 French red wine
26 Prince Valiant's wife
27 "What God has joined together, let ___ put asunder"
29 What a lame joke might elicit
30 Israeli statesman Abba
32 Lesley of "60 Minutes"
33 "Wow!"
34 Like the A B C's
35 Prepare a commemorative plate, say

39 Very close friend
41 Freeze up
42 Condé ___ (magazine publisher)
43 Movable article of personal property
44 Garage occupant
49 Black key material
50 Whack, biblically
51 Fragrant oil
52 What a poor workman blames, in a saying
53 Irish patriot Robert
55 Marching band instrument
56 Common cameo stone
57 The Shangri-___ ("Leader of the Pack" group)
58 Airport screening org.
59 "___ milk?"

by Robert Cirillo

ACROSS

1 Collegiate digs
5 Baby's first word, maybe
9 Provide with funds, as a college
14 Emmy-winning Falco
15 Milky gem
16 ___-Dade County
17 What a dirty person has
20 ___ Gandhi, pioneering female leader
21 Sch. in Baton Rouge
22 Become less bright, as the moon
23 Refrigerated
25 Go down a slippery slope
27 What an embezzler has
33 Hair-raising
35 City where Joan of Arc was burned
36 Espionage org.
37 "If all ___ fails . . ."
38 Feudal workers
39 Machines on cotton plantations
40 Tennis serve requiring a do-over
41 Coffee for before bed
42 Long, arduous walks
43 What a well-connected applicant has
46 Eccentric
47 Aids for disabled cars
48 Kid's summer getaway
51 Bit of Dobbin's dinner
54 Exam taker
58 What a dreamer has
61 Passion
62 Tartar sauce ingredient
63 The "U" in I.C.U.
64 Manage to avoid
65 Blossom supporter
66 "Toodle-oo"

DOWN

1 Actress Moore
2 Valhalla god
3 Orange or watermelon cover
4 Health program for seniors
5 Gazillionaire Trump
6 Suitable
7 Roald who wrote "James and the Giant Peach"
8 Pub quaffs
9 Australia's unofficial national bird
10 Lamebrain
11 Input for computers
12 Portent
13 Telegram
18 Literary twist
19 Oohs and aahs (over)
24 Not beating around the bush
26 Documentary filmmaker Burns
27 Simply must
28 Singer Jones whose father is Ravi Shankar
29 Spot for eating curds and whey
30 Far less friendly
31 Connection
32 Fair maiden
33 Freudian concern
34 Egypt's last ruling Ptolemy, familiarly
38 Forward, as mail
39 Fill with disgust
41 "The butler ___ it"
42 Low-tech hair dryer
44 Honcho
45 Techie's company
48 Paper ballot punch-out
49 Prefix with dynamic
50 Grass-roots org. that fights alcohol abuse
52 Devices you can bank on, briefly
53 "Take ___!"
55 Deli salad fish
56 Fix up, as text
57 "Cómo ___ usted?"
59 Fury
60 Cyclops' distinctive feature

by Lynn Lempel

ACROSS

1 ___ Canaria Island
5 Low man in the choir
9 Too sentimental
14 Frosty coating
15 Tetra- doubled
16 Smoked or salted
17 Hipster's "Understood!"
18 Mekong River land
19 Brainstormer's output
20 Larva-to-adult transition
23 Idle repairman's employer, in ads
24 Egg pouches
25 "___ pig's eye!"
28 ___, zwei, drei . . .
30 Sports show-off
32 Dawn goddess
35 Be monogamous, among animals
38 Mont Blanc, e.g., to locals
40 Windows program suffix
41 Either "Fargo" co-director
42 Leader on the field
47 Solidify, like Jell-O
48 Main lines
49 Ways to go: Abbr.
51 Sound of rebuke
52 Composer Bartók
55 Use Google, e.g.
59 Spam or sausage . . . or a hint to the starts of 20-, 35- and 42-Across
62 Manuscript sheet
64 Big Ten or Big 12 org.
65 Glass piece
66 Ill-mannered sorts
67 Underworld V.I.P.'s
68 Kerfuffles
69 "Golly!"

70 Stick around
71 Refusenik's refusal

DOWN

1 Brothers' name in children's literature
2 "___ Crooked Trail" (Audie Murphy western)
3 Peaceful relations
4 Cancel
5 Italian city after which a deli offering is named
6 "___ in every garage"
7 Subway map points
8 Skater Cohen
9 Clip out, as a coupon
10 BMW competitor
11 Spanish fortresses
12 Pod item
13 Rushing stats: Abbr.
21 Incapacitate

22 ___ Rios, Jamaica
26 Checking account come-on
27 Worker in real estate, e.g.
29 Assembly instructions part
31 Pampering, for short
32 Really bother
33 Nondairy spreads
34 Ignition system device
36 Phone no. add-on
37 Cause of quaking
39 Defib operator
43 Freight train's "office"
44 "Wait just ___!"
45 "Like taking candy from a baby!"
46 It may be urgent
50 Yangtze River boat
53 A library does it
54 Fancy neckwear
56 "___ or not . . ."

57 Vacation rental craft
58 Mushroom cloud maker, for short
60 Bar mitzvah or bris
61 Yemen's capital
62 Sitcom diner waitress
63 Response from the awed

by Paul Hunsberger

ACROSS

1 Smart ___ (wise guy)
5 Persian tongue
10 Roadies carry them
14 Sandwich spread
15 Sandwich spreads
16 Ark builder
17 Bakery fixture
18 Nickname for Andrew Jackson
20 Island east of Australia
22 Says hello to
23 Treasure chest
27 Trap
28 Mao ___-tung
31 The "R" in RCA
32 Shorebird
33 Depressed urban area
35 Former vice president Quayle
36 Word that can precede the starts of 18-, 20-, 53- and 58-Across
39 Smart ___ (wise guy)
42 Any member of a classic punk rock band
43 Morales of "La Bamba"
47 ___ New Guinea
49 Brian of Roxy Music
50 What the nose picks up
51 Pharaoh's realm
52 Dreary
53 Dangerous thing to be living on
58 First prize at a fair
61 Force felt on the earth, informally
62 Civil rights pioneer Parks
63 Cockpit occupant
64 Zippo
65 Aid and ___

66 Make ___ (do some business)
67 Carrier to Tel Aviv

DOWN

1 Surrounded by
2 Shirley's friend in 1970s–'80s TV
3 Goggles and glasses
4 People's worries
5 Jesters
6 It means everyone to Hans
7 Comedian Foxx
8 TriBeCa neighbor
9 "Beauty ___ the eye . . ."
10 Turkey's capital
11 Neigh : horse :: ___ : cow
12 Number on a golf course
13 Wallflower-ish
19 Lemonlike fruit
21 Dined
24 Like 1, 3, 5, 7, etc.
25 By way of
26 Long stretch of time
28 Parts of a bride's attire, for this puzzle
29 ___ Hall Pirates (1953 N.I.T. champs)
30 Prefix with -centric
33 "Today" rival, for short
34 1-1 or 2-2, e.g.
37 Daniel Webster, for one
38 Opal or topaz
39 Gorilla
40 What mattresses do over time
41 007, for one
44 Original
45 Oakland's county
46 Law-breaking

48 Optimistic
50 Caesar whose forum was TV
52 Al ___ (cooked, yet firm)
54 Kelly of morning TV
55 Sluggers' figs.
56 Syllables before "di" or "da" in a Beatles song
57 Winter coat material
58 Push-up provider
59 High tennis shot
60 Have no ___ for

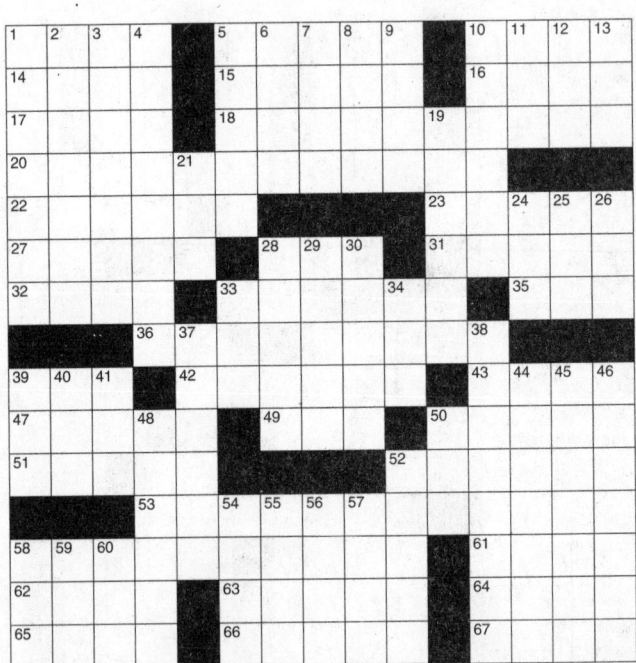

by Steve Dobis

ACROSS

1 Soprano Nixon
6 Infielders' stats, for short
9 Software prototype
13 Demanding instructor's cry
14 "Love the skin you're in" sloganeer, once
17 Part of DKNY
18 Make heads or tails of something?
19 Undergrads' Greek leadership society
21 ___, Straus and Giroux (publisher)
22 Actress Hatcher
23 ". . . like THAT!"
26 Magical
27 Front cover?
29 Turkish capital
31 Steering system part
34 Roman 209
35 Warren Buffett's sobriquet
39 Gazillions
40 Many a nursery chair
41 Racy, say
44 Line part: Abbr.
45 Blood-typing letters
48 Garden party?
49 Target of many a New Yorker cartoon
52 Sent
54 You need to raise your hand to receive this
56 Drunkard
59 Doesn't include
60 Pulitzer-winning novel by Willa Cather
61 Mixed bags
62 ___' Pea
63 What "-" means in a Google search
64 First course?

DOWN

1 Financial scammer Bernie
2 Old Greek markets
3 Was used up
4 S.F. footballer
5 How a fatwa might be issued
6 Tip politely
7 Pre-episode
8 Dirtball
9 ___ Burger (veggie patty)
10 "Turn to Stone" grp.
11 Skater Babilonia
12 Author Rand
15 "The Makropulos Affair," for one
16 "Oliver Twist" creep
20 Bay window
23 Composer with 20 children
24 Song on a stage

25 Top (out)
28 ___ Rabbit
30 1981 Chrysler debut
31 ___ Gallery
32 Tic-tac-toe line . . . and a hint to this puzzle's theme
33 R.A.F. awards
35 Patron saint of Norway
36 Repetitive learning
37 Vermont ski resort
38 Big bust
39 It might come after you
42 Tom Thumb, for one
43 Five to one, e.g.
45 Keys of music
46 Invite
47 "Potemkin" port
50 Olympic snowboarding gold medalist White

51 2009 U.S. Open winner Juan Martin del ___
53 "___ to Pieces" (Patsy Cline hit)
54 Cousin of an English horn
55 Suffix with song
56 Aegean tourist mecca
57 Fort Myers-to-Tampa dir.
58 Wide shoe spec

by Elizabeth C. Gorski

ACROSS

1 See 26-/28-Down
8 See 26-/28-Down
15 Banned medicine used to treat asthma
16 Spray
17 Pinchas Zukerman, e.g.
18 Where "Lucrezia Borgia" premiered
19 Ocean ring
20 Baccarat alternative
21 5/29/1917, for J.F.K.
22 Fish by letting the bait fall lightly on the water
23 ___ Brothers
26 When doubled, a 19-Across
27 Hired thugs
29 "Drawing is putting a line round an ___": Henri Matisse
30 1976 Pulitzer winner for "Air Music"
31 Sports bar fixture
33 Mother ___
34 Big stretch?
35 Ma or Pa in a Steinbeck novel
36 Steinbeck, e.g.
39 Dark
42 Nods
43 Passion
44 Org. that combats illegal file sharing
46 Buffalo-hunting Indians
47 "Easy there!"
49 Approximate year in which Eric the Red was born
50 Big lotto prize, for short
51 Is unused
52 1986 rock autobiography
54 On the mend, say, as one's arm
56 Stephen of Joyce's "A Portrait of the Artist as a Young Man"
58 Pecan, e.g.
59 Senators' place
60 See 26-/28-Down
61 See 26-/28-Down

DOWN

1 See 26-/28-Down
2 "The best is yet to come," for Frank Sinatra
3 Screamed and hollered
4 Scream and holler
5 "Swan Lake" swan
6 Ones on the right track?: Abbr.
7 "Kitty ___" (Beyoncé song)
8 Syllables following "Strike the harp and join the chorus"
9 Doctor whom Nixon called "the most dangerous man in America"
10 Roughly
11 Bird of myth
12 ___ Freleng, creator of Bugs Bunny and Daffy Duck
13 Actual name of Nabokov's Lolita
14 See 26-/28-Down
20 Stew
24 Dealer's accessory
25 It's depicted on the Sistine Chapel ceiling
26 & 28 Theme of this puzzle
30 Unembellished
32 Some necklines
33 TV character who said "Him a beauty. Like mountain with snowsilver-white"
35 Don ___
36 See 26-/28-Down
37 Royal attendants
38 Person who's out of step with society
39 Tailors
40 Island in the Mediterraneo
41 Chairman of the Senate Armed Services Committee, 1987–95
43 Throat soother
45 See 26-/28-Down
47 Second-generation Japanese-American
48 Ream out
51 Pioneering puppeteer Tony
53 Sour
55 D.C.'s Kennedy ___
56 Dark
57 Prefix with warrior

by Brendan Emmett Quigley

Note: When this puzzle is done, connect the four V's with a square, the three K's with an upside-down L, and each K diagonally to the nearest V. Then draw a circle around the only X.

ACROSS

1 Temporary homes for refugees
6 Weekly reading for drs.
10 Wail
13 Scare slightly
14 "Sadly . . ."
15 Supermodel Wek
17 ___ dish
18 Brewskis
19 The way the cookie crumbles
20 Cry heard at a 37-/40-Across
23 Philosopher Watts
24 New Deal inits.
25 French city with a 1598 edict
28 Colorado Springs's ___ Air Force Base
33 Galoot
34 Cuts
36 Let (up)
37 With 40-Across, casino fixture
39 Canterbury can
40 See 37-Across
41 Vatican tribunal
42 Six, at a 37-/40-Across
44 Spearheaded
45 Large-scale wickedness
47 Kitchen items that ding
49 2008 U.S. govt. bailout recipient
50 "Now I see!"
51 Cold, at a 37-/40-Across
59 Dudley's love in old cartoondom
60 Sprinkler attachment
61 Totaled
62 Roof's edge, often
63 Wilson of "Wedding Crashers"
64 Ailey of dance
65 Sidekick
66 Careful phrasing, perhaps
67 Hostess who inspired "Call Me Madam"

DOWN

1 Six of these make a fl. oz.
2 Olympic blade
3 Punishment for a teen, maybe
4 Clawed
5 Like some hot dogs
6 Husband of Medea
7 Grad
8 Fixed, as dinner
9 Proclaims
10 Refuge
11 Norway's patron saint
12 ___ noire
16 Boy toy?
21 Alternative to credit
22 Novelist Harper
25 Inlay material
26 Kitchen wear
27 "Super!"
28 Stockholder's substitute
29 Antidiscrimination agcy.
30 Expensive fur
31 Sir William who wrote "The Principles and Practice of Medicine"
32 "Pressing" things
35 Plenty
38 Euclidean geometry's ___ postulate
40 Laurence Sterne's "___ Shandy"
42 Honcho
43 Olympians, e.g.: Abbr.
46 "O Sole ___"
48 Esprit de corps
50 Cut taker
51 Snake eye (as this completed puzzle depicts)
52 Tide type
53 Edison's middle name
54 Herbert Hoover's home state
55 Minute part of a minute: Abbr.
56 Mailers: Abbr.
57 Squabbling
58 Kind of coffee

by Peter A. Collins

ACROSS

1 Nailed
5 Portland's Rose Garden, e.g.
10 "Twelfth Night" sir
14 Trademarked spray
15 Work divided by time, in physics
16 "Gotcha"
17 Greek god of fake tans?
19 Chain "links": Abbr.
20 Outer layer of the cerebrum
21 "Gotcha"
23 Of yore
24 "Galifianakis wants you to call him back"?
28 Twangy-sounding guitar
30 Java flavor
31 Irksome response to "You're avoiding the question"
34 Sign in the middle of town
37 Selma Lagerlöf's "The Wonderful Adventures of ___"
38 Madhouse at a G.O.P. convention?
41 Do as Dürer did
42 Where credit is given
43 "I should ___ die with pity, / To see another thus": King Lear
44 Find new tenants for
46 Get the word out, perhaps
48 Informal erotic reading?
51 Figurative device
55 Dictator's underling
56 Band with three self-titled albums (1994, 2001 and 2008)
57 "At the Movies" bit
59 Famous Amos, e.g.?
62 Falafel bean
63 Lightning Bolt
64 New Zealand : Kiwi :: Costa Rica : ___
65 Drawing pair, perhaps
66 Gets a break, maybe
67 Tiresias, e.g., in Greek myth

DOWN

1 Brand with a torch in its logo
2 Number of holidays?
3 Greeting on a computer?
4 In need of some hammering out
5 Pinnacle
6 Cartoonist Chast
7 Dolly, for one
8 Surgical specialty, informally
9 Bad match result?
10 China has only one
11 Freeze out
12 Bernanke of the Fed
13 "All right!"
18 High-tech map subject
22 Perfect instance
24 A party (to)
25 Magical land
26 Tech-savvy "24" woman
27 Sports
29 Biting comment
31 Biting
32 "Psycho" setting
33 Nonsexist, in a way
35 Swizzles
36 Brown of Newsweek/ The Daily Beast
39 Batch holder
40 Decorative neckline insert
45 Philosopher Mo-___
47 Puts up
49 Arouse, as someone's wrath
50 Tight rope?
52 Smith in Cooperstown
53 What two fingers may signify
54 Overthrow, e.g.
56 First part of a record
57 Head of cabbage?: Abbr.
58 Permissive
60 Western treaty grp.
61 Drummer's setup

by Joon Pahk

ACROSS

1 Parting word
5 Subject with limits and functions, informally
9 SALT concern
13 Dashboard accessory
15 Nothing more than
16 Food product whose name is an example of "foreign branding"
18 Straw in the wind
19 Big A.T.M. maker
20 Frank
21 Thousand-dollar sums, slangily
22 What 16-Across has?
24 Quark-binding particle
27 Hobby farm denizens
28 Guest worker, e.g.
34 Anonymous surname
35 Mower maker
36 Annie Oakley had a good one
39 What 28-Across has?
44 Proactiv treats it
45 Swiss 5-Across pioneer
46 Ribbon-cutting event
52 Back 40 unit
53 A villain might come to one
54 WWW access option
57 Oscar winner Kedrova
58 What 46-Across has?
60 Give ___ to (approve)
61 Really out of it
62 Some chevron wearers: Abbr.

63 ___ breve
64 Messes up

DOWN

1 "All the Way" lyricist
2 Computer serviced at Genius Bars
3 Way out there
4 Online "Unbelievable!"
5 Jackal or coyote
6 Extra
7 Former NPR host Hansen
8 Hoodwink
9 Sid's sidekick of early TV
10 Fastener for basement flooring, perhaps
11 Greyhound and others
12 Top-2% organization
14 Projectionist's task of old
17 Mme. counterpart
22 ___ polloi
23 Moo goo ___ pan
24 [I'm mad!]
25 Actor Gorcey
26 Sleazy salesman's site, stereotypically
29 N.Y. summer hrs.
30 Largest U.S. union
31 Business card abbr.
32 Sound from a Yorkshire terrier
33 Aloha shirt accessory
37 Having four sharps
38 Boss of a sales staff: Abbr.
40 Diamond complements
41 Leftorium proprietor on "The Simpsons"
42 Shylock, for one

43 Big ape
44 Proceeding like a lob
46 Some fund-raisers
47 Piece of kabuki costumery
48 Bamboo muncher
49 Ford who was the son of Henry Ford
50 Noel who played Lois Lane
51 Home of Bollywood
54 Peephole's place
55 Urge on
56 Not including
59 Last word of Romeo or Juliet

by Jeffrey Wechsler

ACROSS

1 Explorer Abel who discovered New Zealand
7 Band with the 1994 platinum record "Always"
14 Lease period, often
16 Pacific
17 Purplish drink
18 "Pete ___ Greatest Hits" (1967 release)
19 "It looks that way to me!"
20 *Let off some steam?
21 Casting need
22 Accompany musically, maybe
24 Walks off with
28 *___ soup
30 *Not get some Z's?
33 *Birthday secret
34 Kind of dye
36 Capital whose name means "big tree" in Arabic
38 Hockey's Tikkanen
39 Title for this puzzle . . . which the answers to the eight starred clues will help explain
42 Tic-tac-toe loser
44 Suffix with concession
45 Make out
46 *Workshop sight, perhaps
48 *CD part
50 *Providence campus for aspiring artists, for short
53 "___ My Sugar Standing in the Rain" (1920s hit)
55 Sea-___ Airport
57 "Hud" Oscar winner Patricia
59 *It may be pumped or bumped

62 Port on the Tyrrhenian Sea
64 Fantastik, e.g.
67 Causing to wear away
68 Not false
69 Big name in pizza
70 Noodle strainers?
71 Smoothie flavor

DOWN

1 Words sung "with love"?
2 Wreath for the head
3 Martial arts instructor
4 1942 musical starring Rita Hayworth
5 Ethereal
6 Two-time Oscar nominee J. Carrol ___
7 Big blowout

8 "The ___ Love" (1987 hit)
9 Big blowout?
10 Puzzle type
11 Be shy
12 Alternative spelling: Abbr.
13 Collection agcy.
15 French Fauvist Dufy
23 Athletic conference for Grinnell, Ripon and Beloit
25 Chicken ___
26 Suffix with heir or host
27 Doo-wop syllable
29 Baum princess
31 The first "S" in S.S.R.: Abbr.
32 Pursuits of some candidates, for short
35 "The Wizard ___"
37 New World abbr.
39 Water bearer?

40 Night that "Dallas" aired for most of its CBS run: Abbr.
41 Checked
42 Benedict ___ (pope beginning in 2005)
43 Salad topping
47 Rub away
49 Checked out
51 Sister of Venus
52 Yogurt brand
54 Points at the table?
56 Fake chocolate
58 Mucho
60 Spanish muralist
61 Uno y dos
63 ___ Linda
64 TV show with Dr. Ray Langston
65 Kind of license: Abbr.
66 One who's often looking down in the mouth, for short?

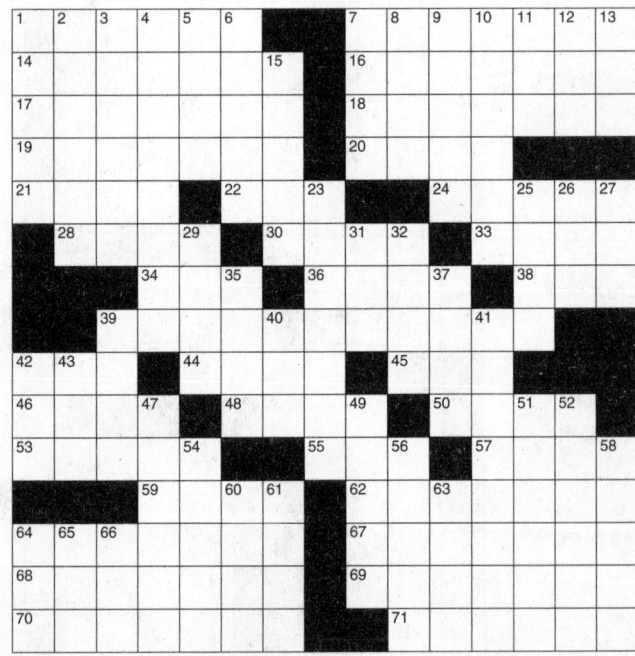

by David Steinberg

ACROSS

1 Aerated beverage
5 Bering Sea port
9 Common ankle injury
15 Domitian's "you love"
16 Eastern sultanate
17 Forerun
18 Grand Central Terminal sight
20 Historical region of France
21 Including 38-, 41- and 60-Across, a description of this puzzle's theme
23 Jalisco article
24 Kröller-Müller Museum artist
25 La.-to-Mich. dir.
27 Middle-earth creatures
29 "No Love (But Your Love)" singer, 1958
32 Often-misused possessive
33 Pa. accident site of 1979
36 Quake
37 "Red Storm Rising" grp.
38 Second part of the description
41 Third part of the description
43 Under 100 mg per deciliter of this is considered optimal
44 Verse oneself in
47 When to take off: Abbr.
48 Xavier Cugat film "___ Were Never Lovelier"
49 YM or Us output
51 Z is the last of them
55 Act humanly
56 Because
59 Curve
60 Description's end
65 Emerged
66 Facet joints connect them

67 Greets at the door
68 Harper's Bazaar illustrator of the 1910s–'30s
69 "It must've been something ___"
70 John McCain ranch locale
71 Katharine of "The Graduate"
72 Lost no time

DOWN

1 "Moo" makers
2 Native Nebraskan
3 Overpermissive to the extreme
4 "Pshaw!," to a Valley girl
5 Québécois's "our"
6 Ruminant's third stomach
7 Sacred words repeated in prayer

8 Take too long
9 Unit for a chairmaker
10 Vivacious
11 Words per minute, e.g.
12 Xmas tree activity
13 "You're wrong!"
14 ZIP codes, e.g.: Abbr.
19 Auntie, to Mom
22 Body of principles
26 Conductor ___-Pekka Salonen
28 Dominique, e.g.: Abbr.
30 Elba, for one
31 Filth
34 Guinea's neighbor to the northeast
35 Hot-weather treats
38 Incapable of being detected, in a way
39 Just left a dusting, say
40 Knows the answer
42 LeShan who wrote child-care books

43 More common name for caustic soda
45 Not stay within the allotted time
46 Online option since 1998
50 Polos, e.g.
52 Quite an injustice
53 Result in
54 Speech that harangues
57 Throws in a chip
58 Ungulate's hoof, essentially
61 Veal dish ___ bucco
62 Words after let or count
63 "X-Men" actress Paquin
64 Yount had 1,406 of them
65 Zebra relative

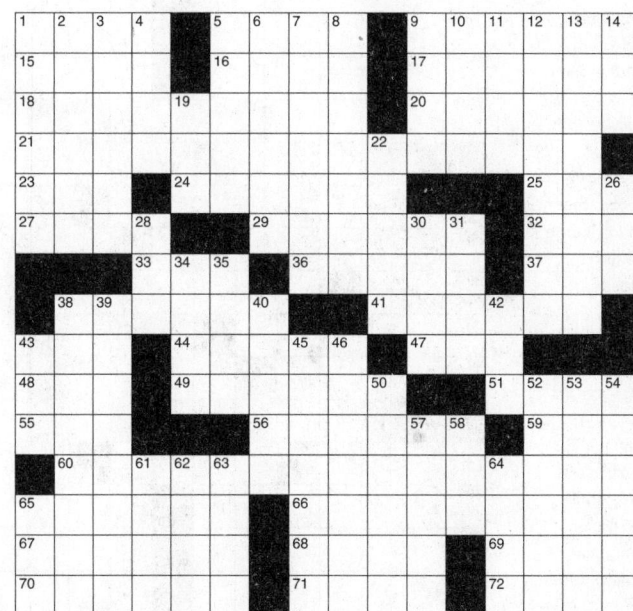

by Tim Croce

ACROSS

1 Persian Gulf sight
8 Getty, e.g.
15 Rear end
16 Trap
17 Early French settler in North America
18 Plants native to mountain summits
19 Off
20 City that's home to the U.S. Brig Niagara
22 Flag support
23 [I'm not happy about doing this]
25 Result
27 Day spa offering
30 Ministre d'___
32 Fatty acid source
36 Locked (up)
37 Pine-___
38 Some bettors bet on them
39 Do some theater work, informally
40 Environmental woes
42 Albanian money
43 Scanty, in Salisbury
45 Mai ___
46 Country where Bambara is the main spoken language
47 Kind of dish
48 Seine feeder
49 Part of N.C.A.A.: Abbr.
50 Like a ballerina
52 "Spring forward" hrs.
54 ___ Bator
57 "You bet!," south of the border
59 Dagger parts
63 Eponymous associate of Stalin
65 Send
67 Nutty confection
68 Time for a show
69 Asian cooking staple
70 Response to 40-Across . . . or what can be done to 12 answers in this puzzle without affecting their clues?

DOWN

1 Garage container
2 Kind of shell
3 Like ___ out of hell
4 "Definitely"
5 Leveling in a ring
6 Spanish "that"
7 ___ Furterer, line of French hair products
8 Canvas coat
9 Hearth decorations
10 "I reckon"
11 Add a bit of support during a conversation
12 Wife of Charlie Chaplin
13 World Cup sounds
14 Fit (inside)
21 Stone-cold truths
24 "Steppenwolf" novelist
26 Astounding Stories subjects
27 Crankcase part
28 Take in again
29 Take a 31-Down off, in a way
31 See 29-Down
33 Albino in "The Da Vinci Code"
34 They may give you a lift
35 Outer-layer protection
38 Worked steadily at
40 Gulf of Mexico sight
41 ___ Piedras, P.R.
44 It's often found in bars
46 Young Roald Dahl title character
48 Greek salad ingredient
51 "That ___ for the record books"
53 County abroad
54 Calls a game
55 Handed-down wisdom
56 "Ah, well . . ."
58 Apple product
60 There may be great interest in this
61 Article to take a spin in?
62 Part of a flight
64 Tebow who won the 2007 Heisman Trophy
66 Not do well?

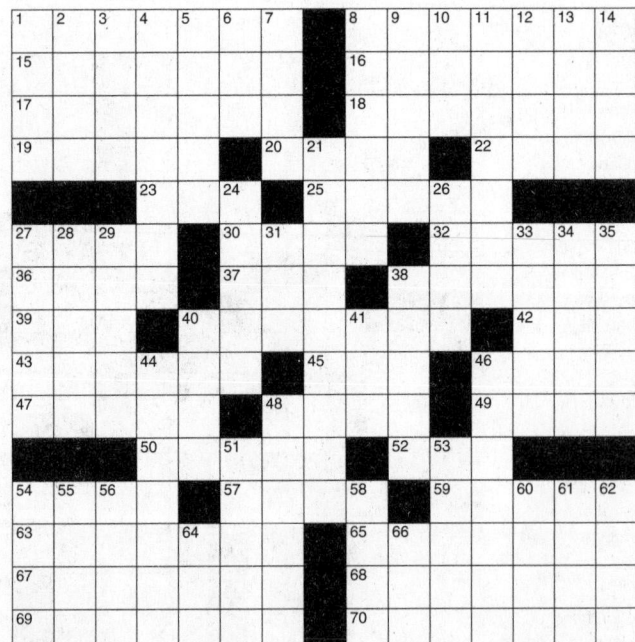

by Ian Livengood

ACROSS

1 Inclined
6 Didn't sink
10 Place to order a stack, say
14 Fund
15 Georgetown athlete
16 Chambers of commerce?
17 Balding person's directive to a barber?
19 French tire
20 Yemeni leader ___ Abdullah Saleh
21 Peeved
22 "Lido Shuffle" singer Boz
24 Knocking sound
26 Like geysers
27 Meandering trip from Kingston to Montego Bay?
31 Green option
34 Boomers' followers
35 Commercial suffix with Cray-
36 Henry ___, first secretary of war
37 Bygone Las Vegas casino
39 ___-Pacific
40 "Lord, is ___?"
41 State bordering the Pacific, informally
42 Construction piece
43 Covered stadium that's off-limits to bands?
47 Kapellmeister's charge
48 Famous last words?
52 Whalebone
54 Strings of islands?
55 Drone, e.g.
56 Acknowledge
57 Protection for a fairy-tale dwarf's brain?
60 "Little Women" woman
61 "Jane ___"
62 Canvas holder
63 Bounce back
64 Paul who co-starred in "I Love You, Man"
65 Argentine soccer hero Maradona

DOWN

1 Old Renault
2 "Waterworld" girl
3 Open a door to
4 Head, slangily
5 Somewhere between excellent and poor, as a restaurant
6 January 2nd?
7 Didn't go straight
8 When repeated, a cry at sea
9 Alternatives to Butterfingers
10 Damage
11 Chill
12 Cassini of fashion
13 "Not only that . . ."
18 First name in linguistics
23 Bamboozles
25 "Iliad" figure
26 Breezed through
28 "No siree!"
29 Inter ___
30 Sir's counterpart
31 Kind of mark
32 Not tricked by
33 Ascetic's wear
37 "A Perfect Day for Bananafish" writer
38 A little open
39 Help with a job
41 Fraternal grp.
42 "Oops!," to a shooter
44 "Tommy" rockers
45 Considered
46 1960s TV boy
49 Bullying, e.g.
50 Pequod co-owner
51 "You there?"
52 Honey
53 Tours "with"
54 One "a-leaping" in a Christmas song
58 Big Apple sch.
59 Chiang ___-shek

by Tony Orbach

ACROSS

1 They may be called
7 2005 Tony winner for Best Musical
15 Horse-drawn vehicle
16 *"Got it! You want me to play Dorothy's aunt!"
17 Artificial
18 Chocolaty treats
19 Slangy turndown
20 Federal Reserve, e.g.: Abbr.
22 Beatty of "Superman"
23 A-line creator
25 *"Get in line, Ms. Gorme!"
31 Register
33 Unlocked?
34 Cub #21 of the 1990s–2000s
35 "The Rules of the Game" filmmaker, 1939
37 Uno y dos y tres
39 Certain world std.
40 *"Ms. Myers, shall I pour?"
43 Is down with
46 Nine, in Nice
47 Good smoke
51 To whom God said "You are dust, and to dust you shall return"
53 Peeler's target, informally
55 Whitman's dooryard bloomer
56 *"Supermodel Macpherson, I presume?"
59 Ruckus
60 1966 gold album by Herb Alpert & the Tijuana Brass
61 "___ bite"
63 Bolivian president Morales
64 "Six Feet Under" creator

69 "The Queen" Oscar winner
71 *"Sly insect!"
72 Like some winter weather
73 Surfer's handle
74 Oxen may pull plows in this

DOWN

1 Bartender's appliance
2 Newman of early "S.N.L."
3 Still woolly
4 Its approval is often sought: Abbr.
5 Domino, e.g.
6 Snack cake since 1961
7 Noted Scrooge portrayer
8 "Don't do drugs!" ad, e.g., for short
9 ___ Lingus
10 Intermediate, at law
11 Sister's homes
12 Sled head
13 Thomas Moore's "Come ___ the Sea"
14 They often accompany logos: Abbr.
21 Backup
24 Crucifix
26 Affording rest
27 1997 Oscar-nominated title role
28 Head of costume design
29 Doctrine
30 Tuck away
32 Property lawyer's concern
36 Kyle ___, "The Terminator" hero
38 Bin Laden hunter
41 Con
42 Alamo rival

43 Allergy source
44 Ruckus
45 Chorizo or merguez
48 Let out, perhaps
49 Greenness
50 Basis of the answer to each starred clue, commonly
52 Eliot's Silas
54 Mid sixth-century year
57 Rocker Hitchcock
58 Horror movie locale, for short
62 Reader's Digest co-founder ___ Wallace
64 Prefix with puncture
65 ___ Noticias (New York Hispanic paper)
66 Law grp.
67 Old NASA vehicle
68 Actor Bruce
70 Stimpy's TV pal

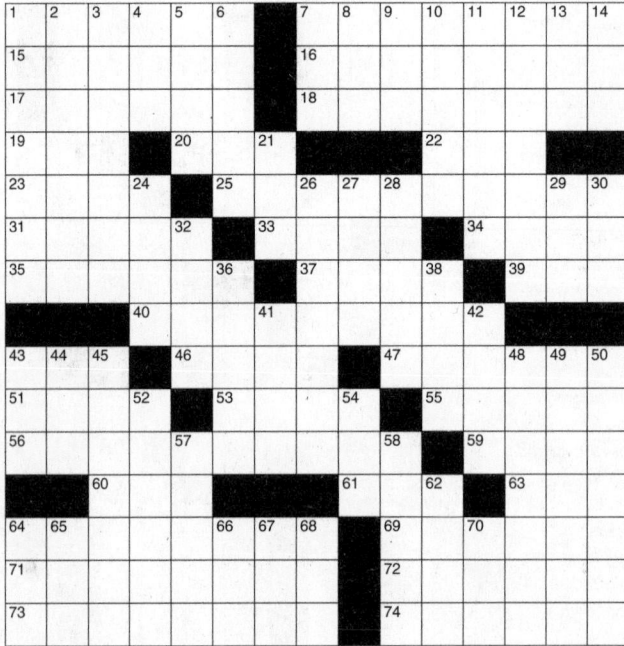

by David Poole

ACROSS

1 Degrees of excellence?
5 Book that begins "Now in the first year of Cyrus king of Persia . . ."
9 Bumbling
14 Architect Saarinen
15 Fly high
16 Legendary battlers
17 Rub elbows with an expert on some Japanese cars?
20 Beginning
21 180's, slangily
22 How the sun proceeds . . . and how to read the answers to 17-, 37- and 56-Across
26 Johnny with a guitar
30 Like much social interaction nowadays
31 Put on the back burner
32 Show on TV
35 Honorary law degree: Abbr.
36 Pageant wear
37 Notice light-colored MacBooks?
41 Local dialect
42 "___ Lay Dying"
43 A.A.A. suggestion
44 ___ Gay
45 Marks on a ranch
48 Meat request
49 How the jet stream proceeds . . . and how to read the answers to 17-, 37- and 56-Across
53 Landing place for Santa
55 Come together
56 Comment like a "Seinfeld" character?
62 Premier

63 "We're ___!"
64 Gives a good whuppin'
65 Hulu offering
66 Meat request
67 Suffix with towel

DOWN

1 Tea type
2 Decorative tattoo dye
3 Smelting byproduct
4 Johannesburg township
5 Abbr. on a city limit sign
6 Place to see lions and sea lions
7 Gamma follower
8 Excite
9 Words before "tomato" or "potato"
10 Show on TV
11 Outer: Prefix
12 "The tongue of the mind," per Cervantes
13 Tongue-produced sound
18 Memo abbr.
19 Asian holiday
23 Spicy stews
24 Source of some power?
25 Makes lovable
27 Detest
28 Was a bad night watchman
29 "Steppenwolf" author
31 Shoe attachment
32 According to
33 Colgate competitor, once
34 Wind turbine part
36 Martin or Louis
38 Put up with
39 Singer/actress Zadora
40 It might give you legal problems: Abbr.
45 Transpire
46 Gloomy
47 Setting for some oratory
49 Stir-fry pan
50 Shoot for
51 Artery implant
52 Like Hemingway's prose
54 Twistable treat
56 Al Sharpton, e.g.: Abbr.
57 Wallach of "The Good, the Bad and the Ugly"
58 Prefix with life or size
59 Golfer's concern
60 Actress Gardner
61 Burns behind a camera

by Peter A. Collins

ACROSS

1 What some prices and spirits do
5 Delay
8 Cause of weather extremes
14 Certify
16 "Ta-ta"
17 Piece for orchestra and soloist
18 Disagreeably direct
19 Carry, as a burden
20 ___.com (Google competitor)
22 Anatomical passageways
23 Hunter's need: Abbr.
25 Author Jong
27 Use for sustenance
30 Sight from St. Peter's Square
34 "This one's ___"
35 Traffic sign literally violated 12 times in this puzzle
37 Mugger?
38 Give lots of love
40 Fr. holy woman
41 Strip alternative
43 Nephew of Abraham
44 It's a blessing
47 Christian denom.
48 Gives the oath
50 Sea spots
52 Add some cushioning to, perhaps
53 Entirely
54 "Art is the triumph over ___": John Cheever
57 Grp. of Ducks and Panthers
59 One's pawns on a chessboard, e.g.
63 Birthplace of many stars
65 Winter item sold in pairs
67 Skilled hoops player, in slang
68 Jiminy Cricket declaration
69 Origami feature
70 ___ Party
71 Something received with a ticket

DOWN

1 Pouches
2 Internet shortening to introduce a different view
3 6, for C
4 Happen again
5 Paper size: Abbr.
6 Lead-in to boy or girl
7 Result of being left out in the cold
8 Flow back
9 One who has a way with words
10 Transmitter, of sorts
11 About, on a memo
12 Koh-i-___, once the world's largest known diamond
13 Doesn't rent
15 Prefix with comic
21 1990s TV neighbor
24 "American Morning" airer
26 Juno, e.g.: Abbr.
27 Newborns in stable condition?
28 Bestow
29 Hardly suppress one's feelings
31 "If all goes well . . ."
32 Restraining order?
33 Make ___ of things
36 Legendary Gaelic bard
39 Exits
42 Statistical shape
45 Medium power?
46 Vardalos of "My Big Fat Greek Wedding"
49 Awaken
51 A sports highlight may be seen in it
54 "Mad Money" airer
55 When doubled, a cry of approval
56 Qualified
58 Unconvincing
60 "Star Trek: T.N.G." counselor Deanna
61 "Thou soft-flowing" stream of literature
62 Strike out
64 Before, in verse
66 Genetic material

by Caleb Rasmussen

ACROSS

1 Start of a URL
5 Neon ___ (fish)
10 They're hooked behind the back
14 Two-dimensional extent
15 Suits
16 Stop
17 Large order of morning drinks?
19 1970s–'80s group with a palindromic name
20 Interim ruling group
21 It helps a pitcher get a grip
23 Activity for a hyperactive barista?
26 Vegetables whose skins may be cooked and eaten separately
30 Gomer Pyle's girlfriend
31 It can be a major turnoff
33 English racing town
38 Bona fide
39 Connect with
41 Subtle show of emotion in the eyes
42 Maud Adams, twice
43 Regulars, or what they'll have
46 Lend, informally
47 Interactive features of starbucks.com?
52 Southern belle's cry of surprise
53 Harasses, as a fraternity pledge
58 Times or Century
59 Classic Mike Myers "S.N.L." sketch . . . or an apt title for this puzzle
62 Herr's wife
63 ___ Cologne
64 "You've Really Got a Hold ___" (1963 hit)
65 Cry of alarm
66 Tony Randall title role
67 Feline line

DOWN

1 Pilgrimage to Mecca
2 Drop ___
3 College freshman, typically
4 Later than
5 Stereotypical cowboy's nickname
6 Button abbr. on a scientific calculator
7 Is overcome by emotion, maybe
8 Dr Pepper alternative
9 Welcomes at the door
10 Hallucinogenic beverage
11 Yeshiva instructor
12 Composer Berg
13 Legendary football coach Amos Alonzo ___
18 Words before and after "what"
22 Hard up
24 ___ Bator
25 ___ of the Rock (Jerusalem landmark)
26 Burglar who really gets cracking?
27 Jump with an extra half-turn
28 It's bigger than a Nano
29 "Set phasers to ___"
32 Morning ___ (bathing, combing the hair, etc.)
34 Napoleon and Snowball, in "Animal Farm"
35 Do a little barbering
36 Other: Sp.
37 Take off one's coat?
39 Lacquered metalware
40 The "I" of R.P.I.: Abbr.
42 Portending evil
44 Zoned (out)
45 Rumpus
47 Sec
48 Have a thing for
49 Susceptible to bribery
50 Make a nuisance of oneself
51 That miss
54 The H, H or O in H_2O
55 Western writer Grey
56 Patron saint of sailors
57 Distort
60 Govt. approver of new meds
61 Fair-hiring abbr.

by Joon Pahk

ACROSS

1 Crew and others
7 Surface, as anger
13 Support, as a weak wrist
14 Completely cut off
16 County of Utica, N.Y.
17 Where to find a date
19 Good behavior
21 Cool
22 Oil amts.
23 Berry used as a dietary supplement
24 Sound on a trail
26 Wise words?
27 It's snapped on a gridiron
30 "Who?," e.g.
31 Stevie Wonder's "I Was Made to Love ___"
32 Blood's counterpart
33 " "
34 Top hat, cane or monocle
35 Thigh muscle, informally
36 It might result in a wrongful lockup
39 Classic Nestlé brand
40 Neat freak's condition, e.g., for short
43 Madison Ave. figure
44 "Oh, that's definite"
46 Betty ___
47 Topic for debate: Abbr.
48 It has boys aged 13 to 18
49 He said "Art is a fruit that grows in man, like a fruit on a plant"
50 Who, in France
51 Good behavior . . . or a hint to two lines of letters in this puzzle
54 Some Carnegie Hall performances
57 "Certainly, Monsieur!"
58 Crossword editors, some say
59 PC communications link
60 One not with the Church of England
61 Like some bad driving conditions

DOWN

1 Stand
2 Flamboyance
3 Like a classical Greek theater
4 Control
5 Cheekiness, slangily
6 Lightly box
7 Marcel Marceau character
8 How some ground balls may be fielded
9 Town on the south shore of Long Island
10 Group (together)
11 Last: Abbr.
12 Decorative floor
15 Call it a day
18 Awards show for athletes
20 Money substitute
25 What cats do . . . or sit on
26 Q.E.D. part
28 Treat for Spot
29 St. Pete ball field, with "the"
30 California worry
33 Call it a day
34 Test ___
35 Cereal with a propeller-headed mascot
36 "Histoire de ___," first in a popular series of children's books
37 Digs
38 Enlarged letter at the start of a chapter
39 Canadian prov.
40 Bested
41 Low-stakes game?
42 Mass divided by volume
44 Winter layers
45 Doting
47 Prefix with judicial
50 Wax remover
52 Ones often calling the shots?
53 Jean who wrote "The Shelters of Stone"
55 The Gem State: Abbr.
56 Display at the Intrepid Sea-Air-Space Museum, for short

by Brendan Emmett Quigley and Ian Livengood

Note: When this puzzle is done, you will find that the ends of the answers to the five starred clues, when in the 15-/67-Across, comprise a 1-/71-Across.

ACROSS

1 [See blurb]
6 Grows old
10 "Easy to Be Hard" musical
14 Boxing locale
15 [See blurb]
16 First word of the "Aeneid"
17 Requested gift in "A Christmas Story"
18 From a distance
19 Shepherd who co-wrote "A Christmas Story"
20 *Midwest conference
22 *Pancake
24 "___ not my fault!"
25 Long Island university
27 Wait
29 Show disdain for, in a way
33 Creatures
38 A star may have a big one
39 *1951 Bogart/ Hepburn film
43 Suffix with front
44 Weaver of tales on the big screen
45 Warfare
49 Limerick's land
50 One-named female singer with the 2002 #1 hit "Foolish"
53 French dance
56 *Billy Crystal's "Memories of Me" co-star
59 *Shooting star?
62 Kind of mail
63 Wander
65 Medicinal shrub
66 When the nude scene occurs in 10-Across
67 [See blurb]
68 Hall's partner in pop music
69 Dancer's strap?
70 Ring results, briefly
71 [See blurb]

DOWN

1 One of three people walking into a bar, in jokes
2 Go around
3 Safecrackers
4 ". . . some kind of ___?"
5 Lovers' ___
6 Simile's center
7 Faux pas
8 "Kill ___" (Metallica's triple-platinum debut album)
9 One of the highest order of angels
10 Pilgrims to Mecca
11 Domain
12 Computer that once came in Bondi Blue
13 Captain, for one
21 Low point
23 Greek symbol for the golden ratio
26 Lucy's husband and son
27 Sheep's sound
28 Like Beethoven's Symphony No. 8
30 Spotted
31 James who co-wrote the script for 39-Across
32 Playwright's prize
33 Ear-related
34 Prefix with -stat
35 It might make you sick
36 Former telecom giant
37 Bob of "Full House"
40 Waterwheel
41 "___ transtulit sustinet" (motto of Connecticut)
42 Coffee container
46 Shoot off the backboard successfully
47 Pop a question
48 Strong desire
51 Actress Aimée of "La Dolce Vita"
52 Mystery writer Marsh
53 Zulu, e.g.
54 Dermatologists' concerns
55 Dog restraint
56 Cracked
57 Time founder Henry
58 Opposed to
60 "It ___ no concern"
61 "Keep it ___"
64 Peaks: Abbr.

by Peter A. Collins

ACROSS

1 Traditional March birthstone
7 Three-pointers: Abbr.
10 Hoop alternative
14 What might be a knockout?
15 Meal preceder?
16 ___ salad
17 French writer with snaky hair and a petrifying gaze?
19 Sportscaster Andrews
20 Dissolve a relationship
21 Antelope of southern Africa
23 Swerves
26 In favor of the first book?: Abbr.
28 Joint custody parties
29 Rich
30 A to Z, e.g.
31 Unisphere, e.g.
32 "The Bridge at Narni" artist
36 & 38 Deli purchase . . . or a description of the answer to 17-, 26-, 47- or 55-Across
39 Troubled
40 From the start
43 Food label abbr.
44 Like some bars and beaches
46 Green gourd, informally
47 One trying to shake a leg, for instance?
50 Seuss character who "speaks for the trees"
51 Provoke
52 ___ One
54 Mech. whiz
55 Mom's special road-trip corn bread?
60 Put out, with "off"
61 Australian sprinter

62 It's developed during training season
63 Buried treasures
64 Swim
65 "Baby" singer Justin

DOWN

1 Nudge
2 Receiver of private letters?: Abbr.
3 ___ Barton, first Triple Crown winner, 1919
4 Obsolescent communication devices
5 Short jackets
6 Tear
7 Service that requires no shoes
8 Hoedown participant
9 Make fast
10 Common work boot feature
11 Engine type
12 Marriage
13 Comment preceding "Gern geschehen"
18 Nada
22 Bigwig
23 Compact Nissan model
24 Rejoice
25 Start of a children's rhyme
27 29-Down, down South
29 See 27-Down
31 "Beat it!"
33 Come to mind again
34 City of 2½+ million at the mouth of the Yodo River
35 Fax predecessor
37 Mewing passerines
38 Walgreens competitor

40 N. African land
41 Fortifies
42 Courtier who invites Hamlet to fence with Laertes
45 Common undergrad course of study
46 Zombie, essentially
47 Deceive
48 Hidden
49 1985 N.L. M.V.P. Willie
50 "Vive" follower
53 Sharp put-down
56 "What a good boy ___!"
57 Pony players' parlor: Abbr.
58 Formerly, name-wise
59 Drop the ball

by Michael Sharp

ACROSS

1 Univ. with the cheer "Roll Tide!"
5 Indiana Jones accouterment
11 Rachael on the Food Network
14 "Ars Amatoria" poet
15 Draws out
16 Like
17 Groom?
19 Rocky peak
20 "___ is nothing but perception": Plato
21 Will-o'-the-wisp feature
23 "Captain! The engines canna take ___ more!" (line from Scotty on "Star Trek")
24 Installs new thatch on, maybe
25 Verbal exchange about a harsh review?
30 Bottle marked "XXX" in the comics
31 Separation
32 Homes for some colonies
35 Water-resistant wood
37 Seasonal songs . . . or a hint to 17-, 25-, 46- and 59-Across
40 City at the confluence of the Ouse and Foss
41 Skinny sort
43 Muckraker Jacob
45 One-eighty
46 Demand during a roadside negotiation?
50 "Fa-a-ancy!"
52 "My gal" of song
53 Eerie 1976 movie with an Oscar-winning score
54 Biblical name meaning "father of many"
58 "I tawt I taw a putty ___"

59 Stylish Lionel?
61 Leandro's love, in a Handel cantata
62 Visigoth king who sacked Rome
63 "Runaround Sue" singer, 1961
64 Grandmaster Flash's music
65 Pursue again, as an elected position
66 French word whose opposite is 2-Down

DOWN

1 Things to draw
2 French word whose opposite is 66-Across
3 Certain skirt
4 Number next to a +
5 Encloses
6 Nose (out)
7 French nobleman

8 Autumn colors
9 Old Spanish silver coins
10 Trademark forfeited by Bayer under the Treaty of Versailles
11 Distributes stingily
12 Detached
13 Paul Bunyan tales, e.g.
18 Where Francis Scott Key saw bombs bursting
22 "Here, piggies!"
25 Super Bowl XXXVI champs, to fans
26 Actor Guinness
27 In second place, say
28 Overseer of corp. accts.
29 Gestation locations
33 Wynken, Blynken and Nod, e.g.
34 Slant
36 Mexican artist Frida

38 Architect Maya
39 Relaxes, in a way
42 The problem with these clue?
44 Emmy-winning Lewis
47 Flamenco cheer
48 Stand-up comic Sykes and others
49 Safari antelopes
50 Boon's "Animal House" buddy
51 Maureen of "Miracle on 34th Street"
54 Singer India.___
55 First Chinese dynasty
56 Very long time
57 The Dolomites, e.g.: Abbr.
60 Uno + due

by Bill Thompson

ACROSS

1 Dig
5 Ten Commandments verb
10 "___ Lake"
14 Baltic Sea feeder
15 Villainous monk in "The Da Vinci Code"
16 "Now I get it," facetiously
17 Fizzle
19 Refill when you don't really need to
20 Irks
21 Hoe and weed, e.g.
23 Anatomical dividers
24 Met the qualifications
28 Env. enclosure
30 Shared with, as a secret
31 Scottish hillside
34 Regarding
37 ___ élémentaire
38 Director Jacquet of "March of the Penguins"
39 Pay sudden attention to
41 Actor Johnson of "Plan 9 From Outer Space"
42 Taken
44 This, in Toledo
45 Big Ten athlete
46 Films, of a sort
48 "Curb Your Enthusiasm" shower
50 Confronts
53 Record store section
57 Amateurish
58 Warning often shouted too late
60 Some hairstyles
62 Prove lacking
64 Suffer from
65 Old Olds
66 Starting point for un inventeur
67 Pygmy couple?
68 Greek island where Zeus was said to be raised
69 Starting point

DOWN

1 Five-time A.L. batting champ
2 Like a great deal
3 Prince's partner
4 Peanutty candy
5 Indication of deflation
6 Message on many a stadium sign
7 How Rubik's Cube is best solved
8 "Mighty ___ a Rose"
9 Airborne African menace
10 Like the Harvard Lampoon
11 It may be the only thing in a bar
12 Crawling African menace
13 Over
18 Peachy
22 Peripheral
25 Flying
26 Sadness
27 Union requirement, maybe?
29 Thor Heyerdahl craft
31 Little things on screens
32 Quickly approach
33 Slightly better than
35 Bothers
36 Overseer of schools: Abbr.
39 Ships
40 "Good one!"
43 They may be cleared with a spray
45 Daredevil's challenge
47 Trash receptacle
49 Fancy wraps
51 Citizen rival
52 New Mexico county
54 Wear down
55 ___ show
56 Michael who directed the Bond film "The World Is Not Enough"
59 Tomato and vegetable
60 Beat and how!
61 Time piece?
63 Pay back?

by Alan Arbesfeld

ACROSS

1 Transact business on the Internet
6 TV/radio host John
10 Turkey club?
14 Treatment coverage provider
15 Toss in a chip
16 Touched down
17 Tricky driving condition
18 Tax-exempt educ. groups
19 Times Roman, for one
20 Traditional use for henna
23 Tackle-to-mast rope on a ship
24 Tiny bit
25 Typist's key: Abbr.
28 Transmitter of waves
31 Train stop: Abbr.
34 Tear-gassing cause
36 Tevye's "good"
37 The Beatles' meter maid and others
39 Team in the A.F.C. South
43 Tallow sources
44 To the ___ degree
45 Trouble with a lid?
46 Time period on a financial stmt.
47 Takes a step toward biting?
51 Took a chair
52 Trap or record preceder
53 Teleflora competitor
55 Tilt-boarding
63 Techie's address starter?
64 Topic lead-in
65 Take as a given
66 The U.N.'s Kofi ___ Annan
67 Tranquilizer gun projectile
68 Two-color horse
69 Tensed
70 Terminal approximations: Abbr.
71 Towel ends?

DOWN

1 Toward sunrise
2 The "T" of TV
3 "Time to rise!" ("Up and ___!")
4 Tending to bungle things
5 Tito Jackson's sister
6 Toledo tidbit
7 Theater's ___'acte
8 Take the night off from partying, say
9 "The Ten Commandments" star
10 Three-country agreement of '94
11 Tons
12 Two-time All-Star Martinez
13 "The Touch of Your Hand" lyricist Harbach
21 Tears
22 Tempest game maker
25 Trying to look cultured
26 Title for Sulu on "Star Trek": Abbr.
27 Tempered, with "down"
29 Talking-___ (scoldings)
30 Track meet component
31 TDs and interceptions
32 Tucker with the #1 country hit "Here's Some Love"
33 Thing of value
35 "The Closer" airer
38 T.G.I.F. part
40 "Terminal Bliss" actress Chandler
41 Third-person ending of old
42 Thug's crime, often
48 TD Waterhouse online competitor
49 Torments
50 Treeless tract
52 Time-honored Irish cleric, for short
54 Tout ___ (straight ahead: Fr.)
55 To the extent ___
56 "Tell Mama" singer James
57 Traitor's rebuke
58 Tomás's "other"
59 Tykes
60 "This ___ what I expected"
61 TV's Nick at ___
62 "Three deuces and a four-speed" cars of old

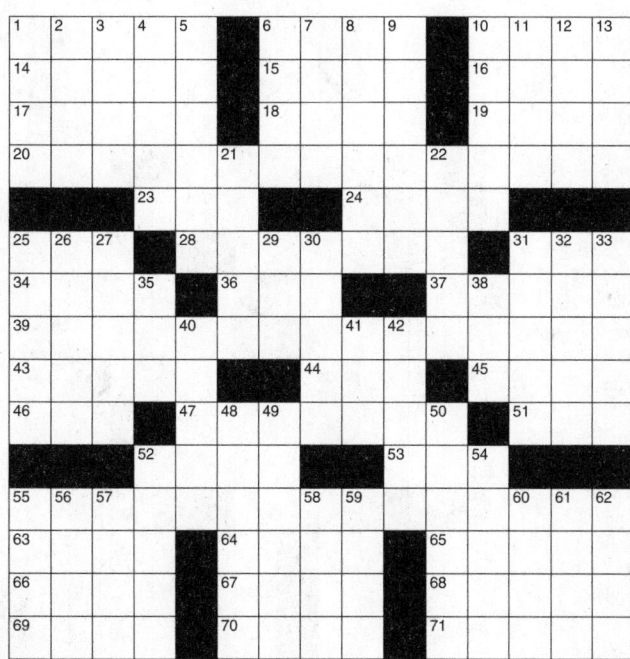

by Paul Guttormsson

ACROSS

1 Boosts
4 Perfect balance
10 Award named after a TV network
14 Philadelphia had the first one in the U.S. (1874)
15 One hanging around a party?
16 "Do I ___?"
17 Some ballpark hits
19 One who might wear slippers
20 Prosaic
22 Provider of some outdoor entertainment
27 Broadcasters
30 John Wayne had a distinctive one
31 Palme ___ (film award)
32 Go home, maybe
33 Nick name?
34 Traffic cop's org.?
35 Group out of the mainstream
36 Allocates, with "out"
37 "Hair" composer MacDermot
38 Theologian Johann
39 Tusked animals
40 "Kitty ___" (1940 movie romance)
41 Kind of fly, briefly
42 Beginning to knock?
43 Chucked
44 "Star Wars" and "Battlestar Galactica"
46 Blue hue
47 Comic's forte
50 Painted the town red, in a way . . . or successfully completed this puzzle?
55 It might come out of a small speaker
56 Naval group

57 Not from a Scot
58 Boundary of myth
59 Liquored (up)
60 Lamb's kin

DOWN

1 Shooter named for its inventor
2 Skating venue
3 ___ bed
4 Ghost of Jacob Marley?
5 Floor specialists
6 French Literature Nobelist Gide
7 KLM alternative
8 "Lord, is ___?"
9 Grainy places to dig
10 Apprehensive
11 Youthful time
12 Nuptial starter
13 "You wanted to see me?"

18 Use a "caret and stick" approach on?
21 It's a tradition
23 I operation?
24 Spun things
25 Girl with a festive-sounding name
26 Gave a keynote, say
27 Eyeball
28 Cold cover?
29 Sugar in large crystals
33 "So cool!"
36 Quarters for quarters?
37 TMZ fodder
39 Support
40 Mattress covering
43 Old vacuum tube
45 Allen in history
46 Record label for Otis Redding

48 Musical with the song "Be Italian"
49 Really bother, with "at"
50 Dict. fill
51 Have a beef?
52 2001 World Series winner, on scoreboards
53 "Beyond Peace" author's monogram
54 "Well, I'll be!"

by David J. Kahn

ACROSS

1 Coach Ewbank who led the Jets to a Super Bowl championship
5 Sturdy mountain climber?
9 English derby site
14 Pac-12 team
15 Circular dance
16 Iroquoian people
17 Place for a sweater?
19 Composer Stravinsky and others
20 A Mexican might sleep under it
21 Totally wrong
22 "Peer Gynt" mother
23 La ___ Tar Pits
24 Sheets for scribbling
29 30- or 60-second spot
33 Three, in Rome
34 Mideast moguls
35 Not just mislead
36 Pocahontas's husband
38 Hogwash
39 When a right turn may be allowed
40 "You have my word on it"
41 Suitor
43 Certain fraternity man, informally
44 Antifur org.
45 Ice cream holder
47 ". . . or so ___ say"
49 "A New World Record" grp.
50 Put down
53 Beau
58 Full-bosomed
59 Fairway clubs . . . or a hint to the starts of the answers to 17-, 24- and 45-Across and 10- and 37-Down
60 "The Surrender of ___" (Diego Velázquez painting)
61 Whitaker's Oscar-winning role
62 "Zip-___-Doo-Dah"
63 Poe's middle name
64 Root beer brand
65 King with the immortal line "Who is it that can tell me who I am?"

DOWN

1 Scaredy-cat
2 Outside: Prefix
3 K–6 sch. designation
4 Entreaty to Bo-Peep
5 Earlyish teatime
6 Uncouth sort
7 Suffix with buck
8 Bump in bumper cars, maybe
9 Rat in "Ratatouille"
10 Playground lingo
11 Possible cause of school cancellation
12 Storybook character
13 Superlative adverb
18 Emma of "The Avengers"
21 Music sheet abbr.
23 Annual city-magazine theme
24 "Peanuts," for one
25 "Gladiator" star
26 Like a candle night after night, say
27 Breathing space
28 90 is a pretty high one
30 Left-hand page
31 Used the dining room
32 "Gunsmoke" setting, informally
35 Legendary siren of the Rhine
37 Fizzless drink
42 High dice rolls
45 Tie the knot
46 O.K. place?
48 Mr. Universe, e.g.
50 "Fernando" group
51 Small knot
52 Figure skater's leap
53 Succotash bean
54 "Amores" poet
55 Presage
56 Fit for service
57 River of Flanders
59 Goldfish swallowing in the 1920s, e.g.

by Elizabeth C. Gorski

ACROSS

1 Took off
5 Princess in a Nintendo game series
10 Ones trying to increase circulation, for short?
14 So-called Family City U.S.A.
15 It might have an attachment
16 One who 26-Across
17 3, 6, 11, 18, 27 . . .
20 "Caught ___!"
21 Ship's doctor, in slang
22 Joint U.S./Canada military org.
23 Journalist on a mission?
25 Jacket part
26 Bugs
28 Some chip dip, informally
30 Small, low island
31 Totally baked
32 Casting director?
34 4, 2, ⁴/₃, 1, ⁴/₅ . . .
40 Supports, with "up"
41 Part of a slalom run
42 Lens holder, for short
45 Setting for Genesis 2:8–25
46 Scoffed
48 Aladdin's home
50 Pop's ___ Vanilli
51 Isn't lazy, say
52 Gem
54 Alias
57 8, 1, -18, -55, -116 . . .
60 First major publisher of board games in the U.S.
61 Instruction sometimes followed by "repeat"
62 Vehicle for Calvin and Hobbes
63 Smart

64 Neuters
65 Uncle ___

DOWN

1 Classic theater name
2 Thereabouts
3 Any of the clues for 17-, 34- or 57-Across
4 Bird whose name is a Midwest school's initials
5 Complete losers
6 Improve
7 Put on
8 Uncool sorts
9 "___ right"
10 Printer brand
11 Standard of assessment
12 A language of South Africa
13 Fuddy-duddy
18 Apt name for a nun?
19 Org. that won the 1965 Nobel Peace Prize
24 Hindsights?
25 "The Wizard Of Oz" co-star
26 ___-rock
27 The time for action, often
28 Presumption, in math
29 Inhales, perhaps
32 Front for "front"
33 Brightest star in Orion
35 Belief in something bigger than oneself
36 Speaker of "Luke, when gone am I, the last of the Jedi will you be"
37 In the answers to 17-, 34- and 57-Across, it was replaced in turn by 1, 2, 3, 4, 5 . . .
38 Common French word with two accents
39 Signed as an illiterate would
42 Cause of feline friskiness
43 Show up
44 Down East native
46 Some spellings?
47 Monopoly util.
49 Ending with wilde- or harte-
50 Old-fashioned
52 Do some barbering
53 ___ salad
55 Gung-ho
56 Contributes
58 Form letters?
59 Kind of port

by Parker Lewis

ACROSS

1 "Big Brother" host Julie
5 Milky Way maker
9 "Oh, get off it!"
14 "The Godfather" score composer Nino
15 Riding on
16 Toothpaste brand once advertised with Bucky Beaver
17 "___ framed!"
18 Org. with Spartans and Trojans
19 Drug that treats panic attacks
20 M/C Hammer?
23 Verdi's "___ tu"
24 ___ in queen
25 Raking in
29 Closing bid?
31 Suspense novelist Hoag
33 ___ de guerre
34 Literally, "reign" in Hindi
36 Like Mendeleev's table
39 W/C Fields?
43 Former Ford minivan
44 Risk damnation
45 ___ tough spot
46 Mlle., across the Pyrenees
48 Summer camp shelter
52 Have the blahs
55 Emergency contact, often: Abbr.
57 Whichever
58 L/L Bean?
61 "Oops!"
64 Sac flies produce them
65 "___ be in England": Browning
66 Big Apple mayor before Koch
67 "Outta my way!"
68 Jockey's handful
69 "You're killin' me!"
70 Goes with
71 Brouhahas

DOWN

1 Yalta's locale
2 Stooge surname
3 List ender
4 Pelé's org.
5 Powerful ray
6 For neither profit nor loss
7 Have a hearty laugh
8 Sci-fi travelers
9 Studio behind "Up" and "Wall-E"
10 Engender
11 Chinese dynasty name
12 Santa ___ winds
13 You might put your stamp on it
21 Comes to
22 Scottish landowners
26 Intro to Chinese?
27 Film ___
28 Yukons, e.g.
30 Hence
32 Not connected
35 Tea in Boston Harbor, once
37 Yule decoration
38 A Chaplin
39 Ragamuffin
40 Russo of film
41 "Of wrath," in a hymn title
42 Sail supports
47 Hit it big
49 Took a dip
50 Ab ___ (from the start)
51 L'eggs wares
53 Andean wool source
54 First Catholic vice president of the U.S.
56 Someone ___ (another's)
59 "An ill wind . . ." instrument
60 Director Ephron
61 Deg. held by George W. Bush
62 Tree with cones
63 Kapow!

by Michael Black

ACROSS

1 Traditional keikogi accessory
4 Apple types
9 Manic
15 One regulated by the F.E.C.
16 It's enough to take you for a ride
17 "Sleepers" co-star, 1996
18 Literary source of "Bless us and splash us, my precioussss!"
20 With force and much noise
21 Memorable ship
22 Literary inits.
24 City on the Rhône
25 Peeling potatoes, perhaps
27 Env. contents
29 Nature worshiper, of a sort
31 Onetime NASA booster
33 Pill bug, for one
35 Stop: Abbr.
36 Anticipate
38 Call, in a way
39 Part of an Asian capital's name
40 Often-cited distance between things . . . or what's hidden in this puzzle
43 Collections
46 Geom. figure
47 Epithet for the mouse in Burns's "To a Mouse"
51 Nav. leader
52 State of Grace
54 Judo move
55 Apparel
57 Jim Beam product
59 River of York
60 China ___
61 Lacto-___-vegetarian
63 Creature in Dr. Seuss's "If I Ran the Zoo"
65 From where
67 Writer featured in the memoir "Dream Catcher"
71 Reduced
72 Narnia hero
73 Center start?
74 Cool red giants
75 Himalayan legends
76 Many an old T-shirt, now

DOWN

1 Reject, with "out of"
2 "Pshaw!"
3 Source of some cubes
4 Folder, sometimes
5 With 52-Down, English-born cabaret singer
6 Hit Brit sitcom
7 Announcers
8 ___ record
9 Modern records
10 Fixed, as tiles
11 ___ and a leg
12 Notable violinist
13 1990s Mexican president Zedillo
14 Its rising signaled the flooding of the Nile in ancient Egypt
19 Cool factor
23 News deliverer
25 Ox
26 Vietnam's ___ Dinh Diem
28 Connected with
30 Free
32 "___ was saying . . ."
34 Assn.
37 Parolee, e.g.
39 Tuba
41 Period of years
42 Take in
43 Writes poorly
44 – – –
45 Most overused
48 Weary walker
49 Aegean island near Naxos
50 Farm milk provider
52 See 5-Down
53 Game stick
56 Noted test provider
58 Zhou ___
62 August 15, 1945
64 One from Germany
66 Some TV drama sites, for short
68 PC key
69 Green grp.
70 Fix

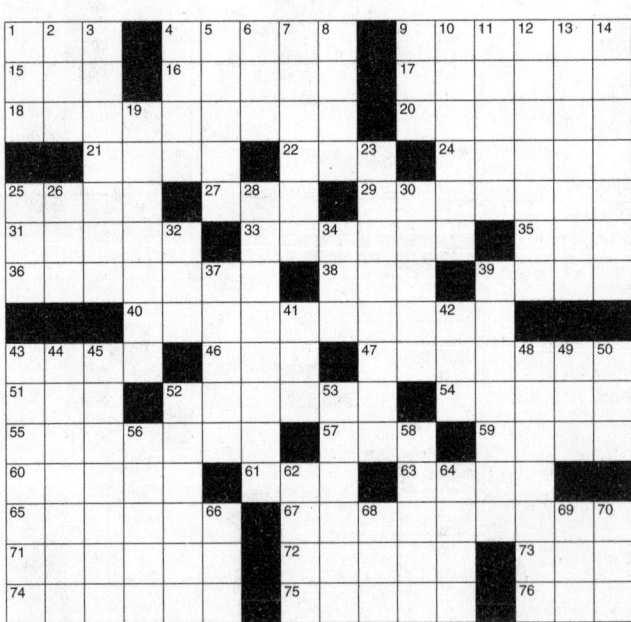

by Kevan Choset

ACROSS

1 Holiday time, in ads
5 Detection devices
11 One way to stand
14 Bunk bed feature
15 Fester and Vanya
16 Shipment to a smeltery
17 Physical therapist's assignment?
19 Postal worker's circuit: Abbr.
20 Gossip, to an Aussie
21 Friend of François
22 Engaged
23 The Forbidden City
24 Blackened seafood?
26 Some small power supplies
27 Facilities, informally
29 Lift up
30 La ___ Tar Pits
32 Kind of arrest
36 Castaway's day in court?
40 Enter slowly
41 Spread selection
43 Mete out
46 It may come in a blanket
48 Bionic part of the Bionic Woman
49 Lure for Popeye's sweetie?
53 ___ Kea
55 After midnight, say
56 "Go on . . ."
57 Maliciously done
58 CPR pro
59 Choosing between pounds and kilos?
61 Funny Charlotte
62 Hang back
63 Uncool
64 Georgia, once: Abbr.
65 Customary practices
66 Hydrocarbon suffixes

DOWN

1 Medical dept. room
2 Exotic dancer executed in 1917
3 Homes for drones
4 Food-stains-on-shirt sorts
5 River to the Rhine
6 Whatever amount
7 1983 Mr. T comedy
8 1836 siege site
9 Frankincense or myrrh
10 GPS heading
11 Wife of Brutus
12 iTunes search category
13 Chew on a baby toy, say
18 Thunder sound
22 Result of a '55 union merger
24 Dance around
25 Information for a oenologist
28 Reason to use Retin-A
31 Dinette spot
33 Union ___
34 Headache for a snow shoveler
35 "Give ___ thought!"
37 Johnson of "Laugh-In"
38 Like Unalaska
39 1989 movie featuring principal Joe Clark
42 Good sources of vitamin C
43 Many I.M. recipients
44 Wool-yielding pack animals
45 Runt's group
47 Auto financing org., formerly
50 Causes of ruin
51 Man's feminine side
52 Med-alert bracelet, e.g.
54 Shackle site
57 Standings column
59 Neighbor of Braz.
60 Eskimo ___

by Kelsey Blakley

ACROSS

1 See, say
6 ___ pyramid, four examples of which are seen in this puzzle
10 Real-estate abbr.
14 French affair
15 Friend of Zoe and Abby
16 "Don't you know there's ___ on?"
17 Loudly berated
19 "Say ___" (1940 hit)
20 Fanny
21 Lena who played Irina Derevko on "Alias"
22 Tech company in the Dow Jones Industrial Average
23 "Signs point to ___" (Magic 8 Ball answer)
24 Go home empty-handed, say
25 Welding bands?
26 Lepidopterist's tool
27 Whack
30 Tailors' allowances
33 1971 Tom Jones hit
35 Has no doubt about
36 Ben-___
37 Patty Hearst alias
38 Pioneer carrier
40 Harold of the Clinton White House
41 How many stupid things are done
42 Abbr. after N. or S.
43 Backsplash unit
44 Some talk on political talk shows
46 PC key
49 John who starred in Broadway's original "Carousel"
51 Break down, in a way
52 Fair
53 All at the front?
54 Conductor's place
56 Foreign farewell
57 Old Testament king
58 Shoddy stuff
59 Part of N.C.A.A.: Abbr.
60 "South Park" boy
61 Tennis great born in Serbia

DOWN

1 Fresh
2 Compère
3 Ephron and Roberts
4 Ingredient in some English puddings
5 Laundry detergent brand
6 Has a hunch
7 "Some Enchanted Evening," e.g.
8 Gulf of ___
9 Flyspeck
10 Straightforward fashion choice
11 Site of many clandestine accounts
12 Gender abbr.
13 Charlie's Angels, e.g.
18 Like some points
22 Like many a Malkovich
24 Dietary dictum for one with hypertension
25 Lou Gehrig's disease, for short
26 Reissue
27 Michael of "Superbad"
28 Falco of "Nurse Jackie"
29 Scandinavian rugs
30 Kitchenware brand
31 Presently
32 Light classical pieces
33 Clog, e.g.
34 O, symbolically
39 Otto - cinque
42 Embassy worker: Abbr.
44 City whose name sounds like a fish
45 "___ the Conqueror" (Max von Sydow film)
46 Do well
47 Zone (out)
48 Blush stoppers
49 Almond ___ (candy brand)
50 "The Pregnant Widow" author Martin
51 "King Kong" co-star, 1933
52 Heroine who says "I resisted all the way: a new thing for me"
54 Shaming sound
55 Mad people, e.g.: Abbr.

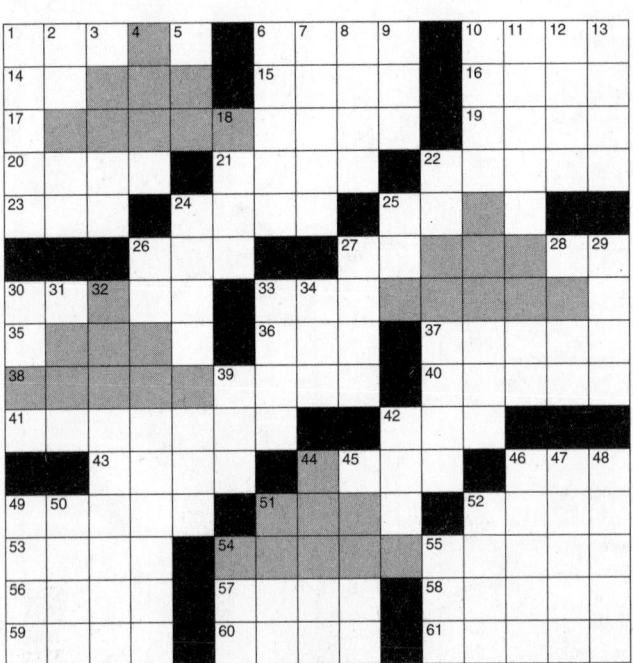

by Patrick Blindauer and Francis Heaney

ACROSS

1 Reindeer herder
5 Sprites, for instance
10 With 64-Across, 1963 Beach Boys hit
14 Lysol target
15 Fairy tale figure
16 Do some computer programming
17 1965 Beach Boys hit
20 "That doesn't bother me anymore"
21 Gumshoe
22 Gulf of ___
23 With 49-Across, 1965 Beach Boys hit
27 ___ Retreat (1970s–'80s New York City club)
30 Trouble
32 Mideast carrier
33 Fall guy?
34 1922 Physics Nobelist
35 It has feathers and flies
36 Egg: Prefix
37 Smitten one
40 Thrilla in Manila outcome
41 Wrestling victories
43 Prefix with -polis
44 Tend, as plants
46 "Cómo ___?"
47 Vote against
48 Dance accompanied by castanets
49 See 23-Across
51 Victim in Camus's "The Stranger," e.g.
52 Minor player, so to speak
53 Rich fabrics
57 1963 Beach Boys hit
61 "___ Ben Adhem" (English poem)

62 African capital
63 "It must've been something ___"
64 See 10-Across
65 "Let It Snow! Let It Snow! Let It Snow!" composer
66 Lotion ingredient

DOWN

1 Sets of points, mathematically
2 Man without parents
3 Kind of shirt named for a sport
4 One following general directions?
5 Packs away
6 Sen. Hatch
7 With 30- and 53-Down, 1964 Beach Boys hit
8 Thrilla in Manila winner
9 Lays on thick
10 Like some eaves in winter
11 Oslo's home: Abbr.
12 Year of Ronsard's "Odes"
13 Vote for
18 Sinatra topper
19 "You sure got me"
24 Nebraska river
25 Surveyor's stake, typically
26 Corrida combatant
27 Polite
28 Rich
29 Like
30 See 7-Down
31 Home of the Rock and Roll Hall of Fame
34 ___ Raton, Fla.

38 Ball club V.I.P.'s
39 Like some plays
42 Refuge
45 Neighbor of Montenegro
48 One of three literary sisters
50 Capital of the U.S.: Abbr.
51 Suffix with parliament
53 See 7-Down
54 Zest alternative
55 Outer: Prefix
56 ___-Ball
57 Choreographer Lubovitch
58 Native Nigerian
59 Overly
60 Didn't get used

by Peter A. Collins

150 MEDIUM

ACROSS
1 It's loaded
5 Atlantic Records, e.g.
10 Blowout
14 Deprecate
15 From the start
16 It connects to the wrist
17 Eco-unfriendly coal sources
19 Auto slogan beginning in 2000
20 "Did you ___ that?"
21 Acts frugally around the holidays, say
23 Deep Blue's opponent in chess
28 One rising at dawn
29 The Gay Nineties and others
30 Idols
35 Tell
38 Hanna-Barbera output
39 Never, in Nuremberg
40 Place ___
41 "Stop avoiding responsibility!"
43 Like sandpaper, typically
44 "Vous êtes ___"
45 It's never finished, only abandoned, per Paul Valéry
46 Southern California college
48 Instruction on a box
51 Pipsqueak
52 Pro ___
53 Place to get a date
56 Secretary of state between Marshall and Dulles
60 Bogey beater
61 Looney Tunes sound
62 It may be hard to change
68 Quaint sign word
69 Accustom
70 Pacific capital
71 Part of a tennis serve
72 Prepare to go on Facebook, say
73 Pace in dressage

DOWN
1 Modern-day tech purchases
2 Like some points
3 Tie up, in a way
4 "Funny running into you here!"
5 Not so cool
6 Some
7 ___ mot
8 "Do I ___!"
9 Frets (over)
10 Paging, say
11 Standoffish
12 One who's standoffish
13 Twin gymnasts Paul and Morgan
18 ___ Tour
22 "Seems to be the case"
23 "Time's fun when you're having flies" speaker
24 Something straining credibility
25 Negotiations of 1977–79
26 Ad Council output, for short
27 Clean, in a way
31 Off
32 Traveling, maybe
33 Feinstein of the 34-Down
34 See 33-Down
36 Holders of reservations?
37 Descendant of Standard Oil
42 Like associates, on some e-mails
47 TV star who once appeared in WrestleMania
49 Much Mongolian geography
50 Some ancient scrolls
54 Filled (with)
55 Brief look inside?
56 Literally, "father"
57 Singer Green with multiple Grammys
58 Follows
59 10^{-9}: Prefix
63 Needle
64 Part of a sched.
65 Onetime name in late-night TV
66 Brand in the freezer
67 Carrot or beet

by Joel Fagliano

ACROSS

1 Job for a cleanup crew
5 Fasten, in a way
11 PC "brain"
14 Place for a pavilion
15 Wild child
16 Cauldron stirrer
17 Sing-along direction
20 Masago, e.g., at a sushi bar
21 Writer Chekhov
22 Team nicknamed the Black Knights
23 Obey
25 Frank with six Oscars
28 River ferried by Charon
29 Children's game
33 Direction to an alternative musical passage
36 Become fond of
37 Fertility lab stock
40 Chase scene shout
42 "___ who?"
43 Figure of many a Mayan deity
45 Before dawn, say
47 Pursue a passion
49 Spreadsheet function
53 Neuters
54 Word missing from the answers to 17-, 23-, 29-, 40-, 47- and 62-Across
56 Worthless sort
58 One of 22 in a Krugerrand
61 "Agnus ___"
62 Do as a mentor did, say
66 Home of the Tisch Sch. of the Arts
67 First-timer
68 Play ___ (enjoy some tennis)
69 Longtime mall chain
70 Times for showers
71 Modest response to kudos

DOWN

1 Some urban transit systems
2 Urge on
3 Quick
4 Turn on the waterworks
5 Knocks for a loop
6 Oxygen ___
7 Sacramento's former ___ Arena
8 Singer whose "name" was once a symbol
9 Chaney of film
10 Dyne-centimeter
11 Game with many "points"
12 Lifeline's location
13 Like a 16-Across
18 Thole insert
19 Netanyahu's successor, 1999
24 Prefix with biology
26 The constellation Ara
27 Cultured gem
29 ___ Maria (liqueur)
30 Misanthrope, e.g.
31 Balmy time in Bordeaux
32 "Frasier" role
34 Lesley of "60 Minutes"
35 Tiny bit
37 Acapulco "eye"
38 Transportation for many a rock band
39 Demographic division
41 Whiskas eater
44 Apply to
46 Fashion monogram
48 Invite, as trouble
50 Guinness superlative
51 Richard with a much-used thumb
52 Like pretzels, typically
54 Clotho and sisters
55 Game extenders: Abbr.
56 Throw a barb at
57 "And Winter Came . . ." singer
59 Isao of the Golf Hall of Fame
60 Stir up
63 Sports stat that's best when low
64 Bribe
65 ___ chi

by Jim Hilger

ACROSS

1 He played Joe Palooka in the 1934 film "Palooka"
9 Elite
15 Like the trades
16 Press agent?
17 Able to be drawn out
18 National park whose name means "the high one"
19 Bunny fancier
20 Itch
21 Like Jesus
22 Hot chocolate time, maybe
24 "Horrors!"
25 Author of the 1968 work named in the circled letters (reading clockwise)
28 Cinéma ___
30 Cartoon "Yuck!"
31 1950s political inits.
32 Perfume, in a way
35 Subject of the 1968 work
39 Source of the saying "The gods help them that help themselves"
40 Detectives look for them, briefly
41 Emulate Don Corleone
42 Castle part
44 Leader of the 35-Across
45 Archer's wife in "The Maltese Falcon"
48 Like ruckuses or roadster roofs
50 Like some poker betting
52 ___-ray
53 1950s–'60s political inits.
56 Secretaries used to make them
57 "Ciao!"
59 Will words

60 Italian scientist who lent his name to a number
61 Hauled (off)
62 Like summer school classes, often

DOWN

1 MacFarlane who created TV's "Family Guy"
2 Amount ignored in weighing
3 Org. with the ad slogan "It's not science fiction. It's what we do every day"
4 More quickly?
5 Make more presentable, as a letter
6 More twisted
7 "No way!"

8 Nevada county containing Yucca Mountain
9 Seconds
10 Loners
11 Actress Anderson
12 Related on the mother's side
13 "The Color Purple" protagonist
14 Double-cross, e.g.
21 Georgia was one once: Abbr.
22 Something new
23 Some bagel toppers
25 Steno's stat.
26 Cup ___ (hot drink, informally)
27 Neon sign, e.g.
29 Recommendation letter, maybe
31 Valued
33 High ___

34 Language from which "spunk" is derived
36 "I played already"
37 Willing to consider
38 Writer in cipher, maybe
43 Slowing down, in music: Abbr.
44 Workable if awkward solution to a computer problem
45 Like Hindi or Urdu
46 Last word in a showman's spiel
47 Let out, e.g.
49 A flower is pretty when it's in this
51 "Leave ___ that!"
53 "Episode VI" returnee
54 Meeting places
55 Noted gang leader
57 Swabbie
58 Man of tomorrow

by Matt Ginsberg and Pete Muller

ACROSS

1 Foe of 71-Across in Mad magazine
4 Slaps on
9 Mass seating
13 Some round components
15 "There, there"
16 Stack server
17 Genetics-or-environment debate
20 Utensil drawer compartment
21 Like guns and dump trucks, over and over
22 Brewskis
24 Shade of blue
25 "And ___ Was," 1985 Talking Heads song
28 Decathlete's implement
30 Brute
35 Discovery Channel survival show
38 "___ Theme" (1965 soundtrack tune)
39 Piedmont wine town
40 Neighbor of St. Kitts
42 Pack down
43 Wozniak or Jobs
45 Home-seeker's decision
47 Usher in
49 ___ avis
50 Bourbon and Beale: Abbr.
51 Get too much sun
53 Standing O, say
55 Chewbacca and kin
60 Saint of Ávila
64 2004 movie featuring a clash of sci-fi species
66 ___ diagram (logic illustration)

67 Wearing a disguise, informally
68 Oz creator
69 John Lennon's "Dear ___"
70 Like some rich soil
71 Foe of 1-Across in Mad magazine

DOWN

1 Went under
2 ___ B
3 Hairy legend
4 Decreases gradually
5 Off-roader, for short
6 "Evil empire" initials
7 Our 206
8 Moves furtively
9 Falafel holder
10 Israel's Olmert
11 Sported
12 Rushed
14 Some 4WD rides
18 Opts not to be discharged
19 Word before pain or treatment
23 More cagey
25 Chart-topper
26 Rush
27 Reply to a knock
29 Young migratory fish
31 Brewery lineup
32 Many Semites
33 Full range
34 Cable TV sports awards
36 South-of-the-border cheer starter
37 Washington of jazz
41 Generalship
44 Pixieish
46 Like a windmill
48 Austin Powers foe
52 Kind of question on a survey
54 Ho-hum
55 Like moiré patterns
56 Land O'Lakes product
57 "Old MacDonald" sound
58 Popular bar game
59 Adoption advocacy org.
61 Itinerary data, briefly
62 Alternative to salad
63 Camp group
65 CD-___

by Jeff Chen

ACROSS

1 It's better than prison
8 #1 on Bravo's all-time "100 Funniest Movies" list
15 Latitude
16 They may be grilled
17 Give back
18 Italian red
19 Country Music Mo.
20 Mine, in Milan
21 Squirreled away
22 Alphabet trio
23 X
25 Adams behind a lens
27 Good call letters for Radio Disney?
28 W.W. II attacker
30 Suffix with hotel
31 Emmy-nominated sitcom of the early 1970s
32 Lacking bargaining power, maybe
34 Waiter
35 Prominent location to build on (as suggested by this puzzle?)
37 Mathematical subgroups
40 You can't go through with it
44 Dough
45 Rear
46 Farm letters?
47 When the French toast?
48 Kind of cell in biology
50 Big name in balls
51 One on either side of the St. Gotthard Pass
52 1900s, e.g.: Abbr.
53 Where the Ringling Brothers circus began: Abbr.
55 Org. employing Ethan Hunt in film
56 "Anything but!"
58 Mount Holyoke graduates, e.g.
60 Seven-time major-league All-Star Alfonso
61 Sailing enthusiast, informally
62 Help
63 Place of learning

DOWN

1 Always going outside?
2 ___ Observatory, home of the world's largest single-aperture radio telescope
3 Has as a base
4 Subject of many lab tests
5 Biblical kingdom
6 Tiny groove
7 Publication with a 1997 headline "Drug Use Down Among Uncool Kids"
8 Zodiac symbol
9 Nothing
10 Scholar's reference abbr.
11 Start of a confession
12 Who wrote "Wealth is the product of man's capacity to think"
13 Leaves alone
14 Vacationer's help
24 Big eyes, metaphorically
26 Six Nations tribe
27 Kind of candidate who's rarely successful
29 It matures in 1 to 10 yrs.
31 Place to live
33 Org. supported by the 16th Amendment
34 End of some scores
36 Missing persons
37 Gets rid of everybody, say
38 Forecast
39 Royal rod, in Britain
41 Investigate
42 Speedy delivery
43 Place where people work for beans?
45 Hymn leader
48 Baseball general manager Billy
49 Lavender
52 Fellow
54 To so high a degree
57 Wed
59 Conductance unit

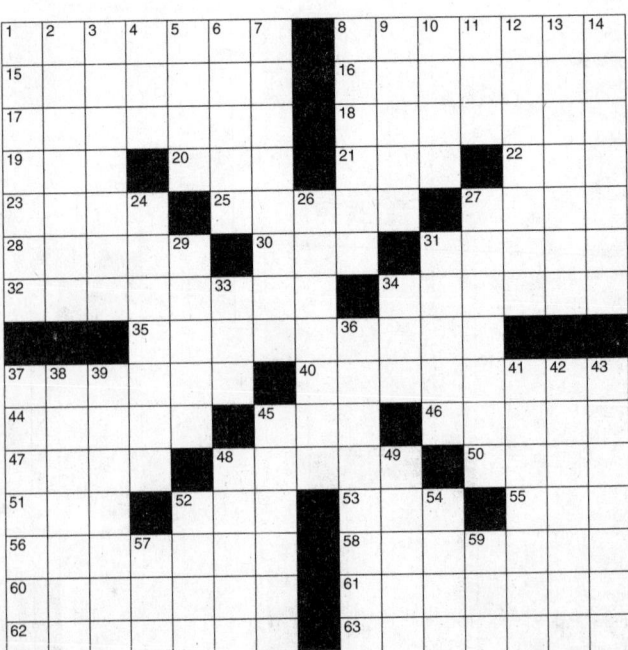

by Samuel A. Donaldson

ACROSS

1 Humped ox
5 Indo-European language speakers
11 Longtime Elton John label
14 "___ (So Far Away)" (1982 hit by A Flock of Seagulls)
15 Cut some more, maybe
16 "Atonement" author McEwan
17 California home of the Crystal Cathedral
19 Something that's burned
20 Morlock's counterpart in science fiction
21 It may be felt by a blackboard
23 Hums
26 California locale just south of Camp Pendleton
29 Flightless flock
30 Home ___
31 Israeli arms
32 Positive
34 Backside
37 Two out of nine?
38 California State University campus site
41 "Ere Heaven shall ___ her portals . . .": Byron
43 Guy's girl
44 Bordelaise and others
47 Traditional Christmas purchases
49 They play in front of QBs
51 Part of rock's CSNY
52 California's Sonoma County seat
55 Concise
56 Wound up
57 Shopping site
59 Ocasek of the Cars
60 Urban areas (as hinted at by the circled letters in this puzzle's grid)

66 "Naughty!"
67 Rests atop
68 "At Last" singer James
69 Urban grid: Abbr.
70 Obfuscate, in a way
71 Pringles alternative

DOWN

1 Turn one way before turning the other
2 Prohibition ___
3 Rare site during Prohibition
4 Like scuba diving
5 View from the Leaning Tower
6 Neighborhood
7 "___ out!" (shout by a 24-Down)
8 Hubbub
9 Skin care product name
10 Severe
11 Toyota Camry, e.g.
12 Collapsed
13 Ursula of "The Blue Max"
18 Trains to Wrigley
22 Sch. in Jonesboro
23 Little, in Lyon
24 See 7-Down
25 Causes of some traffic slowdowns
27 Cousins of girdles
28 Sufficient, informally
30 Thing
33 Alias
35 The Rolling Stones' "___ You"
36 ___-green
39 Puerto ___
40 Ornamental crescents
41 After a fashion
42 One who deals in rags?
45 Last of the Mohicans?
46 Sow or cow

48 Part of S.O.P.: Abbr.
50 Flintlock accessory
53 Nimble
54 Kidney secretion
55 Start of some cycles?
58 Trouble spots?
61 Japanese supercomputer maker
62 That, in Tabasco
63 Cousin ___ of 1960s TV
64 H
65 Coltrane blew it

by Peter A. Collins

ACROSS

1 Vitamin C source from Southeast Asia
10 Songwriter Jimmy and Senator Jim
15 It has just 16 rules of grammar
16 Western language historically written in the Cyrillic alphabet
17 London newspaper
18 Mork's TV companion
19 Sea eagles
20 TV network since 1970
21 Bomb, e.g.
22 Alphabet trio
23 Turkey's location
27 It may be turned against you
28 Hammer's partner
29 ___ Street, main thoroughfare in "Peyton Place"
30 J.F.K. watchdog
31 Training ___
32 Jacob who wrote "How the Other Half Lives"
33 Taking one's sweet time
37 Daly of "Cagney & Lacey"
38 It's beside a sideburn
39 Muscles covering some 32-Down
40 Actress Gasteyer
41 Barrister's deg.
42 Credit figs.
44 Singer with the hit country album "Backwoods Barbie"
47 Sketch show that launched 40-Across's career, in short
50 Gist
51 It's located between two Plymouths: Abbr.
52 Scott of "Joanie Loves Chachi"
53 Mr. ___

54 "Gotcha," formally
56 Author Calvino
57 Skating venue
58 Staff up again
59 After U2, highest-grossing concert band of all time, informally

DOWN

1 Ritual in which bitter herbs are dipped
2 Three Ivans
3 "___ of sweat will save a gallon of blood": Patton
4 Fam. members
5 Lie in the sun with suntan oil
6 Wheelchair-accessible
7 No-can-do
8 Formal acknowledgment

9 "My mama done ___ me"
10 Traded beads
11 Cuban name in 2000 news
12 Win whose money, in a bygone game show?
13 Baseball commissioner starting in 1992
14 Sloppy place
23 Oven part
24 Hall-of-Famer Yastrzemski
25 30-Down, sometimes
26 Apt. parts
27 Fisherman's relation?
30 Course closer
31 It may be sandy or candy
32 See 39-Across
33 1970s sitcom catchword
34 Dog sound

35 Pop for a young person?
36 Fisherman's relation?
37 Wee bit
41 English author Edward Bulwer-___
42 Prime minister before and after Churchill
43 Coral creatures
45 Boxer Ali
46 Jon ___, at 6'11" the tallest player in Major League Baseball history
47 Old Scratch
48 Family relation
49 Mined finds
52 String tie
53 Source of some paper pulp
54 Dah's go-with
55 Member of a D.C. nine

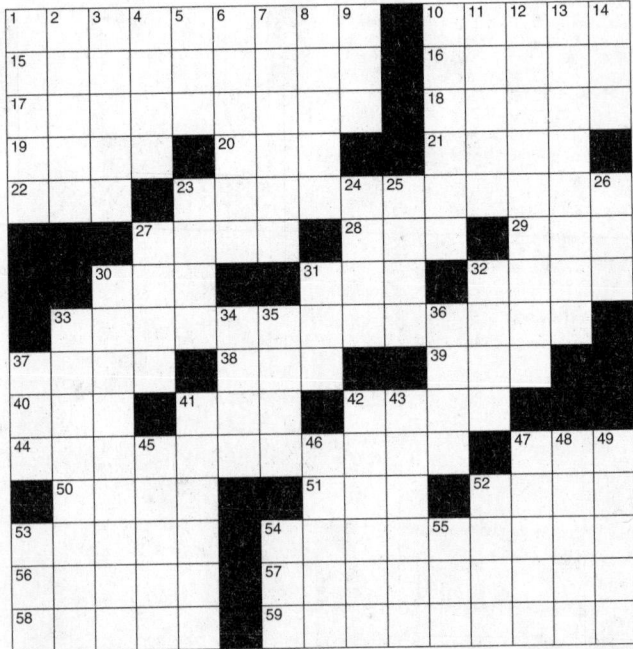

by Jeff Dubner

ACROSS

1 1960s "Bye!"
6 ___ de Boulogne (Paris park)
10 Web site with a "Buy It Now" option
14 Trip planner's aid
15 Way back when
16 Miser's cry
17 Angle symbol, in trigonometry
18 Mark in a margin
19 Have ___ (lose it)
20 Iodine in a barber's first-aid kit?
23 Ultimate degree
24 Passbook abbr.
25 Vamp Negri
26 Doofus given a pink slip?
31 Root used as a soap substitute
34 Balancing pro
35 Philosopher Mo-___
36 Dim bulb, so to speak
39 Hobby kit with a colony
42 Sans affiliation: Abbr.
43 Muff
45 Caffeine-laden nuts
46 One modifying goals?
51 Texas ___ M
52 One with a 6-yr. term
53 Tokyo, to shoguns
56 Cronus and Rhea's barbecue remains?
60 Official proceedings
61 Municipal laws: Abbr.
62 Like some checking accounts
63 Title in an Uncle Remus story
64 Unlucky number for Caesar?
65 Influence . . . and a hint to 20-, 26-, 46- and 56-Across
66 Anti-snakebite supplies, e.g.
67 Superheroes of comics
68 Well-versed

DOWN

1 Party spread
2 One of the Coens
3 Argus-eyed
4 Odds-and-ends category
5 Son of Isaac
6 Ordered (around)
7 Germane
8 Home of the Eyjafjallajökull volcano: Abbr.
9 Eighth-inning hurler, often
10 Many résumé submissions, these days
11 Like a New York/Los Angeles romance
12 In a bit
13 Bow wood
21 Results of most 100-yd. returns
22 You, to Yves
27 Serpent's home
28 Curative locale
29 Cornell of Cornell University
30 2012 Charlotte conventioneers: Abbr.
31 Sarah McLachlan hit
32 Bond that's often tax-free, for short
33 Rembrandt, notably
37 Player of a TV junkman
38 Hoopster Erving, to fans
40 End-of-fight letters
41 Predicted
44 "The Satanic Verses" novelist
47 Much of Libya
48 Mayo is part of it
49 Greets at the door
50 What might make molehills out of a mountain?
54 Willem of "Platoon"
55 Best
56 Spread unit
57 At one's fighting weight, say
58 Machu Picchu builder
59 Paving stone
60 Gym rat's "six-pack"

by Steve Salitan

Note: Two hints for 17- and 57-Across and 11- and 26-Down appear somewhere in this puzzle.

ACROSS

1 Easy catch
6 Site of some Galileo experiments
10 "The ___ lama, he's a priest"
14 Dutch princess who's the daughter of Queen Juliana
15 Air show sound
16 Grievous
17 [See blurb]
19 Year St. Augustine of Canterbury died
20 Org. with a targetlike mark on its flag
21 School yr. section
23 Time for a pique-nique, maybe
24 Honeybun
28 Ming jar, e.g.
30 Second bananas
31 Kind of knife
32 Bugs
33 Seventh heaven
36 N.L. West team, on scoreboards
37 Fairy tale
38 Reporter's aid
43 Best-selling PC game released in 2000
47 Hot
48 Simple ski lift
49 Learned ones
51 Analgesic
52 Scot's negative
53 Service award?
54 Upper body: Abbr.
55 Sphere
57 [See blurb]
63 Enamored (of)
64 Home for Samuel Beckett
65 Language known to native speakers as "te reo"
66 Reverse
67 Esposas: Abbr.
68 Tries

DOWN

1 Glutton
2 Bomber pilot in "Catch-22"
3 Green globule
4 German connection
5 British aristocracy
6 Claim
7 ___ exchange
8 Link in the food chain?
9 #33 on a table
10 ___ duck
11 [See blurb]
12 Baritone piece sung by Renato
13 New Orleans sight
18 Sondheim's Mrs. Lovett, e.g.
22 Range parts: Abbr.
24 Airer of hearings
25 "In ___," Nirvana album
26 [See blurb]
27 Prison staple
29 Suffix with real or surreal
34 One who says a lot in a game
35 "___ can" (campaign slogan)
39 The Depression, e.g.
40 Runners do it
41 Occasionally
42 Hopelessness
43 Wrecks
44 Puts an edge on
45 Curie, Kelvin and Fermi
46 But: Lat.
49 Major mess
50 Sorkin who wrote "The Social Network"
56 Shakespearean stir
58 La-la lead-in
59 Bath ___
60 Flapper wrapper
61 Sphere
62 French flower

by Ben Fish

ACROSS

1 Volcano output
4 Prospects
10 Dash
14 Person with a corner ofc., maybe
15 The Scourge of God
16 Queen in "The Lion King"
17 "The Godfather" actor
18 The 21st Amendment, e.g.
19 Sting
20 Knight ___ (former newspaper group)
22 "Falcon Crest" actress
24 Awakening
26 "How ___ Your Mother"
27 Some cons
29 It might be golden
33 Final words?
36 Dockworkers' grp.
37 Allergy-afflicted dwarf
38 Car with the numeral 9 in all its model names
39 Pro baseball level . . . or a hint to 12 answers in this puzzle
41 River across the French/German border
42 Speed skater Eric who won five gold medals at the 1980 Winter Olympics
44 Location of the quadriceps
45 Enterprise captain prior to Kirk
46 Dangerous snake
47 Raspy
49 Captain of sci-fi
51 Newborn
55 Language of Cape Town
59 Antitank artillery operator, e.g.
60 Grill
61 Jungle vines
63 It may be eaten with tikka masala
64 Itch
65 Like Jimmy Kimmel and Jimmy Fallon
66 Here, in Québec
67 ___ Turing, a founding father of computer science
68 Annual event in Los Angeles
69 Summer, in Québec

DOWN

1 Capital of Ghana
2 It's said to be salubrious
3 1953 John Wayne film
4 City or lake in northern Italy
5 Repeated step
6 The Racer's Edge
7 "___ yellow ribbon . . ."
8 Singer Morissette
9 Low bow
10 Give a right to
11 ___ de Triomphe
12 Jai ___
13 Carquest competitor
21 Make dirty . . . or clean
23 ___ Lewis with the 2008 #1 hit "Bleeding Love"
25 Doozy
28 Painter Picasso
30 He loved Lucy
31 Walton who wrote "The Compleat Angler"
32 Jane of literature
33 Producer of workplace regs.
34 Bleated
35 Footnote abbr.
37 Set apart
39 Shortstop Jeter
40 Put pressure (on)
43 Inhabitant
45 New York's ___ Station
47 Fine-tuning
48 Drunkards
50 It has its moments
52 "___ Get Your Gun"
53 Boston Harbor event precipitator
54 ___ Macmillan, classmate of Harry Potter
55 Blue-green
56 Roll up, as a flag
57 Gulf of ___, arm of the Baltic
58 Room in una casa
62 "Born on the Fourth of July" setting, familiarly

by Barry Boone

ACROSS

1 Go off course
4 Natural
10 Enjoy a pleasant situation
14 Foreman fighter
15 Symbol of Middle America
16 Fighting
17 Start of a silly underwear joke
20 Wine region of Italy
21 Extinct kin of the kiwi
22 "The Scarlet Letter" heroine
23 Joke, part 2
26 PC linkup
27 Leftovers
31 Popular bit of candy
34 Suffix with symptom
36 Final, say
37 Previously
38 Joke, part 3
41 Satisfied
42 Gordon of "Harold and Maude"
44 Small bottle
45 Wear
47 When many alarms go off
49 Good name for an investor?
50 Joke, part 4
55 Five iron
58 Browning who directed "Dracula," 1931
59 Exposed
61 End of the joke
64 Eastern nanny
65 "No way!"
66 Something not good to have on one's face
67 Sylvia who played the Queen Mother in "The Queen"
68 Fake
69 Literary inits.

DOWN

1 When tripled, et cetera
2 Elite
3 B, C or D, at a shoe store
4 Wall St. debut
5 Mad face?
6 At all
7 Geometric figures
8 Aunt, in Acapulco
9 Standard-issue item for a Secret Service agent
10 What some teens do to earn money
11 Soon
12 Render open-mouthed
13 Flier with a ground connection?
18 Farm measure
19 The second "A" of A.M.P.A.S.
24 Symbol of gentleness
25 One of the archangels
28 Sampler
29 Took advantage of
30 Major closing?
31 Maker of 31-Across
32 Fit of shaking chills
33 Child's punishment, maybe
34 Grisham's "___ to Kill"
35 Pan Am rival
39 Gradually disappear
40 Lover of brain games
43 Sinister laughs
46 Service leader
48 One who's easily duped
49 Behind on payments
51 British guns
52 Major artery
53 Country club employee
54 Leftovers
55 Corp. recruits
56 Host
57 Kingdom in "The King and I"
60 Best, but barely
62 Card game for two
63 Moroccan topper

by Alan Arbesfeld

ACROSS

1 "That's all right, ___" (lyric from Elvis's first single)
5 Knife
9 Flat floaters
14 Pearly gem
15 When said three times, a W.W. II cry
16 One who's called "the Merciful" and "the Compassionate"
17 Laugh uproariously
19 Brighter than bright
20 "Hee ___"
21 Like the word 16-Across
23 Dinner scraps
24 A Gershwin
25 Perspire mildly
27 Poindexter type
29 Guarantee
30 Crest alternative
32 Preferred way to proceed
35 "___ your request . . ."
36 Pay cashlessly
39 Blocks from the refrigerator
42 One of the Fitzgeralds
43 Poet who wrote "Heard melodies are sweet, but those unheard are sweeter"
47 Medieval infantry weapon
49 TV show set at William McKinley High School
50 Begin to grin
56 High point of a Swiss vacation?
57 Novelist Philip
58 Tulsan, e.g.
59 Mudroom item
60 "The Mill on the Floss" author
62 Boogie
64 Fruit related to cherry plums
65 Italian wine center
66 Change a sentence, say
67 ___ 500
68 Laura of "Rambling Rose"
69 Speeds (up)

DOWN

1 Punk rock concert activity
2 Jacket and tie, e.g.
3 It might give you a virus
4 Boxer with an allegiance to 16-Across
5 Fab Four name
6 Ancient Romans' wear
7 Dutch-speaking Caribbean isle
8 Dyed fabric
9 Sleazy paper
10 Permits
11 Recurrence of an old problem
12 Steak ___ (raw dish)
13 Business cheat
18 Keyboard key
22 Michael who starred in 39-Down
26 Small bag of chips, maybe
28 It always starts on the same day of the week as Sept.
31 Elevator background
32 Bud
33 Watch readout, for short
34 "So that's it!"
37 Longhorn's school, informally
38 Bud holder?
39 "The ___ File," 1965 film
40 Flower part
41 Jubilance
44 One way to serve pie
45 Mediterranean port
46 Disney's dwarfs and others
48 Came back
51 Eminem rap with the lyric "Guarantee I'll be the greatest thing you ever had"
52 Computer option
53 Wordless song: Abbr.
54 Admit
55 Onetime feminist cause, for short
61 Cough syrup meas.
63 La Méditerranée, e.g.

by Gary Cee

ACROSS

1 Darted
6 Grasp
12 Natl. economic stat
15 Full tilt
16 Proceeding without thinking
17 Place for clover
18 Film about how to win a MacArthur Fellowship?
21 Aoki of the P.G.A.
22 One of the 30 Dow Jones industrials
23 Ancient Anatolian land
24 Like some drugs, briefly
25 Film about a biblical serpent?
29 Winging it?
32 Conspicuously consume
33 Barq's rival
34 Trouble makers
36 Soup vegetable
38 Film about Ali/ Foreman's Rumble in the Jungle?
43 Slave
44 Goes off script
47 Word in the names of four state capitals
51 Viking king, 995–1000
54 Skin: Suffix
55 Film in which Moe, Shemp and Curly show their flexibility?
58 Lobster trap
59 Title town in a 1945 Pulitzer winner
60 "The Cat in the Hat Knows a Lot About That!" subj.
61 Mid sixth-century year
62 Film about earworms?
67 Official lang. of Ghana and Grenada
68 Judicial decision
69 Jaipur royal
70 Madrid royal
71 Vows
72 Mushroom maker, briefly

DOWN

1 Spot that's never seen
2 Figure in a Leonardo mural
3 Passage of grave importance?
4 Sound effect
5 Heavy-metal singer Snider
6 400 list-maker
7 ___ magnetism
8 Graffiti signature
9 "Say what?"
10 First N.L.'er to hit 500 home runs
11 Unifying theme
12 Good witch
13 Didn't approve
14 Heathens
19 One that might catch a double dribble?
20 Did some garden work
26 Toni Morrison novel
27 Not kosher
28 "Anna Bolena" or "Anna Nicole"
30 Rock's ___ Fighters
31 Flanged fastener
35 Waited in line, say
37 Jason of the N.B.A.
39 Art collector's collection
40 Undesirable roll
41 Progressive Field team, on scoreboards
42 Stew container?
45 Appropriate title for this puzzle?
46 Imitation fabric
47 Second drink at a bar
48 Element in disinfectants
49 Like some country music
50 Jerry who co-founded Yahoo!
52 Become an increasing source of irritation
53 "
56 Sports no-nos, informally
57 Quit running
61 "Darn it!"
63 Like ___
64 It's very cool
65 Heat org.?
66 One piece of a two-piece

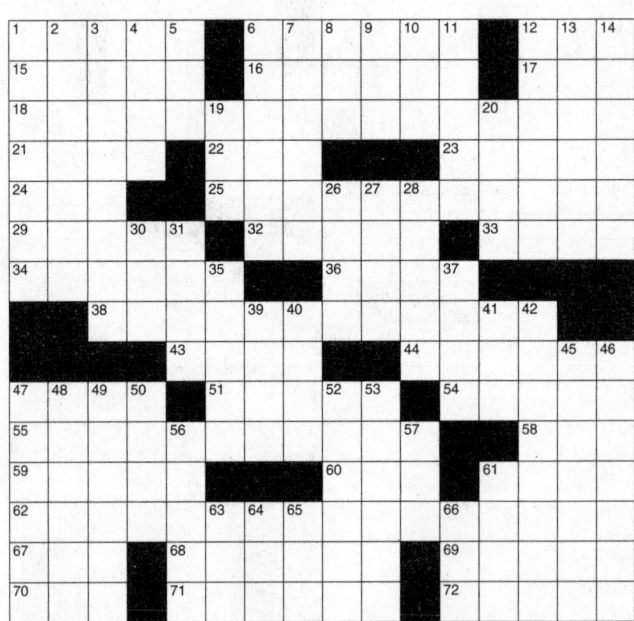

by John Farmer

ACROSS

1 Steamy places
5 "EastEnders" network
8 Toothpaste ingredient
12 Some soot
14 Fellah or fedayee
16 The Venerable ___ (old English historian)
17 Then, to Thierry
18 Insincere flattery, in slang
20 Request to an interviewee
22 "Harry and Tonto" star
23 "___, 'tis true I have gone here and there": Shak.
24 Burlesque bit
25 1980s Rowan Atkinson sitcom series set in various historical periods
28 Material you might look through
29 Every last bit
32 Items wrapped in friction tape
33 Many arcade-goers
34 Gift upon arrival, maybe
35 Winged god
36 Like zebra crossings
37 Livery delivery
38 Follow a pattern, say
39 Jimmy of "The West Wing"
40 Title role for Joe Pesci
41 House sitter?
42 Mates
43 Best Supporting Actress nominee for "Five Easy Pieces"
44 Sticks out
45 Eat in style
46 Biased
49 Pod-bearing plant
53 Started one's shift
55 Hunger enhancer, sometimes

56 Typical romance novel love interest
57 "What rotten luck!"
58 Nest-building pests
59 It's whipped to make mousse
60 Bud drinker?
61 Former life

DOWN

1 Sarcophagus lid
2 Like Death's horse
3 One of the Minor Prophets
4 Butter knife, e.g.
5 Nurslings
6 Fastener in a punched hole
7 Pink-slip
8 Famously polite Old West stagecoach robber
9 Unreactive element
10 Sedgwick in Warhol films
11 Bank
13 January department store events
15 Iconic AC/DC album with the song "You Shook Me All Night Long"
19 Filed things
21 Organic sealant
24 Bird feeder tidbits
25 Cover-up
26 Mann of rock
27 Go under
28 Volcano features
29 Unlucky in love, say
30 Country singer Rimes
31 Untainted by corruption
33 Call option?
36 Some nerve tissue
37 It's worthy of condemnation

39 Gumption
40 Woman of letters?
43 Sorento manufacturer
44 Star of 2010's "Gulliver's Travels"
45 Packed with ideas, as an essay
46 Soreness
47 Shot of liquor
48 Protracted
49 Snack
50 Novelist Jaffe
51 First-aid experts, briefly
52 Defender in a bridge column
54 Lightly apply

by Patrick Berry

ACROSS

1 Hanging open
6 Cousin of an ax
10 Near Eastern V.I.P.'s
14 Doesn't have a second to lose?
15 Boutique fixture
17 Exhibited perfect braking
19 Native Nebraskan
20 Followers of nus
21 "For me? You shouldn't have . . ."
22 Nicest room on a ship, probably
27 Toward the back
28 E.T.A.'s for red-eyes
29 Here, to Henri
32 Foofaraw
35 Aloe additive?
37 "Heavens to Betsy!"
38 Cashier's error, as suggested by 17-, 22-, 47- and 58-Across?
41 Henry who made a Fortune?
42 Baby taking a bow?
43 Befuddled
44 Baton Rouge sch.
45 Peace grp. since 1948
46 "___ loves me . . ."
47 Certain loaf
54 Frigidaire competitor
56 Bumbler
57 Réunion, e.g.
58 Being frugal
63 Strongly praised
64 Goose bumps-producing, maybe
65 Funnywoman Martha
66 Actress Naldi of the silents
67 Kickoff

DOWN

1 N.A.A.C.P. part: Abbr.
2 Must, slangily
3 Something to be thrown for
4 Top 40 fare
5 Medium capacity?
6 Contribute to the mix
7 Impurity
8 Eastern state?
9 That, in Tijuana
10 "___ there yet?"
11 Handy IDs in the hood?
12 Unwanted spots
13 Kind of terrier
16 Slows down traffic, say?
18 Sign by stairs, often
23 1,000-foot-deep lake that straddles a state line
24 Many miles away
25 Game with a maximum score of 180
26 Apple offering
30 Zoo keeper?
31 Noodle product?
32 Over the ___
33 Burden
34 Number of people in a room
35 Numbered thing in the Bible
36 Friendly introduction?
37 Faster's opposite
39 Bring in
40 "Yeah, right"
45 Gerald Ford's birthplace
46 Muslim mystic
48 Theodore Roosevelt, to Eleanor
49 Man of many words?
50 Press conference component, briefly
51 Arena sections
52 Carl's wife in "Up"
53 Bowling alley button
54 On ___ with (equal to)
55 Sheet mineral
59 "There is no ___ team"
60 Name placeholder in govt. records
61 Many a Fortune profilee, for short
62 "Jeopardy!" whiz Jennings

by Milo Beckman

ACROSS

1 Visibly scared out of one's wits
9 "You're ___ trouble!"
14 Alternative to a home meal
15 "___ Fall in Love" (1961 hit by the Lettermen)
16 Got comfortable with
17 1957–91 king of Norway
18 Food-stamping org.
19 Opposite of flushed
21 Dundee denial
22 Classic 1921 play set partly in a factory
25 Atlanta-based cable channel
26 In ___ (undisturbed)
27 Helps for autobiographers
31 Make available
33 Spooky sound
34 For two
36 Up
37 Befuddle
38 Having spirit?
40 Olympic entrant: Abbr.
41 "A Passage to India" woman
43 Cut back
44 Contest in which the rules must be followed to the letter?
45 1990 title role for Gérard Depardieu
47 Fictional character who says "I wear the chain I forged in life"
49 Caesar's "these"
50 Tuna type
52 On the other hand
53 Ritual garment
54 X-File subj.
55 One of the Castros
59 Cubbies, e.g.
61 Tibetan terrier
66 Altoids alternative
67 "Most certainly!"
68 Stage direction
69 1984 film whose soundtrack had a #1 hit with the same title

DOWN

1 Brake parts
2 Slightly
3 Italy's ___ Islands
4 Certain M.D.
5 Senesce
6 Lay turf on
7 Self: Prefix
8 Result of a boom and bust, maybe
9 Lucky lottery player's cry
10 Senator's org.
11 Toy collectible of the late '90s
12 Enamors
13 Cash in one's chips
14 Glace, after thawing
20 Fed. bureau
23 Jazz fan, probably
24 The scarlet letter
25 Something of earth-shaking concern?
26 Part of a band's performance
27 Tiny possibility
28 Who wrote "It's not that I'm afraid to die, I just don't want to be there when it happens"
29 "Life Itself: A Memoir" autobiographer, 2011
30 Start another tour
32 Make by interlacing
35 Additional, in ads
39 Mysterious: Var.
42 Fond du ___, Wis.
46 Buffoon
48 Major discount brokerage
51 Trinity member
54 Cold war inits.
56 Copycat
57 Plays for a fool
58 City near Ben-Gurion Airport
60 Artery: Abbr.
62 New Test. book
63 The Sun Devils, for short
64 Auntie, to Dad
65 Word with black, red or white

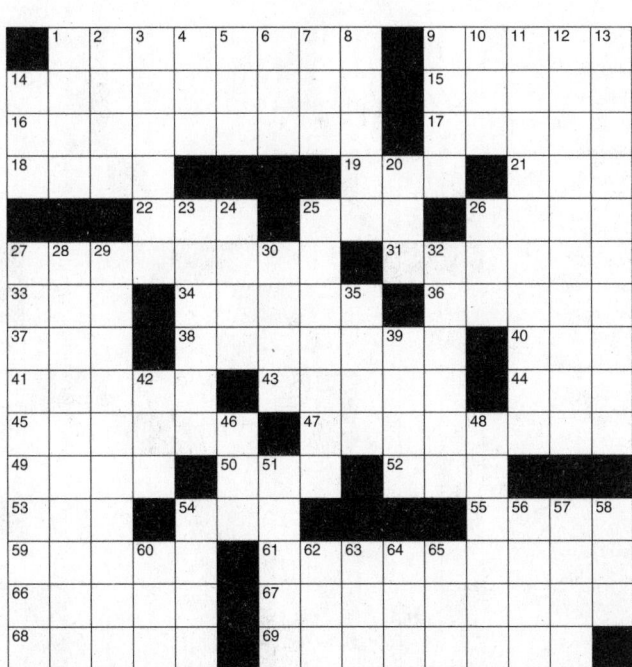

by Kurt Mueller

ACROSS

1 Astronomer Sagan
5 Final preceder
9 Like E.T.'s voice
14 Sounder of the tuning note at the start of an orchestra rehearsal
15 Gillette ___ II
16 Apple communication tool, once
17 See 37-Across
19 Palace employee
20 Appeal
21 "Aren't you special!"
22 Caleb who wrote "The Alienist"
23 See 37-Across
28 Provider of a jawbone to Samson
29 G.I. address
30 Traffic caution
31 "Stat!"
34 Clingy wrap
36 London's ___ Gardens
37 Grammatical infelicity . . . or what 17-, 23-, 48- or 60-Across is?
41 Part of R.S.V.P.
42 Runaways
43 Linear, briefly
44 "___ tu" (Verdi aria)
45 Foot soldiers: Abbr.
46 TV extraterrestrial
48 See 37-Across
54 Neck of the woods
55 Crones
56 A hand
58 Where the brain resides, slangily
60 See 37-Across
62 "Ask me anything"
63 Part of Georgia is in it
64 Sound
65 "___ Doone," 1869 historical romance
66 Alpine capital
67 Food safety org.

DOWN

1 Some prison furnishings
2 Circa
3 Official state sport of Wyoming
4 Wahine wear
5 Bar lineup
6 Weasley family owl, in Harry Potter books
7 ___ Picchu (Inca site)
8 Put away
9 Pasta variety
10 Honda division
11 Shiny suit fabric
12 Score to aim for
13 Stock page abbr.
18 Part of R.S.V.P.
22 Hearings channel
24 Big ___ (nickname of baseball's David Ortiz)
25 "We'll always have ___" (line from "Casablanca")
26 Student in 25-Down
27 Planted
31 It's a plus
32 Vice president Agnew
33 Pricey belt material
34 Smokeless tobacco
35 At the back of a boat
38 Ambitious track bet
39 Ancient Aegean region
40 Elegantly dressed bloke
46 Crocheted item
47 Simpson girl
49 1970s–'90s film company
50 "Along ___ lines . . ."
51 P.L.O.'s Arafat
52 Goodbyes
53 Cede
57 Actress de Matteo of "The Sopranos"
58 Communication syst. for the hearing-impaired
59 However, for short
60 Bar bill
61 Fifth of seven: Abbr.

by Barry Franklin and Sara Kaplan

ACROSS

1 Certain lamp goo
5 Home
10 Subject of an exhaustive E.P.A. study?
14 Give ___ up
15 Thoroughly enjoy
16 Monarch moniker, for short
17 Part of an equine pedigree
18 California's Santa ___ University
19 Cemetery sights
20 Nearly impossible target, literally
23 Apt name for a crime boss
24 Gist
25 One who's enraptured, say, literally
31 Ship navigation hazard
33 Detected
34 Equatorial land
35 Promenade
37 Weenie
40 Caboose
41 "It must be ___ news day"
43 Some jeans
45 Young ___
46 Inadvertently destructive sort, literally
50 Mardi follower
51 Five pairs
52 Something rapidly deteriorating goes to it, literally
59 A good one is cracked
60 "Bye-bye, mon ami"
61 Something that's just for starters?
62 "The Lord of the Rings," e.g.
63 Set the volume of to zero
64 "Chocolat" actress Olin
65 Weasel relatives
66 Chimpersonators?
67 Purpose of many a doctor's visit

DOWN

1 Pirate's punishment
2 Inter ___
3 First part of an I.P. address?
4 A chair usually has one
5 Rose
6 Treadless
7 Like faces, typically
8 Bread
9 Cleared
10 One without a title
11 Chicago exchange, informally, with "the"
12 Porcine protest
13 Division units, for short
21 Ages upon ages
22 Job to do
25 Stringed instruments
26 Wood used in Voldemort's wand
27 Sound at a funeral
28 Top
29 Film private
30 They may ring or have rings
31 Jobs plan, once
32 Convert, in a way
36 Certain beer bottle
38 Sushi staple
39 Intimates
42 ___ of the state
44 2000 World Series locale
47 Grand ___ Island
48 Depleted
49 Marked down
52 Neighbors of the Navajo
53 Similar
54 Having less fat
55 Uninviting look
56 Building toy brand
57 Italian mount
58 ___ U.S.A.
59 Scout's brother

by Parker Lewis

ACROSS

1 Sting figure
5 Car dealer's starting point: Abbr.
9 Old Buckeye State service station name
14 Chewy candy treat
15 Old buffalo hunters of the Great Plains
16 Work that gives the illusion of movement
17 Needing no invitation
19 Safety ___
20 Like a successful marathoner?
22 Late-night beverages
23 1960s teach-in grp.
24 Bit of crying
27 Same: Prefix
28 Helsinki hoosegow?
32 Himalayas, e.g.: Abbr.
34 "___ me my Highland lassie, O": Burns
35 Pulitzer nominee for the novels "Black Water" and "Blonde"
36 Accommodating person? . . . or a hint to 20-, 28-, 48- and 57-Across
40 Bat cave deposit
43 It's part of the gene pool
44 Intentions
48 Call of a siren?
52 Chess champion Mikhail
53 It may be green or black
54 Seek damages
55 Warm and comfy
57 Jaded ale drinker's question?
61 Pied-à-___
63 Like many a whisper
64 Rugged rocks
65 Pro's foe
66 Some readouts, briefly
67 Not realized
68 For fear that
69 They may be announced en route: Abbr.

DOWN

1 Darken
2 Most downcast
3 French city associated with lace
4 Gianni's grandmother
5 Lesser-known astrology symbol
6 Missing women?
7 Massage deeply
8 Longtime Democratic House leader
9 Tapless tap-dancing
10 Mayberry moppet
11 Construction worker
12 Org. with auditors
13 Giant legend
18 Little slapfest
21 Takes too much, briefly
25 Alternative to I, you, he or she
26 Gives the nod to
29 Suffix with peace
30 Food and shelter
31 Home in a Mitchell novel
33 ___ Fein
37 Registering the most on the applause-o-meter
38 Music producer Brian
39 Women's businesswear
40 Prime meridian std.
41 Slangy reversal
42 Chemical agent for climate change
45 "You're on!"
46 Title woman in a Harry Belafonte song
47 Duplicity
49 Many a rosary carrier
50 Good-humored
51 Prod
56 Like an acrobat
58 Prod
59 Non-P.C. suffix
60 They're taken in high sch.
61 Home of the Horned Frogs: Abbr.
62 Directional suffix

by Paula Gamache

ACROSS

1 Snowmen and snowwomen?
6 Analogy words
10 Fraternity characters
14 Word akin to "-ish"
15 "Absolut nicht!"
16 River to the Arctic Ocean
17 Get an A, say
18 Vulnerable parts
20 Iago
22 Half of a 1955 merger, for short
24 "Alea iacta ___": Julius Caesar
25 Poet Elinor
26 Ion
31 Wind up
32 "If I were king of the forest . . ." singer
33 Gave pills, e.g.
35 Iams, say
42 It might hold you back
43 "Such is life"
44 Med. unit
47 lamb's place
51 "In bad company," per Ambrose Bierce
53 Boxcar
54 Ones getting base pay
55 Feature replaced in four clues in this puzzle
60 Locale for some diving
61 Touches
64 "My Life" autobiographer, 1975
65 Clip
66 Trouble
67 The Ponte Vecchio spans it
68 Approximately
69 Cicely of "Roots"

DOWN

1 Dollar coin figure before Susan B. Anthony, familiarly
2 "Ain't gonna happen!"
3 Strip
4 Dome light?
5 One may be smooth
6 A part of, as a gang
7 Comprehended
8 Mexican kin
9 Cleaning a mess in a mess, maybe
10 Roman writer who originated the phrase "with a grain of salt"
11 Beyond reason?
12 Fills, as black squares
13 Like many windows
19 "Compromise is the best and cheapest ___" (saying attributed to Robert Louis Stevenson)
21 PC key
22 Roping target
23 Myth ending
27 Things picked out of the earth
28 Take in
29 Passeport info
30 Picking up things?
34 Call
36 Spring break locale, casually
37 Order member
38 They may do write-ups, for short
39 Hard-to-clean floor covers
40 Big name in luxury hotels
41 "___ Declassified School Survival Guide"
44 City on Commencement Bay
45 Assassin
46 Comes calling unexpectedly
48 Experienced with
49 Gradually slowing, in mus.
50 Still around
52 "Explosive" roller coaster at Six Flags Great Adventure
56 Mythical ship with a speaking oak beam
57 Angle iron
58 Hawaiian handouts
59 Where Al Yankovic bought a "Dukes of Hazzard" ashtray, in song
62 "The way"
63 Depot: Abbr.

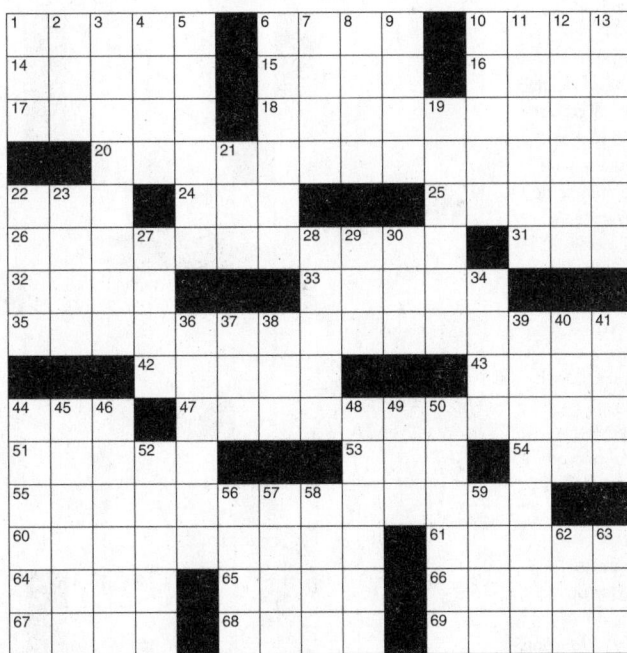

by Tim Croce

170 MEDIUM

ACROSS
1 Some undies
5 Go unhurriedly
10 January 1 game
14 Half court game?
15 Joyful tune
16 Ibuprofen target
17 Common result of a lane closing
19 Pronoun in hymns
20 Looking intently
21 Symbol of sturdiness
22 Vilify
23 Outdoor affair
26 Computer for one who's on the go
30 Nationality suffix
31 Nondairy dairy aisle item
32 Address the flock
36 Abbas's grp.
39 Large, fun quantity, in a saying
42 Word that appears eight times on a dollar bill
43 Baseball star nicknamed Godzilla
44 Missing roll call, say
45 Avian source of red meat
46 Gives a thumbs-down
48 Performer with sinuous moves
54 Some golf clubs
55 Stephen of "V for Vendetta"
56 Reach the Top 40, say
61 Mozart's "___ Fan Tutte"
62 Shot follower, often . . . and a hint to the starts of 17-, 23-, 39- and 48-Across
64 Blissful spot
65 Anesthetized
66 Singles bar delivery
67 What's tender in Mexican restaurants?
68 Mean-spirited
69 Writing on the wall

DOWN
1 Cake with a kick
2 Journal on YouTube, maybe
3 Flash drive filler
4 ___ bath (therapeutic treatment)
5 Breeze through
6 Lord's home
7 Slicer input
8 Social contract theorist John
9 Fraternal member
10 Penguin's nemesis
11 Earthy tone
12 ___ penny (pre-1959 cent)
13 Smelling a rat
18 Building block brand
22 Warren ___, baseball's winningest lefty
24 Heap kudos on
25 Kind of salad made famous by Julia Child
26 Timber wolf
27 ___ Freed, 1960s payola figure
28 ___ Noël (French Santa Claus)
29 Rocky hill
33 Go to seed
34 Abysmal grades
35 ___ Darya (river of central 58-Down)
36 Hymnals' storage spots
37 City on the Rhône
38 Nobel Institute city
40 TV honors
41 Bandleader Kyser
45 Phenomenon named for the infant Jesus
47 Keystone's place
48 Muscle strengthened by curls, informally
49 Chip away
50 Shakes, so to speak
51 Kind of football with eight-player teams
52 Requisites
53 Insertion indicator
57 Soccer segment
58 See 35-Down
59 Monopoly payment
60 Lineage depiction
62 Hamburger helper?
63 Get blubbery

by Gary Cee

ACROSS

1 Repulses, with "off"
6 Bruise preventers
10 Kind of converter
14 Opinionated Dr. ___
15 Lie next to
16 Like a pro rata division, say
17 Roof detour
19 Without following up, say
20 Tea-grading term
21 Gas up?
23 One mo
26 Duplex mail
28 Game fish in northern lakes and streams
30 Co. follower, sometimes
31 Girl's name meaning "loved"
32 They're not as heavy as stones
33 "___ in good health"
35 "Stronger title" for this puzzle
40 Rarity on the other end of a help line, nowadays
41 "See ___ Play," classic Pink Floyd song
43 Pick, with "for"
46 Bee: Prefix
47 Spring opener
49 Rear garden
52 D-Day refuges for the wounded, for short
53 House of Tudor woman
54 Watts of "21 Grams"
56 Makes sore
57 Mad manager
62 Glare preventer
63 Figures
64 Lighter choice
65 They have 225-min. 34-Downs
66 Part of N.E.A.: Abbr.
67 A Coen brother

DOWN

1 Rapper ___ Rida
2 French word that sounds like a letter of the alphabet
3 Flake
4 Painter's appurtenance
5 Untouchable?
6 Release, in a way
7 Egypt's Gamal ___ Nasser
8 Kind of date for a woman
9 Item that's mostly mesh
10 Ere
11 Bilingual country
12 Authoritative pronouncement
13 Halloween-ish
18 "I suppose"
22 Gets going
23 Parrot's cry
24 Yachting need
25 Magazine that serialized Simone de Beauvoir's 1967 "La femme rompue"
27 Sendai seasoning
29 Chesapeake Bay, e.g.
33 Seal's grp.
34 Certain cut-off point
36 Savory turnover from south of the border
37 Puddle source
38 Penpoints
39 Overfill
42 Two of these make a fathom: Abbr.
43 Runs rings around?
44 Average Town, U.S.A.
45 On-air personalities, in the biz
47 The 40th since 1789
48 Something lost in the wash?
50 Recesses
51 Swarms of them are called clouds
55 Building plan with many doors, say
58 "Illmatic" rapper
59 Dashboard fig.
60 Cleanup org.
61 "The Godfather" title

by Patrick Merrell

ACROSS

1 Some confessions
5 Quite
9 Yearned (for)
14 Economist Smith
15 Arthur who often raised a racket
16 Home to Bates College
17 "Later"
18 Fan sound
19 Grain disease
20 *1982 hit by the Clash
23 64-Across, for one
24 "You are not!" retort
27 "___ durn tootin'!"
28 *1994 World Cup final site
30 Cul-de-___
33 Off-kilter
35 Part of A.D.
36 Spanish uncle
37 *Fortuneteller's bit
40 M.D.'s reading
41 Stuff to be loaded
43 1953 John Wayne film
44 Teetotaling
45 *Popular drinking game
48 Sounds of woe
50 Shut up
51 Trapdoor concealer
55 Ordinary . . . or what the beginning of the answer to each starred clue is?
58 Ritzy
60 Cutting put-down
61 Salon employee
62 Taken for ___
63 Blue shade
64 Colossal statue outside ancient Rome's Colosseum
65 Church council
66 Big name in locks
67 Bogotá bears

DOWN

1 "___ bleu!"
2 Cut to the chase, say
3 Org. co-founded by W. E. B. Du Bois
4 Bear with a hat
5 Carpenter's aid
6 Program distributor
7 All the rage
8 Goddess whose name is an anagram of her mother's
9 Single-celled creatures
10 South-of-the-border cry
11 Pretentious
12 Record producer Brian
13 Ford Field team, on scoreboards
21 Pick up the tab
22 Family nickname
25 One of the capitalist class
26 Science
28 Register anew
29 ___ Glendower, last Welshman to hold the title Prince of Wales
30 Attempts
31 Singer Mann
32 "Huh?"
34 France's Dominique Strauss-___
38 Eliciting an "aww," maybe
39 Room with a closet, often
42 Florida getaway locale
46 Sat (up)
47 Roulette bet
49 Declined
51 Singer Lavigne
52 Spanish kings
53 In ___ (unborn)
54 Sidewalk vendors' offerings
56 Parent company of Shopping.com
57 Grandma
58 An original member of the Star Alliance
59 Twisted

by Ian Livengood

ACROSS

1 Titles of respect
5 Rum-laced cake
9 Fictional character who declares "Sleep? . . . I do not sleep, I die"
13 Bills, e.g.
14 It may be assumed
15 Feeling stood-up, say
16 Real estate figure
17 Try to win
19 Put on again
21 Draftsman's need
22 True
23 Pranks, in a way, informally
26 Mrs. Forsyte in "The Forsyte Saga"
27 Not vary from proper procedure
29 Parts causing paper cuts, say
30 Period with a tilde?
31 ___ time
33 German direction
34 Follow everyone else
38 "That's revolting!"
40 Piglet's pal
41 Gerard of "Buck Rogers in the 25th Century"
42 Prosecutor's burden
45 Deteriorate
50 Vodka drink, informally
51 Scrape (out)
52 Jet pilot's wear
53 Anchorites
55 Dr. No's org.
57 Take things way too far
60 Cantina vessel
61 Send private messages?
62 Stravinsky and Sikorsky
63 Transportation mode
64 Juanita's "this"

65 Canceled . . . or a hint to answering 17-, 27-, 34-, 45- and 57-Across
66 Much of a flock

DOWN

1 Ancient Egyptian talisman
2 Almost never
3 Searcher's cry
4 Abduct
5 Wasted
6 Transportation mode
7 Be in a lineup
8 Queens stadium name
9 Heavenly home of the Norse gods
10 Pokey
11 TV's Francis and others

12 Standard means of recovery from an illness
14 Chargers' org.
18 Tribe that lent its name to a canal
20 In regard to
24 S-shaped holder
25 ___-Ball
28 Nobelist Niels
32 Alphabet quartet
34 Waiting room query
35 Carryall
36 Feudal lord
37 Something to settle
38 Practically in one's face
39 Musical cuts?
43 Italian code of silence
44 Old West trading post
46 Gems, precious metals, etc., in Spain

47 Billy the Kid or Jesse James
48 Hardly like a he-man
49 Moves furtively
54 Soccer injury site
56 Letter addendum, for short
58 I, in old Rome
59 Enclothe

by Sharon Delorme

ACROSS

1 Time in some want ads
4 Shutout spoiler
8 Globetrotter's woe
14 Tuba sound
15 Language of Pakistan
16 Plaza Hotel moppet
17 Washington and ___ University
18 Team on the receiving end of a prank?
20 Seams' contents
22 "Arrivederci"
23 "E," "pluribus" or "unum"?
27 Comeback?
31 Bother no end
32 China's Sun ___-sen
35 "Come again?"
36 Call that might result in a 27-Across
38 Much bigotry
40 Athletic trainer for Neanderthals?
43 Some summer fare
44 At full tilt
45 Send packing
46 SAT company
48 Like Cup-a-Soup
52 Items in many lists of ingredients
54 West Coast punk rock group?
56 Kind of computing using remote servers
59 Wolf's look
60 Entered pie-eyed?
66 Guinness Book suffix
67 Not in any key
68 Running ___
69 Start of some California place names
70 Stereotypical bum's place
71 Police setup
72 Addition to 18-, 23-, 40-, 54- and 60-Across

DOWN

1 Self-assurance
2 Denmark's ___ Islands
3 "Period!"
4 Candy store purchase
5 "___ y plata"
6 Stir
7 Kind of eclipse
8 Yoda, notably
9 Choice word
10 Chef's topper
11 Imprisoned Peace Nobelist ___ Xiaobo
12 Simile center
13 Goal for some H.S. dropouts
19 Whitewater phenomenon
21 "Later!"
24 De Carlo of "The Munsters"

25 Most inclusive
26 Olive genus
28 In vogue
29 "Shut your mouth!"
30 Its symbol is omega
33 Things understood by few
34 Eastern belief
37 Letters on some N.Y.C. baggage tags
39 Playground retort
40 Like a proverbial 10
41 Arborist's study
42 Oil-rich ruler, perhaps
43 "Way cool!"
47 Say "Offisher, I am completely shober," e.g.
49 Dundee who trained Ali
50 Gov. Rockefeller
51 Sleeping sickness transmitter

53 Public spectacle
55 X-rated
57 When doubled, a 1997 Jim Carrey movie
58 Just
60 Chew the rag
61 Ear: Prefix
62 Diva's demand
63 Nick, say
64 Overseer of N.Y.C. bridges
65 "I reckon so"

by Rolf Hamburger

ACROSS

1 Table staple, of sorts
7 You might find one at a sawmill
14 Times going onto a secure site
15 Delivery expediters
16 Open
17 Chronicler of events
18 Bad spells?
20 Gentle decline?
21 One of a Jewish biblical trio
24 Party mixer
25 Actor Penn of the Harold and Kumar movies
26 Show instability
30 Untested
31 Make no bones about
34 Grandparent, often
36 & 39 Apt title for this puzzle
42 Flimflammed
44 Terra ___
46 Big inits. in bowling
49 Diversion with 81 squares
52 Some meditation
53 Coffin cover
55 Bounce back and forth quickly
58 Before surgery, briefly
60 "Meet the Fockers" co-star
61 Blankets
63 More unctuous
67 Bistros
68 Part of a meter
69 One in a corner
70 Figure often mentioned by meteorologists

DOWN

1 Ray preceder
2 Chaney or Chaney Jr.
3 Dept. of Justice chiefs
4 Pointed to
5 Soup brand
6 Eschewer of fat
7 1971 Bond girl ___ Wood
8 Certain porcelain piece
9 Thom ___ shoes
10 Some ties
11 Leading record label of the early 1900s
12 Domicile
13 Stick pulled from a pile
15 Got clean
19 Bandage trademark
21 Some Caribbean music
22 Pilgrimage near year's end
23 ___ mater
27 Playground user
28 Addis Ababa is its capital: Abbr.
29 Coral formation
32 I, in Innsbruck
33 Too many hits might result in them, for short
35 One hit might result in it, for short
37 Sch. in Pocatello
38 1998 film "Waking ___ Devine"
40 Type of pasta
41 Marvel characters
43 Druggies
45 Director Lee
46 Brandy made from cider
47 Singer Carey
48 Run for
50 Blood
51 British standard
54 Schlemiel
56 "Good ___!"
57 Person propelling a punt
59 Nonlibrary reading
60 Harts and hinds
62 Go (for)
64 Court affirmation
65 Loop loopers
66 Abbr. after many a military title

by Elizabeth A. Long

ACROSS

1. Had down
5. Chips go-with
10. Lineage-based women's org.
13. Person dressed in black
14. Wolfed down
15. Isao of golf
16. *What an EEG reads
18. Peat or propane
19. Stahl of "60 Minutes"
20. Dish alternative
21. "Time to get moving!"
24. Reinvest, as winnings
25. Some, but not much
26. ___-nez
27. Many a turkey
28. *Back to the beginning
33. Justice Kagan
36. Enclosure with a ms.
37. Newbies
38. *Up-and-comer
41. Polo Grounds great
42. Way up or down
43. Decides one will
46. Pig roast spot, briefly
48. Mimics convincingly
50. Boxing's Brown Bomber
51. Drive like a drunk
52. Midget car-racing org.
53. Tools for ESP researchers (whose symbols are found at the ends of the answers to the five asterisked clues)
57. Ankara native
58. Half-witted
59. "Gotta run!"
60. Unified
61. Lose one's marbles
62. Small-screen award

DOWN

1. Putin's former org.
2. Scand. land
3. Capt.'s guess
4. As long as, old-style
5. Removes, as a branch
6. Whatsoever
7. Like a pool table, ideally
8. Chop ___
9. H.S. courses for coll. credit
10. *Act of betrayal
11. "The Jungle Book" wolf
12. Easy life, personified
15. Much removed (from)
17. Sleuth Wolfe
20. "Zip your lips!"
21. "Gotta run!"
22. Christ's literary stopping place
23. *Scene of an annual ball-dropping
24. Shot
26. ___ bargain
29. 1-Down's land
30. Long. partner
31. Bunch of, casually
32. These, in Toledo
34. Sweat the small stuff, in a way
35. Diarist Nin
39. "Skedaddle!"
40. Sister of Snow White
44. Tiny fraction of a min.
45. Bridge combo
46. Wooer of Olive Oyl
47. Merchant ship officer
48. ___ Games (quadrennial event)
49. Boxing venue
51. Prefix with -zoic
53. Part of a slalom's path
54. What a swish shot doesn't touch
55. Hydroelectricity structure
56. Faux meat base

by Julian Lim

ACROSS

1 Gambol about
7 [See circled letters]
14 Tart, in a way
15 Schubert masterpiece
16 Renée of silent films
17 '84 Super Bowl victor
18 [See circled letters]
20 Pinches
21 It comes in a chicken variety
22 Niña's title: Abbr.
25 Prefix with center
26 "Psst!"
27 Dash reading: Abbr.
30 Blotto
31 S'pose
33 Emotional outburst
35 [See circled letters]
37 Uncivilized
40 Headquarters for UBS and Credit Suisse
44 Flock female
45 Sequence with two hyphens: Abbr.
46 Anderson who directed "Fantastic Mr. Fox"
47 Bird sound
48 Very willing
50 Half-___ (coffee order)
51 Rockefeller Center muralist
52 [See circled letters]
57 Went downhill
59 Neighbor of Suriname
60 Male gland
61 Santa's little ___
62 [See circled letters]
63 Rendezvous

DOWN

1 Less convoluted
2 Bureaucratic hoops
3 Roundish with an irregular border
4 They're standard
5 Online tech news resource
6 Epiphanies
7 Fire drill activity, briefly
8 So so?
9 Old Apple product marketed to schools
10 Gets perfectly
11 Ward worker
12 Einstein's "never"
13 Good listener?
15 "A Clockwork Orange" narrator
19 N.H.L. great Patrick
23 "My country, ___ . . ."

24 Balance provider, for short
26 Parts of el día
27 Big D cager
28 Struggle over a purse
29 Start of a spelling?
32 Anti-Bond org.
33 ___ Park (Pirates' stadium)
34 Gen ___
36 A in German class?
37 Do a dog trick
38 Cobbler's need
39 It has many rods
41 Ones at the pole positions?
42 Princess' headwear
43 Active military conflicts
46 W.W. II female
49 Use a divining rod
50 Algonquian tribe

51 How a card sharp plays
53 Bit of dust
54 Jason who sang "I'm Yours," 2008
55 90° from sur
56 Violinist Leopold
57 No. with a decimal
58 Celestial body

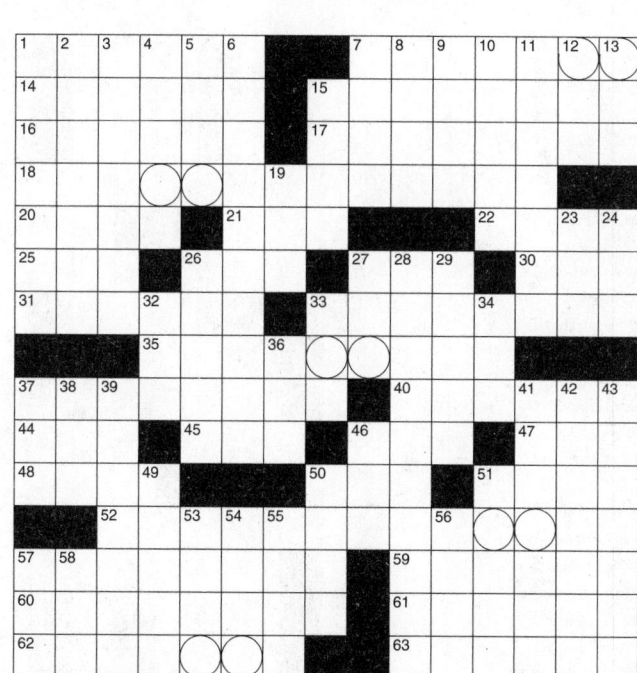

by Daniel A. Finan

ACROSS

1 Metrosexual's tote
7 "Doesn't thrill me"
10 Top awards at los Juegos Olímpicos
14 Cuneiform discovery site
15 Geisha's tie
16 Backing strip
17 Transplants, in a way
18 Make note of, with "down"
19 Cornell of Cornell University
20 Mesopotamia?
23 Role in "Son of Frankenstein"
24 Kind of fly, informally
25 ___ Paese cheese
28 Inconsistent root beer brand?
34 Red wine of Spain
36 Santa ___, Calif.
37 Qaddafi's rise to power, e.g.
38 Vintners' prefix
39 Consumer products giant, briefly
41 "Gotcha!"
42 Close by, in poems
43 "Yoo-hoo!"
44 ___ Quested, woman in Forster's "A Passage to India"
45 Local ascetic?
49 Camera type, in brief
50 Barker and Kettle
51 Pizzeria chain, informally
53 Some Mideast laptops?
61 Helen's city
62 "Proved!" letters
63 Fish-eating raptor
64 Regarding, on memos
65 "Hänsel ___ Gretel"
66 President who said "Mr. Gorbachev, tear down this wall!"
67 Like a D-

68 U.F.O. crew
69 Movie camera settings

DOWN

1 Trade center
2 C.S.A. part: Abbr.
3 Vintners' valley
4 Adrien of "The Pianist"
5 Barbuda's island partner
6 Alphonse's comics partner
7 Voodoo charm
8 Black, to bards
9 Run into unexpected trouble
10 Soapmaking compound
11 Motorola cell phone brand
12 ___ vez (again: Sp.)

13 Hoopster with six rap albums, for short
21 Ill temper
22 "Chocolate" dog
25 Horse to be broken
26 Sequence sung by kids
27 "Rude" sound
29 Chekhov uncle
30 Put the kibosh on
31 Pasadena posies
32 Put down, as a riot
33 Hurled weapon
35 "No Such Thing" blues rocker
39 Mr. America's pride
40 W.W. I mil. group
44 Wakens
46 Sealer's stuff
47 Holy city of Iran
48 At a cruise stop, say
52 Annual parade honoree, informally

53 Popular swab
54 The New Yorker cartoonist Peter
55 Ring foe of Manolete
56 Euro fraction
57 They may be even, ironically
58 Descartes's "therefore"
59 Get, as profits
60 "Cease" and "desist," e.g.: Abbr.

by Tim Croce

Note: Parts of 15 answers in this puzzle are missing, in a manner for you to discover.

ACROSS

1 Company's numero uno
7 Bit of dance attire for Fred Astaire
10 Elite
14 Toyota sedan
15 Recipient of three consecutive Hart Trophies
16 About
17 Arsenal, so to speak
19 Opening word of many an Italian letter
20 Kind of coach: Abbr.
21 Reveled in
23 Bypass
26 Bitter and sweet
28 Key ___
29 & 30 They started in 1969
34 Some shot targets
36 User of night vision
37 One-named pop star
38 Oil source
39 Midnight to 4 a.m., at sea
41 In the 40s?
42 Whups
44 Debt doc
45 Harriet Beecher Stowe novel
46 ___ verte (green earth pigment)
47 Early 26th-century year
48 Certain joint
49 Wrigley product
51 Certain gifts in "The 12 Days of Christmas"
53 Trademarked sanitary wipes
56 Word with belt or tape
58 Michigan college
59 Boom-causing, perhaps
64 Fabulist
65 ___-pitch

66 What Cowboy legend Tom Landry sported
67 Often-flooded locale
68 Hit a low point
69 Starfish or sea cucumber, e.g.

DOWN

1 Writing in a box
2 Many a Monopoly property: Abbr.
3 Pile
4 Following ___
5 Like the origin of the names for some days of the week
6 Pantry problem
7 ___ polloi
8 Check
9 Nottingham's river
10 Dish often served in a shell
11 "My word!"
12 To be, at the Louvre
13 Way less traveled
18 Capital whose name comes from an Algonquin word for "to trade"
22 Jump on a stage
23 Drug drawback
24 1958 hit that won the first-ever Grammy for Song of the Year
25 Rehab candidate
27 Like the highest high
29 Disseminates
31 Fictional plantation owner
32 Kowtows, say
33 One way to ride a horse
35 Port alternative
37 Feng ___
40 Overindulge

43 Words after count or let
47 "Star Trek" helmsman
50 Painter's preparation
51 "Check it out"
52 Lyric poem
53 Tire part
54 "The South-Sea House" essayist
55 No friend of the bootlegger
57 "Carmina Burana" composer
60 What a big hand often grabs?
61 Make a little mistake
62 Source of heat
63 Brandy cocktail

by Jim Hilger

ACROSS

1 Hold back
5 Egg pouches
9 Bus. cards in commercial mailings, e.g.
14 Janowitz who wrote "Slaves of New York"
15 Dept. of Labor agency
16 "M*A*S*H" setting
17 "Little Caesar" gangster
18 Movie about La Brea Tar Pits' formation?
20 Sharp-tongued
22 Does a post-meal chore
23 Movie about a Nobel-winning chemist?
26 Our sun
29 Word after Farm or Live
30 Craving
31 Humble oneself
34 Curtain material
36 Surfer wannabe
37 Movie about Wall Streeters' excesses?
42 So far
43 Bridge bid, briefly
44 Wild West badge
47 William Tell's canton
48 Brit. military honor
51 ___ Tomé
52 Movie about the early life of Lassie?
55 ___ Creed of A.D. 325
58 Nonsense word said while pointing a finger
59 Movie about the memoirs of the Duke?
63 Saint Philip ___
64 Packing heat
65 The "a" in a.m.
66 Baseball analyst Hershiser
67 "Siddhartha" author
68 River through Belgium
69 Seasonal song . . . or a phonetic hint to 18-, 23-, 37-, 52- and 59-Across

DOWN

1 Geologic layers
2 Meditative exercises
3 Acted the host
4 New Zealand native
5 Boozehound
6 Bat wood
7 "S.N.L." alum Oteri
8 Texas/Louisiana border river
9 Ticker tests, for short
10 Snoop (around)
11 Bygone Toyota sedan
12 Jeans brand
13 Syrup base
19 "Young Frankenstein" woman
21 Certain protest
24 Soft ball brand
25 Put in stitches
27 "The Plague" setting
28 Bygone Fords
32 Precarious place, metaphorically
33 ___ death (overwork)
34 Dams and does
35 Unit now known as a siemens
37 Musical with Mungojerrie and Jennyanydots
38 Home to billions
39 Prim and proper, e.g.
40 Plenty, informally
41 Garr who played 19-Down
45 Knuckle draggers
46 Takeoff site
48 Do-re-mi
49 Evening affair
50 "The Iceman Cometh" playwright
53 Lowly laborers
54 Mortise's mate
56 Supermodel Sastre
57 Hand over
59 Cartoon baby's cry
60 "Chances ___," 1957 #1 hit
61 Address abbr.
62 ___ Spiegel

by Ron and Nancy Byron

ACROSS

1 ___-Frank Wall Street Reform and Consumer Protection Act, 2010
5 Playlet
9 Small spade, maybe
14 Mideast bigwig: Var.
15 1951 historical role for Peter Ustinov
16 "Nope!"
17 Beaut of a butte?
18 Minnesota's St. ___ College
19 Autumn shade
20 Uncool Eskimo?
23 Original Beatles bassist Sutcliffe
24 Sound on Old MacDonald's farm
25 Title comics boy
29 "The Big Chill" director
31 Part of a baseball
33 Khan married to Rita Hayworth
34 Percussion instrument owned by a New York newspaper?
37 7/5/75 winner over Connors
39 Who wrote "It was many and many a year ago, / In a kingdom by the sea . . ."
40 Depose
41 Close-knit group at a popular island destination?
46 Topic of Objectivism
47 Company car, maybe
48 Aphrodite's love
51 Lite
53 Champagne chum
54 Mo. of the hunter's moon
55 Werewolf, e.g. . . . or the one responsible for 20-, 34- and 41-Across?
59 "Shine On, Harvest Moon," e.g.
62 Fair
63 Opera that premiered on Christmas Eve of 1871
64 Red-haired ogress of film
65 Brim
66 Nothingness
67 Pink ___
68 It can make the face red
69 Early Beatles tune subtitled "Go to Him"

DOWN

1 Reversible fabric
2 Code of silence
3 Olympic event dating back to ancient Greece
4 "Phooey!"
5 Carnival treat
6 Chief of medicine on "Scrubs"
7 "The Hurt Locker" locale
8 Food that wiggles
9 Kid's art project
10 Shine
11 The Wildcats of the America East Conf.
12 Roller coaster part
13 Cyclone part
21 Worship leader
22 Popular source of antioxidants
26 Inkling
27 Drugs and crime, e.g.
28 Security Council vote
30 Per ___
31 Soup base
32 ". . . ___ saw Elba"
35 Go at it
36 Court plea, for short
37 Biblical brother
38 State symbol of Utah
42 In the near future
43 Writer François ___ Rochefoucauld
44 Make forcefully, as a point
45 Year of the Battle of Pollentia
49 Immobilized by a storm, maybe
50 Italian road
52 Hit TV series starring Gary Sinise
53 Part of a mountain forest
56 Sponsor of ads famous for nudity
57 Not jud. or leg.
58 Kind of bean
59 Slightly askew
60 Wee
61 Scooby-___

by Kristian House

ACROSS

1 Roommate, informally
6 Parade honoree, perhaps
10 Brewer's need
14 Big name in handbags
15 Withdrawn apple spray
16 James who won a posthumous Pulitzer
17 Gift to an outgoing member of Congress?
20 Hanukkah pancakes
21 Billing cycle, often
22 The University of the South, familiarly
25 Em, to Dorothy
26 Y sporter
27 Rancher's land
30 Camera type, for short
31 Plant anew
33 Like some elephants
36 Dialect coach's slogan?
41 Tot's wheels
42 "The usual," say
44 A Bush
47 Carl Sagan book
50 "Michael Collins" org.
51 Too firm, perhaps
54 Modern crime, briefly . . . or a hint to 17-, 36- and 59-Across
56 Computer screen lineup
57 He "was here"
59 European gin mill?
64 Romain de Tirtoff's alias
65 Hence
66 Hale who won three U.S. Opens
67 Nostradamus, e.g.
68 Small songster
69 Spoke sweet nothings

DOWN

1 Radar's rank on "M*A*S*H": Abbr.
2 ". . . Mac ___ PC?"
3 Cured fare
4 Miss Quested of "A Passage to India"
5 "You shouldn't have said that!"
6 Cyber-nuisance
7 Sommer on screen
8 Speaks ill of
9 Notable #4 on the ice
10 Grand Lodge member
11 Most major-leaguers have them
12 Campbell's variety
13 Restrain, in a way
18 Sun Bowl Stadium sch.
19 Grounded avian
22 Sun. talk
23 Zeno's home
24 Cheesehead's state: Abbr.
25 1998 Sarah McLachlan hit
28 Moves carefully
29 Mountain ___
32 Leaf-turning time: Abbr.
34 Pontifical
35 D.C.-based media giant
37 Riviera city
38 Bout ender, briefly
39 Pop singer Brickell
40 Soft ball material
43 Wharf pest
44 Breakfast offerings
45 Shout at a concert
46 Literary family name
48 Poet who wrote "They also serve who only stand and wait"
49 Wroclaw's river, to Poles
52 The "I" of ICBM
53 Tire letters
55 Prefix with foil or phobia
57 Deborah of "Tea and Sympathy"
58 "Bus Stop" playwright
60 Just out
61 1945 battle site, briefly
62 Go head to head
63 What this is, fittingly

by Louis Zulli

ACROSS

1 Wagner heroine
4 Eagerly expectant
8 Street ___
12 Opportunity maker?
14 Hello and farewell
15 With 37-Down, complete
16 Facile
17 Start of a brainteaser whose answer appears in order, from top to bottom, in this puzzle's circled squares
19 City in the San Gabriel Valley
21 Complete
22 John XI's successor
23 War of 1812 battle site
24 Schedule abbr.
27 Part two of the brainteaser
30 One of the Chaplins
31 Home state of the 1964 and 2008 Rep. presidential candidates
32 Part three of the brainteaser
38 Debate (with)
39 10th- to 12th-century Chinese dynasty
40 Part four of the brainteaser
48 Muckraker Tarbell
49 Harsh
50 1944 Sartre play
51 Lays the groundwork for?
52 Inventory
53 End of the brainteaser
57 Harem rooms
58 Nifty
59 Trifled (with)
60 Spanish muralist
61 Russia/Ukraine's Sea of ___

62 They can be batted and rolled
63 '60s radical grp.

DOWN

1 Communist Friedrich
2 Rudy with a megaphone
3 "The End of Eternity" author
4 Zoological wings
5 Certain cat
6 Start of many a bumper sticker
7 Peppermint ___
8 At the home of
9 Old bus maker
10 Suffix with Euclid
11 W.W. II gen.
13 Greater than
14 10,000, for 4, in base 10, e.g.
18 Person who's groundbreaking?
20 Curtain fabric
23 Online merchant
24 When tripled, a 1970 war movie
25 One who may say "I say" a lot
26 Woodworker's tool
28 Blowup: Abbr.
29 Cry from a crib
32 Popular tablet
33 Zola best seller
34 Coastal flier
35 Half a strawful, say
36 Like a house that's of interest to ghost hunters
37 See 15-Across
38 Subj. of three of the six Nobel Prizes
41 Aerosol target
42 As yet

43 Restaurant gofer
44 "How to" explanations
45 Rust and quartz
46 Person with a conical hat, maybe
47 Bikini explosions
51 Onetime show for John Candy
52 Composition of Polynésie
53 ___ sense
54 Part of a French face
55 ___ Tomé
56 "g2g" follower

by David Steinberg

184 MEDIUM

ACROSS
1. With 14-Across, breakfast order?
5. U.F.O. crew
8. See 16-Across
14. See 1-Across
15. Romanian "dollars"
16. With 8-Across, world's oldest subway system?
17. Show greed or impatience
18. Fat-mouth
19. Pontiac, for one
20. ___ by Google
22. "Left!"
24. Like
25. Condemned
29. With fervor
31. Away from the mouth
32. Good cholesterol, for short
33. Raccoon relative
34. With 42-Across, bogey?
36. Put up
41. Put on a show
42. See 34-Across and 45-Across
43. Coconut oil source
44. "___ Eyes" (1969 hit)
45. With 42-Across, birdie?
46. Implied
47. Winner of the first World Cup: Abbr.
49. Sickening
51. Answer angrily
54. Entry at a hippodrome
55. Like some answers
56. When repeated, it might accompany a finger wag
58. Longtime TV inits.
59. 15th-century pontiff who was the only pope to write an autobiography
61. Weapon in "The Terminator"

63. Confidante, say
67. See 70-Across
68. Actor Moody of "Oliver!"
69. With 72-Across, motto of a fitness trainer?
70. With 67-Across, dreaded words from a cop?
71. "___ bad!"
72. See 69-Across

DOWN
1. Result of a certain med. test
2. Long-nosed fish
3. Govt. office supplier
4. Lovers of luxury
5. Parisian palace
6. What the Mad Hatter pours on the Dormouse to wake it up
7. Turban wearer
8. Was radiant
9. Balderdash
10. Ready
11. One of a Western political family
12. "Keep dreaming!"
13. "CSI" topic, often
21. Split
23. Stalwart supporter
25. Coin in "The Merchant of Venice"
26. Eocene, e.g.
27. Jalopy
28. Classless group?
30. Run for it
35. Tandoori-baked bread
37. Traditional Easter entree
38. Florida tourist attraction
39. Bookstore section
40. Spud
48. Many an Australian bird
50. "Twelfth Night" duke
51. Dick's partner
52. Pacific republic
53. Not like a landlubber
57. Mathematician Gödel
59. Subject of union negotiations
60. Neighbor of Syr.
62. Morning ___ (radio format)
64. Puccini's "O ___ babbino caro"
65. Neighbor of Ill.
66. Joseph who co-founded an ice cream company

by Clive Probert

ACROSS

1 Veracruz's capital
7 Its motto is "Semper paratus": Abbr.
11 Bonobo, for one
14 You can count on it
15 Kelly of "Live! With Kelly and Michael"
16 Word with band or sand
17 Command to a French composer at an intersection?
19 Conciliatory gift
20 Pen
21 Tickle response
22 Uccello who painted "The Battle of San Romano"
24 Don Corleone
25 Loading locale
27 City south of Luxor
30 Command to a Hungarian composer at the piano?
34 Activities
36 Jacques Cousteau's middle name
37 "Tippecanoe and Tyler ___"
38 Move like mud
39 Sophia of "Marriage Italian-Style"
41 Fringe benefit
42 Sch. supporter
43 Author who famously ended a short story with the line "Romance at short notice was her specialty"
44 Cell on a slide
46 Command to a German composer on a baseball diamond?
49 Lessen, as fears
50 Jay Gatsby's love
51 Mayberry boy
53 Leaf holders
55 Czar of Russia between Feodors
57 Initials at sea
60 Snap, Crackle or Pop
61 Command to an Austrian composer on a scavenger hunt?
64 Freudian concept
65 Adm. Zumwalt, chief of naval operations during the Vietnam War
66 Word before a sentence
67 Guerra's opposite
68 Does, e.g.
69 "Woo-hoo!"

DOWN

1 Injures with a pencil, say
2 Somewhat
3 Unlike a go-getter
4 Point of no return?
5 Green skill
6 Plus
7 What an addict fights
8 Symbol of simple harmonic motion
9 Tax pro, for short
10 Bachelorette party attendees
11 Hard core?
12 Game involving banks
13 Fair
18 Denny's competitor
23 Talent agent ___ Emanuel
24 Roof topper
26 Relative of an aardwolf
27 Make one's own
28 Truth, archaically
29 1939 title role for Frank Morgan
31 Like much poetry
32 1964 title role for Anthony Quinn
33 Hungarian wine
35 Hearty helpings of meat loaf, say
40 "Go ahead"
41 It may be + or -
43 Moved, as a horse's tail
45 "But of course!," in Marseille
47 Symbol of strength
48 Device making a 53-Down
52 "Little" digit
53 Sound made by a 48-Down
54 Kurylenko of "Quantum of Solace"
56 Febreze target
57 Succor
58 Parcel (out)
59 ___ terrier
62 Hearty quaff
63 Take in slowly

by Will Nediger

ACROSS

1 Athletic shoe manufacturer
7 Some camcorders
11 Arabic characters
14 Sister city of El Paso
16 Bygone Chrysler
17 Straight
18 Asti ___
19 Desserts in Rome
20 ". . . kissed thee ___ killed thee": Shak.
21 Umps
23 Greenpeace subj.
24 "Georgy Girl" star Lynn
26 Spot to moor
27 "Jane Eyre" et al.
29 Summer drinks
30 Diminutive tree
33 "Who's Next?" singer/songwriter/ satirist
35 Venice Film Festival locale
36 Rhythm band instrument
38 Deal breakers, on occasion
39 Laboratory sessions
43 Aforementioned
44 Relative of Thos. or Wm.
45 Noteworthy name in lens care
46 Gyro inventor
48 Suffer from high humidity, e.g.
51 Choice
52 Professional filmgoer
53 Remove skin from, as whales
54 Neon sign on many diners
55 Pieces of work?
56 Fitted together

DOWN

1 Tropical avians
2 Construction site conveyance
3 Contaminated
4 Judged
5 Forces to answer an indictment
6 Bygone pitching star Johnny
7 Viking letter
8 Transportation on tracks
9 Prefix with triple digits
10 Dispatched (to)
12 Venice premiere of 1853
13 Jacket part
14 Liquor containers
15 Scrabble 10-pointers
22 Gave in to exhaustion
25 Wander
28 Church offshoot
30 Rudy Giuliani turf
31 Dash instrument
32 Punk facial decoration
34 Forehead border
35 Thinks ___ (disesteems)
37 Brad of "Sleepers"
40 Uprights on staircases
41 Really bother
42 Employer of Clouseau
44 Newton fraction
47 "ER" doctor
49 Like each answer in this puzzle—also each word in each clue—in length
50 TV palomino

by John Farmer

ACROSS

1 "Roger that" sayer
5 Cakes with a kick
10 "A ___ on you!"
13 ___-kiri
14 Laughing gas, for one
15 Mixologist's instruction
16 Fine-tune, as a script
17 Finland-based communications giant
18 Wee bit
19 "Yada yada yada"
20 Ironic weather forecast?
22 KFC servings
24 Alluringly slender
25 What to do at a drive-thru window
26 Do some cardio
29 Thin as ___
30 It's under a foot
31 Bullet-point item
33 Ironic marriage plan?
38 Grows darker
39 Ride for Hawkeye or Radar
41 Chipped in
45 "Making something out of nothing and selling it," per Frank Zappa
46 Like dogs in packs
47 Carrier crew
49 Classic Sinatra topper
50 Ironic exam schedule?
54 Nellie who circled the world
55 "How could ___ this happen?"
56 Agent Swifty
57 Dust jacket bits
58 Ruing the workout, maybe
59 Where élèves study
60 Prom night worry
61 Helpful connections
62 Overhauled
63 Army NCO

DOWN

1 Orange munchies
2 Ball field error
3 Monty Python member
4 Unpopular mobster
5 Boss's good news
6 Neural transmitter
7 Stephen ___, subject of "Cry Freedom"
8 Point before "game," maybe
9 Clothes lines
10 Sometimes-dyed dog
11 Bested at Nathan's on July 4, e.g.
12 Got an inside look at?
15 Yearning sort
20 Stock unit: Abbr.
21 Cameo shapes
23 Turned right, like Dobbin
26 Midrange Volkswagen
27 None of the above
28 All skin and bones
31 Paternity test factor
32 Quarterly payment recipient, for short
34 Of yore
35 Spun 45s, say
36 Gym class set to music
37 Like many magazine subscriptions
40 Jungle gym, swings, etc.
41 Home of St. Francis
42 "S.N.L." alum Kevin
43 Home runs, in slang
44 Be melodramatic
46 Palin parodist
48 Buc or Niner
49 Got along
51 Where "They're off!" may be heard
52 Preppy shirt brand
53 "The Persistence of Memory" artist
57 Many undergrad degs.

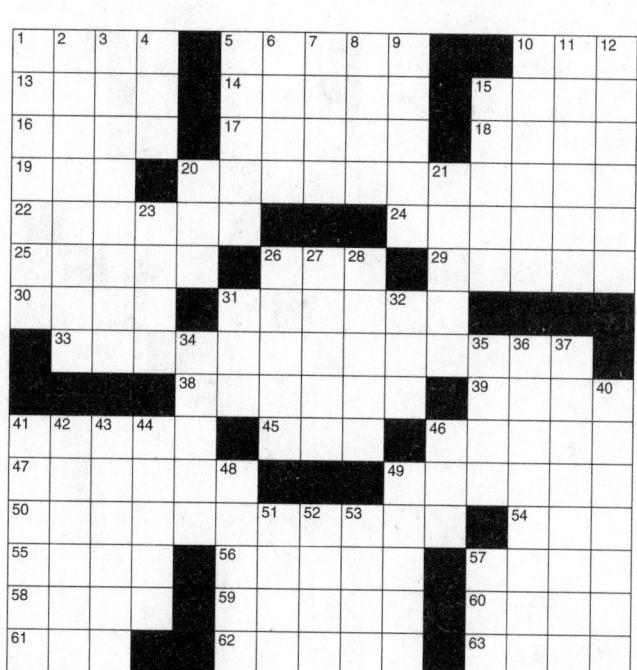

by Michael Black

ACROSS

1 Thing with four digits
4 Unfirm
8 Target, as a receiver
14 Small business's dream, for short
15 Sets in geometry
16 Colorful summer treat
17 After 66-Across, Batcave feature
19 Popular headlights
20 Shift one's focus
21 After 66-Across, anonymous Valentine sender
23 After 66-Across, participant in a gift-giving activity
24 Vex
25 Some Ferraris
28 "You know better than that!"
30 Mideast city that is the capital of the world in H. G. Wells's "The Shape of Things to Come"
31 Coniferous trees
34 Hot tub sound
35 After 66-Across, election standard
36 Kitchen gadget brand with a rotationally symmetric logo
37 What for
38 Muffin choice
39 Agosto to agosto
40 After 66-Across, classic 1911 children's book, with "The"
42 Janis Ian, Billy Preston and George Carlin were its first guests
43 Champion's shout
44 Boozehound
45 Four-time Yankee All-Star Paul
47 Places where connections are made: Abbr.
48 Literary character who says "For hate's sake, I spit my last breath at thee"
49 After 66-Across, spy
53 After 66-Across, exposé subject
55 Squarepants
56 Sorry soul?
58 After 66-Across, marketing gimmicks
60 Old TV "Uncle"
61 Irish pop star
62 1970s supergroup, for short
63 "V" extras
64 Jiang's predecessor
65 Lo-___

DOWN

1 Docks
2 Sleep lab study
3 "Der Ring des Nibelungen" war god
4 Beasts of burden
5 One in an accelerated program?
6 Cormac who wrote "No Country for Old Men"
7 Bake sale container
8 Sprite
9 Big PC maker
10 Dakar's land
11 Judicial area dealing with athletes
12 Host
13 Photo finish?
18 Photographer Herb
22 ___ Day, Jan. celebration
26 Chief Joseph ___, after whom a Maine college town is named
27 Squelched
29 "Clue" actress Madeline
30 Hit
31 Options at a gym
32 Elevate
33 Person who doesn't know when to quit
35 2,100-square mile island with six volcanoes
37 Lilliputian
38 Individually
41 Dig up
42 Gobbled
43 Labor grp.
45 "What's all this?"
46 Maxim, e.g.
48 Still
50 Certain fisher
51 Football Hall-of-Famer Greasy
52 Dosage amts.
54 River that's the site of Javert's demise in "Les Misérables"
56 Member of a Latin trio
57 Tessellation piece
59 Artist Rembrandt van ___

by Brendan Emmett Quigley and Patrick Blindauer

ACROSS

1 "Impression, Sunrise" painter
6 Gives the thumbs-up
9 DreamWorks's first animated film
13 Site of some rock shows
14 End of a boast
16 Pitcher Derek
17 A heap
18 Flair
19 Subject of many Georgia O'Keeffe paintings
20 Disaster
23 Skill
24 Woman's name meaning "weary" in Hebrew
25 Of this world
27 Swelter
30 Word before and after "for"
32 Airport info: Abbr.
33 Maryland athlete, for short
34 They're often eaten with applesauce
38 Bard's "below"
40 Place to put a bud
42 Like J in the alphabet
43 Flirtatious one
45 See 53-Down
47 Suffix with Brooklyn
48 Made tidy, in a way
50 Bibliographic abbr.
51 Experience a mondegreen, e.g.
54 Agenda unit
56 ___ carte
57 Lover's woe . . . or something found, literally, in the 4th, 5th, 8th and 11th rows of this puzzle
62 Brass component
64 When doubled, popular 1980s–'90s British sitcom
65 Alexander the Great conquered it ca. 335 B.C.
66 Appendices with some studies
67 SAT taker, e.g.
68 Don
69 Genesis man
70 Date
71 Editors' marks

DOWN

1 Like bueno but not buena: Abbr.
2 Filmdom's Willy, for one
3 "Cool beans!"
4 It's ultimate
5 French cup
6 "Psst!"
7 Metric prefix
8 Pretty vistas, for short
9 The Greatest
10 Singer Jones
11 Pirouette
12 Full of spice
15 Rope for pulling a sail
21 Lacking spice
22 Mess-ups
26 French bean?
27 French bench
28 Uh-Oh! ___ (Nabisco product)
29 Where many a veteran has served
31 Distinct
33 Information superhighway
35 Make a sweater, say
36 "At Last" singer James
37 Poet/illustrator Silverstein
39 Rear
41 Slow alternative to I-95
44 Rip into
46 Breadth
49 Lower class in "1984"
50 Manage
51 Protegé, for one
52 Poem with approximately 16,000 lines
53 With 45-Across, largest city in California's wine country
55 Sends by UPS, say
58 Painter Paul
59 Chip or two, maybe
60 Real knee-slapper
61 Bronzes
63 Video shooter, for short

by Oliver Hill

ACROSS

1 Pups' complaints
5 *Jackson 5, 1970
8 Soupçon
13 Time it is when daylight saving time ends
16 Dirt accumulator?
17 Salsa partner?
18 Gave up
19 Capital whose name is Urdu for "place of peace"
20 Year of the Great Fire of Rome
21 Unagi sources
22 *Usher feat. will.i.am, 2010
23 Gutter site
24 Informal denials
26 "Harlequin's Carnival," for one
28 Nostalgist's opening words
33 More substantial
35 Bouquets
36 Shortest title of any #1 hit on the Billboard Hot 100 [Britney Spears, 2009]
37 "I swear!"
38 Book of Judges judge
40 Greeted deferentially
41 Foul mood
42 "Network" director
44 Taft and Bush, collegiately
46 *Michael Jackson, 1972
47 Catch, as flies
51 Gospel singer Winans
52 Earliest million-dollar movie role
55 Wooden-soled shoe
56 Gypsum variety used in carvings
57 Worshiping figure
58 What a talent scout looks for
59 Authority
60 *Frankie Avalon, 1959
61 Numerical prefix

DOWN

1 Hanna-Barbera bear
2 Occupied
3 "Positive thinking" exponent
4 Setting for "The O.C.," for short
5 Longest book of the Book of Mormon
6 Faux pas
7 Workshop device
8 Bike
9 Check over
10 United
11 Subject of the 1997 best seller "Into Thin Air"
12 *Michael Jackson, 1987
14 Wheels inside a car
15 Small anchors
24 Like the first of May or the end of June?
25 "Smoking!"
27 "For here ___ go?"
28 Kids
29 "Fame" actress
30 1864 battle site that was the source of the quote "Damn the torpedoes! Full speed ahead!"
31 They often begin with colons
32 *Edwin Starr, 1970
34 *Flo Rida feat. T-Pain, 2008
36 Length of the eight runners-up to 36-Across [as of 2010], all of which are answers to starred clues in this puzzle.
39 Outer covering for some nuts
40 Unworthy of
43 Tone down
45 Brawl
47 Stretch over
48 Can't not
49 Lofty story
50 Word repeated before some relatives' names
53 Succumb to mind control
54 Janis's comic-strip husband
55 *Rihanna, 2006

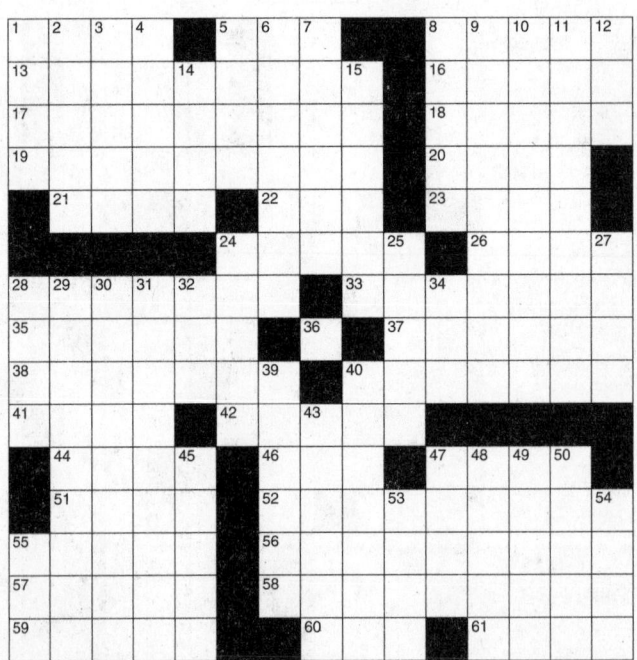

by Jeremy Horwitz

ACROSS

1 Declines, with "out of"
5 Professor says "Stocking stocker," pupil suggests . . .
10 Badlands formation
14 Mata ___
15 Model glider material
16 Still unfilled
17 With 27-, 49- and 63-Across, the story behind 5-, 36-, 39- and 70-Across
20 Public commotion
21 Like much Vegas stagewear
22 Postgraduate field
23 Ramirez of "Spamalot"
25 1040 entry
27 See 17-Across
32 Ready to rock
33 Neighbor of Arg.
34 Bonny young girl
36 Professor says "Qualifying races," pupil suggests . . .
38 MGM motto ender
39 Professor says "Ax wielder," pupil suggests . . .
43 Buzzard's fare
45 Suffix with Brooklyn
46 Biblical witch's home
49 See 17-Across
52 Simple bit of plankton
54 Some reddish deer
55 "___ liebe dich"
56 Has in view, archaically
60 "Twice as much for a nickel" sloganeer, once
63 See 17-Across
66 Hodgepodge
67 Like limousines
68 Un-P.C. suffix, to many
69 "Hud" Oscar winner

70 Professor says "Equine restraint," pupil suggests . . .
71 Those, in Toledo

DOWN

1 Resistance units
2 Parisian picnic spot
3 Goes for a spot on the team
4 Prepare to turn
5 Kobe sash
6 Turned state's evidence
7 "Play it, Sam" speaker
8 Genesis twin
9 "Amazing" magician
10 Soccer or hockey follower
11 Feature of TV's "The Fugitive"
12 Halvah ingredient
13 Respond to a knock
18 Ex-Spice Girl Halliwell
19 Force units
24 Fighting it out
26 Docket item
27 Directly
28 ". . . ___ mouse?"
29 Earth, in sci-fi
30 "___ ride" ("Don't change a thing")
31 Poet whose work inspired "Cats"
35 Ed of "The Bronx Zoo"
37 Kilt wearer
40 Signs of leaks
41 Jocular suffix with "best"
42 Flying Cloud automaker
44 Came about
46 "Speaking machine" developer

47 Paris's "The Simple Life" co-star
48 Mexico's national flower
50 Beatlesque dos
51 Tiny
53 Anne of "Archie Bunker's Place"
57 Life sci. course
58 Gait slower than a canter
59 Pentagonal plate
61 Madrid Mlle.
62 Fateful day in the Roman senate
64 Solid geometry abbr.
65 Onetime U.A.R. member

by Howard Baker

ACROSS

1 Take in
6 With 55-Down, where to get oysters
9 Big East team
14 Decorative fabric
15 Milk source
16 "Be-Bop-___"
17 Enchanted world in "Return of the Jedi"
18 Golf groundskeepers' tools
20 Added conditions
21 Reservoirs
22 Broncos' home, once
26 "What did I tell you?"
27 Stopover
28 "Nice!"
29 Prefix with -nomial
30 [Snap snap]
31 Unilever soap brand
32 Rural musical instruments
33 Chef's hat
36 Here/there separator
37 "The Basement ___" (1975 Dylan album)
38 Rest on
39 Internet giant
40 Flying Tiger Line hub, for short
41 Mauna ___
42 Tach measure
43 It came out of Cicero's mouth
44 Rested
47 Place for an N.H.L. logo
51 Roseau is its capital
52 Blue-roofed chain
53 "Keep your eyes open!"
55 Battle of Blue Licks fighter, 1782
56 Showed
57 "Baudolino" novelist
58 Napping
59 River through Glasgow
60 To be, in Baja
61 Moves, briefly

DOWN

1 Starting groups
2 ___ Walsh, N.B.A. executive
3 With 44-Down, educational stage . . . or a hint to the contents of 18-, 22-, 47- and 53-Across
4 "The pot's all yours"
5 Dutch painter Gerard ___ Borch
6 Bow out
7 Inundated
8 Fell apart, as a deal
9 Casino chain founder William F. ___
10 Chan portrayer in film
11 Has some laughs
12 Bath suds?
13 Carrier that had a pioneering transpolar route

19 Get clean
21 Quitting time in Québec, maybe
23 Cow cover
24 Press
25 Whiff
30 Worded
31 Titter in a tweet
32 N.F.L. team with teal jerseys, for short
33 Rash treatment
34 High-pitched wind
35 Bind
36 Some contenders
37 Shout made with a raised arm
39 Fourth of 12
40 "Mi Vida ___," gritty 1994 drama set in L.A.
42 Like "King Kong" and "Psycho"
43 Airplane heading

44 See 3-Down
45 Hoopster Mourning
46 Plain homes?
48 Flirted (with)
49 Sorceress on the island of Aeaea
50 ___ Oro
53 Kind of fly, for short
54 Up to, quickly
55 See 6-Across

by Peter A. Collins

ACROSS

1 Part of un archipiélago
5 Urban commuter's aid
11 "My dear ___"
14 Gorged, gorged and gorged some more, informally
16 Blow away
17 Unwritten reminders
18 "Top Gun" target
19 Zen enlightenment
20 Wimbledon do-over
21 RC, e.g.
22 Sail support
23 The Pirates of the N.C.A.A.
25 ID entered on every I.R.S. form
26 "My ___ Private Idaho," 1991 film
28 Lip-puckering
29 Robert Frost poem about a snowfall
32 Anything to talk about
36 Clock face
37 Shaped like pizza slices
40 "99 Luftballons" band, 1984
41 Shopaholic's indulgence
43 It may have wire binding
45 Trees loved by squirrels
48 Sch. in Columbus
49 Halves of qts.
50 Oranges, reds and golds
54 Busy bee
56 Impolite
57 Comic Charlotte
58 Pageant crowns
60 Swearing-in phrase
61 Petrify . . . or what five alternating words in 17-, 23-, 29-, 43- and 50-Across can do?
63 Number after many a state postal abbr.
64 Many a Twitter message
65 Taxonomy suffix
66 Undemanding courses
67 Nothing, in Nantes

DOWN

1 Big name in pet food
2 The Titanic, for one
3 Was a sounding board
4 Road runners
5 Neighbor of Java
6 Dept. of Defense branch
7 Embezzled, e.g.
8 Mozart's "Ave Verum Corpus" and others
9 Playground retort
10 Residents of 10 Downing St.
11 Part of the U.S. south of the Equator
12 Volunteer's cry
13 Fit for the throne
15 Dolly who sang "9 to 5"
21 Time: Prefix
23 Dagger in "The Mikado"
24 Fanatic
25 Norms: Abbr.
27 Egypt-to-Niger dir.
30 Enthusiastic flamenco cry
31 N.F.L. stats
33 Alternative to mushroom or sausage
34 Spellbound
35 Wham-bam-thank-you-ma'am types
38 1960s band with a car-related name, with "the"
39 "Sounds good!"
42 Break a fast
44 One with no tan lines
46 Czech currency
47 Some drums
50 Humid day hair problem
51 It's mastered in a studio
52 Rx for Parkinson's
53 Minuscule, informally
55 Western, in slang
58 Oceans
59 Viewed
61 Stiff ballet shoe part
62 Reason for a service break at Wimbledon?

by Elizabeth C. Gorski

ACROSS

1 Denounce
8 Painters Frank and Joseph
15 Its official bird is the great northern loon
16 Nasty fall
17 1983 Jean Shepherd film memoir
19 Out of concern that
20 Doth speak
21 Year of the swine flu epidemic
22 Last name in ice cream
24 Summer refuge
26 Botch
29 Pompous sort
30 Canon competitor
34 Wall St. happening
35 Hindu noble
37 Kind of code
38 Preserve
39 Noxious
41 Slapstick prop
42 Temper, as metal
44 Place for a pot
45 Silver of the silver screen
46 "The Palindrome" Symphony composer
47 Popular 1980s arcade game based on simple geometry
48 Minnesota city where part of "Fargo" was filmed
50 Really enjoyed
52 "Either you ___ . . ."
53 Bergdorf competitor
56 Finish cleaning, say
58 Branch of Islam
62 Segue
65 Halo
66 What the circled parts of this puzzle comprise
67 Knobby
68 At great length

DOWN

1 Kentucky resource
2 First word of "The Raven"
3 Unspecified degrees
4 Moved like a minnow
5 Verdi's "___ tu"
6 Young girl
7 "___ chance!"
8 What lawn mowers make
9 ___ B'Av, Jewish day of fasting
10 Some records, for short
11 "Open up!"
12 Hang over
13 Hearing: Prefix
14 Milton called it "The flood of deadly hate"
18 It runs through the middle of the 66-Across
23 Inactive
25 Dentist, at times
26 Prophet who prophesied that the Savior would come from Bethlehem
27 Classic toothpaste brand
28 One of the Corleones
29 Literary olio
31 Italian tourist destination
32 Whom Artemis loved and unwittingly killed
33 Coyote relative
36 Not be well
37 French court event
40 This and that
43 "Rich Man, Poor Man" Emmy winner
47 In Bartlett's, e.g.
49 Cast off
51 Actor Hirsch of "Into the Wild"
52 "Another ___, Another Show" ("Kiss Me, Kate" song)
53 One way to go to a party
54 Make ___ for it
55 ___ Zor-El, Supergirl's birth name
57 L'___ Vogue, Italian fashion magazine
59 Got a move on
60 "___ doing . . ."
61 Memo heading
63 G
64 iPhone, e.g., briefly

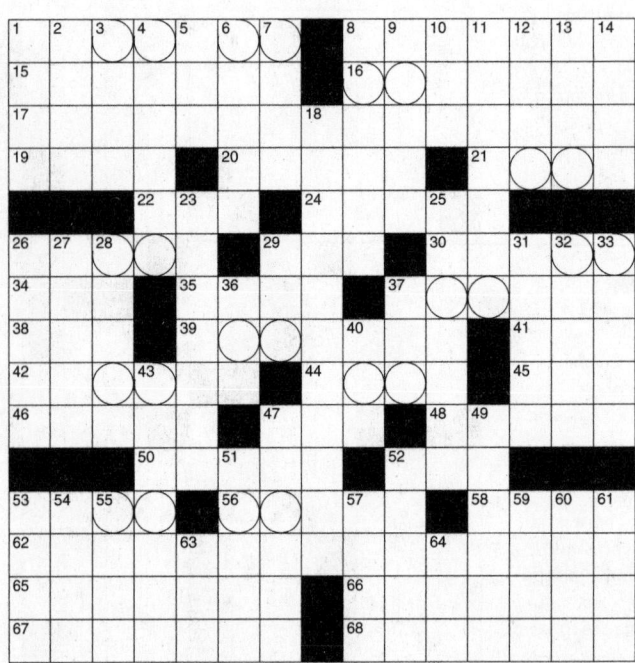

by Gary J. Whitehead

ACROSS

1 "Attention please . . ."
5 Mensa figs.
8 F.B.I. operation involving a nonexistent sheik
14 Nattily dressed ad figure
16 Queen's Guard workplace
17 Want badly
18 Going nowhere, jobwise
19 Early second-century year
20 Took advantage of
22 Suffix with bleacher
23 Dickens character who says "Something will turn up"
28 Lupino of "High Sierra"
29 Dogpatch diminutive
30 Philosopher Descartes
31 Mineral in tailor's chalk
33 Toy with an axis
35 Jim Crow-fighting org.
39 Wisecracking dummy of old radio
43 Mandel of "Deal or No Deal"
44 "Stifle!"
45 Plod along
46 Lessen, as difficulties
49 Yahoo! competitor
51 Shirt part
52 Dorothy L. Sayers's bon vivant sleuth
57 Therapists' org.
58 Kind of collar
59 Bucolic setting
60 Colbert or Stewart specialty
62 Giggling nervously
67 Moon of Neptune
68 Items worn by 14-, 23-, 39- and 52-Across
69 Any of a comedic trio

70 59-Across grazer
71 One of a Roman septet

DOWN

1 First daughter of 1977–81
2 Charlemagne's realm: Abbr.
3 DDT-banning org.
4 Maker of Zocor and Fosamax
5 G37 automaker
6 Status ___
7 Play lightly
8 Pricing word
9 Part of many a bank robber's outfit
10 1974 kidnap org.
11 Native encountered by Columbus
12 Sharp
13 It's fed at curbside

15 Smithery sight
21 Title for Mick Jagger
23 Broom-Hilda, for one
24 Home to part of Yellowstone Park
25 Steven Bochco TV drama
26 Plumlike fruit
27 Is tiresome
32 Sang the blues
34 Meir and Rabin, briefly
36 Big name in tires
37 Milking the cows, e.g.
38 Tiny tribesman
40 Jumping game
41 Blacken
42 Mess queue
47 Greek moon goddess
48 Saison on the Seine
50 Be dishonest with
52 Hangs in there
53 Some eyeball benders

54 Track odds, e.g.
55 Wonderland cake words
56 Success on TV's "Concentration"
61 "Am ___ believe . . ."
63 Blow the socks off
64 New Haven student
65 Fam. member
66 Fashion monogram

by Ed Sessa

ACROSS

1 Stop on it
4 Caffè go-with
9 Like some 21-Acrosses
14 Headbanger's instrument
15 Stadium sign
16 Traveler who carries his own bag
17 See 38-Across
19 "Give it ___"
20 "___ to Kill" (Sandra Bullock movie)
21 Certain stampeder
23 Agents' handfuls
24 Mid sixth-century year
25 Et ___
26 Starting pitcher
27 Ming of the N.B.A.
29 Common costume for a costume party
31 Lab blowup: Abbr.
32 Top 10 singer born in Nigeria
34 Question before "And how!"
36 Life
38 73-Across, in 17-Across
41 Vacation vehicle
44 ___ Christiansen, founder of the Lego company
45 Verb with "thou"
49 Reply to Captain Kirk
50 Quantum Computer Services, today
52 Chemical suffix
54 "Phooey!"
55 Fire
57 Cong. established it in 1958
59 Well feature
61 Focuses (on)
63 ___ deux
64 Transmission conduits, of a sort
65 Responder to 38-Across on 4/15/1912
68 Rightmost column in the periodic table
69 Indo-___

70 The Yankees play on it during the summer: Abbr.
71 What might do a foul tip?
72 Talk show host Gibbons
73 See 38-Across

DOWN

1 Beach shelters
2 Strange things
3 Came (from)
4 Rinky-dink
5 Singer Ocasek of the Cars
6 Rock genre
7 Runway user
8 Joni Mitchell song with the lyric "She was swallowed by the sky"
9 "On the double!"
10 White House girl
11 Asthmatic's need
12 Yom Kippur activity
13 One way to dress
18 Scot's "wee"
22 Rushed
24 Part of the "De Camptown Races" refrain
28 New wings
30 Terminate a relationship
33 Cuts and splices film, e.g.
35 Snake's place
37 Mrs. Woodrow Wilson
39 Longtime Chicago Bears coach
40 Mexico's national flower
41 "The Great Gatsby" setting
42 Prerequisite for many a prescription

43 Flower named for its smell
46 Embarrasses
47 Married
48 Ultimatums, say
51 Like some church matters
53 Neighbor of Francia
56 Typical Clint Eastwood role
58 Catch
60 Many a gang symbol, for short
62 Swedish actress Persson
66 Catcher's place?
67 Goal of las Naciones Unidas

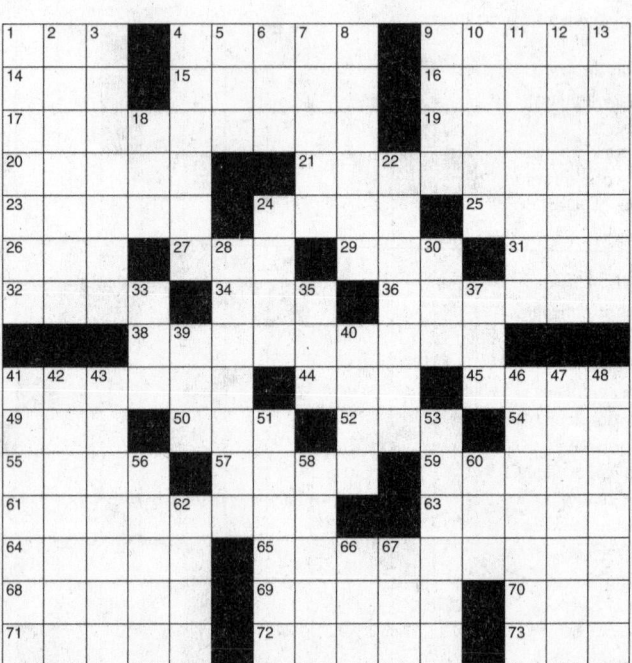

by Barry Boone

ACROSS

1 Barnyard female
4 X
7 Like Shakespeare's sonnets
13 TV schedule abbr.
14 Nonfiction films, for short
16 Mafioso's code of silence
17 One who breaks the 16-Across
18 Mourning comic book mutants?
20 Ed with the 1967 hit "My Cup Runneth Over"
22 Toto's creator
23 Bending easily
24 Event that includes Snowboarding Charades and Motocross 20 Questions?
27 Source of perspiration
28 Set on
32 One way to play
34 Speak with folded hands, say
37 "You Are My Destiny" singer, 1958
38 Classic Fiat model
39 Result of a phobia of medical pictures?
42 Integral
43 Business major subj.
45 Tina's "30 Rock" co-star
46 North Africa's ___ Mountains
48 Travel in the bush
50 Cousin of a foil
51 Curious person's video game console?
57 Endor natives in "Return of the Jedi"
60 Barnyard females
61 "The great instructor," per Edmund Burke
62 Diabolical graph line?
65 X

66 In a fair manner
67 Sci-fi novel made into a 1984 cult film
68 Word before booster or tripper
69 Has a premonition of
70 It may get whipped in the kitchen
71 Fled

DOWN

1 Part of a football helmet
2 First president whose name ends in a vowel other than E or Y
3 Safe for the 40-Down
4 XLI × X
5 Dude
6 Glacier climber's tool
7 It's charged
8 Moseys
9 Etheridge who sang "Come to My Window"
10 Imp
11 Desire
12 Birthday order
15 Cozy
19 "___ Gigolo"
21 Nickelodeon opening
25 Large African antelope
26 Poet Angelou
29 Rug rat
30 Acronymic store name
31 Potato chip brand owned by PepsiCo
32 Club bill
33 Member of an empire founded by Manco Capac
34 Bud
35 Bread for a Reuben

36 "Happy Days" network
40 Precipitation
41 Refreshers
44 Table cloths
47 Send a quick update, in a way
49 Have a backwoods brawl
50 Facilitating
52 "Be Kind Rewind" co-star Mos ___
53 Outstanding
54 Vaudeville offering
55 The end
56 Gas used in flash lamps
57 Former flames
58 Breaker, e.g.
59 Plow pullers
63 Jewish laments
64 Relay part

by Alex Boisvert

ACROSS

1 Dish that might come with mole sauce
5 Item sometimes having an elbow
10 "L'Amour avec ___" (French love song)
13 ___ open road
14 Lover of Orsino in "Twelfth Night"
15 Actor La Salle
16 *One on safari
18 Alternative to a B.L.T.
19 Rat in "Ratatouille"
20 *Part of stage scenery
22 Just got (by)
25 Staples of holiday displays
26 *What a cell doesn't need
29 Inclined
30 Objectivist Rand
31 Kind of lighting
32 Some R.P.I. grads
33 Impetuously . . . or what can go on each part of the answer to each starred clue?
36 Popular cleanser
38 "Calm down, big fella"
39 Want to take back, say
42 Surgical tube
43 *Absolutely
46 2003 Christopher Paolini fantasy best seller
48 Figure in red
49 *Cut off from water
52 Chief justice before Hughes
53 Rat Pack nickname
54 *Person with a baton
58 Force felt on earth, for short
59 The Joker, to Batman
60 Common computer instruction
61 Things read by 41-Down
62 Host Gibbons of "Hollywood Confidential"
63 Recess

DOWN

1 Dress (up)
2 "___ is the only slight glimmer of hope": Mick Jagger
3 Best Director of 1997, and Best Director nominee of 2009
4 Kind of army or show
5 "Law & Order: ___"
6 Part of bronze
7 Spoils
8 How the helm might be put
9 Targets of salicylic acid
10 Arboreal marker
11 Garage refuse
12 Measure of brainpower
15 Renowned
17 Ballyhoo
21 Hardly measures up
22 Hydrotherapy spot
23 Town outside of Buffalo
24 Circuit components
27 Words on some diet food labels
28 "___, the Man," 1940 biopic starring Spencer Tracy
33 Abject
34 Laud
35 Hall-of-Famer Sandberg
36 Carriers from northern Manhattan to Far Rockaway
37 Actresses Crain and Tripplehorn
39 Like the last Beatles concert, 1969
40 Heavy overcoats
41 Those who read 61-Across
42 Scarcely
44 "At Last" singer James
45 Topnotch
47 Prize won by Einstein and Yeats
50 Prop for Winston Churchill
51 Banjo site?
55 No man's land, briefly
56 One-named singer of the 1998 hit "It's All About Me"
57 Hwy.

by Kristian House

Note: This crossword is unusual in a certain way. Can you identify how?

ACROSS

1 Ali ___ of "The Arabian Nights"
5 French bench
9 Strikebreaker
13 Big blast maker, for short
15 "Able was I ere I saw ___"
16 Letters on beach lotion
17 Southern cousin of bouillabaisse
18 Basics
19 Lb. or oz., e.g.
20 Locale of Britain's first Christian martyr
22 Subsidiary route
24 Flows back
25 Helps in a bank heist, say
26 Bodega setting
29 Not be able to stomach
31 Former New York mayor Beame
32 Uneven, as fabric
34 The Beatles' "Eleanor ___"
38 His ___ (the boss)
40 Its beat may accompany a fife
42 Cowboy's tie
43 Baseball's Rusty
45 Old stringed instrument with a narrow body
47 Buddy
48 Bovine nickname
50 Cribs hold them
52 Scrubber
54 Neuwirth of Broadway
55 ___ of bad news
56 Research group associated with many Nobel Prizes in Physics
60 Kebab meat
61 Above, in Berlin
63 Bendable body part
64 ___ Longa, where Romulus and Remus were born
65 Opposite of badly: Fr.

66 Raymond's wife on "Everybody Loves Raymond"
67 "___ your best behavior"
68 Juice brand
69 "Born from jets" sloganeer

DOWN

1 Pocketbooks
2 Border on
3 Capital of the former Belgian Congo
4 One walking comfortably
5 Baked ___
6 Priests' robes
7 Brian Williams's network
8 Citadel, in Arabic
9 Barbecue item
10 Actor Sebastian

11 P.L.O. bigwig Mahmoud
12 Shakespeare or Browning
14 Ribbon holder, maybe
21 Bring ___ (cause)
23 ___ City (Tampa neighborhood)
26 Prohibitions
27 Before long, after "in"
28 Sitcom with the character B.J.
29 Setting for Umberto Eco's "The Name of the Rose"
30 Part of an invitation to an imbiber
33 Beer places
35 Expanse south of Ulan Bator
36 Bawdy
37 Rowdies, in British slang
39 Beyond the city limits
41 Disobedient sort

44 Big name in speakers
46 Sent a message before fax machines, say
49 Bougainvillea and others
51 Ball girls
52 Memphis street with many jazz clubs
53 "First Blood" protagonist
54 Capital SSW of Basel
55 Babble
56 English broadcaster, with "the"
57 "SOS" band
58 When doubled, a Polynesian island
59 Shipboard mop
62 Life, briefly

by Clive Probert

ACROSS

1 Actress ___ Pinkett Smith
5 Sports page fill
10 Derisive response to "She thinks she's going to be homecoming queen"
14 Virus named for a river
16 Texas' South ___ Island
17 Spicy tea
18 Where to see X's and O's
21 "CSI" field
22 See
23 Balance
24 Meadowlands squad
25 "Angélique" composer
27 College bigwigs
31 Comfy-cozy
32 Like 007's martinis
33 "___ time"
35 Where to see X's and O's
39 Journey segment
40 Flaring garb
41 Shade providers
42 Followed
44 Medical breakthroughs
46 Draft choices
47 Fluffy stuff
48 Sharpness
51 Bing Crosby hit in which "your branches speak to me of love"
56 Where to see X's and O's
58 Rice on a shelf
59 "There's many ___ 'twixt . . ."
60 Halloween option
61 You might sweat it out
62 Year-end celebrations
63 Tibetan herd

DOWN

1 One of the acting Bridges
2 Peek follower
3 "Let's Make a Deal" choice
4 Doppelgänger
5 Alley oops?
6 Soothing sprinkle
7 Tosses in
8 Numerical prefix
9 It's affected by global warming
10 Not this way
11 Big section of Bartlett's: Abbr.
12 "___ Strange Loop," 2007 Douglas Hofstadter book
13 Symbol of revolutionary power
15 Capp lad
19 Staffer: Abbr.
20 Fisherman's jubilant cry

24 Routine material
25 Central
26 Move slightly
27 Ring
28 Carried on
29 Sir or madam
30 Florist's waste
31 Season on the Seine?
32 Squinter's eyes
34 Ones with rings: Abbr.
36 Imperfect
37 Shortcut in a chase scene, maybe
38 Period of the Cenozoic Era
43 Breezed (through)
44 V as in Versailles
45 Whole
47 Talks like Daffy
48 Captain with a "regal overbearing dignity of some mighty woe"

49 Traffic marker
50 Arm part
51 Survey
52 Jon Arbuckle's pooch
53 Met melody
54 Spoon
55 Probes
57 Nebraska rival, for short

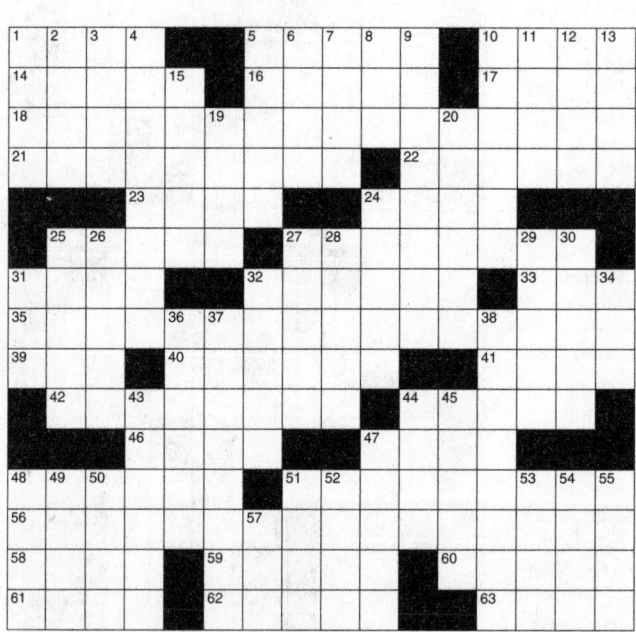

by Henry Hook

ACROSS

1 Lost-and-found containers
5 It has ringers on its team
9 Brown shade
14 "Got it"
15 Sauce brand
16 Subway station sight
17 Like a sunken treasure?
20 Third of December?
21 Grp. with the platinum record "A New World Record"
22 Systems of principles
23 Ice cream flavor, briefly
26 Receptionist on "The Office"
28 High place near Aberdeen?
34 One in custody
35 Breakfast cupful
36 Like most bathrooms
37 Spanish bear
38 "The Wizard of Oz" weather event
41 Eastern V.I.P.
42 "Amazing!"
44 One fawning
45 Gift tag word
46 Restraints for writer Flagg?
50 James who sang "A Sunday Kind of Love"
51 Like some textbooks
52 Complain
55 Grecian art object
57 Creepy
61 Cooking instruction hinting at this puzzle's theme?
65 Thingy
66 A.L. or N.L. division
67 ___-a-brac
68 Look of superiority
69 Cry from Charlie Brown
70 When sung three times, part of a Beatles refrain

DOWN

1 Places for double dribbles?
2 Golfer Aoki
3 Hasbro product
4 Not yet paid for, as a mailed package
5 Shot put's path
6 Kilmer of "Real Genius"
7 Kind of arch
8 Centers
9 Consume
10 Tablets site
11 Partner of pieces
12 Part of 51-Across: Abbr.
13 Some wines
18 Number after sieben
19 Honker
24 Eight: Prefix
25 Singer with a Best Actress Oscar
27 Loving
28 Olympic skater Cohen
29 Bonk
30 2008 Beijing Olympics mascot
31 Irish county north of Limerick
32 Building set
33 Mild cheese
34 Pound sound
38 Dweeb
39 Super-duper
40 25%-off price, e.g.
43 What Shakira or 25-Down goes by
45 Passes quickly
47 French CD holder
48 "Silas ___"
49 Julia Child, for one
52 High-performance wheels
53 Thor's father
54 Wood shaper
56 Org. with Divisions I, II and III
58 Exceptional
59 Pelvic bones
60 Mark permanently
62 ___ favor
63 Pres. initials
64 Periods of extra mins.

by Mike Torch

202 MEDIUM

ACROSS
1 Skins
6 It's hardly haute cuisine
10 Miracle-___
13 Go over again
14 "___ girl!"
15 Active volcano near Messina
16 ___ Gay
17 Move text around
18 Not a dupe: Abbr.
19 On the ___
20 Goddess of discord
22 Late-night beverage
23 Season opener?
24 Start of instructions for solving this puzzle
27 Winter air
28 Relative of -esque
29 Helicopter part
32 A number one
34 Misses
38 Instructions, part 2
41 Aids for police detectives
42 Lake bordered by four states
43 Female, formally
44 Dashiell Hammett hero ___ Beaumont
45 Nautilus leader
47 End of the instructions
52 Voyage kickoff?
55 Brand of wafers
56 Height: Prefix
57 Suffix with ranch
58 Cross
59 Word from a Latin lover?
61 Matriculate
63 The Blue ___ (Hank Azaria's "Mystery Men" role)
64 Penthouse pinups
65 Rover
66 Figs.
67 Circus trainer's prop
68 Divisions politiques

DOWN
1 Bombards with e-junk
2 Lots of "Deck the Halls"
3 Professeur's place
4 Poet's time of day
5 Ones whose work is decreasing?
6 Denis, to France
7 Flexible weaving material
8 British co.
9 "Sprechen ___ Deutsch?"
10 Not neat
11 Prelate's title: Abbr.
12 All-natural sparkler
15 John who co-starred in "Sands of Iwo Jima"
21 Prefix with metric
22 "This might be of interest," on a memo
25 Stage
26 College sci. class
27 Overhead cost for an artist?
29 Bldg. units
30 "Alley ___!"
31 Angular prefix
33 ___ curiam (like some court rulings)
34 Constellation next to the Dragon, with "the"
35 Much-discussed initials of a 1967 Beatles song
36 Bibliographic suffix
37 Pinup feature
39 It bugs bugs
40 Green rocks
44 Opposite of remove
46 Bit of A/V equipment
47 Performance fanfares
48 1988 Olympic track star, informally
49 Online financial services company
50 One way to N.Y.C.'s Penn Sta.
51 Prefix with -path
52 Bellini opera
53 Words after "whether"
54 Designer Geoffrey
59 Abbr. on a cough syrup bottle
60 ___ Z
62 Kind of bran

by Patrick Blindauer and Andrea Carla Michaels

ACROSS

1 Prefix with bucks
5 iPhone user's purchase
8 Wings it
14 Came to rest
15 Pot-au-___ (French stew)
16 Sign near roadwork, maybe
17 Flashy display
19 "Water that moves you" sloganeer
20 Org. in "Burn After Reading"
21 Brand with an iconic cowboy
23 Where pastrami may be put
25 Golf's ___ Pak
26 Toss high up
30 Passover meals
32 Dutch-based financial giant
34 Test for Ph.D. wannabes
35 Having a razor injury, say
38 Like Rod Serling tales
40 Asleep . . . or a hint to this crossword's theme
43 La ___ (San Diego area)
44 Patron of sailors
45 Nile slitherer
46 Matchsticks game
48 Marks up or down, perhaps
52 Rock trio known for its bearded members
54 "This just in . . ." fare
57 Earth, in sci-fi
58 Copycat
61 Element with the shortest name
62 Tested, as on "The $64,000 Question"
65 1892 Kipling poem
67 "Key Largo" actress
68 Prefix with dermis
69 He sang about Alice's restaurant
70 Iced rum cocktail that's stirred with a stick
71 Mr. ___ (old whodunit game)
72 Orbison and Bean

DOWN

1 Imelda, the shoe lover
2 "Seinfeld" gal
3 Giblets component
4 7-Eleven convenience
5 Shaving lotion brand
6 Compote fruits
7 You're doing one
8 Juxtapose
9 Snookums
10 Maj.'s superior
11 Paper in a poker pot
12 Caffeine-induced state, slangily
13 Eastern honorific
18 Like apple pie, in a saying
22 Game with a dummy
24 1983 Streisand title role
27 Big brute
28 Bad hair day problem
29 Kicker's aid
31 Coll., e.g.
33 Euclid's subject
36 Destiny
37 Otoscope user, for short
39 Gush on stage
40 Part of COLA
41 Bowser's bowlful
42 Camera type, briefly
43 Newport festival music
47 Out of gear
49 Conductor Toscanini
50 Yellowstone sighting
51 Some plasma TVs
53 Zest
55 Nilla cookie
56 Dimwit
59 "Momma" cartoonist Lazarus
60 Harriet's mate
62 Eli and Peyton Manning, for two: Abbr.
63 Motor City labor org.
64 Here, to Henri
66 Collect-all-the-cards game

by Tracy Gray

ACROSS

1 Surrounded by
5 Work with singing Egyptians
9 Lower septet of black squares in this grid, typographically
14 "Late Show" host, colloquially
15 Crossed, say
16 Clear, as a windshield
17 Three scruples
18 Higher septet of black squares in this grid, typographically
20 Bone on the pinkie side
21 Be mousy?
22 Actor Wheaton
23 McCarthy associate Roy
24 Fancy duds
25 Hat worn in "Casablanca"
26 Octet of black squares in the middle of this grid, typographically
30 Intrinsically
31 React to something striking?
32 Salon solutions
33 Green lights
34 Groan trigger
35 Much-read book of 150 poems
39 Containers on desks
44 Units of chains × furlongs
45 Nonet of black squares in this grid, typographically
46 Miss, south of the border: Abbr.
47 Bearded beast
48 Hothouse plant
49 Word before and after "yes"
50 Bouquets
53 Stun, in a way
54 Higher pair of black squares in this grid, typographically

56 Skip
57 "Work ___" (Beyoncé song)
58 Enthusiasm
59 Rend
60 Lower pair of black squares in this grid, typographically
61 Greek god who figures in an annual holiday
62 River to the North Sea

DOWN

1 Brings together, as two parts of the body
2 "Shakespeare in Love" role
3 Arthur Sullivan opera
4 Calls for
5 Fundamentals
6 Modern locale of ancient Ur
7 Delegates

8 Versailles valedictions
9 Wounded Knee's locale: Abbr.
10 Lithe swimmer
11 Watching people
12 Sun block?
13 Nervous ___
19 Duty
25 "Toy Story 3" character
27 Electron-swathed nuclei
28 Competitor of Bloomie's
29 First periods in H.S., often
30 Pilfer
32 Musical scales, e.g.
34 It may be split at a restaurant
35 New Jersey city, river or county
36 Classic pencil brand
37 It has drawers at school
38 Michele of "Glee"

39 More well-fed, say
40 Expressive of 61-Across, e.g.
41 They often hang around delis
42 Wearing
43 Outdoor summer pest, slangily
45 Siesta, say
47 [This is frustrating!]
50 "___ girl!"
51 "Got it," jocularly
52 Math items represented using { and }
55 Math item represented using + or Σ

by Kevin Wald

ACROSS

1 Org. known for drilling?
5 Masseur's target
9 Soap operas, essentially
14 Offshore
15 What adolescents may fight
16 Bit of dental work
17 Where lead weights grow?
19 Horatio who wrote about down-and-out boys
20 How babies may be carried
21 Bit of a Coleridge poetry line?
23 Takes it easy
26 Nine-digit ID
27 Harvard degree earned by J.F.K. in 1956
30 10 of them make a thou
32 "Take a Chance on Me" group
36 Little battery
37 "Let's call it ___" ("We're even")
38 S O S's, essentially
39 Ammo for idiots?
42 Bert's "Sesame Street" buddy
43 Actress Stewart
44 ___ mater (brain cover)
45 Cheeky chatter
46 Surgical inserts
47 What's up?
48 Gulager of "The Virginian"
50 "Saturday Night Live" segments
52 "Shut up!" . . . or a phonetic hint to this puzzle's theme
56 No-good sort
60 ___ wait

61 Toy house door support?
64 Verdi aria
65 German port
66 ___ Minor
67 "Marat/Sade" playwright Peter
68 Pushing the envelope
69 Singer Perry with the 2010 #1 hit "California Gurls"

DOWN

1 Enthralled
2 Munch Museum's locale
3 German: Abbr.
4 Certain cigarette
5 Capital of Nepal
6 Big name in A.T.M.'s
7 Single
8 Ball supporters
9 Sends cyberjunk
10 Everything considered
11 Lady ___
12 "Lemme ___!"
13 Balkan native
18 Wedding gown fabric
22 Long-eared farm animal
24 Layout
25 Equine areas
27 Works as a stevedore
28 Object of Petrarch's passion
29 Curses
31 Only coach to win both N.F.L. and A.F.L. championships
33 Prompts on answering machines
34 Hand-dyed fabric
35 Analyze
38 Bandage, across the pond

40 Dog treats
41 Not expected
46 Take to court
49 "Peanuts" boy with a blanket
51 Pat of "Wheel of Fortune"
52 Muffed
53 Homeland of Joyce and Yeats
54 Helen Mirren's crowning role, informally?
55 It takes a toll: Abbr.
57 Astronaut's letters
58 Cry during a recess game
59 Web site with a "Buy It Now" option
62 Help
63 Accurate throw

by Zoe Wheeler

ACROSS

1 Dive
6 Kind of screen
10 Guarantor of many bank loans to cos.
13 First Greek-American vice president
14 Condé Nast title
15 Retro hairstyle
16 Site of a memorable 1989 impromptu performance by 50-Across
18 Lake ___, head of the Blue Nile
19 "Didn't I tell you?"
20 Stocking stuffer?
21 Famous Olde Tyme brand
22 Prized possession of 50-Across
26 Actress Anne
29 Option after six months, say
30 What le gendarme enforces
31 Joyful damsel's cry
33 Director of "Eat Drink Man Woman"
35 Approval indicator
36 City on the Arkansas River
38 Off
41 Isn't alert
43 Its symbol is "X"
45 Top-notch
47 Ogre
49 "I'll see you in the parking lot!"
50 20th-century master of the [circled letters]
53 Lots of, slangily
54 Tolkien's Treebeard, e.g.
55 "Ti ___" ("I love you," in Italian)
58 Tommie of the 1969 World Series Mets
59 Birthplace of 50-Across
63 Polonius, for one

64 Loch Lomond lovely
65 Charleston or lindy, once
66 Live
67 Shanghai's ___ 2010
68 Stan Getz's instruments

DOWN

1 Pointed comments
2 Arch type
3 About
4 "___ mezzo del cammin di nostra vita": Dante
5 Forum for 140-character messages
6 "No lie!"
7 "Cry ___ River"
8 The works
9 Former sports org. with the teams Hitmen and Rage
10 Puppeteer with 12 Emmys
11 Ghost in "Macbeth"
12 Sports legend with the autobiography "Open"
15 "You are here" symbol
17 Neither's partner
21 Sob
22 Beach home?
23 Gives a hand
24 Places for guests
25 Home of Bally's and the Venetian
26 Horatio Nelson's ___ Victory
27 Observe
28 "Bullitt" has a famous one
32 Alamogordo's county
34 The so-called "blue marble"
37 "___ and away!"
39 Early Fox rival
40 £ : pound :: ¥ : ___
42 River through Castile and León
44 Some tiny mints
45 Force defeated in 1588
46 Old Mercury
48 Really
51 You, once
52 Like Brahms's Piano Trio No. 1
55 Greek warrior
56 Big garden project
57 Till compartment
59 Pintful, perhaps
60 Slate-cutting tool
61 Ability to pick things up
62 401(k) alternative

by Joey Weissbro

ACROSS

1 Dweller on an Asian peninsula
6 Ballgoer, for short
9 Steamed
14 Whack-___
15 Org. doing atmospheric tests
16 Meeting point
17 Gifts for divas
18 Shoreline indentation
19 Has only half-servings, maybe
20 *Turn-of-the-millennium explorer
23 Saudi "son of"
24 Punk rocker ___ Vicious
25 Immobile
28 Hounds
30 *1996 Grammy winner for the album "Falling Into You"
34 "Not a chance!"
36 Kind of place to the left of the decimal point
37 1,055 joules: Abbr.
38 *Treaty of Versailles signer
43 "Give ___ little time"
44 Pitcher Maddux who won four straight Cy Young Awards
45 Cleopatra held it close
46 *Point in a planet's orbit that's closest to the sun
50 Attract
53 Expensive violin, for short
54 ___ pad
56 Before, to Byron
57 Subject of a children's song associated with the vowels in the answer to each starred clue
61 Overly thin
64 Fertility clinic samples
65 Put on, as cargo
66 Sleep disorder
67 "___ the ramparts . . ."
68 "Mr. Belvedere" actress Graff
69 Brenda of comics
70 Promgoers: Abbr.
71 Risked

DOWN

1 Catch that might be mounted
2 It multiplies by dividing
3 Becoming discouraged
4 Beth preceder
5 Some survey responses
6 Ridicule
7 Like some battles
8 Sounds heard by 57-Across
9 World's fourth-most populous country
10 Restricted, with "in"
11 Tool used by Hansel and Gretel's father
12 King ___
13 What's extracted from soil to get oil?
21 Singer Ocasek of the Cars
22 Tendon
26 Tool used in thoracic surgery
27 Kansas canine
29 Carrier with a hub in Copenhagen
31 Second in line?
32 Abbr. on a bank statement
33 Carmelite, for one
35 Sanctuary fixture
38 Any singer with Gladys Knight
39 Delivery persons' assignments: Abbr.
40 Judicial title role for Stallone
41 Slippery swimmer
42 It was dropped in the '60s
47 Worker whose job always has a new wrinkle?
48 Hollywood treasures
49 Silent assent
51 Francis of "What's My Line?"
52 Kind of bliss
55 Nonliquid state
58 Sounds heard by 57-Across
59 Maintain
60 "The Lion King" role
61 Nonliquid state
62 Likely
63 Italian article

by Peter A. Collins

Note: When this puzzle is completed, the circled letters, starting at 21-Across and reading clockwise, will reveal the first part of 17-Across.

ACROSS

1 Like many a cellar
5 "The Usual Suspects" setting
9 Peddle
13 Suit material?
14 Unwanted spots
15 Ireland's ___ Islands
16 Come next
17 Musical work in four parts
19 Went off on a tangent
21 Sugar
22 Letters between a name and a nickname
23 Hebrides isle
24 Meet, as expectations
26 Turkey
27 With 6-Down, genetic carriers
29 Divining rods
31 Somme time
32 ___ Kramer, 2010 Dutch Olympic gold medalist in speed skating
34 Practice
35 Attendee at a 17-Across performance
39 Bottom line
41 Boomers' kids
42 What you might need after a breakdown
45 Clog up
49 Savings vehicle
51 Decide
52 ___ Rouge
54 Eat like ___
55 Hosp. test in a tube
56 Letters on a crucifix
57 Yankee ___ Howard, 1963 A.L. M.V.P.
59 Singing voices in the 17-Across
62 "___ Mio"
63 All over

64 Parcel (out)
65 First company to successfully manufacture bubblegum
66 Bother
67 In ranks
68 Trueheart of the comics

DOWN

1 Patronize a bistro, say
2 It may be excused
3 Kind of network
4 Artist Paul
5 It might get tips
6 See 27-Across
7 Strapped
8 Smooth and connected
9 Mudder's fodder
10 Pac-Man centers
11 "Die ___" (second part of the 17-Across)
12 Folds, presses and stretches
13 Met maestro James, longtime conductor of the 17-Across
18 Exult
20 Motivation
25 "Happy Birthday" writer, say
28 Medium strength?
30 Big ___
33 Kvetch
35 "Yikes!," online
36 Spice Girl Halliwell
37 Down ___ knee
38 No. after a no.
39 Singing voice in the 17-Across
40 Peppy
42 Sneaks (around)

43 Birds with hanging nests
44 Composer of the 17-Across
45 Fighting
46 Issue
47 County next to Napa
48 Hurt's "Body Heat" co-star
50 Bother
53 Mislead, and more
58 Artist's pad?
60 W.W. II site, briefly
61 Clinch, with "up"

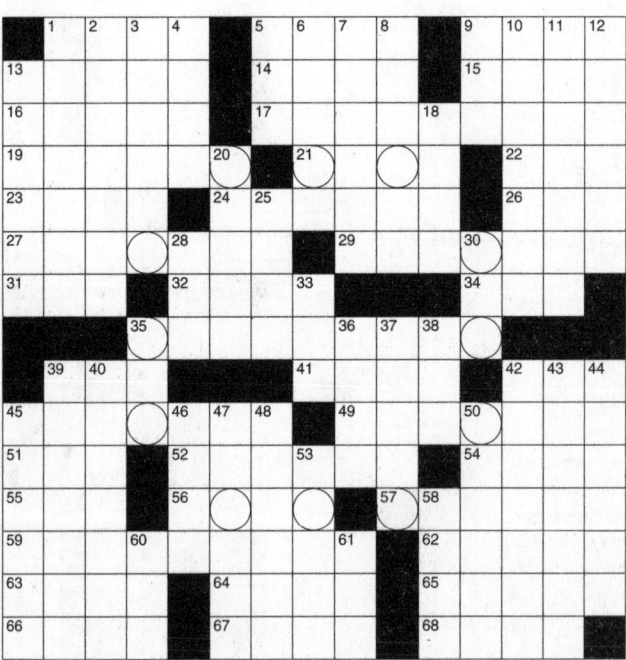

by David J. Kahn

ACROSS

1 Supply with more ammo, say
6 Term of endearment
10 Bits of land in la Seine
14 2003 Sandler/ Nicholson comedy
17 1940 Crosby/Lamour/ Hope film that was the first of a "travel" series
18 Yalies
19 Part of NATO: Abbr.
20 "Mad Men" extras
21 Conducted
22 Actor Bert
24 Mystery writer Deighton
25 It may make a ewe turn
27 Big name in baseball cards
30 Starters
33 Gelatinous ingredient in desserts
34 First X or O, say
37 1971 film that was Cybill Shepherd's debut, with "The"
41 1954 Elia Kazan Oscar winner
42 Bout stopper
43 Author Philip
44 Some razors
45 Ergo
46 Pugilists' grp.
47 Blood-typing syst.
49 Mystery writer Edward D. ___
51 Ode title starter
54 World Cup chant
57 Singer/actress Zadora
58 Lomond, e.g.
59 2008 film derived from Dr. Seuss
62 1986 film for which Paul Newman won his only Oscar
63 Inauguration Day highlight
64 Proverbial heptad
65 Addicts

DOWN

1 Less well done
2 ___ Gay, historic plane displayed by the Smithsonian
3 "Encore!"
4 N.L. Central team
5 "I pity the fool" speaker
6 Mideast city whose name, coincidentally, is an anagram of ARABS
7 1935 Marx Brothers romp
8 Proscribe
9 Drivers (on)
10 Drives
11 Sierra ___
12 Bankrupt company in 2001–02 news
13 Fr. holy women
15 Lettuce or kale
16 Corrode
23 Ne'er-do-well
25 Setting for candlelit romance
26 Current unit
28 Henry VIII's sixth
29 Like some suburban homes
30 Scads
31 Go south
32 "___ perpetua" (Idaho's motto)
34 Thursday's eponym
35 College in New Rochelle, N.Y.
36 100-lb. units
38 Triumphant cry
39 Fisherman's 10-pounder, e.g.
40 Mex. miss
45 The sauce
46 Fisherman's spot
47 Lei-person's greeting?
48 Covering for la tête
50 Pietro's ta-tas
51 Olde ___ (historic area, quaintly)
52 Orangish shade
53 Shipboard cries
54 "___ be in England . . ."
55 Old card game with forfeits
56 Photo blowups: Abbr.
58 Vientiane's country
60 Implement in a Millet painting
61 Dallas sch.

by Charles E. Gersch

ACROSS

1 Sci-fi role starting in 1966
8 Keach of "W."
13 Marked by dignity and taste
15 He played opposite Jones in "Carousel" and "Oklahoma!"
16 With 24-Across, "Uh-uh!"
17 Reversals
18 Map line: Abbr.
19 Like the devout
21 Wagering locale: Abbr.
22 Some socials
24 See 16-Across
26 Backdrop for many a Winter Olympics
27 Wayne or Lee
28 It may be square
29 It gets the juice out
31 Destination for a Near Eastern caravan
34 "Uh-uh!"
36 "Uh-uh!"
40 Brand associated with Everyday Knee Highs
42 Unanimously
43 Island in the Tyrrhenian Sea
46 "That's amazing!"
48 Deut. preceder
49 "Uh-uh!"
52 ___ Harker, wife in Bram Stoker's "Dracula"
53 Dorm V.I.P.'s, for short
54 Part of a winter stash
55 Letters on the road
56 Behind
58 "Uh-uh!"
62 "You think I won't?!"
63 Put under
64 Girl in "Waterworld"
65 Guinness superlative

DOWN

1 Year Michelangelo began work on "David"
2 VCR button
3 Bridge need
4 Shows disappointment, in a way
5 Heraldic band
6 Mail order option
7 Style of fighting
8 Nymph pursuer
9 Fort Worth sch.
10 Arid region's watercourse
11 Shout in a playground debate
12 "I'll grant you that. However . . ."
14 Greek philosophical group
15 Pack carrier
20 One who's definitely not in the in-crowd
22 Nasty remark
23 Zeno's locale
24 Sale table notation
25 Actress Alexander of "The Cosby Show"
27 Eliot protagonist
30 European fashion capital
32 Betray
33 "Don't have ___!"
35 Disco phrase
37 Hardly a picky eater
38 8-Down's Roman equivalent
39 Low-cost home loan corp.
41 Some broken glass
43 Brokerage name since 1992
44 Like the Dalai Lama, historically
45 Spot for a bite
47 Emerge on top
50 Fate
51 Teen breakout
52 Feature at an auto show, in two different ways
55 Webmaster's lingo
57 Sushi fish
59 Jazz group, for short
60 Mag. edition
61 New Year festival overseas

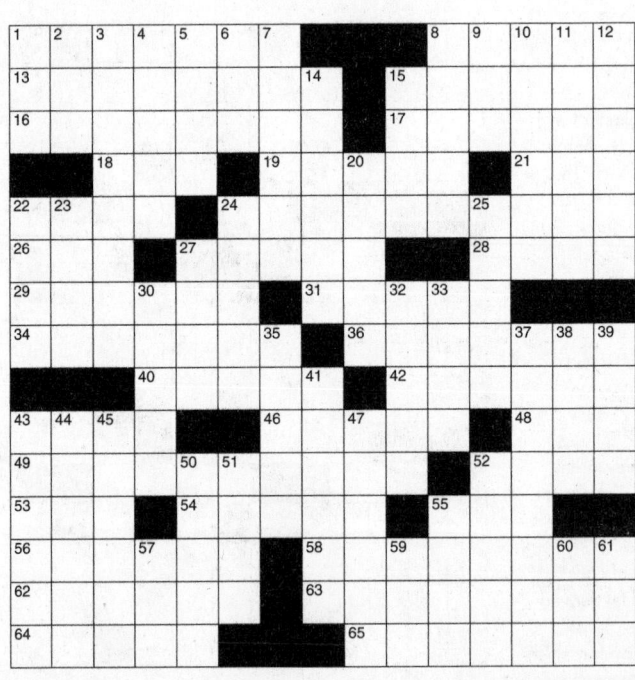

by Victor Fleming

ACROSS

1 Red October detector
6 Mystified
11 Support grp. for the troops
14 Pong maker
15 Hardly chic
16 Black goo
17 1970 James Taylor hit
19 Egg cells
20 See 2-Down
21 Go over
22 Mischievous rural pastime
25 Kind of agent
30 "I can ___"
31 Hatch on the Senate floor
32 Start of a dog owner's sign
35 Keeping your elbows off the table, e.g.
40 Surrounded by
41 Basslike fish
42 Complaints, informally
45 Renter
46 Classic Dana Carvey character, with "the"
50 Eastern discipline
51 Bygone warship
57 1989 play about Capote
58 Sound of capitalism? . . . or a hint to the starts of 17-, 22-, 35- and 46-Across
60 Orders at a restaurant
61 Restaurant order, with "the"
62 Tempt
63 Bus. card info
64 Luxurious
65 Building material in "The Three Little Pigs"

DOWN

1 Bombproof, say
2 Big name in the 20-Across business
3 Undercover buster
4 Turf
5 Iranian money
6 Supplement
7 "Presumed Innocent" author
8 Brainy
9 Prefix with dermis
10 Rand who wrote "Civilization is the process of setting man free from men"
11 Best of all possible worlds
12 Idiot ___
13 "High," in the Homeland Security Advisory System

18 Common crystals, chemically
21 Body organs associated with anger
23 "The Hurt Locker" setting
24 Browse
25 Mail-order option
26 ___ Gold, agent on "Entourage"
27 Samovar
28 Singer honored on a 2008 U.S. postage stamp
29 Lacking brio
32 Flower's home
33 Frequent Weekly World News subjects, briefly
34 Wordplay, e.g.
36 Full of calories
37 How-___

38 Nail holder
39 Just make (out)
42 Swath maker
43 Chest
44 Lordly
45 Boston suburb
47 Capt.'s inferior
48 Ball's partner
49 Valentine embellishment
52 Capt.'s inferiors
53 "Ri-i-ight!"
54 Sweets
55 Designer Schiaparelli
56 Ton
58 "___ Father . . ."
59 Tire abbr.

by Ian Livengood

212 Medium

ACROSS

1 It began commercial service in '76
4 Chinese dynasty at the time of Christ
7 Cartoon featured in 23 best-selling books
13 1983 Randy Newman song
15 Brazier
16 Thingamajigs
17 Partly paid back
19 Fair-hiring inits.
20 Silverstein who wrote "The Giving Tree"
21 Backbreaking
25 Mattress brand
28 In America
31 Splinter group
34 Quaker product
35 "Star Wars" surname
36 Like "be": Abbr.
37 Figure that shares a property with this puzzle
39 Mercury or Saturn
40 Harmonic singing style
42 Member of the Be Sharps on "The Simpsons"
43 Equestrian's grip, maybe
44 Page of music
46 Michelin Man makeup
48 "___ Anything" ("Oliver!" song)
51 Reggae relative
54 Where marmots and chamois live
57 Hearten
61 Composer Antonio
62 Nixon policy
63 Came out
64 ___ Peres (St. Louis suburb)
65 Work of Alexander Pope

DOWN

1 Outdoor retail promotion
2 Oodles
3 Feldshuh of "Brewster's Millions"
4 Disturb a stand-up routine
5 Malt beverages
6 Nimbus launcher of 1964
7 Number that looks like the letter yogh
8 Step on it
9 Withdraw
10 Carrier overseer, for short
11 "Roméo et Juliette" section
12 Stat starter
14 Most repellent
18 Type of terrier
22 Express romantic interest in
23 Powerful kind of engine
24 "___ Can Cook" (former cooking show)
26 Critic who's a real thumb-body?
27 Quick expression of gratitude
29 Caesar dressing?
30 Like ink, poetically
31 Graze, in a way
32 Olympic archer
33 Be exultant
37 Uto-Aztecan language
38 Valedictorian's pride: Abbr.
41 Punster
43 Above the ground
45 Lord and lady
47 Foreign dignitary
49 Muralist Rivera
50 One way to turn right
51 Southwestern rattler
52 Had down
53 Palio di ___ (Italian horse race)
55 Like some clothing
56 "The ___ Game" (1965 Shirley Ellis hit)
58 Put down, in a way
59 Colts, on a scoreboard
60 Rural env. abbr.

by Patrick Blindauer

ACROSS

1 "The Da Vinci Code" priory
5 Disgusting-tasting
9 The first to stab Caesar
14 Feminine suffix
15 Key point
16 Gordon and Ginsburg
17 Dog in whodunits
18 Fine-tune
19 Register
20 Place with a "You Are Here" map
23 Brew source
24 Dermal opening?
25 Fleet letters
26 Packed away
28 Left at sea
30 Anchor-hoisting equipment
33 Go straight
35 Howard who parodied Adolf
36 Affirmative actions?
37 Longtime Greenwich Village music venue, with "the"
40 Source of bubbly
43 The other army
44 Innumerable
48 Protection for Pelé
51 Slowly, to Solti
52 Ground breaker
53 Breakfast orders at a 55-Down, briefly
54 Altar agreement
56 Muslim convert in 1964 news
57 Glen Campbell hit, the last word of which is this puzzle's theme
61 Half of diez
62 Verve
63 Instrument played with a mallet
64 "I don't care if they do"
65 Learning by flash cards, e.g.
66 Seek out
67 Decrease, as support
68 Poll closing?
69 Badlands locale: Abbr.

DOWN

1 Five-pointed creature
2 Like most gym rats
3 Keeping up with
4 Tide type
5 TV blocking device
6 Having a twist
7 One getting an inspiration?
8 Will figure
9 Actor Richard of "Rambo" films
10 Unpaid sitter, perhaps
11 Like some dirty windshields
12 "Through the Looking-Glass" laugh
13 Hand communication: Abbr.
21 Lab dish inventor
22 Hold in regard
27 Some R.P.I. grads
29 Batpole user
31 Mideast leader: Var.
32 Core group
34 Japan's highest point: Abbr.
38 Wedding reception participants, often
39 Hose material
40 Smokestack emission
41 More ostentatious
42 Connect with
45 Sulky
46 Emory University's home
47 Hanging in there
49 "Beat it, kid!"
50 Get wider
55 Where hash is "slung"
58 E-mailed a dupe to
59 Jillions
60 Orders at a 55-Down
61 A.L. Central city

by Alan Arbesfeld

ACROSS

1 Gangbusters
5 Some Spiders, informally
10 Part of a frame
14 Sweeping
15 Petrified weeper of myth
16 Member of a pit crew?
17 Border names
19 Big do
20 With 40-Across, coloring advice . . . and literally so
21 Stink
23 Half a dance
24 Owner of the Titanic
28 Old ___ Bucket (Big Ten conference football prize)
30 Worrying comment from a surgeon
31 Ultimate goal
33 1959 hit with the lyric "Did he ever return? No, he never returned"
34 Fictional villain whose given name is Julius
36 Antique asset, often
40 See 20- and 58-Across
43 It might be rolled up on a farm
44 Prefix with meter
45 "And we'll ___ a cup o' kindness yet": Burns
46 Paying guest
48 Head of Haiti
49 Live in the past?
52 Unblockable shot
55 The New Yorker cartoonist Chast
56 "___ Es el Amor" (classic Spanish-language hit)
58 With 40-Across, infer something . . . and literally so
59 Skinned knee, say, to a tot
61 Factory output
66 Start of an old boast
67 Malfunction
68 Frozen drink brand
69 Elysium
70 Appliance button
71 Warehouse

DOWN

1 Gender abbr.
2 Abbr. in many car ads
3 Go away
4 Big name in lawn care
5 Some male dolls
6 2018 Super Bowl number
7 Sexy babe
8 On
9 Thrill
10 Butcher, baker or candlestick maker
11 One way to be taken
12 ___ Arens, former Israeli defense minister
13 Irish writer Brendan
18 Rob Roy's refusal
22 "Color me impressed!"
24 Sonogram targets
25 Tourist locale
26 Clingmans Dome is its highest point: Abbr.
27 Round request
29 Prefix with meter
32 Zenith
34 Commit
35 Thatching material
37 Head off
38 "Super-duper!"
39 Crooked
41 Wisher's spot
42 "___ goes!"
47 Pressing concern for an astronaut?
48 Start of a clarification
49 Was the designated one?
50 Amazed
51 Internet publication
53 Hit the roof
54 Gumshoe
57 Box a bit
60 A as in Austria
62 Some game enders, for short
63 Directly
64 Antipoverty agcy.
65 Mint

by Jim Hilger

ACROSS

1 City SSW of Jacksonville
6 Physics units
10 First of two before-and-after pictures
14 Mannerly
15 Stir (up)
16 "No prob"
17 *Megadeth's music genre
19 "Now!"
20 European tongue
21 Cornerstone abbr.
22 Green bug
23 Increase in increments, with "up"
25 Sign in the bleachers
27 *"The Lion King" song
31 Enlightened Buddhist
34 ___ the beginning
35 Neighbor of Hung.
36 You may take one before dinner
37 Swedish-based international clothing giant . . . or a hint to the answers to the six starred clues
39 Dr. Johnny Fever's station, in 1970s–'80s TV
40 Hi-tech heart
41 Spanish bath
42 Kind of buddy
43 *Hilton head, e.g.
47 One of the three original Muses
48 Knocked someone out, say
52 Viking training camp?
54 "The Godfather" composer Nino
56 "I finished"
57 Who once remarked "You can't stay mad at somebody who makes you laugh"
58 *The Father of American Public Education
60 Extra: Abbr.
61 German word slangily used to mean "extremely"
62 Circle measures
63 Germany's ___ Canal
64 Internet ___ (viral phenomenon)
65 English race site

DOWN

1 Autumn hue
2 Old Olds
3 "Stop, matey!"
4 Real-time online conversation
5 Prince ___ Khan
6 1974 Mocedades hit
7 Film director Martin
8 Politician's greeting
9 Partner of poivre, in French seasoning
10 It's "short and stout" in a children's song
11 *Lines on a football field
12 Morales who played a 13-Down officer on TV
13 See 12-Down
18 Docile
22 Part of a Latin 101 trio
24 Symbol of a position
26 Shi'ite leader
28 Sheer fabric
29 One seeing red?
30 Like 12-hour clocks
31 "The Nazarene" author Sholem
32 "___ Man"
33 *Society
37 2004 Olympics gymnastics star Paul or Morgan
38 Organism that doesn't require oxygen
39 Colorful almanac feature
41 Ran
42 Busy type
44 Sign up
45 Rubbernecking
46 Auto financing co.
49 A lot
50 Film composer Morricone
51 Material in a "Canadian tuxedo"
52 Criticism
53 Lightsaber wielder
55 Utah city
58 What fans do
59 Poetic preposition

by Finn Vigeland

ACROSS

1 Rock blaster
4 Shredded sides
9 Blackballs
14 "Fantasy Island" prop
15 1944 murder mystery directed by Otto Preminger
16 Jazz pianist with 20 Grammys
17 Hagen of Broadway
18 Footnote abbr.
19 Flexible conjunction
20 "Wow!"
21 Butcher's roast cut
23 Spill
25 More fervent
26 Border line?
28 Not a copy: Abbr.
29 Trendy
32 O's overseas
35 Pax ___ (uneasy peace)
38 Temporary lapse of memory
39 Neighborhood get-togethers
40 Metal casting housing automotive cylinders
41 It displays the connections between system components
42 Incessantly
43 Like many squares in a French crossword
45 Pout
47 Newbie rollerblader's sore spots
52 Filling holders
57 N.B.A. Hall-of-Famer Hayes
58 Certain 1920s faddist
60 Anise-flavored liqueur
61 Scheme
62 Bronx cheers
63 1963 role for Liz
64 E-mail folder
65 Stop on the Métro?
66 Cigarette that once advertised the "health benefits" of its Micronite filter

DOWN

1 Fraternity benefactors, for short
2 Rock music genre
3 Cabinetmaker's hardware
4 Neatnik's opposite
5 In the ___ the gods (left to fate)
6 What a hammer may hit
7 Author's bane
8 Zen enlightenment
9 Close call
10 Pay tribute to
11 Language of Islamabad
12 Old Dodge
13 Reddish-brown gem
22 What screaming may exacerbate
24 Jelly thickener
27 Start of some addresses
29 It'll grow on you
30 Fit for duty
31 Land under Down Under: Abbr.
32 Harbinger
33 ___ mosso (less rapid, in music)
34 Hoagy Carmichael's "___ Buttermilk Sky"
36 Soothsayer
37 Subj. of a 39-Down reminder
39 See 37-Down
43 Smash hit
44 Bit of comic strip text
46 Kind of board
48 The 2×2 black square near the middle of this puzzle's grid, e.g., which is part of eight answers
49 Fertilized item
50 Shrivel from age
51 Condescending one
52 Third afterthought in a missive: Abbr.
53 Princess loved by Hercules
54 Dash
55 Small price to pay
56 Bone-dry
59 Queue after Q

by Dan Naddor

ACROSS

1 Director Lee
4 Big name in sport shirts
8 Dispute
14 Little dipper?
15 Film style
16 Makes less than a killing
17 Cholesterol abbr.
18 Nut with caffeine
19 Grand grounds
20 Comment on life by 52-Across?
23 Like some straw
24 Hangs around
28 Deposit and withdrawal site for 52-Across?
32 Lamebrained
33 Musical Reed
34 Displaying more violence
35 Result of an encounter with 52-Across?
40 Seize for ransom
41 Capek play
42 Mole, e.g.
43 Crib plaything for a young 52-Across?
49 Buffy the Vampire Slayer, e.g.
51 Stiffness
52 See 20-, 28-, 35- and 43-Across
56 Vampire story, e.g.
59 Deuce follower
60 Frozen water, to Wilhelm
61 Hebrew name for God
62 Part of a vampire
63 ___-Foy, Que.
64 Pied Piper's sound
65 Nipper
66 Down

DOWN

1 Like the heart during a horror movie
2 "Sorry, Charlie"
3 Frozen treat
4 Way to pay someone back
5 ___-suiter
6 Like mechanics' hands
7 Void of any va-va-voom
8 Poem title start
9 Ill-fated ship of film
10 Spot to pick up Spot
11 Spanish she-bear
12 Bar fixture, maybe
13 Squeeze (out)
21 Fierce sort, astrologically
22 Sort
25 Awesome, in slang
26 Stink
27 Neighbor of Turk.
29 Tiny bump on a graph
30 ___ Center (Chicago skyscraper)
31 Commercial lead-in to Sweet
34 "Cootie"
35 Carpet feature
36 Month before Nisan
37 Having clean hands
38 Like some parks
39 QB's utterance
40 Speed meas. in Europe
43 Big ___
44 Popsicle choice
45 Pen with a cap
46 "Um . . . O.K."
47 1955 novel that was made into 1962 and 1997 films
48 Obliterated
50 Racy film
53 1920s chief justice
54 Subject of the book "Six Armies in Normandy"
55 N.H.L. venue
56 No. on a map
57 Tokyo, once
58 Melted chocolate, e.g.

by Jay Kaskel

ACROSS

1 Bucko
4 Berlin cry
7 George Washington and others
14 Burning issue
15 ___ Greene, "The Godfather" gangster
16 "The poison of life," per Brontë's Rochester
17 With 27- and 35-Across, a Halloween riddle
19 Set apart
20 Online store option
21 "Punk'd" cable channel
22 Club for swingers
23 Bar, at the bar
25 Poet's Muse
27 See 17-Across
32 Coral reef dwellers
33 Prefix with comic
34 Check out
35 See 17-Across
38 Be sociable
41 Bottled spirit
42 Go for the gold?
43 With 60-Across, answer to the riddle
48 Soft drink brand
49 Fresh
50 Seat holders
51 Italian TV channel
54 Sniffler's supply
58 Bibliophile's concern
60 See 43-Across
61 Dovetail with
62 "Tell ___ story"
63 New York or Wisconsin, in D.C.
64 Yankee manager who wore #37
65 African menace
66 Base ___

DOWN

1 Bryn ___ College
2 "Off the Court" autobiographer
3 Elaine ___, George W. Bush's only labor secretary
4 In the center of
5 Math groups
6 Be told about
7 Spilling point
8 Staff symbol
9 "That issue is in the past"
10 Capital of the U.S.?
11 Reach for rudely
12 What you will
13 Mind
18 Lock
24 QBs, often
26 Kia model
27 "Whaddaya know!"
28 "Whaddaya know!"
29 Ring cry
30 Sign of a winner
31 Bomber pilot in "Catch-22"
35 Pre-election activity
36 Chemical suffix
37 "My dear fellow"
38 War stat
39 Barnard's ___, locale in "Great Expectations"
40 Crossed (out)
41 Understood
42 Debbie who won three swimming gold medals at the 1968 Olympics
43 Picaroon
44 Like some job training
45 Washington city, river or tribe
46 Nurses take these
47 Top-of-the-world topper
48 Feudal domains
52 Learning method
53 Hydroxyl compound
55 In order
56 Projecting edge
57 2000 Hugh Jackman movie
59 Component of bronze

by David J. Kahn

ACROSS

1 The two together
5 In fighting trim
8 Sparks's state
14 Quick as a wink
16 For all, as a restroom
17 Online university staff?
18 Trig function
19 Anthem contraction
20 Phone no.
22 Body designs, informally
23 What Nashville sunbathers acquire?
27 One to hang with
28 Special attention, for short
29 Golf ball's position
30 "Not on ___!"
32 Hasty escape
34 Ballplayer with a 40-Down logo
39 Sign prohibiting sunshades?
43 At attention
44 Sgt. or cpl.
45 Like many fast-food orders
46 Bailed-out insurance co.
49 Local govt. unit
51 Make public
52 Salon jobs from apprentice stylists?
57 Zinging remark
58 Coffee, slangily
59 Nest egg letters
60 Where to find a piece of Turkey
62 "Stop that!" . . . and a hint to the answers to 17-, 23-, 39- and 52-Across
67 Chips away at
68 Seinfeld's eccentric relative
69 Many a Little League rooter
70 "Go team!"
71 Sunbathers catch them

DOWN

1 Coal holder
2 Indivisible
3 Demolitionist's aid
4 Biker's invitation to a friend
5 Former Big Apple mayor La Guardia
6 Global currency org.
7 Lab jobs
8 Atomic centers
9 Brian of ambient music
10 Scenic view
11 Like most Turks
12 Body shop jobs
13 Graph lines
15 1545–63 council site
21 Moray, e.g.
23 Drum accompanying a fife
24 École attendee
25 Emotionally damage
26 Blue-green hue
27 Plexiglas piece
31 Muscle spasm
33 AOL alternative
35 W. C. Fields persona
36 Bar closing time, perhaps
37 Philbin of TV
38 "P.U.!" inducer
40 See 34-Across
41 "Hamlet" has five
42 Fastball in the dirt, say
47 Kiddingly
48 Prefix with thermal
50 Jeopardy
52 Michelle's predecessor as first lady
53 Goof
54 "Humble" home
55 Come back
56 Zagat, to restaurants
57 Microwave sound
61 Porker's pad
63 Old-time actress Merkel
64 Suffix with pay or plug
65 Driver's one-eighty
66 How-___ (handy books)

by Tracy Gray

ACROSS

1 Office device appropriate for this puzzle?
7 Await
11 Rte. suggester
14 Setting for many a fairy tale
15 Assistant played by Charles Bronson in "House of Wax"
16 Drama set in Las Vegas
17 Command agreement
18 "That's of little importance"
20 Out of service?: Abbr.
21 Road hazards
23 Fence builder's starting point
24 Small doses may come in them
26 "Charlotte's Web" girl
27 One half of an old comedy duo
28 Like the Paris Opera
31 Airport need
34 Substitute
37 I.R.S. 1040 line item
38 They might give each other French kisses
39 Way to get around something
40 No longer interested in
41 Undecided: Abbr.
42 Album half
43 Space under a desk
44 End of a perfect Sunday drive?
46 Grill
48 Impulse path
49 33-Down's group, with "the"
53 Kitchen tool
55 Physicist Bohr
56 Jim Beam product
57 Like some patches
59 1940s British P.M.
61 Times in classifieds
62 Game played on a world map

63 Quick outing for Tiger Woods . . . or what this completed puzzle contains
64 Violin cutouts
65 What a peeper uses to peep
66 Can't stand

DOWN

1 Game item usually seen upside-down
2 Check writer
3 Is of ___ (helps)
4 Some Windows systems
5 The Cutty Sark, for one
6 Lifesavers, say
7 Features of homemade cameras
8 Big ones can impede progress
9 Montréal or Québec
10 Window dressing
11 Feigns ignorance
12 Play ___ (perform some songs)
13 Seal's opening?
19 Conflicted
22 Photography aid
25 Portable info-storing devices
26 Below-ground sanctuary
29 Almond or pecan
30 Batting helmet feature
31 Filthy place
32 Prefix with valent
33 See 49-Across
35 Pre-schoolers?
36 Light-blocking
39 Part of a home security system?
40 French eleven
42 Ones who sleep soundly?

43 Alley behind a bar on TV?
45 They're drafted for service
47 Higher ground
49 Topographical feature formed by underground erosion
50 1957 hit for the Bobbettes
51 Parts of masks
52 "Thou ___ I have more flesh than another man": Falstaff
53 Role for which Marion Cotillard won a 2007 Best Actress Oscar
54 Vest feature
55 Like a quidnunc
58 Feature of many a ballroom dance
60 "We Know Drama" channel

by Mike Nothnagel

ACROSS

1 The old man
5 Bare minimum
10 Arias, e.g.
14 "Thirteen" actress ___ Rachel Wood
15 Ob/gyn test
16 Eliot Ness and cohorts
17 "anyone lived in a pretty how town" poet
19 Manassas fighters
20 Modular, as a home
21 Author better known as Saki
23 Fakes, as figures
26 Whopper topper
27 "Star Trek" director, 2009
30 "The Thrill Is Gone" bluesman
31 "Bad, bad" Brown of song
32 Banking nos.
34 Cameo gem
35 Juice box go-with
36 Big Indian
40 Animals in a Western herd
41 Neighbor of Chad
42 Big name in mail order
46 "The Monkey's Paw" author
48 Heroine in Bizet's "The Pearl Fishers"
49 Not real
50 Creator of Eeyore
52 One of a winter pair
56 Some med. scans
57 2007 A.L. Cy Young winner
60 Years, in Rome
61 "___ dead!" (worried teen's words)
62 Srs.' lobby

63 Cookbook instruction
64 Grid play starters
65 ___' Pea

DOWN

1 Slightest sound
2 No longer disturbed by
3 Eight minutes/mile in a marathon is a good one
4 Ornamental tobacco holder
5 Letter resembling an inverted "V"
6 ___ Group ("big four" record co.)
7 One of Heart's Wilson sisters
8 Heaved sounds
9 Brit's "Baloney!"
10 "The Elements of Style" co-author
11 Subtitle of 1978's "Damien"
12 Former Cavalier James
13 How Broadway characters may break out
18 TV host Povich
22 Crowds around
24 Hurdles for M.B.A. hopefuls
25 Third-party accounts
27 "Selena" star, familiarly
28 Aniston, in tabloids
29 Suffix with vision
30 "Incidentally," to texters
33 Eager kids' query to parents
35 Ugly as ___
36 Ravioli fillings
37 Back in time

38 Brother of W.
39 "___ Poetica"
40 Jezebel's god
41 Gymnast Comaneci
42 Andean wool sources
43 Found out, British-style
44 Fountain of Youth site, it's said
45 "L' ___ d'Amore" (Donizetti opera)
47 747 and Airbus A380, as jets go
49 Praline nut
51 CBS military drama
53 Warming trend
54 Limerick's land
55 Target of a rabbit punch
58 Wee, to Burns
59 Cleopatra biter

by Samuel A. Donaldson

ACROSS

1 French clerics
6 President after Tyler
10 Medicinal amts.
14 General's cry
15 This and that
16 Stimulate
17 Game maker starting in 1972
18 Actress Carrie and others
19 Like wetlands
20 *Antimicrobial bit in mouthwashes 90°
22 *Like wizards' caps 90°
24 ___ volente (God willing)
25 Really thin person
27 Tornado
30 Judgment
32 Food thickener
34 Undivided
35 #1 hit by the Byrds . . . or directions for reading the answers to this puzzle's starred clues (always clockwise as indicated)
38 Mai ___ (drinks)
41 Wine: Prefix
42 "Comin' ___!"
43 *Apollo 11 and 12 180°
48 Given the nod
49 Dance at a Jewish wedding
50 Showing signs of disuse
54 Iranian city of 1.2+ million
56 Masculine side
58 Insurance plan, for short
59 *Marriage, say 270°
61 *Specification in a burger order, maybe 270°
63 Attorney General Holder

65 Endure
67 Dessert cake
68 [I'm kidding!]
69 Nobelist Wiesel
70 Dipsomaniac
71 Jumpy
72 LP or 45
73 Biblical dry measures

DOWN

1 "She's the Man" actress Bynes
2 Washes
3 Longest river in Texas
4 Off-white shade
5 Tibetan dog
6 Kind of scheme
7 West Coast brew, for short
8 Place
9 Dweller in Pristina
10 Like many TV movies: Abbr.

11 Public mention
12 Candy that comes in more than a dozen flavors
13 Farm structure
21 Short person?
23 N.F.L. coach Jim
26 St. Louis's arch, symbolically
28 "Just you wait, ___ 'iggins . . ."
29 TV warrior princess
31 Formal/informal response to "Who's there?"
33 Ben ___, "Treasure Island" pirate
36 "The Big Sleep" film genre
37 Shooters
38 General ___ chicken
39 Egyptian cross

40 Treating, in a way, as table salt
44 Bygone sovereign
45 Three sheets to the wind
46 Of little ___ use
47 Should
51 Five-time Olympic gold-medal swimmer
52 One overacting
53 Catnappers
55 Tumultuous
57 Old pyramid builder
60 District of Colombia?
62 Camera feature
63 Animal often seen with a bell around its neck
64 Clear (of)
66 Family girl

by Andrew Zhou

ACROSS

1 Home, slangily
5 Rio Grande city
11 In the manner of
14 Rhein tributary
15 Food storage area
16 Mick Jagger's title
17 Signs of elation → marathon segments
19 Liberal arts maj.
20 Prefix with skeleton
21 Italy's side, once
22 Melt ingredient
23 Put down
25 Sign of trouble → commercial writers
27 Greedy sort
28 Certain offshoot
31 Lech of Poland's Solidarity
32 Beehive State Indians
34 "Born from jets" automaker
36 Watch readouts, for short
37 Pigtail → cause for a siren
40 Hydrotherapy sites
42 Squandered, as a lead
43 Courtroom attention-getter
47 Like some phone minutes
49 Furry sci-fi creature
51 That, in Tijuana
52 Toaster food → dazzling designs
54 Smoothly, on a score
56 Spanish counterpart of a mlle.
57 "Dies ___"
60 Rotund Wolfe
61 Ore suffix
62 Fireplace part → fall color
65 TV spot, often
66 Katharine Hepburn's foursome

67 États-___
68 What a farmer in Del. works on?
69 Surgeon's probe
70 Bog product

DOWN

1 Locomotive part
2 Cheesy dish
3 First millennium B.C., roughly
4 Worrier's handful
5 Chi-town rails
6 Holy man in an Ogden Nash verse
7 ___ fixe
8 Forgo the script
9 Plaything for two
10 Places for scrubs, for short
11 Like an alias
12 Disney's Nala, for one
13 Deep secrets
18 Performs
22 El Greco's city
23 Satyajit Ray's "The ___ Trilogy"
24 First name in '50s TV comedy
26 Painter of dreamscapes
29 Prepare for a marathon, say, with "up"
30 Set aside
33 Cascade Range peak
35 Make stout
38 On the ocean blue
39 A.F.B. truant
40 Showed contempt for something
41 Soldier's shelter
44 The start of time
45 Where Skype was invented
46 Wild scene
47 Positive aspect
48 Having the least vermouth
50 Ranges of knowledge
53 Comics character with a wrist radio
55 Fancy duds
58 Asia's ___ Sea
59 To be, to Brigitte
62 Jolly sounds
63 Prez who said "If you can't stand the heat, get out of the kitchen"
64 Ballpark fig.

by Robert W. Harris

ACROSS

1 Fighter in the "Iliad"
5 Excellence
10 Similarly round
15 Sumptuousness
16 Onetime name at the Taj Mahal
17 Apt
18 OPEC dignitary, maybe
19 It might be run in a hospital
20 Annoyance, in British slang
21 Microsoft debut of 2001
22 Common result of high humidity
23 Located
24 Infrequent blood type, informally
26 Like some doors
28 Keeps going
33 Modern sum?
36 Stone work
39 Blue hues
40 Drank heavily
43 What this puzzle is, orthographically
46 Spanish ___
47 Head of the class, in slang
48 Dressing tool
49 1990 autobiography subtitled "Baseball, the Wall and Me"
50 "Hold on . . . what's going on here?!"
53 Basketball's Isiah Thomas, to fans
55 Suitable for teen audiences
58 Gets set
61 Some child-care center sites, for short
66 Plug
68 Prepare for battle
69 Like the Addams Family
70 ___ Croft, Angelina Jolie role
71 Optimistic
72 Hall-of-Famer Michael of the Dallas Cowboys
73 "Semper Fidelis" grp.
74 Model Cheryl
75 Judges
76 Longest-lived first lady

DOWN

1 "A Clockwork Orange" lead role
2 Extra-large
3 Hypothetical fundamental particle
4 Persepolis king
5 Put out
6 "If I ___ . . ."
7 Sitarist Shankar
8 Don Juan's mother
9 "Me" follower
10 "Lawrence of Arabia" city
11 Sweetening
12 Mediterranean harvest
13 It's about 90 yards of a football field
14 Eliminated from a boxing match, in a way
25 Sentry
27 "St. Matthew Passion" composer, for short
29 Loudly voice one's objections
30 Male sheep, in Britain
31 Noted Finnish chair designer
32 "___ little silhouetto . . ." ("Bohemian Rhapsody" lyric)
34 Locale of a much-visited mausoleum
35 Flagon contents, perhaps
36 Presidential inits.
37 Alecto, Megaera or Tisiphone
38 Hindu god of desire
41 ___ pursuit
42 Part of Korea, for short
44 Brilliant
45 Manhandle
51 Geezer's cry to a young 'un
52 Tech-savvy school grp.
54 Awards show with a Best Play category, with "the"
56 Stage
57 "Bugs"
58 Witticism
59 Distant leader?
60 Crescent shape
62 Abraded
63 Coastal feature
64 Actor Tamiroff
65 Thesaurus contents: Abbr.
67 W.W. II group

by Peter Wentz

Note: When this puzzle is done, read the eight circled letters clockwise, starting with square #24, to identify this puzzle's theme.

ACROSS

1 Crept (along)
7 Word with Orange or Peach
11 Car that was the subject of a 1964 top 10 hit
14 Sesame seed-based sauce
15 Eye area
16 Put out
17 Passes
18 #2
20 Mid 12th-century year
21 Hosp. areas
23 Cantankerous
24 ___ Valley
26 At the home of, to Henri
27 Hoist
29 Infomercial host Gibbons
33 Co-star of Hanks in "Forrest Gump"
35 Puts away
37 Cambodia's Lon ___
38 Carry on
39 Singer Studdard who won the second season of "American Idol"
41 Sunroof or moonroof alternative
42 What rings reveal about a tree
43 Funeral fire
44 "___ Be Stupid" (1985 Weird Al Yankovic album)
46 Performer dubbed "The Great Dane"
48 Like a next-door neighbor's lawn, or so it seems
50 Just sitting around
52 Tool
55 W.W. II battle cry
58 Qxe5, e.g., in chess
59 Way in Québec
60 #5
62 Kind of kick
64 Fish-fowl nexus
65 Old space-launched rocket
66 Still on the shelf
67 Envoy's bldg.
68 Gazpacho, e.g.
69 Team with a big B on its helmets

DOWN

1 Twosomes
2 Folk singer Griffith
3 #3
4 Hawaiian Punch alternative
5 Lures
6 #4
7 Tampa Bay gridders, for short
8 Lacto-___ vegetarian
9 Laura Bush's maiden name
10 Symbol of victory
11 Andy with the #1 hit "Shadow Dancing"
12 "Lou Grant" paper, with "the"
13 Give a thumbs-up
19 It may be hedged
22 Mozart's "___ donna a quindici anni"
25 Tennis's Nastase
26 Grammy-winning Winans
28 Italian waterway
30 #1
31 ___ suit
32 Mighty Dog rival
33 Q-tip, e.g.
34 "I am not what I am" speaker
36 #6
40 Exhort
41 Dos follower
43 Nitpicking types
45 Dish alternative
47 City with the Great Sphinx
49 Prefix with hazard
51 Certain printing process, briefly
53 "September 1, 1939" poet
54 Does some yardwork
55 Ruin
56 Orbit site
57 Workers' rights agcy.
58 Letters on a car sticker
61 Letters from a debtor
63 Aspen or Tahoe

by Allan E. Parrish

ACROSS

1 The Divine, in 23-Across
4 "M*A*S*H" co-star
8 Get started
14 Woman's name that means "messenger of God"
16 Simple hydrocarbon
17 *Omaha-born human rights activist
18 Mauled
19 Pick ___ (quibble)
20 Supérieur et Érié
22 Baum princess
23 Ligurian capital
25 Having harmony
28 Suffix with ball
29 Physics unit
30 Tee follower
32 1955 Platters hit
34 Plunk preceder
35 Follows
36 *Today's kids, demographically speaking
38 Plessy v. ___ (landmark Supreme Court decision)
40 Gate opener for Apollo
41 Afternoon services
42 Drew Barrymore hosted this show at age 7: Abbr.
43 Est., e.g., once
46 Approximately 946 of these make a qt.
47 Bouquet : pheasants :: covey : ___
49 Volkswagen model
51 Hockey's Phil, to fans
53 Hubbub
55 "Dianetics" author ___ Hubbard
56 How some gym instructors stand
59 *Brand with the challenge to lose one inch from your waist in two weeks

61 Many a campaign fund-raiser
62 Sweet wine
63 It goes in front of a coal tender
64 Hayes portrayer in "The Mod Squad," 1999
65 Number of tiles per Scrabble set for the letter at the end of the answer to each starred clue

DOWN

1 Split or crack
2 More asinine
3 Viewing with elevator eyes
4 ___-pitch
5 It may be good or free
6 Con
7 Mexican silver center
8 Trick
9 Chiwere-speaking tribe
10 "And ___ the field the road runs by": Tennyson
11 Courtroom cry
12 Feeling gloomy, say
13 Lockjaw
15 ___-1 ("Ghostbusters" vehicle)
21 Part of a pig
24 *"What Do You Do With a B.A. in English?" musical
26 ___ régime
27 *Performer born James Todd Smith
31 Mocedades hit subtitled "Touch the Wind"
33 Urges
34 Gunpowder holders

35 Japanese surname follower
36 Comprehending
37 Latin lover's bouquet, maybe
38 Where the N.S.A. is headquartered
39 Some wallet material
42 Blunder
43 Prefix with cumulus
44 Like some kisses
45 Irk
48 "Hello ___" (Todd Rundgren hit)
50 Director Kazan
52 Bygone science/sci-fi magazine
54 Sued party in a legal case: Abbr.
57 Michael Jackson's first #1 solo hit
58 Calif. neighbor
60 Hosp. units

by Bill Thompson

ACROSS

1 With 66-Across, subject of this puzzle
6 "Maude" star Arthur
9 With 64-Across, 1-/66-Across movie of 2005
14 "If memory serves . . ."
16 Dress in the Forum
17 . . . of 1987
18 Some tomatoes
19 Faux pas
21 Winter hrs. in St. Louis
22 . . . of 1990
26 ___ exchange
27 It's high on the pH scale
28 Silents actor Novarro
29 . . . of 1979
31 Asian nurse
32 Dorothy's state: Abbr.
33 "Too bad!"
34 . . . of 1971
36 . . . of 1973
40 Be up
41 Mayo is in it
42 ___ land
43 . . . of 1977
47 Par ___
48 Part of l'été
49 A mean Amin
50 . . . of 1983
51 Nelson Mandela's org.
52 Shaded passageway
55 Verdi's very
57 . . . of 1978
62 Close, in verse
63 Feverishness
64 See 9-Across
65 Raiders make them, informally
66 See 1-Across

DOWN

1 Something played out in a theater
2 Spanish she-bear
3 Geometric suffix
4 Demoisturized, in commercial names
5 Palace workers
6 Flock sounds
7 Heavenly
8 Hall-of-Famer Walter who was a Dodger manager for 23 years
9 No. on a car
10 ___ Z
11 Male with whiskers
12 Top-level
13 Get a move on
15 Early fifth-century year
20 Surround with a glow
22 Sheik's mount
23 Spiritual guide
24 One-named 1970s–'80s supermodel
25 Live together
27 Vitamin involved in cell metabolism
29 "Keep them coming, Juan!"
30 Amazement
32 TV's ___ Lee
35 Scot's not
36 Show announced by Don Pardo for 30+ years, for short
37 Construction worker's lunch container
38 H. G. Wells people
39 Phoned
41 Neatened, in a way
43 Certain travel guide
44 "Stop! You've got it all wrong!"
45 Centers
46 Unmoored
47 Hank with voices on "The Simpsons"
52 Left side
53 Places where the Daily Racing Form is read, in brief
54 Celtic sea god
56 Get bronze
58 Excellent, slangily
59 Lube (up)
60 Way: Abbr.
61 Dict. listing

by Caleb Madison

ACROSS

1 Orient
8 Orient
15 Ace
16 Ace
17 Lower in stature
18 Lower in stature
19 Part of B.C.E.
20 Shakes
22 Runnin' ___, 1944 N.C.A.A. basketball champs
23 Party favorites?
24 Onetime sponsor of Richard Petty and Mario Andretti
26 Uses a needle
29 Dummy
31 Epitome of simplicity
34 I, for one
38 I, for one
40 Understanding
41 Understanding
42 Tire
43 Tire
44 Tax form datum: Abbr.
45 Major sight in the sky?
47 Ballet bend
48 East end?
49 Sweater woes
53 Raw side?
56 Sway
57 "Nonsense!"
60 Loose
63 Loose
65 Mean
66 Mean
67 Bristles
68 Bristles

DOWN

1 What some things do in the sun
2 Profess
3 Latvian capital
4 Elephant's-___ (plant)
5 Whatever
6 "Me too!"
7 Lock
8 They're good for crying out loud
9 Serpent tail?
10 Good companion for an ace in Vegas
11 Burn through
12 Pit-___
13 Lug
14 Old English letters
21 J.F.K. posting
23 Ed of Hollywood
24 Froth
25 Lure
26 Gushes
27 Coastal fliers
28 Odin, to the Germans
30 Lulu
31 Old Russian co-op
32 Religion with an apostrophe in its name
33 River through Glasgow
35 "___ Own," 1989 #2 hit by Bobby Brown
36 Possible response to a driving mistake
37 Trawlers' gear
39 Brothers of the Wild West
46 ___ result
48 Vessels by basins
50 Lake bordered by Malawi, Mozambique and Tanzania
51 Moving
52 ___ body (cell part)
53 Denigrate, in English slang, with "off"
54 In the flesh
55 Aid's partner
56 Something that's fun on the coast?
57 Person under the Union Jack
58 Fuji rival
59 Startled cries
61 Winning Super Bowl XXXIV player
62 Turkish title
64 Response: Abbr.

by Joe Krozel

ACROSS

1 Shade of green
5 Workplace watchdog, for short
9 "That ___ my question"
14 Each
15 Mrs. Frisby's charges in "The Secret of NIMH"
16 See 26-Across
17 Home of Eastern Michigan University
19 Rodeo rope
20 Harry Belafonte's specialty
22 "___ natural"
25 U.N. workers' grp.
26 One may be lit on a 16-Across
27 Veer off track
29 Pole, for one
31 It might precede a collection: Abbr.
32 Guns' partner
33 Rapper parodied by Weird Al Yankovic in "Amish Paradise"
35 1979 film with Capt. Willard and Col. Kurtz
40 Universally known
41 "Idylls of the King" lady
43 Motocross racer, for short
46 Skating maneuver
47 P.F.C.'s punishment
49 Some prayer clothing
51 My ___, Vietnam
52 ___-wolf
53 Undercover operatives . . . or what are hiding in 17-, 20-, 35- and 58-Across?
57 Onetime TWA competitor

58 Leaf-eating insect scourge
62 Hundredth: Prefix
63 Gray ___
64 Tot's injury
65 Couldn't stand
66 Garden divisions
67 Post-baby boomer group, for short

DOWN

1 Homer Simpson's middle name
2 iPad download, in brief
3 First of a pair of lists
4 Awesome
5 How some medications are taken
6 Big name in Japanese electronics
7 URL start
8 Sale condition
9 35-Across, for one
10 North Pacific islander
11 Immobility
12 Longtime local
13 Finder of missing persons
18 Cubs' place
21 Most toilet seats
22 Turkish title
23 Result of trauma, maybe
24 Pack (down)
28 Bark
29 Russian space program started in the 1960s
30 Takes the top (off)
33 Medical condition treated by thrombolysis
34 Lacking width and depth, for short
36 Screening aid
37 Something that can't be missed
38 Burden
39 ___ child (pregnant)
42 Hair salon stock
43 In and of itself
44 Title location in a Hemingway novel
45 Like rooms to rent
47 Where Manhattan is
48 Unfortunate circumstance
50 Correspond
51 Cartoon stinker
54 Food thickener
55 Greek deli specialty
56 Urban woe
59 Be short
60 Cookie holder
61 Do voodoo on

by Mike Nothnagel

ACROSS

1 Opposite of race
5 Pyramid schemes, e.g.
10 Its scores are used in selecting Natl. Merit Scholars
14 For all grades
15 Shanty
16 Prefix with -pod
17 Comical Martha
18 Actor Hirsch of "Into the Wild"
19 See 44-Down
20 Five Jacksons
22 *Dramatically expose
24 *Home near a shore
26 Prevaricate
27 Patron saint of Norway
28 They're shown in a beauty pageant
32 Madam
35 Just out
37 Where to find eBay and Google
38 Govt. watchdog since 1970
39 Miller products?
41 Big Ten sch.
42 Co. bought by Verizon
43 One leading a cheer, perhaps
44 1998 Roberto Clemente Award winner
45 Like a vampire's victims
47 Classification for some popular Spanish music
48 Push
49 Mount Whitney's range
51 Et ___
53 'Fore
54 *Massachusetts college
59 *1975 Southern rock hit stereotypically requested at concerts
61 Words mouthed to a camera
62 Pro team?
63 Beef type
65 Tropical vegetable also known as elephant's-ear
66 "I ___ dead!"
67 Part of 41-Across
68 Short race, briefly
69 Paula of TV news
70 Whom Raskolnikov confesses his crime to in "Crime and Punishment"
71 Word that can combine with the ends of the answers to the six starred clues

DOWN

1 Stool, perhaps
2 Southwest plain
3 Words to a kidder
4 Fresca, e.g.
5 Maroon 5's "___ Will Be Loved"
6 Dos that are don'ts?
7 St. Teresa's place
8 Youngest Hall-of-Famer (at age 22) to hit 100 home runs
9 Whole bunch
10 Baked entrees
11 *Porch feature
12 Lots
13 Nerf ball, e.g.
21 Sinuous swimmer
23 Pueblo pots
25 Outlaw's accessory
29 Late Soviet diplomat Dobrynin
30 Italian poet who was the subject of a Goethe play and a Donizetti opera
31 ___ car
32 Turkeys
33 PC character set
34 *Hillbillies' put-down
36 Baylor's home
40 Kantian concern
43 Oberon of "Wuthering Heights"
44 With 19-Across, U.S.C.'s marching band
46 Checks the fit of
50 Literally, "way of the gods"
52 I, to Wilhelm I
55 Silent film accompaniment
56 Certain rial spender
57 More peeved
58 Word that can combine with the starts of the answers to the six starred clues
59 Org. criticized in "When the Levees Broke"
60 See 64-Down
62 Bosox legend
64 With 60-Down, big Chilean export

by Byron Walden and Caleb Madison

ACROSS

1 Friends and neighbors
5 Bend one's elbow, e.g.
9 Cornered
14 Start of an incantation
15 Wash up
16 "On the Beach" author
17 Hard-boiled crime genre
18 Aesir ruler
19 Perfect Sleeper maker
20 Athlete who has pigged out on snacks at a bar?
23 Interstate-championing prez
24 Strippers' tips, often
25 Explosive of old
28 Special treatment, for short
29 "___ geht's?" (German "How are you?")
30 ___ pro nobis
31 Chief heckler?
36 Skewer
37 Place for a Dumpster
38 Juan's "what"
39 Lavender, for one
40 Pesky arachnid
41 Skydiver's amended plans?
43 Troop-entertaining grp.
44 Cara ___ (Italian term of endearment)
45 Performer yukking it up
46 Friend from afar
48 Tickled
50 Indy letters
53 Insulation from jokes?
56 Rodeo ride
58 Astronomy's ___ cloud
59 Brand for woofers, but not tweeters?
60 Cultural prefix
61 Purple shade
62 Sound from a steeple
63 Core belief
64 Critic's unit
65 Primordial stuff

DOWN

1 Japanese writing system
2 Old Apple laptop
3 Brief moment
4 "Listen!," old-style
5 Walk with jerky motions
6 Chili server
7 Escapees from Pandora's box
8 Alien: Prefix
9 Take on
10 Angle symbol, in trigonometry
11 Explode like a puffball
12 "Boston Legal" fig.
13 Truly, in the Bible
21 Unwise undertaking
22 Brand once advertised with the jingle "We wear short shorts . . ."
26 Circular gasket
27 Barista's offering
28 Back into a corner
29 Boo-hoo
31 Copier malfunction
32 Beethoven dedicatee
33 "Rocket Man" rocker
34 Pastel hue
35 Scat syllable
36 Bernie Madoff's hedge fund, e.g.
39 Parasol's offering
41 Leave high and dry
42 Say "Hey, batter batter batter" and such
44 Mr. Met, for one
47 Tubular pasta
48 Mosaic artist's material
49 Spanish poet García ___
50 Fifth-century canonized pope
51 Birthstone for many Scorpios
52 Working stiff
54 The old man
55 Banjo accessory
56 Double or nothing, e.g.
57 Tpke., e.g.

by John Lampkin

ACROSS

1 "Caro nome," for one
5 Gov. Faubus in Arkansas history
10 Black
14 Bryn ___
15 Unsuspecting
16 Second to ___
17 *"I don't know yet"
20 Comment put in by Putin, perhaps
21 Ballet headliners
22 Decide to take, with "for"
24 *1968 #2 hit heard in "Easy Rider"
27 Grp. at home on the range?
28 To ___ (just so)
29 English fashionista Bartley
33 Air or ami preceder
34 Biblical verb with "thou"
36 Aligns
37 "Yo te ___"
38 Ill-fated . . . or a hint for answering the six starred clues
40 Hit Jerry Bruckheimer TV drama
41 Scorch
43 Boozer
44 Sportage maker
45 Applies
47 They may be boxed
49 Over there
50 *1924 Isham Jones/ Gus Kahn song
52 Interview part: Abbr.
53 Hollywood's Anderson and Reed
56 Diamond on a record player
58 *"No way!"
63 Character in "Beowulf"
64 Alternative to hash browns
65 Through
66 People mover since 1853
67 Vintner's need
68 What a rake may do

DOWN

1 Tsp. or tbsp.
2 When repeated, excited
3 *Memorable movie quote of 1932
4 Like many a gallerygoer
5 Length in years of a lenient sentence, maybe
6 Head of the Egyptian god Amun
7 Through
8 Arthur Miller play "___ From the Bridge"
9 Soup variety
10 Person with special access
11 Good name for someone born on Dec. 25
12 What might give a physical reaction?
13 Wishes
18 Old WB sitcom
19 Substance in a chemistry experiment
22 In a position to steal
23 Blend before using
25 Vaquero's rope
26 Snug, as in bed
30 *Like someone who's had a narrow escape
31 Wound
32 Chinese, e.g.
35 Sweet wine of Hungary
38 Irk
39 Certain English poetry scholar
42 Feels a loss
46 Hirsute
48 Took to court
51 "That's ___ subject"
53 Fire starter?
54 Follower of juillet
55 San Francisco's public transit system, with "the"
57 Favorite
59 ___ Maria
60 Pawn jumpers: Abbr.
61 Formerly
62 [Mumble, mumble]

by Charles Deber

ACROSS

1 *Cry at the start of a vote
6 Tree in California
10 Soulful Redding
14 Duane ___ (New York City pharmacy chain)
15 Land west of the Pacific
16 "This is terrible!"
17 Greased
18 "Believe" singer, 1999
19 Liberals, with "the"
20 *"Soon enough, my friend"
22 Big mess
24 "Bien ___!"
25 Former "S.N.L." comic Gasteyer
26 French theologian who wrote "Sic et Non"
28 Jean Sibelius, for one
29 Seat of Albany County, Wyo.
30 Biggie ___ (rapper a k a Notorious B.I.G.)
33 Bennett of "What's My Line?"
34 "Am ___ risk?"
35 Women's rights pioneer Elizabeth ___ Stanton
36 *As a package
37 Old man: Ger.
38 Here, in Juárez
39 Bomber type
41 More agile
43 Relinquish, as arms
45 Move from site to site?
46 Hall of TV fame
47 Oslo Accords party, for short
48 One way to sway
51 Many a Justin Bieber fan
52 *Completely imagined
54 Restaurateur Toots

55 Kirk's foe in a "Star Trek" sequel
57 Lofty dwelling
58 Unadulterated
59 Alveoli site
60 "I love you," in a telenovela
61 Sacred chests
62 Tense
63 Poker phrase . . . or what's needed to complete the answers to the six starred clues

DOWN

1 Aristophanes comedy, with "The"
2 Alphabetic pentad
3 Bravery
4 Took too much
5 Common North American hawk
6 Iconic chomper
7 New York stadium eponym
8 Taradiddle
9 Classic candy with nougat
10 "How luxu-u-urious!"
11 *Top-rated TV series of 1971–76
12 Madden
13 Lush
21 Quaint lodgings
23 Brand of 45-Down balls
26 Direction at sea
27 Block
28 Pass muster
30 Where "Otello" premiered, with "La"
31 General played by Fonda (in 1976), Peck (1977) and Olivier (1982)
32 *To be expected

33 MSNBC competitor
36 Vintner's prefix
37 Terrier's sound
39 Exemplar of dryness
40 Glimmer
41 U.S.S. Enterprise helmsman
42 How some wages are calculated
44 Popular tractors
45 See 23-Down
48 Untamed
49 Sam who directed "Drag Me to Hell"
50 Classic theater
52 Masculine side
53 Cad
54 Where the robed are rubbed
56 Movie for which Patricia Neal won Best Actress

by Michael Sharp

ACROSS

1 "___ time"
4 Originator of the phrase "rosy-fingered dawn"
9 Last picture in an alphabet book
14 Lay
15 Adult
16 Ducks, in "Peter and the Wolf" productions
17 What to use to spell 30-Down, according to George Bernard Shaw, reputedly, Part 1
20 Shout into a canyon
21 Still
22 Notorious 1999 computer virus
25 Conservative philosophy in Britain
28 Actress Lupino and others
29 They're usually white or brown
31 Letters from a mathematician
32 Books often read on Saturday
34 One of the five counties of Hawaii
36 Part 2
40 Beginning of a saying about evil
41 Object of Andy's affection in "The 40-Year-Old Virgin"
42 Flight board abbr.
43 Workplace for a 23-Down
44 Goals
48 Intro
52 Lion's home
54 Like some eyes and soup
56 Prefix with -pathy

57 Part 3
61 Zero, in slang
62 Lips
63 Nod, perhaps
64 Noisome noise
65 The Tower, e.g.
66 Flight board abbr.

DOWN

1 Panama and Suez
2 Snickered
3 Designer McCartney
4 Alternative to Ring Dings
5 A little peculiar
6 Spoil
7 They may be deal breakers
8 Opposite of invoices
9 One fighting urban sprawl, say
10 Black
11 Shop

12 Like some gas: Abbr.
13 Memento from an old flame?
18 Shine
19 Grp. with the platinum album "Out of the Blue"
23 Worker on a 43-Across
24 Lab gel
26 Reggae/dancehall artist ___ Paul
27 Century-starting year
30 "Fish"
33 Tic-tac-toe win
34 Ring results, for short
35 One of the Five Colleges
36 Abbr. on an old map of the West
37 Shout at the top of a roller coaster

38 Who'll "talk 'til his voice is hoarse," in a 1960s sitcom
39 Good radio station for a bride?
40 Simpleton
43 Find (out)
45 Spot
46 Fade
47 High
49 "Peace out"
50 Of service
51 High-___
53 A goner
55 Jedi with a big forehead
57 Big inits. on cable
58 Old Chinese dynasty
59 Boss: Abbr.
60 Prefix with conservative

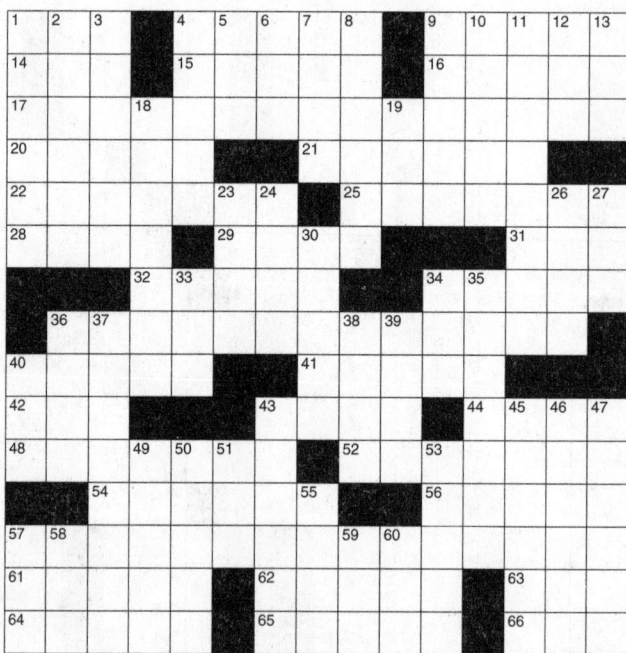

by Oliver Hill and Eliza Bagg

ACROSS

1 Jettisoned compartment
4 Update, in a way
10 Noise in a comic book gunfight
14 Expert
15 Key of "The James Bond Theme"
16 Bathe
17 Big __
18 Margarita alternatives
20 Spanish for "the meadows"
22 Mexican bloom
23 Like telemarketing headsets
24 Bit of a climb
26 They're caught in Chicago
27 What a cheeky one's cheek might get
29 Screen role for Skippy the dog
31 Pit-__
34 Cook Island carving
36 Card game of Spanish origin
40 Salsa verde ingredients
43 Barrio outsider
44 At 30° W 30° N, e.g.
45 Lock part
46 Goals against, e.g.
48 "What __ be done?"
50 Certain Protestant: Abbr.
53 Golfer Aoki
55 Reason for an evacuation
59 Baja buddies
61 Like traditional Mexican music
63 Procrastinating words south of the border
65 Castor __ (old comic strip character)

66 Subj. involving cells
67 Be altruistic
68 Mustachioed "Simpsons" character
69 Kournikova of tennis
70 They might be knee-jerk reactions
71 Carbohydrate suffix

DOWN

1 "Tortilla Flat" character
2 Jersey Shore county, appropriately
3 None too swift
4 Officially annul
5 Go from home to home?
6 One of a 15th-century trio
7 "With the jawbone of __ . . ."

8 Comfy footwear, briefly
9 Slowly disappears
10 Bor-r-ring
11 Soup kitchen server
12 Use
13 Tijuana tables
19 One turned off for takeoff
21 Virgins of ancient Rome
25 Island capital of 2.6 million
28 It requires one who's blind with a bat
30 Two-handled vase
31 1977 double-platinum album by Steely Dan
32 Sweeping shot
33 Medit. land
35 Flattens, for short
37 Arthur of "The Golden Girls"

38 $200 Monopoly properties: Abbr.
39 Gift in "The Gift"
41 Crone's concoction
42 White House ceremony site
47 Syrian presidential family
49 Helping for the very hungry, maybe
50 "La __"
51 At full speed
52 Evergreen with edible nuts
54 Psi follower
56 Cheap, in adspeak
57 "But of course"
58 Mark used four times in this puzzle's solution
60 Pricey event
62 Yucatán years
64 Soak (up)

by Patrick Merrell

ACROSS

1 Dull shade
4 Road caution
7 Place for a hammer
12 One in on the founding of a company
15 River of York
16 Record label of the Beatles' "Ain't She Sweet"
17 Spy sent by Moses into Canaan
18 Production site chief
19 Wonder of note
21 Yes ___
23 One getting a bouquet?
28 Makes fun of
31 Profess
32 It flows near the Piazzale Michelangelo
33 Workplace where there are many openings
35 Sorento and Sedona
36 "Our Gang" approval
37 Plentiful
38 Song played at the school dance in "Back to the Future"
41 Kind of year: Abbr.
42 Chinese for "black dragon"
45 Officially
49 Schubert's "Eine kleine Trauermusik," e.g.
50 1996 Gwyneth Paltrow title role
51 River in a 1957 hit film
52 Warning to intruders
53 Young fish that has migrated from the Sargasso Sea
54 Rubble maker, for short
55 Some Windows systems

DOWN

1 Rent-___
2 Synagogues
3 Attacks
4 Cholesterol medication
5 Helper's offer
6 Sea menace
7 Certain pie toppers
8 Big bug
9 Fit
10 Thomas Moore's "___ Ask the Hour"
11 Eye, to poets
13 Some passport applicants
14 It's all the same
20 Something that's stamped
22 Green
24 Town on Lake Geneva opposite Lausanne, Switzerland
25 Too: Fr.
26 Hydroxyl compound
27 Setting for "Coriolanus"
28 One may be running over time
29 Headquarters for Polynesian Airlines
30 Schnapps flavor
31 Legal cases?
32 Judo maneuvers
34 Highlander
36 Song words accompanying "Sherrie" and "Susanna"
39 Nervous laugh
40 Enter an Ivy League school, maybe
41 Many a French business partner
42 "The Suze ___ Show"
43 Kind of situation
44 Award
45 Half-wit
46 Airing
47 Pre-___ (take the place of)
48 Pad
49 Ft. Myers-to-Orlando dir.

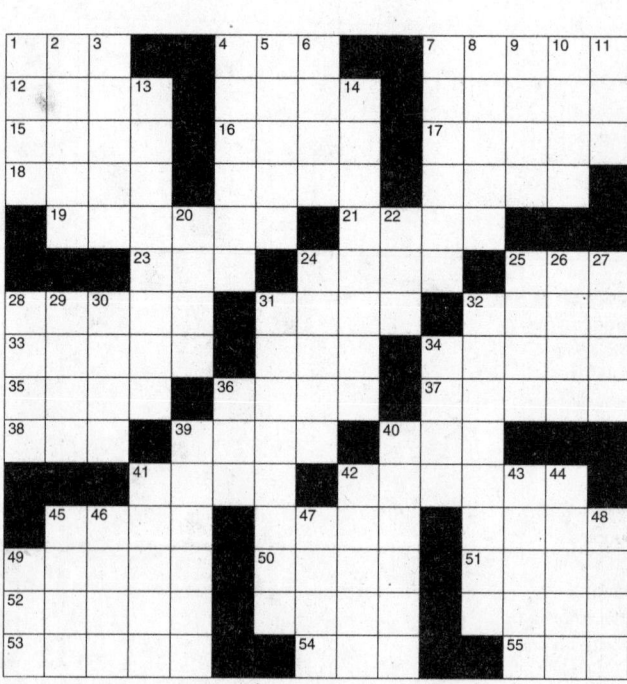

by Joe Krozel

ACROSS

1 Add a new article to, maybe
6 Sweat units
11 Prime meridian std.
14 Zellweger of "Leatherheads"
15 Not yet reached
16 Evergreen tree
17 Race energetically past?
19 What an athlete may turn
20 It sometimes depicts a dragon or tiger
21 Rides
23 Keys on the side of a keyboard
26 Last word of a January 1 song
27 Mozart's "___ Fan Tutte"
30 Yellow one
33 Todd who directed "I'm Not There," 2007
36 More bohemian
37 East ender?
38 Like King Solomon . . . or an oral hint to 17- and 62-Across and 11- and 29-Down
40 "___, verily"
43 Nonchalant
45 Adjusts to one's situation
47 Games involving picks
50 Sch. groups
51 River to the Mediterranean
52 Dust collector
55 Stonewall, say
58 Popular sandwich bag
61 Smoke detector batteries, often
62 Native African's musical beat?
66 "I said . . . out!"
67 Banana-loving zoo critter
68 "With this ring ___ wed"
69 What every inning has three of?
70 Native of India in the British army
71 They might get shingles

DOWN

1 Thin bark?
2 Soften
3 Grammy winner for "Amarantine"
4 Occupies, as bushes or trees
5 Sonar's measurement
6 Bribe
7 Photo blowup: Abbr.
8 Singer Winehouse
9 Red ink
10 Eyelid annoyance
11 Where an old wanderer is interred?
12 Sister of Venus
13 Like some short tennis matches
18 Louis XIV, e.g.
22 ". . . so long ___ both shall live?"
24 Fishing boat
25 Garment in Gujarat
27 2008 title role for Benicio Del Toro
28 Trireme propeller
29 What Romeo and Juliet had to do?
31 "___ date!"
32 Went kaput
34 Luxury
35 Arc on a music score
39 Made, as a wager
41 Sorority letter
42 Blockhead
44 Tiny bit
46 Try for a job at
47 "Gil Blas" novelist
48 Secure
49 Alignment of celestial bodies
53 Former space station
54 Biblical land with "ivory and apes and peacocks"
56 Debuts on Wall St.
57 Rochester's love
59 Roman emperor after Galba
60 Contestant on a Bravo reality show
63 Breach
64 6 on a phone
65 Enero, por ejemplo

by Julian Lim

ACROSS

1 Heebie-jeebies
8 They may have titles
14 Landing
15 Expensive way to the hospital
16 Enemy encounter
17 Unlikely section in a religious bookstore
18 Last word in "Oh! Susanna"
19 "The Glass Bead Game" novelist
21 Lead
22 High flier, once
23 Teacups, e.g.
24 Asks (for)
25 Bashes
26 Web ___
29 Bashes
32 Absolutely terrific
37 Japanese flower-arranging art
39 Selfish, as an attitude
40 Gets upset
42 Plundering opportunity
43 D-back or Card
44 Biscuit holder
45 Appearance of O or W
49 Locate, as Waldo
51 Narrow inlet
54 "Say ___"
55 See 11-Down
57 An Ivy
58 Pole position?
60 Unpopular ones
62 Congenital
63 Name-dropping, maybe
64 Stored compactly, in a way
65 See 57-Down

DOWN

1 10 superiors
2 Fetters
3 Citi Field mascot
4 See eye to eye
5 Gardner of "Mogambo"
6 His 1959 album "Heavenly" was #1 for five weeks
7 Set upon a slope, say
8 A Dumas
9 Hullabaloo
10 "See what I mean?"
11 Big brand of 55-Across
12 Something that might work on a full stomach?
13 Optical readings
15 "___ amis . . ." (start of a French oration)
20 Trig function
23 Cash in the music business
24 "Shut up already!"
25 Actress Olivia of "Law & Order: Criminal Intent"
27 Soupy Sales and others
28 Former Japanese P.M. Shinzo ___
29 Yankee fighter
30 Letters between two names
31 Yours may be asleep while you're awake
32 Fluster

33 Ali, the ___ of God
34 CBS newsman Bob
35 NATO founding member
36 Trough location
38 Goose egg
41 Once, once
44 Picadors assist him
45 Cry at a poker game, maybe
46 Title film character who's idolized by a boy named Joey
47 Some Balkanites
48 Full-length
50 Georges with the best seller "Life: A User's Manual"
51 Arise anew
52 Many a freshman course
53 Photographer Adams
55 Like eights in crazy eights
56 Don't just sit there

57 With 65-Across, extermination . . . or what can be done to 10 answers in this puzzle without affecting their clues?
59 Distinctive Dilbert feature
61 M.L.K. Day month

by Xan Vongsathorn

ACROSS

1 Pond film
5 Relaxed
11 Candy in a dispenser
14 Noted archbishop
15 Cigarette additive?
16 Like
17 Author of "The Sea, the Sea"
19 One likely to be taken in
20 Films have them
21 Harvard and Yale, e.g.
23 Internet address ending
24 Friction fighter
25 [It's chilly!]
28 Henry James heroine
34 Regretted
36 English facilities
37 Immune system agent
38 Playground retort
40 Mid sixth-century year
41 Morton who founded Morton's steakhouses
42 Latin stars
43 College in New Rochelle, N.Y.
45 Plains Indians
46 Noted mother of nine
49 Notations on some game scores
50 Unit of cultural information
51 Anatomical duct
53 Francis' home
56 Unsolved crime
61 Something you might jump for
62 Certain wedding participants . . . or a hint to 17-, 28- and 46-Across?
64 Massachusetts' Cape ___
65 Gretzky's team from 1979 to 1988
66 Dart
67 Marks (out)
68 Band aide
69 Jot

DOWN

1 ___-fry
2 Fix
3 Elec., e.g.
4 Paris's ___ d'Orsay
5 By tradition
6 Tucker (out)
7 What circles lack
8 From ___ Z
9 Pelvis part
10 Early trial presentation
11 "Qué ___?"
12 Airline whose meals are all kosher
13 Microwaves
18 Org. with a "Designate a Driver" program
22 Zipper alternative
24 Certain amino acid
25 Prickly shrub
26 Gibson's "Ransom" co-star, 1996
27 Flat rates?
29 First-aid item
30 Ancient lawgiver
31 Slowly
32 "Silas Marner" author
33 Like non-oyster months
35 Start of a musical series
39 Assumes to be
44 Opposed
47 James Bond antagonist ___ Largo
48 Masculine side
52 Film genre
53 Role in "Troy"
54 Loudness unit
55 Dict. offerings
56 Was in the red
57 Actress Gilpin of "Frasier"
58 Folkie Guthrie
59 Narrow cut
60 It is, in Peru
63 Suffix with Victr-

by Kevan Choset

ACROSS

1 Paris Hilton catchphrase
9 "The Country Girl" playwright
14 Be for, in an argument
15 Nazione di Napoli
16 Like a poison pen letter?
18 "The Office" unit
19 Prefix with -zoic
20 End of a quiz?
21 "Fly Me to the Moon" and others?
26 Abbr. on every original Beatles song
29 South Australia's ___ Bay
30 Prefix with political
31 Ham operator's "Hurrah!"?
35 They come and go
39 Huskies' home
40 Writer Chinua Achebe, by birth
41 Suffer ignominy
42 "Do ___!"
43 Yes-man's biography?
45 Not there, to 11-Down
47 Gold stds.
48 Host of the 1970 and 1986 World Cup: Abbr.
49 Like a superlatively sneaky sleuth?
55 Sumac from Peru
56 Silk: Fr.
57 Not having gone pro?
61 TV movie interruption . . . or feature of 16-, 21-, 31-, 43- and 49-Across?
66 Garden structures
67 Time on the Enterprise
68 "___ Hope," long-running ABC soap
69 Black gold

DOWN

1 Ukase issuer
2 Obscure
3 Recipe direction starter
4 Contract fine print
5 Host of the 1912 Olympics: Abbr.
6 Bill Haley and ___ Comets
7 They may follow last periods, for short
8 This puzzle's is revealed at 61-Across
9 He played Lord Jim in "Lord Jim"
10 ___ Terr., 1861–89
11 Henry's pupil
12 Put on, as a roof, maybe
13 ___ slip
15 "We're on"
17 Miss out?
22 Drudge
23 U.N. figure: Abbr.
24 Tchotchke
25 Like some yogurt, informally
26 Fabergé cologne
27 It might come with the mail
28 Kelly Clarkson, once
32 Sound, say
33 Litigators' grp.
34 Ingredient in a salty dog
36 Volume 1 of a two-volume encyclopedia?
37 Not just serious
38 Hit 1970s–'90s band with a mythological name
41 "Happy Motoring" sloganeer
43 The Three ___
44 Pay stub abbr.
46 Stage equipment
49 One way to go
50 American university where Desmond Tutu taught theology
51 Bossa nova kin
52 [That's what it says]
53 Job in "Ocean's Eleven"
54 Little Orphan Annie and others
58 Swell
59 Thames gallery
60 Retail giant from 5-Down
62 Jamaican fellow
63 Ingested
64 Loose
65 Supporter, of sorts

by Caleb Madison and J.A.S.A. Crossword Class

ACROSS

1 Stingy
5 Phrenologists read them
10 Not shut all the way
14 What to call a crown
15 Chris with the 1991 hit "Wicked Game"
16 Common mixer
17 Roofless home
18 It creates a small vacuum
20 Personal account
21 "Now I see!"
22 Art buyers' worries
23 Parts of double-blind trials
28 Baby sitter's bane
29 Where flocks feed
30 Word unlikely to end a sentence
33 Sauce prepared in a mortar
36 Daughter of Laban, in the Bible
37 1856 Stowe novel
38 Aspirant's motto . . . or, phonetically, what 18-, 23-, 47- and 57-Across each consist of
41 Clancy hero
42 Gives succor to
43 Clear, as a loan
44 Salt
45 Contralto James
46 Elusive swimmer
47 What national banks oversee
53 Not too ___
55 Tapped-out message, often
56 Reach the end
57 Chinese menu option
61 Show-off's shout
62 "The Gong Show" regular Johnson
63 It can be worth up to 20 points
64 "Pardon me"
65 Unappreciated worker
66 Seize, to Caesar
67 Like the "Saw" movies

DOWN

1 Rachel Maddow's network
2 Children's song refrain
3 Flame blame, sometimes
4 Post-tax amount
5 King's neighbor
6 Fully expected
7 OS X runner
8 Too rehearsed
9 Perform a wedeln, e.g.
10 No problem at all
11 Guy's means of support
12 Literally, "by two"
13 They often include samples
19 "The Sum ___" (Russell Crowe movie)
21 Hard wear?
24 Nashville-based athlete
25 Actresses Farrell and Jackson
26 Goes from cover to cover
27 Kailua Bay's setting
31 Vengeful goddess
32 Swirl
33 Left to the captain?
34 Popular singer born in County Donegal
35 Overrun
36 Body that's not the clergy
37 Harp (on)
39 Fruit growing at an oasis
40 Gets ready
45 Opposite of exo-
46 Heroic poem
48 Frequently
49 Take over
50 Western potato
51 Large duck
52 Run-down
53 Cash-free transaction
54 Modeled
58 Grp. that meets in the Situation Room
59 Upscale hotel offering
60 Boathouse item
61 Cry before "You're it!"

by Trip Payne

ACROSS

1 "Don't take offense at that"
9 Was free
13 Some fairly difficult odds
14 1983 Gary Busey comedy
16 Major role in "Troy"
17 Performer in a seven-million-gallon tank
18 Affirmations to pitchers
19 Univ. helpers
21 Dustup
22 Stick on a pub wall
23 Put off till tomorrow, say
27 It may have a big mouth
28 Since Jan. 1
29 Ballad's end?
30 "We shun it ___ it comes": Emily Dickinson
31 It's not to be believed
32 Microscope part
34 Wide of the mark
36 What this puzzle's theme does?
38 Occurring relatively soon
40 Haven
41 Brevipennate bird
42 Cat on the prowl
44 British character in "Zorro"
45 1992 hit "Life ___ Highway"
48 Struck (out)
49 Hardly fops
51 Lambert Airport's home: Abbr.
52 Speaker in the Hall of Fame
54 What might charge a going rate?
55 Brand at a checkout counter that's also the name of a Phoenix radio station
56 Seven-footers' jeans sizes, say
58 Green mold in the fridge
62 Pueblo pottery
63 "Seinfeld" co-star
64 Loan lure, maybe
65 Daring person's cry

DOWN

1 Eat an entire cake, say
2 Sidestepped
3 Bedtime phenomena
4 Véronique, for one: Abbr.
5 ___-pah band
6 Vote in Vichy
7 Make ___ of
8 Delaware tribe
9 Alternatives to downloads
10 Newspaper publisher Arthur ___ Sulzberger
11 Shoulder blades
12 Rain forest monkey
13 Free of bells and whistles
15 "Swish!"
20 Author of the 1965 biography "Kennedy"
23 Disney's dwarfs and others
24 "It's game time . . . !"
25 ___ the Midget, regular on "The Howard Stern Show"
26 50 mythical sea nymphs
32 Sinclair Lewis novel "___ Mr. Wrenn"
33 Corp. manager of day-to-day affairs
35 Things with xings
36 Authoritarian Spanish leader
37 Bulldoze
38 A nominal fee
39 Ring rock
43 Dough
45 Tristan's love
46 Opera house attire
47 Betting option
50 Wedding dress fabric
53 Part of many a KFC order
55 Numbers game
57 Application datum: Abbr.
59 On a map it may be colored bleu
60 Program file extension
61 XK or XKE, for short

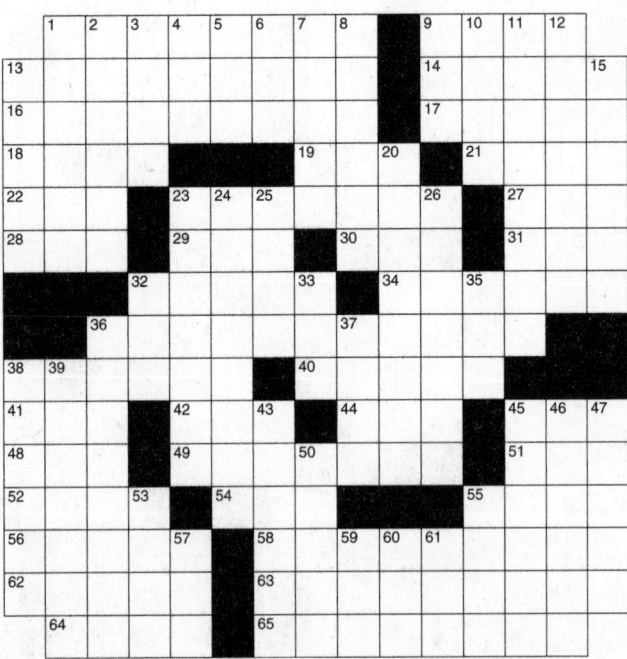

by Elizabeth C. Gorski

ACROSS

1 Intimate inn, familiarly
6 Actor David of "Rhoda"
10 Common rhyme scheme
14 Cara of "Fame" fame
15 "Damn Yankees" woman who gets what she wants
16 Mug spray?
17 What helps pay the governor's salary in Austin?
19 Suffix with convert
20 Mother's urging at the dinner table
21 Like some sums
22 Pay
24 "It's a ___"
25 Hudson and LaSalle, once
26 Try to telephone some snowbirds?
31 Monopoly purchases
32 Modern addresses, for short
33 Broadway play about Capote
34 Major in astronomy?
35 Calendario span
36 "Put ___ writing"
37 Back of a soccer goal
38 Con
40 Whimsical roll-call response
42 Be familiar with a city near White Plains?
45 Be grandiloquent
46 Journalist Paula
47 Deli offering
49 Explore Yosemite, perhaps
50 Pickle
53 It may be sprung
54 Some film work Down East?
57 Rebuke from Caesar

58 Vogue competitor
59 Unthinking servant
60 Have a bawl
61 Hollywood constructions
62 Journeys

DOWN

1 Fall for something
2 Figure in geometry
3 On deck
4 Kind of sample
5 "Hush!"
6 "My pleasure!"
7 Classic theater name
8 Corrida cheer
9 Knows people, say
10 Key of Beethoven's "Für Elise"
11 Occasional role for a 30-Down, maybe
12 Rights grp.

13 Audible warning on the road
18 Spats
23 Platte River people
24 Earth goddess
25 Retro hairstyle
26 Quiz show scandal figure Charles Van ___
27 "You had your chance"
28 Unpleasant encounter
29 Have trouble passing the bar?
30 Family member
31 Playgirl calendar type
35 Perfectly, after "to"
36 Airs
38 Composer Khachaturian
39 Daily since 1851, briefly

40 "Are you ___?"
41 From memory
43 Finish
44 Online reads
47 Worry (over)
48 "Laugh-In" comedian Johnson
49 Sword handle
50 Agree
51 Wild
52 Team Gil Hodges both played for and managed
55 Bass, for one
56 Neither's partner

by Alan Arbesfeld

244 MEDIUM

ACROSS

1 Lounging sites in lounges
6 Chocolat au ___
10 Pump, in a way
14 Hatch at a hearing
15 The Mountain of Fire, to 23-Acrosses
16 "Come ___ these yellow sands, / And then take hands": Ariel in "The Tempest"
17 Scalding castle weapon
19 Gas brand that's also an Italian pronoun
20 Former Saturn
21 En ___ (on tiptoe)
22 Prefinal game
23 Person of olden times
25 Like stocks and reference books
27 About
28 Four-bagger
29 Spinal parts
31 Airs
35 It's not Occidental
36 Coarse-woven cloth
37 Influence
38 Not direct at all, as gossip
40 Follows
41 Square, maybe
42 Source of many a bead
43 Like a crucifix
46 Not normal, as a gene
49 A gun, slangily
50 Chooses
52 Follower of harvard. or yale.
53 ___-food industry
54 What 17-Across and 10- and 24-Down all conceal
56 ___-Aryan
57 "The Dark at the Top of the Stairs" playwright
58 ___ a time

59 Foreshadowing
60 Villain
61 Bathhouse wear

DOWN

1 Queen of Spain's Juan Carlos I
2 Acrylic fiber
3 The last Holy Roman emperor
4 Marksman's skill
5 Some marksmen
6 Kosher
7 Lots
8 Approved, in a way
9 Having star potential
10 Resigned response to tragedy
11 Emasculate, say
12 Response to "Who's there?"
13 Animal-like
18 What the "poor dog" had in "Old Mother Hubbard"
24 A pharaoh vis-à-vis Horus, in Egyptian myth
26 Advent mo.
28 Size two, say
29 "What's up wit ___?"
30 Suffix with freak
31 Talking silly
32 It may help close the deal
33 Wee bit
34 M.O.
36 "Star Wars" droid, informally
39 Passbook abbr.
40 Real somebody
42 Not go for a drive?
43 1894 opera set in Egypt
44 59-Acrosses, in Italian
45 Head of government?
46 Lonette of "The Cotton Club" and "Malcolm X"
47 Mitchell of Apollo 14
48 Common nickname for a cowpoke
51 Hwy. planner
55 Suffix with mescal

by Raymond C. Young

ACROSS

1 Infamous motel of film
6 Son of Seth
10 Dual-___ engine
14 "___ Jubilee," weekly 1950s country music program on ABC
15 Serenader's subject
16 Baseball family name
17 Amish conveyance
18 ___ fixe
19 Main point
20 Parental order #1
23 "Darn tootin'!"
24 Inauguration Day words
25 Rte. 66, e.g.
26 Co. split off from Time Warner in 2009
27 Dr. with several Grammys
28 Actress Benaderet of "Petticoat Junction"
31 Parental order #2
36 Stallion-to-be
37 Sculler's need
38 ___ of lamb
39 Parental order #3
44 Place for a mudbath
45 Seasoning for pommes frites
46 Hubbub
47 Govt. investigation
48 Rapper with the #1 hit "Empire State of Mind"
50 Put on
53 Reply to the question in 13- and 57-Down
57 "___ #1!"
58 Emphatic type: Abbr.
59 Wheel on a spur
60 "Flower power" musical
61 Newcastle upon ___, England
62 One of a Disney septet
63 Big laughs
64 Marked, in a way
65 Ranee's wrap

DOWN

1 Coventry cop
2 Fair-weather hue
3 Touch base after a fly-out
4 Joule fractions
5 Abdul-Jabbar's trademark shot
6 Silas Marner's creator
7 Slangy "That's obvious!"
8 ___ easy
9 Like a sheer nightie
10 Cautious, as a reply
11 Touched down
12 ___ Hashanah
13 With 57-Down, possible response to 20-, 31- or 39-Across
21 River to Korea Bay
22 Vessel by a basin
26 Part of a Spanish play
27 All-nighter site, perhaps
28 Wild tusker
29 Flemish painter Jan van ___
30 "Fire away!"
31 Inside dope
32 Kovalchuk of the N.H.L.
33 Science fiction writer Frederik
34 7'6" N.B.A. star
35 1982 Disney cybermovie
36 Some Amazon.com mdse.
40 Alma mater for Adm. Richard Byrd: Abbr.
41 Give in return
42 "Slow Churned" brand
43 Some Hogwarts students
47 Patisserie artisans
48 Astrologer Dixon
49 Was green around the gills
50 Exchange of TV smears, maybe
51 River of Grenoble
52 John who loved Pocahontas
53 Steady guy
54 Estrada of "CHiPs"
55 Charon's river
56 Where James T. Kirk was born and raised
57 See 13-Down

by Kristian House

ACROSS

1 Launch time?
9 Found to be legal, in a way
15 Voicer of Underdog on TV
16 Voicer of Ego in "Ratatouille"
17 Children's song that's based on an old work song melody
18 Like many countries' rulers
19 The unwashed
20 She hid Zeus from Cronus
22 Suffix with señor
23 Generic addressees
24 Chilly shower setting?
27 Kind of milk
28 Set upon
29 "King Richard II" lord
30 Subject of a museum in eastern Colorado
31 Is no longer
33 Without any embroidery
35 Passes out slowly
39 Misanthrope who says "We are all born mad. Some remain so"
45 In ___ (embryonic)
46 Alternative to being tapped
49 It might make drinkers blush
50 Convention lengthener?
51 Great ape?
53 It often goes out with a bang
54 "I think," briefly
55 Literally, "barley"
56 They're no rain-makers
57 Many a khan
59 Wheatworm, e.g.

62 Crate
63 Chemist's relatives?
64 Thought
65 Other side

DOWN

1 Exchanges
2 Ease
3 Winner of gold in four consecutive Olympics, 1956–68
4 Set for juggling
5 They're seen on both sides of bridges
6 More than talk
7 Confounded
8 Like effort and influence
9 Wakes
10 Superior group
11 Gobbledygook
12 Tasty triangle
13 Superior groups

14 They might provide coverage for racecars
21 Track meet event
24 Coll. acquisitions
25 Mediterranean or Baltic: Abbr.
26 Kind of pie or cake
28 They can be saturated
32 Really thin
34 Biblical 912-year-old
36 Spinning device giving the illusion of motion
37 Principal player in "Grease"
38 Superlatively sad
40 Spun
41 Brand of munchables
42 Composer Vivaldi
43 Do stuff

44 Part of the underground economy?
46 Ready
47 She had a 1959 hit with "I Loves You, Porgy"
48 Wall fixture
52 Laissez-faire
53 Keep hush-hush
56 Foe of Caesar
58 What a floozy might show off
60 Picking up power?
61 Job for a barber

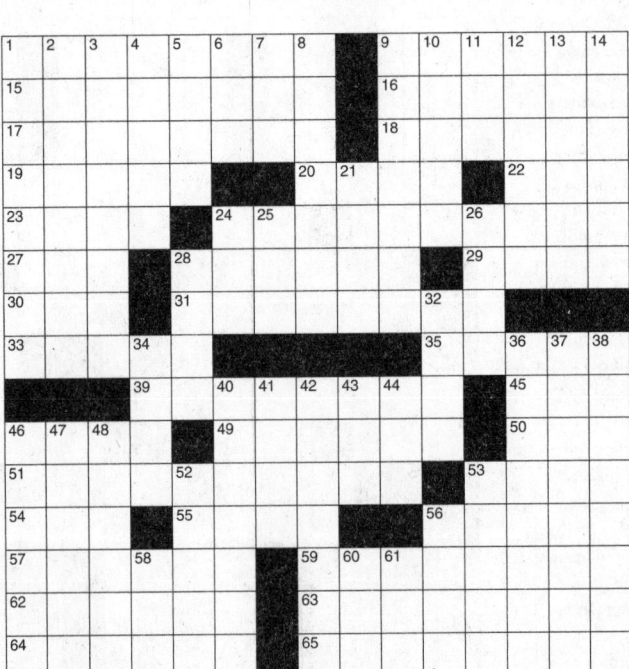

by Jeffrey Wechsler

ACROSS

1 Deer ___
5 Lush performance setting?
15 One with a neck, mouth and lip, but no eyes
16 First names
17 Utility bill datum
18 "Dream on!"
19 Walt Disney's record collection
21 Sticker of the past
22 Kind of synthesis
23 Transkei native
24 Get through dull work
25 Source of some extracts
26 Classic film featuring Captain America
28 Bank security feature
29 Target of a 1972 ban in the U.S.
30 Info from some captains
31 Imitate
32 Ancient Egyptians revered it
33 It may be spinning
34 Is part of the cast of
37 Historic French region
38 One with uma auréola
41 Indication to put something in
42 Risky funding source
44 Lead
45 Addition to the 33-Across
46 Foxes' neighbors, once
47 ___ Fresnos, Tex.
48 Pike lookalikes
49 Riot
50 He fell in love with a fire hydrant on "Sesame Street"
53 Home to some notable cast-iron architecture in N.Y.C.
54 "Seems possible"
55 French singer/actor Rossi
56 Opposite of duck
57 Indication to leave something in

DOWN

1 Duped
2 Cry after being duped
3 It's lowered by 14-Down
4 Flattering to a fault
5 Home of McConnell A.F.B.
6 Trouble
7 Scraps in the sticks
8 "Für Elise" setting
9 Like a galley
10 Often-replaced part
11 City near Arnhem
12 Support for cold feet?
13 Fictional Prince Edward Island community
14 Some incentives
20 Dish that often includes ale
24 Droids, e.g.
25 Go well (with)
27 Rub ___
28 Explodes
31 Nuisance
32 "The fog has lifted"
33 Shooting goal
34 Strong approval
35 ___-conscious
36 Words to a doubter
37 Forwent modesty
38 Followed through on something
39 Weaver of myth
40 "I'm ready for your questions"
42 Ochoa who won the 2007 Women's British Open
43 Pulls up
45 Maugham's prostitute
48 Van ___ (oil producer)
49 In a day, say
51 Kind of hay
52 ___ pardo (grizzly, in Granada)

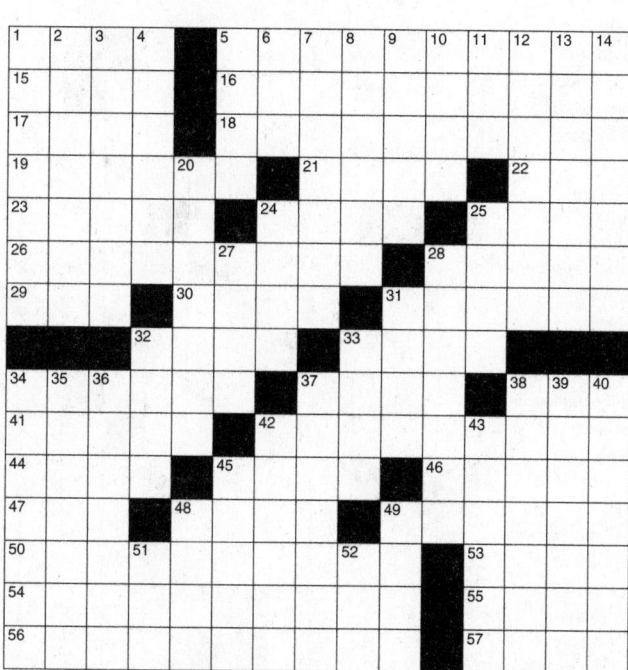

by Frederick J. Healy

ACROSS

1 It uses liquid from a pitcher
9 Cloud maker
14 Resolve a longstanding disagreement
16 ___ 8
17 Political entity of 1854–1900
19 Tree-defoliating insect
20 Tries to ensure a hit
21 One with big hips, maybe
22 Bounces
25 They're thrown in anger
29 What keeps a camera rolling?
30 Old English recorder
31 Day break
32 Pirate's hiding place, possibly
33 "Poor Richard's Almanack" tidbit
34 Maintenance
35 Roadbed inset
36 Like the ancient Greeks
37 "Beyond the Sea" singer
38 Ones offering pass protection?
40 Designated
41 Membership list
42 Jazz trumpeter Baker
43 Largest land animal
50 Popular June program?
51 Mid 19th-century president
52 Site of Goodfellow Air Force Base
53 Spheres
54 1950s million-selling song that begins "The evening breeze caressed the trees . . ."

DOWN

1 Chance to win
2 Shave
3 Tolstoy character ___ Ilyich
4 Arm of the sea?
5 Typical of urban life
6 Special Forces units
7 Artists' stories, maybe
8 It's at the end of the line
9 Hockey stat
10 Role in a drawing-room mystery
11 Flame Queen ___ (famous gemstone)
12 Having multiple layers of self-reference
13 Southern contraction
15 Swampland swimmer
18 Rob Roy or Shirley Temple
22 Cuts a line, say
23 Animated girl-group leader
24 Actress Corby who played Grandma Walton
25 Short-lived republic founded in 1836
26 Take a piece from
27 Madame Tussaud's first name
28 Devote
30 Elaborate spectacles
33 Cocktail often made with pineapple juice
34 Queen Dido's home
36 Handle, as paperwork
37 Where one may take the plunge?
39 Game show fodder
40 Oedipus, for one
42 Copy
43 Alan who won an Emmy for his role on "The West Wing"
44 "That little darkroom where negatives are developed," per Michael Pritchard
45 Major party
46 Conseil d'___ (French government body)
47 Make known
48 "Little" Dickens character
49 Where Patroclus met his end

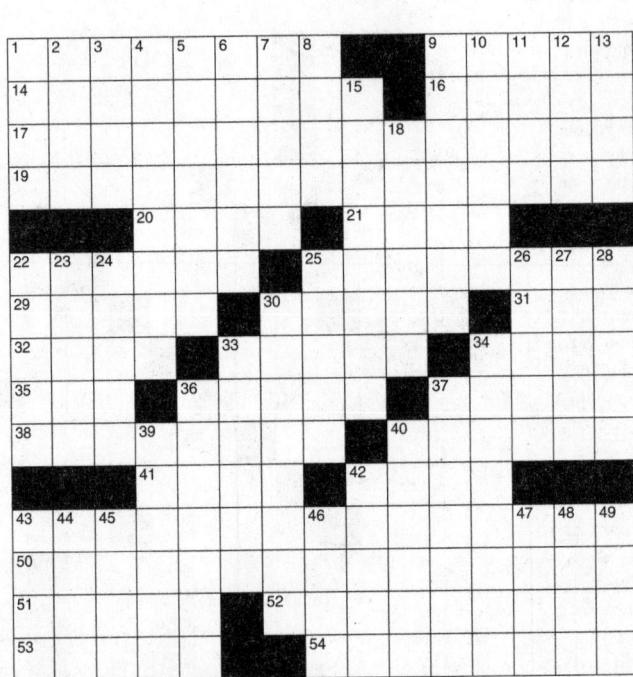

by Patrick Berry

ACROSS

1 Service with many followers
8 Kettles, e.g.
15 Hair-raising stuff?
16 Where it never rains
17 With 53-Across, classic Kipling poem ending
19 Plane wing component
20 Pro team with a horseshoe logo
21 Many trial subjects
22 ___ penny (very common, in British lingo)
23 "White Writing" painter Mark
24 Penny ___
25 Quagmire
27 Unit of fun?
28 Challah form
29 Fresh
31 Attempt to enter dead space?
32 Kind of identity
36 Like many gems
37 Gershwin's first hit
38 "Ewww!"
39 Curve creators
40 Tangier location: Abbr.
41 East Coast city where tourism peaks in October
46 "___ Is Betta Than Evvah!" (1976 album)
47 Creamer who won the 2010 U.S. Women's Open
49 In case
50 Duke's setting: Abbr.
51 Talk, talk, talk
52 Barneys rival
53 See 17-Across
56 Small, simple flute
57 Casanova's first name
58 At the movies, say
59 "Without further ado . . ."

DOWN

1 Getaways that people try to get away with
2 Like some 8-Downs
3 Creature in a Tennessee Williams title
4 Dental concern
5 Potential play prolonger
6 Put into 13-Down
7 Started over, in a way
8 One deserving a hand?
9 Apprehensive
10 Suffix with grape
11 Field work that was award-winning
12 Ruling
13 The way things are done
14 One way to take drugs
18 Brachium's end
26 Wings, e.g.
28 St. Pauli Girl alternative
30 It's between Obama and Robinson
31 Holder of eggs
32 Give a thumbs-up
33 Activate, in a way
34 Orange neighbor
35 Scored due to an error
36 Leave
38 Y.M.C.A. section?
40 River through Toledo
42 Strasbourg is its capital
43 Bait
44 Like the language Kalaallisut
45 Vt. ski resort
47 Big name in aircraft engines
48 Miss Hannigan's charge, on Broadway
54 Spanish name suffix
55 Alligator ___ (underwater menace)

by Gary Cee

ACROSS

1 Cause of a paradigm shift
12 Prepare for pain
14 It takes a lot to get one upset
16 Stadium support?
17 Antiquity's antithesis
18 "Vox populi, vox ___"
19 Disney animator Johnston who received the National Medal of Arts
21 Civil Rights Memorial designer
22 Like some milk
24 ___ Bonn Airport
25 One of a sailing trio
27 25-Across part
28 Opting not to strike out?
30 German/Polish border river
32 24-Across article
33 Smithereens
34 Longtime guitar brand
37 "I'm with you"
41 Little belts
42 Have ___ on (monitor officially)
44 Plane figures?
45 Philosopher Kierkegaard
47 She, in São Paulo
48 Unpolished
49 Grp. with a "decent work" agenda
50 They often get incorporated into the body
53 Follower of many a mineralogist's name
54 Tendency to overcompensate for a perceived shortcoming
57 Hunter with rough hair
58 Spoke up with one's head down?

DOWN

1 2007 Disney princess
2 Fig. at the bar
3 ___ Liebe (Dear, in Dresden)
4 To be overseas
5 Waiters in a mess
6 "World of Magic" Emmy nominee
7 Without
8 Party bowlful
9 Brief explanation
10 The Liberty Tree, for one
11 Gears up
12 X-box setting?
13 Immune system circulators
14 Doctors
15 Words that'll get you carded?
20 Extreme
23 High-tech scam artist
25 Singer with a short-lived 1950s sitcom
26 Manga set in motion
29 Image on some joke T-shirts
31 When French fans circulate?
33 Gymnast, often
34 Not righteously
35 Place for cultural studies?
36 Regarding
37 "Psycho" feature
38 Site-specific merchant?
39 Scan lines on a monitor
40 New Jersey county whose seat is Newark
43 Accessory for Sinatra
46 Actress Nita who never made a talkie
48 Prius alternative
51 Owning evidence
52 Pseudonym of a noted Freud patient
55 3,600 secondi
56 Amount to be divided

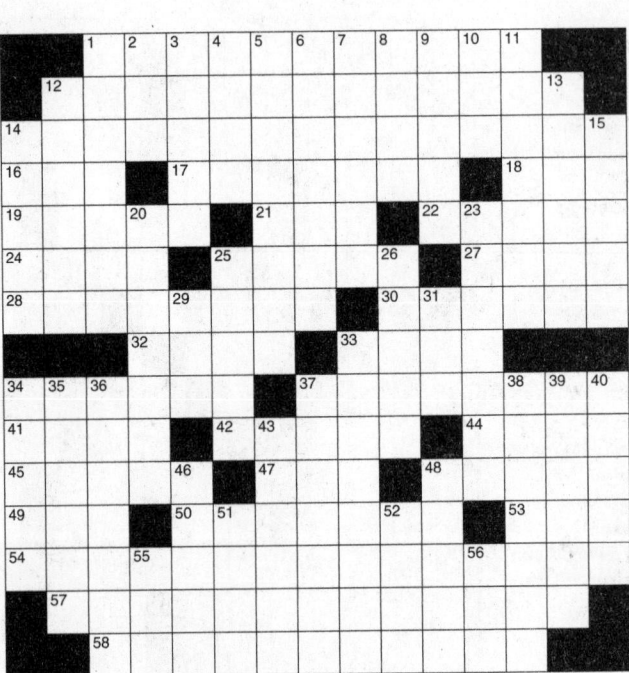

by Paula Gamache

ACROSS

1 Outclass one's peers?
11 Round bodies
15 Stressed
16 Nutty stuff
17 Providing relief, but not a cure
18 Retreat
19 Flooring specialist?
20 Poetic work with an account of Ragnarok
21 Right on
22 "The Franchise Affair" novelist
23 It's about 5 mL
26 Pushover
28 Numbskull
29 "Too rich for my blood"
31 1,000,000,000 years
32 Fox Sports reporter Andrews
33 See 7-Down
36 Like some insurance
38 Not at all loose
39 Scottish doctor/ explorer John
41 Teresa's home
42 "Pushover" singer James
43 Straight out of the dryer, perhaps
46 Sop for aloo palak
47 Cost-of-living no.
48 Norman __, coach in "Hoosiers"
49 It goes from one vessel to another
51 One in 100
57 Bar closing?
58 City on the Ohio
59 __ incline
60 "Snow-Bound" setting
61 Creatures with electrocytes
62 Spots

DOWN

1 Takes night courses?
2 Chip, as flint, in Britain
3 Baseless
4 Athlete nicknamed "O Rei"
5 Desiccated
6 "My pleasure"
7 With 33-Across, confirmation, e.g.
8 Live
9 Religious observance
10 Its entrance was barred with a flaming sword
11 Give the twice-over?
12 Ceaseless drinking or gambling, say
13 Certain control freak
14 Artificial alternative to the sun

23 1811 battle site
24 Android runner, e.g.
25 Like rankings
26 Stop: Abbr.
27 Generative music pioneer
28 Wally's bro
30 Sch. whose alumni constitute the Long Gray Line
34 [I'm not happy about this]
35 Brandy
37 Elfin
40 Issuing forth
44 Largely green kingdom
45 Show
50 Impulses
51 Works on one's jumper, say
52 "Lift __ Voice and Sing" (old hymn)

53 Group of pages
54 Home of the ancient Olympic games
55 Author/architect Buzzi
56 Romeo or Juliet

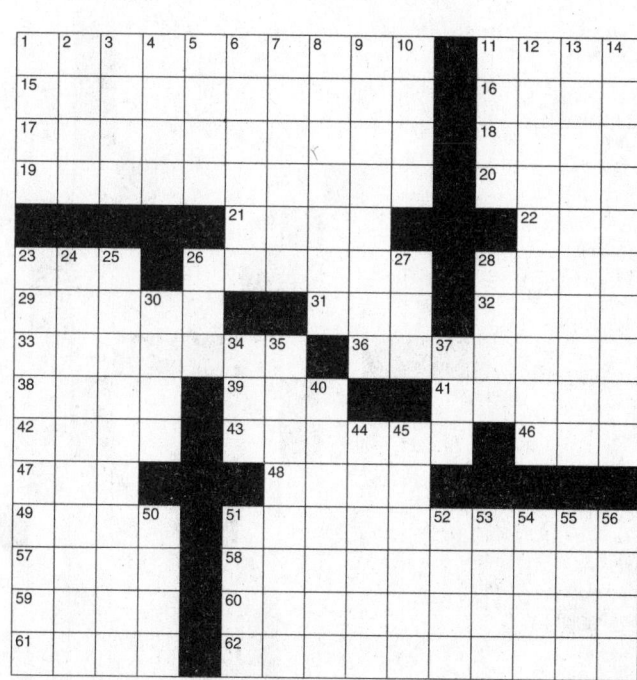

by Joon Pahk

ACROSS

1 "Try not to stand out"
10 Call ___ to (stop)
15 Words after an insult
16 Jason who directed 2011's "Arthur"
17 Beatles song with a complaining title
18 Utah State athlete
19 I. M. Pei's alma mater, for short
20 War hero who killed himself with a onetime rival's sword
21 Rapid descent on skis
22 Hail ___
24 Unrestricted music plan
26 Burdened
28 French waters
29 "Bloody"
30 Ticket
31 Honorary deg. for many a writer
32 They're found in rock bands
33 End of a flick?
35 Letters at the beach
37 Absorbed
40 "Here comes trouble!"
44 Some stars
48 Plot segment
49 Tons of
50 Cover
51 Words accompanying an arrow
54 Kind of twin
55 Like some glasses
56 Professor 'iggins
58 Gray
59 Admit
60 Prepared
62 Levels
63 "Told you so!"
64 Suit material
65 Remedy for a tizzy

DOWN

1 Some cracker shapes
2 Wacky
3 Fiesta food item
4 $$$ head
5 Old Spice rival
6 Conductor Ozawa
7 Like a first-time tournament player, usually
8 Type of reproduction
9 Was up
10 ___ plane
11 Very recognizable
12 Bony, as a face
13 Work's opposite
14 Locks
21 Titillating transmissions
23 One stage of development
25 Rapa ___ (Easter Island)
27 "Der Ring ___ Nibelungen"
34 Moist
36 Smartphone, e.g., for short
37 Discombobulates
38 Carry out
39 Press user
41 Cheated
42 Rule for free samples
43 Sonata maker
45 Composer known as the Red Priest
46 First name of two first ladies
47 Calf part
52 Detect
53 Old "Go from flat to fluffy" sloganeer
57 Term of address in the South
60 Open ___
61 Fire

by Milo Beckman

ACROSS

1 Adroitness
5 22-Across product
10 English Leather alternative
14 Interjections from the obtuse
15 Searches for signs in a hospital
16 Queen with a degree from Princeton
17 ___-Z
18 Its shadow is often cast
19 Decoration
20 "Gnarly waves, dude!"
22 Pabst brand
23 Foil
24 Like some exchange rates
26 Less like nuts?
27 Where to get a citation while surfing
28 Like two Kennedy brothers
30 Portions
31 Hang-up
34 Watt-hour fraction
35 Small team
36 You might get a charge out of it
37 Secure the aid of
39 They're lined up on a neck
41 Kind of test associated with the null hypothesis
43 Practice with the Wheel of the Year
47 27-Across, e.g.
48 Wet behind the ears
49 Directive obeyed by Alice
50 City where "Smokey and the Bandit" begins
52 Fit to finish?
53 Like many dreamers

54 Pap's son, in literature
55 La., e.g., once
56 Like la nuit
57 Scored together?
58 Brand that has Dibs
59 Former telecom giant headquartered in Denver
60 Fork-tailed flier

DOWN

1 Subjects are expected to follow them
2 Polar region phenomenon
3 Greet and seat
4 Things some cons are pros at
5 Preceded, with "to"
6 Impulse carrier
7 Van Gogh threatened him with a razor blade
8 Keep from spilling over, in a way
9 U leaders?
10 St. John's is its capital
11 Like some conclusions
12 Grooming routine
13 Missiles may be delivered in one
21 Tom Stoppard's "Travesties," e.g.
22 Chief Sassacus led one side in it
25 Nettle
27 Easily changeable locks
29 Pianist Schnabel
31 Play
32 Like many swimming pools
33 Severely sunburned, say
35 Producer for 50 Cent, familiarly

38 Atomically related compounds
39 Prize in Cracker Jacks, e.g.
40 Part of morning dress
42 Ad imperative
44 Rains in a studio
45 Go along (with)
46 Arouse
48 Massachusetts Maritime Academy student, e.g.
51 MTV generation
53 It may be judicial: Abbr.

by Barry C. Silk

ACROSS

1 It often contains "lies"
8 Person making a cameo, say
15 Start of a big 1975 sports event?
16 Tending to bring together
17 Florida's ___ Park Race Track
18 Some photography equipment
19 Priest at Shiloh
20 Genetic stuff
21 It may be pinched
22 "Do Ya" band, for short
23 Winthrop's affliction in "The Music Man"
25 One taking orders
27 Title girl in a 1990s–2000s MTV cartoon
29 Fishing tool
31 Like many blog comments, informally
33 One of eight in chess
34 2008 World Series athlete
36 Cousins of blackbirds
38 Pro-Church of England position
40 Creamlike paint shade
42 French article
43 ___ land
44 Aforementioned
46 "A little ___ do ya" (1950s–'60s slogan)
50 London borough with Wembley Stadium
52 'Vette option
54 Tart plum
55 Eastern band
56 Big East Conf. member
58 1-Across accompanier
60 Mama grizzly, south of the border
61 Crazy Horse, e.g.
63 Causes to take hold
65 Chanel fragrance "pour homme"
66 Astronaut's favorite dessert?
67 Indicates
68 Overruns

DOWN

1 Rosenberg and Roosevelt
2 An apostle
3 Declaration at a poker table
4 The Everly Brothers' "(___) I Kissed You"
5 34-Across, e.g., for short
6 Alternative fallback position
7 "You think you're so funny!"
8 Popular hair care product
9 Prefix with -derm
10 Hyper
11 Normandy was in it: Abbr.
12 What's not right?
13 Story from Joyce's "Dubliners"
14 Wets again
24 Like some politics
26 Class with Browning and Golding, say
28 Home of the 42nd U.S. president
30 Salad tidbit
32 Kind of chart
35 Ja and da
37 Squalled
38 Structural piece bent 90° along its long dimension
39 Sheet music notations
40 Jostled
41 Claptrap
45 Moolah
47 Hardly line drives
48 Went bonkers
49 Papers on pads?
51 Plot element
53 New Mexico's state tree
57 Yea or nay
59 Classy sort?
62 2016 Olympics host
64 "___ moment"

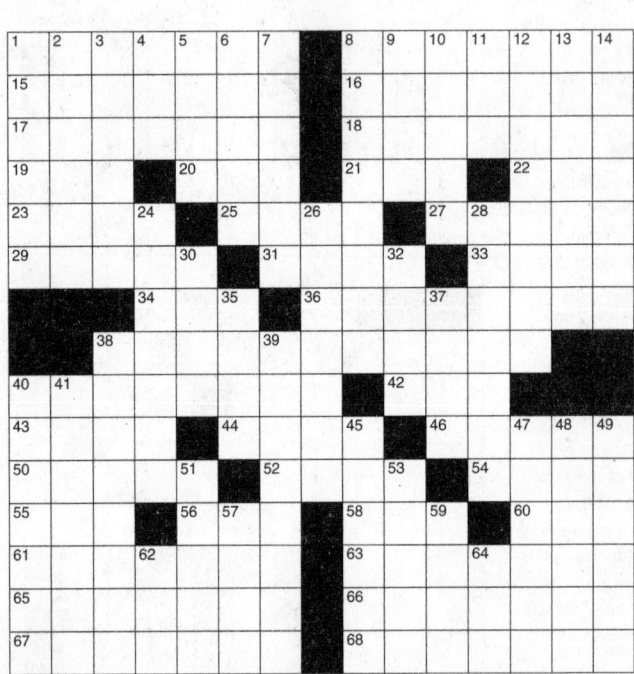

by Chris A. McGlothlin

ACROSS

1 Makeshift mask
9 Old Navy's owner
15 Lingua di Livorno
16 Ford from long ago
17 Home of minor-league baseball's Sea Dogs
18 23-Across representing a user
19 Join
20 Rte. through 17-Across
22 It may be groove-billed
23 Desktop item
24 "Mama's Special Garden" brand
25 Old Maltese money
27 March Madness souvenir
28 Literature's Dolores Haze, familiarly
30 Most arias
31 38-Down, to a 14-Down
32 Drive in N.Y.C.
33 What may appear after washing or baking
34 Oppose authority
39 Reaction to bad news
40 Giant rival, briefly
41 Tag for some grandchildren
42 Kept in
43 Patrol boats patrol them
45 Stat on some guns
48 Casino winner, often
50 Man ___
51 Driver's alert
52 Like "Spring" from Vivaldi's "The Four Seasons"
53 Use as a crash site?
55 Where Paul and Silas were sent, in Acts
56 Stage name of entertainer David Adkins

58 Stage name of entertainer Stanley Burrell
60 Yet
61 Chemistry Web site?
62 Faulkner family name
63 "Don't believe it for a second"

DOWN

1 Supply, as elevator music
2 Straightaway
3 Ape
4 Singer at Diana's funeral
5 Streamlet
6 Cry of shear fear?
7 Tomato or pea, e.g.
8 Don Juan's self-description
9 Bootlegger's bugbear
10 Dumpy dwelling
11 Writer LeShan
12 Cry to the overly amorous
13 "The Four Seasons" director
14 Métro area resident
21 One-up
24 Violinists' cake ingredients
26 Some nonnative Hawaiians
28 Coin whose original portrait was Alexander the Great
29 More affected
31 Most Prestwick Airport patrons
34 Fallacious reasoners
35 It has unbelievable news
36 Part of many a smear campaign
37 Kings Beach sits on it

38 Embroidered word, at times
44 Vaquero's charge
45 Young follower
46 Runs a bill through
47 Cry for attention
49 Really pick up
51 Bonne ___ (cooked simply)
54 13th, at times
55 Spots for shots
57 Like Bill Clinton or Jimmy Carter: Abbr.
59 ___ characters (common Chinese writing)

by Joel Fagliano

ACROSS

1 Like some nationalism
8 Fruit-filled snack
15 30°, for 0.5
16 Hoards
17 Crystal-rubbing type
18 Gets by
19 The great Gatsby
20 Tall bloomer with candelabra-shaped branches
22 One of two opposing forces
23 A.M.A. member?: Abbr.
25 Fix, as a bowline
26 What some performers lip-sync in
27 Shower scenes?
29 Córdoba's land: Abbr.
30 "The Pearl Fishers" soprano
31 Droid's rival
33 School paper a student shouldn't write himself
35 They deliver
37 One taking a pounding
38 Footballer who co-starred in "The Dirty Dozen"
42 Winter fishing aid
46 Has left the office, e.g.
47 Prefix with sensitive
49 Breakout company
50 Telecom hookups
51 Flock members
53 Frugivorous creatures of sci-fi
54 Knight who hosts a country music radio show
55 Soprano Josephine
57 Plus exercise
58 They're often flashed
60 Amontillado's darker relative
62 Cutting down
63 Barely touched, as a meal
64 Plus or minus
65 Commensurate

DOWN

1 Most-spoken language in Pakistan
2 Hostel handout
3 "Mowing" painter, 1907
4 "___ precaution . . ."
5 Hard-to-park vehicles
6 Close, once
7 Norway's second-largest city
8 Many a dreaded native?
9 To love, Italian-style
10 "Shortfin" or "longfin" fish
11 24th Russian letter
12 Old Fertile Crescent land
13 Tries to get through anew
14 Whom Kerry succeeded in the U.S. Senate
21 Sewage co., e.g.
24 Yellow feature of Brazil's flag
26 Drain
28 Bull's sound
30 Big name in lenses
32 Alternative style to goth
34 ___ sabaki (martial arts movement)
36 Certifies
38 Imaginary number?
39 Emphatic refusal
40 Dweller around Port Hercules
41 Show with a "Los Angeles" spinoff
43 Stain-removing stuff
44 Kinsey Institute subject
45 Modern-day video game controller
48 Ink jet producers?
51 Dockworker
52 One of the Seven Sages of Greece
55 Cracker topper
56 Vessels seen over fires
59 Shop dresser
61 Abbr. next to a blinking light on a camcorder

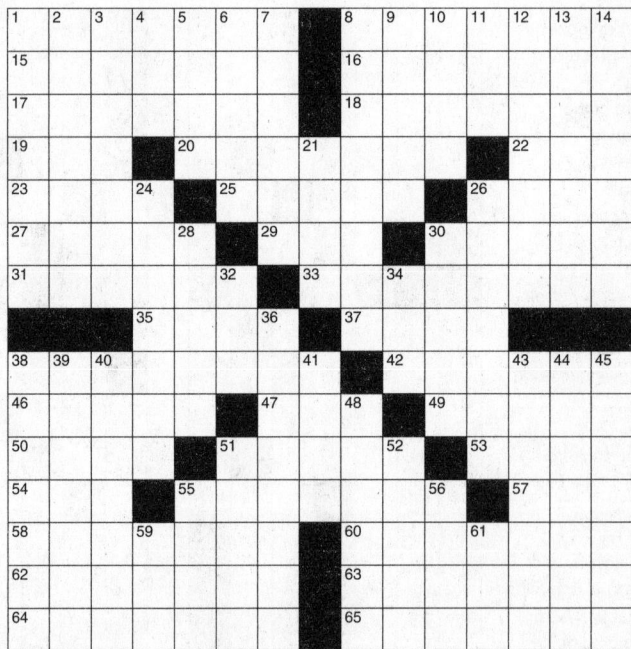

by Brendan Emmett Quigley

ACROSS

1 Pick for a pendant
5 In reserve
9 Jets used to make touchdowns there
13 Stinky
14 Group with a 1977 hit banned by the BBC, with "the"
16 Polo alternative
17 The basics
18 Narc's measures: Abbr.
19 Perniciousness
20 1982 A.L. Rookie of the Year
21 Go on and on
23 Sucker
24 "Wait for it . . ."
30 Windfall
31 Deadening agent
32 Media inits. since 1970
33 Coin with two stalks of wheat on its reverse
35 Mouse handler's aid
36 Row
38 "I hated it"
39 Is significant enough
42 Titanic-taloned terrorizers
43 Film starring Elliott Gould as Philip Marlowe
46 U.N.C. Charlotte's athletic conf.
47 "We're on!"
49 Writer and director of "Julie & Julia," 2009
52 Take advantage of a broken line
54 "Forget it!"
55 Radially symmetric creature
57 Plot element?
58 It may be combed for hairs
59 Lean

60 Beat reporters?: Abbr.
61 640 57-Acrosses: Abbr.
62 Catonian infinitive

DOWN

1 Bellatrix's constellation
2 It may spin overhead
3 Qur'an part
4 Set the bar
5 Mann's title
6 It has its problems
7 Breakable records
8 Upset
9 Corner item
10 Ham option
11 Actress Sommer
12 N.E.A. member?: Abbr.
14 Chain using lots of 2-Down
15 "Tropic Thunder" director and co-star
19 Line on a jumper
22 Earworm, e.g.
23 "I'd be delighted!"
25 Question the truth of
26 Sixth-century Chinese dynasty
27 Soreness causes
28 Sporty ensemble?
29 Kite kin
30 Polo alternative
34 Environmental transition area
37 Downtowns, e.g.
40 Knot-tying result
41 "Obviously"
44 They used to play at the Big A
45 Tippler's trouble

48 Aster relative
49 Suffix with 1-Across
50 Private jet, e.g.
51 "Caveat: Realism, Reagan and Foreign Policy" writer
52 Scanning work, often
53 10 in un decennio
56 John Wayne cop film
57 Were present?

by Caleb Madison

ACROSS

1 Dispense with courtesy
16 1970 film with much Sioux dialogue
17 Game that kids fall for
18 They often need polishing
19 Dark time for bards
20 Reggae artist ___-Mouse
21 Fugitives' flights
24 Situation in which nobody is up
26 "Kathy Griffin: My Life on the ___" (Emmy-winning reality show)
30 According to
31 Direction for a whaler?
33 Craze of 2005–06
34 Sharp turn
35 Diverts, in a way
37 Word often pig-Latinized
38 Put up with
40 Get out of
41 Red state?
42 Digital camera maker
43 Penpoint
44 Makes a scene?
45 Epidemic
47 Basics of learning, briefly
49 Some firebirds
57 Government grant?
58 Tons to do
59 Is absurd

DOWN

1 Zoo keepers?
2 Issue
3 Frederiksberg resident
4 Artist with a self-named museum in Montauban, France
5 Run from a pianist
6 Very eager, informally
7 University near Burlington
8 Lie-abed
9 Thought about the Louvre?
10 Money making hits
11 School board output?
12 Nora's husband in "A Doll's House"
13 Wood-cleaving tool
14 Amer. ally in W.W. II
15 Simon who wrote "The Death of Napoleon"
21 Talent agent Swifty
22 Out for a trial
23 Potter's field?
24 ___ Mahal
25 Like some dinars
27 Counterpart of covalent
28 Evade
29 They often come with vests
31 Wyndham alternative, familiarly
32 Lay low
33 Runner for the hills
36 Den delivery
39 Family in a Dickens novel
43 Former AOL competitor
44 Diamond pattern
46 Boxing ploy
47 Pancreatic enzyme
48 Isn't clear in speech, maybe
49 Fokker foe
50 Home of Steamboat Spgs.
51 Hyacinth relative
52 Lake ___ (Blue Nile source)
53 Film director Keshishian
54 Style
55 Metaphorical low points
56 "Luff, you lubber" speaker of literature

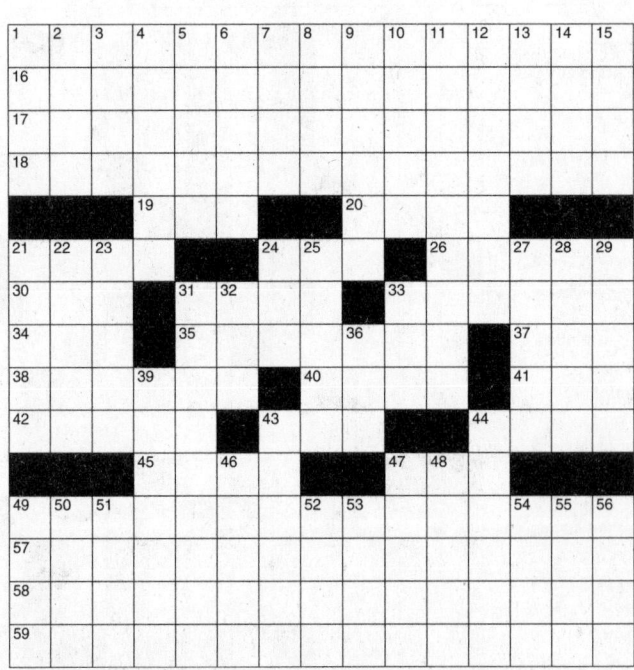

by Martin Ashwood-Smith and Joe Krozel

ACROSS

1 Mechanisms not meant to be handled
7 I.B.M. processor type found in Nintendo's Wii
14 Cheap T-shirt feature
15 Fly on a line
16 Chinese tree considered a living fossil
17 Sponsor of old radio's "Little Orphan Annie"
18 Man-made habitat
19 Possibly a result of
20 A, in the hexadecimal number system
21 Coattail riders
22 One drawn to igloos
24 Swinging, say
25 It's shown to a caller
27 Thus far
32 Not working
33 Big ox
34 Its first issue featured Mia Farrow on the cover
35 Shakespeare's collaborator on "The Two Noble Kinsmen"
36 One way to fall
38 ___ Ocean, Julia Roberts's "Ocean's Eleven" role
39 Like some short-lived romances
43 Place to wash up
44 Follower of St. Francis
45 Recurring subjects
48 Some software purchases
49 His statue once graced the Cortile del Belvedere

50 Unscientific means of getting results
51 Literary character fathered by an incubus
52 Uncomfortable place to be
53 Bank statement data

DOWN

1 Litter producers, in two different senses
2 Ontario's Fort ___
3 Famous relief worker?
4 Like the water in inflatable kiddie pools, typically
5 Wolverine's alias in "X-Men"
6 "He who meanly admires mean things," per Thackeray
7 Covering a lot
8 Target of a mealybug
9 Clearly didn't enjoy the show
10 Dimethyl sulfate, for one
11 Busts
12 Sporting a coat of many colors
13 Political rival of Pericles
15 Where Samuel Goldwyn was born
21 Engage
22 Class of tools?
23 Isolated
24 Be completely clueless
26 Ensure an accurate reading of
28 Their word is law
29 Home of the Biltmore Estate
30 Inexpensive pro shop buys

31 Makes a bad call
33 Road map abbr.
35 Green acres
37 Current
39 Flatten
40 Gloria in "Madagascar," e.g.
41 Product of a mold
42 Destinations for some wires
43 Leisurely gaits
45 "Baby ___" (2008 comedy)
46 Dart along
47 Pearl S. Buck's sequel to "The Good Earth"

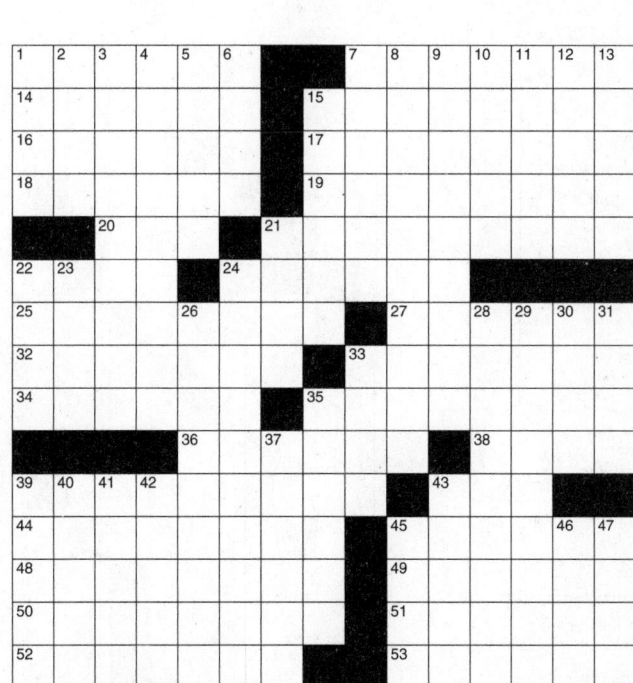

by Patrick Berry

ACROSS

1 California river, county or mountain
7 Vegas Strip hotel
15 Spirits
16 Redolent
17 "Well, perhaps . . ."
18 Business card info
19 Waste of an election?
20 Cuts (down)
21 Persuade
22 "Look!," in Latin
23 Manipulate data
24 Championship game
25 ___ moment
26 Peewee
28 2003 movie involving Christmas Eve robberies
30 Come back again
34 Depend upon, as a decision
35 It's signaled with a white flag
36 Counterfeit
37 Peewee
38 Co-writer of Michael Jackson's posthumous hit "This Is It"
40 Pizza option
41 "Your Precious Love" duet singer Terrell
44 Charge
45 What you might be rushed to get out of?
46 Concerning
47 Colon, e.g.
48 ___ Bird, daughter of L.B.J.
49 Natural
51 Office attachment
52 It often includes a colon
53 Select as a successor
54 R-rated element
55 Card table error

DOWN

1 Like deli meats
2 Small diner location?
3 Pool exhibitions
4 It's blue in an old song
5 Trash
6 "___ Grammatica" (classic work on Latin)
7 Island where Rafael Nadal was born
8 Development
9 Packs
10 Setting for BBC reports, in brief
11 Movie box set?
12 "Tuesday ___" (Count Basie tune)
13 Nabisco brand
14 Big battery type
20 The "1" in 1/2, e.g.
23 He wrote "All war is deception"
24 ___ Bowl
26 Umbrella holder, perhaps
27 Family in John Grisham's "Skipping Christmas"
29 Bargain hunters' events
31 Hassle-free fashion item
32 Gambling
33 Filming process for multiple aspect ratios
35 Second pope, following St. Peter
37 Procter & Gamble hair-care line
39 Watch
41 Patio pieces
42 Style on Japanese screens
43 "Fantastic" figure of children's lit
45 James who invented the Dual Cyclone vacuum cleaner
47 Gambling aids
48 Single
50 D.M.V. issue
51 Course objective

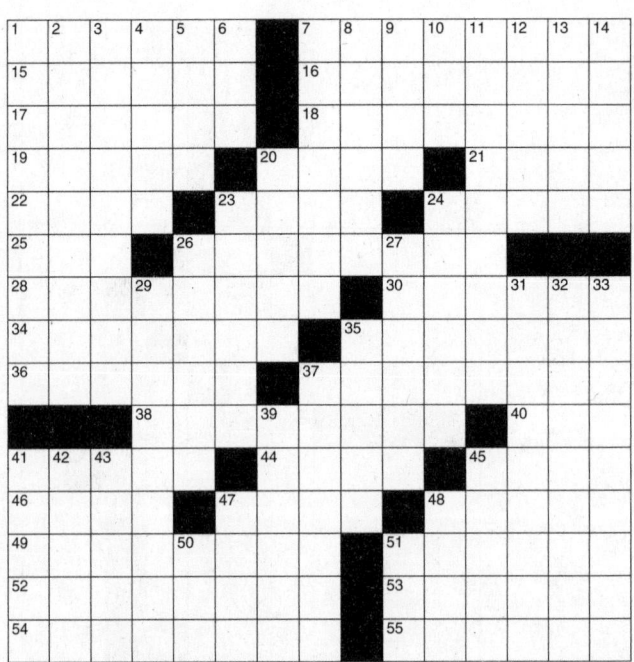

by Todd McClary

ACROSS

1 It's a blast for some balloonists
10 "This is a disaster!"
15 Asian symbols of wisdom
16 Like longship sailors
17 A dodger might cook one
18 Begin some revising
19 Maker of life-and-death decisions, briefly
20 Provider of a hot spot at a coffee shop?
21 Responded to wisely
22 Alexander's need
23 They may be shared during a show
25 Prohibition
29 Offices may require them
30 Town council president, in Canada
31 Big mystery during the summer of 1980
35 Dish component
36 Bent to do nothing
37 String shortener
38 Become known
40 "Friendly" things, in old ads
41 Composition of many sports courts
42 "A dish best served cold"
44 A dish best served cold
47 Waterloo marshal
48 N.H.L. team and former N.F.L. team
49 Casino action
51 Pec pic, perhaps
54 Courier alternative
55 Bit of décor at Trader Vic's
57 Change around the Thames
58 What a ham may use
59 Double-___
60 Hypnotized

DOWN

1 "Grand" or "petit" dance move
2 Ancient rival of Assyria
3 Cell composition
4 Silver ___, Md. (Wash. suburb)
5 It was Obama's self-professed favorite TV series
6 Place on a scale
7 Sufficient, informally
8 Two of hearts?
9 ___ Explorer (Web browser)
10 Here
11 Baloney
12 Yard stick?
13 Native of the central Caucasus
14 What thoughts may become
21 Ruin . . . or great success
22 Plagued
24 Pig, at times
25 Previously archaic?
26 She resigned after the Yom Kippur War
27 Much too bright
28 Giving a hoot?
32 Biblical mount where Aaron died
33 PC image acronym
34 Beau's buy
36 Design info
39 Like many a fishing line
40 Relatively sylphlike
43 Get on base?
44 Come unglued
45 Hit the waves?
46 Giant in astronomy
50 Soup thickener
51 1982 high-tech film
52 Plug possibilities
53 What you used to be?
55 "That's more than I wanted to know," in brief
56 Andean vegetable

by Tom Heilman

ACROSS

1 Lethally poisoned ruler, familiarly
5 22- and 38-Across
10 Pipeline accident investigator: Abbr.
14 Saab competitor
15 How deli meat may be served
16 Item in a "lick race"
17 Pregame rituals, for some
20 Opposite of swell
21 What some lawns cover
22 Ham's place
23 Kind of sheet
25 Jan. honoree
26 Like many salts
28 Introduction
30 Princess ___ (Disney duck)
33 Capturer of fin-de-siècle Paris
36 Barker who pitched a perfect game in 1981
37 Field of 33-Across
38 ___-twist
39 ___ poco (soon, in Sorrento)
40 Opinions about books
44 Singer with a wide range
45 Wags
46 Tick, e.g.
47 Maker of calls
49 Twist-___
50 "___ man!"
51 Compose together
54 Tire shop employee, at times
58 It can make for fruity kisses
60 Elaine ___, first female Asian-American cabinet member
61 Brush up on?

62 Lock or luck follower
63 Line from Penn Sta.
64 Some columns
65 They're subject to inflation and deflation

DOWN

1 Tigers, e.g.
2 Occasion to use a cooking pit
3 Tasteful bedclothes?
4 Engine leakage preventer
5 Washer/dryer unit
6 Borrower's protection
7 Field fare, briefly
8 How some things are brought back
9 Parker who was one of the original faces at Facebook
10 Chicken feed

11 Activity of some ghosts
12 One reading signs
13 Giant in audio equipment
18 Player's job
19 Dreamer's activity
24 Old ___ (Civil War eagle mascot)
26 Counselor-___
27 French sister
28 Hardy red hog
29 Weight factors
31 Quaint complaint
32 With ___ of thousands
34 Straw source
35 Maker of calls
41 Off
42 What a guru might be called
43 Showing some polish?

48 Provider of material for some wreaths
50 One going to school?
51 Mid-century year
52 "I wasn't expecting you!" lead-in
53 Unlucky strike?
55 Doesn't decline, with "in"
56 Prefix with -morph
57 Bygone theaters
59 Move it

by Paula Gamache

ACROSS

1 Another name for hardtack
12 Do Not Call Registry org.
15 Often-retractable car part
16 Can of Prince Albert?
17 Selfish
18 Acknowledge
19 Something seen on a pad
20 Italian bread
21 Two teaspoons, e.g.
22 Recover from a nap
24 Lilac or rose
26 Nickname popularized by a New York Morning Telegraph sportswriter in the 1920s, with "the"
27 Adamantine
28 Name that means "princess" in Hebrew
29 What "the lowing herd wind slowly o'er" in a Thomas Gray poem
30 Like cranberries
31 Detective work
32 Determine the age of, in a way
33 Hieroglyphic symbol
34 Legally binding
35 They make up a chapter
36 Medicated lozenge
38 Rolling landscape features
39 Source of most of the names in "The Lion King"
40 Italian seaport that's home to Saint Nicholas's relics
41 "I wasn't expecting that!"
42 Chats at a high school reunion, maybe
47 Wee drink
48 Earlier
49 Unkindly
50 Site of the War of 1812 Museum
51 Ball point?
52 Spot treatment?

DOWN

1 Part of a legionnaire's costume
2 Fox News political commentator
3 Proofreading abbr.
4 Something to clean one's teeth with, maybe
5 Common condo feature
6 Central
7 Mushroom stem
8 Flying Eagle, for one
9 Regrettable, as consequences
10 It's hard to get a reaction out of it
11 Smidge
12 Aircraft that doesn't need a runway
13 Officials who may issue licenses
14 TV family that popularized the term "parental unit"
20 Animation
23 Cry that's often tripled
24 "Sit yourself down"
25 What a stratigraphist might take
26 "Goin' to Chicago Blues" songwriter
27 Picks up the pace
28 Lending "lady"
31 See who's there, say
32 Big sports venue
34 The first manned Apollo mission
35 Guatemala's national instrument
37 Word used three times in the first four lines of the Lord's Prayer
38 Beat it
40 Towlines are tied around them
43 Self-referential, informally
44 Find fault to a fault
45 Brand with Toaster Swirlz
46 Loft-y place?
48 No. on a bottle, maybe

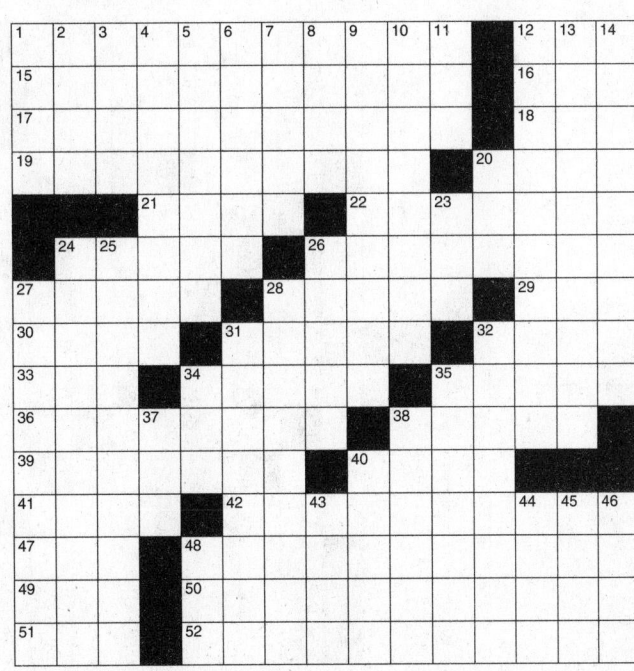

by Patrick Berry

264 HARD

ACROSS

1 Historic U.S. place in the shape of a five-pointed star
12 Present time?: Abbr.
15 Russet Burbank, e.g.
16 Leader of leaders?
17 Tryst spot
18 Outfit's biggest suit
19 What might send Rover right over?
20 Directly
21 Is catlike
23 Newbery Medal-winning author Lowry
25 Has a seamy job?
28 Rush
29 Bright
31 Scaling challenge
33 Cicero's servant and secretary
34 Red Man rival
36 First #1 Billboard hit by an Australian artist (1972)
38 Hospital gown go-with
40 Small yarn?
43 Occurrences between springs
46 Fishing spot
47 Strike authorizer
49 Camaro options
51 Campus home for mice
53 Area near Manhattan's Union Square
55 First name in mysteries
56 Eponymous Greek island
58 Festive cry
60 Tobacco holder
61 NASA fine?
62 Natal setting
66 Single opening?
67 Handler of intelligence agents
68 Kickback site?
69 Researcher's audiotapes and such

DOWN

1 Campus stress source
2 Nose-noticeable
3 Canary
4 & 5 What iconoclasts break
6 79, say
7 Students might clean up in it
8 The Lorraine Campaign was part of it: Abbr.
9 Red rival, briefly
10 GPS choices: Abbr.
11 Whites' counterparts
12 Give a passionate recital
13 The Doors' record label
14 Seal, as a deal
22 Current
24 Frequent catch on TV's "Deadliest Catch"
26 E-mail, say
27 "Move your mind" sloganeer
30 Half a fathom
32 Old pulp fiction hero
35 ___ of Judah
37 N.Y.C.'s PBS station
39 Persian for "place of"
40 Express approval
41 Expression of approval
42 Wallet material
44 Classical Greek temple feature
45 Old-fashioned film editor
48 "What a girl" lead-in, in an Eddie Cantor hit
50 Based on the number six
52 Hershey's alternative
54 King surnamed Tryggvason
57 Rocket
59 Pair of buffalo?
63 Stars represent its constituents
64 Letterhead abbr.
65 Slowing, in mus.

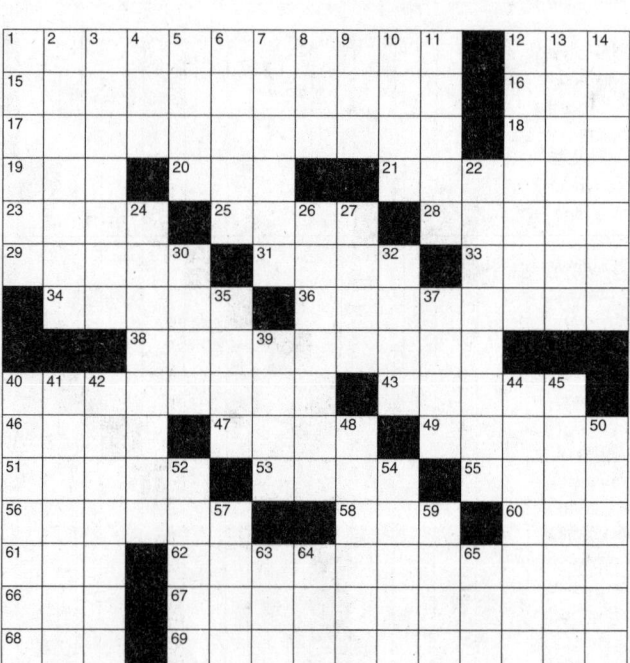

by Barry C. Silk

ACROSS

1 Wants, with "to"
8 It may be held in battle
15 1977 Jacqueline Bisset movie
16 Literary critic Broyard
17 Acted unfairly
19 Aluminum foil alternatives?
20 Quite
21 Liability-limiting words
22 Natl. Humor Month
23 One in Germany
25 Slough
27 One may be called in court
29 Holiday time
31 It might go for big bucks
32 Equestrian's command
33 Bit of evidence in court
35 Concertedly
37 21st-century epidemic concern
40 Flibbertigibbety
42 Hymn words before "beyond all praising"
43 Get hush money from, for instance
46 It's "not master in its own house," said Freud
47 Family: Abbr.
49 Stop-press order?
51 Kind of 6-Down
53 Lord's domain
55 It once stretched from France to Russia: Abbr.
56 Shakespearean words following "Speak, hands, for me!"
57 "___ well"
59 ___ rage

61 "Not to my recollection"
64 Scholar
65 "The Morning Show Murders" novelist
66 Bleach component
67 "Happy" sorts

DOWN

1 Deep down
2 U.P.S. customer
3 Easter character
4 "___ delighted!"
5 Candy brand
6 One that swims with a current?
7 Cuddle, in a way
8 Broadway smash whose poster image consisted of just two eyes
9 Like some nursing
10 ___ Bo
11 Being tried
12 Registers surprise, say
13 National Book Award-winning novelist named after Emerson
14 "Hmmm . . ."
18 Never
24 Motor add-ons?
26 Patron saint of carvers
28 Biblical endings
30 Prefix with -phile
34 Bad way to go
36 Refuse at a mill
38 Name abandoned for Rochester
39 Skirt
40 Ruses
41 "Understood"
44 Dine at another's house
45 Some deals
48 Took out
50 Maintain

52 TV detective Peter and others
54 One spared in a sacrifice
58 Superman's mother
60 Blue-roofed chain
62 It's declared after the last hit, for short
63 Grp. in 1974 news

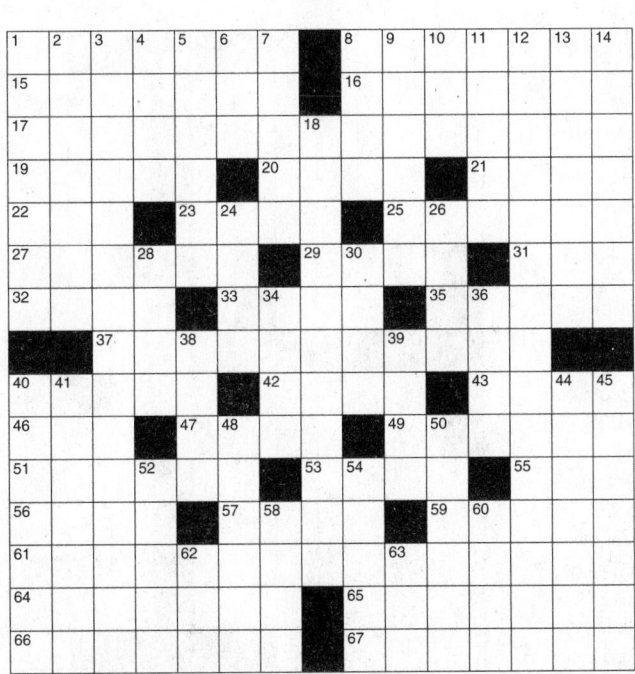

by Joe Krozel

266 HARD

ACROSS
1 Officers
6 Award show category
11 In haste
14 Derided
16 It might help you catch your breath
17 Kind of pickup
18 "St. Martin and the Beggar" painter
19 Tenth Commandment subject
20 "Just this time . . ."
21 Upbraided
22 Lascivious sorts
24 Beans and others
25 Go on
26 Having more bites, say
28 Word from a waiter
29 Language with no word for "hello"
32 Sloven
35 Enthusiast
36 One wiping out
39 Pitt athlete
41 Mercurial
43 Former
44 Subject of the Fujita scale
45 British dish with an American version called a Hot Brown
46 Polka relative
47 Fathers, of a sort
48 Lachrymose
49 Attacked
50 What the cogent make

DOWN
1 Summary
2 Need replenishing
3 Silverish
4 "My" girl in a 1979 hit
5 Knee cap?
6 Coins for Cicero
7 College student's request
8 Judge
9 Varmints, in a classic cartoon line
10 Extra
12 Big name in wafers
13 Creator of "The Simpsons"
14 Blubber
15 Having a hard time connecting?
23 Missouri metro
27 It may come down after a win
28 Native to a certain region
29 Like some spirits
30 It's typed with the left pinkie
31 Check
32 Echoes
33 "That makes 50-Across"
34 Lie in the sun
35 Start of a Christmas refrain
37 :-(
38 Equestrians
39 It may be screened
40 Softens in water, in a way
42 Thicket of trees

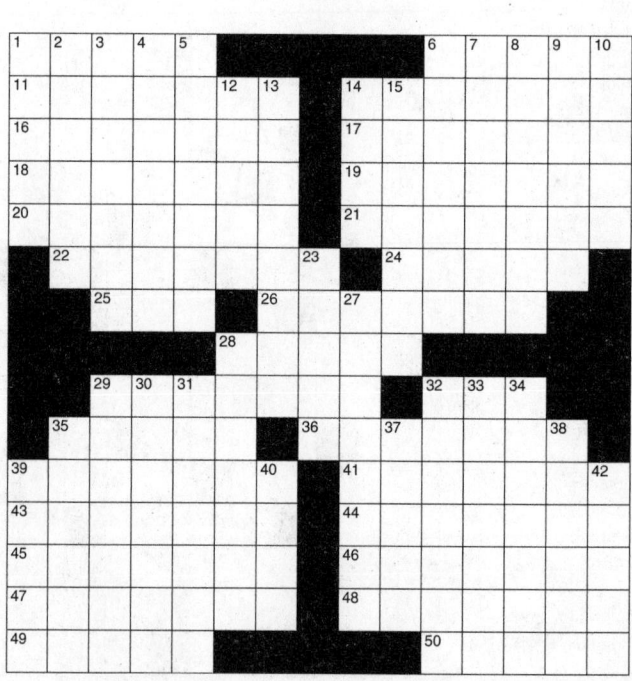

by Julian Lim

ACROSS

1 Lit
6 Up to one's old tricks
15 Trigger-happy sound?
16 Propositions
17 In a main location?
18 Like newly available products
19 Take care of the spread
20 Winnebago relative
21 New Mexican, e.g.
22 It's raw
23 "That's it"
25 "Singin' in the Rain" co-director
26 Unlike aristos
28 Allspice and clove's family
30 Ki ___ (legendary founder of Korea)
31 City representatives?
32 Letters in some church names
33 Walk-___
35 Pastoral prophet
36 It worked from a prompt
38 Allowing peeking, perhaps
42 Viroid composition
44 Offensive time?
45 Splendid
46 See 62-Down
49 Like old AM radio
51 AM or FM specification
52 Make a measure
54 Clear wrongs
56 Jacques Cousteau, e.g.
57 Am or Fm stat
58 Sci-fi writer Frederik
59 Go all the way through
61 Fifth in a series of seven old comedy films
63 Her temple was adorned with cows' horns

64 Extravagant way to live
65 Set up
66 View on a clear night
67 Gets down to the ground?

DOWN

1 One you don't want to have a crush on you
2 Order to curtail public bussing
3 Not block out
4 Arch type
5 Slip site
6 MoMA and Epcot, e.g.
7 Mind-numbingly exhausted
8 "That made no sense to me"
9 "SCTV" segment?
10 Polymer finish?
11 "You couldn't be more wrong!"
12 Install in an office
13 Its logo features two eighth notes
14 Zip
24 Yardbirds hit of 1965
25 Place for a retreat
27 Red giant, once?
29 Clay target?
34 9–5, e.g.
37 It's concerned with ports
39 Follower of Arlo Guthrie at Woodstock
40 Come out with
41 Duck, emu, etc.
43 Baby beef?

46 Finds on a bed
47 Digging something
48 Godzilla creator Tomoyuki ___
50 They call their native language "te reo"
53 Many a software company employee
55 Comforter material
58 Like tailgated drivers, often
60 Red giant in Cetus
62 With 46-Across, prehistoric animal preserver

by Tim Croce

ACROSS

1 Actual title of the 1979 #1 hit known as "The Piña Colada Song"
7 "Family Guy" mayor, or the actor providing his voice
15 Dump truck filler
16 Deliver
17 Shameless yes-man
18 1984 film starring Tom Selleck as a jewel thief
19 Front covers
20 Fashion magazines, e.g.
21 Trespasses
22 Higgins's pupil in elocution
23 Abbr. rarely seen at the start of a sentence
24 One rudely put out?
25 Satellite community?
28 Small brawl
33 Removes from a spool
34 Ignoring copyrights, say
35 "In the Night Kitchen" author
36 Lady famous for piemaking
37 Cash in
39 Vegas hotel that hosts the World Series of Poker
40 Nighttime assignment, often
44 "Star Trek: First Contact" villains, with "the"
46 Girl's name meaning "messenger of God"
47 Second run
49 Foot-stomping music

50 Unfazed by
51 Top-quality
52 DVD box set purchase
53 Wild West show headgear
54 Place to sit, ironically

DOWN

1 "___ in Berlin" (1960 live album)
2 Mineral used as chalk by tailors
3 One born on Christmas Day
4 Enlargement
5 Unskilled laborers
6 Newton-meter fractions
7 No more
8 Kind of box for input

9 Moral theory that doesn't allow for shades of gray
10 Old-fashioned letter opener
11 You might keep a watch on it
12 Weird Al Yankovic's first Billboard hit
13 What tuning forks are made of
14 Clipped
22 Sleep, in British slang
23 Skinny-legged trotters
24 Had one do through persuasion
26 Outlaw Kelly of Australian legend
27 Like Lincoln before his presidency
29 1950s–'70s senator Ervin

30 Added to the soup, say
31 Pressed one's suit?
32 Return a call?
34 Little game, perhaps
36 Falling rocks
38 Company behind the 1960s yo-yo craze
40 Fishing hooks
41 Dark
42 Mesoamerican plant
43 Ran into again
44 Hemmed in
45 "No good ___ plot can be sensible . . .": W. H. Auden
47 Former Wisconsin senator Feingold
48 Dispose of

by Patrick Berry

ACROSS

1 Indian home
6 Store
15 Gloucester and Kent, in "King Lear"
16 1822 Walter Scott novel about Capt. Clement Cleveland
17 Its calling code is +39
18 President Harding's Laddie Boy and others
19 Elvis's and Mariah's record number of weeks at Billboard's #1
21 Big mouth
22 Carmen Sandiego cover-up?
23 8 on the Beaufort scale
24 Until June 25, 2011, its first three digits had geographical significance: Abbr.
25 "Tempest" Golden Globe nominee Julia
26 Purple
27 Lived in King James's era?
29 "Jason Lives," e.g.
30 Notes in passing?
33 Like the word "its," often
34 Crows
35 Ice cream case selections
36 Take what one oughtn't
37 Weapon that comes in easy-to-carry and hard-to-carry varieties
38 Lacuna
41 Snarling, say
42 Ursi maritimi
45 Place that shows placing and showing: Abbr.
46 Miami or Amsterdam, for example

47 Uniform shade
49 "Let's ___ there"
50 Something one might be forced to wear at work
51 Top
52 Deal incentive
53 Some of them are flukes

DOWN

1 Withdrawals that may incur substantial penalties?
2 Tom Mix vehicles
3 Second Commandment word
4 Wrench handle?
5 "It's Gonna Be Me" band of 2000
6 Emergency directive?
7 Become sparse
8 From above

9 Blown
10 Mask
11 Constellation between Scorpius and Triangulum Australe
12 Supercenters, e.g.
13 More than gnawed at
14 Celebratory chant at Chicago's Grant Park on 11/4/08
20 Basketball long shots
23 Mavens
26 In a bad place?
27 Sweet, to Scipio
28 Dating
29 Sebastián ___ (president of Chile beginning in 2010)
30 Reprimands
31 Gary Cooper played one in "Man of the West"

32 Certain ATV
33 Dickens character whose first name is Wilkins
35 Blonde picked up at a bar?
37 "We feel your pain" sloganeer
38 Ankle covering
39 Kind of eraser
40 "Hearts and minds" activities, in military slang
42 Luke's mother in "Star Wars"
43 Already
44 Tightwads' prefix
46 Exploit
48 Capital of Victoria

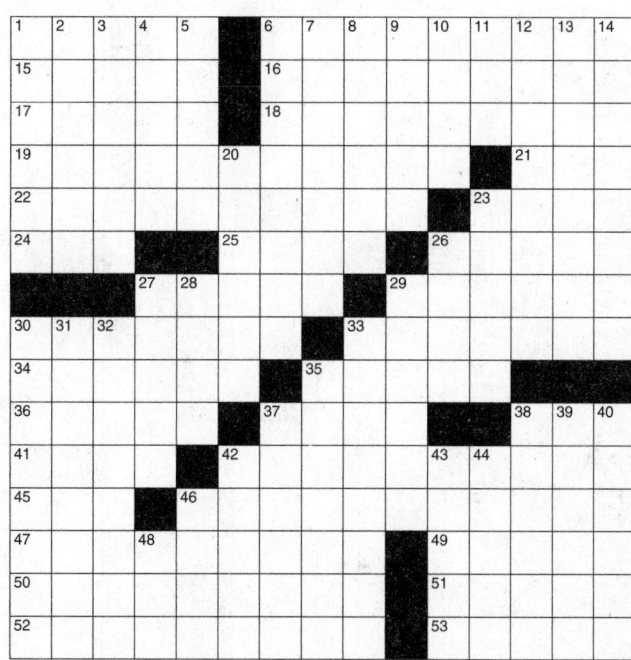

by Byron Walden

270 HARD

ACROSS

1 Like a snap
9 With 46-Down, strike zones
15 Kind of stew
16 Role Enrico Caruso was preparing for when he died
17 Eye openers?
18 He said "I never think I have finished a nude until I think I could pinch it"
19 Glossy scarf fabrics
20 Japanese mat
21 Well and good finish?
22 Like Hollywood
24 Landing place
26 Yardbird
27 "Here's Johnny!" memoirist
31 Line in the sand?
35 Give a hand
36 Think that just maybe one can
37 Put down in writing
39 Deep orangish hue
40 Take in
41 One code-named Renegade by the Secret Service
43 Hundred Years' War leader
46 Colonial group
50 A destroyer may be in one
51 "Forget I said that"
54 Like pupils that are too small
55 Big, purple Hanna-Barbera character
56 Take stock?
57 Go mano a mano
58 Discharges
59 Romulus and Remus, to Rhea Silvia

DOWN

1 1956 movie monster
2 What some dictators end up in
3 What may hold a world of information?
4 Good earth
5 Inside opening?
6 Like many ports
7 "Absolutely!"
8 "Absolutely!"
9 Rich dessert
10 Elite soldiers
11 Dollar store?
12 Show poor sportsmanship about, say
13 Waste
14 Like Life Savers
23 Cowboys compete in it: Abbr.
24 Tiny amount
25 Aid in gaining an edge
27 Start of the 16th century
28 "1984" activity
29 Played
30 Turns off
32 Very early 2-Down
33 Hardly seen at the Forum?
34 Sign of assent
38 E.R. status
39 "Goodbye, Columbus" co-star, 1969
42 Intelligent
43 ___ Oliver, a k a the Naked Chef
44 Certain foot specialist
45 Trivia quiz fodder
46 See 9-Across
47 Just ducky
48 Court gimme
49 Correction corrections
52 Language spoken on Pandora
53 Not settled

by Brendan Emmett Quigley

ACROSS

1   It may be seen in a 3-Down picture
10 Times up?
15 Like bending over backward
16 Lowest deck on a ship
17 Feign concurrence
18 Words of concurrence
19 Bit of consolation
20 Google rival
21 Scriveners
22 Yesterday, to Yvette
24 "Gomer Pyle, U.S.M.C." star
26 Their lines have ties: Abbr.
27 It's taken while waiting
29 "Le Roi d'Ys" composer
30 Lumpkin
31 Bible supporter, often
33 One may be suckered
35 Hedonist's opposite
39 Unwanted tail?
40 Black-and-white
42 W.W. II agcy.
43 Bottom of the ocean?
44 Group sharing a coat of arms
46 Feeds on the farm, maybe
50 Offensive time?
51 City that lost its "tallest building" distinction in 2007
53 Not apart, in scores
54 Club alternative
56 ID figures
58 ID issuer
59 Match
60 "Let's roll!"
62 Long

63 Very close game, e.g.
64 Bloody Sunday march site
65 Like some skiing and swimming

DOWN

1   "The tenth Muse," per Plato
2   Oblong temptation
3   Beyond suggestive
4   Far from forward
5   Quatrain scheme
6   Author of "America by Heart"
7   Missing a key?
8   Dope
9   Lines coming from the heart, briefly?
10 Gardeners' aids
11 One letting off steam
12 1970s music genre

13 What the Faroe Islands were granted in 1948
14 Frumpy loner, stereotypically
21 "Now!"
23 Undo
25 Accented cries
28 Out of practice?: Abbr.
30 Line forgetter's substitute
32 Magick worker
34 It causes lights to go out
35 Camels' resting places
36 Sponge alternative
37 Kind of awareness
38 Title locale in a 1998 Notorious B.I.G. hit
41 The Notorious B.I.G., e.g.
45 Tabloid nickname
47 Ripley's love

48 Pound
49 Very bad
51 Singer ___ Marie
52 Fireplace
55 Shoulder
57 Displays disconsolation
60 Like Beethoven's Sixth
61 Black-throated ___

by Ashton Anderson

ACROSS

1 Sensitive information is often shared on it
16 Thing rolled in a classroom
17 Continue cordially despite differences
18 Cousin of a canvasback
19 Scapola or clavicola
20 It gets lapped a lot
21 Potential mouth choker
23 Agricultural Hall of Fame locale: Abbr.
24 Certain X or O
25 It includes an analytical reasoning sect.
27 ___-80 (old computer)
29 Nascar Hall of Fame locale: Abbr.
32 A good defense may result in it, briefly
34 A wee bit
36 1968 title role for Vanessa Redgrave
40 "Thinking . . ."
41 Chihuahua assent
42 Idyllic place
43 ___ suspension (ear drops)
44 "And that sort of thing": Abbr.
46 Evidence of some growth
49 One-third of nove
51 "Configuration" artist
53 Enrich
55 Not as experienced
57 Earth as an organism
59 Place for a rip
61 Like real danger
64 Toiletries and such
65 Feature of many a residential neighborhood

DOWN

1 Ingenious
2 Ball's lack
3 Continental pass provider
4 Common flashlight fillers
5 South Korea's Roh ___ Woo
6 Cartoon busman Mann
7 Small business site
8 Gives a passing acknowledgment
9 Piquant sandwich base
10 "Time ___ . . ."
11 Firing result
12 Kandahar cash
13 Dust-laden winds
14 Soprano player Robert
15 Hook accompanier
22 Hit lightly
26 Painful struggle
28 Look bad?
30 Put down
31 Movie heroine Norma ___ Webster
33 Dumas hero
35 Some cashless commerce
36 Prefix with -meric
37 Get on the bottom?
38 Seemingly
39 Cut
45 Protect
47 Six-Day War figure
48 Attic locale
50 Owl in Harry Potter tales
52 Brought (in), as music
54 He met Charon in the underworld
55 Return request: Abbr.
56 A, Jay or Ray
58 Boxer rebellion cries?
60 ___ Mary's (L.A. college)
62 Black bird
63 Young pond dweller

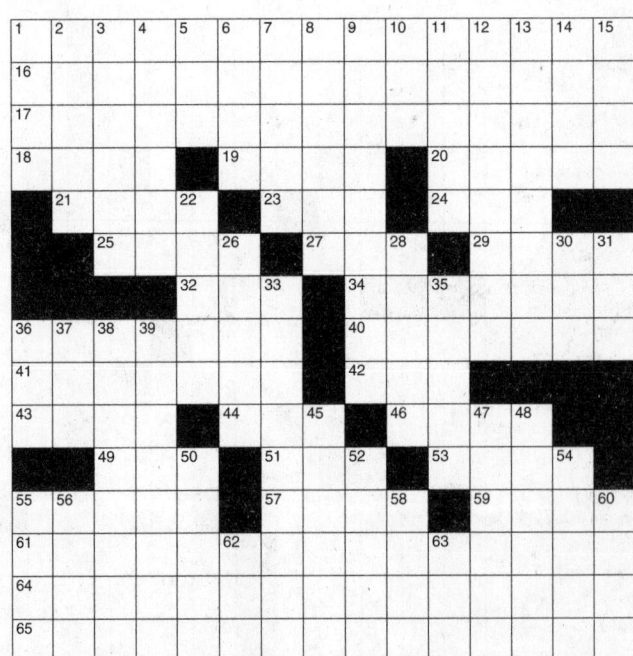

by Tim Croce

ACROSS

1 "Star Wars" villain
6 Broken thing in "Gimme a break"
15 Perform "All of Me," say
16 Performing perfectly
17 Chili container
18 Pirate's implement
19 Sapporo's home
21 Nobel-winning economist James
22 "Would you look at that!"
23 Inventor of the battery in 1800
26 Extinct wingless bird
27 Birth city of Mother Teresa
30 It's acquired in the sun
33 A little too quiet, perhaps
34 Gruff rejoinder
35 Brewmaster's science
37 Term for some morning deejays
41 Having been tainted, as a drink
43 United hub
44 Noted role for 46-Down
47 Many domes
48 Great Society inits.
49 __ Park
51 "That's awful!"
52 "David __," Edward Noyes Westcott novel
55 Ninnies
58 It stirs things up
61 About to happen
62 Gathering place for animals
63 Glandular opening?
64 They're thrown over the shoulder
65 Ready for another play

DOWN

1 Former 'N Sync vocalist and judge on "America's Best Dance Crew"
2 Pointer for a computer user
3 Bibliolater
4 Dark quaff
5 "Tonight My Love, Tonight" singer
6 Little fella
7 Absorb
8 Sliver
9 Former org. for Azerbaijani president Heydar Aliyev
10 Poisonous lily
11 Moved with force
12 Cleanser with the logo of a chick emerging from an egg
13 Photographer who once collaborated with Capote
14 Brushed up on
20 "__ changed"
24 Excited state
25 U.K. highway connecting London and Dover
28 Ninth successor of St. Peter
29 Beef product
31 Screamingly funny
32 Part of a mudslide, maybe
34 "The Tinker's Wedding" playwright
36 Japanese capture after Pearl Harbor
38 Projects, in a good way
39 "Grey's Anatomy" actor
40 Chink in the armor
42 Relatives
44 Fashion strip?
45 "The __ Diaries" (2007 best seller)
46 Actor Pat
47 Sponge
50 They're added in some infrastructure upgrades
53 Conference USA sch.
54 "The Sands of __" (Arthur C. Clarke's first science fiction novel)
56 Window coating?
57 German fantasy writer Michael
59 Article in hip-hop
60 Org. against doping

by Peter Wentz

ACROSS

1 Starting point for a ferry ride to Alcatraz
16 Ways to avoid traffic jams
17 Many people can make this claim
18 See 55-Down
19 It's less than premium: Abbr.
20 Drilling type: Abbr.
21 Be unable to get the rest?
28 Battling something, say
29 Mock
30 North American singers with raspy notes
39 Bozo's suggestion
40 As a hobby
41 Not overseas
42 "That so?" reply
43 Beggar's receptacle
44 Result of prolonged worry
51 "Aloha nui ___" (warm greeting in Waikiki)
52 From ___ B
53 Going, going, going
62 Appalachian, e.g.
63 1953 hit for Mitch Miller

DOWN

1 Side
2 "Any volunteers?" reply
3 Some wild parties
4 Attendees of 3-Down
5 Unscripted utterances
6 Makeup of some strands
7 Large-scale
8 When some retire
9 Snow on les Alpes
10 Sign of a good show
11 Like some hands and hearts
12 Czech religious reformer Jan
13 Carry ___
14 Tend to again, as an injured joint
15 Shooting setting
22 Cause to pull over
23 "Imagine that!"
24 Mr. Cub and others
25 More together
26 One may take your heart
27 Run
30 Things traveling on sound waves?
31 Ear part
32 Quit lying
33 Ice cream shop request
34 Plains homes: Var.
35 "Away! you are ___": Shak.
36 Head of design
37 Cancel
38 Saint-___ (Delibes contemporary)
45 Dissolve out
46 Tough question
47 It's not a long shot
48 Local theaters
49 Anatomical aqueducts
50 "___ Alice" (1971 antidrug book)
53 Home of Sun Devil Stadium, for short
54 Stopping-off point: Abbr.
55 With 18-Across, no-goodnik
56 Santa ___
57 Service address
58 Opening for birds?
59 Last article of the U.S. Constitution
60 Dijon toasting time?
61 Roads with train tracks: Abbr.

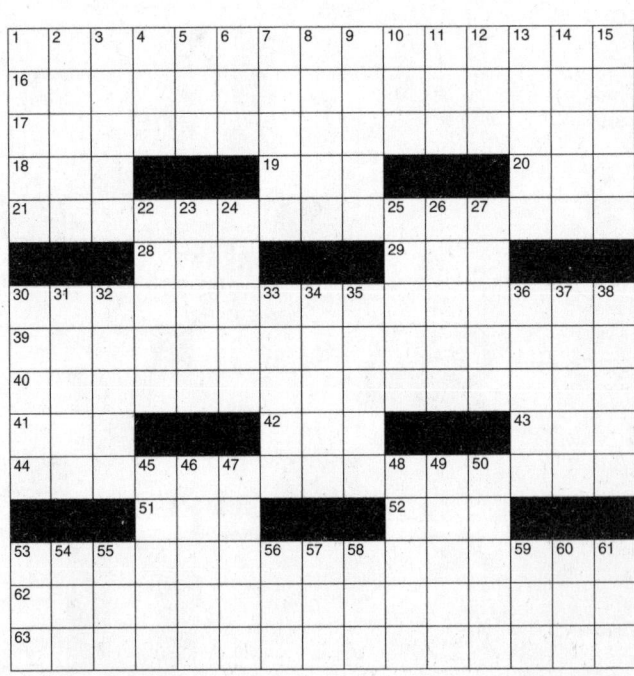

by Joe Krozel

ACROSS

1 Only song on Rolling Stone's "500 Greatest Songs of All Time" list that is not sung in English
8 Midweek
15 Unitedly
16 See
17 Humor
18 Goes back and forth, in a way
19 Bread pudding ingredient
20 Subject on a wanted poster
22 NPR's Shapiro
23 "A God in Ruins" novelist
25 Man of steel?
26 Gridiron cues
27 Reduces
29 Country music's ___ Brown Band
30 Line up
31 Shady, say
33 Frequently disputed court call?
35 Map abbr.
37 First name in auto racing
38 Transfer
42 Concedes
46 Island near Ayr
47 It ended in 1947
49 Welcome to paradise?
50 Tower
51 Charybdis, e.g.
53 Source of some highly prized 19-Acrosses
54 1940s–'60s world leader
55 Where one's head is
57 Robitaille of the N.H.L.
58 #1 in sports
60 Northern air

62 Sometimes-banned work
63 State of anarchy
64 Misters abroad
65 Setting of many plots

DOWN

1 Some boots
2 Name on the highest award of the American Society of Plant Taxonomists
3 Diamond handler?
4 Had
5 Keyboardist Saunders who played with the Grateful Dead
6 Mongolian for "hero"
7 "A Perfect Peace" novelist
8 Drink in a mug
9 Wolf pack member
10 U.S.M.C. E-8
11 Tuning device
12 "Stop Whining, Start Living" author
13 Turned away
14 "That is clear"
21 Boarder's aid
24 Rising time, for some
26 Writer on whose work Woody Allen's "Sleeper" is loosely based
28 Setting for a set
30 Basilica de San Vicente setting
32 Home of Pyramid Lake: Abbr.
34 Christian ___
36 Balustraded locales, often
38 Honors

39 Major export of Brazil and Australia
40 Marketing giant with a portmanteau name
41 Bust
43 "Hot!"
44 "Poetry makes nothing happen" writer
45 It's unfortunate
48 2002 horror sequel
51 Many an heiress
52 Lure
55 Bergman's last role
56 Response to the '08 financial crisis
59 Pou ___ (vantage point)
61 Void: Fr.

by David Quarfoot

ACROSS

1 Reduce to bare bones
10 "Hey you!"
15 1990 Clint Eastwood cop film
16 Studio sign
17 Likely to take chances
18 Figure on a bridge score sheet
19 Money competitor
20 Was up to date, with "out"?
21 They may work for both sides
22 Pitlik who directed "Barney Miller" and "Mr. Belvedere"
24 Toledo-to-Columbus dir.
26 Shut (up)
27 Reaction of thirsty people
31 Firm
33 Wallace who wrote "Angle of Repose"
34 Stolen
35 Old "One mission. Yours." sloganeer
36 Miss ___
37 Worse than awful
41 Blowout
46 Small night creatures
47 Reckless smuggler of sci-fi
48 Area close to a hockey net
49 Abbr. before "Co." in some company names
51 Suffer from the heat
52 Having less coverage
54 Go down again, so to speak
58 Frost relative
59 "Get ___ on!"

60 "Generally speaking . . ."
62 Hit the bottom of?
63 Spread quickly over the Internet
64 Laments
65 Put one's feet up in neighborly fashion

DOWN

1 Series
2 Become sparse
3 Change one's image, in a way?
4 Needle
5 ___ wheelie
6 Actress Diana
7 "Enough already . . . relax!"
8 Blushes, say
9 Has trouble getting started
10 Piles of chips, say
11 Stir-fry vegetable
12 Pronounced
13 Matte finish?
14 Met on the down-low
23 Certain meas. of economy
25 Kings prophet
28 Getting dragged along
29 Minnesota home of Martin Luther College
30 Semiterrestrial bug-catchers
32 Sap
37 Alice Cooper's appropriately titled theme song for "Friday the 13th Part VI"
38 Morse who sang "Cow-Cow Boogie"

39 "From my perspective . . ."
40 Much less than that
42 Australian state: Abbr.
43 "Is it worth the chance?"
44 Criminal
45 Recovered
50 Explorer John Cabot's birthplace
53 Some M&M's
55 "I'm busy then"
56 Eye part
57 Powers (up)
61 Big swing

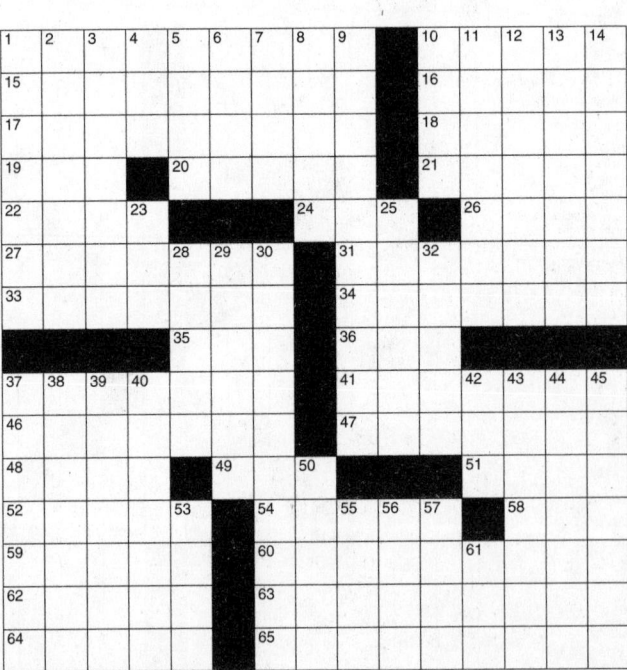

by Joe DiPietro

HARD 277

ACROSS

1. Singer/songwriter Scialfa
6. ___ student
9. Banjo accessory
14. Cause for some spatial relationships?
17. Debut at the 1979 Frankfurt Auto Show
18. It can heat up Roquefort
19. Smooth
20. One with nothing to hide
21. Wallop
23. Last movement of a sonata
25. Like bath beads, typically
28. Show one's stamped hand, perhaps
32. Can't take a bit
33. Bear essentials?
35. Relatives of the Iowa
36. They're in the vicinity: Abbr.
37. Sartre's "Les Jeux Sont ___"
38. Box office need
39. Got things down
40. Damn
41. Like 14-Across
42. Tool handle strengthener
44. Member of a very early union?
46. Titan after whom one of the oceans is named
48. Silver checker
49. Some time
52. Choice job
54. Lid around a loch
57. Suffered serious consequences
60. Groups aiming for good returns
61. Smoking and heavy drinking
62. Security demands
63. They go with uppers

DOWN

1. Surface
2. Over and over
3. One spending a long time in the bathroom?
4. Drug in a sci-fi novel series
5. What swallows swallow
6. Suits often hold them
7. Landscaping aid
8. Like some balances
9. Memphis hospital, familiarly
10. Like sashes
11. Indian flatbread
12. Some marching bands
13. Math is part of it: Abbr.
15. Benefiting from Vivarin
16. It's shown on TV monitors at many airports
22. Tips, often
24. Is a spellbinder
25. Bundle of a sort
26. 51-Down division
27. Alexandria is in it
29. Coming down hard
30. Net sales
31. Spur part
34. Tulipe relative
37. Maximum
38. Numerical prefix
40. Pirate's appurtenance
41. Grandfathers, e.g.
43. Speakeasy scourge
45. Blow
47. "The primary factor in a successful attack," per Lord Mountbatten
49. Capital near Faleolo International Airport
50. "The Joy Luck Club" director, 1993
51. Busy place
53. Magnifier
55. Lofty place
56. Hoarder's problem
58. "I think you overshared," briefly
59. Locomobile competitor

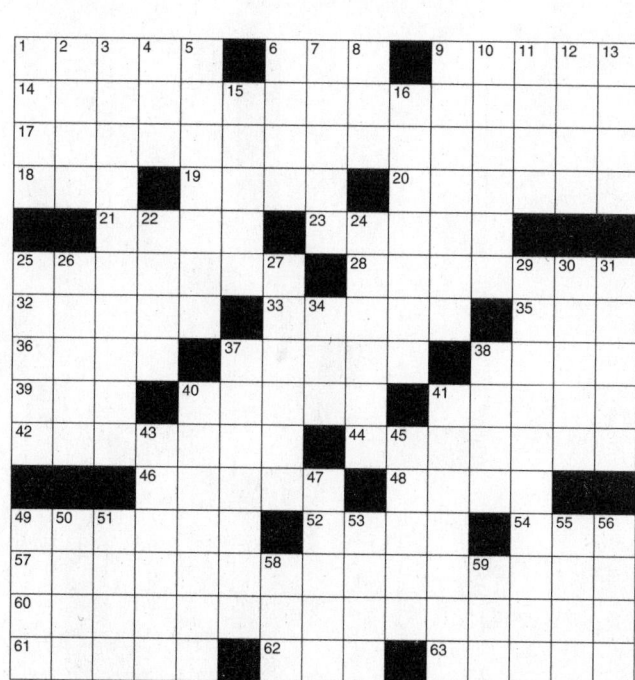

by Peter A. Collins

ACROSS

1 It has rock bands
6 Pooh-pooh
14 ___-toothed
15 Informal show of approval?
16 Stroll
17 Factor affecting Google search results
18 Juicer detritus
19 Modern proofs-of-purchase, for short
20 Takes for a ride
21 Many gamblers have them
23 Self-help book
24 Gaston who wrote "The Phantom of the Opera"
25 Include as an extra
28 ___ Lady (decades-old commercial creation)
29 Movie credits, usually
31 Collision sound
34 "Dominus illuminatio ___" (Oxford University's motto)
35 Validate
36 "___ Como Va" (1971 hit)
37 It makes a lot of connections
38 Give a slant to
39 Follower's response
40 In many cases
41 Worries
43 Last report on the evening news, typically
46 Deny
48 Give a good rubdown
49 Blue shade
51 Providers of directions

53 Admitted
55 The Temptations' "Since ___ My Baby"
56 Leisure
57 Spitting mad
58 Something a drunkard is liable to hit
59 Turns brown quickly

DOWN

1 Before all else
2 Series ender, sometimes
3 1969 #1 album for 11 weeks
4 Betrays, in a way
5 1974 lyric repeated after "Como una promesa"
6 Plea from the self-conscious
7 One looking for a deal?
8 Some blockers
9 Old Tokyo
10 Diamond substitute
11 Grant
12 7-Down, for one
13 Many a sculpture
15 Like some Olympic races
22 Not counting
23 Multitude
24 Asian spiritual guide
26 One who's gone but not forgotten
27 Muscles strengthened by squats
30 Put on a scale
31 Music style derived from samba and jazz
32 Agreement from one's mate?
33 Big competition
35 Aficionado
39 Phrase used to 46-Across
40 Proposals
42 Forgers' tools
43 He famously asked "Why didn't you burn the tapes?"
44 Vinegar quality
45 Attachments to pronator quadratus muscles
47 Botanical balm
49 Object frequently painted by Degas
50 Grand
52 Some govt. issuances: Abbr.
54 Employer of many a 7-Down

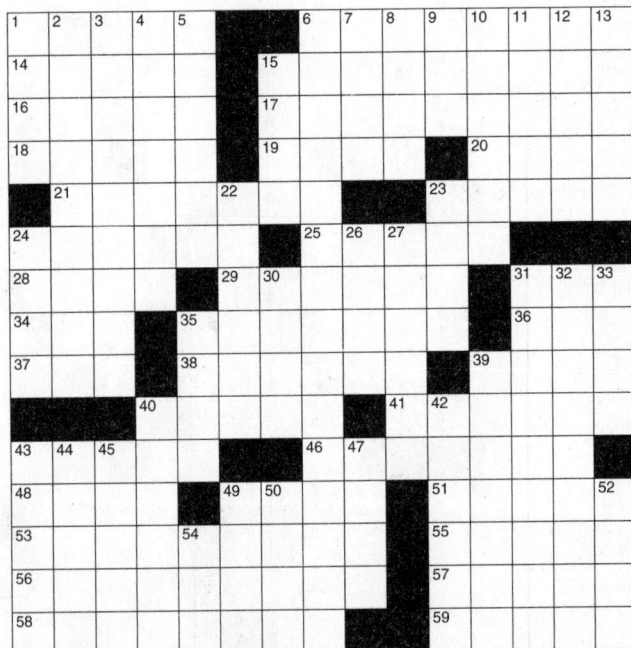

by Mike Nothnagel

ACROSS

1 Bit of miner's gear
9 Go for first
15 Take pains
16 Where it's at
17 Upbeat
18 Much of Micronesia
19 Use a Zen garden
21 Gloating cry
22 Disallowed FedEx destination
25 ___ Aarnio, innovative furniture designer
26 Put on cloud nine
27 Spacewalks and moonwalks, briefly
28 Put back in order?
29 Direction for a boxer
30 Tip for a writer
31 Creator of many 38-Across
35 Response to "Thanks so much"
37 Once-common urban skyline sights
38 Many 31-Across characters
40 Free
41 See 42-Across
42 With 41-Across, discuss
43 Kellogg's brand
44 Wrigley sticks?
46 Characteristic governor
47 Bakers' dozen, maybe?
48 Mars, e.g.
49 Title for Wallis Simpson
51 Opening for the wrist or the back?
53 Attend the lectures of
57 Curve-cutting line
58 She played Jane in "Fun With Dick and Jane," 2005
59 Where traditional bloomers gather
60 Aim for

DOWN

1 Cool, once
2 "Warszawa" instrumentalist
3 Much e-mail
4 Martian moon
5 Glove material
6 Like noisy fans
7 Place to witness a big scene?
8 What a bar mitzvah recently was
9 "Apology" author
10 Drills that can bore
11 Conscious beginning?
12 Bum rap
13 Astronaut Ochoa
14 Fix, as ribs?
20 Nude showers?
22 Kind of code
23 Like ones that are fleeced
24 Bum rap?
26 Aye-aye relative?
28 Certain
29 Sean Connery and Roger Moore, e.g.
31 End it with suddenly
32 Be mephitic
33 Associate (with)
34 Kind of PC command
36 Certain crosses
39 Ice-T or Ice Cube persona
43 Plane, e.g.
44 Nova preceder
45 Composer nominated for an Oscar for "Blues in the Night"
46 Lavatory label
47 Circular windows
49 Make more efficient
50 "___ at the pane": Robert Browning
52 Mate
54 ___-eyed
55 Fictional creature whose name is Old English for "giant"
56 Museu do Índio site

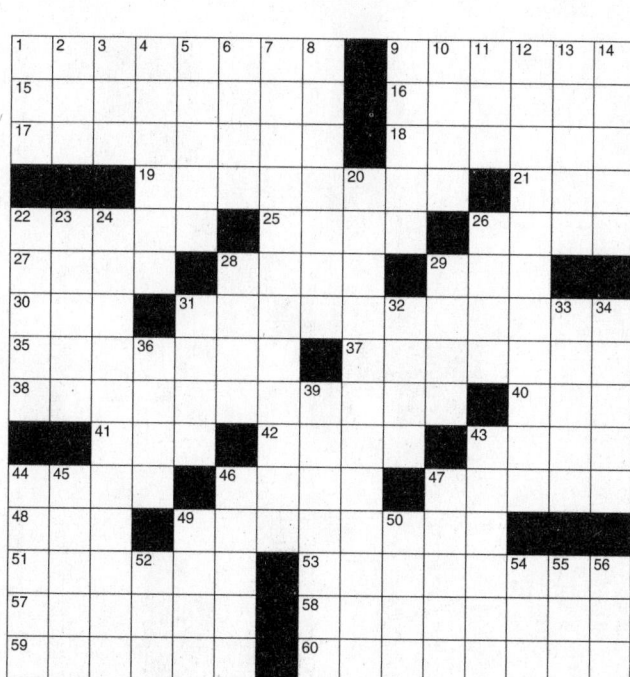

by Jeremy Horwitz

ACROSS

1 Many viviparous births
8 Where many beads are formed
13 Pretty good result for a golf round
14 Without incident
15 Coyote, say, to a Western rancher
16 Subject of the 2001 book subtitled "The Shock of the Century"
17 Stumble
18 Like many resorts
20 Expression of praise
21 Clouds
23 Toppers popular with jazzmen
25 1958 Pulitzer-winning novelist and family
26 His character had the signature line "Book 'em, Danno"
27 Territory on a Risk board
28 Like stools and many benches
29 Event for many a dashing young man
31 Having been overexposed to the sun, maybe
32 Unrefined sort
36 Officially starts work
37 "Nature's lay idiot, I taught thee to love" penner
38 Sea food
39 Points of view?
40 "Chariots of Fire" co-star Charleson
41 Doesn't go away
43 Thing to drive off of
44 Choices for snaps
46 Like some Internet searches
48 ___ monkey
49 Least desirably
50 Sounds from a 3-Down
51 They're far from stars

DOWN

1 Slight show of affection
2 Going ballistic
3 One producing 50-Across
4 Petty recording
5 Boots
6 "___ Most Wanted" ("best-of" compilation of a popular TV cop show)
7 Miss hitting a piñata?: Abbr.
8 Bauhaus artist and teacher
9 "___ I had heard of Lucy Gray": Wordsworth
10 "La Loge" and "La Grenouillère"
11 Skipped over
12 General George at Gettysburg
14 Performed brilliantly
16 Warehouse workers
19 Job for some wall fixers
22 Deuterium has one
24 London letter getter
26 Twenties
28 Wheelie supporter
30 Daredevilish
31 Muleta material
33 Four years as governor, say
34 Like most apartments
35 Minds
36 Danes featured in films
37 Renounce
38 Little digit?
39 Prefix with type
42 Israel's first U.N. delegate
45 Orthodontist's concern
47 Mauna ___

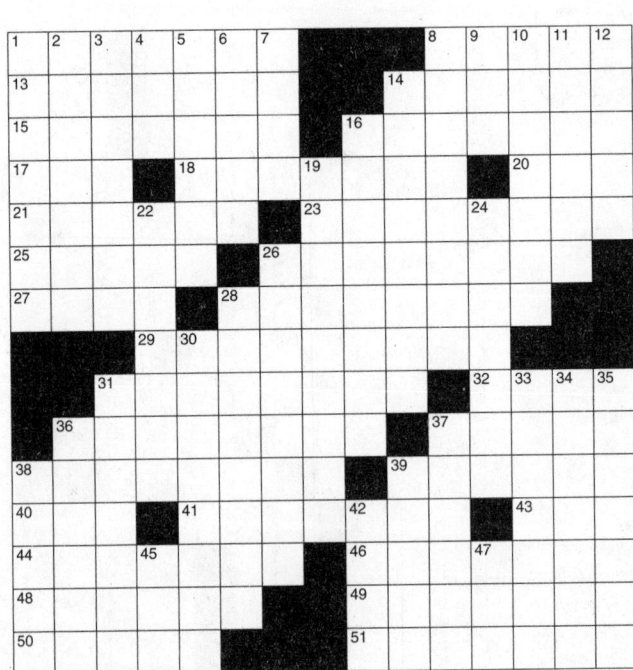

by Joe Krozel

ACROSS

1 Subject of search engine optimization
9 Changing place
15 It may involve the colon
16 Investment option, informally
17 Right part of a map
18 Portmanteau wear
19 Arsenal decommissioned in 2005
20 "The Play About the Baby" playwright
22 Ease
23 Volunteer's offer
25 City of the Altiplano
27 Abandon
28 Certain adjustments
30 Flying Dutchman captain of film
32 Fictional character whose first name is Kentaro
34 One vertex of the Summer Triangle
35 Big name in confectioneries
36 "Delightful!"
38 E-5: Abbr.
39 My country's follower?
42 Ignition trouble
44 Library spot
46 Way to see the big picture?
50 Kind of card
51 French singles
52 Foil alternative
54 Spiced quaffs
55 North Atlantic catch
57 ___-Obama Proliferation and Threat Reduction Initiative (2007 law)
59 Footnote abbr.
60 Rung
62 Time for Conan, informally

64 He played Mandela on TV's "Mandela"
65 Joins, redundantly
66 Movie genre named for a food staple
67 Starbucks offering

DOWN

1 "Step aside, I'll help"
2 Bit of green in a wallet
3 Side in an epic battle
4 Letters for college-bound students
5 Annual romance writer's award
6 Place ___
7 "I'm impressed!"
8 Bit of in-line skating gear
9 Price abbr.
10 Canadian singer with three #1 Billboard hits

11 Growing concern for a surgeon, informally?
12 Transportation to Sugar Hill, in a 1941 song
13 Get to
14 They're positive
21 Collection sites, of a sort
24 Romantic introduction?
26 Company behind the popular social network games FarmVille and CityVille
29 Commercial prefix since the 1950s
31 "Romeo Must Die" actor, 2000
33 Bounces
37 Good
39 Where some write checks
40 "Bingo!"
41 Censor's target

42 Free
43 Anarchy
45 Atlanta's ___ Center
46 Angry lover's dismissal
47 Beverage nickname, with "the"
48 Product of Bordeaux
49 Olympics site that introduced snowboarding
53 Smart
56 Bucks and bucks
58 Casting need
61 Hospital grp.
63 Kind of card

by David Quarfoot

ACROSS

1 Brainchild of 57-Across
5 1998 Sarah McLachlan hit
9 1972 Bill Withers hit
14 Some documentary workers
16 Film studio spearheaded by 57-Across
17 Brainchild of 57-Across
18 Parade V.I.P.
19 Post-PC ___
20 Thimbleful
21 Finest example
23 Focus of some prep work
25 Ulan-___ (Siberian capital)
26 Slogan associated with 57-Across
32 Flatterer
33 Bitmap images
34 Tyler of "The Lord of the Rings"
35 Hole punchers
36 Huffs
38 Singer Simone
39 Head
40 Like some Arabians
41 Reacted to an unveiling, say
42 Frequent description of 57-Across
46 Wheeler Peak locale: Abbr.
47 Many an early computer user
48 "Doonesbury" cartoonist
52 Anderson who directed "Rushmore"
53 ___ drive
56 Cover again, as terrain?
57 This puzzle's subject
60 Company co-founded by 57-Across
61 Rocket parts
62 Prepared to be shot
63 E-mail heading: Abbr.
64 Company founded by 57-Across

DOWN

1 "Have a Little Faith ___" (1930 hit)
2 Onetime host of "The Tonight Show"
3 One seeking to catch some rays?
4 Soft & ___
5 "Sic 'em!"
6 Thingamajig
7 Return letters?
8 ___ Stadium, sports venue since 1997
9 They're positive
10 Junior watcher
11 Site of some unveilings
12 Term of address for a lady
13 "Symphony in Black" artist
15 "Friends, Romans, countrymen, lend me your ears" speaker
22 Patisserie offerings
23 YouTube content, for short
24 One of many from 57-Across
26 "Prelude ___" (1942 Frank Capra film)
27 Split, in a way
28 Tailor's concern
29 Root of diplomacy
30 Good diving scores
31 Show stopper?
32 Baby powder ingredient
36 Hindu god often depicted meditating
37 All Saints' Day mo.
38 Mitchum's genre
40 Got into hot water?
41 "Hold on"
43 Speedy Gonzales shout
44 Film in which the Marx Brothers join the gold rush
45 Gridiron group
48 Golfer's concern
49 Unwanted collection
50 Ones who might cry foul?
51 "From knowledge, sea power" org.
53 Tract
54 Mountain climber
55 Cheater's whisper
58 Tater ___
59 Pianist Nakamatsu

by Kevin G. Der

ACROSS

1 Accessories for some suits
16 It's often popped on a shoulder
17 Assassinated leader called "the Liberator"
18 Part of many a chain
19 Blow off
20 Go off
21 Largest city in Nordrhein-Westfalen
22 Like many dyed eggs
24 They may be networked
25 Supermarket chain
26 Predecessor of Pope Hilarius
28 It's often enough
32 Kind of memory
34 Permanent, in a way
37 Unquestioning adherents
40 Stigma
41 ___ nitrite
42 Its minimum score is 60, briefly
43 End of the lion
45 ___ Lingus
46 Old political inits.
48 Quality of the queen's jewels?
50 Set, as the sun
54 Opposite of "Happily . . ."
56 Quarter-millennium year
57 Singer called "The Jezebel of Jazz"
58 Jails
62 Shows oneself
63 Responded to some rapping

DOWN

1 Certain fabric worker's work
2 Richard ___, 2002 Pulitzer winner for the novel "Empire Falls"
3 Ever
4 Existentialist Kierkegaard
5 Kind of request in Burns's "To a Mouse"
6 ___-pros
7 Grandpa player in "Look Who's Talking," 1989
8 Like some clothing ensembles
9 Savanna grazer
10 Big brand of writing instruments
11 The Taurus replaced it
12 "Xena: Warrior Princess" role
13 Parts of some pay-as-you-go plans?
14 "Giant Brain" of the 1940s
15 Sounds like a broken record
22 Sound investment
23 21-Across refusal
27 Cleaning the mess?
28 Stamps, say
29 With 50-Down, fair
30 Ones holding wraps in restaurants
31 "Dream-Children" author, 1822
33 What's caught during a tumble?
35 Long reign, e.g.
36 Reason for a late shift?: Abbr.
38 Plant in the pea family
39 "___ Pastore" (Mozart opera)
44 Like some vertebrae
46 Hayek of Hollywood
47 Hoops Hall-of-Famer Jerry
49 Where it's at
50 See 29-Down
51 Fictional Sicilian town in a 1944 novel
52 Member of a crack team?
53 Bandleader with the hit "Three Little Fishies"
55 Twist
59 From Bakersfield to LA., say
60 Kind of power
61 "Forgot About ___" (2000 Grammy-winning rap)

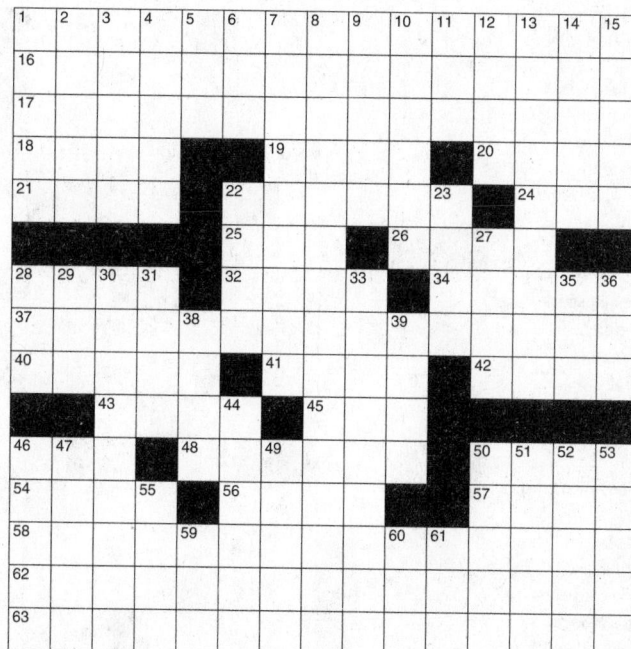

by Tim Croce

ACROSS

1 Bologna is in it
7 Look out for, say
11 Pilot's point?
14 Player of Duke Santos in "Ocean's Eleven," 1960
16 What may come between two friends?
17 Co-writer and star of "Bridesmaids"
18 Part of the former U.A.R.: Abbr.
19 Blocks of history
20 One concerned with blocking
22 More reasonable
24 Caucus call
25 Sports org.
26 Coal-rich valley
28 "Are you up for it?"
32 One helping with filing, for short
35 Momentary disruption
37 "Gotcha"
38 Where to see the writing on the wall?
41 A. J. who wrote "The Citadel"
42 Will of "Jeremiah Johnson"
43 Lou Gehrig's disease, for short
44 Abnormally small
46 Little middle?
48 Terre Haute sch.
49 Cousin of the cassowary
51 Messing around on TV?
55 Melodious birdsong, maybe
59 Composer Khachaturian
60 Peabody Museum patron, perhaps
61 Wind instrument?
63 Abbr. after several examples
64 Playwright who became a president
65 Big hits, for short
66 Artist whose moniker is the pronunciation of his initials
67 Vice president from Tennessee

DOWN

1 Official in the Clinton White House
2 ___ nullius (no man's land)
3 Like about 25% of legal U.S. immigrants
4 Gals across the pond
5 N.Y.C. subway inits.
6 Father of Harmonia, in myth
7 Distributor of Nutrilite vitamins
8 Sandy shades
9 City on Presque Isle Bay
10 ___ party
11 It "isn't what it used to be," said Simone Signoret
12 So to speak
13 William ___, 1990s attorney general
15 One side of the Detroit River
21 Part of U.S.C.: Abbr.
23 Hopper
27 Exclusively
29 New worker
30 Dear
31 "Vous ___ ici"
32 Ozone destroyers, for short
33 Liking
34 Sound system?
36 Env. alternative
39 Lassitude
40 1968 Julie Christie movie set in San Francisco
45 Extract the essence of by boiling
47 Cartoon villain who sails the Black Barnacle
50 Filmmaker Louis
52 Applause accompanier
53 More bloody, so to speak
54 Big
55 Easily imposed upon
56 Mass gathering place
57 Tour de France setting?
58 Source of venanzite
62 The Stars may play the Blues in it, briefly

by Caleb Madison and J.A.S.A. Class

ACROSS

1 Bibelot
11 Overweening
15 It really sucks
16 1997 Home Run Derby champion Martinez
17 One-way flights?
18 Not again
19 1973 Nobel Peace Prize decliner Le Duc ___
20 Singular
21 Has to repeat, maybe
22 Get the best of
24 Rodin's thinker?
25 Germany's University of Duisburg-___
26 Wore
28 Like depleted uranium
30 Lao-___
31 House party?
33 One who's got no hope
35 Frito-Lay product
39 Sets at ease
40 Island state in a 1964 merger
42 Explorer's need
43 Places for cutters, for short
44 Star
46 Try to bite
50 What a mail carrier might use in self-defense?
52 ___ Nordegren, ex-wife of Tiger Woods
54 They're counted at meals: Abbr.
55 Growls
56 Cousin of a cutter
58 Nasdaq listing: Abbr.
59 Minotaur, e.g.
60 "You said it!"
62 Formally appeals

63 Malady that typically worsens in the spring
64 You need only scrape the surface to get it
65 1940 cartoon in which Woody Woodpecker debuted

DOWN

1 Beef producer?
2 Home of Daniel Webster College
3 "Brrr!"
4 Reviewer of books
5 Letter before lima in the NATO phonetic alphabet
6 Dog topper
7 Cleared
8 Decided not to run
9 Went without control

10 Gold meas.
11 Sides of some ancient temples
12 Tend
13 Steely-gazed pointer
14 Flips
21 Consumes
23 Funny George
27 Classifieds, e.g.
29 Whiz
32 Gray area?
34 "It's ___!"
35 Leon ___, McKinley's assassin
36 Vituperation
37 Catches up
38 They do better when they close early
41 Chile ___ (Mexican dish)
45 Superhuman, in a way
47 Afghani tongue

48 Language family including Mongolian
49 "You shouldn't have"
51 Waveform maximum
53 Unacceptable
57 Chops in a kitchen
60 "Don't ___"
61 When repeated, hero of children's lit

by Joon Pahk

ACROSS

1 "King Kong" co-star, 2005
10 Magazine subtitled "The Horse Owner's Resource"
15 Son or daughter, usually
16 Aachen appetizer
17 Fictional king with an enormous appetite
18 "Passion" actress, 1919
19 It had "three deuces and a four-speed and a 389," in song
20 Yachting event
22 Thousandth of a yen
23 Has a yen
25 Showy
26 One hanging around the house
27 Napoleon biographer Ludwig
28 Maker of a small purchase, sarcastically
30 Buttonwood
32 Bakery gizmos
33 Fire
34 Writer Jaffe
36 Like some antes
39 Arboriculturist
43 "The Fearless Vampire Killers" actress
46 First name in design
47 More than plenty
48 Claptrap
49 Turkish province or its capital
50 Some income: Abbr.
51 Unfair
53 Opened
54 "Dilemma" rapper
56 Superlatively stout
58 Newsman Roger
59 Fiancée, say
60 Popularity
61 Operation in 1998 news

DOWN

1 Shakes
2 All the things you are
3 Prolonged
4 It's tapped
5 Chutzpah
6 Propositional phrase?
7 Cry to an obedient dog, maybe
8 Heart
9 African livestock pens
10 Feudal worker
11 Lab. neighbor
12 Better model
13 Opposite the current
14 Some fishing boats
21 It's often put on backward
24 Bakery gizmos
26 Protected
28 Campy wear
29 A single, in Stuttgart
31 "Love ___" (1964 hit)
34 Contributions to them are not tax-deductible
35 It may have a lead part
36 "Memed My Hawk" director and star, 1984
37 Cell assignment: Abbr.
38 What a toddler might pull
39 What a scammer might pull
40 Brewed bit
41 Former Mexican president Zedillo
42 Drivers' duty
44 Its members may be seen traveling: Abbr.
45 Sluggish
49 ___ nothing
51 1944 Pulitzer correspondent
52 "Look ___!"
55 N.Y.C. school
57 N.Y.C. subway

by David Bunker

ACROSS

2 Bring joy to
5 Like some store-bought nuts
6 Country singer Gibbs glided a short distance?
9 Old West gun crossing over?
11 Doing time
12 Nautical leader?
13 Illegal copying
16 Corporate treadmill
19 Org. with a draft
20 Where somebody might be spotted
21 Nitwit
22 Lady's attendant
26 Radio switch
28 Trip director, for short
31 Chemist's container
34 What Newton's first law of motion concerns
35 Cowboy Rogers as part of a posse after some younger namesakes joined up?
36 Poisonous gilled mushroom, crossing over?
39 Like a roast
40 Presenters' bits
41 Offense
43 Every mirror image has one
45 Prelapsarian home
46 L.A. winter hrs.
48 Common female middle name
50 Source of much plywood
52 Like a crown's gems, maybe
55 Resolve
56 Stressful tests
58 Matter barely worth mentioning
60 Leasable tropical locales aren't truthful?
64 Simon Templar's creator, crossing over?
65 Slip around
66 Reach the top

DOWN

1 Sleep-preventing sound, perhaps
3 Poetic contraction
4 Bookkeeping notation
7 First name in despotism
8 Plant with fiddleheads
10 Learn the hard way?
14 "The ___ Daba Honeymoon" (1914 #1 song)
15 Language in which "yes" and "no" are "baat" and "te," respectively
17 Knock
18 Give out
20 Free Web-based correspondence service
22 "This Week in Baseball" host Allen
23 "As You Like It" setting
24 Particular
25 Piece in the game Othello
27 Whimsically odd
28 Letter from school?
29 What the "Surgeon's Photo" supposedly depicts
30 Distressed
32 Impact point for a spoons player
33 "Dear me!"
37 1976 Broadway musical based on Henry VIII's life
38 "Henry & June" author
42 Banker's recommendation, for short
44 TV show with the most Emmy nominations, informally
46 Pet sound
47 Torrent
49 Part of NBC: Abbr.
50 Takes to the cleaners
51 Off-___ (sturdy bikes)
52 Natalie Portman's birthplace
53 Heat generator?
54 Grad sch. composition
55 Overused plot device
57 Chaim Potok's "My Name Is Asher ___"
59 Winter protection?
60 TD Garden team
61 Curtis of hair care
62 Chilling, say
63 Set of channels?

by Will Shortz

ACROSS

1 Theory related to eugenics
16 What good competitors may give one
17 Part of many confessions
18 Old Testament book before Neh.
19 Some services
20 Composer of "1/1," "1/2," "2/1" and "2/2"
21 Some HDTVs
23 Noodle
24 Guidebook listings for the budget-conscious
32 Gossips
33 Winter cry in New York
34 Riddle
36 Like some cross-dressers
38 Stoker who wrote "Dracula"
39 "Hooked on Classics" company
41 "That's the spot"
42 Pacific, perhaps
49 Here, in Juárez
50 Fictional maker of earthquake pills and elephant bullets
53 Feature of the ideal path
54 Some I.T. experts

DOWN

1 More prudent, say
2 "The People and Its Leaders" muralist
3 Tangy pie fruit
4 Amsterdam-based financial giant
5 Pitch ___
6 It means nothing
7 De Matteo of "The Sopranos"
8 Note passers?
9 Korean War leader
10 Filling yarn
11 "Look at me, ___ helpless . . ." (first words of "Misty")
12 What may come before so much?
13 How Ginger Rogers danced
14 Taken for
15 "Discobolus" sculptor
22 New York's ___ Building, designed by Mies van der Rohe
23 Crazy way to go?
25 Jerry in the Basketball Hall of Fame
26 Polo and others
27 Go out with ___
28 Some Parisian income
29 Walter ___, two-time winner of golf's U.S. Open
30 Echo, e.g.
31 Short
34 Some rodeo bulls
35 Doesn't lay off
36 Actress Ullman
37 Boil down
38 Some idols
40 Heat divisions
42 Part of a Molière work
43 Abram of "This Old House"
44 Oh so
45 Res ___ loquitur
46 "How's it ___?"
47 ___ Minor
48 Like some monuments: Abbr.
51 Wilfred Owen poem "Dulce et Decorum ___"
52 Scotland's longest river

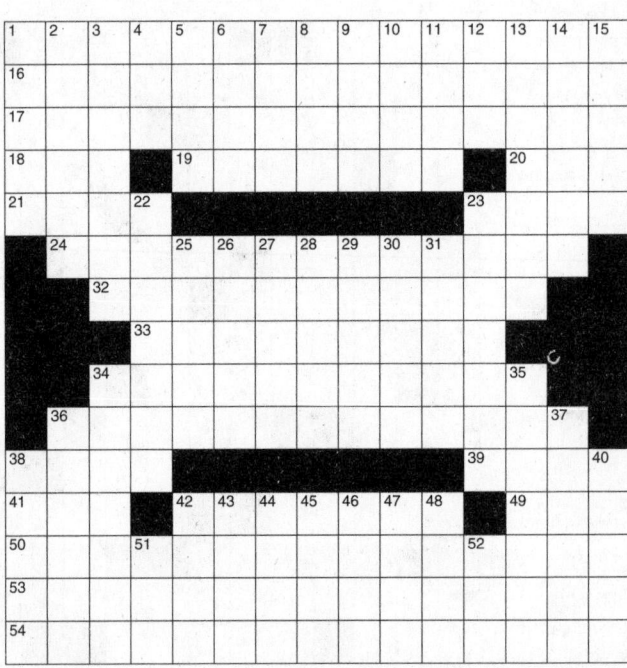

by Tim Croce

ACROSS

1 Coffee shop, often
12 "Sid the Science Kid" network
15 Stops being infantile
16 Pianist Stein
17 Producer of shooting stars
18 Ado Annie, e.g.
19 Pentagon-to-Lincoln Memorial dir.
20 Aid in relieving xerostomia
21 Breaks up
23 Bullish declaration
25 What has made some people miss the mark?
28 Pungent dressing
29 Barely visible art collection?
31 Polynesian port, when doubled
33 Game player's concern
34 Stopped being infantile
36 Part of the Buchanan High faculty
38 Certain preserved strips
40 Shape preserver, of a sort
43 Not so stuffy
47 Banks with many spreads
48 Pack of lifesavers?
50 With 1-Down, good thing to have for a tornado
51 Does some piece work
53 "Mottke the Thief" novelist, 1935
55 Music critic's concern
56 Scored very quickly?
58 It holds the line
60 British big shot
61 Love
62 Its title character is Manrico

66 Contact info spec.
67 March locale
68 Clinton was its first gov.
69 Attachable bulletin

DOWN

1 See 50-Across
2 "Ditto"
3 Base in Anne Arundel County: Abbr.
4 Metaphor middle
5 "Wayne's World 2" actor James
6 How orchestra members enter
7 Band
8 Subj. of the Privacy Act of 1974
9 Holder of notes
10 Look like a sleaze
11 Mrs. Mulder on "The X-Files"
12 Gorges
13 It has many tangible points
14 Having more four-letter words
22 Fink
24 Pop trio with the 1964 hit "Bread and Butter," with "the"
26 Aircraft propellers without moving parts
27 Damsel distresser
30 Cake makeup for a feeder
32 Southern side
35 Old man of Orléans
37 Ado Annie, e.g.
39 Damage-assessing grp.
40 King with revolting subjects
41 Like citric acid and lactic acid
42 Points
44 Resolve
45 Land above the Rio Bravo
46 Cousin of kvass
49 Splits for cooking, as fish
52 Mushroom supporter
54 Shack
57 Wang Lung's wife, in literature
59 Playground provocation
63 Italian TV channel
64 Some kind of nerve?
65 Rattle holder

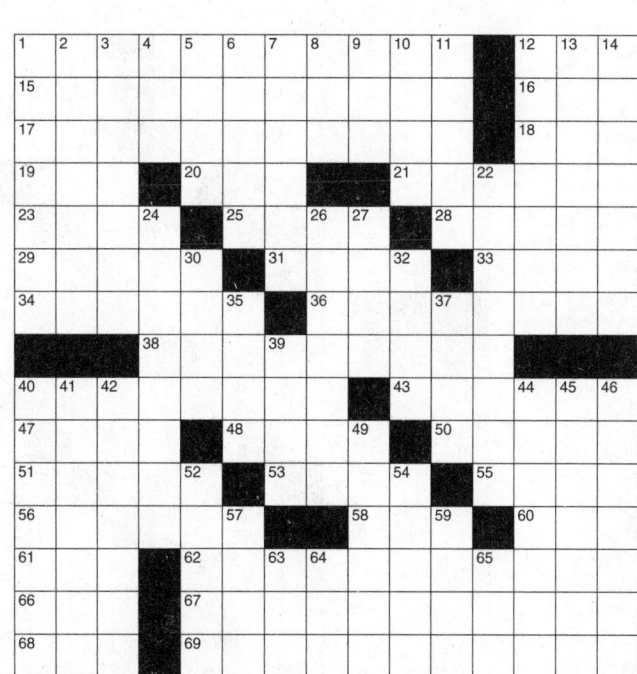

by Barry C. Silk

ACROSS

1 Leave the pad, say
9 Rustle up some food
15 ___ Brewster, beleaguered nephew in "Arsenic and Old Lace"
16 Grammy-winning 1996 Beck album
17 How some legal conversations are held
18 Newly christen
19 Touch up
20 African migrators
22 "The Amazing Race" network
23 Born earlier
24 Neeson of "Taken"
25 Decision
26 Some distillery products
27 Lunchtime queueing spot
28 Metaphorical crowd
29 Dodges, as an obligation
32 Gets bent out of shape
35 Shirt or skirt
36 R&B "drinking song" covered by Ray Charles
38 Shoots in the foot, say
39 Yarn unit
40 Buddyroo
44 "You've got a deal!"
45 OS X runners
46 What a cookie cutter cuts
47 Large amount
48 What stars might indicate
49 Foul ball's landing spot, often
50 The DC-10 was one
52 While
54 "Gone With the Wind" actor Howard
55 1994 sci-fi film about an alien artifact
56 Controversial one-act play by Mamet
57 Visited a vacation house, maybe

DOWN

1 Bach's "Mass in ___"
2 Unfrequented
3 Establishment with children's quarters?
4 Leading ladies?
5 Proctor's need
6 Sign
7 "___-de-Lance" (debut of Nero Wolfe)
8 Warning on a box
9 Discussion venue
10 High-flown tributes
11 1990s cartoon dog
12 Without sides, you might say
13 Take the risk of
14 Marching order
21 Shooters on the boards?
24 Symbol above the comma on a keyboard
25 Amount scarcely worth arguing over
27 Confounded
28 Ruptured
30 Ninth-largest body known to orbit the sun
31 La Jolla's ___ Institute for Biological Studies
32 Doctor in Hugh Lofting tales
33 Lovestruck
34 Doctrine associated with Betty Friedan
37 Contemptible fool
41 Craft store?
42 Bit of new info
43 Blundered, with "up"
45 Out of the game, in chess
46 One tracked by radar
48 Curb
49 Close with a bang
51 2001 album featuring "Love Don't Cost a Thing"
53 ___ Redman, hero of Stephen King's "The Stand"

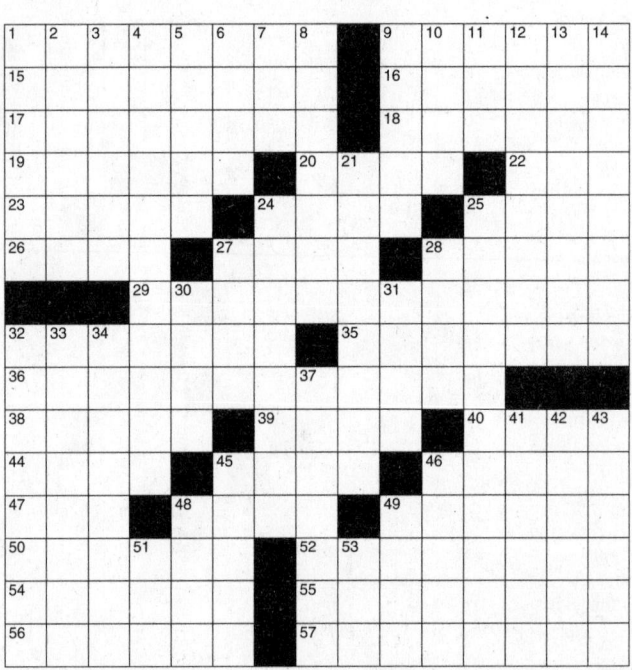

by Patrick Berry

ACROSS

1 First name in eroticism
6 Confab
9 Queen ___ (Maryland county)
14 Relative of a bobolink
17 Friendly
18 Minor despot
19 It has a crosspiece for a head
20 One in a Biergarten?
21 Title role for Omar Sharif or Benicio Del Toro
23 "Ulysses" star, 1967
26 Like some outlets
28 One is often said to be dead
30 Not notched
31 Plays with masks
32 Gets out in the open
33 Current event around Christmas?
35 With 39-Across, street fair fare
37 19th dynasty's founder
38 Take
39 See 35-Across
40 Composition of some stars
41 Symposium offering: Abbr.
42 Commuter's annoyance
44 Popular tech news site
45 Massachusetts town near the New Hampshire border
47 Like some survey boxes
48 1970s radical grp.
49 Frittata alternative
51 Options for building torpedoes
55 1930 Laurel and Hardy film
58 What a lessee often gets back less of

59 Gives a "Yoo-hoo!" on Facebook
60 Vous, over the Rhine
61 Part of a beehive

DOWN

1 "Take ___" (1994 Madonna hit)
2 Family nickname
3 Creator of much suspense
4 Biased, in a way
5 Kinsman of Jesus
6 Visa offering
7 Man's name that spells another man's name backward
8 Like losers
9 Half of a sci-fi name
10 TV producer's concern
11 1960s–'70s foe
12 Wahoo, for one

13 22-Down, in Dijon
15 It was last inhabited in 2000
16 15-Down went around one
22 Matching pair designation
24 Wee: Var.
25 Apply chrism to
26 Tony's boss on "Who's the Boss?"
27 Armstrong blew it
28 Specialty
29 Obviously not happy
32 KO connection maker
34 KO connection?
36 2004–06 Haitian P.M.
37 Shoulder holder
39 French key
43 Wields
44 Hullabaloo
46 Glassware ovens
48 Was quiescent

50 Bank of China Tower designer
52 The 4th of November?
53 Sister of Nephthys
54 Former high fliers
55 Possible cause of paralysis
56 Liberal leader?
57 Memo opener

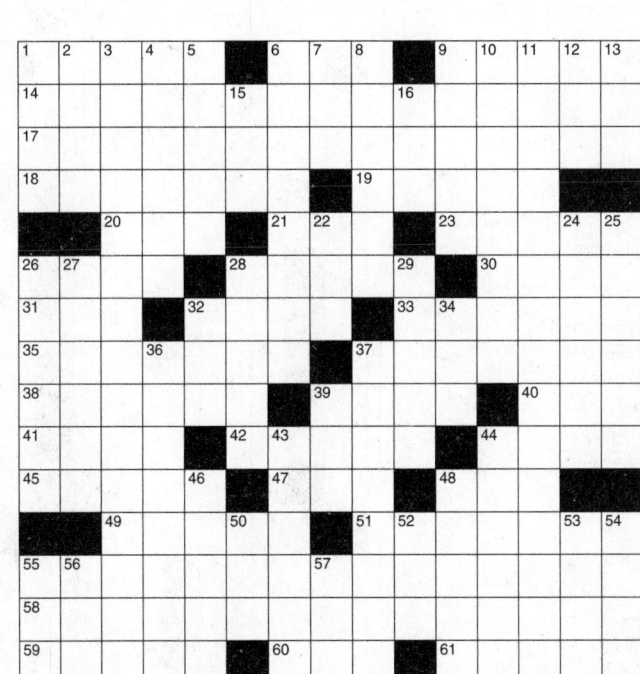

by Kurt Mueller

Note: This crossword was originally published on 11/11/11.

ACROSS

1 __ scan
4 Media inits. since 1927
7 Music genre of the Mighty Mighty Bosstones
10 Solid rock center?
13 It's shown on a topographical map
15 Disheveled
17 Family members
18 Parents, e.g.
19 Prefix with -matic
20 Google search object
22 First name in auto racing
23 Cousin __
24 "Well done!"
25 Actress Merrill
26 Bygone espionage org.
28 Biology div.
30 Cry of repugnance
31 Morales of "Gun Hill Road"
32 Hot spot
33 First name in auto racing
35 Philadelphia landmark
36 Denigrates, in British slang
37 Over
38 Reverse
39 Things gotten with a credit card, often
40 Get beat
41 Atlanta sch. with 30,000+ students
42 Publication that clicks with readers?
43 "Star Trek" extra: Abbr.
44 Carrie Chapman __, founder of the League of Women Voters
45 Buttocks
46 1974 Gould/ Sutherland spoof
48 W.W. II rationing org.

49 Norse equivalent of Mars
50 Death on the Nile cause?
51 Female charmer of myth
55 Montana neighbor
59 Rockefeller Center is built in it
60 More rich, as soil
61 Meeting
62 Breaks

DOWN

1 Year the first Rose Bowl was played
2 1940 Crosby/Lamour/ Hope comedy
3 Irregularly
4 It might make you jump
5 Rotary Club members
6 Outlawing

7 Medical bigwigs
8 Place for a pad
9 Wanted letters?
10 Carnegie Hall debut of 1928, with "An"
11 Building safety feature
12 Befuddled
14 Familia member
16 Wipes out
21 It's not a dream
27 Recuse oneself from, say
29 Some services
31 Layer of green eggs
34 "Concentration" pronoun
44 Flat ones are not good
47 Wrangles (with)
52 Glamour types, for short
53 Gift on a string

54 Prefix with car
56 __ cit. (footnote abbr.)
57 Dickensian cry
58 Record label inits.

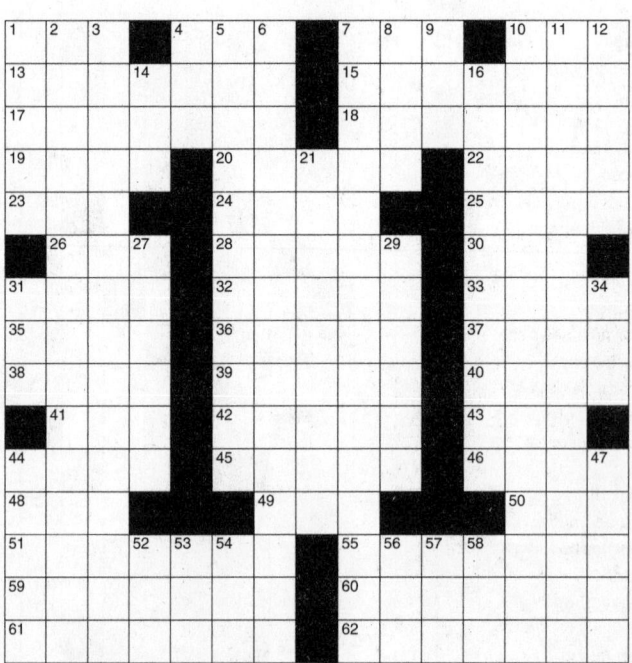

by Alex Vratsanos

ACROSS

1 Musical great whose grave went unmarked for nearly 150 years
7 Bombing, e.g.
15 Pôrto ___, Brazil
16 One whose crush was caped
17 Frank
18 Player of the evil Blofeld in "Never Say Never Again"
19 Make more efficient
21 All-inclusive
22 All targets
23 Troubled
24 Pulitzer-winning sports reporter Berkow
27 Sight-seeing need in Spain?
28 What a weaver may be guilty of, briefly
29 Inner city, e.g.
35 Words of betrayal
36 Cheese ___
37 Eat
39 495
42 It's cut and dried
43 One often seen in drag
44 Dir. from Gramercy Park to Central Park
45 Stage part
48 One side in a 1960s civil war
51 Record producer Talmy
52 People who see what you're saying?
56 Didn't approve
58 Some dishwashers
59 Prescription proviso
60 Herald
61 Quaint introduction
62 Picks up

DOWN

1 Awesome parts of a Museum of Natural History display
2 Cut
3 See 24-Down
4 Georgia's ___ Scott College
5 Tyra Banks, vis-à-vis "America's Next Top Model"
6 Lead-in to some royal names
7 All-Star Dark of the 1950s Giants
8 Masked scavengers
9 Sticker on a plate
10 "Inglourious Basterds" org.
11 Boxing class
12 Relatives of arroyos
13 Part of an ignitron
14 Keep from drying out
20 2005 Emmy winner for "ER"
23 17-Across supporter
24 With 3-Down, Bud product
25 Coll. elective
26 Broadway acronym
28 The "me" in "nothing can stop me now," in a 1962 #1 hit
30 Place for some car fluid
31 Shocker, perhaps
32 Al-___ (one of the names of God in Islam)
33 Grass roots development?
34 Form of "John"
38 Good looker?
40 Form of "John"
41 North Platte feeder
45 Name of father-and-son world leaders
46 Period
47 Palacio resident
48 Junkyard dog, probably
49 They may help people tune out conversations
50 Turkish city or province
52 California wine locale
53 Many a Lockheed Martin employee: Abbr.
54 Pavement pounder
55 ID theft targets
57 Video game letters

by Barry C. Silk

ACROSS

1 Certain chip feature
6 Billboard once named her "Female Entertainer of the Century"
15 Food item with layers
16 "Here's what they said . . ."
17 "Dum spiro, ___" ("While I breathe, I hope": Lat.)
18 Veal dish
19 Partner of ciencias
20 Second person in the Bible
21 Second person in the Bible
22 Old man
23 Bull: Prefix
24 MS. dos?
26 Part of A.S.T.: Abbr.
27 Deceitful ones
29 Behind
31 Moving like hummingbirds
35 Pollux and Aldebaran
36 Certain fisherman
37 Capone portrayer, 1959
39 What's hot
40 Flags
42 Cry repeated in "The Whiffenpoof Song"
43 It causes many people to scratch
46 Big maker of consoles
47 Big East team
48 Cortés's quest
49 Kind of film
50 "___ It," 1979 top 10 hit
51 Missed curfew, say
54 Still in the game
55 Simple golf putt
56 Appeal of New York, e.g.?
57 Something transparent
58 ___-cross

DOWN

1 Onetime boycott instigator
2 How 1-Down's act was conducted
3 Reduced fare?
4 Runs through
5 Grandson of 21-Across
6 Sneak
7 Increase slowly
8 Stuck
9 Start of a call for help
10 Environmental datum of concern to asthmatics, for short
11 Place to get stuck
12 Radiates, as confidence
13 Either co-founder of Apple
14 1991–92 U.S. Open winner
23 Wound tighter
24 Easy ___
25 Showing life
27 ___ Valente (clothing line)
28 1955 Belmont and Preakness winner that shared its name with a U.S. city
30 "Love Sneakin' Up on You" singer, 1994
32 How some calorie counters eventually want to look good
33 Demerits
34 Lead-in to an exciting announcement
38 Paraphrase
39 Duds
41 Usher, e.g.
43 Visit, as a site, with "to"
44 Hockey East town
45 Venerated symbol
47 More chalky
49 Schedule
50 Fashion designer Jacobs
52 Suffix with solid
53 Rejections

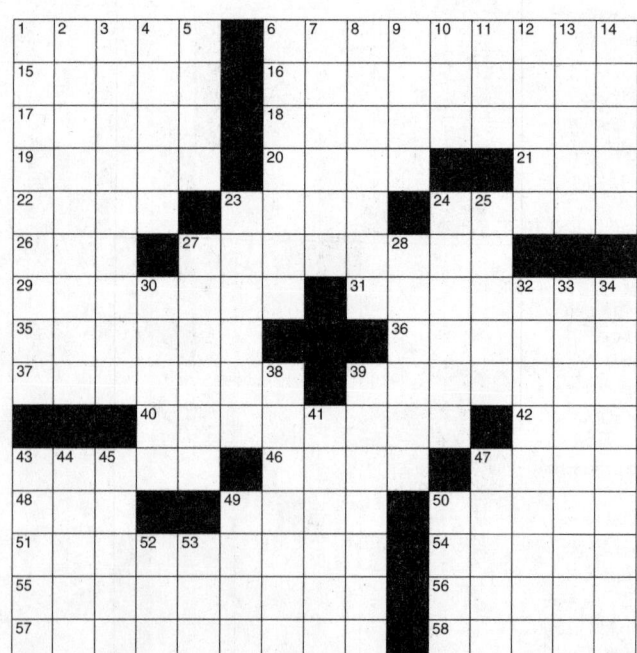

by Joe DiPietro

ACROSS

1 Where a lecture may be given
5 Biology class topic
10 One trying to eliminate bad notes
14 French possessive
15 Beauty
16 ___-American relations
17 Cook's final setting
20 Eager
21 Desperate
22 Charge
23 Graffitist's trademark
25 Like much home improvement, for short
26 "The answer ___"
28 Drew back
30 One who brought together many couples
33 Accompaniment for oysters
36 Actress Graynor
37 "Tell ___ Mama" (2009 Norah Jones song)
38 With 52-Down, a "grand" place
39 Biology class topic
40 One with a growing hobby
44 What a jumpy person is on
45 Steel worker?
46 St. Louis landmark designer
47 Substantially
49 Sound that might indicate hunger
50 Maid employer
51 Dovetail part
54 Select smokes
58 Snap
60 County west of Wyoming
61 "Northward Over the Great Ice" writer
62 Kite's kin
63 Suffix with adipo-
64 Gives some air time?
65 U.K. decorations

DOWN

1 Crack response
2 Part of a loving threesome?
3 It may be picked first
4 Link
5 Honeybee genus
6 It helps show you when something is done
7 Suffix with Mozart
8 Symbol of pork
9 "Ran" preceder
10 Sovereign of yore
11 Social admonition
12 "You ___" (2004 Celine Dion hit)
13 One can get stuffy
18 Test the patience of
19 City in the Plain of Sharon
24 Land in a stream
26 Projected thing
27 Originated
28 Grinch's expression
29 Vermeer's home
31 Having a spotty situation to face?
32 Learns (of)
34 "Thimble Theatre" surname
35 Something with many arms
41 Source of an essential oil with medicinal properties
42 Phiz on a five
43 Superficially updated
48 Setting for Hitchcock's "Notorious"
50 Pianist Pogorelich
51 How long it takes light to travel 186 mi.
52 See 38-Across
53 Org. in "Monk"
55 Actress Poehler and others
56 Dating word
57 Women with auréoles: Abbr.
59 Asian affirmative

by Paula Gamache

ACROSS

1 Puts in a seat
9 Like vinyl records
16 Fills all the seats for
17 Faith-based initiative?
18 Most likely
20 Capital 7,200 feet above sea level
21 Poltergeist output
22 It's south of Sp.
23 Tree line stats.
24 Sought the opinions of, in a way
25 ___ other (matchlessly)
26 "Is ___?"
27 Keebler's head elf and others
28 Dressing holder
29 Levels with sticks?
31 Sitcom sports agent Michaels
32 What goes around at a hoedown?
33 Big Dipper star
34 Bath hub?
35 Sowing pioneer
38 Court whizzes
39 Some smokes
40 Peace Nobelist Kim ___ Jung
41 Italian novelist Morante
42 Bellyacher
43 47-Across personnel: Abbr.
44 Screened city dweller?
45 Tennis's Fraser and others
46 High-profile defendant of 1992
47 "Dracula" and "Frankenstein" producer
50 Clio maker
51 Struggling to get
52 What MapQuest requests
53 Some opinions

DOWN

1 "Again . . ."
2 Opposing team's turndown
3 Suggest subliminally, perhaps
4 Cantina cookware
5 Gran Bretaña, e.g.
6 Start of the second half?
7 Make like
8 Sting participant
9 First and last quarters, e.g.
10 Dressed like 27-Down
11 Participants in the annual Safety Dance
12 One of four in Mississippi: Abbr.
13 Revealing issue
14 Pine
15 Some building weakeners
19 They were black and yellow in old medicine
24 Tough thing to swallow
25 Jimmy Johnson title comics character and others
27 10-Down commanders
28 "Help!" and such
30 Senate stars?
31 ___ nothing
33 Social time at the lodge
34 Bard's break
35 Brown-tinged Hawaiian crow
36 Like some station wagons
37 Cuts it out
39 Doesn't work hard
42 Blackbirds
43 Skirt
45 ___ Zürcher Zeitung (leading Swiss daily)
46 Magazine contents
48 Dictionary abbr.
49 "___ so appalling — it exhilarates": Dickinson

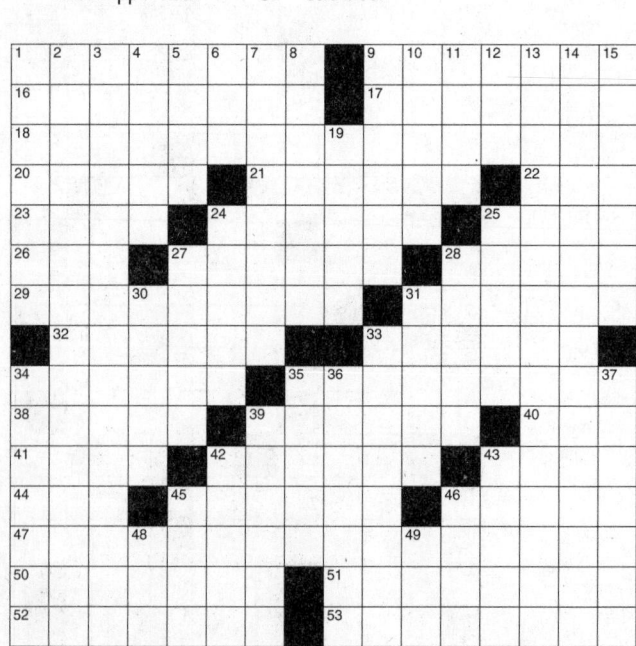

by Joe Krozel

ACROSS

1 Park ranger?
7 Several "Beowulf" scenes
13 Princess who was a sister of Napoleon Bonaparte
14 Fails to factor in
16 Aims
17 "Peanuts" surname
18 Sports champion with a palindromic name
19 & 21 Like many rivers in winter
22 Literary title character with a palindromic name
23 French twists, e.g.
25 Feta maker's need
26 Genre of "The Set-Up," 1949
28 Picked-up pickup, perhaps
30 Long seen on TV
31 Where natural gas accumulates
34 "Few can be induced to labor exclusively for ___": Abraham Lincoln
35 Popular sea menaces of film
41 Where I-15 meets I-86: Abbr.
42 Flawlessly
43 Dickens heroine ___ Trent
44 Banned aids?
46 1974 Best Picture nominee directed by Bob Fosse
48 Big name in Modernism
49 Nothing but
50 ___ Emperor (Taoism figure)
51 Roger's "77 Sunset Strip" co-star
53 "___ Country" (James Baldwin novel)
55 Rope-ladder rung on a ship
57 It's also called a "way car"
58 Forwarding e-mail addresses
59 Latin tongue
60 Yarn with a rubber core

DOWN

1 She's tried often
2 Spent
3 High spirits
4 Pitched blade?
5 "The ___," next-to-last song on "Abbey Road," ironically
6 Place with higher speeding fines, often
7 Army post unused since the 1950s
8 Minced oath
9 "Roman Holiday" princess
10 Lethargy
11 Golfer nicknamed "Supermex"
12 Containing element #34
13 Losers of the Battle of Meloria, 1284
15 Run out of clothes?
20 Like Arcadia's inhabitants
24 Magic word
25 English city that's home to the Spartans football club
27 Ready enough
29 Appeared
32 Tokyo Imperial Palace features
33 Hero of many Clancy novels
35 Nova Scotia's Lake ___, named for an Indian tribe
36 Near the kidneys
37 Uhuru Park locale
38 Second appearance on a soundtrack
39 It may be offered with a blessing
40 Besmears
45 Back
47 Cryptozoological creatures
50 "___, meine Freude" (Bach motet)
52 One way to be turned down
54 Appropriate in an inappropriate way
56 Imitating

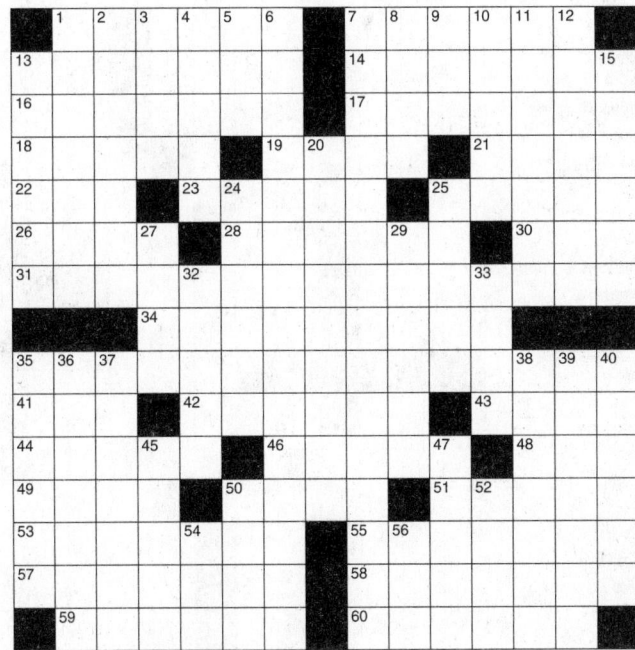

by Patrick Berry

ACROSS

1 Stock maker's addition
9 Field's pair
15 Site of a college stadium that seats over 100,000
16 Skier's spot
17 Not taken in
18 Stick on, in a way
19 Count on greens
20 You might have one after spraying yourself
21 Kvetch
22 It's above 90
23 Share letters?
24 Big hand
26 Endings to some letters, for short
27 Mr. ___ (old mystery game)
28 Intense excitement
29 Fulfillment
30 Looney Tunes animator Friz
33 Pugilists' org.
36 Up
37 Firing squad?: Abbr.
38 Spots before one's eyes?
41 Big pistol maker
43 1950s car feature
44 Reads
46 Grassy areas
48 Repaid
49 Storied gift givers
50 Inability to get A's or B's?
51 Detective's question
52 Aspirin and such
53 Learn about, with "on"
54 Element of radon or xenon
55 Some reserves

DOWN

1 Continues
2 Rating numbers
3 Not followed
4 "Ah, But Your Land Is Beautiful" novelist, 1981
5 Discontinued
6 London weekly, with "The"
7 Terrible twos responses
8 Up until
9 Book size
10 Upset
11 Play the jester
12 Fixture in a pub
13 Marks up, say
14 Precious ones, possibly
20 Descriptive of Snow White
22 Artist's place
25 Swore
31 Badminton dinks
32 Gradually corroded
33 Beneath one's self-respect
34 Making ends meet?
35 Modern places for groups of groupies
38 Balls with bands
39 Peace-loving
40 Handled
41 His last film was "The Harder They Fall," 1956
42 Extremely
45 Possible reaction to a pretense
47 Miss by ___
49 Second person in Genesis
51 Chicago cable station

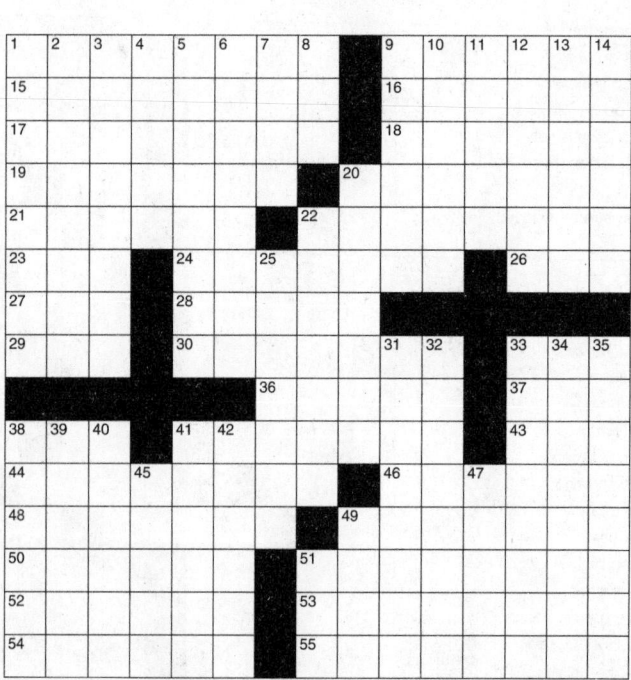

by Joe DiPietro

ACROSS

1 Counter act
5 One reported to the Better Business Bureau
9 Woe for the unwary
14 "___ quiet!"
15 Like many indies
16 Attack as a young boxer might
17 One side in the Battle of Cold Harbor
18 Very small parts
20 Meteorology, e.g.
22 Go caving
23 Cry from a stuck-up person?
27 Chicken George player in "Roots"
29 Like some hush puppies
30 "Donnie Brasco" grp.
32 Near midnight, say
34 "Brokeback Mountain" role
35 Eschew exertion
37 Bad lover?
39 Bearer of trumpet-shaped flowers
40 Branch of zool.
42 Find another tenant for
44 "Lo! in ___ brilliant window-niche . . .": Poe
45 Female adviser
47 Seize again
49 Snake intake
51 Carting fee
54 Online reference for all things "Star Wars"
56 Buzz sources
59 Some police officers: Abbr.
60 Subject for un poeta
61 Baker's accessory
62 Myoglobin component
63 Game with half-elves, informally

64 Word in many cruise ships' names
65 10-time Silver Slugger Award winner, familiarly

DOWN

1 Dermatology topics
2 Not built to last
3 Short-term?
4 Oh Henry! maker
5 "Golf Begins at Forty" writer
6 One involved in bowling balls
7 Husband of Gudrun
8 Lee ___ (transmission repair chain)
9 Icy treat
10 Skittles
11 Easily taught
12 Bit of motivational speech
13 Some "Space Patrol" characters, for short
19 Hooked on
21 Pitch
24 Guinness's "most fearless animal"
25 Society of Jesus founder ___ López de Loyola
26 Last words of Kipling's "If"
28 Alternative for now
30 Old Dubble Bubble maker
31 It's not played with sticks
33 Alexandria is in it
36 Its page numbers are often Roman numerals

38 Airplane seat features
41 Studied some, with "in"
43 Corner
46 Small matter?
48 H. Rider Haggard heroine
50 Hardly pores over
52 U.S. facility in Cuba, for short
53 Made smooth
55 First name in 1970s tennis
56 Gnarly
57 Janeane's co-star in "The Truth About Cats & Dogs"
58 Back-to-sch. time

by Mel Rosen

ACROSS

1 Bed bottoms?
12 Letters for a duke
15 Bauxite or cryolite
16 Winning lineup
17 One whose shots reveal lots
18 The Tigers, for short
19 Worked on peanuts?
20 Tricksters
21 Passes over
23 Many mgrs. have them
24 Pointed artwork?
25 Concordia University locale
28 One of a grand trio
29 Preceder of his name?
30 End of a tile game's name
31 It may be boiled in Bordeaux
32 Hydroelectricity providers?
33 Pulls a switcheroo on, perhaps
34 One might be caught near a beach
35 Is for more than one?
36 Behaves like a loon
37 Attendance count
38 Put right
40 Really bother
41 Father of the Blues
42 Vint ___, Father of the Internet
43 Former chocolaty Post cereal
44 "Fanny's First Play" playwright
45 ___ Poke (candy on a stick)
48 Visionary 1921 drama
49 Its contents may get strained
52 One making a scene?: Abbr.
53 Be shellacked
54 Slob's environment
55 Very early morning, in slang

DOWN

1 Sunblock ingredient
2 Put down
3 Record player, briefly
4 French sweet
5 Short coach
6 Like some instincts
7 Shell collection?
8 Biblical shepherd
9 Betray inattention
10 Nursery IDs
11 One side of traffic
12 Call waiting line?
13 Bouquet greenery
14 Extra mouth to feed, maybe
22 I.B.M. event of 1915
23 Gymnastics school supply
24 Home Depot display
25 They often fly out during an explosion
26 2003 spy thriller starring Al Pacino and Colin Farrell
27 Amontillado, e.g.
28 Like some rafts
30 Swinging
33 Feeder filler
34 Grimm villain
36 "Stay"
37 British home of Cow Tower and Dragon Hall
39 Way of the world?
40 Be serious
42 Gymnastics school supply
44 Line of combat?
45 Excite
46 Period of abstinence
47 Period of indulgence
50 ___ price
51 Runner given the boot?

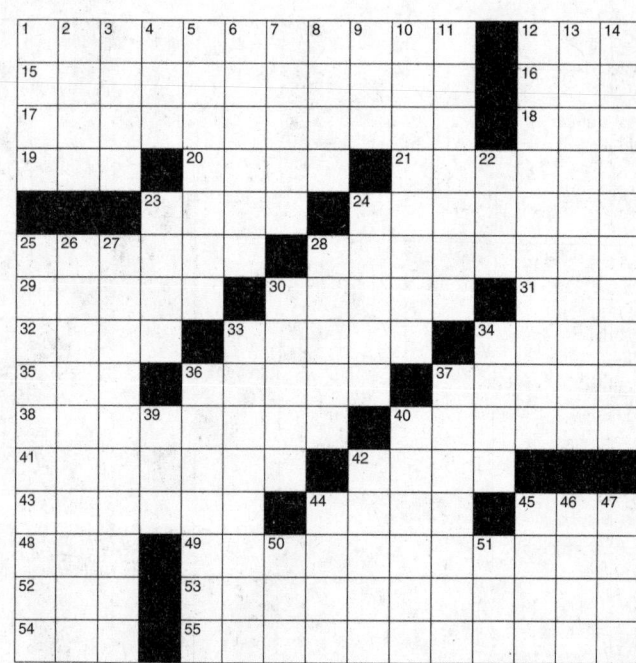

by Mark Diehl

ACROSS

1 Fearsome Foursome teammate of Jones, Olsen and Lundy
6 Alternative
11 Jean ___, 1969 Oscar-winning title role for Maggie Smith
12 "That's ni-i-ice!"
14 Gilded Age tycoon with a legendary appetite
17 Actor Auberjonois
18 Chaney Sr. or Jr.
19 One of about 14,500 in Manhattan
20 Fort named for a Civil War major general
21 Dulcify
25 ___ Motors
26 Grade sch. class
27 Shop-at-home method?
28 Wasn't off one's rocker?
29 Eye, ear and nose
31 Whom the Romans defeated at the Battle of Aquae Sextiae, 102 B.C.
33 Sporcle.com feature
34 Nub
35 Hint
38 Visits
41 Scuba tank meas.
42 2002 Emmy winner for lead actress in a comedy
44 First to come?
45 Exchanges that may come with emoticons, briefly
46 People born on February 29, colloquially
47 Barack Obama's mother
48 58-Across leaders
50 Interregnum
51 Pother

52 In a precarious position
57 Mulligan, e.g.
58 See 48-Across
59 Ranch in the 1956 film "Giant"
60 Growing area of commerce

DOWN

1 Christ's visitor in a tale from "The Brothers Karamazov"
2 Home of the Arch of Constantine
3 When repeated, cry often made with a hand up
4 Brahms's "___ Deutsches Requiem"
5 Ted Kluszewski's team when he won the 1954 N.L. home run title
6 Indicate
7 Actor Herbert of the "Pink Panther" films
8 Mass apparel
9 First capital of Japan
10 Subject of "Eight Men Out"
11 Writer of "Happiness, n. An agreeable sensation arising from contemplating the misery of another"
13 N.F.L. rushing star Peterson
14 What's discarded
15 Frank Zappa rock opera "___ Garage"
16 "Easter, 1916" poet
21 Unmoved
22 Dangerous place to be
23 12th Amendment concern

24 Cell transmitters
30 "___, bro?"
32 Male sheep
35 Two-time running mate of Richard
36 Onetime teen idol who later hosted "Pyramid"
37 Metaphor for a flood of tears
38 It's a start
39 Harmless
40 Matchmaker for Tevye's daughters
43 "I'm such a ___!" (klutz's comment)
49 Brogue, e.g.
51 Part of a convoy
53 ___ Air (carrier to Taiwan)
54 Not working: Abbr.
55 Tripe
56 Dama's title: Abbr.

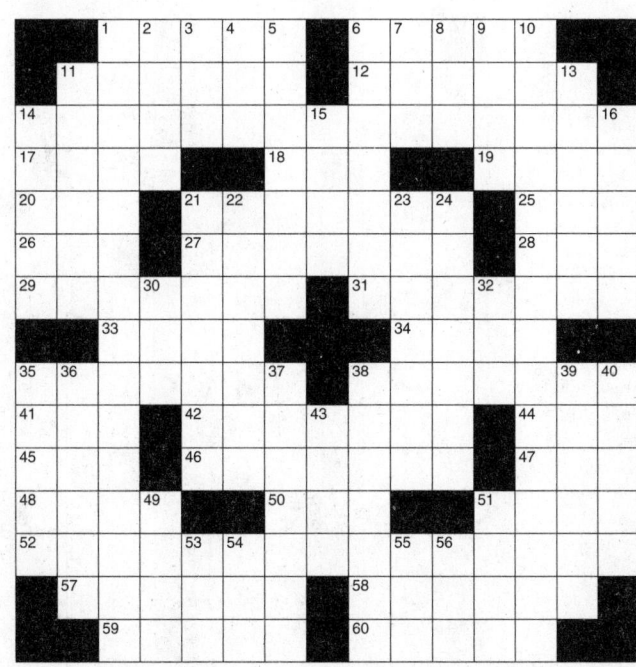

by John Farmer

ACROSS

1 Some Guinness Book listings
7 Sources of woods used for saunas
13 Literary character whose name is said to mean "laughing water"
14 Nonabrasive leather
16 Grandma or grandpa
17 Went back to the buffet, say
18 Norwegian violinist ___ Bull
19 Two-___
21 Figure depicted in une église
22 Mind
24 Server's edge
26 Besmirch
27 Advocacy
30 Smooth
32 Film studio stock
34 Raptor 350 and others
35 Pucks
38 Founding member of the Washington Freedom
40 Many mail-order items, briefly
41 Singer Jackson
43 English word that comes from Tswana
45 Tomfoolery
47 Places to unload
51 Alpha or beta follower
52 Jewelry store feature
54 How fried foods are fried
55 Hydrocarbon endings
57 1992 Elton John hit
60 Sessanta minuti
61 Missouri site of the Scott Joplin Ragtime Festival

63 Fellow with no monetary woes
65 Place for barkers?
66 What you may have while solving this puzzle?
67 Adolescence and others
68 Civic alternative

DOWN

1 Nice girls
2 Seriously committed
3 Workers with 64-Downs, for short
4 Embarks
5 You, once
6 Hot spot
7 Hurt
8 "Hidalgo" co-star, 2004
9 Digs
10 Classic novel that ends with two weddings
11 When two hands meet
12 Tennyson hero
13 Yellowstone sight
15 Figure in the Iliad
20 Seat of Leon County, Fla.
23 Add
25 Con's call
28 Actor who played Scrooge in "A Christmas Carol," 1951
29 Settled
31 Appeared in, as a TV show
33 Literary pirate
35 Awe
36 Old royalty
37 Didn't do seriously

39 N.Y.C. travel letters
42 Springer's org.
44 Watched closely from a distance
46 "Fahrenheit 451," e.g.
48 Paying guest
49 Capital midway between Rome and Istanbul
50 Editorial feature
53 ___ Rebellion
56 Palacio part
58 Some Siouan speakers
59 Handle
62 One with a supporting role
64 Colleague of 3-Down

by David J. Kahn

ACROSS

1 Christmas trifle
16 Like bar codes
17 Cup holders and such
18 Femmes mariées, across the Pyrenees: Abbr.
19 Glaciation products
20 Tailor's concern
21 Joined the swarm
23 Knockout
24 Actress Edelstein of TV's "House"
25 "___ Femme Mariée" (Jean-Luc Godard film)
26 Convened anew
28 Walnut, e.g.
29 Nag
31 90 proof, say
32 Quahogs
34 Potential game stoppers
37 Wig out
41 Rare equine hybrid
42 See 36-Down
43 Flight ticket abbr.
44 ___ McCawley, Ben Affleck's role in "Pearl Harbor"
45 Airport patrons often avoid it
46 Series finale
48 ___ heap
49 "Aww"-inspiring
51 Bounce
52 It was put on decades ago
55 Elaborate
56 Tip over, say

DOWN

1 Bad traffic accident
2 Bullish
3 Musical series
4 Drew a lot, say
5 Amanti maker
6 User of a record-keeping device called a quipu
7 Dead, as tissue
8 Ones concerned with sustainable design
9 Quatrain's longer relative
10 Real stunner
11 Japanese salad plants
12 "___ out!"
13 Dangerous thing to leak
14 "Have mercy," in a Mass
15 Result of jumping the gun
22 Overcast
24 Mucho
27 Goes off
28 Total
30 Ross, Lennox or Angus, in Shakespeare
31 Smooth over
33 Epithet for an annoying roommate
34 Decrease in vitality
35 Undersize keyboard
36 "Jeux d'___" (42-Across keyboard work)
38 One of the seven hills of Rome
39 Free of hormones, say
40 Have words
42 C_4H_8
45 Started on a course
47 Masur's New York Philharmonic predecessor
49 Italian sweet?
50 Sage exiled on the planet Dagobah
53 Sports supporter
54 Abbr. that might appear above "e-mail"

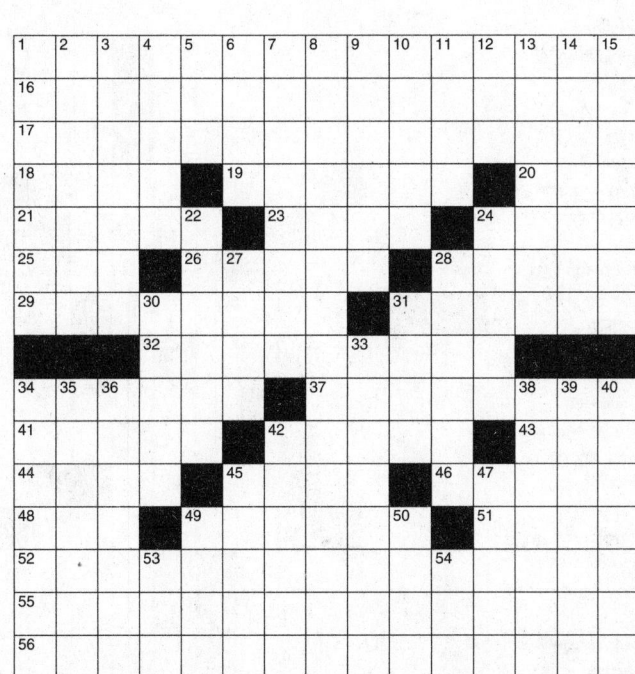

by Kevin G. Der

ACROSS

1 It may measure 16" x 16" x 2"
9 It was sung in Rocky Balboa's neighborhood
15 Septic tank resident
16 Accidentally uninked embossed stamp
17 "___ to Power" (Frederick J. Sheehan's exposé of Alan Greenspan)
18 1987 All-Star Game M.V.P. Tim
19 Center opening?
20 "My bad!"
22 Forward-moving occasion?: Abbr.
23 Suffer the effects of a haymaker
25 Tony's portrayer on "NYPD Blue"
26 Measure of support?
27 26-Across attachments
30 Traditional gathering place in old Europe
31 Literary character whose first word is "'Sblood"
32 Least dignified
34 Like the rarest rhino
35 Preventers of many thefts
38 Holder of ornaments
40 "And Absalom rode upon ___": II Samuel 18:9
41 New Age mecca in the Southwest
43 Word whose antonym is its own homophone
44 Legend locale
45 Ready
49 Like arroyo areas
50 Legal hearing
52 Interior designer Aarnio
53 Whit
54 One of his aliases was Theo. LeSieg
57 Frequent sound at a wine tasting
58 Bed riser?
60 "My comment was serious"
62 Philippine port
63 Occurrence after the fall
64 Used
65 Pitching target

DOWN

1 Researchers' output
2 Miffed
3 Comparatively clownish
4 London Zoo opening?
5 His chariot was drawn by fire-emitting horses
6 ___ Park (B'klyn neighborhood)
7 Extremely upscale?
8 Possible result of vitamin A deficiency
9 Catcher Fletcher of the 1990s Expos
10 Big name in anti-aging products
11 One getting waisted in Tokyo?
12 National park in South Dakota
13 Coffee specification
14 Shelve
21 Didn't just opine
24 Pigeonholed
26 The Plame affair, informally
28 Window shopper's selection
29 Retired runway model
33 Some nonfiction
34 Doe being defended
35 Coating of cheese
36 City mentioned in "Route 66"
37 National monument near Flagstaff
39 Deck (out)
42 Jabber in a mask
44 "Good ___" (quaint greeting)
46 Infected
47 Musical work whose name means "valiant"
48 Billboard's best
51 One may circulate quickly
54 Word often written in red
55 Ward with awards
56 Reason to scold a kid
59 Have the best time, say
61 Last in a series

by Barry C. Silk

ACROSS

1 Prepares for the trophy room, say
7 "That greeny flower" in a William Carlos Williams poem
15 Husband of Denmark's Queen Margrethe
16 Italian cooking style
17 Maker of Emporio White perfume
18 Dr. Eric Foreman's portrayer on "House"
19 Con artist's crime
20 Carol king
21 Cheap roofing material
22 Wartime bridge builder
24 Prevailing character
25 Sargasso Sea spawner
26 Undomesticated
27 Justicialist Party founder
28 Arid area agriculture
30 A belligerent arguer may grab them
31 "Los Olvidados" director Buñuel
32 El Misti's location
33 Limited release
36 Walks aimlessly
40 Crack
41 Tibiae
42 Delighted expression
43 Pushes (off)
44 Ambulance chaser's prize
45 The Fighting Tigers, for short
46 Item first marketed under the name Snurfer
48 She won three Grammys for her 1989 album "Nick of Time"

50 What phorid flies are imported to prey on
51 Green stuff
52 Accurate
53 Got ahead of
54 Not worry
55 Oktoberfest souvenirs

DOWN

1 Given a raw deal, slangily
2 Popular rat-baiting dog in Victorian England
3 Weak and craven
4 ___ Blücher (forbidding "Young Frankenstein" character)
5 Is critical
6 Word with pole or jump

7 They reproduce via mitosis
8 ___ cake (marzipan-covered dessert)
9 Follow the leader?
10 A leveret is a young one
11 Bruce Springsteen ballad
12 Censure
13 Catalán relative
14 Moderates
20 Goes up a degree or two
23 Like freakish coincidences
27 Pete Dexter novel whose title character is an unrepentant murderer

29 It sometimes covers first-time performers
30 Singer Rimes
32 Dug for gossip
33 Appear to be, to most eyes
34 Base found in DNA and RNA
35 "So's your old man!" and others
36 Seeking relief from a pitcher?
37 Composer who tutored Mozart's son
38 Roll film inventor
39 They're home 24/7
41 Schoolhouse needs of yore
44 Kind of line
47 Display
49 Michelangelo work
51 Salon selections

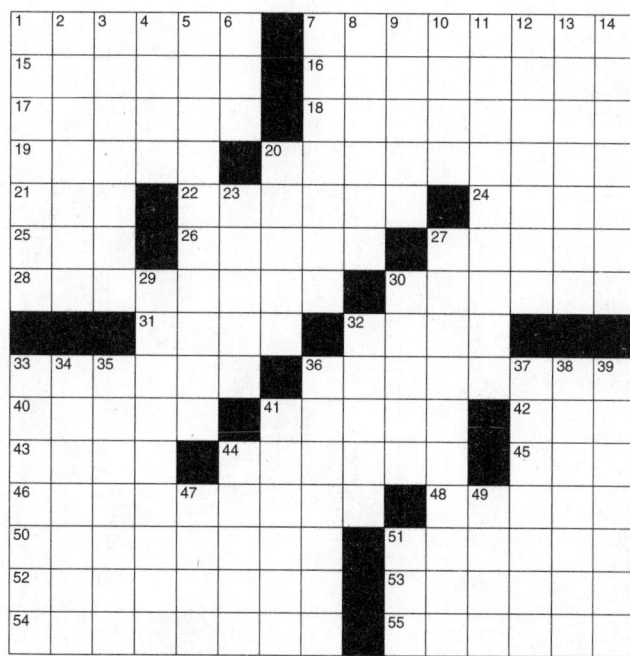

by Patrick Berry

ACROSS

1 Seeks
8 Throttle: Var.
15 Some literati
17 Unlikely to be pressed
18 The Sakmara feeds it
19 Clipper supporters
20 Singer with the 4 × platinum album "Watermark"
21 Help-wanted indication
22 Knowing what's what about
23 Big name in Top 40 countdowns
24 Contemporaries
26 GIF or JPEG alternative
27 Longtime "Column One" printer, briefly
28 Port alternative
29 Proverbial certainty
30 Some kitchen waste
31 Bit of biblical "writing on the wall"
32 Eggheaded experts
33 Old autodom's Model M or Model T-6
35 Columnist and graphic novelist Jonathan
36 They're often screened
37 Jazz flutist Herbie
38 Uncomfortably tight wrapper?
39 ___ column (concrete-filled steel cylinder)
40 Lacking luster
41 "This one's incredible!"
43 More lean and muscular

44 Aid in understanding some old pictures
46 Court no-no
47 It may offer a variety of oils
48 Former "20/20" co-anchor John

DOWN

1 Charge
2 One making a special delivery?
3 Host's invitation
4 Leaning, in a way: Abbr.
5 Bulg. relative
6 Many ascetics
7 Ranchero dressing?
8 Vivacity
9 Noted ring family
10 Football linemen: Abbr.

11 Shown up at a restaurant?
12 Souls' post-death passages
13 It's better than life
14 Imprint: Sp.
16 Occasional bullet stoppers
22 Five-time "Hill Street Blues" Emmy nominee
23 "But the ___ not my son" ("Billie Jean" lyric)
25 Is sociable, in a way
26 Potential burglary deterrents
28 Oozing testosterone
30 Dirty
31 "Bewitched" spinoff
32 Pikeperch
34 Length of some shorts

36 Leading to something
37 Tuesday in Tijuana
39 Novelist Mario Vargas ___
40 Muff
42 Musical settings: Abbr.
43 Emergency room concern
45 Some surfers' needs

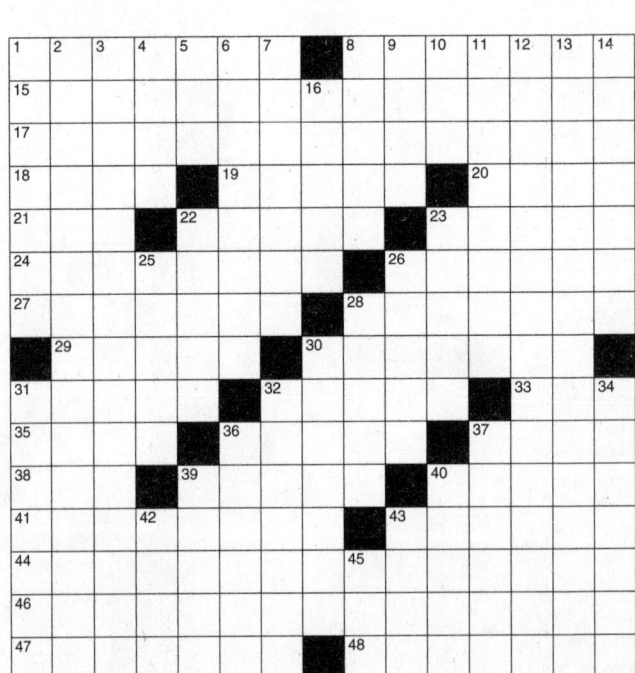

by Joe Krozel

ACROSS

1 Homo found in 1891
8 Mother who never had a delivery?
15 Noted password user
16 Start of a form to fill out
17 Deceive
18 Extras
19 "Chéri" novelist, 1920
20 Foments
21 One of its groups is rec.puzzles
22 Have covered
23 Alternatives to Civics
25 Dirty campaigner
26 Fangorn Forest race
27 What may make you bats?
29 Literary title character called "a pure woman"
30 Ball-bearing article
31 Alarmist's topic
35 Midpoint of morning watch
37 Port container
41 Empty, at a port, say
43 As a welcome change
45 Brown, then red, then brown again, maybe
46 Use for support
47 One not seated?
49 Start up, as electronic equipment
50 Meat curer
51 Get moving
52 Like tractors
53 Stole
54 Like many seals
55 Trees, hills, etc.

DOWN

1 1898 Émile Zola letter
2 1953 A.L. M.V.P. who played for the Indians
3 Wroth
4 Withdraws (oneself)
5 Be able to nail
6 Adjacency
7 It's often cleaned up by a barber
8 Preceder of a bit of bad news
9 Was a joint tenant?
10 1939 Giraudoux play
11 Tries to make out
12 Clerical clipping
13 Gets through
14 Combining workers
24 Like some bedding
25 Unit for 14-Down
28 Handle on a ranch
31 Entertainer with the gag reply "What elephant?"
32 A pound of Turkey?
33 Person getting way up there?
34 Kind of campaign
35 Calms down
36 Dumb
37 Company whose logo is a lantern
38 Whatever happens, after "at"
39 Two-wheeler
40 Castro's "enemy to whom we had become accustomed"
42 Put down
44 Make some new connections in
48 ABC newsman Potter and others
49 Dads, in dialect

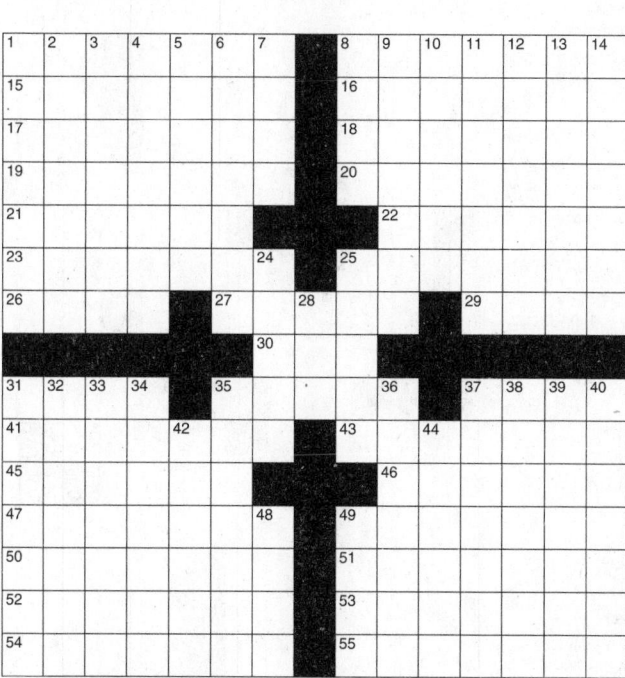

by Manny Nosowsky

ACROSS

1 Pound of flesh?
9 Difference between winners and losers?
15 1967 Simon & Garfunkel hit
16 Armor plate protecting the hip and thigh
17 One in a million
18 Fix
19 Rock-___
20 Furtive observations
22 Only word spoken in Mel Brooks's "Silent Movie"
23 Hirsute sitcom relative
25 O.K.
27 It may be classified
28 ___ Martin
29 Mining samples
30 Hard to ignore
32 Shake or rattle, but not roll
33 Some concert pieces
34 Cheated, in slang
38 "Be More Chill" novelist Vizzini
39 Weeper
40 "World News Now" airer
43 Conversation piece?
44 Kind of accent used by Ado Annie
45 Reduced to nothing
47 Like a mirror image: Abbr.
48 Lao-___
49 Go wild
52 Some temple utterances
54 Makes a lasting impression
56 Hypersonic plane engine

58 One who splits the bill?
59 Longstanding issue
60 Tootsie
61 Most difficult to manage

DOWN

1 Baccarat alternative
2 What "Arrivederci!" is spoken in
3 "The ___ Story," Jimmy Stewart baseball movie
4 Dijon drink
5 Madre's treasure
6 "Munich" arms
7 Man of one's dreams?
8 Stands above the crowd?
9 Follow too closely
10 Softies

11 Ray Bradbury's "___ for Rocket"
12 One of Austen's Dashwood sisters
13 "Take it from me, elections matter" speaker
14 Chain offering Moons Over My Hammy
21 Whichever
24 Port on Italy's "heel"
26 Bowl filler for a bowl game, maybe
27 North Dakota's ___ Lacs National Wildlife Refuge
28 Drag
31 It's all downhill from here
32 Filmmaker Apatow
34 Fermion or boson

35 1949 Humphrey Bogart/Sessue Hayakawa movie
36 Lawn care equipment
37 Gloria Estefan hit whose title is Spanish for "Listen!"
39 Cousin of a custard apple
40 Some pyramid builders
41 Award
42 Christmas scene
43 Landed
46 Wipes clean
50 Municipal regs.
51 Job
53 Leave without changing
55 It may leave a noticeable plot hole
57 Verizon acquisition of 2006

by John Farmer

ACROSS

1 Objet d'art at auction in "Octopussy"
11 Queens's ___ Stadium
15 Torn
16 Grps. sponsoring many book fairs
17 What a lift may get you out of
18 Languishes in the lockup
19 Big print: Abbr.
20 Not procrastinating
21 Rosaceous ornamental
23 European princely dynasty name
24 Ancient dynasty name
25 Newspaper section
28 Phil Mickelson specialty
29 Shake, as a tail
30 Sweat blood
31 Bit of bread
32 Make less flamboyant
33 What a V may indicate
34 Doesn't look normal
35 Its HQ is in D.C.'s Federal Triangle
36 Origination point for many fireworks
37 Dogged
38 It's played with 144 pieces
40 Reading-and-feeding occasions
41 Heir, legally
42 Cosmetic extremes?
43 Strands on a branch, perhaps
44 Org. that subpoenaed Abbie Hoffman
45 He outlawed 38-Across because it promoted gambling
48 Rambos might wield them
49 Lampshade blemish

52 "The Labors of Hercules" painter
53 Simple trattoria dressing
54 What people are on during a nail-biter
55 Common feature of a Dracula mask

DOWN

1 Put in the archives
2 Like many forum postings: Abbr.
3 Not just sniffle
4 Masthead figs.
5 "Touché!" elicitor
6 Effects created by 43-Across
7 Unexplainable, maybe
8 Discharge
9 Std. in chronometry
10 Pilot's setting
11 Folks are often fooled when these arrive
12 Magazine
13 Prejudicial propagandist
14 What cribs might be used for
22 Venerated visitor
23 Himmel und ___ (apple-and-potato dish)
24 Niche
25 Still developing
26 Like men, women and children
27 Topping
28 Fannie who wrote "Fried Green Tomatoes at the Whistle Stop Cafe"
30 It has a diagonal rib

33 Plywood cutter
34 Hospital administration, briefly
36 A boxer may work on it
37 Triangular nut producers
39 Daughter in "'night, Mother"
40 Creature with a paddlelike tail
42 "Antiques Roadshow" item
44 You may hear Muzak when you're on it
45 ___ soprano
46 Soprano ___
47 Assent to relent
50 Hollywood techie's field, briefly
51 Disorderly do

by Brad Wilber

ACROSS

1 Kind of mouse
8 Indicator that you're back to your own words
15 Nearly shot
16 Sew up a hole?
17 Winter weather hazard
19 Dresses down . . . or butters up?
20 Scratch
21 Maccabiah Games setting: Abbr.
22 Defense secretary after Cheney
23 Backpack alternative
24 Jacket material
25 Game with trumps
26 See 27-Down
27 "Five Weeks in a Balloon" author
28 Surface for the Olympische Winterspiele
29 Antisubversive grp. of old
30 Jubilant cry
31 Group that may be hounded?
35 Headache cause
36 Hub for Air Caraïbes Atlantique
37 Do some course work
40 Primates vis-à-vis humans
43 Barrie's "oddly genial man"
44 Tot's plea
45 Stand-up comic's fear
46 Latitude
47 Like some joints
48 Suffix with cartoon
49 "Rhapsodie Hongroise" composer
50 Cobwebs may be a sign of it
51 Part of many a daily supplement
54 Like the midafternoon hours, typically

55 Foggy
56 Takes over
57 Waved a knife at, maybe

DOWN

1 Wrong
2 Go down a slope with a chute
3 Do wrong
4 "Save the explanation"
5 Flimflam
6 French cordial flavoring
7 Perfect-game pitcher Barker
8 Many a software download
9 An operator may call on one
10 Stick in a cabinet
11 Snack food brand

12 More like the Blob
13 Certain Tornado Alley resident
14 Ageless, ages ago
18 He said "I was married by a judge. I should have asked for a jury"
23 Star ___ (big name in exercise machines)
24 What ribs are delivered in
26 Go time in a game
27 With 26-Across, "Amen!"
29 Bit of evidence for a sleuth
30 Ivy with deep roots
32 Fulda feeder
33 Food chain part
34 Princess Najla player in Broadway's "Flahooley"

38 Endlessly adjustable, as clothing
39 Diversified
40 Native of the Lake Superior region
41 Checkout correction
42 Render harmless, in a way
43 Falls like 17-Across
44 Where Family Day is observed
46 Good thing for a medic to find
47 Trig ratio
49 Mountaineer's goal
50 Complement of Dante's circles of hell
52 Title of Dickens's Defarge: Abbr.
53 Punch

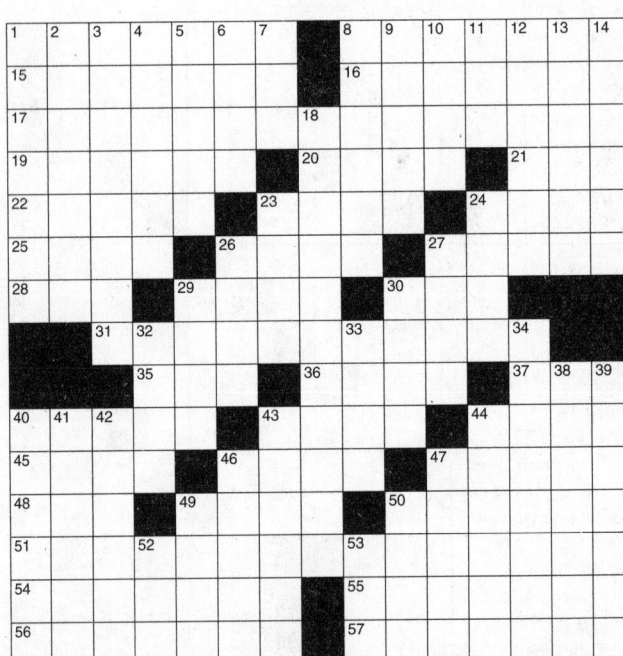

by Barry C. Silk

ACROSS

1 Lanai's county
5 Five-spots
9 Deep-sea exploration pioneer
14 & 17 Encouragement for a trailing team
18 Normal muscle tension
19 Search
20 It originated at Zurich's Cabaret Voltaire in the 1910s.
21 Get blitzed
22 Ignored, with "out"
24 Actress Chandler and others
26 Occasions to use pepper?
31 Caesarean section?
34 See 46-Down
35 A.A.A. listings
36 Parts of e-mail addresses
38 Baking need
39 Tiki bar order
40 Golfer who turned pro at age 15
41 Things locked into place
42 Newswoman Lesley
43 Wharf fare?
45 1948 Literature Nobelist
47 Vienna-based grp. with no European members
50 Opposite of yours, in Tours
54 ___ 'acte
55 Apothecary's stock
57 & 60 Risky "Jeopardy!" declaration
61 Out with the junk, say
62 It's risky to build a house on this
63 In case

DOWN

1 A baker might have a hand in it
2 Massachusetts city called Tool Town
3 "I swear I ___ art at all": "Hamlet"
4 Give the flavor of
5 Court fig.
6 Gives a shot in the arm
7 Hurricane survivor, maybe
8 Lots are in lots
9 Something to take a pass on
10 Often-referenced but never-seen wife on "Scrubs"
11 Site of Vulcan's smithy
12 Stars' city, informally
13 The bride in Wagner's "Bridal Chorus"
15 Relief providers
16 Slugger Sandberg
23 Transporter of heavy loads
25 Lydman of the N.H.L.
27 Like many laid-up Brits
28 Concert halls
29 Apparatus for pull-ups?
30 They had Machmeters, briefly
31 Pedigree alternative
32 Recap figure
33 Java setting
35 Java, e.g.
37 One might make waves
38 Venomous venting
40 Put to paper
43 Types a little to the left
44 Bright spots in the sky
46 With 34-Across, slag furnace input
48 1960s Joint Chiefs of Staff chairman Wheeler
49 Things pieced together
50 1985 Oscars co-host with Fonda and Williams
51 Nut part
52 Its products go up and down
53 1-Across, for one
56 Send explicit come-ons by cell phone
58 R&B singer with the hit "It's All About Me"
59 R&B group with the hit "Ain't 2 Proud 2 Beg"

by Corey Rubin

ACROSS

1 ___ soup
5 One ___ (kid's game)
9 Floor support?
13 Former Israeli P.M. Olmert
14 Beast on Botswana's coat of arms
16 Running gear component
17 One might perform behind bars
19 The wind unwinds it
20 They let people off
21 Gentleman's partner?
23 Really smell like
25 Hangs
26 Cutting edge of science?
29 Grabs and runs, say
30 Words before "You're on!"
35 Out of town
36 Avoids
38 Style of Duchamp's "Fountain"
39 Light limiter
41 It's often remotely controlled
42 Bits
45 Literary character who's "always good-tempered" and "not very clever"
49 They're good at breaking things
50 Twitter
52 Danger for small watercraft
55 Drop without warning
56 Kind of line symbolizing a cultural boundary
58 Able to see through
59 Arab, maybe
60 Historic town on the Vire
61 Rigging handler, briefly
62 Fresh lines?
63 They can be piercing

DOWN

1 Drive units, briefly
2 Chain with many links
3 Alternative to a cup
4 Product associated with the annual Rotten Sneakers Contest
5 Range near Wal-Mart's headquarters
6 Pixelate, say
7 Epitome of simplicity
8 Cube root of veintisiete
9 Comedian Smirnoff
10 What some traitors end up in
11 Stopping point for a train?
12 Ball-bearing types?
15 Ancient Athenian magistrates
18 Thinks
22 Feature of Africa . . . and some of its denizens
24 Angel player of the 1970s
26 Bond girl Kurylenko
27 Shut (up)
28 Drummer Starkey
31 Throw out pitches?
32 Number system used by the Babylonians
33 An old couple fell in it
34 Some lasting art, in slang
36 Yo-yos
37 It's between Bern and Graubünden
40 Bolshevik foe
41 Unable to escape, in a way
43 Features in many Fra Angelico paintings
44 Fixes
45 Not the most stimulating work
46 Record label named after an animal
47 Has a list
48 "The Ruffian on the Stair" playwright
51 Three-time grid champs of the 2000s
53 Relief
54 1980 TV spinoff
57 Source of rays

by Xan Vongsathorn

ACROSS

1 Question the morning after
9 What can be a turnoff?
15 "That makes two of us"
16 "So chic!"
17 Under control
18 Aids to privacy
19 Sire
20 Ricky ___, frontman for bluegrass's Kentucky Thunder
21 Fassbinder film "___: Fear Eats the Soul"
22 "Hip Hop Is Dead" rapper
24 What any of the Four Horsemen symbolizes
25 Jeremiad
27 It drops on the way home
31 Avow
33 They may have your number
34 Auto marque of the 1980s–'90s
35 Total: Abbr.
36 "See if I care!"
40 Fault finders?
44 Far-off discoveries in astronomy
46 "Perpetual Peace" thinker
47 Prefix with air or field
48 Co-producer of "Beautiful Boy (Darling Boy)"
49 ". . . but no more like my father / Than ___ Hercules": Hamlet
50 Russets, often
54 Secured the rights to
58 Paris's partner on "The Simple Life"
59 Fragrant white wine
60 Voice of Moe and Apu on "The Simpsons"
61 Legendary Spanish bullfighter
62 See 53-Down
63 Ropes in

DOWN

1 High and low indicators
2 Part of England in the time of Alfred the Great
3 "___ that!"
4 Cut
5 Pique
6 Fervor
7 Hall with a posse
8 Capital that was the scene of 2009 mass demonstrations
9 Breaks down
10 Annual journalism award, informally
11 Mother of Romulus and Remus
12 More than a turf battle
13 Cigarette brand that once used the slogan "Not a cough in a carload"
14 Part of some strippers' attire
23 Kind of boot
26 Touch base
27 Tiny opening in a leaf
28 Some cheeses
29 Its uniform includes a red serge tunic and a Stetson: Abbr.
30 Dyeing art
32 Spinner
36 Formative
37 Get rusty
38 Pop-top spot
39 1970s Bowie collaborator
40 Idealist
41 Volcano in a national park
42 Understanding
43 Fuddy-duddies
45 It's big in Bordeaux
51 Crescent moon feature
52 Scramble
53 With 62-Across, subject of "Beautiful Boy (Darling Boy)"
55 Till compartment
56 "The race ___!"
57 Bit of pottery

by John Farmer

314 HARD

ACROSS
1 Fishing gear
12 Hollywood acronym
15 Company mascot introduced in the 1930s that has never been put out to pasture
16 Group with the '79 double-platinum album "Discovery"
17 Stance in a fashion magazine
18 Up to, informally
19 ___ milk
20 Bench warrant, e.g.
21 Walk to the gate, perhaps
23 Baseball stat
24 Lamented
25 Zeros, in sports slang
28 One who's smart?
29 Switch positions
30 "Lost" actress Raymonde
31 Liszt's "___ Préludes"
32 Hardly traditionalists
33 ___ Sisters (daughters of Atlas)
34 Popular spectator sport that's not in the Olympics
35 Money market currency abbr.
36 The Abominable Snowman, for one
37 Block
38 Babe-in-arms alternative?
40 "___ Really Matter" (Janet Jackson song)
41 John Wayne
42 It's hardly a smash hit
43 Kindle, say
44 Impotent
45 E-2 Marine
48 Utter doofus
49 Apathetic person's words
52 John L. Lewis was its first pres.
53 Laptop tested aboard the Endeavour
54 Home of Smallville: Abbr.
55 Swift retreat?

DOWN
1 Adjures
2 Gallic greeting
3 "Well!"
4 Title guy in an animated HBO sitcom
5 Aid to King Hrothgar, in literature
6 Some driving school practice
7 Rock on a stage
8 Didn't go stale
9 Friendly intro?
10 Adds
11 Comic strip adoptee
12 Course load?
13 Like the 1974 rope-a-dope fight
14 Kiawah Island, for one
22 Hellenic character
23 Calls
24 Got into port
25 Incentive to buy a CD, maybe
26 Number of folks?
27 Excuse
28 Sing vibrato, say
30 Hides on a frame
33 Luxurious wrap
34 Grope for
36 Tekka-maki sushi source
37 Promoter of the 13-Down fight
39 "How ___ . . ."
40 Phone headquarters
42 City of 15+ million whose busiest street is Chandni Chowk
44 Steam engine pioneer
45 Parental term of endearment, in Spain
46 Frequent party planner, for short
47 Opt to drop
50 Hosp. units
51 Contents of some books: Abbr.

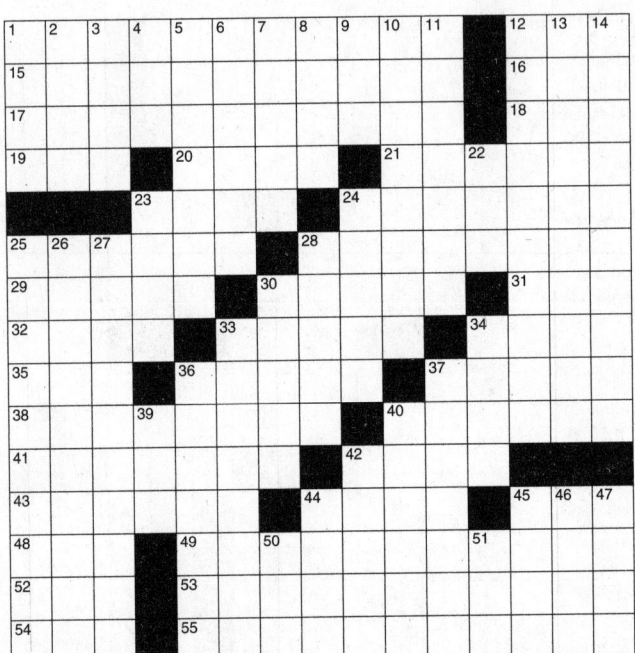

by Mark Diehl

ACROSS

1 Hot dogs
9 It's all ivory and no ebony
15 NyQuil ingredient?
16 Change the boundaries of
17 "Speak of the devil!"
18 Opposite of abridge
19 Racked (up)
20 Some westerns
22 Class with graphs, for short
23 Danger for a king
26 Its max. score is 240
27 Leonardo's "The Aviator" co-star
28 Sported
29 Crotchety cries
30 ___ acid (microscopic staining compound)
31 Hayseed's greeting
34 Luther opponent Johann
35 Derek who played Claudius in "I, Claudius"
38 Walks in the park
40 Havana greeting
41 1995 platinum rap hit that starts "To all the ladies in the place with style and grace"
45 Polish capital
47 Formal girl
48 Salma of the screen
52 Big name in retail jewelry
53 Structures near cell walls
54 Trash-talks
55 Golden Globe winner Sommer
56 "Leaving Brooklyn: ___!" (Williamsburg Bridge sign)
58 One with notions
59 What's going on
61 Fiji rival
64 Briefs, e.g.
65 Literally, "sweet song"
66 Bygone currency
67 Visual aids?

DOWN

1 Really let have it
2 Response to sarcasm
3 Theorized
4 Swift gift
5 Decisive periods, briefly
6 Tammy ___ of 1970s–'80s TV
7 Was a turkey
8 Like a wet Nerf ball
9 Roadrunner feature
10 Code for Latin America's busiest airport
11 San Diego State team
12 Much-maligned mascot
13 Warned
14 Hillbillies' cousins
21 What a sleuth tries to close
24 Alaskan salmon
25 Tuberous
30 Punches
32 Boom Blox console
33 Fist bump
35 With added spice
36 Without any help
37 Nerd-rejecting high-school group
39 Ancient fertility god
42 Victorian's greeting
43 Be everywhere in
44 Burial rite
46 Very small, as a bikini in a 1960 hit
49 Washington city or county
50 2009 Grammy winner for "Relapse"
51 Orange dwarfs
53 Nova lead-in
57 Time to visit a lot of trees
60 Confound
62 Buddy
63 Pickle

by Peter Wentz

ACROSS

1 1956 film that earned an Oscar nomination for 11-year-old Patty McCormack
11 Bond girl opposite Lazenby
15 Victorian conveyance
16 Lofty beginning?
17 Campaign setting for Moshe Dayan
18 Grant consideration
19 Follower of directions
20 What a lei person might pick?
21 Sneeze triggers
23 Trees in the mint family
25 Player of Clouseau's superior
27 Yoga posture
28 A catnap may not provide it
31 "McMillan & Wife" network
32 Protagonist bound for Mordor
34 Basis of many positive IDs
35 The Warta's outlet
36 It often messes tresses
37 "Candid Camera" co-host Jo Ann
39 Ancient humor
40 Situation a teen wants cleared up?
41 "__ maior, minor cessat"
42 Boot
44 Eldest of an Alcott quartet
45 Strongly protesting
47 Whitewater navigator?
49 Post-Manhattan Project org.
50 Hardly wholesome
54 Boho-chic accessory
56 "__ plaintive anthem fades": Keats
58 Try one's suit on?

59 Film critic Gleiberman
60 One often picked up after a split
63 Become inseparable
64 Person not credited for a save?
65 East End greeting
66 High point of 1980 news

DOWN

1 Hospital room fixture
2 3,600 secondes
3 Classmate of Felicity on "Felicity"
4 Name attached to some 1836 "Sketches"
5 Like defendants
6 Dagger
7 What barkers bark
8 Some wiring whizzes: Abbr.
9 Paste container?
10 First name in '50s comedy
11 They're often closed in an emergency
12 Like the Great Geysir
13 What may encircle a rising chopper?
14 Churchyard, quaintly
22 Budgeting concern
24 Coin with the monogram of King Harald V
26 Traditional
29 Handle final details of
30 Itching
32 First-class flight amenity
33 Trigger familiarity
35 Struggling with middle management?
36 Emphasizes with vehemence

38 One on a big case
43 Playwright who co-founded the Abbey Theatre
45 L.A.-based music magazine
46 Misbehave
48 Many a Beethoven work
51 "That's a shame"
52 Emulate Electra
53 Shows great instability
55 Jack-in-the-pulpit, e.g.
57 "What the . . . ?"
61 Some four-year degs.
62 FedEx rival

by Brad Wilber

ACROSS

1 Japan's Prince Hirobumi ___
4 Five-time N.B.A. All-Star Chris
10 2001 #1 album with the hit "Love Don't Cost a Thing"
13 "Easy peasy!"
15 Christian with many robes?
16 Over the top
17 ___Ring (birth control brand)
18 Over
19 Vessel over heat
20 "Leaving on ___ Plane"
21 Perfect-record breaker
22 When all one's planning is put to the test
23 Company outing, for short?
24 River of Devon
25 Sch. for the preordained?
26 Photoshop, say
29 Literally, "different lizards"
32 Descartes found this truth to be self-evident
34 Colorful stage performers since 1987
35 There are 50 in a keg of Newcastle
36 Home of Polar Bear Prov. Park
37 One of about 3,000 in Shakespeare's plays
40 It starts with el primero de enero
41 "Wassup, ___?"
43 One might lose it in a crisis
44 Tee off
46 Where you might see some initials
47 Break down, in a way
48 Prefix with angular
49 Like some love
51 Opine
52 Put off retirement?
53 Spec for a roomy flat?
54 O.K.'s
55 Subj. in "The Electric Kool-Aid Acid Test"

DOWN

1 Scarf down
2 Home for Barbie and Ken, perhaps
3 Counter
4 Tediously went (on)
5 Flag
6 Autumnal event so called because it helps hunters kill their prey
7 "Twilight" protagonist
8 "Bones" actress Deschanel
9 Jay-Z's ___-Fella Records
10 Practice with locks and pins?
11 Troubadour's creation
12 Ones happy to give you their addresses?
14 Makes roar
15 Kind of profiling
22 Some sorority women
25 Lowlifes
26 Sea grass grazer
27 "Indoors ___?"
28 Where two branches of a curve meet, in math
29 Sun exposure, for one
30 Part: Abbr.
31 Certain navigational aids
32 Company that gets a lot of its money from foundations?
33 Defunct
34 "It's my fault"
37 Door
38 Reasons to use Pepto-Bismol
39 Compulsory
41 Il Poeta
42 Decoration for Gertrude's room in "Hamlet"
43 When repeated, exuberant cry
45 "Ptui!"
46 Tied up
47 Litter, maybe
50 36-Across neighbor

by Jonah Kagan

ACROSS

1 45, e.g.
5 Founding member of Public Enemy known for wearing large clocks around his neck
15 "___ at Duke's Place" (1965 jazz album)
16 2007 satirical best seller subtitled "And So Can You!"
17 ___ de Caña (Nicaraguan rum)
18 First British group since the Beatles to have two albums in the U.S. top 10 at the same time
19 "That's a great price!"
21 Strained
22 ___ sauce (sugary purée)
23 Run for it
25 Bygone medical ventilator
28 Hikes
32 Perfectly
33 Bldgs. with community courts
35 Building support
36 Area worth the most bonus troops in the game Risk
38 Literary captain who says "It's better to sail with a moody good captain than a laughing bad one"
40 About
41 Solid
43 More solid
45 Defunct ministry initials
46 Hatted bell ringers
48 "Relaciones Espirituales" writer
50 Fish also called a Jerusalem haddock
52 Site of a noted ancient league
53 Caustic soda, symbolically
56 One may cause your dinner to be spoiled
59 Out of it
61 Wet bar, maybe
63 2009 Lady Gaga hit
64 Oread in love with her own voice
65 One of an evil fairy tale duo
66 Three-player game

DOWN

1 "Fo' sho"
2 Distresses
3 What some plays are shown in
4 List quickly?
5 Alternative to a shake
6 Bachelor party entertainment
7 Date in France?
8 Spanish cows
9 Breakfast dish
10 Pump abbr.
11 9-Down variety
12 Money in the banca, once
13 Org. since 1920 with many staff lawyers
14 Sweeping
20 "For Better or for Worse" matriarch
24 "___ sine scientia nihil est" (Latin motto)
25 "Not for me"
26 Certain Afrocentrist
27 Bashes
29 Board game grande dame
30 Attempts to sink
31 Lady Liberty garb
34 Topic in artificial intelligence
37 Variety of zither
39 Age
42 Minor hit
44 Brand in contact lens care
47 Makings of a hero?
49 Some salon jobs
51 Papa Bear of Chicago football
53 Bills
54 Gut course?: Abbr.
55 Adjective for a coach house inn, maybe
57 "___ pis!" ("Too bad!," in France)
58 Nelson's catchphrase on "The Simpsons"
60 ___ Banos, Calif.
62 Where the chips fall where they may?

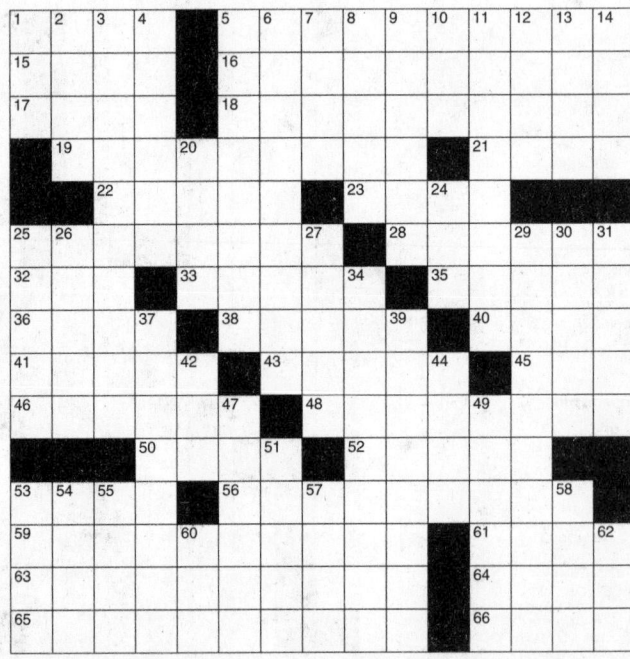

by Natan Last

ACROSS

1 Construction zone sign
12 Band pieces
14 Jean Rhys opus
16 Psychoanalyst Fromm
17 Affix securely
18 Coroner's subj.
19 Deli option
20 Performed as a minstrel, maybe
21 Ones doing lab exams?
22 Ain't right?
24 Dixie rival
25 Ball in a socket
26 Saw
28 Big inits. in photography
29 Possible IV pusher
30 1971 Tony-winning actress ___ Allen
31 Atlanta-based org.
34 She quipped "I've been in more laps than a napkin"
36 Night that "Dynasty" aired for most of its run: Abbr.
39 Curse out
41 ___ de Noyaux (almond-flavored liqueur)
42 Anathema
43 Line up
45 Slightly
46 Island off the coast of Tuscany
47 Vague
49 God, with "the"
50 Aid to researching 35-Downs by topic
52 Ganging up on, in basketball
53 What patients may need patience to get

DOWN

1 Throw off
2 Puts up
3 Knockout
4 Hagen of stage and screen
5 Carl Icahn or T. Boone Pickens
6 Attracts
7 September happenings, often
8 Tip preceder, maybe
9 Oil support
10 Escapist reading?
11 Firedome and Fireflite
12 David of "St. Elsewhere"
13 "Black Beauty" author
14 Hair extension
15 Some choice words
19 Touchdown locale
23 Sideboard collection
26 Peach
27 Cannon, e.g.: Abbr.
31 First blond Bond
32 Actor Mulroney of "The Wedding Date"
33 End of many a driveway
35 Free cookie distributor
36 They sometimes create a scene
37 Sportscaster Dick
38 "My pet"
40 "My little" girl of early TV
42 Get lost
44 Dog park noises
48 Invader of Rome in 390 B.C.
49 Credits date for "Cinderella" or "All About Eve"
51 ___ de parfum

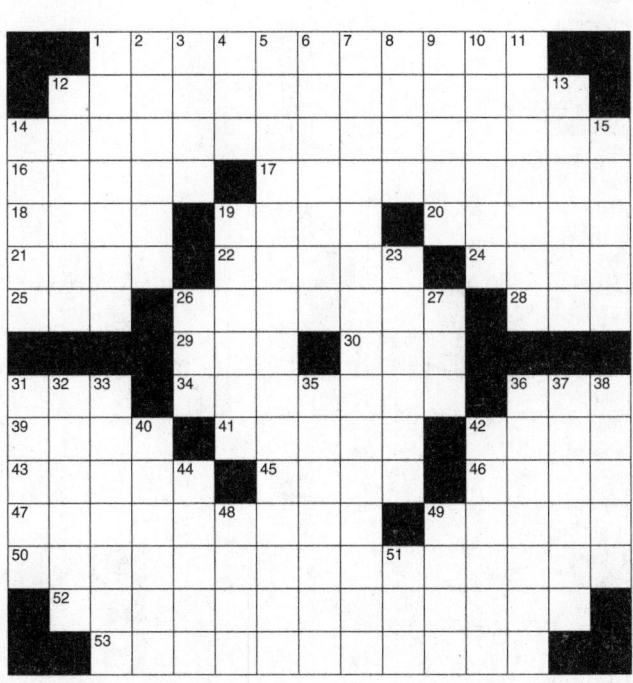

by Mark Diehl

ACROSS

1 Masonry that requires little mortar
7 "Duck" call?
15 Mr. or Mrs. Right
16 ___ Shelly, writer/director/co-star of "Waitress," 2007
17 They might grab something to eat
18 Draws inspiration from, maybe
19 1965 top 10 hit for the Dave Clark Five
21 Mushroom parts
22 Big name in agribusiness
23 British actor Postlethwaite
24 Hank Williams's home state: Abbr.
25 Heavy metal, e.g.
26 Maker of rifles and revolvers
27 Total producers
29 Personal problems
30 Birds said to feed their young with elephants
31 Instrument capable of glissandi
32 Withdraw
35 Table of values
38 Compact container?
39 Common number of spots on a ladybug
40 Crime novelist McDermid
42 Shade akin to lavender
43 Specialty of Charlie Parker
44 There might be one for depression
45 California city with a statue of Jack Benny
48 Practically
49 Made a hash of, with "up"
50 Reluctant risers
51 Computer program subsection
52 "Unfortunately . . ."
53 Attachable by pressing

DOWN

1 Ancient land on the Aegean
2 1974 top 10 Al Green hit subtitled "Make Me Happy"
3 Takeoff spot for many a traffic reporter
4 Attractiveness
5 James I's queen consort
6 Requirement for running for political office
7 1960s–'70s group originally known as the Teenagers, with "the"
8 Prize
9 Short ride?
10 Make an example of
11 Alternatives to furnaces
12 Active
13 Left over, possibly
14 Tough questions
20 Cares for
25 Sparkly rock
26 Showed, as a classic
28 Tails
29 Oasis sights
31 Devastation
32 Increases alarmingly
33 The majority of people live here
34 Drew back
35 "L'Enfant Prodigue" composer
36 Balances
37 Juicy fruit
39 Two-time Grammy winner Jon
41 Sluggish
43 Seems to indicate
44 It may be smoked in a supermarket
46 Depression-era traveler
47 Sentimentalize

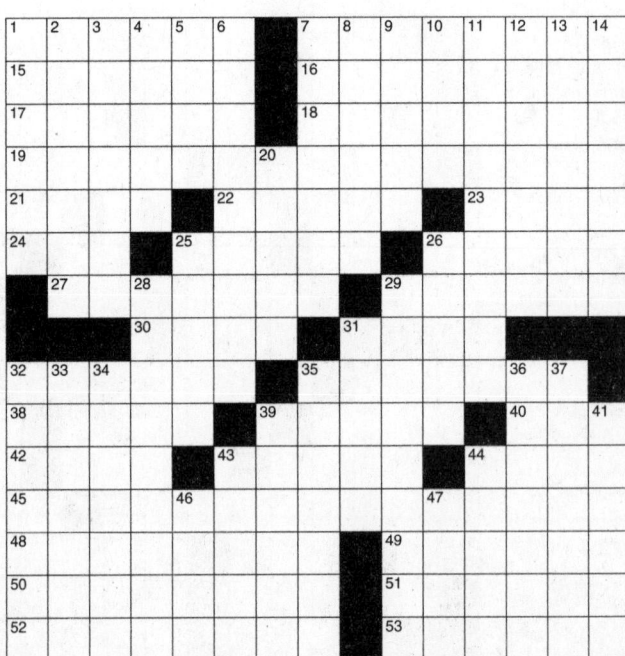

by Patrick Berry

ACROSS

1 Monte Leone, for one
4 Secy., e.g.
8 Henry Fielding title heroine
14 Hebrew leader who rebuilt the walls of Jerusalem
16 40-Across activity
17 Troublemaker
18 Big home run hitter, in slang
19 Director Riefenstahl
20 Likeness
22 "___ heard"
24 White, in a way
26 Sp. misses
30 "House" actor
32 Statesman of old Athens
34 "Comin' ___ the Rye"
35 British diaper
37 Pony or alligator
39 Funny Philips
40 Memorable 10/1/75 event
43 Tobacco holder
44 Like some anteaters
45 Brewer Bernhard
46 Humdinger
48 Bugger of Bugs
50 Take out
51 Change, as a watch
53 Kind of printer
55 Atmosphere: Prefix
56 Giant
58 History
60 Bed piece?
63 Nickname for racer Dale Earnhardt Sr., so called because of his stubbornness
67 With 62-Down, 40-Across loser's nickname
68 Generosity
69 Does 85, say

70 "___ up!" (game cry)
71 40-Across ending, for short

DOWN

1 "Wheel of Fortune" purchase
2 Advantage, with "up"
3 Where the 40-Across was held
4 Big appliance maker
5 March alternatives
6 Brazil's ___ José Bay
7 40-Across, familiarly
8 Pop group whose first Top 40 album was, appropriately, "Arrival"
9 Musical equipment popularized in the 1960s
10 Pro

11 The Louisville ___ (40-Across winner's nickname)
12 Carol ending?
13 Cabinet dept.
15 Time spent on la Côte d'Azur
21 Silvery fish
22 Cicero or Publius
23 Iridescent
25 164-foot-tall movie star
27 40-Across winner's nickname
28 Tee shirt opening
29 Balm
31 Block letters?
33 A.T.M. maker
36 Decade parts: Abbr.
38 Flunking grades
41 Big lug
42 "___ be my pleasure"

47 Second shot
49 Bang or boom
52 Meek
54 The Rockies, e.g.
57 Gets some color
59 "___ Walks in Beauty" (Byron poem)
60 Letter endings: Abbr.
61 Speaker's place
62 See 67-Across
64 Published
65 Expect (of)
66 "In excelsis ___"

by David J. Kahn

322 HARD

ACROSS
1 Onetime J.F.K. visitors
5 Tangy treat
14 Furtive look
15 Orange's place
16 Eastern dignitary
17 Blue, say
18 Not settled up
20 Monthly expense: Abbr.
21 Producer of hits
24 Like good explanations
25 Squad booster
26 Prime meridian hrs.
29 Lottery mix-up?
30 She's a problem that needs to be solved, in song
32 Need for des poissons
33 Its members are represented by stars
34 Activity for folks in the pits?
36 Style guru Gunn
37 With 4-Down, German equivalent of Time
38 Tricked cunningly
39 Cry of consternation
41 Part of Awacs: Abbr.
42 Cellular opening?
43 "Hast thou ___ like God?": Job 40:9
44 Supposed aid in curing neurosis
48 Show a yellow card, e.g.
50 Rodent that may weigh over 100 pounds
51 Worn
54 Shaft entrance
55 Senate cry
56 Chimera, in part
57 Fare often folded in half
58 -trix kin

DOWN
1 Garnish amount
2 Irish playwright who wrote "Cock-a-Doodle Dandy"
3 Value of a U.S. coronet head coin, minted from 1838 to 1907
4 See 37-Across
5 Takes on cargo
6 Get around
7 Cool number?
8 With regularity, to Whitman
9 Organization nickname that plays off the group's secrecy
10 Loyalty
11 Millennio divisions
12 Streamlet
13 It flows from a loch to a firth
15 Provide courses for
19 Coke product maker
22 "Get a little closer" brand
23 Picnic problem
26 Sense
27 Legendary outlaw's companion
28 Product of some relief pitches?
29 Ones to hang with
30 Words to live by
31 Commercial ending with Power
35 Commercial ending with Pasta
40 What's at your disposal?
43 In line with
44 Alberto VO5 rival
45 Make ___ for
46 Newswoman Logan and others
47 Certain finish
48 Big blow
49 R&B singer India.___
51 While, for short
52 Not dis
53 Play favorites?

by Barry C. Silk

ACROSS

1 Use a joystick
6 Biblical figure who received the curse of Ham
12 Somewhat astringent, as wine
14 What a yo-yo might make
15 City where A.A. was founded
17 Like collision avoidance systems
18 "Driving Miss Daisy" setting
19 Conservative pundit with a daily morning radio show
20 Popular bar since 1946
22 "I never ___ moor": Emily Dickinson
23 Delivery that may floor you
24 One doing laundry, often
25 Wrap in sheets
26 They're on the books
27 The great Pretender?
31 Things to come to grips with?
32 Sound made while working on a mop
33 Basketball shooting game
34 Maximally intense
37 "Alice ___ It Again" (Noel Coward song)
38 Pantry
40 What a compact often lacks
42 Green
44 Reply to a pushy person
45 Think worthy of doing
46 Change, at times
47 Turned down
48 What big projects are usually done in
49 Tough row to hoe?

DOWN

1 One way to go to a party
2 Lead-in to bath or powder
3 Join
4 Massive, in Marne
5 Country standard that begins "Love is a burning thing"
6 Quail flock
7 Words of clarification
8 Strip teaser?
9 Toughened
10 Seemingly
11 Workers may be drawn to them
13 What can give you a heads-up?
14 Big shot
16 Some pilgrims
21 Lake Chapala's state
24 Ordered programming
26 Bleached
27 Like an owl's eyes
28 Set of cursive Japanese symbols
29 Fix, as a bow
30 Toughened
31 Big name in home theaters
34 ___ Energy (big natural gas utility)
35 Elegantly groomed
36 It's worth a couple of bucks in Canada
38 Acoustics measures
39 Soft, now
41 His vet is Liz Wilson
43 Rolls out for sale at a nursery

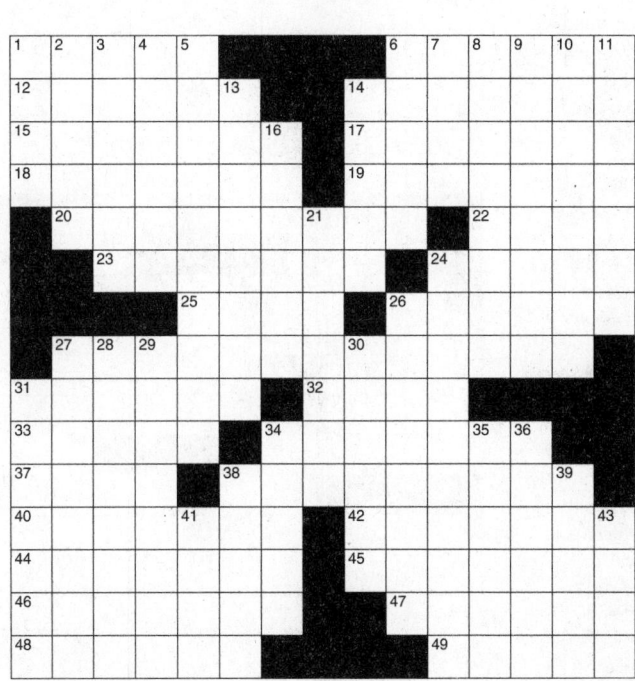

by Brendan Emmett Quigley

ACROSS

1 Was proven innocent
16 Merger alternative
17 Drive to drink?
18 Stops striving
19 With 12-Down, turns down
20 Ready for assault
21 Agricultural labor grp.
22 Become useless, as a 26-Down
27 Ukraine/Moldova border river
32 Debtor's option, briefly
33 It often includes tax
35 "Do ___ else!"
36 River through Dresden
37 Where Citigroup and JPMorgan Chase are headquartered
39 Pizza joint in "Do the Right Thing"
40 Potential poster boy
41 Dancing technique
44 New Orleans setting: Abbr.
45 Food preservative, briefly
47 Banda ___ (2004 tsunami site)
49 Bombshell revealed shortly before Election Day
57 Didn't judge a group fairly
58 An employee may accept a package for one
59 Met a body

DOWN

1 Not just brown
2 Like a maverick
3 Rough figs.
4 Quintessentially
5 Cut along the grain
6 Football Hall-of-Famer Hirsch
7 Actor Richmond and singer Jackson
8 Early Roman emperor
9 Mrs. Boris Yeltsin
10 "La Dolce Vita" actress
11 Earth-shaking beginning?
12 See 19-Across
13 Reebok rival
14 "Is it just ___ . . ."
15 Kite relatives
21 Lacking the resources
23 Order at Long John Silver's
24 "___ your hearts faint": Deuteronomy 20:3
25 In a tangle
26 Inflation target
27 Tony Randall title role
28 Brake fluid brand
29 Without flaws
30 Soyons is a form of it
31 Symbol of St. Barnabas, whose saint day comes at hay harvesting time
33 Daring exploit
34 PC connection
38 Firm cheese, for short?
42 Where brothers and sisters hang out
43 1677 Racine tragedy
46 Issued pound notes?
47 Coq ___
48 10 million rupees
49 Grp. that rolls out the barrels?
50 Woodwind instr.
51 Hawaiian staple
52 Olive kin
53 Japanese Peace Nobelist of 1974
54 Willow variety
55 Text message status
56 Job preceder: Abbr.

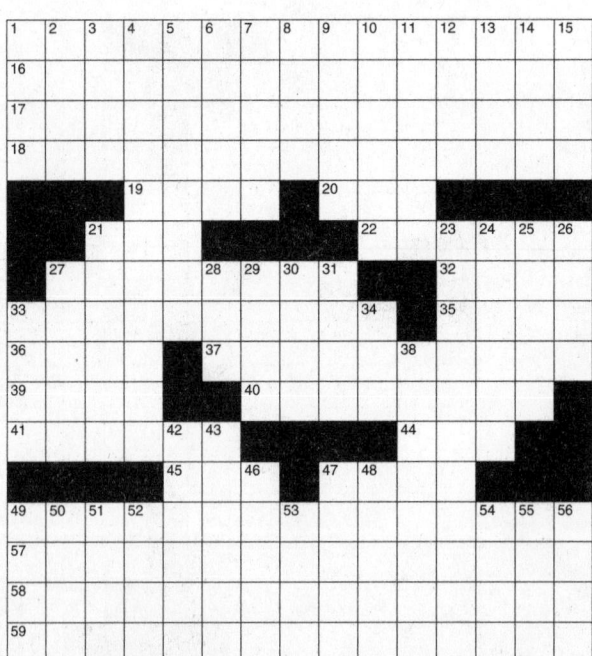

by Joe Krozel

ACROSS

1 Party bowlful with zing
9 Joint
15 "No problem!"
16 Bad way to carry something
17 Pitchman who said "It has more seats than the Astrodome!"
18 Peripheral, e.g.
19 They may be fluid: Abbr.
20 Covenants
22 ___ Prairie, Minn.
23 Sporty ride
26 Its final production was released in 1959
27 Cat of comics
28 One of the Home Counties
29 Thing picked up at a water cooler
31 Year China's Liang dynasty began
32 Part of some cultural nights out
34 "___ Mine" (track on "Let It Be")
35 Total bore
38 Large pieces of cabbage?
40 Humana offering, briefly
41 Unlike a type A
45 Letters for enlistees' letters
46 "The Lamp-Lighter" painter
47 ___ Spring
51 Solidified
53 Relative of "Apt."
54 Paradigm of piety, in Pamplona
55 Have down
56 In the middle
58 English composer/ pianist Lord
59 Pitcher López or Vázquez

61 "No problem!"
64 Port named for a Norse god
65 Setting for half of Chopin's 24 preludes
66 Thrust oneself heedlessly
67 Flimflams

DOWN

1 "I swear!"
2 With 6-Down, gets bombed
3 Parts of many role-playing games
4 Technology for "Avatar," e.g.: Abbr.
5 Noel syllables
6 See 2-Down
7 He had Atahualpa executed
8 High-hat
9 They're normal: Abbr.

10 "Hop-Frog" writer
11 Flame
12 Controversial O. J. Simpson book
13 Camera hog's concern
14 Fans may be worked into them
21 One with an extra-wide spine
24 Half of oct-
25 Let out, in a way
27 Crick who co-discovered DNA's structure
30 Cousin of a blackfish
33 Eddie who inspired "The French Connection"
35 Nut
36 South-of-the-border snack
37 Grabbed the reins

39 Soup thickener
42 Childish rejoinder
43 Many went bust after booming
44 Cause for an alarm
48 What only a select few might get
49 Person firing a locomotive
50 Uses cajolery on
52 1992 Dream Team member
56 Ebenezer Scrooge's nephew
57 Noted reader of headlines
60 Official conclusion?
62 ___-hoo
63 Nickname for Dwight Gooden

by Peter Wentz

326 HARD

ACROSS

1 Licks
8 Plant production
14 In a position of prominence
16 Hydrocarbon with two carbons
17 City founded by Shiva, according to legend
18 Reasons to presoak
19 Reform
20 One in a crowded delivery room
22 Soup thickener
23 It may be written in code
24 Overdo the tanning
25 Information on wine bottles: Abbr.
26 Insufferable guests
27 Mobile home dweller
29 Fish catchers
30 Puerto Rican seaport
31 Expressions of affection made with the eyes
35 First name of a 1978 Peace Nobelist
36 Renew old connections?
37 Shows anger publicly, say
38 Throw in together
39 Kahn of Broadway
42 1940s musical innovation
43 Drill item
44 Unhappy influence
45 Not fully reliable, as evidence
48 Viola da ___ (old stringed instrument)
49 Mideast dough
50 William Cullen Bryant poem that begins "Yet one smile more, departing, distant sun!"
52 Like many songbirds
53 It's more than just a game
54 Monologue writers?
55 Fill up

DOWN

1 Literary adulteress's surname
2 Bewitch
3 Father of Agamemnon
4 "I appreciate it," in text messages
5 Transport
6 Meryl's "Prime" co-star
7 It's also known as a maypop
8 Forest homes
9 Shakespeare rebuke
10 Get rough
11 Crayfish features
12 Creator of the Mayfair Witches
13 Makes over
15 Architect interred in Arlington National Cemetery
21 Russian Orthodox substitutes for palm branches on Palm Sunday
23 ___ dire
26 Case load?
27 Staple of gothic architecture
28 Slim win margin
29 "At once!"
31 Island nation with a trident on its flag
32 Supporter of the North
33 British coin introduced in 1971
34 One of many lost by Charlie Brown
39 Smallest republic on the African mainland
40 Begin disrobing, possibly
41 English illustrator who created the "St. Trinian's" cartoon series
43 Anniversary order
44 "___ Meets Godzilla" (classic 1969 cartoon)
46 First son
47 1962 title film character played by Joseph Wiseman
48 Mannerly man
51 Through

by Patrick Berry

ACROSS

1 What a wink often means
10 Words that prevent firing
15 Gunpowder ingredient
16 "A Season in Purgatory" novelist Dominick
17 Romanov family member
18 Former Brazilian president Luiz Inácio Lula da ___
19 Job description detail
20 Repetitive composition
22 Get out of the field
23 Chorus heard at some retreats
24 Let one's god down?
25 Old Asian title
27 Havens for folkies?
29 Thick
31 Brand written about by Hawthorne
32 Davis of Hollywood
33 Stadium thrillers: Abbr.
34 Creator of the currency system consisting of galleons, sickles and knuts
37 Time of the fall: Abbr.
40 Racing form data
41 Hot partner?
45 Like financial statements and hospital patients
47 "Sorry, too busy!"
48 It may be handed down
49 Sob story subject
50 Corporeal case
51 Host of the 1974 Asian Games
52 Begin's partner
55 "La Légende des Siècles" poet
56 Congressional feminist of note
58 "Avalon" band
60 Chilled, so to speak
61 Court star being courted?
62 Hissies
63 Compound combinations

DOWN

1 ___ Sharp, founder of Four Seasons Hotels
2 Let go
3 Gabbers' gathering
4 Opposite of 55-Down, informally
5 Vaccine combo
6 Sweets
7 Row announcement
8 Cologne contradiction
9 Former Lenin adherent?
10 Items checked before flying
11 Offbeat
12 Let go
13 Saxon or Celt, once
14 Big-eared china
21 Certain Bedouin
24 Becomes understood
26 Literary classic featuring the jester Wamba
28 Once-in-a-lifetime trip, for some
29 Stuck (to)
30 Elusive types
32 Stick
35 Equipment near a horse
36 Ready to be totally remodeled
37 They appear in installments
38 Almost in the sticks
39 Grand Canal sights
42 Exploits
43 1970s peace anthem
44 Concentrates, in a way
46 It often includes a trio
47 "Hold on"
49 Like some realistic statues
53 Pound racket
54 Small fishing vessel
55 Monster
57 They're peddled: Abbr.
59 Chinese game name starter

by Scott Atkinson

ACROSS

1 Couples' activity once considered scandalous
9 Tilting setting
15 Chicken's comment
16 Track
17 "You're doing it all wrong!"
18 Green goof
19 Like a moonstone
20 Fealty swearers
21 Circus tent raiser?
22 Binding agent
23 Like overdramatic spoken-word versions of pop songs
28 Campaign creations
31 Not moved much
32 They're plopped down
33 Old New Zealand natives
35 Sends up
37 "__ Love — not me": Dickinson
38 "I'm gone"
40 Farmhands, at times
42 1969 Peace Prize grp.
43 Athlete stripped of a 1994 national title
46 Something to get a round in
47 Side in a 1948 war
51 Many of his subjects were kings
53 Activity requiring three walls
55 "84 Charing Cross Road" author Hanff
56 Maximally kinky
57 Fendi rival
58 Lemony dessert
59 Conservative commentator Peggy
60 Place of discreet punishment

DOWN

1 Red lovers, perhaps
2 Assume
3 The Pineapple Island
4 Chat room annoyances
5 Climbers' goals
6 Not excluded from
7 Squat
8 It's "tachin' up" in a 1964 song
9 Cause of many a split
10 Farm stirrer
11 Like baboons' eyes
12 Subject of the 2008 book "How to Break a Terrorist"
13 Toots
14 Milk sources
20 Like some shirts
22 Part of Scotland's coat of arms
24 Deposit box?
25 How someone may try
26 Territory in Risk
27 Shell alternative
28 Part of a Latin succession
29 Part of Mauritius's coat of arms
30 Fire man?
34 Lecithin source
36 Guru's title
39 Zebra zone
41 Moved along slowly
44 Above or below preceder
45 Earnestly pursued things
48 Letter resembling an ox's head
49 "King Joe" composer
50 Positioned
51 Part of a comparison
52 Heart recipient, perhaps
53 2007 Best Picture nominee with a mythological name
54 Talos hurled huge stones at it
56 Avian call

by Will Nediger

ACROSS

1 Fixes, as some fairways
7 Charm the pants off
15 Missile that sank a British destroyer in the Falklands War
16 Words before many a foolish act
17 "I'm not listening . . ."
18 April shower?
19 I love the classic way?
20 Causes of breakdowns
22 Old Asian capital
23 Capital of Shaanxi province
25 Far from a sure thing
26 Lingerie shop specification
27 Ancient empire builders
29 Abbr. of politeness
30 Bit of wishful thinking
31 Company at the forefront of the dotcom boom
33 Home of Lewis-Clark State Coll.
34 Like brutal tactics
35 Not so tenuous
39 One with a small nest egg?
40 Make purr, as an engine
41 Poisonous mushroom producer, briefly?
44 Club cousin
45 Star in the Swan constellation
46 Shield border
47 It's worn while driving
49 Top: Prefix
50 "Sk8er ___" (2002 top 10 hit)
51 Locale for an Olivier Award winner
53 One may suffer a blow
54 1980 Maxwell Smart film, with "The"
56 Extract
58 Clearing
59 Really lit
60 "Hang in there!"
61 Copied a capo

DOWN

1 In a hammock, say
2 Many a patient
3 Ones with the motto "One for the road"?
4 Andean tuber
5 Strike
6 See 7-Down
7 With 6-Down, common sight outside a school building
8 Mingo player of 1960s TV
9 Sawyer's successor in Chicago
10 Longtime enemy of Wonder Woman
11 Discipline symbolized by a painted circle
12 Style associated with washboards
13 Stuff
14 It covers 2% of the earth's surface
21 Lighter option
24 The court's Bucharest Buffoon
26 Latte alternative
28 Opposite of ample
30 Wasn't employed
32 Quick to get things
33 Plasma bit
35 Join, as a table
36 Quaint humiliator
37 Pep up
38 Responded to a crash, maybe
40 No posh hotel
41 Hang (with)
42 51-Across unit
43 Uses shortening on?
44 State surrounded by Lower Saxony
47 Complete, informally
48 "How pallid, chill and ___!": Keats
51 Alternative to a carpet lift
52 Part of the Tuscan Archipelago
55 Apnea diagnoser, briefly
57 They, in Calais

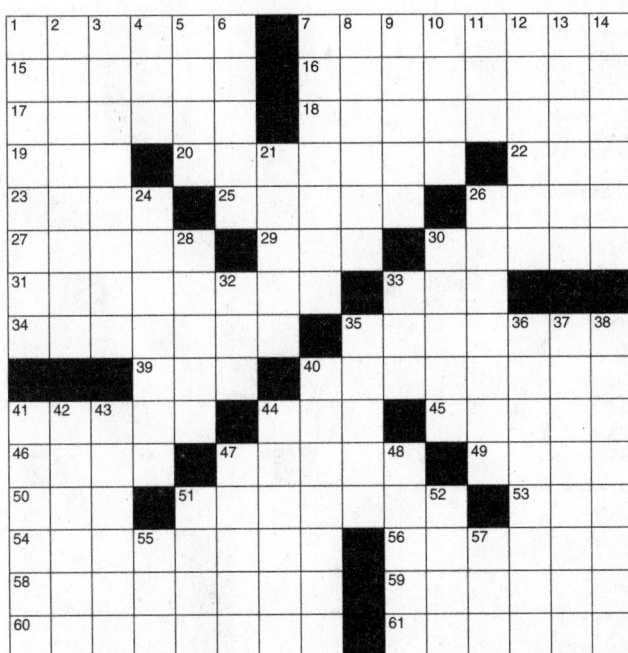

by Barry Boone

ACROSS

1 Treaty of Fort McIntosh signer, 1785
9 Taste test need
15 Can't do without
16 William Herschel discovery of 1787
17 Comment while hemming
18 Has an impressive address
19 Local listings
20 Coin collector's classification
22 De Gaulle's predecessor
23 Part of the Kingdom of the Netherlands
24 Contrivance for taking people for a ride
25 440 yards, for many runners
27 They often want to settle: Abbr.
29 Ad conclusion?
30 "What's New, Pussycat?" co-star, 1965
32 Antigen attacker
34 Least likely to turn tail
37 Automobil site
39 Bethlehem's region
40 Pump alternative
42 Subway inspection org.
43 Empathic counselor of sci-fi
45 Has a loan from
49 What a webmaster may master
51 Gulf of Aqaba city
53 Eats
54 Monomaniacal
56 Group 13 member, in chemistry
57 Mistreating

58 Common salad ingredient
60 Confederate
61 Eponym of an Australian Open arena
62 Surgeons' insertions
63 Deliverers of product lines?

DOWN

1 Big name in oil
2 El Cid player
3 Lead-in to someone else's words, after "and"
4 What a crush might be
5 Marks in a casino
6 Leandro's partner
7 River to the North Sea
8 Kind of reproduction

9 Not skilled in
10 Magician's opening
11 Browses (through)
12 They're in rags
13 They may be treated in a spa
14 Pieces together?
21 American Lung Assn. recommendation
23 Blood drive spec.
26 Distressed
28 One stuck in a float
31 Holy Roman emperor, 973–83
33 Florida city on the Caloosahatchee
34 Singer with the 1966 hit "I'm So Lonesome I Could Cry"
35 Area with aging factories
36 Water

38 Compete in the Breeders Crown
41 Some Olympians get them
44 Covers over, in a way
46 Freed from guilt
47 Stonemason's chisel
48 They have rights
50 Comintern creator
52 "The Frogs Who Desired a King" author
55 Editorial reconsideration
56 "Oklahoma!" set piece
59 Year the Visigoths invaded Italy

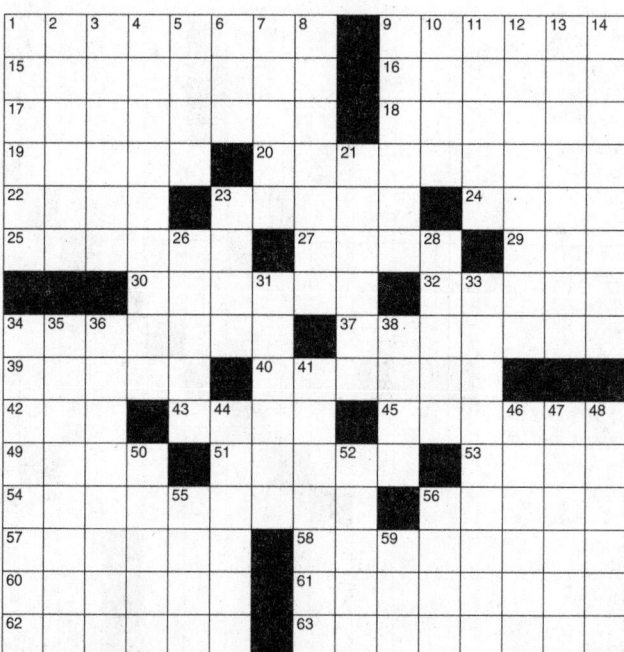

by Barry C. Silk

ACROSS

1 ___ hole
7 Early film star who wore lipstick in the shape of a heart
15 Severe sales restriction, informally
16 Plunge
17 City that's home to Parliament Hill
18 Has a service break?
19 Reqmt. for giving someone the third degree?
20 Some compact light sources
22 Try to fit a square peg in a round hole, e.g.
23 With 8-Down, takes a lot of shots, say
24 Non-union?
25 Suggest for the future
26 ___ B (first step)
27 Sweltered
28 ___ Farm, setting for a George Orwell story
29 Member of a campaign staff
31 National Wear Red Day mo.
32 Came out of a hole, say
33 Continues, as a band
37 Its first two vols. covered 43-Across
38 Top-level commands, collectively
39 Hard to discern
42 Pin in a hole
43 See 37-Across
44 "Dinner's ___"
45 Measures of volume
46 House of prayer
47 Spirited response?
48 Runs up
49 Farm shelter

50 "Uh-huh"
52 Iberian city that lends its name to a variety of wine
54 It's not useful in a long shot situation
55 Food writer Nigella
56 Extremely touching?
57 Noted TV twins

DOWN

1 "You played well"
2 Maryland's historic ___ Creek
3 Litter pickup place?
4 South's declaration, perhaps
5 Mint
6 Like rulers
7 Toronto landmark
8 See 23-Across
9 Solicited
10 Actor Roger
11 Things that pop up annoyingly
12 Crunch
13 Go too far
14 One in an outfit
21 Approved, as a contract
25 Subject of a 1980s surrogacy case
27 Produce
28 Not accidental
30 Coin with a hole in it
31 Goes it alone
33 Worker with street smarts?
34 Fish whose male carries the eggs
35 Starting point?
36 Bundles of bound quarks
38 Something from which something else is taken away

39 As an example
40 "Star Wars" name
41 Brew
42 "Way to be, man!"
45 [Bo-o-o-oring!]
46 Junk vehicles
48 Peculiar: Prefix
51 In addition
53 Bud

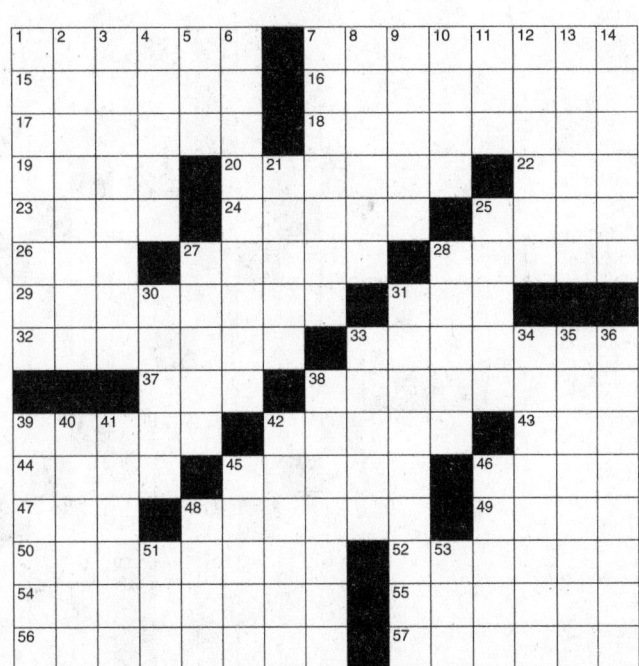

by Mike Nothnagel

ACROSS

1 Baseball All-Star's nickname . . . or a popular food product
7 Music that may make you get down
15 Crazy Horse, e.g.
16 Kooky
17 Physically show elation
18 U.S. Civil War starting point
19 Financial report abbr.
20 Coming up on the hour
22 Old Chicago Outfit frontman
23 Go for
25 Actor Rogen and others
27 Register indicator
28 Like monster trucks or their spectators
30 Hardly inclined
32 Commuting options
33 Macaque or marmoset
35 Many a benefit tourney
37 Axel alternative
39 Argumentative
43 Cause of a rash reaction?
45 Reel revolution
46 Settings for much stitching, briefly
49 Capital near Lake Titicaca
51 Capital near Green Peter Lake
52 NOW head?: Abbr.
54 Buns may cover them
56 Cheese portion
57 Bolt
59 John's neighbor
61 Oslo Accords grp.

62 Treats served toasted and buttered
64 Triple-platinum 1982 album with the #1 hit "Africa"
66 One drawing many blanks
67 Rodin worked in it
68 Past paranoia producer
69 At that place

DOWN

1 Wear after a serious spill
2 Signature song of Peter Allen
3 Delightful
4 Lt. col.'s inferior
5 Put down
6 Aviary supply
7 Feature of many a Jeep
8 Producer of simple chords
9 Woe while getting clean
10 Floor
11 Like some resistance
12 Vex
13 Fictional woodcutter's daughter
14 Character traits?
21 "Regnava ___ silenzio" (Donizetti aria)
24 Flip response?
26 Bore
29 Dadaist Hausmann
31 They may appear over icons
34 "___ of Her Own" (Clark Gable film)
36 Western scenery
38 One with a notably hard bed

40 Wheel-powering reservoir
41 Put on a pedestal
42 Cover-up unlikely to fool anyone
44 "Got it?"
46 G.M. system with a "Virtual Advisor"
47 Poinciana feature
48 42-Down unit
50 Part of an English wizard's spell?
53 Doctors with spirits
55 Reserve for future use
58 Like 60-Down: Abbr.
60 Zodiaco animal
63 Rondo producer
65 Host

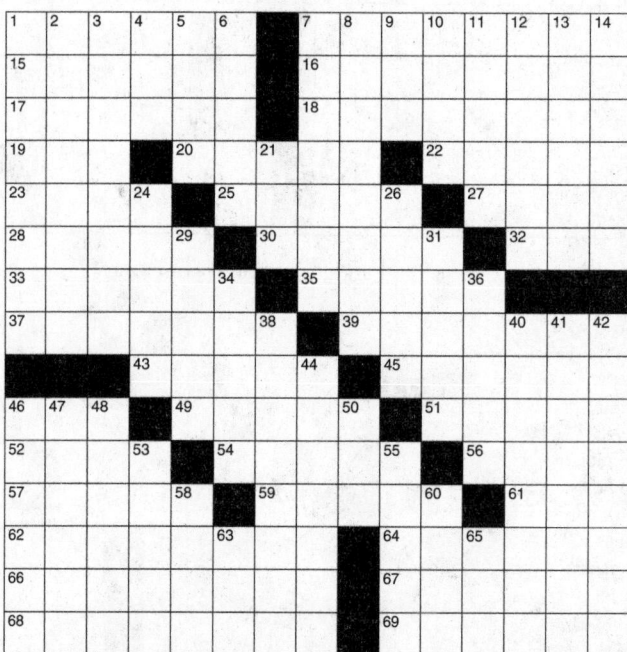

by Brad Wilber

HARD 333

ACROSS

1 One "standing by the ocean's roar," in a 1963 song
11 Fall times: Abbr.
15 Newton alternative
16 "The Battle Hymn of the Republic" lyricist
17 Traveler's check
18 It might cross 1st, 2nd and 3rd
19 What's gained after taking off: Abbr.
20 Most fetching
22 Letters of discharge?
23 Trough's opposite
25 No slowpoke
27 Division indicator
30 Ross Perot's birthplace
32 Ancient resident of Mexico's Cholula
34 Choir practice?
35 Chronological threshold
36 Backwash creator
38 Put away
39 It's often in a sling
41 Was present
44 Fruit-ripening gas
46 Crassus defeated him
48 Like jugs
49 TheraFlu alternative
50 Nürnberg or Neu-Ulm
52 Stock page abbr.
53 Monotonous beating sound
55 Expert on plays
58 Piece of cake?
60 "Don't mention it"
63 División del día
64 Birth of a notion?
65 "Idylls of the King" figure
66 Quartzite and such

DOWN

1 1997–99 N.L. strikeout leader
2 Russia's ___ Airlines
3 Robbed, old-style
4 Scarecrow, to Batman
5 External: Prefix
6 Early car company co-founder
7 Lose one's shirt
8 1960s R&B backup group, with "the"
9 Chafe
10 1983 #1 hit for David Bowie
11 Omega, to a physicist
12 Aid for not losing one's shirt
13 Like some fighters
14 Civic rival
21 Not scattershot
23 Midwest setting: Abbr.
24 Slot car controller
26 With 45-Down, unisex topper
27 Abbr. in many Québec addresses
28 Preparation that makes folks hot?
29 Grandson of Catherine the Great
31 Top of many a timepiece
33 Maze full of dead ends?
37 Sport, for short
40 Jarrett of Nascar
42 Old N.Y.C. elevated operator
43 Bunny collector?
45 See 26-Down
46 Means of splitting stalks?
47 Hard to stir
51 Periods of prayer?
54 Pioneering woman lawyer Bradwell
55 Make unusable
56 Contemporary of Ngaio
57 Some badge flashers
59 "Outstanding, man!"
61 Put-on
62 "The Big C" airer, briefly

by Barry C. Silk

ACROSS

1 Calisthenics for show-offs
12 Plaintive cry
15 Saturn, for one
16 Diminutive Spanish name suffix
17 European neolithic monument
18 Lawyer's thing
19 Doctors
20 Least
22 Pablo Neruda's "___ to Common Things"
23 ___ tie
24 Go after
25 Bit of centurion gear
27 G.E. unit: Abbr.
28 Something a father may hear
32 Play at recess
34 Coal holder
36 British form of 33-Down
37 Hint
39 Widows' allowances
40 Many a character on "The Big Bang Theory"
41 Web site with the subheading "Merchant Services"
43 Overthrew, e.g.
45 Samosa ingredients
46 Some fishing gear
50 Import/export business concern
52 Air traveling over snow?
53 Actor Somerhalder of "Lost"
54 Rental for many an apartment dweller
56 Freon initials
57 Like critics
58 "Animal Farm" locale
59 Kitschy stuffed toys

DOWN

1 Red cocktail, for short
2 Played some dulcet tones
3 Square things
4 Isn't settled
5 U. V.I.P.
6 Supermarket lines, for short
7 Loafer, e.g.
8 Five Norwegian kings
9 Exposes
10 Trophy, of sorts
11 Firewood measure
12 Kind of wheel
13 Took something in at night?
14 They may take you in at night
21 Back to back
23 Engage in a bachelor party activity
25 Zen Buddhists, e.g.
26 Hamilton and Hunt
28 Study making sound judgments?
29 Rapid transit?
30 It's just not normal
31 Penned in
33 See 36-Across
35 Frenzied
38 Sign meaning "Let this be our little secret"
42 Footnote word in Latin
44 Shows at an expo
46 P.M. before Sharon
47 Stand and deliver?
48 Menace in the air, maybe
49 Moves along tirelessly?
51 Middle management?
52 Didi of "Grease" and "Grease 2"
55 Word accompanying "Much," "Little" and "Late" in a 1978 #1 hit

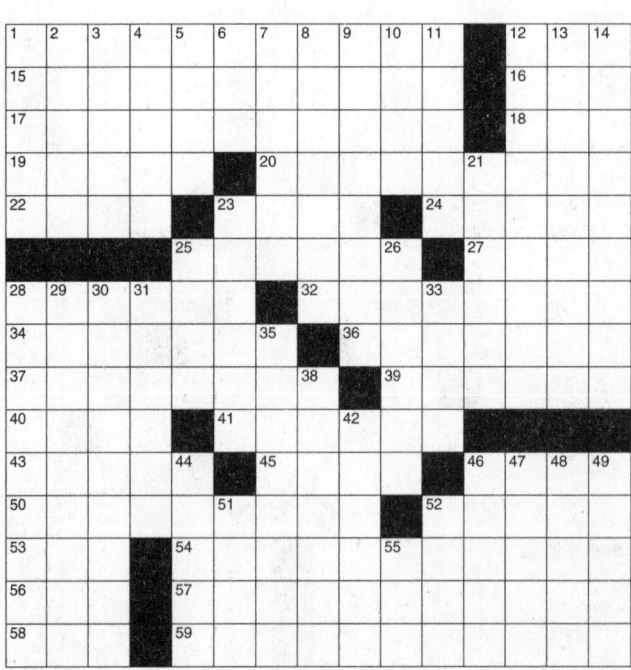

by Mark Diehl

ACROSS

1 Locals make them often
6 Pic
10 ___ pros. (court record abbr.)
13 Actress Roberts
14 Bridge unit
15 Nixon pal Rebozo
16 It's high when it's red
17 Stage part
18 At sea
19 1980s–'90s women's magazine
20 Rockies rangers
21 Períodos de 52 semanas
22 "Moses" novelist
23 Setting for a roaster
24 Massage locale
25 Start a scrap
27 Enjoyed a British tradition
29 Lemon on a baseball field
30 Tops at the dinner table?
31 Heat sources
34 Barbers
35 Legislation station?
37 Done to ___
38 Did as suggested in a Gershwin musical?
39 Relatives of 20-Across
43 Spring times
44 One who might have an original imitation
46 Heavyweights face off in it
47 Crab Key villain of book and film
48 Ciliary body setting
49 Locale shrouded in mystery?
50 Bodily channel
51 Basis
52 Joined
53 Digging for dirt?
54 Succotash bit
55 Place for a small flag
56 Some racecars
57 Police dept. figure
58 Ones being shot at

DOWN

1 Compound used in wartime
2 "A Writer's Life" autobiographer, 2006
3 Like Sartre's "No Exit"
4 Win offset by losses
5 Their scores may be on transcripts
6 Colonial stinger
7 Old Greek coins
8 Gets on the phone, say
9 They're often lying in beds
10 Kind of ward
11 Superseded
12 Doesn't challenge
15 A state symbol of Maryland
23 Neither nails it nor blows it
24 In one's cups
26 Trig symbols
28 Dispossession
31 Very hot
32 Deep-fried mouthful
33 Transparency
36 Not excise
37 Tour guide?
40 Grand tour setting
41 2009 Grammy winner for "Relapse"
42 Miss America host after Bert Parks
45 Salon jobs
48 Aptly named hybrid
49 Something to weave

by Victor Fleming

336 HARD

ACROSS

1. Word that keeps the same meaning if "cap-" is added at the front
5. Group whose 1968 album "Time Peace" was #1
15. They burn
16. Could still have gotten
17. Some people with sports M.B.A.'s: Abbr.
18. Subject of 1987 Congressional hearings
19. N.Y.C. neighborhood
20. Pharaoh's head?
21. Bibliophile's suffix
22. Mayo setting: Abbr.
23. Charlemagne, e.g.: Abbr.
24. Back
30. Coach Mike of the 1994 Stanley Cup-winning Rangers
31. ___ Poly, school nickname
32. What-___
35. Platinum-group element
37. Delete from copy
39. Basketball Hall-of-Famer Holman
40. "Come ___?" (Italian greeting)
41. Yelena ___, Soviet dissident and wife of Andrei Sakharov
42. Flooring option
45. Short lines at checkout?
48. Diminutive suffix
49. Costume party costume
50. Tiny, valuable beads
55. Wide-headed fastener
56. "Shhh!"

57. Classic football rival of Notre Dame: Abbr.
58. Hero whose statue appears in front of Chicago's Tribune Tower
59. Not an orig.
60. Expressionless
61. Like some friends

DOWN

1. Oscar-winning actor with the autobiography "Halfway Through the Door"
2. Time past
3. Give the business
4. ___ Blue (old kerosene brand)
5. "Insane!"
6. African capital of 1.5+ million
7. Fess Parker's TV co-star
8. Objurgation
9. "East River" novelist, 1946
10. Place to put a tap
11. Hustles
12. "___ Zoo," 1967 hit
13. Super Bowl XIV competitor, for short
14. Forever ___
25. Share of responsibility
26. Mrs. Gorbachev
27. Number in a pack?
28. No-good
29. "The Sacred Wood" writer
32. Highly seismic area off the Greek coast
33. Tank-to-carburetor conduits

34. Graffiti, e.g.
36. Whole world in one's hands?
38. Basic cable inits.
43. It can follow two hips
44. One may be dominant
45. On drugs
46. Bee's landing place
47. Item of sports equipment worn on the wrist
51. Three of these make an O
52. Free TV spots, for short
53. Start of a children's rhyme
54. Long
55. Gang land

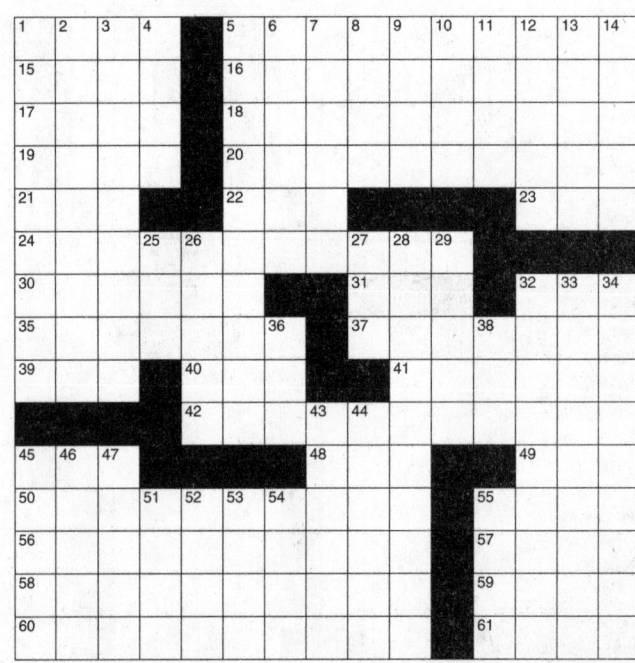

by Joe DiPietro

ACROSS

1 Showed great discomfort
8 Turkey tots?
14 Lamont Library locale
15 Like some expense reimbursements
16 1968 Rock Hudson action film
18 They can make waves
19 It's out of bounds
20 H.M.O. personnel
21 Grow together
22 One way to be in love
24 "Dressing Rich" author Feldon
25 Heartbeat
26 Sights in an intensive care unit
27 "___ of Roses" (1995 adult contemporary album)
28 Green Monster's squad
29 One on board an outboard
30 1940 Tyrone Power adventure film, with "The"
32 Strongly realistic
34 Dweller along the Skunk River
35 1935 Pulitzer-winning biography
36 Take over
37 Many a prof
40 "Aida" chorus subject
41 Where Hausa and Djerma are spoken
42 Adonis' undoing
43 Sitter's charge, maybe
44 Big bank investment?
45 "She's Got You" singer, 1962

46 1937 Ronald Colman adventure film, with "The"
50 Political tactic
51 Thing under a tumbler
52 Transplants
53 Without any gas?

DOWN

1 Egg beaters
2 County south of Milwaukee
3 Peaceful
4 Show case?
5 They have crowns
6 Big time
7 It's been banned in the U.S. since 1972
8 Wise leader?
9 Italian side dish
10 Ulan-___, Russia

11 Book
12 Like a clover leaf
13 Atom ___
15 Crawl spaces?
17 Telephone dialer?
22 Like some perfume
23 "Bug ___" (1999 Destiny's Child hit)
24 Wise up
26 Calorie-rich dessert
27 Ingredient in artificial gems
28 Katharine Lee ___, writer of "America the Beautiful"
29 Garden shelter
30 Revolutionary War groups
31 Neighborhood
32 Vise
33 What things may be held in

36 Conrad who wrote "Ushant," 1952
37 ___ shoes (ballet wear)
38 "Ezio" composer
39 Gray
41 Young hijos
42 Smile upon
44 Darer's cry
45 Powerful person
47 Tampa-to-Ft. Myers dir.
48 Time of much raking: Abbr.
49 One to counter

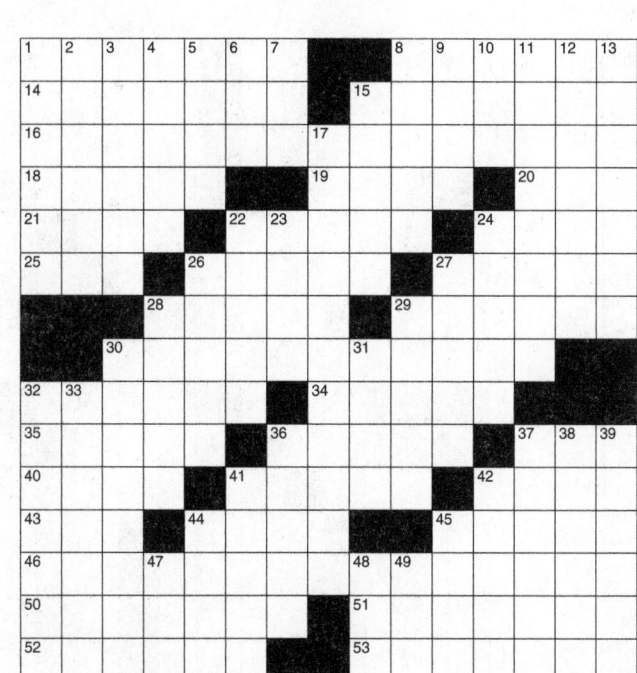

by Gary Steinmehl

ACROSS

1 Reaction from one who has a bone to pick?
7 Duel action
15 Confusion
16 Working class's antithesis
17 Game with tricks
18 Literally, "small wheel"
19 Word on a scale
20 Old dirk
21 Tony winner Caldwell
22 High-class affliction?
25 Patent-Motorwagen inventor
26 Historic institution near Slough
27 Buzzes
28 "Check it out!"
29 Poll fig.
30 Nabokov novel
31 Casual remarks?
32 Show in which many pots disappear?
38 Took back, as words
39 Ticked
40 Moose Drool or Trout Slayer
41 Send a Dear John letter
44 Like some eyes
45 Turtle's eye, often
46 See 33-Down
47 Bouncer in a sports stadium?
49 Bond girl player Green
50 District in southern Kazakhstan
51 Ryan of "Star Trek: Voyager"
52 Mediterranean appetizer
54 Novelist Diamant and others
57 It uses 20 different end rhymes for "ore"
58 Aging establishment
59 Float maker
60 Felt

DOWN

1 Something to be struck with
2 Ping-Pong or dancing, for short
3 Harmony spoiler
4 "Quickest way to Harlem," in song
5 Back in
6 Like some chickens
7 Defeated contestant in a face-off
8 Male doll
9 Turns sharply
10 TV segment
11 N.F.L. cornerback ___ Bly
12 Alternatives to Triscuits
13 Show opener
14 Allergy symptom
22 Deux into quatorze
23 Do some impressive work?
24 "Gotcha"
25 Chowderhead
28 Deprive of vitality
30 British leader in the Seven Years' War
31 Features of some bear traps
33 Cost to get out of 46-Across
34 Dinar earner
35 Something intended to move fast
36 "Old China" essayist
37 Like many offs.
41 Red-cards, say
42 Adjective-less language
43 Got on the horn
44 Kite, often
45 Iconic building?
47 Unlike chickens
48 Kids' rhyme starter
50 Setting of Mozart's only clarinet concerto: Abbr.
53 Neighbor of Scorpius
55 Is for you?
56 Folk rock singer Straw

by Xan Vongsathorn

ACROSS

1 German superhighway connecting the Ruhr with Berlin
5 Where the Beatles opened their 1965 North American tour
9 Mountain climber?
13 Sleuth's quest
14 Hang loose
15 Our genus
16 Like some communication
18 Shady group?
19 Going ___
20 Weight or freight
21 Road hog?
23 Computer action of last resort
25 Definitely not a company man?
26 Endangered Arctic presence
27 Cabbageheads
29 How a toddler eats
31 Knit alternative
32 Out
35 Spade, e.g., for short
36 1959 Broadway hit with the song "All I Need Is the Girl"
37 Rolling stone?
38 "The powerful scent of real clean" sloganeer
40 They're set in place settings
42 Edible clam
46 Put right?
47 What snake oil is, supposedly
48 Chucked out
49 Pointed encouragement
50 Largest labor union in the U.S.
51 "___ quote . . ."
52 Game time?

55 Angel Cheryl
56 Elizabethan barmaid
57 What some hearts are made of
58 Or ___
59 Ambassador of old autodom
60 Home of a Big 12 school

DOWN

1 Service centers?
2 Home on the range
3 Shipyard worker fired in 1976
4 Lyricist's offering
5 Young hog
6 Back
7 2010 title role for Denzel Washington
8 13-, 20-, 49- and 57-Across, commonly?
9 Where Persia defeated Sparta in 480 B.C.
10 Bungle
11 Evaluators of current events?
12 Positive
14 Walking the dog and others
17 Found a job for
22 Tentacle
24 They won't wait, in a phrase
25 Tom of "Animal House"
27 They're put on many cars
28 Rocky, really
30 It may help you make big strides
32 W.H.O. concern
33 Reasoned
34 Oxymoronic chances
36 Haitian currency

38 Define clearly
39 Game played with a dotted ball
41 Get it
43 Victorian taxi
44 Soccer cheer
45 Secretive group?
47 Beach souvenir
48 It may be tied up in farmwork
49 Washington, Grant and others: Abbr.
53 Snow ___
54 Ottoman officer

by Matt Ginsberg

ACROSS

1 Capital NE of the Gulf of Trieste
10 Housemate in Steinbeck's "Tortilla Flat"
15 With nothing on
16 Outfit
17 Fiery rhetoric
18 "You're nothing but a pack of cards!" speaker
19 Becomes fixed
20 File stuff
22 Sparkle
23 With 3-Down, collectively
24 Fringe group?
26 Easter egg design
30 Spell
32 Stop running
33 Victoria's "Dallas" role
35 Some shirt pocket problems
37 Presbyterian-founded Michigan college
38 Stir
40 Puma rival
41 Mrs. Dalloway in "Mrs. Dalloway"
43 Treasure
45 Get down
46 Kitchen mishap
48 Not flowery
49 Dress down like a sailor?
51 Co. with many keywords
53 Wrong
54 Wind sounds
56 Monarchy since the 1740s
60 Collection of 24 books
62 Russian famously played by an Egyptian
64 Superhighway service site
65 Like many former friends
66 "Days of Our Lives" town
67 It may have you in an awkward position

DOWN

1 Culture development sites
2 De ___ (by law)
3 See 23-Across
4 Smashing sounds
5 Some capts.-to-be
6 Old Isle of Wight settlers
7 Invisible enticements
8 New Mexican?
9 Red flag's purpose
10 Ed supporter
11 "Cafe Terrace at Night" setting
12 Hit the roof
13 Settings
14 "Let me in," facetiously
21 One noted for ingenuity
23 American leader?
25 GPS data: Abbr.
26 "Avatar" craft
27 Home of Whitman College
28 Neither here nor there
29 Can
31 Like some pools
34 Sting in 1980 headlines
36 Brie alternative
39 It has color-coded sections
42 Its highest mtn. is Meron
44 Card letters
47 Birthplace of Günter Grass
50 Floor
52 Tony-winning Tessie
55 Joan followed him at Woodstock
56 Like olives
57 ___ Hari
58 Dating service data
59 Signs an agreement?
61 Stop from running
63 Letterhead abbr.

by Doug Peterson

ACROSS

1 Dealers' dreads
6 Clothes hangers?
15 Plant whose roots are used as detergent
16 Something you can bank on
17 Tart flavor
18 Totally assured, as victory
19 Two-time U.S. Women's Open winner
21 ___ date
22 Like swift streams
23 People who have been 45-Downed
26 Air-gulping swimmer
27 Went wild
28 What flounder flounder in
29 Grp. knocked in "Sicko"
30 Needle point?: Abbr.
31 Alternative title of "Mack the Knife"
33 & 36 "Babes in Arms" tune that's apt for this puzzle
37 Sodium ___ (cleansers)
38 Like some people resisting arrest
39 It might accompany a bar line
40 N.Y.C.'s Washington ___
41 "___ date"
42 Stuck, in a way
47 Kitties
48 99 times out of 100
49 Spot for a tot
54 Stethoscope inventor Laënnec and others
55 Early 19th-century engineering marvel
56 Bill Bradley, once
57 Where cells are of little use
58 Friends and such

DOWN

1 Inventor of logarithms
2 Dualistic Egyptian deity
3 "All right, dude!"
4 Superb
5 What a motto encapsulates
6 Dupes in some mailboxes
7 Part of AIM
8 Part of many an AIM chat
9 P.G.A. Tour Rookie of the Year two years before Woods
10 Femme canonisée: Abbr.
11 Fancy shooters
12 One who surrenders
13 MSG component
14 Apart
20 Tennis's Goolagong
23 Being reserved
24 They may be incubating
25 Accents
32 Like Bach's second violin concerto
33 Author of "Chasing the Dream: My Lifelong Journey to the World Series"
34 Aeschylus trilogy
35 Dogged
37 Appeared on screen, in a way
43 Rich of old films
44 Like some tattooed characters
45 Give a seat to
46 Anchors' places
50 Dupes in some mailboxes
51 Chance
52 Dweller near Central Park's Strawberry Fields
53 Kind of flour

by Elizabeth C. Gorski

342 HARD

ACROSS

1 Abbr. for change
4 One who's just arrived in Mexico?
8 "I got ___"
14 Possible result of high temperature
16 Setting of muchas islas
17 What Tito shows, in opera
18 Recipient's reply
19 Daughter of Alexander VI
21 These, on Ibiza
22 What an aspiring model may read
23 One with star power?: Abbr.
24 Comic with the 1955 album "At Sunset"
25 Open
26 ___-robe (Calais closet)
27 Didn't just ask
28 Ancient amulet inscription
30 19th-century, say
31 Doctored account
32 Bread source
33 Nigerian language
36 "Emma" studio
38 Kodak film used in surveillance
39 Under control
42 Quinceañera treat
43 "___ goes!"
44 Country whose name is occasionally used as an exclamation?
45 Time, to Freud
46 Eddy site
47 What a Yankee is unlikely to have
50 Bit of beachwear
51 Projection creator
53 Sitcom witch
54 Element between polonium and radon on the periodic table
55 They go in and out
56 Wreck-checking org.
57 Matt Dillon title role of 1982

DOWN

1 Flu-fighting org.
2 Blabs, blabs, blabs
3 Did some digging around
4 Backwoods sibs
5 Stern article
6 Thrilling hoops shot
7 One may attach something
8 "This should ___!"
9 A third of veinticuatro
10 Riot control agent
11 One in the closet
12 One way to respond
13 Register message
15 [Brrr!]
20 "The die is cast," to Caesar
21 Boston Garden nickname
25 Midway point?
26 Tittle-tattle
29 Love letters?
31 Hamper part
33 Affirmation of seriousness
34 Military band piece
35 Draft team
36 Tiger Balm ingredient
37 Best bud
38 Security problem
39 Scraps
40 Aggregate
41 Foot-washing ceremony
45 Some Greek sisters
46 1983 Joel Schumacher film
48 Storied slacker
49 Analog oscilloscope parts: Abbr.
52 Playmate for Spot

by Paula Gamache

ACROSS

1 Progress too slowly
4 Joe Btfsplk's creator
8 Effective salesman
14 Tavern
16 Micro wave?
17 Popular name for tolnaftate
18 Things holding up the works?
19 Image that stays with you
20 Traffic reporter, you might say
22 TV show whose opening music is the Who's "Who Are You"
23 Where Alfred Krupp was born
24 Frequent flier
25 What an only child lacks
26 Lump in one's throat?
28 "The Cryptogram" playwright, 1995
29 Noisy vehicles
32 Meeting in which one person is anxious to leave
33 Staples of old police work
34 PayPal transactions, e.g.
35 Lock
36 Welsh word in a Pennsylvania college name
37 Held back
38 "I Just Can't Wait to Be King" singer
43 Subj. of Stansfield Turner's "Burn Before Reading"
44 Attain success
45 A term may end with one
46 Full-blown
48 Declutter
50 Malicious sort

51 Aids in breaking shells
52 Arthur who wrote "The Symbolist Movement in Literature"
53 Part of the American Greetings logo
54 1950 film noir

DOWN

1 Milky drink
2 Cover
3 Bathroom door sign
4 Natural skin moisturizer
5 Caddy, e.g.
6 Clairvoyance and such
7 Means of getting the lead out
8 Ecclesiastical council's formulation
9 Embroidery expert
10 Black ___
11 Lab stock

12 Analyst who leaked the Pentagon Papers
13 Puts up a fight
15 Word on Harry Powell's left fingers in "The Night of the Hunter"
21 Common glow-in-the-dark item
24 Liquid dispensers in laboratories
25 "Vexations" composer
27 Mouse lookalike
28 Canadian singer with a 1995 album that went 16× platinum
29 Language that reads the same backward and forward
30 ___ Man, commercial symbol since the 1950s

31 Dumbarton ___ Conference (1944 meeting that laid the groundwork for the U.N.)
32 Three-time N.B.A. Coach of the Year
33 Monitor toppers
37 High-strung items?
39 Slush Puppie alternative
40 Like horses
41 Comic strip bully
42 Series opener
44 Leave destitute
45 Unimpressive attire
47 1969 bed-in participant
49 Roman I

by Patrick Berry

ACROSS

1 Aid in deep diving
12 One might use Peter Pan, in brief
15 "Casino" Golden Globe winner
16 Sch. with a 60-foot "Praying Hands" sculpture
17 Proverbially newsworthy item
18 Designer of Alabama's Civil Rights Memorial
19 It displays an array of spikes: Abbr.
20 Trunk attachment
21 Basic drive
23 Take on
25 Marine muncher on mangrove leaves
26 Explosion producer
27 Smashes
28 Heroine of Inge's "Picnic"
31 1986 Indy 500 winner
32 Poule's counterpart
33 Sparkle
34 Opposite of frumpish
35 Actor awarded a Distinguished Flying Cross in W.W. II
36 On-target
37 Deltoid ligament attachment point
38 French frost
39 Old Rory Calhoun TV western
41 Disney character prone to spoonerisms
42 Period about a decade before the 34-Down
43 Person in a pool
46 "Saving Fish From Drowning" novelist
47 Fist pumper's cry
48 Spider, Snoopy or Intrepid: Abbr.
50 Football Hall-of-Famer Huff

51 Artwork depicted in Dalí's "The Hallucinogenic Toreador"
54 "Last Train to London" grp.
55 Financial option upon leaving a job
56 Father's alma mater: Abbr.
57 Tag with a message, often

DOWN

1 Woman in all four "Twilight" novels
2 R&B's ___ Khan
3 Pays dearly for one's crimes
4 Astronomical discovery
5 Stain
6 Good way to arrive

7 1972 Bill Withers hit
8 Wreck checker: Abbr.
9 U.S.N. and U.S.A.F. div.
10 Ship with devastating cargo
11 Queenly
12 Like some platforms
13 Engagement party?
14 Queenly
22 "Ridiculous!"
24 Plus or minus, say
25 Israel Philharmonic maestro
27 Après-midi follows it
28 Places to display cuts
29 First mate?
30 Intergenerational MTV reality show
31 Home to Mohammed V University

34 When William Safire worked at the White House
35 One may be Protestant
37 Shalom Meir Tower locale
38 Entered rehab, e.g.
40 Three-day holiday
41 Not just dangerous
43 Inebriate
44 Rival of Yastrzemski for 1960s A.L. batting titles
45 Filled anew, as a flat
47 Chess master Averbakh
49 Hog's desire
52 Book editor Talese
53 CO, e.g.: Abbr.

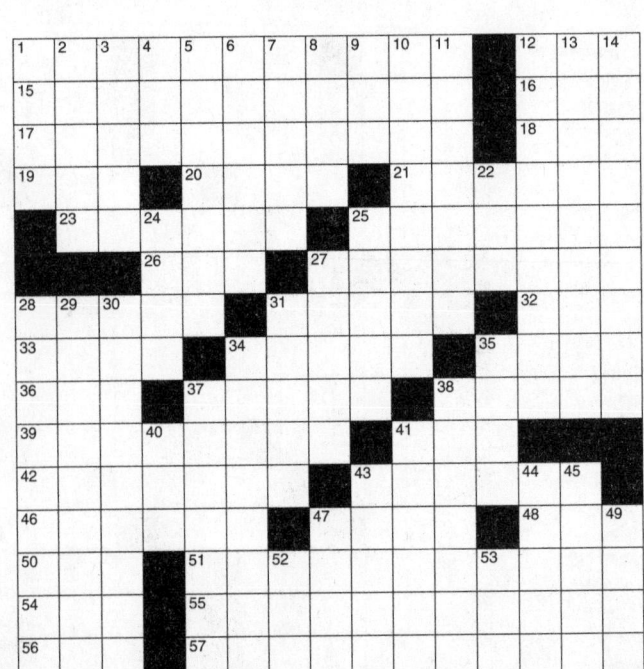

by Brad Wilber

ACROSS

1 Not an ideal answer to "Do these jeans make me look fat?"
4 Chief
8 Something to unscrew on an auto
14 Feu fighter
15 Uncommon, in ancient Rome
16 Land of Papá Noel
17 N N N
18 Carols, often
20 Mr. Hilarious
22 Chair: Abbr.
23 Nonverbal congratulations
24 Scrooge player of film
29 It has 3,750 "steps of penitence"
30 Intimate
33 Down
34 Bird, e.g., once
37 Comment upon receiving a large bill
38 Polar opposites?
42 "___ doing . . ."
43 Cold capital
44 Pique condition?
46 Saw
48 Entered cautiously
51 Time before the present day?
54 Palindromic girl's name
57 With 67-Across, sacred symbol to Zeus
58 TV's Anderson
59 Song of 1859 . . . or what the five circled letters represent?
64 It's taken to calm down
66 It takes place on board a ship at sea in "The Tempest"
67 See 57-Across
68 Be a certain way?
69 Bit of candy
70 Start of something
71 Brief subject

DOWN

1 Game ___
2 Its capital is Nouakchott
3 Score keeper?
4 Inverse trig function
5 Exclamation heard 12 times in Lady Gaga's "Bad Romance"
6 Word on a vin bottle
7 Head of cattle?
8 The Iron Horse of baseball
9 Silvery-gray
10 19-Down employee
11 Rough it, say
12 Lady whom Don Giovanni tries to seduce
13 Over
19 Employer of 10-Downs: Abbr.
21 "___ don't know"
24 Fr. title
25 Per
26 Misinform, maybe
27 #10 on a table
28 Seamstress's aid
31 Chance
32 "Dirty Rotten Scoundrels" setting
35 Lily, in Lille
36 Flat sign
39 Car-racing org.
40 Van follower
41 Tramp
45 Chemical suffix
47 Blue
49 Like many winter roads
50 Peruvian pronoun
52 Ziering of "90210"
53 Burlesque bits
54 Bob Cratchit to Scrooge, e.g.: Abbr.
55 Part of a boast
56 Smart ___
60 Three-in-one M.D.
61 Class-conscious grp.?
62 Princeton Review subj.
63 Part of a snicker
65 Fresh

by Jay Kaskel and Daniel Kantor

346 HARD

ACROSS

1 "The Twentieth Century" producer
8 Point
15 Knock noise
16 Spring
17 How some pranks are done
18 1970s "first mother"
19 Santa ___
21 Security Council veto
22 Makeup of some burgers
23 Stunning
28 Put away
30 Get stuck
33 Off-white shade
34 Sight from the top of the Leaning Tower
35 Out-and-out
36 Santa ___
39 Isn't straight
40 Certain party, in headlines
41 Members of an ancient empire
42 Golf scorecard abbr.
43 Part of the planning for many a surprise birthday party
44 Happy cohort?
45 Company with an I.P.O. in both 1992 and 2009
46 Point
48 Santa ___
56 Stir up
57 Schmaltz
58 Builds a foundation, say
59 Bridge topic
60 Lab procedure
61 Some game show questions

DOWN

1 Big snapper, informally
2 Actor who played the villain in 2009's "Star Trek"
3 Doctor's directive
4 Zip
5 Endnote abbr.
6 Big blender maker
7 Old office worker
8 Place for a ham
9 E.P.A. measurement
10 Tap
11 Fine furniture feature
12 Water carrier
13 Slightly
14 Wiseman who directed "Live Free or Die Hard"
20 Wife of Perseus
23 How distant stars shine
24 Go around
25 Thinks about nothing, with "out"
26 Tennessee's state flower
27 Former U.S. capital: Abbr.
29 Heavy load
30 Oomph
31 "I Love Lucy" executive producer
32 Embarrassing
34 City north of Des Moines
35 Stamp sheet
37 Fawns over
38 Corrosion-resistant plating
43 Circumvolve
44 "Perfection under fire" product
45 Imply
47 Certain chamber piece
48 Uninformative attribution: Abbr.
49 Granada girl
50 Doctor's directive
51 Turner and others
52 Chins or jaws
53 Opponent of the Patriot Act, for short
54 Give a hand?
55 They have all the answers
56 Foot up

by Stanley Newman

ACROSS

1 One likely to die on the road?
7 What something may go down to
14 Foster girl
15 Poster girl
16 Debunked?
17 Response to great news
18 Big tin exporter: Abbr.
19 Beat badly
21 Battle joiner's choice
22 Kind of replication
23 Sticks up for, maybe?
25 Serbian city where Constantine the Great was born
26 Org. with towers
27 Luzón, e.g.
28 Thingamajig
31 Film in which Eddie Murphy voices the dragon Mushu
33 Lit
35 Be revolting
40 Homes within nations
41 San Francisco's Museo ___ Americano
42 Red giants in the night sky
45 Procure
47 Big hit
48 Cross character
49 Not dormant
51 As
52 Ice legend's family
54 Head start?
56 It's often hung illegally
57 "The Humbugs of the World" author, 1865
60 Be coerced
62 Relationship in the 2009 film "I Love You, Man"

63 1974 hit with Spanish lyrics
64 "Got it"
65 The Allman Brothers Band, e.g.

DOWN

1 Creator of TV's "Alias"
2 Blimp navigator
3 Boxer who wrote "Reach!"
4 Switch sides?
5 Some county fair contest entries
6 Folks getting into dirt
7 Bait
8 Bucks, e.g.
9 Rock's Brian
10 Freaks (out)
11 Not going anywhere
12 Carrier of drum cases, maybe
13 First in line, say
15 Over and over
20 Like M&M's
24 Sacrifice fly?
27 Cartoonist, at times
29 64-Across, to a cat
30 Debugger?
32 Court proceedings
34 Freak
36 Self, in a Latin phrase
37 Many users follow its directions
38 "Gentille" one of song
39 Problem for one who's trapped
42 Visit
43 "The Transcendence of the Ego" writer
44 Some muscle cars
46 ___ National Park
50 It may stick to your ribs
53 Language related to Finnish
55 Dummy on a greyhound track
58 Coll. peer leaders
59 Uptown's dir. in N.Y.C.
61 Really try

by Caleb Madison

348 HARD

ACROSS

1 Part of a horse between the shoulder blades
8 Xanax maker
14 Quaint game with a giver and a striker
15 Valerie of "The Electric Horseman"
16 Like broken things
17 Pros at projecting
18 Ready to be fired
19 Pot cover
21 Basketball Hall-of-Famer Holman
22 Resistance leader in Woody Allen's "Sleeper"
23 Eldest of a trio of comic brothers in 1930s–'40s films
24 Neil Sedaka's "___ Ape"
25 Williamson who played Hamlet and Macbeth on Broadway
27 Its chapel was designed by Eero Saarinen, briefly
28 Processing time unit: Abbr.
29 Foul territory?
30 Pas de deux part
33 Dostoyevsky's exile city
34 Coarse, as stucco
36 Plantation creation
39 Dieter's concern
40 Org. whose emblem features an eagle and a crown
43 She's a paradigm of patience
44 Notable head-turner
45 Bouillabaisse go-with
47 I
48 Like some love
51 Time of Obama's swearing-in
52 First Across word in the world's first crossword

53 Einstein, notably
54 Elk's enemy
55 His opening statement is famous
57 Uniform adornment
59 New Testament miracle recipient
60 Great Dark Spot locale
61 Blackmailer's words
62 Record producers

DOWN

1 Some winter wear
2 Sure to be grounded, say
3 Matter of lease concern?
4 Bring bad luck to
5 Coin depicting Louis XVI
6 One with a dreaded style?
7 Play set entirely in a beauty parlor
8 Choate ran with him in 1996
9 Half of a recurring "Saturday Night Live" duo
10 N.Y.C. transportation debut of 1904
11 Movement Herman Wouk called "a single long action of lifesaving"
12 Sets off
13 Do a store chore
15 City hall, often
20 Clown's over-the-top topper
26 Mekong River native
28 Zinger
31 Police blotter abbr.
32 One of Iowa's state symbols
34 & 35 Mocha is on it
36 Mix on the range
37 Far from Rubenesque
38 Put on a pedestal
40 Abductor of the Sabine women
41 Sustaining stuff
42 Obsesses
46 Ascribe
48 Psychotherapy topics
49 Suffuse
50 New Testament miracle recipient
56 Credit card statement abbr.
58 Credit card statement abbr.

by Brad Wilber

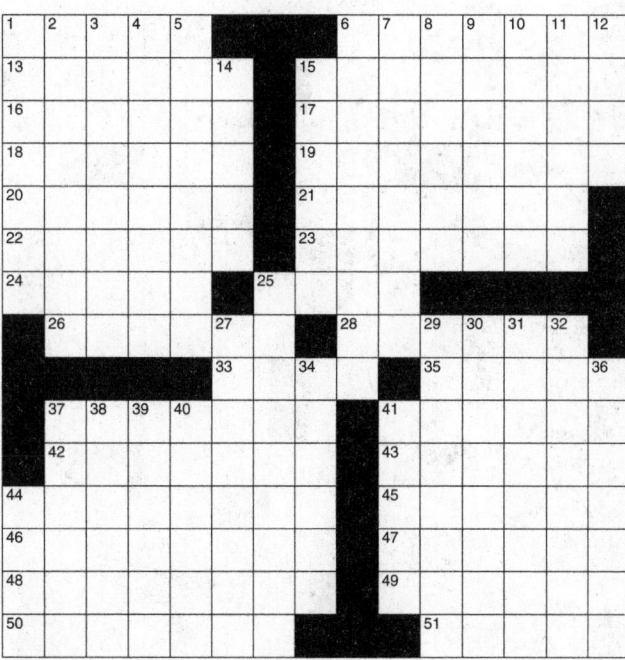

ACROSS

1 Early 1990s first lady's first name
6 Cross
13 Group member from the time of Jesus
15 Chosen as a career
16 Mushroom supporters
17 Without any wood or plastic, say
18 Repetitive rebuke
19 Untrustworthy
20 What goes on?
21 A conductor may have it memorized
22 Units in nuclear physics
23 Serves
24 They may be full of hot air
25 Sigmoid architectural feature
26 Rubber stamp
28 One getting hit on?
33 Skipping syllables
35 Acoustic measures
37 Momentum
41 Play the flute
42 Kings Henry I and Stephen
43 Oxide used in television tubes
44 Spasm-relieving alkaloid
45 Feast
46 Mexican and Indian, e.g.
47 Spinachlike potherb
48 People working with logs?
49 Parents' hiree
50 Folks going through leaves
51 Its openings are often studied

DOWN

1 Fill positions differently
2 With sapience
3 "Really?"
4 Defensive fencing positions in which the top of the blade is pointed at the opponent's knee
5 Arterial problem: Var.
6 They're not green
7 New face on base
8 Congregation location
9 Dapper Dan's doodad
10 Destine
11 They're often drawn on the street
12 Like an 8-Down
14 Eleanor who wrote "The Hundred Dresses"
15 One full of hot air
25 How most sleds are mounted
27 Goal getter
29 Way out there
30 Way to walk
31 Dramatic break
32 Fancies
34 Value
36 Those who put you in your place?
37 Pleasant way to play
38 Swank's co-star in "The Next Karate Kid"
39 Wrote an essay, say
40 Persia, e.g., once
41 Pros' opposites
44 One not allowing a volley

by Robert H. Wolfe

ACROSS

1 Repeat offenders?
5 Cover
11 Ask too much?
14 Sarcastic reply
15 Unsuitable for mixed company
16 Note traded for bills
17 "That's how it looks to me, anyway"
20 Cheers
21 Weak heart, for example?
22 Does badly at the box office
24 Rubber
27 Org. that awaits your return
28 Hightail
31 In the vicinity of
34 John no one knows
35 Like some glasswork
36 13th-century literary classic
37 Night light used by Sherlock Holmes
40 Therapist's comment
41 King defeated at Châlons
42 Disembarrass
43 Cricket match
44 Eye shadow?
45 Put in one's ___ (interfere)
46 Mason's assistant
48 "South Park" boy
50 1950s—'60s actor known as the Switchblade Kid
52 White robe wearers
55 Crows and others
60 French dip's dip
61 Chevy model discontinued in 2001

62 Deadfall, e.g.
63 Jack, for one
64 Docile marine mammal
65 Daring, in a way

DOWN

1 Plame affair org.
2 Things used during crunch time?
3 Extreme exposure
4 Follow closely
5 "Vamoose!"
6 Cheat, slangily
7 Clive Cussler best seller made into a 1980 film
8 Member of Sauron's army
9 Miss ___
10 Dings

11 Charles IX's court poet
12 It may be played for money
13 ___ Ball, quinquennial dance in Harry Potter
18 Irritated reactions
19 1995 thriller about identity theft
22 Chocolate chip, e.g.
23 Stir to action
25 Land
26 Speedy Gonzales cry
29 Words that affect one's standing?
30 Father Time's prop
32 Monk's first name on "Monk"

33 Stopped flowing
38 Thorn, once
39 Acted as an informant
47 Muddies up
49 Carriage trade
50 Goya's "La ___ Desnuda"
51 1989 Radio Hall of Fame inductee
53 Italian boxer Benvenuti
54 Not just nibble
56 Prompter action
57 Practice overseers: Abbr.
58 Not just nudge
59 Invisible ink user

by Patrick Berry

ACROSS

1 Fugitive-hunting Fed
10 2000 U.S. Open winner
15 "E.T." follower
16 Free sample, say
17 Local assessment
18 Plume hunter's prey
19 Antisocial type
20 Type with finesse
22 "How ___ is the candle of the wicked put out!": Job 21:17
23 Like some thin fibers
26 Not quite none, in Naples
27 Yacht spot
29 Reason for a lighter conviction?
30 Like many smoothies
31 View spoiler
33 Chronicle
35 Crutch
36 Social type
37 Get down
41 Where some touchdowns are made
45 Detriment
46 Popular piercing site
48 Orchestra alternative
49 Where organs may be repaired, briefly
50 It stores fish in a pouch
52 Set of utensils
53 It has a dark side, in sci-fi
55 "___ My Family" (Cranberries song)
57 Corral
58 Its logo is a rubber-band ball
61 Spring
62 Counted raised hands, say
63 See 7-Down
64 Like many avenues

DOWN

1 In one's face
2 Pennsylvania Dutch pie
3 Enduring symbol of Canada
4 Last of the Stuarts
5 In once more
6 Lacking
7 With 63-Across, 1972 Rolling Stones "greatest hits" album
8 Knight of medieval literature
9 Defining work
10 What a 9-Down might help you do
11 Galley of myth
12 H_2O, e.g.
13 "For real!"
14 Opposite of destined
21 Smoke that's not thick
24 "The Canterbury Tales" charlatan
25 26-Across and 26-Across and 26-Across
28 The last one begins "Praise ye the Lord"
30 Percival caught sight of it
32 Permian Basin yield
34 Sister's study: Abbr.
37 Met the course standard
38 Bronze Star recipient
39 One of the metalloids
40 Literature Nobelist Derek
41 TV's "___ Ramsey"
42 Collectible card creatures
43 Shake
44 Quit using
47 Try to win
50 Dixie cakes
51 Lite as can be
54 1972 A.L. Rookie of the Year
56 Supreme Hindu goddess
59 One to go up against
60 Memorable 2008 Gulf hurricane

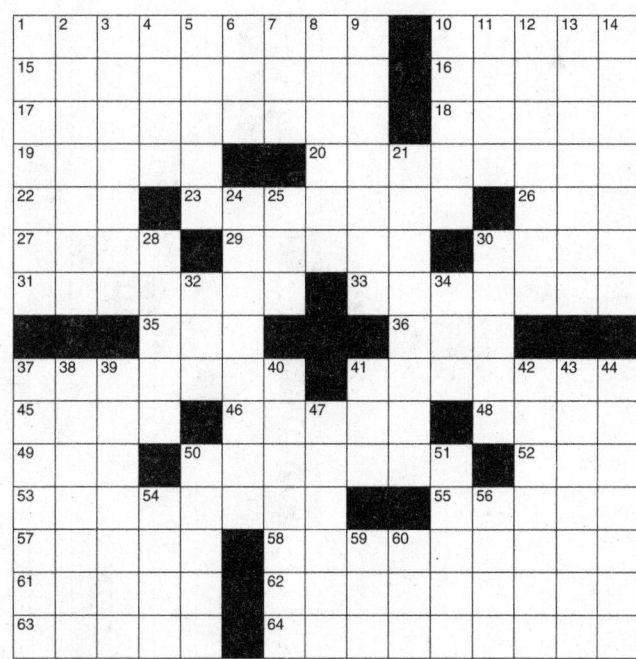

by Chuck Deodene

352 HARD

ACROSS

1 Ticketed
6 Chilled
15 Chilling
16 Constellation once called the Dragon's Wing
17 Tenor Mario
18 The Who's "Quadrophenia," e.g.
19 Microscopic protists
21 Part of a picket fence
22 Docs who've paid their dues
23 Lettuce variety
24 Japanese code word meaning "tiger"
25 Tandoori-baked breads
26 Singer of the Leoncavallo aria "Vesti la giubba"
27 Organ repair sites, for short
28 Like some coats
29 Fine point
30 Land of a Million Elephants
31 Bill
32 Printing press parts
35 A cappella group part
36 Joe-___ weed (herbal remedy)
39 Perfume, in a way
40 Suffix with techno-
41 1930s Royales
42 ___ milk
43 Be fourth in an order
45 Union and others: Abbr.
46 "Well done!"
47 Reveled
49 In Key West it's known as the Overseas Hwy.
50 "You're probably going to get me, but go ahead"
51 They result from catching bugs
52 Set sail
53 Break off a relationship

DOWN

1 School in the Patriot League
2 Well-suited?
3 Bad traits for conductors
4 Aloe target, perhaps
5 Silas who was the United States' first foreign diplomat (1776)
6 Bicep builders' accessories
7 Process of mountain building
8 Walt Disney has more of these than anyone else
9 Great ___
10 Post-punk genre
11 Returns, as from a high level
12 Makeup of some jokes
13 Briefly
14 Stereotypical college drinker
20 OB's perform them
26 Bye for an Italian soccer team?
28 Suffix after kitchen
29 Irk
30 Factor in a more healthful diet, perhaps
31 Food item once used as currency in Mongolia
32 Event with pairs and eights
33 Fresh angle
34 Add gradually, as to dough
35 Virtuoso
36 Certain table tennis grip
37 1941 Glenn Miller hit that spent five weeks at #1
38 Zener cards are used in it
40 City on the Strait of Dover
41 Outs, in a way
43 "The Hobbit" character
44 Draw forth
48 It can come on white, briefly

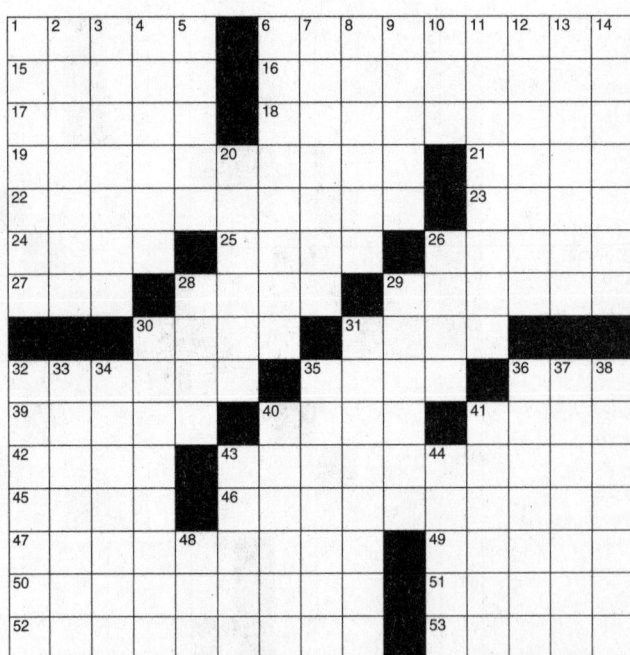

by Joe DiPietro

ACROSS

1 One very concerned with how a kid acts
9 Edible mold
14 Plant disease similar to blackleg
16 Comic actress who co-starred on "Archie Bunker's Place"
17 1968 soul album with the hit "Think"
18 Plague
19 Boarding house?: Abbr.
20 "That's completely wrong!"
22 Medical suffix
23 Got together
26 Like the coats of 25-Down
27 ". . . who hath begotten the drops of ___?": Job 38:28
28 South of Brazil?
30 Not just reworked
31 Lay an egg
32 Driver's problem
35 Limerick scheme
36 A bowl of cherries, in Chelsea
38 Sheets are sold in them
39 Gender-neutral phrase
40 "___ White Season" (André Brink novel)
41 Cost increaser
42 Not even once, to Nietzsche
43 Mil. authority
44 Change (into)
46 Org. that tracks numbers
50 It was split in 1948: Abbr.
51 #1 hit from the album "J.Lo"
53 Mimicking
54 How some foods are packed
56 To the extent that

59 Dividers of 35-Down
60 A caddie may hold it
61 A caddy may hold it
62 Sonnet feature

DOWN

1 Jerk
2 Nutty nosh
3 Troubled
4 Rod
5 End of the Bible?
6 Evidence of paranormal activity, perhaps
7 Speculation follower
8 1919 novel set in Paris and Tahiti, with "The"
9 The ___ Dukes (1960s–'70s band)
10 Go with
11 Dance based on bullfight music
12 "Time was . . ."
13 Carolina natives
15 What an angry employee might give a boss
21 Kansas City-to-Omaha dir.
24 Company man's grp.?
25 Deer stalkers
29 Orderly supervisor, maybe: Abbr.
31 Engages in hydrotherapy
32 Entrepreneur's request
33 They may fall when you're down
34 Jackson Pollock's player in "Pollock"

35 They're fed by venae cavae
36 Neither freshwater nor marine
37 What "+" may indicate
41 Kenyan leader Mboya whom Obama called his "godfather"
44 Biblioteca Ambrosiana locale
45 Sports
47 Sportscaster with the autobiography "Holy Cow!"
48 Cell phone feature
49 ___ bourrée (ballet move)
52 One who minds his manors?
55 Contemporary of Baiul and Yamaguchi
57 Élément #26
58 Exclamation in Ems

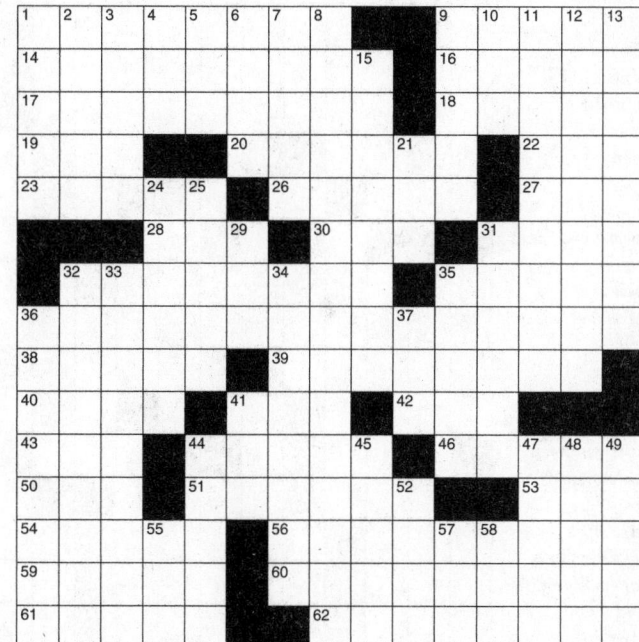

by Ned White

354 HARD

ACROSS

1 Pad producers
12 Name in many suit cases
15 Cry before a disappearance
16 Saturn's wife
17 Something that's just too cool
18 Recharging aid
19 Musician who was a trailblazing Rastafarian
20 European wine center
22 Matching ring recipients: Abbr.
23 Small part of an archipelago
25 Ben Franklin
26 Follower of directions
27 Cry upon being fleeced?
29 Grateful Dead bassist Phil
31 One exploring deeply?
35 Longtime name in auto parts
36 Ramen brand
38 It's sometimes forbidden
39 Free
40 Classic record label for the Bee Gees and Cream
41 M., in Milan
42 Monitor setting, briefly
43 Nickname in pioneering jazz piano
45 38-Across variety
46 "Grey's Anatomy" hookups
49 Hushed
52 Mother of the Gods
53 Big name in flooring?
54 So-called "baby busters"
57 Pronoun in 20-Across
58 Song that mentions "the Father, Son and the Holy Ghost"
59 Unit in astronomy
60 Well-known TV evangelical

DOWN

1 There are 746 in a single horsepower
2 Can't stomach
3 Bun bit
4 Up
5 Producer of some dishes
6 Muscle strengthened in rowing, in brief
7 Opinion opener
8 Skedaddles
9 "Uh-huh"
10 Work that marked the start of musical Romanticism
11 Admitted politely
12 "St. Mark" artist
13 Is like a moonstone
14 Make out
21 Finely tempered blades
23 Item next to a salad bowl
24 Jamaica's St. ___ Bay
26 E.T.'s pal
27 Opposite of clarify
28 The Ponte alle Grazie spans it
30 You may work out its kinks
31 Common crash site?
32 What an art student builds
33 Cabinet department
34 First name in international diplomacy
35 Passed (out)
37 En ___ tiempo (formerly, to Felipe)
41 Help line?
44 Navajo home
45 You're in it if you cry 41-Down
46 Bit of wishful thinking
47 To come, in Cádiz or Caen
48 Instruments in Ravel's "Boléro"
49 Matching
50 Superficial, briefly
51 Vint ___, the Father of the Internet
52 38-Across covering
55 Here, in Honduras
56 Result of exposing oneself at the beach?

by Natan Last

ACROSS

1 Acted impulsively
6 Unofficial "Main Street" of New York's Chinatown
10 They might prevent getaways, briefly
14 He starred as himself in "Cuban Pete," 1946
15 Treat with a "Golden" variety
16 Doubtful
17 Wife of Augustus
18 Smoke with straight sides
20 Like
22 Agenda
23 Wins easily
25 Nest down
26 Archer of literature
28 ___ Plateau (U.S. region)
31 They're in the neighborhood: Abbr.
33 Capital on the island of Viti Levu
34 Source of valuable deposits
35 Self expression?
37 Responses of confusion
39 One may be in stitches
40 Chairmen often call them: Abbr.
42 Calls
44 Potential hiding places
46 Respectful greeting
48 Stern playing?
50 Old song with the lyric "When he would ride in the afternoon / I'd follow him with my hickory broom"
55 Not withdrawn
56 1-Down counselor Ann
57 Hot
59 Living proof?
60 Italian well
61 River with historic flooding in 1966
62 Goober
63 A.M.A. member?: Abbr.
64 B'way buys
65 Inclines

DOWN

1 "ER" replaced it on NBC's schedule in 1994
2 "Traffic" actress Christensen
3 Aid in forging
4 One canvasing?
5 Gyro sauce
6 One with a replaceable head
7 Their addresses are moving
8 Near the hour
9 Grunting, slimy-skinned swimmer
10 Fielding and Menotti title heroines
11 Lenin's body
12 Lenin, for one
13 Saves, say
19 Some emergency services
21 It has hundreds of thousands of meanings: Abbr.
24 Curt summons
27 Swimmers do them
28 Resistor measures
29 "Chicago" Oscar winner
30 Book of Common Prayer readers
32 Actress Allen
36 Kid with no hometown, often
38 Scene of horror and confusion
41 Instrument played with a spatula
43 Major pest in the South
45 Block
47 One of a loving trio?
49 "Oh, no!"
51 Court figure
52 K. T. of country
53 Do some green maintenance
54 11-Down dissents
55 Nagasaki noodle
58 Takes down

by Karen M. Tracey

356 HARD

ACROSS
1 Red choice
10 Decide to use
15 "The Hitch-Hiker" director, 1953
16 Old Indian infantryman
17 Resin sources
18 Weenie
19 Appropriate game
20 Ram
22 Dostoyevsky's exile city
23 Dessert fruit
24 It's grounded on the Sabbath
26 Many reality shows
29 Star followers
32 Precious
33 Streaked
34 Nat stat
35 Endures
38 Spare part?
39 Pat makeup
41 Sir ___, foster brother of King Arthur
42 Hero described as "Eyeless in Gaza"
44 "Are you nuts?!"
46 Right fielder, on a scorecard
47 It merged with Tanganyika in 1964
49 Get down quickly
53 Managed to obtain
55 One thing on top of another?
56 It has 95 printable characters
57 Not currently
59 Tubular snacks
60 What might come as a relief at night?
61 Tracking aid
62 Noted Volstead Act enforcer

DOWN
1 Diddly
2 Hit the ceiling, say
3 Spoilers, often
4 Like a strawberry roan's coat
5 Bibliography abbr.
6 "Science Friday" carrier
7 Motor ship driver
8 Hostile
9 City near San Jose
10 Breathtaking condition?
11 Most childishly pure
12 Results of some labor laws
13 Computer connection
14 Four for for, for one
21 Loud drill bit?
23 Vodka cocktail
25 Electronic gag reflex?
27 The Jimi Hendrix Experience, e.g.
28 A diagram bears his name
29 Parts of it may be revealed in biology class
30 Fit
31 "Übermensch" originator
32 "Watch it!"
36 Confirm
37 Chicken tikka go-with
40 Keynote, e.g.
43 4.184 petajoules
45 Win the support of
46 Campania's capital, in Campania
48 Tear-resistant synthetic rubber
50 Worth keeping
51 Has a hitch
52 Metric system output?
53 Words of support
54 Org. with a SportsMan of the Year award
55 Digs cash?
58 Conservative front?

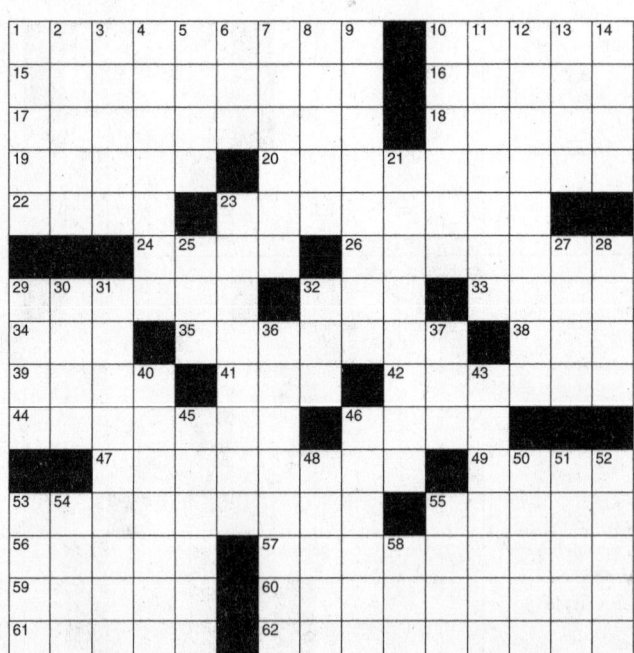

by Doug Peterson

ACROSS

1 Allergy source
9 "Steve Canyon" cartoonist
15 Small planted bulb
16 Lacking a signature, say
17 Diamondback, for one
18 Church room
19 Group whose 1972 debut album "Can't Buy a Thrill" went platinum
21 Plenty
22 Robin Hood, the ___ of Huntington
23 Indian barter item
25 No. usually figured to two decimals
26 Toyota pickup named for a U.S. city
29 Giocondo and Angelico
30 Make a person feel good
33 Shock-and-awe strategy
34 Sources of some Zimbabwean exports
35 Alternative to Beauvais
36 "Who ___?"
37 Substantial hit: Abbr.
38 Hardly balmy
39 Part of una salsa
43 Co-winner of the first Albert Einstein Award, 1951
45 Late entertainer who was known for his laugh
49 Like Chekhov's "The Cherry Orchard"
51 Overthrows, e.g.
52 Head-scratcher
53 Not together
54 Certs ingredient
55 Absents oneself

DOWN

1 Small stand
2 One of the Pointer Sisters
3 Strength of a solution
4 Neighborhood eyesore
5 Navy relative
6 Game with a spotter
7 English horn, e.g.
8 Get ready for chow
9 Ohio pro, for short
10 Worried
11 Little something
12 Limits of some sums
13 Nowhere near an agreement
14 Go by quickly
20 Macduff, to Macbeth
24 California peak
26 The witches in "Macbeth," e.g.
27 Cross of mysteries
28 Pub pull
29 Long row
30 Blame-diffusing words
31 Major employer
32 Pull up
33 Not grounded
34 Relatively hard to pin down
38 Vile
39 ___ States
40 Thackeray's "Vanity Fair: A Novel Without ___"
41 What a loser may be out of
42 First sign
44 Many Caltech grads: Abbr.
46 M.'s counterpart
47 Judging point at a dog show
48 Comfy wear
50 Preserve . . . or get rid of

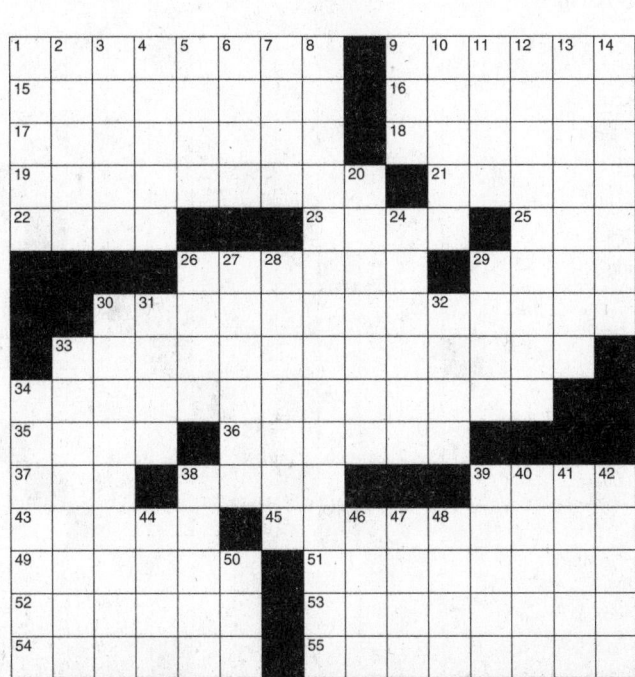

by Mark Diehl

ACROSS

1 Mexican play places
8 Cry of accomplishment
15 Very rarely indeed
17 They're often tipped on sidewalks
18 Home of Samsung Tower Palace
19 Astra and Antara
20 Often-improved thing
21 P.D. rank
22 "Let's take ___"
23 Italian province or its capital
24 Windows options
25 Title town in a 1945 Pulitzer-winning novel
26 Drop by quickly
27 Arrive
29 [Yawn!]
30 They may get belted
31 Lane in a mall
32 Charges
33 Quick surveys
35 "O naked Moon full-___!": Browning
36 Tell
37 ". . . ___ will!"
38 Podiatric problem
39 Heave
40 Spanish conquistadora ___ de Suárez
41 Mgmt. member
42 Loggers' contest
43 "___ of Simple Folk" (Seán O'Faoláin novel)
44 Stored something for future use?

47 Big-top worker with a big responsibility
48 Maid in "The Merchant of Venice"
49 Drawn-out dissertations

DOWN

1 Sign of fitful sleep
2 Summit success
3 Like an extradition transition
4 Start a hole
5 Indochinese currency
6 Bruce Peninsula locale: Abbr.
7 Some tearoom equipment
8 Hardly ignorant of
9 Option for one's return
10 Fourth qtr. enders
11 "That's ___ quit!"
12 Calls for a quick dispatch
13 "Try someone else"
14 "1, 2, 3" lead-in
16 "Gypsy" Tony winner
22 More than capable
23 Unseen surroundings
25 Jamal of jazz
26 1972 Pulitzer winner for Commentary
28 Current device for a cop?
29 Stock option
31 Doesn't buy, in a way
32 Marine Corps candidates, it's said

33 Scarcely visible fingerprint
34 Residents of some campus houses
36 1993 Grammy winner for Best Mexican-American Album
39 Some tomatoes
40 About 90% of people have one
42 Fan sounds
43 Poison apple creator?
45 Something left of center?
46 Compass creation

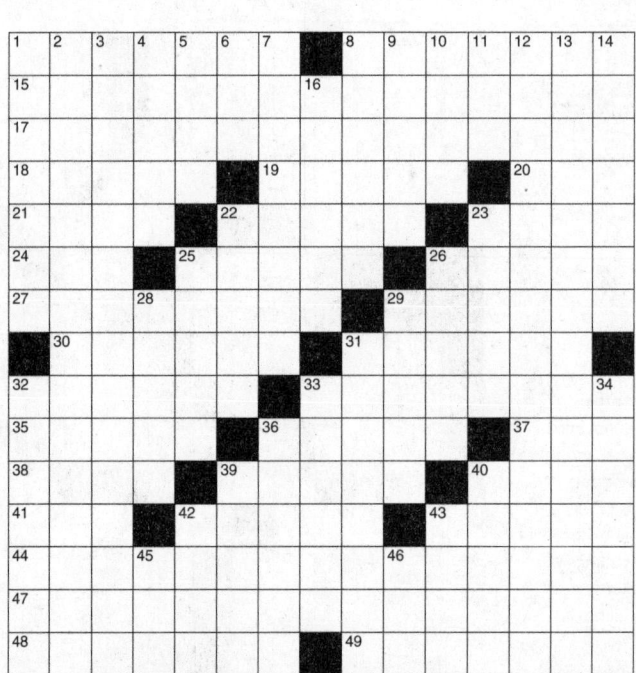

by Joe Krozel

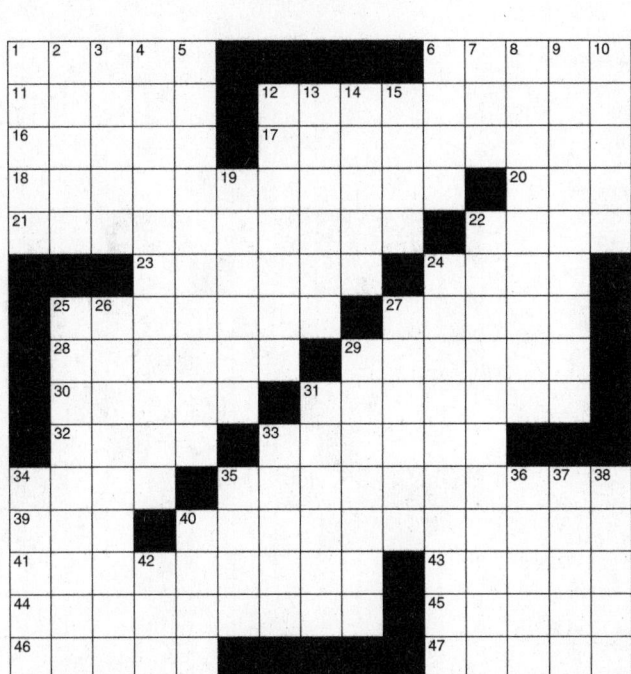

ACROSS

1 Savage
6 Present
11 Alpine feature
12 Get in the can early
16 Tasty torus
17 Heavily corroded
18 "Not bad at all!"
20 Cavaliers' home, for short
21 "Cheers" alternative
22 Calculating bunch, briefly
23 Relief pitcher Craig
24 Day-care charges
25 Like some wrongs
27 "Blue II" and "Harlequin's Carnival"
28 Run on
29 ___ Mae
30 Less approachable
31 Magic acts?
32 Safety org.
33 King's middle name
34 Poison
35 Observance made official by President Wilson in 1914
39 N.F.L. passing stat.
40 Prominently featured
41 "The lady in red" betrayed him
43 Pulitzer-winning poet Mark Van ___
44 Samaritans' doings
45 Have no life
46 ___ año (in the course of the year: Sp.)
47 Socialite who inspired "Call Me Madam"

DOWN

1 Career diplomat Philip
2 Mild-flavored seaweed in Japanese cuisine
3 Denver university
4 Slow an increase
5 Heading for classified information?
6 Grant consideration
7 Goose, in Spain or Italy
8 Lacking sufficient desire
9 Levee breaches
10 "Hairspray" mom and others
12 Iron-handed one?
13 Hasty
14 Ruhr Museum locale
15 Lines: Abbr.
19 A dead one looks like something else
22 Place to get milk
24 Whit
25 Opposite of sluggishness
26 Something to build on
27 Lothario
29 Confession receivers
31 Stopped being a 38-Down, with "out"
33 What opens easily?
34 Scout's honor
35 Mysterious word repeated in Daniel 5:25
36 Isn't too yellow
37 Chemical ___
38 Blabbermouth
40 Killer ending?
42 C.E.O., e.g.: Abbr.

by Frederick J. Healy

360 HARD

ACROSS

1 $9 + 3 + 1 + \frac{1}{3} + \frac{1}{9} + \ldots$, e.g.
16 Dating service questionnaire heading
17 Seminal naturalistic work
18 They're dishwasher-safe
19 Main character?
20 Tree-line tree
21 Some 21-Downs
25 Tir à ___ (bow-and-arrow sport: Fr.)
27 Punch lines?
30 Thunderstorm product
31 Fit by careful shifting
32 Help in hunting
33 Routine statement?
36 ___ francese
37 Puttering
38 Fish garnish
39 Novelist who was a lifelong friend of Capote
40 Ducky
41 What the ugly duckling really was
42 Tipping point?
43 Where one might keep time?
44 Heart and brain
53 Doesn't hedge
54 A lot may be on one's mind
55 13-time Grey Cup winners

DOWN

1 Hoods may conceal them
2 German "genuine"
3 "Cup ___" (1970s Don Williams song)
4 Trend in 1970s fashion
5 "Sure, but . . ."
6 10-kilogauss units
7 Potato preparation aid
8 California's Mission Santa ___
9 Milk holders: Abbr.
10 Spares
11 Sizzling, so to speak
12 Point (to)
13 "This ___ . . . Then" (Jennifer Lopez album)
14 Citation abbreviation
15 Govt. database entries
21 One with subjects
22 Nitrogen compound
23 Physicist James who contributed to the laws of thermodynamics
24 He had a #4 hit with "It's Time to Cry"

25 Hanukkah nosh
26 Visibly horrified
27 Odysseus saw him as a shade in the underworld
28 Animated character who likes "Hello, Dolly!" songs
29 Lane pain?
31 Sci-fi's Chief Chirpa, e.g.
32 One of the Palins
34 Creator of some illusions
35 Time of awakening
40 Dan ___, 1994 Olympics speed-skating gold medalist
41 "Alistair ___ America" (1973 book)

42 Need for some shots
43 Top-___ (sports brand)
44 To be in a faraway land
45 Basis of development
46 Compliment's opposite
47 Hand ___
48 Lightman who wrote "Einstein's Dreams"
49 1958 Best Song Oscar winner
50 "Lemme ___!"
51 Chile child
52 Fleet fleet, once

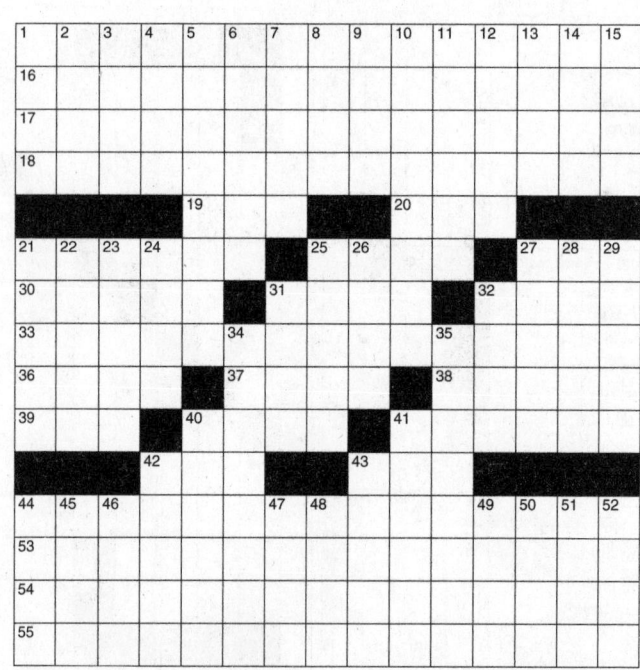

by Kevin G. Der

ACROSS

1 1968 hit musical with the song "Life Is"
6 Former transportation regulation agcy.
9 Hot: Fr.
14 "Caesar, now be still: / I kill'd not thee with half so good ___": Brutus
15 Whirl
16 Stop from running, maybe
17 One making waves in the news business?
20 What 36-Acrosses and 7-Down appreciate
21 Gray and others
22 Sworn ___ (officially given the role of)
23 Charter of Punta del Este grp.
25 Omne vivum ex ___ (all life [is] from eggs: Lat.)
26 "For the life ___ . . ."
30 Make plans to tie the knot
34 Like Cuba and Venezuela, e.g.
36 You, e.g.
38 Clear out
39 Mozzarella alternative
40 Cavort
41 Pen
42 Community coll. prerequisite, maybe
43 Big Utah export
45 It's written right to left
48 Ones with reading schedules
55 "It was the best of times, it was the worst of times . . . ," e.g.
56 50-Down holder
57 John who pioneered time-lapse photography
58 Some porcelain
59 Patisserie order
60 Intelligence grp.
61 Parties with a whole lot of shaking going on

DOWN

1 Cup holder
2 Man ___
3 Endure difficulties, with "out"
4 Paradise
5 Welcome to paradise?
6 "Was ___ hard . . . ?"
7 You and others
8 Rostand hero
9 Santa ___
10 Long way?
11 It's west of the Sea of Okhotsk
12 Former part of 11-Down: Abbr.
13 Feeble-minded
18 Certain H.S. teams
19 Draft org.
23 Academy offering
24 ___ di linea (flier to Italy)
25 Iowa relative
26 Pot on a fire
27 Like an old English coin worth 105 shillings
28 Reagan cabinet member
29 Conqueror of Northumbria in 946
31 Express letters?
32 It ends in the fall: Abbr.
33 Dazzle
34 It's sometimes seen in the corner of a TV screen: Abbr.
35 Prune
37 ___ mother
41 Brand for the bath
43 Singer profiled in "Sweet Dreams"
44 Vintner's prefix
45 Holder of a "leaf-fringed legend," to Keats
46 Honey badger
47 Sch. in Madison, N.J.
48 ___ of all
49 Prefix with -metry
50 Contents of a 56-Across
51 Questionnaire datum: Abbr.
52 Not fully tested
53 Soft shade
54 Part of a committee sched.

by Ashish Vengsarkar

ACROSS

1 Male gopher
10 People travel only one way on them
15 "The Broken Tower" poet
16 The senior Saarinen
17 "Beautiful" things in a 1951 hit song
18 See 7-Down
19 Orlando's former ___ Arena
20 Capital largely surrounded by high clay walls
22 Sportscaster Collinsworth
23 Uncle ___
24 City at the mouth of the Fox River
26 They make cents.
27 Cards
31 Homage
32 Dress down
33 Cat's-eye relatives
34 Metaphor for a middle-class American
37 Host of a self-titled 1990s talk show
38 Las ___ Filipinas
39 Ancient Macedonian capital
40 Abbr. at the top of a memo
41 Abbr. for the Prince of Wales
44 Hair salon activity
46 New range rover?
47 Freedom fighter, for short?
48 Their faces have spots
51 Secretary on "Hogan's Heroes"
52 Weapon for Wonder Woman

54 When women may get in for less
56 Put through the system?
57 Rush hour, to radio programmers
58 Some flying saucers
59 Fleet type

DOWN

1 "Man alive!"
2 One with growing concerns
3 Displays displeasure
4 "___ my pleasure"
5 Big Apple sch.
6 Ahead of, in verse
7 Parts of planes in which to put 18-Across

8 First to be called up
9 Answerable with a nod or a shake
10 Sherlock
11 They have chocolate relatives
12 Overhead corridor
13 Need for checking people out
14 Applies carelessly
21 Blitzkrieg
25 Ewing player
27 Twist alternative
28 Oregon Shakespeare Festival locale
29 Former AT&T rival
30 Crayola color in a 64-crayon box
32 Encouraging statement start
34 Kind of appointment

35 Like most bars
36 U.S.N. craft
37 Downgrades, e.g.
41 "Whoa!"
42 "___ Sans-Gêne" (Sardou play)
43 Offer?
45 Brightens
46 Sock deliverers
49 Complaint
50 Lou Grant's ex on "The Mary Tyler Moore Show"
51 Not brush off
53 FAQ part: Abbr.
55 It may be added to excess

by Victor Fleming

ACROSS

1 Product with a secret sauce
7 Muff
14 Pitcher's charge
15 Like many student jobs
16 "___ in bloody thoughts, but not in blood": Richard III
17 Like the drummer for rock's Def Leppard, amazingly
18 First Japanese infielder to sign with a major-league team, familiarly
20 Naja naja, familiarly
21 Writer of the 1950 Tony-winning play "The Cocktail Party"
22 Letter after Juliet in a phonetic alphabet
24 ___ Éireann (Irish legislative assembly)
25 Ran-tan
26 Energy converters of a sort
28 Bourbon and others: Abbr.
29 Certain suckling
30 Note from one who's shy
31 Exposure warning?
36 Catchy thing?
37 Some bushes, for short
38 I.M. not sent through AOL?
40 Alcohol or drugs, it's said
44 See 1-Down
45 Be-all and end-all
46 "___ doch!" (German reply)
47 Emasculates
48 ___ Zagora, Bulgaria
50 2008 Olympics sensation
52 Heat
54 Model for Machiavelli's "The Prince"
55 Person making a check mark?
56 Come (to)
57 Nereus and Proteus
58 Bridge problem

DOWN

1 With 44-Across, it may lead to a seizure
2 Perfection
3 Elegantly, to Brahms
4 Burrower with a bushy tail
5 Bugged
6 Superior court writ: Abbr.
7 The Pearl of the Orient
8 Extreme soreness
9 Disconnected, in music: Abbr.
10 Approached purposefully
11 Kettledrum
12 "The Essence of ___," Food Network show
13 Goes by foot, in a way
15 Chardonnay from Burgundy
19 Copenhagen alternative
23 Prayer
26 Liking romantically
27 Talks romantically
29 Neck piece
32 Cartoon hero with a blue cape
33 ___ Spalko, Indiana Jones villainess
34 Words after "The end"
35 Some provocation
39 Tuition classification
40 Breakouts
41 ___ rating
42 "Finding ___," 2008 comedy
43 Participates in a class action
44 James of the court
47 Diminutive chthonic figure
49 Prefix with biology
51 Building piece
53 Foreign exchange abbr.

by Paula Gamache

364 HARD

ACROSS

1 Releaser of "1921" in 1969
7 Author of the best-selling investment book "You're Fifty — Now What?"
13 Participate in drag?
14 Thing turned while speaking
15 Source of the word "avatar"
16 Words of intimidation
17 They get many saves
18 Shout about Paris?
19 Something below the bar
20 Diet of Worms concern
21 Lewis Carroll's birthplace
23 "___ Growing" (Temptations hit)
24 One against another
25 Soeur de la mère
26 One concerned with entrances and exits
31 Stalemate
35 Start of a traditional love story
36 They rock, sometimes
39 Far-away connection?
40 "The Art of Hitting .300" writer Charley
41 A diva may throw one
43 Not splurge on a 48-Across, say
46 Inits. by a dateline
47 Tony's consigliere on "The Sopranos"
48 It's often taken down Broadway
49 Make the rounds?
51 Completely in the dark
52 Cell assignment
53 Sci-fi smuggler
54 R-rated, say
55 Mean

DOWN

1 Band member with a bent neck
2 1946 Literature Nobelist
3 Tennis's Clijsters and others
4 Cause of fitful sleep
5 Sartre's "___ clos"
6 Target of Durocher's "Nice guys finish last" sentiment
7 Body in a case
8 Breaks a bottle on, maybe
9 It ended in 1806: Abbr.
10 Capacious closet
11 Hold
12 Member of the 27-Down group
13 Item used for studio mixing
15 Big break
18 How a gull might feel
21 O.K.
22 What Greece has that Germany doesn't
24 Means of reaching the stars
27 Brothers who sang "Stayin' Alive"
28 Biodiversity setting
29 Period named for an earth goddess
30 Option for a hit
32 Setting for big rigs
33 "Yep, unfortunately"
34 Orchestra section
36 Dairy equipment
37 Remove, as carpet
38 A question of introspection
42 Very hot
43 Go to a lot
44 Very upscale?
45 DuPont discontinued it in 1990
48 Group sharing a coat of arms
50 Utah Stars' org.
51 City with both A.L. and N.L. teams, informally

by Josh Knapp

ACROSS

1 Big-time kudos
9 Film about the Statue of Liberty?
15 Exasperated cry
16 Response to a good dig
17 Hidden danger
18 Preparatory stage
19 Subject of the biography "King of the World"
20 Bright spot in architecture?
22 Saison de septembre, mostly
23 Deal killers
25 Sets right
26 Honoree on the third Friday of Sept.
27 Like many old series, now
29 Grammy-winning Gnarls Barkley, e.g.
30 Bats are smaller than normal in it
32 Disco or swing follower
34 Mascot that's a shell of a man?
36 Slinky and stealthy
40 What's-his-face
41 Demi Moore was in it
43 ___ factor
44 Springtime arrival
45 College football coach Miles
47 Wiesbaden's state
51 Application datum: Abbr.
52 It's under the Host
54 Torpedo
55 Eponymous general
56 Be cut down to size

58 Mute neighbor, maybe: Abbr.
59 Dot-com with an asterisk in its name
61 Words at the outset
63 Picture receiver
64 Moved out?
65 Official's helper
66 Opening used before opening a door

DOWN

1 Lombardia's capital
2 "Operation Bikini" co-star, 1963
3 Robbed of
4 Goal of some candidates
5 Means of forced entry
6 Bad blood

7 Immobilized, in a way
8 What sticks to your ribs?
9 Tops of golf courses?
10 Subtle warning sound
11 It goes through lots of luggage: Abbr.
12 Hot
13 Captain Nemo's final resting place
14 Beseech
21 Things that disappear in the shower?
24 Modelesque
28 Namby-pambies
30 Do school work
31 One concerned with checks and balances
33 Street name lead-in

35 One side of Hawaii
36 Common toy go-with
37 One being printed at a station
38 Customize for
39 Kudos
42 Dog's coat?
46 Still
48 Definitely gonna
49 Film critic Joel
50 Protect, in a way
52 Triumphant song
53 Like some mythology
56 "Laverne & Shirley" landlady
57 Emulate Niobe
60 "Ready" follower
62 Crib note?

by Patrick John Duggan

The New York Times

SMART PUZZLES

Presented with Style

Available at your local bookstore or online at www.nytimes.com/nytstore

 St. Martin's Griffin

ANSWERS

1

```
U S M A   A S O F   L A I R D
P R I X   N A P E   A L T E R
C I V I C D U T Y   N A S T Y
    S U E D E   A D M I R E
C N N   M A I D O F H O N O R
Z O O M I N   G O O
A R S O N   H A L O   S G T S
R A I D   C A D E T   C I R C
S S R S   D I O R   K A Z O O
    A R K   W E T M O P
B A C K C O U N T R Y   O P E
A S Y L U M   L A I U S
S T R U M   W E S T P O I N T
S A U T E   A R T E   F L E W
I B S E N   Y S E R   A L T O
```

2

```
P U L S E S   A C A D   O A K
O N E C A R   M L L E   I L E
S H O R T I S T A L L   L O G
T I N A S   A R M Y   A C E S
S T A B   Q U A D   T A R
    B L A C K I S W H I T E
A G I L I T Y   P E I   S A Y
C I N E M A   U N R I P E
A R S   I R E   C R E A S E D
B L U N T I S S H A R P
    M R S   T W I T   M A M A
Z I M A   M A I L   D U R A N
I D A   L I T T L E I S B I G
O E R   A L E C   O N I O N S
N A Y   M E S H   S E C R E T
```

3

```
R A C E D   W I S P   M A G I
E R A S E   A O K I   O N U S
T A B L E L I N E N   S E A L
A M I   R E T I L E   A C M E
P I N G   D O Z E   A I D
E S S E S   N E T I N C O M E
    N E Z   R O C K S T A R
T I C   X E S   N B A   E Y E
A T H E I S T S   M R I
B A L L S T A T E   A S C I I
    O A T   C O L A   P O N G
W A R P   S C O U T S   C H E
A X I S   P A D D L E B O A T
C E D E   O T O E   A I O L I
O D E S   T O N S   M O N E T
```

4

```
B E D S   T H A T   A G O R A
Y U R I   O O Z E   N I X O N
P R A M   L A T E   T R Y I T
L O W B U D G E T F I L M
A P I A R Y   C H E F   O P T
Y E N   A O L   R O B R O Y
    B L U E M A N G R O U P
E L I A   D E R   A N T E
B U M M E D A R O U N D
A R M A N I   D N A   B O X
N E O   T O S H   I N T I M E
    D O W N C O M F O R T E R
T R E V I   O R E O   I M A X
I B S E N   U S S R   M A R E
L I T R E   T E A M   S P A S
```

5

```
H A S S L E   A R L O     M A Y
A C T U A L   R A I D     O V A
T H I N S K I N N E D     T O N
C O N K S   N O D S     W O N K
H O G   I M P   O T T E R
    M E A L Y M O U T H E D
C H I A   R A E     G L O R Y
H U N T   C Y N I C   A M I E
E L S I E   T S A   N E E D
F A I N T H E A R T E D
    D E C A Y   A O L   A G A
S M E E   M E R E   E R R E D
T A J   L I L Y L I V E R E D
A G O   A L E E   D E P O S E
B I B   B L T S   S N O W E D
```

6

```
V I P S   C P O S   S H A R I
A B L E   U R A L   H E R O N
S O A P O P E R A   E Y E O N
C O N T R O L S T H E J A M
O K S   A L I   I S O
    F L A M E S T H E F A N
D E V I L S   T I S   A D O
R A I N Y   P H D   R I Z Z O
A C C   W I I   E I L E E N
W H I P T H E C R A C K
    R E A   U S O   A V A
    Q U E S T I O N T H E P O P
A U R A L   S W I M S U I T S
S I G M A   L E N A   R A R E
S T E P S   A S S N   O N E S
```

7

```
B O O P   M A K E   A R T E S
A U D I   U L N A   L E E C H
I C O N   P I E S   A D A L E
T H R E E P E A T S   S P A R
    T R E N D   C R E A T E
G O K A R T S   A R O A R
U S E R   P H A T   T R A
A L E   M I X T A P E   I O N
M O P   I D E A   R E S T
    T A C O S   A R O U S E S
I S A B E L   A L O O N
S O B S   S W E A T P A N T S
L A S E R   A S S T   W A I T
A M O N G   Y O K E   A S E A
M I N T S   S P A N   Y A R N
```

8

```
A T B A T   S T U   L A N E S
P R I M O   H E N   I N A N E
P I A P P R O X I M A T I O N
S O S   S E R T   A I E L L O
    C A T   D I S   P A R
    A B S O L U T E Z E R O
A I R A R M   A C E   E L S A
C R E T E   M N O   R O I L S
S E A U   V E G   P E R S I A
    S P E E D O F L I G H T
O F T   X X I   L A S
R E B A T E   D A I S   A N T
A V O G A D R O S N U M B E R
L E N I N   A R K   E I E I O
B R E N T   G A S   D A L L Y
```

9

```
O B A M A   Y A W N S     F L O
P E T A L   E L A T E     L E I
S E A R C H L I G H T       Y I N
    T O U P E E     F L I C K
T H R I V E S     A R E N A S
R O O N E Y     B A D E G G
A N A I S   A L B E E     H E D
M E R S   G L O B E     B O L O
P S I   D U E B Y     T O R M E
    N O O S E S     C H A S E R
Y O G U R T       C A R T E R S
M U L T I   P O O R E R
C S I   T O R C H B E A R E R
A T O   O R A T E     A C U T E
S S N   S I M O N     M E T A L
```

10

```
S C O W L     G L O B     W A S H
O H S A Y   H I L L     A S T I
F U L L S P E E D O A H E A D
A M O N   A T V     O P I A T E
      U N I T     S P I N
D I R T Y R O T T E N E G G O
E X I S T     O U R   S O N S
N I N     T O W N S     G A T
Y O G A   E W E     S P O R E
S N O W B A L L I N H E L L O
      A L M S     B A H N
K R A K O W   H I S   A I D E
N O L E G O T O S T A N D O N
O P E N   R O L E   O C E A N
X E R S   K E Y S   L E A S E
```

11

```
L E G S   B L U R     B A S I L
A L O E   E A S E   A A N D E
S A F E H A V E N     C H A O S
S T E P O N   D O R K   R L S
O E R   U P I   W O R S E
    F R O Z E N T U N D R A
T I D E   L O P     B O R A T
O B I E   E D S E L   O U Z O
M A R D I     O L E   T M E N
B R I E F S U M M A R Y
    G R O A N   O N E   D O H
U Z I   R O O T   O C T O P I
S O B I G   D O W N S O U T H
P O L L O   O R E M   A S I A
S M E L T   S A D E   D E N T
```

12

```
D A I L Y   O M G   G H O S T
O L D I E   F O R   R E C U R
U L E E S   T O I   E N T R E
B E A N I E   C L E A R O F F
L Y L E   A T H L E T E
E S S E   G R E E N L I G H T
    S A L A D   A D I E U
P R O   F E Y   M A W   S E X
I C H A T     M E S N E
E A S T E R L I L Y   R A B E
    T R O U N C E   O C A T
D S T U D E N T     T A T T L E
I T I N A   G T E   R I S E R
F A K E R   E E L   A C O R N
F R I S K   D A Y   M A N S E
```

13

```
L I M O ■ G A B L E ■ M C A T
A R A B ■ O N E A L ■ O H I O ■
C O T T O N C L U B ■ B E D S
E N S U R E ■ ■ D E R I V E S
■ ■ S T R A F E ■ E L Y ■
P U C E ■ S I D ■ M E C C A
A B A ■ S L A V ■ P A S H A S
N O R ■ C A P E C O D ■ A M P
G A S B A G ■ C O T E ■ S E E
S T O R M ■ M C S ■ A E O N
■ N I P ■ A S T R A L ■
S U C T I O N ■ E S K I M O
A L I I ■ C O C O C H A N E L
A N T S ■ T R A L A ■ L O A D
B A Y H ■ A S T E P ■ I N N S
```

14

```
H A I T I A N ■ A P E M E N
A G N O S T I C ■ R E L A T E
L A D Y O F T H E K N I G H T
E R O S ■ ■ R A N ■ C O M E T
■ ■ U P I ■ D I E T A R Y
K N I T P I C K E R ■ ■
R E T O S S ■ H A S B E E N S
I S S U E ■ J A R ■ O L D I E
S T A R T R E K ■ A S I A N S
■ ■ K N I C K N A M E S
R U C T I O N ■ L A S ■
A L L I N ■ E G O ■ T G I F
K N O T F O R E V E R Y O N E
E A G L E T ■ L E V E R A G E
D E S E R T ■ S E D A T E D
```

15

```
A T O M S ■ A C A D S ■ A S H
R O S I E ■ T U L I P ■ F O E
O R A N G E S L I C E ■ F R A
D O G C A R T ■ A T E L I E R
■ S E E ■ I A M S ■ D O L L
■ P I C K L E D O N I O N
A S P I N ■ E S S O ■ A S A
S P R E A D ■ ■ W R I T E R
A L I ■ O H M S ■ E M E R Y
P I M E N T O O L I V E ■
■ T R O I ■ O P U S ■ A R F
L E O N A R D ■ R A I N H A T
I N S ■ C E L E R Y S T I C K
D D E ■ I N U R E ■ M I N E O
O S S ■ N O M A D ■ S T E T S
```

16

```
J A M B ■ P O N T E ■ M U S T
O M A R ■ O D O R S ■ S T E W
S P E E D L I M I T ■ N O V A
■ ■ M A K E A B E T ■ P E N
F A D E R ■ ■ D E E R X I N G
O P E N E N D ■ ■ A M A S S
R E C ■ D I E T S O D A ■
E X I T ■ K E I T H ■ S T O P
■ E V E P L U M B ■ E P A
S T A R E ■ ■ B Y A H A I R
H O S P I T A L ■ ■ B A K E R
O R T ■ L O N E S T A R ■
A Q U A ■ M E N W O R K I N G
L U T E ■ E A T A T ■ E Z R A
S E E R ■ I R O N S ■ D E A D
```

17

```
HAITI   CBS     PINA
ARTICULATE    LOON
MARTINAMIS    UNIT
SLY     SWARTHMORE
    SHEA      ESS
  BIPARTISAN   PHD
NOCAN   MUG    HAI
AWORKINPROGRESS
DEN   DIE    EARTH
ADO   DOLLARTREE
   COO     DAZE
MILKCARTON    WEB
ESAI    THIRDPARTY
ELSE    MOVEDAPART
TATS    SOD   TEPEE
```

18

```
MGM    FELT   STRAFE
EEO    OLEO   TRILLO
DANECOOK     REVLON
IRANI    ELI    EUR
ATMS   DANACARVEY
OILPAN   XTC    INE
   AORTA    COACT
  DAVECHAPPELLE
TENET    AHAND
ALA   IMA   ARTFUL
DICKCAVETT    ONEA
MON    TEN    ORKIN
GENOME   DCCOMICS
BADBOY   ATOZ   NAE
STASIS   TROY   DSL
```

19

```
HIGH   MENSA   FILL
ONEA   ASSAM   IDLE
COTTONSWAB    STAN
KIT   TEA   BIGHAND
  LOVEDIT   LEGOS
   KER   IDEES
RUNNINGMATE    PSI
AVON   INERT   ALAN
JAW   CRACKERJACK
   PHOTO    IAN
SPORE    PITCREW
PINETAR   CEE   FIG
AXIS   KOSHERSALT
RIOT   IBEAM   ARLO
KENO   NEWTS   SEAS
```

20

```
MAIA   AJAR   THIEF
ISBN   CONE   CYCLO
THEGREATPUMPKIN
TOLET   DEAN   NYET
STILES    YUGO
   EASTLA   MOTTOS
ATV   AABA   BIALY
THEFUNKYCHICKEN
MASAI   ESCE    ESC
STOLEN   STEFFI
   LSAT   LIOTTA
ISPS   VASE   DREAR
THEFLYINGTOMATO
CANOE   NOGO   ASAS
HYDRA   TWOD   LYRE
```

21

```
S C O O P █ C R A B █ A L S O
C O N G A █ R O P E █ C I A O
R O A R S █ A L E C █ A M M O
A P P E T I Z E R O R D E R █
P E A █ O N E █ T O O █ R A P
E R R O R S █ B U L B █ I I I
█ █ S A U C E R █ A C M E █
█ B I L L M A Z E R O S K I █
C O M O █ L O S E R S █ █
S T P █ A W L S █ F A N N E D
I S O █ O A S █ L E T █ A L I
█ W U R L I T Z E R O R G A N
Z A N E █ T I E D █ R E S I N
I N D O █ O M N I █ I N A N E
P A S S █ N E O N █ O T T E R
```

22

```
C R O P █ I M A C █ T I L E D
L E C H █ N A I L █ E R A S E
I D E A █ G O T O H E A V E N
C H A S M █ █ C R A T E █
H O N E Y I M H O M E █ I F S
E T S █ E G O █ X M R A D I O
█ █ K Y O T O █ █ D I N O
█ T O W E R O F L O N D O N █
M A M A █ █ T A P A S █ █
I P A N E M A █ D A D █ F D A
T E N █ K I T T Y L I T T E R
█ █ O B E S E █ R E R A N
H I D D E N T E X T █ N O N E
A D E E R █ U N I S █ D O N S
N O M S G █ D Y N E █ S P A S
```

23

```
G A G █ F E E L I N █ S E E D
R T E █ U P D A T E █ A L L Y
O T T █ R I G H T T O L I F E
W H O A █ L E T █ S P A █
L E F T T O D I E █ E M B E D
█ F R O G █ V A N I L L A
A S T I R █ S A I D █ A L F
S T R A I G H T T O V I D E O
O L A █ T A M E █ I R E N E
R E C R O O M █ █ B E A R █
T O K E N █ U P T O S N U F F
█ K I D █ L E A █ I N R E
D O W N T O E A R T H █ N A T
O L I O █ D E C R E E █ E M U
E D I T █ O L E A R Y █ R E S
```

24

```
S A W T O █ C A M P █ L A T H
I M E A N █ O B O E █ E U R O
C O B R A █ R I D E █ S P A R
█ S P R I N T E R U S A I N
A L I █ O N E █ █ S E I N E
M E T A L F A S T E N E R █
O N E A L █ L O L A █ █
S A S H █ A L O O F █ T C B Y
█ █ A S I A █ E R A S E
█ L I G H T N I N G U N I T
S T O N E █ N E G █ D X I
L E A V E S U D D E N L Y █
U L N A █ T R E E █ O O M P H
S L E D █ O G L E █ G R A C E
H Y D E █ W E L D █ S E N S E
```

25

```
Q T I P S ■ A P E S ■ G L O B
T O T A L ■ J U M P ■ R O T E
S U C R E ■ A M I R ■ A N T E
■ T H E P U R P L E O N I O N
■ ■ N T H ■ ■ E N D ■ ■ ■ ■ ■
S P A T ■ O P E N S E S A M E
H I S ■ S H A R I ■ R O L E X
E X T R A ■ P I T ■ U N I T E
L E R O I ■ A C T I N ■ B A R
F L O O D P L A I N ■ S I L T
■ ■ ■ T A R ■ ■ C E L ■ ■ ■ ■
T H E W H O L E S H M E A R
A U T O ■ B E V Y ■ B A G E L
K E R R ■ E V E N ■ E Z I N E
E Y E D ■ D I S C ■ D E N T S
```

26

```
M A W ■ L E C T O R ■ C R O P
A B E ■ A L C O V E ■ A U D I
S R I ■ C L I V E B A R N E S
S I R R E E ■ R A N D D ■ ■ ■
E D D B Y R N E S ■ N O O N E
U G L I ■ O L E O ■ O W E N
R E Y ■ M I L L E B O R N E S
■ ■ D O T ■ ■ I R S ■ ■ ■ ■
D A V I D B I R N E Y ■ R A T
I K E A ■ E A S E ■ C O C O
P A R M A ■ S T B E R N A R D
■ M A R I S ■ L A N D E D
F R O N T B U R N E R ■ M A L
A I N T ■ I M D O N E ■ A G E
N O T E ■ S E A W A R ■ P E R
```

27

```
C L A S P S ■ H B O ■ Y O D A
H A C K I T ■ A R P ■ A L I T
E S T A T E ■ N A E ■ M E R V
W E S T V I R G I N I A ■ ■ ■
S R O ■ I N R U N ■ R H E I N
■ S N A P ■ S P I T V A L V E
■ ■ H E M ■ S A O ■ ■ L A W
D I S H R A G ■ C L E M E N S
A S A ■ R O S ■ D X I
S P L I T V O T E ■ I G O R
H Y E N A ■ D I D S T ■ L A Y
■ A B S O L U T V O D K A
T H A W ■ A M T ■ R I P P E R
V I V A ■ F E E ■ U S E R I D
S P A Y ■ E N D ■ T A L O N S
```

28

```
T A L C ■ M E S A ■ A T T A
A R E A ■ E A G E R ■ I R A S
T R A V E L C A R D ■ R I M S
■ ■ I N G ■ D I E ■ F A I T
J E S T E R S ■ O N C A L L
A L L Y ■ E T C ■ T A R P
B I O ■ S C A R F ■ R E E K S
O T T ■ Z O N E O U T ■ R A W
T E M P E ■ S T O K E ■ I N E
■ A L L S ■ E D U ■ S O Y A
■ S C A L E D ■ S L A N D E R
D A H S ■ L O P ■ E T A
E X I T ■ D O U B L E T I M E
C O N E ■ O Z Z I E ■ C O A X
O N E R ■ M Y O B ■ H U G O
```

29

```
P A W   F L O O D   I G I V E
A H A   L A T T E   A L O E S
R O L L O V E R M I N U T E S
T Y K E   L O O P   T A S E
    G A O L   R O V E
    S I T D O W N D I N N E R
E N C O R E   O A S T   O V A
P O R N O   D R Y   I D T A G
I N A   P S I S   A A R O N S
C O M E H E R E O F T E N
    L Y R E   B R E A
P U M A   I N E S   M A G I
S T A Y O F E X E C U T I O N
S A U N A   E P S O N   D O G
T H I E F   D O S E S   A D E
```

30

```
I B I S   C L U E   E P S O M
S A M M Y C A H N   T R A C E
A D M I S S I O N   H O S T A
S M E L L   C H A K A K H A N
    I D E       O N E A L S
A N I S E   M A S K E D
U T A   S H I N T O   S M E W
T O T   C O N G A M E   O X O
O N E G   M I L T O N   N I K
    R E E S E S   A S S T S
E S S E N E       O I S
J A M E S C A A N   A L G I D
E R I T U   F R E E R A N G E
C A T E R   B I L L Y C O N N
T H E R E   S A L K   E R S T
```

31

```
A R R R   C R O P   A P P S
N O A H   L O V E S   R O O T
D A V Y J O N E S L O C K E R
I R I S E S   R E A M   E M U
    L E A S T   A V A S T
T A L K L I K E A   H E R
A T O I   N I E   M A G O G
B A S S O O N   P E N G U I N
  D E M O N   P A D   I N G A
    N E C   P I R A T E D A Y
B O O T Y   A N K L E
A C T   T I C K   L A A L A A
S H I V E R M E T I M B E R S
I R M A   S A Y S O   B A C H
N E E T   N E O N   A H O Y
```

32

```
C P U S   A P I A   L U C A S
A L P E   N A C L   E R O D E
B U D G E T C U T   A I R E R
A R A   C O M   I N A N
N A T I O N A L A N T H E M S
A L E C   N O A H   S L A W
    E G G   U R A L   I R A
D O L L A R D I P L O M A C Y
A V E   D U E S   F L O
D E F T   M A X I   J E N A
E N T E R P R I S E Z O N E S
    W H E Y   O X O   L A K
A K I R A   R E N T A C A R S
S O N A R   A L T O   A C T I
S I G N S   F O O L   P E O N
```

33

```
S P A T   I T C H   S L A S H
H E S S   N E H I   C O P T O
A R I A   H A I L   O A S I S
Q U A R T E R P O U N D E R S
      H R S     S E E
A D M I R E   F L U   D A T E
B U E N O   B O A R   D U A L
H A L F B L O O D P R I N C E
O N E I   O R L Y   A C T I N
R E E D   R E S   F I E S T A
    E O N     P A S
F U L L M E T A L J A C K E T
U S A I N   E S A I   R A R A
D E N T I   L E S T   A M I S
D R A Y S   L A M A   B A C K
```

34

```
V I A L   T O D D L E   M A R
A C L U   H E R E O N   A M I
C H I C K E N Y A R D   R I M
    C A W   E R N   I O N S
D I G I T A L Y E A R B O O K
O N O   S L I E R   E E N S Y
O D O M   R N S   C P A
R O P E R U G   T O O M A N Y
    T I S   T R U   S L A V
P I P I T   H E I N Z   E S E
A N I M A L I N S T I N C T S
L U X E   E T A   R O E
A R I   C A T C H I N A L I E
C E E   A V E R S E   L A M E
E D S   B E R E T S   E X P O
```

35

```
N I N J A   A P L U S   T A B
A R I E S   B O O S T   E T A
G E T S O N E S W A Y   M D S
    U F O   S E T   C P A S
L E N S   T H E R O Y A L W E
E P A   N E O   D E C E N T
V I D E O   P O P A R T
I C A N T T E L L Y O U W H Y
    A I R S E A   U S A G E
S C A M P I   T N T   I T A
T A L E S O F W O E   A T V S
O V A L   X I I   H E R
L E S   P I T C H I N G W O O
I R K   E D U C E   D U B Y A
D N A   R E P A Y   S E A L S
```

36

```
A C D C   S P O C K   N D A K
T H O R   T I A R A   O I S E
T A M E   U N T I L   I S P Y
N I P S I N T H E B U D
    E S L   A S S   S E E R S
S H R I L L   L E A N I N
P A I D   I R O N E D   T A I
R I G A   R E I N A   K E L P
E R N   M A P L E S   E R T E
A D O R E S   E M P T O R
D O N E N   A C T   I T A
    J U G G L I N G P I N S
M A Z E   A R O M A   A N E W
A L E C   S E W E R   C E R A
P I N T   H E N R Y   E D D Y
```

37

M	A	R			S	O	B	S				C	O	L	T	S
O	B	I			E	R	R	O	R			A	C	E	I	T
C	I	G	A	R	C	A	S	E			T	H	E	T	A	
S	T	O	V	E			C	A	P	E	C	O	R	A	L	
		L	E	N	A			D	O	R	A			S	N	L
C	U	E	C	A	R	D				I	L	K				
H	S	T			C	O	A	T	C	L	O	S	E	T		
I	S	T	O			U	M	A			S	P	C	A		
C	R	O	P	C	I	R	C	L	E			A	R	F		
		T	A	D			C	R	E	W	C	U	T			
S	H	O			R	O	D	S			A	L	I	E		
C	A	M	E	C	L	E	A	N			E	N	S	U	E	
O	S	A	K	A			C	L	A	Y	C	O	U	R	T	
O	T	H	E	R			K	A	P	U	T			I	G	O
T	E	A	S	E			D	A	M	S			T	E	N	

38

L	A	P	T	O	P			N	E	W	S			R	I	M
O	B	E	Y	E	R			A	C	H	Y			A	L	E
L	O	C	K	D	E	V	I	C	E	S			B	I	N	
L	U	K	E			F	E	V	E	R			M	B	A	S
				S	P	A	R	E			E	R	O	I	C	A
A	V	A			R	B	S			T	I	L	T			
C	I	R	C	U	S	A	C	R	O	B	A	T	S			
T	E	C	H	S			C	O	E			C	R	E	P	E
	W	H	I	S	K	E	Y	G	L	A	S	S	E	S		
	I	L	I	E			A	I	G			T	D	S		
O	U	T	L	A	Y			U	L	C	E	R				
P	R	E	Y			C	U	R	I	E			A	L	A	S
T	I	C			J	A	C	K	A	N	D	J	I	L	L
E	A	T			I	S	L	E			S	C	A	M	P	I
D	H	S			M	E	A	L			E	C	H	O	E	D

39

I	D	E	S			R	A	V	E			R	A	T	S
T	I	L	E			A	T	S	E	A			E	R	A	T
A	V	O	N			N	A	I	L	S			D	O	P	Y
L	A	N	D	M	A	R	X			S	A	D	S	A	X
			S	E	M	I			M	E	L	E	E	S	
	A	D	I	E	U			P	I	T	A	S			
B	L	A	N	K	C	H	E	X			S	T	I	N	T
F	D	R			K	A	P	U	T			D	U	E	
F	A	T	W	A			H	Y	P	E	R	L	Y	N	X
		H	U	L	A	S			N	E	I	L	S		
	F	L	A	R	E	S			D	E	A	L			
T	I	E	T	A	X			T	U	M	M	Y	T	U	X
E	R	O	S			U	S	A	G	E			P	O	N	E
N	E	N	A			S	A	T	I	N			A	G	I	N
D	D	A	Y			W	E	N	T			D	A	T	A

40

J	A	B	B	A			G	A	R	B			L	A	I	C
U	N	A	R	M			A	G	U	E			A	N	N	A
S	T	A	R	S	K	Y	A	N	D	H	U	T	C	H	
T	I	S			C	H	E	R			T	A	R	Z	A	N
			B	R	A				L	I	R	E				
P	U	R	E	A	N	D	S	I	M	P	L	E			
E	L	E	G	Y			A	C	M	E			S	A	F	E
R	N	A			D	R	O	P	S			R	A	Y		
M	A	C	S			I	N	R	E			K	A	N	Y	E
		H	U	G	S	A	N	D	K	I	S	S	E	S		
			B	A	B	Y			A	R	K					
I	M	P	A	L	A			A	W	L	S			G	P	A
B	E	E	R	A	N	D	S	K	I	T	T	L	E	S	
E	S	A	U			D	E	E	R			I	N	E	R	T
T	A	R	S			S	W	A	P			E	N	N	U	I

41

```
I S L E   B A L M Y   T B S P
D I E T   I L I A D   R A T A
I N T H E D U M P S   I R A S
  T I E R   M O O   D A R N S
P A T R O L     U T I L I Z E
A X L   D O W N T H E R O A D
P E I   E P E E   E D U
A S E A   B I T   N Y P D
    I A N   G R A B   O L E
O V E R T H E H I L L   G E L
T E A B A L L   F A C I A L
O C T A D   O H S   N A B S
O T I S   U P T H E C R E E K
L O N E   M E T O O   L A D Y
E R G S   A S P E N   A R O D
```

42

```
S I P S   H U S H   I N F E R
C O A L   O H I O   N E I G H
A N N A   N O L O   F A R G O
M I D N I G H T H O U R
S C A T S     A T T   S H A
    M A T T H O U S T O N
M A M A   R O O   R O A S T
A P A R T M E N T H O U S E S
M I N C E   T A E   S H A Y
B A S S E T H O U N D
O N E   S H E   O U T D O
    W H E R E A R T T H O U
C A P R I   B L U E   U R N S
S W E A R   A S K S   R O U T
I N A P T   L E S T   N E T S
```

43

```
A S A P   M E T A   A R M O R
V A I L   A R A B   L O U P E
A L L A T O N C E   I M H I P
    C U R S E   S T P A U L
F L E A B I T T E N   E M M Y
O U T T A   R E A R M
R I P E   C A R N E Y   A C E
U G H   V A M P I R E   D I V
M I O   C R I M E S   C A V A
    N O R A S   S O L I D
B E E S   T H I N K T W I C E
E T H I C S   T O R A H
A H O R A   C A M E R A S H Y
R E M I T   C L A M   N C A A
D R E S S   L O N E   D I T Z
```

44

```
A N A T   N O B E L   J A R S
S E T H   E P O X Y   O M E N
H O M E R E P A I R   C A V A
E N S U E D   S T A C K S U P
    S P L I T   Y E S E S
R E F U S E S   D E N Y
A S I A   O K A P I   S K I
H A R L E M B O Y S C H O I R
M U M   M E A N S   A U T O
    S C A R   P L A Y P E N
E S Q U E   H A I R S
C O A L E S C E   T E E I N G
R U N T   H A I L C A E S A R
U S D A   O P R A H   D A Z E
S E A N   P E S C I   S W I G
```

45

```
S P A S   B A G S   S P A T
W A L K   A U R A L   N A D A
A G E E   P S I L O V E Y O U
P E C L A S S   B E E
    E M O   P T B A R N U M
  R I T E   S O R E L   E N E
S E T O N   T B A R   A B I T
C L A N S   R O D   B R U T E
A I L S   L U X E   A B L E R
L E I   M I N E R   B O A S
P F C H A N G S   O E R
    O L D   P H L E V E L
P G T H I R T E E N   T I D Y
O A H U   O U T G O   U S E R
I T E M   S E A S   M A N E
```

46

```
A B B A   F A S C I A   B R O
F O O L   A T H E N A   O O F
C I N D E R F E L L A   S P F
    N E E   R E A   A T E E
B E I N G B O B B Y B R O W N
A B E T   A B E S   U L N A S
R O B E   R O T   B Y E B Y E
S N L   H E E   R A I S A
    U R A L S   E N T   K O I
O L E A R Y   A H A   V E R T
R E B I D   E L A N   O D E S
B O U N C I N G B A B Y B O Y
I N T S   D R E   R A E
T I L   F L A B B E R G A S T
E N E   R E G R E W   E N O S
D E R   I D E A T E   R S V P
```

47

```
A S E A   A L A M O   P O M P
S A U D   P E T A L   S C A R
S T R I K E G O L D   T A K E
A R E N A   A M E N D   R I T
Y A K   R U T   I O D I N E
S P A R E S O M E C H A N G E
    E N E   I R K   M A I N
W A S P S   O L E   E A S T S
A P I A   I O N   B U S
S P L I T T H E J A C K P O T
S L I D E S   O Y L   E K E
A E C   N A B O B   I S L E T
I P O D   B O W L E D O V E R
L I N E   O R E O S   F I F I
S E E S   Y E N T A   A C E S
```

48

```
K A Z A N   P A X   A P L U S
A L E V E   A L E   T T O P S
R O B E D   L A N C E B A S S
T O U R   C E S A R I O
  F L A V O R   I N A J A M
  O G E E   G E M   T U B E
A B N E R   E R I E   S L O E
C A P   A L D O R A Y   I R S
C R I P   A G U E   O R A T E
T A K E   T E T   J U A N
S K E T C H   H O R N B Y
  S L E E P I N   F R A T
F I S H E R M E N   A R E N A
A C E O F   M E D   D E A N S
T E M P T   A L I   S E M I S
```

49

B	E	H	I	N	D	■	Z	I	T	■	B	L	U	E
A	D	A	G	I	O	■	A	C	E	■	R	O	N	S
B	I	G	O	T	S	■	N	E	A	■	A	T	I	P
E	T	S	■	■	A	V	E	■	B	O	Y	T	O	Y
■	■	S	A	G	O	■	C	A	R	E	E	N	S	■
B	R	O	W	N	E	Y	E	D	G	I	R	L	■	■
R	E	R	A	N	■	A	L	P	S	■	■	E	N	G
I	N	A	N	E	■	G	A	L	■	A	P	N	E	A
T	O	N	■	■	R	I	T	A	■	L	A	Y	E	R
■	■	G	R	E	E	N	E	Y	E	D	L	A	D	Y
A	R	E	A	R	U	G	■	E	T	A	S	■	■	■
B	A	T	M	A	N	■	F	R	A	■	■	B	A	R
A	I	R	S	■	I	M	O	■	L	O	Y	O	L	A
S	N	E	E	■	T	E	X	■	I	N	O	N	I	T
E	Y	E	S	■	E	L	Y	■	I	T	U	N	E	S

50

B	O	P	■	B	A	J	A	■	S	P	A	S	M	S
O	N	O	■	A	L	O	T	■	O	L	D	H	A	T
W	E	M	A	D	E	I	T	■	R	E	M	E	D	Y
I	A	M	B	■	S	N	I	P	■	A	I	D	■	■
E	L	E	C	T	■	I	C	A	N	D	R	E	A	M
■	■	■	T	W	I	N	■	R	E	S	A	V	E	S
C	I	V	I	C	■	L	E	W	■	L	I	R	R	■
B	L	T	■	T	H	E	Y	S	A	Y	■	L	I	P
U	O	F	A	■	I	D	E	■	G	O	O	S	E	■
S	N	I	P	I	N	G	■	K	E	R	R	■	■	■
H	E	G	O	T	G	A	M	E	■	K	I	S	S	Y
■	■	■	U	S	C	■	R	A	N	D	■	N	O	P	E
M	A	R	T	H	A	■	Y	O	U	A	G	A	I	N
F	U	E	L	E	D	■	O	B	E	Y	■	P	C	T
A	S	S	E	S	S	■	R	I	T	E	■	Y	E	A

51

F	L	O	W	■	I	M	A	C	■	H	A	D	A	T
D	I	D	I	■	S	A	R	A	■	O	B	E	S	E
A	M	O	S	■	O	N	A	N	■	F	I	C	H	E
■	■	P	R	E	T	T	Y	B	O	Y	F	L	O	Y	D
■	■	■	G	O	O	■	S	E	E	M	E	■	■	■
G	A	L	U	M	P	H	■	R	A	N	G	I	N	■
U	G	L	Y	B	E	T	T	Y	■	N	E	U	R	O
E	R	A	■	S	T	E	E	P	■	■	L	A	M	■
S	E	M	I	S	■	P	L	A	I	N	J	A	N	E
S	E	A	M	E	N	■	■	S	L	O	E	G	I	N
■	■	■	A	C	E	L	A	■	S	H	E	■	■	■
G	O	R	G	E	O	U	S	G	E	O	R	G	E	■
A	V	O	I	D	■	S	H	I	N	■	I	R	I	S
R	E	U	N	E	■	T	O	N	E	■	N	E	R	O
B	R	E	E	D	■	Y	E	A	R	■	G	W	E	N

52

D	I	S	C	S	■	I	C	E	S	■	C	A	R	S
O	N	T	H	E	■	P	L	E	A	■	U	V	E	A
S	C	R	A	T	C	H	A	N	D	S	N	I	F	F
T	H	A	I	■	H	O	N	■	■	T	E	A	S	E
■	■	G	R	E	E	N	G	O	B	L	I	N	■	■
T	A	G	■	G	R	E	■	R	O	O	F	■	■	■
C	U	L	P	A	■	H	E	M	■	O	L	D	S	■
B	R	E	A	D	C	R	U	M	B	T	R	A	I	L
Y	A	R	N	■	A	Y	E	■	O	M	B	R	E	■
■	■	D	A	T	A	■	D	E	M	■	Y	E	W	■
■	■	B	A	C	O	N	N	U	M	B	E	R	■	■
A	D	O	B	E	■	A	R	M	■	L	I	M	B	■
M	O	N	E	Y	M	O	N	E	Y	M	O	N	E	Y
O	N	E	A	■	O	W	N	S	■	A	P	T	T	O
K	E	R	R	■	D	E	Y	S	■	R	E	H	A	B

53

```
J I B   M A M I E   M A L L S
A R I   A M E N D   S C O O T
P E Z   N A T K I N G C O L E
A N E S T     C Y R U S
N E T P R O F I T S   S E R A
    C A N A L S   R E B U T
E L S A   E S L   E N D A L L
M O P   N I T W I T S   L E A
B R I D A L   A A H   L L D S
E R N E S   B I G A P E
D E A F   N O T O N A D A R E
    L A T E X   S A M O A
N U T C R A C K E R S   A D S
P L A T O   A I M E E   N E E
R E P O T   R A I D S   A O L
```

54

```
S H I L O H   D O S   A S I A
C A S A B A   A S P   U R N S
T R O V E S   F L O U R I S H
V A N I S H   T O N T O
    S E A R   G A R I S H
B A C H   N A S T Y   A M I E
U S A   C A R T A   A S P E N
M I R   C H E R I S H   U S N
R A M O S   F I L C H   R T E
A G E R   T Y P E O   F E A R
P O L I S H   D O D I
    E A R P S   P U N I S H
B R A N D I S H   E L I S H A
A U N T   L I E   R A S H E R
M E T S   L S D   S C H E M E
```

55

```
K U D O S   W A T T   C A L L
E T U D E   A R E A   O B O E
P A P E R T I G E R   V L O G
T H E   M E T O O   L E E K S
    P O S H   F L O R
    C E N T E R F I E L D E R
H A U T   S R A   S W E R V E
A L T E R   E R S   S T E E N
S O U R E D   E T S   T A R T
P E P P E R G R I N D E R
    A V E R   L E E R
A Z U R E   O I L E R   O R B
F O L K   P O W E R M O W E R
A N N E   I V O R   A R E N A
R E A R   P E N S   L E N D S
```

56

```
C R E D O   T E S S   T U F T
H O M E D   I R O N   A L O E
A G I L E   M I R E   K N O X
F U L L S P E E D A H E A D
F E E   S A W   I K O N
    T A D A   D Y N A M I C
F L E W   U R L   E B O N Y
L I M O   A P A R T   A T R A
A L I A S   M I R   C O E N
G A R B L E D   P E C K
    R U N E   T E L   C O S
T H E G A M E I S A F O O T
W H O A   M I L D   M A T Z O
E A R S   E S M E   O T T E R
T I N T   L E S S   R E A D Y
```

57

A	L	T	O		S	T	A	R		D	E	C	O	R
D	O	H	S		O	H	S	O		E	X	L	A	X
Z	W	E	I		L	I	A	M		M	E	E	T	S
	B	E	R	N	I	E	M	A	C		C	A	M	
O	L	D	I	E		F	I	N	E	T	U	N	E	S
L	O	G	S	O	N			E	A	T	S	A	T	
E	W	E		S	H	A	Q		R	E	E	L	S	
		E	S	C	A	P	E	P	O	D				
P	O	S	S	E		J	U	D	D		D	A	M	
T	O	P	T	E	N			Q	U	A	R	T	O	
S	H	O	E	P	H	O	N	E		G	L	E	E	M
	L	I	E		L	A	U	N	C	H	P	A	D	
P	A	L	M	S		T	E	T	E		A	M	I	E
S	L	E	E	K		E	V	E	N		C	O	R	Y
T	A	R	D	Y		S	O	R	T		A	N	T	E

58

C	U	S	P		A	R	C	S		G	A	F	F	E
A	L	T	O		C	O	A	T		U	L	C	E	R
S	T	E	P		H	A	L	E		N	I	C	E	R
T	R	I	P	L	E	M	I	L	E	S				
S	A	N	Y	O		B	A	L	M	O	R	A	L	
			T	H	R	E	E	F	O	R	O	N	E	
A	C	T		A	I	R			K	I	O	W	A	
L	O	W		G	Y	M		P	O	E		S	A	D
O	B	E	S	E		B	O	W			T	R	Y	
F	R	E	E	R	E	F	I	L	L	S				
T	A	N	T	A	L	U	M			P	A	S	T	A
	N	O	M	O	N	E	Y	D	O	W	N			
R	A	B	B	I		I	D	O	L		E	N	I	D
A	D	I	E	U		N	A	S	A		A	N	N	E
T	O	T	E	M		G	L	E	N		L	Y	E	S

59

S	N	I	P		A	R	E	N	A		G	N	A	T
T	O	T	E		L	A	T	E	R		E	I	N	E
E	V	E	R	Y	B	I	T	A	N	A	N	G	E	L
M	A	M	M	A		L	A	P	E	L		H	R	E
		I	C	Y			S	I	N	T	A	X		
H	A	S	T	H	E	H	O	T	S	F	O	R		
E	V	E		T	W	O	T	O		T	R	I	P	E
R	E	E	D		S	T	A	B	S		A	D	A	M
A	S	K	U	P		E	R	I	E	S		E	L	I
	A	B	S	O	L	U	T	E	W	O	R	S	T	
V	A	S	S	A	R			D	E	B				
E	L	Y		T	E	R	P	S		D	R	O	V	E
T	E	L	L	S	I	T	L	I	K	E	I	T	I	S
C	R	U	E		D	E	U	C	E		E	T	A	T
H	O	M	E		A	S	S	A	Y		N	O	L	A

60

M	A	P	S		P	R	A	T	E		B	A	B	A
E	L	O	I		L	O	R	A	X		O	M	A	N
T	E	L	L	M	E	M	O	R	E		B	O	Y	D
O	C	E	L	O	T		A	P	T	S		C	O	O
			M	Y	C	H	E	R	I	E	A	M	O	U	R
C	R	I	M	S	O	N		T	R	U	E			
L	A	C	E		R	C	A		E	D	S	E	L	
O	V	A		J	A	Y	M	O	H	R		T	A	O
D	E	L	T	A		P	R	O		F	E	S	T	
		A	P	A	R		E	N	D	I	V	E	S	
B	E	N	J	A	M	I	N	M	O	O	R	E		
L	E	A		N	A	V	Y		R	E	E	D	I	T
I	R	I	S		L	A	M	M	E	R	M	O	O	R
T	I	L	E		I	L	E	N	E		A	R	N	O
Z	E	S	T		E	S	T	O	S		N	E	A	T

61

```
S M O K Y ■ P I L E D ■ C A B
L A D L E ■ R O A R S ■ I R E
O C E A N B O T T O M ■ N B A
P E S T ■ A W A I T ■ O D O R
■ ■ C O T ■ ■ N I P P E R S
G R A H A M C R A C K E R ■ ■
P A T ■ T A R A ■ G R E B E
A U T O ■ N O I C E ■ A L M A
S L A N G ■ S A L T ■ L O S ■
■ C R Y S T A L P A L A C E
I C K Y P O O ■ A D A ■ ■ ■
T I D E ■ L O E S S ■ S E W S
A D O ■ I D O L W O R S H I P
L E G ■ D E L L A ■ B I L L Y
O R S ■ A R D E N ■ S E E D S
```

62

```
T E M P O ■ D E E R E ■ Z I P
A V I A N ■ E N T E R ■ U S A
C O N T R A C O S T A ■ L E D
I K E ■ E T A S ■ I S S U E S
T E D ■ C O M ■ B R E T ■ ■
■ C O M P U T E R C O D E
O G L E R S ■ S U E ■ R D A S
P O U N D ■ M A S ■ S O I R S
E T A T ■ R E G ■ S H I N T O
C O U R T E N E Y C O X ■ ■
■ U R D U ■ A I R ■ D A M
B I G M A C ■ S H O T ■ O U I
A V A ■ C O M M O N C O L D S
J E W ■ T A B O O ■ U N L I T
A S K ■ S T A G S ■ T E S T Y
```

63

```
S P C A ■ O S L O ■ C L U E S
H O Y A ■ I H O P ■ L E N T O
E N C H I L A D A ■ O D I S T
A I L E D ■ W E L T S ■ ■ ■
V E E D U B ■ S H E B A N G
E S S ■ N O S E ■ O R A T O R
■ S N A P T O ■ R I S E
■ S H O O T I N G M A T C H
D Y A D ■ T A L O N S ■ S R O
A N T O N Y ■ S E C Y ■ S R O
S C H M E A R ■ S W I P E D
■ S P E W S ■ A N O D E
G E T A T ■ N I N E Y A R D S
P R E L L ■ T R I O ■ N E O S
S N A P E ■ S E T S ■ E S T A
```

64

```
A B E D ■ S T O O D ■ R E S T
R A V I ■ T I L D E ■ O L L A
T H E S P E E D O F M U S I C
■ C A N T E R ■ I N E P T
M A E ■ C O H N ■ W E D
A L L R I S E ■ C O N ■ C B S
R O D I N ■ K A R L ■ N A L A
T H E S O U N D O F M O N E Y
H A R K ■ R O D S ■ O V I N E
A S S ■ S I T ■ S T R A N D S
■ L O S ■ B E R T ■ E S T
S A G A S ■ R A D I A L ■ ■
T H E C O L O R O F L I G H T
A O N E ■ A N N U L ■ P E E R
B Y E S ■ B A S T E ■ S E X Y
```

65

P	S	I	■	F	I	E	N	D	■	H	A	T	C	H
T	E	N	N	E	S	S	E	E	■	O	P	I	U	M
B	A	S	E	B	A	L	L	B	A	T	T	E	R	S
O	N	E	A	■	■	L	U	N	A	■	■	■	■	■
A	C	C	R	U	A	L	■	N	A	I	V	E	T	E
T	E	T	■	S	T	O	C	K	P	R	I	C	E	S
■	■	A	M	O	U	R	■	■	■	S	C	A	T	■
U	N	D	E	C	I	D	E	D	V	O	T	E	R	S
R	E	A	R	■	■	D	O	E	S	A	■	■	■	■
S	A	L	O	O	N	D	O	O	R	S	■	S	L	R
A	L	Y	S	S	U	M	■	M	O	O	N	P	I	E
■	■	■	A	T	I	T	■	■	■	T	R	O	I	■
T	H	I	N	G	S	T	H	A	T	S	W	I	N	G
O	U	N	C	E	■	R	E	W	R	I	T	T	E	N
P	E	S	O	S	■	I	O	W	A	N	■	E	L	S

66

I	T	C	H	■	C	Y	R	U	S	■	A	C	R	O
N	E	R	O	■	O	V	U	L	E	■	T	O	E	D
C	L	A	P	■	M	E	T	E	R	■	T	O	M	E
■	B	I	T	E	T	H	E	B	U	L	L	E	T	■
A	T	M	■	O	T	T	■	■	R	E	E	D	S	■
C	H	E	W	T	H	E	S	C	E	N	E	R	Y	■
T	R	A	D	E	■	■	T	I	N	S	■	■	■	■
S	O	T	S	■	E	Z	R	A	S	■	D	A	I	S
■	■	■	A	L	O	E	■	■	■	G	E	N	R	E
S	W	A	L	L	O	W	T	H	E	B	A	I	T	■
O	H	A	R	E	■	■	H	E	R	■	I	S	H	■
D	I	G	E	S	T	T	H	E	N	E	W	S	■	■
I	N	O	T	■	R	E	E	L	S	■	O	N	U	S
U	T	N	E	■	A	L	A	M	O	■	R	I	P	E
M	O	S	S	■	S	E	D	A	N	■	K	N	I	T

67

L	E	A	D	■	A	D	D	U	P	■	L	O	A	D
I	N	S	O	■	N	U	E	V	A	■	L	P	G	A
S	T	E	W	■	I	L	L	E	R	■	C	E	E	S
T	R	A	N	S	M	U	T	A	T	I	O	N	■	■
■	■	■	P	O	E	T	■	■	B	O	O	S	T	S
■	S	C	A	N	■	H	E	S	■	U	L	T	R	A
H	O	O	T	I	E	■	T	U	B	■	J	A	I	L
A	I	M	■	A	L	C	H	E	M	Y	■	N	E	T
S	L	E	W	■	K	A	Y	■	W	A	R	C	R	Y
T	E	T	O	N	■	B	L	U	■	N	A	E	S	■
A	D	O	R	N	S	■	■	R	A	N	T	■	■	■
■	■	P	S	E	U	D	O	S	C	I	E	N	C	E
A	M	A	T	■	Z	I	P	I	T	■	D	O	O	S
N	O	P	E	■	I	R	E	N	E	■	P	L	A	T
G	O	A	D	■	E	E	L	E	D	■	G	O	L	D

68

G	A	M	M	A	■	S	P	E	E	D	■	S	P	A
A	M	O	U	R	■	N	I	E	C	E	■	T	A	N
L	O	O	S	E	C	A	N	N	O	N	■	O	U	T
A	S	T	I	■	A	F	T	■	■	I	D	O	L	S
■	■	■	C	A	S	U	A	L	F	R	I	D	A	Y
A	S	P	I	R	E	■	■	A	L	O	P	■	■	■
M	A	Y	A	N	■	D	E	M	O	■	■	E	M	U
B	U	R	N	O	N	E	S	B	R	I	D	G	E	S
I	L	E	■	■	A	L	P	S	■	R	I	O	T	S
■	■	■	D	I	S	H	■	■	N	A	S	S	E	R
C	A	P	U	C	H	I	N	M	O	N	K	■	■	■
E	X	U	D	E	■	■	O	O	P	■	E	R	O	S
L	I	L	■	T	V	D	E	T	E	C	T	I	V	E
L	A	S	■	E	C	O	L	E	■	A	T	T	I	C
O	L	E	■	A	R	E	S	T	■	W	E	E	D	Y

69

```
G A L O P S   S A S S   Y A M
I D O N O T   O U C H   O B I
S A W E D O F F S H O T G U N
    A C U R A   W R A I T H
I T S L A T E   B I E R
N I L   S L I P O N S H O E S
R E A L T Y   R O N   E R A T
A R L E S   S O S   H E D G E
G R O T   F A D   O O L A L A
S A M E O L D S O N G   I E D
    M U I R   D E C A N T S
E X C I T E   R E M A P
S O U N D S O F S I L E N C E
P X S   I B I D   L L A M A S
N O S   D Y E S   E S K I M O
```

70

```
T B A R S   I N O W   G I S T
S A R A H   S E L A   A S T O
O N E W A Y O R A N O T H E R
S K A   R E P O   N E S T L E
    I P S O   D A D   A E R
D E A D E N D J O B   O R S O
O R S I N O   O C E A N
T A H O E   R R S   N E N E S
    M R B I G   A A R O N S
P S I S   Y I E L D C U R V E
R U G   I F S   I M O N
E L N I N O   U L A N   Z O O
S T O P D R O P A N D R O L L
T A R A   C H O C   A I L E D
O N E D   E O N S   S N A G S
```

71

```
F E N C E   N A P S   I M U P
E N O R M   A L O T   C U B A
Z O W I E   V E R Y   K H A N
    M R N I C E G U Y A N A
H I P P I E   S I S   M G M
A R R   T O A T   A N E M I A
S M O K I N G B A N A N A
P A C E   H O P   I D I G
    O N E M A N B A N D A N A
P E L O S I   E S A U   L O B
A C H   S S N   B A S I N S
J O A N O F A R C A N A
A C R E   I G O R   C L E A R
M A U S   T A M E   E V A D E
A R M S   S T E W   D E T O X
```

72

```
P J S   S F P D   S O M B E R
R I O   I L I E   Q U A Y L E
O F F S T A G E   U N S E A T
    T H U M P   B I C   N I A
P O S Y   B E F O R E L O N G
E T H   S E N I O R   E W E S
W O O E R   S N E A D
    S E C O N D H E L P I N G
    A S O R E   E N I A C
A G A S   T O Y C A R   N I P
R I G H T F I E L D   S T L O
T A L   R O D   O R A T E
I N A N E R   T W O H A N D S
S T R E A M   U N I S   D E O
T S E T S E   E S T O   O W L
```

73

B	I	T	E		E	S	T	H		S	P	R	A	T
A	M	E	X		S	O	L	O		P	R	E	G	O
L	A	M	P		P	F	C	S		E	E	L	E	R
E	X	P	L	O	I	T		P	R	E	S	E	N	T
		O	M	E	G	A		O	D	E	T	T	E	
R	E	W	I	N	D		D	E	L	O	N			
A	M	A	T	I		I	D	Y	L		T	R	A	P
H	M	S		A	D	D	R	E	S	S		E	N	L
M	A	H	I		R	E	E	D		A	C	U	T	E
		N	C	A	A	S		E	L	O	P	E	D	
V	I	A	C	O	M		S	A	X	O	N			
I	N	C	E	N	S	E		C	O	N	S	O	L	E
G	L	A	N	D		D	O	I	T		O	V	E	R
G	E	S	S	O		A	U	D	I		L	A	S	T
O	T	T	E	R		M	I	S	C		E	L	S	E

74

P	O	E	M		H	U	S	H		S	P	I	E	L
A	L	A	I		A	R	I	A		P	I	N	K	O
P	E	R	K		M	I	L	L		A	N	G	E	L
	S	P	E	C	I	A	L	F	O	R	C	E	S	
		M	O	T	H		A	S	H					
A	R	E	Y	O	U		S	A	T	E		N	B	C
F	E	V	E	R	P	I	T	C	H		C	O	R	A
R	E	A	R	S		R	E	M		J	O	N	E	S
O	D	D	S		L	I	V	E	R	E	M	O	T	E
S	S	E		B	A	S	E		A	T	E	S	T	S
	S	R	I		G	I	L	A						
	S	A	T	U	R	D	A	Y	N	I	G	H	T	
H	U	N	A	N		E	B	R	O		A	I	R	S
A	R	T	I	E		A	L	O	U		I	D	E	A
H	E	I	D	I		R	E	S	T		N	E	E	D

75

P	O	N	D	E	R		D	A	N		G	E	N	S
P	R	I	O	R	I		A	L	E		A	B	E	T
P	U	P	P	E	T	S	H	O	W		M	O	R	E
	A	C	U	T	L	E	T	A	B	O	V	E		
A	R	T		T	A	Y			H	I	K	E	R	
L	O	O	S	E	L	E	A	F	L	E	T			
I	N	K	E	D		P	O	E	M		S	A	G	
E	D	E	N		P	A	R	E	D		W	A	G	E
N	O	N		M	I	N	I		S	H	I	R	E	
	R	I	N	G	L	E	T	T	O	N	E	S		
T	R	E	E	S		S	U	R		T	E	E		
E	A	V	E	S	D	R	O	P	L	E	T			
E	T	A	L		R	A	I	N	S	T	O	R	M	S
T	I	D	E		A	I	L		A	T	O	N	A	L
H	O	E	D		Y	D	S		N	O	T	A	R	Y

76

C	O	O	P	S		E	K	E	S		I	B	E	T
A	C	H	O	O		T	A	L	K		N	E	M	O
B	E	A	R	W	I	T	H	M	E		S	T	I	R
L	A	R	K		P	A	N	E	L		E	T	T	E
E	N	A	C	T	S		R	E	P	A	Y			
	H	O	O	T	S		T	O	M	B	O	Y		
A	M	N	O	T		E	P	S	O	M		O	N	A
L	O	O	P		B	R	O	W	N		D	O	C	K
E	T	S		C	L	A	R	A		W	I	P	E	S
S	H	E	R	P	A		E	P	S	O	N			
	D	A	R	C	Y		T	O	O	H	O	T		
F	A	I	R		K	O	A	L	A		S	O	L	O
L	I	V	E		S	U	G	A	R	D	A	D	D	Y
I	D	E	S		O	R	E	O		A	U	G	I	E
P	A	S	T		X	E	R	S		B	R	E	E	D

77

E	R	E	C	T		O	D	E	S			T	I	C	K
S	U	S	H	I		U	R	S	A			W	I	R	E
S	E	Q	U	E	N	T	I	A	L		I	N	O	N	
		T	R	A	D	E			O	R	S	O	N		
R	I	T	Z		B	O	R	D	E	R	L	I	N	E	
A	D	A	P	T	S		E	T	D		S	E	D		
T	O	R	A	H		I	N	A	N	E		T	R	Y	
		H	E	A	D	S	T	A	R	T					
Z	I	P		A	L	L	A	H		E	A	T	U	P	
A	D	E		T	O	E			E	D	M	O	N	D	
M	I	N	O	R	E	R	R	O	R		P	O	O	F	
B	A	D	G	E			E	V	I	T	A				
O	M	A	R		B	R	E	A	K	A	B	L	E	S	
N	I	N	E		L	A	S	T		C	A	I	R	O	
I	N	T	S		T	H	E	E		T	Y	P	E	D	

78

D	R	O	P		B	A	S	E	R		A	G	A	S	
R	A	V	E		A	C	C	R	A		E	L	L	A	
J	E	A	N	S	S	M	A	R	T		R	E	I	N	
			A	H	E	M		F	I	A	N	C	E		
D	O	G	G	I	E	S		V	I	N	T	N	E	R	
E	R	R	A	N	D		M	I	N	C	E	S			
L	E	A	P	T		W	O	N	K	A		C	H	I	
V	O	C	E		D	A	R	N	S		G	L	A	D	
E	S	E		G	U	T	S	Y		M	O	O	R	E	
		S	T	A	N	C	E		S	I	E	S	T	A	
I	P	S	W	I	C	H		P	O	S	S	E	S	S	
P	O	L	I	T	E		T	A	U	T					
O	D	I	N		C	H	I	C	S	Y	O	U	N	G	
D	I	C	E		A	I	M	E	E		A	S	I	A	
S	A	K	S		P	E	E	R	S		K	E	P	T	

79

B	I	L	B	O		B	M	O	C	S		A	M	A	
A	S	I	A	N		E	A	R	T	H		N	I	P	
B	U	T	T	E	R	F	L	Y	S	H	R	I	M	P	
A	Z	T		S	O	O	T			E	M	I	L		
R	U	L	E		C	R	A	W	L	S	P	A	C	E	
		E	R	A	S	E		E	A	T	A				
O	M	E	N	S		D	E	C	A	Y	I	N	G		
R	E	V		S	T	R	O	K	E	S		D	I	E	
I	R	A	N	I	A	N	S			I	R	E	N	E	
			O	S	S	A		R	E	S	I	N			
B	A	C	K	I	S	S	U	E	S		A	T	O	N	
A	G	R	I			N	A	T	O			I	P	O	
B	R	E	A	S	T	O	F	C	H	I	C	K	E	N	
Y	E	T		A	W	A	I	T		L	O	I	R	E	
S	E	E		P	A	R	T	S		S	E	T	A	T	

80

L	O	L	A		S	E	E	S	A	W		D	E	S	
I	M	A	C		S	T	R	O	K	E		A	L	L	
P	I	T	C	H	E	S	A	F	I	T		F	I	E	
O	T	E	R	I			S	A	T		O	O	Z	E	
		C	A	T	C	H	E	S	A	B	R	E	A	K	
G	O	O		S	H	E			S	O	N				
A	L	M	A		A	M	I	S		P	A	B	L	O	
F	I	E	L	D	S	A	Q	U	E	S	T	I	O	N	
F	O	R	M	A		N	S	E	C		E	G	G	Y	
			O	N	T			D	O	M		T	E	X	
B	A	T	S	A	N	E	Y	E	L	A	S	H			
R	I	O	T		O	L	E			M	A	R	I	A	
U	S	A		S	T	E	A	L	S	A	K	I	S	S	
I	L	S		H	E	N	R	Y	S		E	L	L	A	
N	E	T		A	S	A	S	E	T		S	L	A	P	

81

C	A	W	S		W	O	O	L		B	I	P	E	D
A	S	I	T		I	N	K	Y		U	T	E	R	O
R	I	F	E		N	O	R	M		S	E	A	R	S
P	A	I	R	A	G	R	A	P	H	S		R	O	E
			E	N	S			H	I	T	H	A	R	D
H	O	P	O	N	P	O	P		D	O	O	M		
O	R	E		S	A	T	I	N		P	L	O	W	S
C	A	R	B		N	O	P	A	R		D	U	A	L
K	N	E	A	D		S	E	P	I	A		N	N	E
	A	R	R	S		D	E	P	L	E	T	E	D	
S	A	M	B	A	E	D		A	P	U				
P	L	O		P	A	R	E	A	P	H	R	A	S	E
A	C	U	T	E		A	D	D	A		O	K	A	Y
C	O	R	E	R		M	E	I	R		P	I	N	E
E	A	S	E	S		A	N	A	T		E	N	D	S

82

S	E	T	U	P		S	A	P	O	R		E	T	E
A	D	O	R	E		N	U	R	S	E		C	O	L
F	I	R	S	T	L	A	D	I	E	S		O	N	O
E	T	N	A		E	P	I	C			F	L	I	P
			S	T	A	T	E	P	O	L	I	C	E	
	E	L	D	E	S	T		T	A	R	O			
S	L	O	O	P		H	A	N	G	O	V	E	R	
H	E	R	O		M	O	O	G	S		R	A	V	E
O	V	E	R	H	A	N	G			S	I	N	E	W
			D	I	C	E		L	E	T	T	E	R	
P	O	L	I	C	E	S	T	A	T	E				
E	R	I	E			I	R	M	A		L	O	I	S
T	A	N		L	A	D	I	E	S	F	I	R	S	T
A	T	E		A	B	E	T	S		E	S	T	E	E
L	E	S		C	A	D	E	T		U	P	S	E	T

83

P	E	R	U		D	R	A	G		U	N	C	A	P
C	R	O	P		I	O	N	E		N	E	H	R	U
S	A	Y	B	Y	E	B	Y	E		D	W	E	L	L
		R	O	O	T	S		S	S	E		R	E	L
P	R	O	W	L	S		N	E	A	R	M	I	S	S
L	O	G		K	O	K	O		C	P	U			
E	L	E	V		D	O	T	E		A	S	S	E	S
A	F	R	I	C	A	N	A	M	E	R	I	C	A	N
D	E	S	T	E		A	S	I	P		C	O	R	E
			A	R	M		T	R	I	M		O	L	E
A	P	P	L	E	P	I	E		T	A	M	P	E	R
F	R	O		M	S	N		K	O	R	A	N		
L	I	N	G	O		D	O	N	M	C	L	E	A	N
A	D	D	O	N		I	D	E	E		E	C	H	O
T	E	S	T	Y		A	D	E	S		S	K	A	T

84

S	L	A	M		B	A	M	A		G	A	I	N	
C	A	P	O		S	A	L	O	N		O	N	T	O
O	M	A	N		A	L	E	R	T		A	J	A	R
T	E	C	T	O	N	I	C	P	L	A	T	E		
I	N	H	E	R	E			H	E	R		L	O	P
A	T	E		A	L	T	A		R	E	S	I	D	E
			F	L	Y	I	N	G	S	A	U	C	E	R
A	L	O	E			E	G	O		M	A	S	T	
F	I	F	A	W	O	R	L	D	C	U	P			
R	A	F	T	E	D		E	S	A	S		C	H	I
O	R	S		A	D	S			P	E	A	H	E	N
		H	O	L	L	Y	W	O	O	D	B	O	W	L
F	L	O	P		O	R	I	O	N		O	K	I	E
D	A	R	E		T	I	T	H	E		V	E	N	T
A	X	E	D		S	A	S	S			E	R	G	S

85

J	A	N	E	T	S				L	A	B	R	A	T
I	N	A	H	E	A	P		F	E	B	R	E	Z	E
M	A	R	S	A	L	A		A	P	R	O	P	O	S
			S	T	P		K	E	A					
P	S	S	T		S	A	B	E	R		M	G	M	T
A	H	Y	E	S		D	A	D		M	A	Y	E	R
J	U	N	C	T	I	O	N		S	I	E	R	R	A
A	T	E		J	A	C	K	S	O	N		A	I	G
M	O	R	M	O	N		J	U	L	I	E	T	T	E
A	U	G	I	E		J	O	N		S	T	E	E	D
S	T	Y	X		C	O	B	R	A		E	D	D	Y
			N	O	N		O	R	E					
S	E	P	H	O	R	A		O	C	T	O	M	O	M
N	O	V	O	T	E	S		F	E	R	T	I	L	E
L	E	C	T	E	R			D	E	C	L	A	W	

86

U	M	P	S		O	H	A	R	A		M	Y	R	A
S	I	R	E		A	M	B	E	R		P	E	E	P
U	S	E	D		F	O	S	T	E	R	H	O	M	E
R	E	M	A	P			E	A	U		M	A	X	
P	R	I	N	C	I	P	A	L		S	C	A	R	E
E	L	S		S	T	I	L	L		S	I	N	K	S
D	Y	E	S		S	N	L		A	I	R			
		S	U	M	M	E	R	P	L	A	C	E		
			P	I	E		I	I	I		A	L	E	S
W	I	R	E	S		M	S	N	B	C		O	N	E
I	N	E	R	T		R	E	S	I	D	E	N	C	E
I	S	P		E	S	T			S	A	G	A	S	
F	I	E	L	D	H	O	U	S	E		T	A	R	O
I	D	L	E		O	A	S	I	S		E	T	T	U
T	E	S	T		O	D	O	R	S		N	E	A	T

87

M	I	M	I	C		M	U	S	T		S	H	I	P
E	V	I	T	A		O	S	H	A		P	I	S	A
M	A	K	E	R	B	R	E	A	K		A	T	T	U
O	N	E	M	O	R	E		G	E	R	I	T	O	L
			M	E	L	T		S	A	N	E			
F	I	B	B	E	R		R	I	O	T		R	H	O
A	L	O	U	D		G	E	N	U	S		M	A	N
L	I	O	N		S	L	A	N	T		D	I	R	K
C	A	M		S	T	U	D	S		P	O	S	S	E
O	D	E		C	A	M	O		S	L	O	S	H	Y
		R	O	O	T		N	A	P	A				
R	E	B	A	T	E	S		M	U	S	T	A	R	D
A	B	U	T		L	O	V	E	R	M	O	N	E	Y
G	O	S	H		A	L	A	N		A	B	O	D	E
A	N	T	S		W	E	L	D		S	Y	N	O	D

88

B	A	L	M		M	A	T	E		B	O	W	I	E
A	L	O	E		A	V	I	D		A	D	H	O	C
B	O	O	M	E	R	A	N	G		D	E	A	T	H
E	F	F	O	R	T		T	E	A	K		M	A	O
S	T	A	R	L	I	T		S	P	A	S	M		
			Y	E	A	R	S		P	R	A	Y	T	O
T	A	B		N	A	P	E		M	A	B	E	L	
S	T	A	R	T	S	W	I	T	H	A	B	A	N	G
A	R	M	O	R		L	E	T	O			R	D	A
R	A	B	I	E	S		L	A	T	C	H			
		O	L	S	E	N		S	T	R	A	N	G	E
E	M	O		P	E	E	R		O	U	I	O	U	I
P	I	Z	Z	A		P	O	W	D	E	R	K	E	G
I	S	L	E	S		A	M	I	D		D	I	S	H
C	O	E	N	S		L	A	Z	Y		O	A	S	T

89

```
R A L L Y . P A P A . B E A R
A V O I D . R I O T . A N N A
T O R E S T O R E S A N I T Y
S I R S . O M B . T R A D E S
. R E T R O . A L U M . . .
. . O A F . L A D Y L U C K
N B A . T A I L S . A R E A
C O L B E R T . S T E W A R T
A R T E . S T O R M . L A Y
A N A T H E M A . E M B . .
. . A L E G . M A R C H
S T A N Z A . T W O . I H O P
T O K E E P F E A R A L I V E
A R I A . S E A R . A L T E R
B E N T . E M M Y . R O A R K
```

90

```
S T O I C . P I N U P . K F C
S W I R L . A N D R E . E R E
W A L K I N G C A N E . Y I N
. . S Q U E A K . P A B S T
S P R O U T S . S H E I K S
T H A M E S . F A V O R S .
A L I E . A R P E L . C O G
L O S . C O C A I N E . A G O
L X I . O R A N G . B Y R D
. N I M I T Z . B O R N E O
R A G T A G . D O P I E S T
E X C O N . S T O N E S .
A L A . C I T I Z E N K A N E
P E I . H A U T E . E L D E R
S S N . E N D O N . R Y D E R
```

91

```
B B S . I B M P C . A T O M
E L O . R A T I O . M A K O
D U D E R A N C H . B R O W
E T O N . . K O D I A K S
W H I T E R U S S I A N .
. . S K I S . T A N T E S
A R I . C E E S . C I A O
P A R D O N M Y F R E N C H
O B O E . E N D O . O H O
P E N P A L . C I N Q .
. J U L I U S C A E S A R
A L A T E E N . . I A G O
K I W I . D R E S S I N G S
I D E E . T E V Y E . D I E
N O D S . O P A R T . Y E S
```

92

```
A R C . A L A M O . J E A N S
R I O . R E S I N . O W L E T
A T L . S E I Z E T H E D A Y
B A D G E . S E D A N . A P E
. W A N T . G U S T . .
G R A B A B I T E T O E A T
O E R . L A C E . N A T A L
S L E W . R E A P S . M A M A
H I R E S . S E A L . L P N
. C A P T U R E T H E F L A G
. T A T E . L A I C
S P A . S E D E R . D R O V E
C A T C H P H R A S E . S I X
A G R E E . O S K A R . T A P
M E A L S . T E E N S . S L O
```

93

```
H E P   ·   S I M P   ·   T E R P S
A M I   ·   G E M M A   ·   I D I O T
D I E S E L O I L   ·   P I C K Y
J R R T O L K I E N S T H E
·   I L S A   ·   E Y E
M A L L   T Y C H O   D R E D
S T E T H O   L A N D   E L I
N O T S O   H O W   E G E S T
B O G   S E W N   B R A V O S
C L O P   B Y E A R   R E L Y
·   Y A R   ·   T E E M
·   L O R D O F T H E R I N G S
P U R I M   A M A Z O N A N T
D A N T E   V A N E S   D A Y
Q U E E N   A N D S   A W E
```

94

```
A R F A R F   A S S   I N R E
B U R G E R   E L O   C O O L
A S I A G O   R O D   E R O S
S T E T S   R O T O   C A K E
E S S E   K A S H M I R
·   S T E N O S   R E T R O
R O O   R A I L   S O A R E D
O I L P A N S   M A N M A D E
I N L O V E   D E L I   Y O S
S K A T E   D E T A C H
·   A L A R M E D   A B L E
M E A T   D I O R   C L E A R
A L T O   O F T   N O V A T O
S L O E   R T E   F R A N K S
H A M S   E S S   L E S S E E
```

95

```
I N F E R   S C O F F   O W E
R O U S E   M O V I E   P O M
M E N T A L I M A G E   T O M
A L D O   O R A L   D A I L Y
·   N I C K S   P O B O Y S
G O F I S H   L I N E N
O N E A L   S P I N   P S U
T U R N E D T H E T A B L E S
H S T   D A I S   G E A R S
·   I D T A G   B R E Y E R
S A L A R Y   P I L A F
P R I M O   D I N O   S A G A
A D Z   O C E A N B O T T O M
D O E   P L A N E   D E N T E
E R R   S E N O R   S W O O N
```

96

```
M A T S   M E S A S   A G E S
A T R A   A L E R T   R O T E
S E A N   D E W A R   L I S A
C A N A D I A N B A C O N
O S C A R S   S N L   G A T
T E E   N O S H   G A D F L Y
·   M O N T E R E Y J A C K
C O M A   E R A   E R S E
I T A L I A N B R E A D
T I M I N G   S E R F   S P F
E S A   N I C   N A S C A R
·   B O S T O N L E T T U C E
R U E D   A R I E S   E L K S
A T A D   T O L E T   A L E C
H E R S   O T E R O   K Y R A
```

97

I	N	C	A		B	A	R	D		E	F	L	A	T
N	O	E	L		I	S	A	Y		J	O	Y	C	E
F	U	L	L	H	O	U	S	E		E	U	R	O	S
O	S	T	E	O			P	I	T	C	R	E	W	S
		G	W	E	N		N	O	T	A				
T	H	R	E	E	K	I	N	G	S		C	H	U	M
R	O	O		L	E	N	O		S	M	E	A	R	Y
A	S	S	T	S		O	W	S		A	S	I	G	N
P	E	E	W	E	E		A	W	A	Y		K	E	A
P	A	S	O		R	O	Y	A	L	F	L	U	S	H
		P	A	I	N		B	E	A	U				
I	T	S	A	D	E	A	L		I	T	I	S	I	
R	A	P	I	D		P	O	K	E	R	H	A	N	D
E	X	E	R	T		A	L	E	X		E	G	A	L
D	I	D	S	O		R	A	N	T		R	O	P	E

98

I	D	L	E		B	O	S	H			N	O	A	H
R	E	A	D		E	X	P	O		G	E	N	R	E
A	L	B	S		L	E	A	P		E	W	E	R	S
Q	U	E	E	N	A	N	N	E	S	L	A	C	E	
W	I	L	L	I			I	S	P		G	O	S	S
A	S	E		K	I	S	S	O	F	D	E	A	T	H
R	E	D	S		D	O	H		A	N	T	S	Y	
		H	E	A	D		B	A	N	D				
F	O	C	A	L		S	O	Y		A	C	C	T	
T	R	A	F	F	I	C	C	O	N	E		H	A	I
D	A	R	T		S	O	U		R	E	A	L	M	
	C	R	E	A	M	O	F	T	H	E	C	R	O	P
S	L	E	D	S		P	F	U	I		A	G	R	A
H	E	R	B	S		E	L	B	E		R	E	I	N
O	S	A	Y		R	E	E	D		D	R	E	I	

99

C	A	L	F		A	R	O	D		B	E	G	I	N
O	R	A	L		N	I	C	E		A	M	A	Z	E
A	L	M	A		Y	V	E	S		R	O	T	O	R
T	O	P	S	T	H	E	L	I	S	T		O	D	D
		K	Y	O	T	O		T	A	D				
D	O	C		P	O	S	T	N	O	B	I	L	L	S
I	N	U	S	E		S	E	M		P	E	A	S	
S	T	O	P	O	F	F		O	P	T	S	O	U	T
K	A	M	A		R	U	R		H	O	N	D	A	
S	P	O	T	R	E	M	O	V	E	R		E	E	R
		S	A	D		S	I	N	U	S				
J	A	G		P	O	T	S	O	F	M	O	N	E	Y
E	Q	U	I	P		S	I	L	O		C	O	R	E
S	U	A	V	E		A	N	I	L		A	V	O	W
T	A	M	E	R		R	I	N	D		L	A	S	S

100

C	A	J	U	N		L	I	P		P	A	S	T	
O	R	A	T	E		A	M	A		A	C	M	E	S
L	I	K	E	D		S	H	I	P	S	H	A	P	E
E	D	E	N		P	E	E	R	A	T		R	E	A
		S	H	A	R	P	S	H	O	O	T	E	R	
A	R	T	I	E	S			R	A	M				
S	H	E	L	L	S	H	O	C	K		F	O	B	S
C	E	L		P	A	R	T	I	I	I		N	E	A
H	A	L	T		S	H	O	R	T	S	H	E	E	T
		M	O	O				E	L	A	Y	N	E	
S	H	E	E	P	S	H	E	A	R	E	R			
Y	A	M		T	H	O	R	N	S		D	A	Z	E
S	H	O	E	S	H	I	N	E		S	H	R	E	W
T	A	R	S	I		S	I	R		S	A	C	R	E
	S	E	E	N		T	E	A		E	T	H	O	S

101

I	R	A	Q		M	A	P	L	E		R	I	N	K
N	A	N	U		I	W	I	L	L		O	M	A	N
C	H	I	E	F	T	E	X	A	N		A	P	S	E
	M	E	E	T		M	I	S	D	E	A	L		
S	T	A	G	E		G	I	A	N	T	B	I	L	L
E	A	T		L	A	U	D		O	I	L			
R	B	I	S		B	I	O	S		L	O	C	O	S
F	O	O	T	B	A	L	L	M	A	T	C	H	U	P
S	O	N	A	R		T	I	E	R		K	A	T	E
	G	Y	M		Z	A	C	H		M	I	A		
J	E	T	P	A	C	K	E	R		U	P	P	E	R
A	R	R	A	N	G	E		P	L	E	A			
R	O	A	R		R	A	M	C	H	A	R	G	E	R
E	D	I	T		A	C	R	I	D		I	N	F	O
D	E	N	Y		W	H	I	G	S		L	E	G	O

102

J	E	T	S		R	I	S	E	N		M	A	P
A	T	O	P		R	E	T	I	N	A		I	L	L
N	E	T	E	A	R	N	I	N	G	S		N	B	A
	E	S	S	E	N		S	L	E	E	T		
S	C	U	D	S		W	A	S	T	E	A	R	E	A
C	A	S	S	I	O		H	O	R	N			
A	D	O		G	R	A	D	E	R		A	S	A	P
D	E	F	I	N	I	T	E	A	R	T	I	C	L	E
S	T	A	N		O	S	I	R	I	S		U	L	T
	I	S	L	E		D	E	B	B	I	E		
W	Y	A	T	T	E	A	R	P		T	R	A	N	S
H	E	S	S	E		E	R	A	S	E			
E	L	K		P	L	A	N	E	T	E	A	R	T	H
A	L	E		P	O	M	E	L	O		S	U	R	E
T	O	W		E	X	P	E	L		T	E	A	R

103

M	O	R	A	L		P	E	W		C	H	E	S	S
E	L	O	P	E		O	D	E		L	E	G	A	L
S	E	L	E	S		W	I	L	L	I	N	G	L	Y
H	O	L	D	T	H	E	F	L	O	O	R		
	A	U	R	I	S	T		Y	E	A			
	H	I	T	T	H	E	C	E	I	L	I	N	G
M	I	N	E		D	E	T	O	X		R	E	T
O	T	H	E	R	S		N	I	K	O	N	S	
P	E	A		P	O	S	S	E		A	L	T	O
	C	L	I	M	B	T	H	E	W	A	L	L	S
	H	E	C		B	E	A	R	E	R			
	E	X	E	R	C	I	S	E	R	O	O	M	
S	U	N	S	T	R	O	K	E		N	O	R	M	A
O	N	A	I	R		I	L	S		A	T	E	A	T
D	O	N	N	A		D	E	T		S	H	O	N	E

104

L	E	A	P		M	C	C	O	O		R	E	S	T
O	S	L	O		A	R	A	I	L		O	T	T	O
C	A	T	S	C	R	A	D	L	E		T	H	A	I
H	U	S	T	L	I	N	G		Q	U	I	L	L
	M	O	N	K	E	Y	S	U	N	C	L	E	
M	R	H	A	N	E	Y		A	T	A	D		
B	E	E	N	E		A	D	A		A	F	A	R
A	M	A		D	O	G	S	A	G	E		A	C	E
S	O	L	O		Z	A	P		Z	A	I	R	E
	S	E	M	I		U	M	P	I	R	E	D	
E	L	E	P	H	A	N	T	S	E	A	R		
P	E	A	R	S		R	E	A	S	S	I	G	N
S	O	R	E		L	I	O	N	S	S	H	A	R	E
O	N	L	Y		A	R	I	E	L		O	G	O	D
M	E	S	S		P	A	S	T	Y		W	O	W	S

105

R	E	A	C	T		O	P	T	E	D		T	I	N
A	L	L	A	H		L	L	A	N	O		H	B	O
P	L	A	N	E	B	O	A	R	D	S		I	S	M
T	E	N		K	E	R	N		A	S	S	E	S	
		M	I	N	D	B	L	O	G	G	I	N	G	
S	E	C	A	N	T		O	D	E	T	S			
P	L	A	N	K		E	R	E	I		T	B	A	
C	H	R	I	S	T	M	A	S	C	L	A	R	O	S
A	I	R		Y	E	N	S		A	M	U	S	E	
	Y	E	A	R	N		I	C	I	E	S	T		
B	L	O	T	T	E	D	W	A	T	E	R			
L	A	N	C	E		I	T	A	R		I	L	E	
O	R	B		A	D	A	M	S	L	A	N	D	E	R
O	V	A		S	N	A	P	E		T	I	L	E	S
M	A	G		E	A	S	Y	A		E	X	E	R	T

106

B	A	T	M	A	N		R	P	M		S	E	E	
A	R	O	U	S	E		A	E	R	O		T	A	X
B	E	N	C	H	W	A	R	M	E	R		A	T	A
S	A	S	H		S	C	A	L	A		L	I	L	
		C	A	S	H	P	A	Y	M	E	N	T		
S	T	O	P	U	P		T	S	E					
M	I	L	L	E	R	L	I	T	E		R	A	R	E
U	N	D	I	D		E	R	E		U	M	I	A	K
T	E	E	N		R	I	V	E	R	S	E	D	G	E
		T	O	E		T	E	N	S	E	S			
N	A	S	H	R	A	M	B	L	E	R				
I	Z	E		C	R	E	E	P		W	O	K	E	
P	U	T		H	E	R	E	S	J	O	H	N	N	Y
P	R	O		I	N	I	T		E	D	I	T	O	R
Y	E	N		D	D	T		D	E	M	O	T	E	

107

S	H	E	L	F		S	G	T		S	N	A	R	E
L	E	V	E	L		P	O	E		T	O	N	E	S
A	R	E	N	A		O	W	E		A	S	I	D	E
M	A	R	A	T	H	O	N	M	I	N	I			
		T	A	N	S		S	C	R	A	M	S		
S	C	A	R	E	D		E	T	E		V	I	E	
M	A	R	I	N	E	S	U	B		S	M	I	L	E
E	N	C	L		S	A	R	A	N		C	A	E	N
A	A	H	E	D		F	I	N	E	E	X	T	R	A
R	P	I		I	S	E		H	A	L	E	S	T	
S	E	E	S	A	W		F	O	R	T				
		P	R	E	C	I	O	U	S	S	E	M	I	
A	T	A	R	I		A	R	M		O	I	L	E	D
M	O	V	I	E		I	S	P		U	T	I	L	E
S	T	A	G	S		N	T	H		T	E	S	T	S

108

G	A	M	E		S	C	R	A	P		L	E	M	S
A	V	O	N		P	I	E	T	A		S	M	E	E
S	O	U	R	G	R	A	P	E	S		D	E	L	A
	C	R	O	N	Y		R	U	S	H		R	I	B
M	A	N	N	A		T	O	P	B	A	N	A	N	A
O	D	E		W	A	H		Y	I	E	L	D	S	
S	O	D	A		L	O	O	T		T	A	D	A	S
		B	E	A	R	F	R	U	I	T				
A	B	H	O	R		N	A	E	S		O	O	H	S
T	R	A	V	I	S		S	A	G		N	O	T	
L	E	M	O	N	L	A	W	S		O	C	A	L	A
A	W	S		S	A	S	H		B	R	A	D	Y	
R	E	T	D		C	H	E	R	R	Y	P	I	C	K
G	R	E	Y		K	O	R	E	A		O	M	O	O
E	Y	R	E		S	T	E	A	M		S	E	W	S

109

S	C	O	F	F		T	B	A	R		S	L	O	W
A	U	D	I	O		R	I	T	A		K	E	P	I
S	T	O	R	E	D	E	T	E	C	T	I	V	E	S
H	E	R	E		A	V	E		I	O	D	I	N	E
		D	R	N	O		S	E	E					
S	N	A	R	E	D	R	U	M	S		D	U	M	A
W	A	R	I	L	Y		B	U	T		A	S	I	N
E	V	I	L	S		F	O	G		B	R	I	N	K
D	E	A	L		P	E	A		C	L	E	N	C	H
E	L	L	S		O	U	T	E	R	E	D	G	E	S
			R	E	D		L	O	D	E				
A	F	L	O	A	T		P	I	C		V	I	S	A
T	E	A	C	H	E	R	E	D	I	T	I	O	N	S
I	T	C	H		S	O	R	E		A	L	L	A	H
T	E	E	S		S	T	U	D		O	S	A	G	E

110

W	A	V	E	R		J	A	M	S		B	A	S	H
E	C	O	L	I		E	M	I	R		O	M	O	O
B	R	I	D	G	E	T	O	N	O	W	H	E	R	E
B	E	D	E		D	L	I	I		H	E	X	E	D
				R	H	E	A		S	T	E	M		
F	I	L	L	I	N	G	S	T	A	T	I	O	N
O	B	E	Y	S			W	E	D		A	T	O	N
G	M	C		S	A	H	A	R	A	N		T	R	E
S	P	A	N		N	A	M		A	T	O	M	S
	C	R	O	W	N	V	I	C	T	O	R	I	A	S
			T	H	E	E		O	A	H	U			
A	G	G	I	E		A	P	E	X		M	B	A	S
B	R	A	C	E	S	F	O	R	I	M	P	A	C	T
B	A	L	E		W	I	S	C		A	E	T	N	A
A	B	E	D		E	T	T	E		E	T	H	E	R

111

L	O	B	E		A	P	P	T		A	R	B	Y	S
O	K	R	A		P	A	A	R		H	E	R	O	N
C	O	O	T	I	E	P	I	E		A	L	O	H	A
A	K	I	S	S		A	R	E	S		I	N	O	R
		L	A	R	R	Y		A	M	E	C	H	E
A	F	E	W		F	A	M	I	L	Y	F	O	O	D
B	A	R	A	C	K		A	M	E	N				
E	A	S	Y	A		O	M	S		A	S	S	E	T
			S	C	A	B		A	S	T	E	R	S
F	O	S	S	I	L	F	O	O	L		A	R	G	O
A	H	C	H	O	O		P	A	I	G	E			
T	S	A	R		G	A	S	P		V	E	N	T	I
C	U	R	E	D		B	O	O	T	Y	M	A	R	K
A	R	E	W	E		B	A	S	E		O	D	I	E
T	E	D	D	Y		A	P	E	X		M	E	G	A

112

S	O	L	I	D		P	O	M	E		B	I	K	E
S	P	A	R	E		E	L	A	L		U	S	E	S
R	E	N	E	W		R	A	C	E		D	E	E	P
	C	A	N	I	B	U	Y	A	V	O	W	E	L
			E	T	A		W	A	K	E				
A	R	G		T	R	A	P		T	A	I	C	H	I
M	E	R	C		S	U	R	V	E	Y	S	A	Y	S
I	C	A	H	N		L	E	O		S	E	P	A	L
C	O	M	E	O	N	D	O	W	N		R	O	T	E
I	N	M	A	T	E		P	S	A	T		S	T	S
			T	I	V	O		T	H	O				
	T	H	E	P	A	S	S	W	O	R	D	I	S
B	E	A	D		D	A	L	I		E	E	R	I	E
O	R	Z	O		A	K	I	N		E	T	A	T	S
X	M	E	N		N	A	M	E		D	O	N	U	T

113

```
A C M E   A S P E R   S S N S
T R A M   D O L E D   O T O E
B I N O C U L A R S   B A M A
A T A   R E I N   D I G I T
T I N G E   D E T E R G E N T
S C A R A B S   E S E   M A L
    A S I   A C T   C O T E
  N A M E O F T H E G A M E
B O T S   L A M   E A U
A S T   P A Z   S M U S H E S
H E A R T B E A T   G E E S E
A D I O S   R A Z E   L A D
M I N I   Q U E S A D I L L A
E V E L   B R A I N   A N E T
N E D S   S I S S Y   N O N E
```

114

```
H U N G   A T A L E   H I E D
O L E O   B O G E Y   T O F U
O N E R   A T O N E   T W O S
P A R E N T   B A L L P A R K
      D A T A   S E E
S T P   C O L O   T E S T E D
T R A S H I E S T   H O S E
P A R F O R T H E C O U R S E
A L E C   A E R O M E T E R
T A R S A L   A I D A   S S E
      L O C   S I N S
P A R A B O L A   F I E S T A
O N E S   M E R C I   P A R D
U K E S   E A G L E   T W O D
R A F T   D R O I D   S S T S
```

115

```
B O T H   M I N T   E S Q U E
A T R A   I D E A   V A U N T
C O U N T D O W N   A L I C E
H E S S I A N   S A D I E
  S T O P I T   D E N T E D
  L T R   T A O   A T N O
T A B O O   S I L L   S I G N
I R A   P A C E O F F   M E N
D I C E   D A R T   A D E L E
A S K S   H R S   T R E
L E T S G O   S E R B I A
  R E A C H   N E A T N I K
P L A N T   O P E N H O U S E
B O C C E   L A R S   R I L E
J O K E S   A R T Y   S T E P
```

116

```
R A M I S   S T E E L   K A T
A L A C K   N O W A Y   W O E
P I C K Y E A T E R S   I N N
I N A Y E A R   S M O C K E D
D E W   S E W   A L O E
  S S T   H U R   O M S K
J A V A N   R I C K I L A K E
A V I L A   E N L   A C R E D
W I K I P E D I A   M A T E S
S A K E   M S N   F A T
  I N R E   G R O   M R E
L E C T E R N   E X C L A I M
E R A   M I C K E Y M O U S E
A I R   E T A I L   O G D E N
H E R   T A R T S   N O E N D
```

117

```
L I S A   H E A R   A P A R T
O N C E   E L L E   T Y L E R
S A U R   L I E S   T R A C E
S P L I T D E C I S I O N
E E L E R     N H L   A C E
S T Y   E A R S   H A L L O W
    B A S I C S   A D Z E
D I V I D E D H I G H W A Y S
E G A D   S M O R E S
C O G E N T   O N O N   P O R
I R A   O E D   N I O B E
  B R O K E N H E A R T E D
S T O A S   R A I L   W A Y S
T E N S E   M E G S   I S E E
E D D A S   A S H E   N H R A
```

118

```
M B A S   M E G A   S E X Y
E U R O   A S O F   S A C R O
S T O L E N C A R   C L O A K
A T W O R K   D I C E   L Y E
    N I L   C O N F E S S
B O I L I N G W A T E R
A G R E E D T O   Y I E L D S
G R O G   H O T   S U C K
S E N A T E   D E L I C A C Y
  T A B A S C O S A U C E
P A L O M A R   S N L
L U I   A Y E S   D E A R M E
A D V I L   T H I R D R A I L
N I E C E   H I K E   N I C K
B O D Y   A P E S   O N E S
```

119

```
P S A T   C A V A   U P S E T
H E M I   O D E S   P L A Y A
I M A M   R O T O   T A X E D
L I S B O N B O N B O N
E S S E N C E   A P E M A N
  R O O   G E T A   E L O
S O B E R B E R B E R   D E M
T H A D   T O A   I O T A
A B S   I N C A N C A N C A N
H O I   C A H N   H U T
L Y C E E S   S A T I A T E
  B O T T O M T O M T O M
L T G O V   U N I T   A T O M
A S O N E   B Y T E   T A L E
S A T Y R   A X E L   E R S T
```

120

```
D O R M   D A D A   E N D O W
E D I E   O P A L   M I A M I
M I N D I N T H E G U T T E R
I N D I R A   L S U   W A N E
  C O L D   S K I
H A N D I N T H E T I L L
S C A R Y   R O U E N   C I A
E L S E   S E R F S   G I N S
L E T   D E C A F   T R E K S
F O O T I N T H E D O O R
  O D D   T O W S
C A M P   O A T   T E S T E E
H E A D I N T H E C L O U D S
A R D O R   M A Y O   U N I T
D O D G E   S T E M   T A T A
```

121

G	R	A	N		B	A	S	S		S	A	P	P	Y
R	I	M	E		O	C	T	A		C	U	R	E	D
I	D	I	G		L	A	O	S		I	D	E	A	S
M	E	T	A	M	O	R	P	H	O	S	I	S		
M	A	Y	T	A	G		S	A	C	S		I	N	A
			E	I	N	S			H	O	T	D	O	G
E	O	S		M	A	T	E	F	O	R	L	I	F	E
A	L	P	E			E	X	E			C	O	E	N
T	E	A	M	C	A	P	T	A	I	N		S	E	T
A	O	R	T	A	S			R	T	E	S			
T	S	K		B	E	L	A		S	E	A	R	C	H
	P	R	O	C	E	S	S	E	D	M	E	A	T	
F	O	L	I	O		N	C	A	A		P	A	N	E
L	O	U	T	S		D	O	N	S		A	D	O	S
O	H	G	E	E		S	T	A	Y		N	Y	E	T

122

A	L	E	C		F	A	R	S	I		A	M	P	S
M	A	Y	O		O	L	E	O	S		N	O	A	H
O	V	E	N		O	L	D	H	I	C	K	O	R	Y
N	E	W	C	A	L	E	D	O	N	I	A			
G	R	E	E	T	S					T	R	O	V	E
S	N	A	R	E		T	S	E		R	A	D	I	O
T	E	R	N		G	H	E	T	T	O		D	A	N
			S	O	M	E	T	H	I	N	G			
A	S	S		R	A	M	O	N	E		E	S	A	I
P	A	P	U	A		E	N	O		S	M	E	L	L
E	G	Y	P	T					D	I	S	M	A	L
			B	O	R	R	O	W	E	D	T	I	M	E
B	L	U	E	R	I	B	B	O	N		O	N	E	G
R	O	S	A		P	I	L	O	T		N	A	D	A
A	B	E	T		A	S	A	L	E		E	L	A	L

123

M	A	R	N	I		D	P	S			B	E	T	A
A	G	A	I	N		O	I	L	O	F	O	L	A	Y
D	O	N	N	A		F	L	I	P	A	C	O	I	N
O	R	D	E	R	O	F	O	M	E	G	A			
F	A	R	R	A	R		T	E	R	I		B	A	M
F	E	Y		B	I	B			A	N	K	A	R	A
			T	I	E	R	O	D			C	C	I	X
	O	R	A	C	L	E	O	F	O	M	A	H	A	
A	L	O	T			R	O	C	K	E	R			
R	A	T	E	D	R			S	E	G		A	B	O
E	V	E		W	A	S	P		M	A	I	L	E	D
		O	A	T	H	O	F	O	F	F	I	C	E	
I	N	E	B	R	I	A	T	E		L	A	C	K	S
O	N	E	O	F	O	U	R	S		O	L	I	O	S
S	W	E	E			N	O	T		P	L	A	N	A

124

N	E	W	Y	O	R	K		F	L	O	R	I	D	A
E	P	H	E	D	R	A		A	E	R	O	S	O	L
V	I	O	L	I	S	T		L	A	S	C	A	L	A
A	T	O	L	L		F	A	R	O		D	O	B	
D	A	P		E	V	E	R	L	Y		B	O	R	A
A	P	E	S		I	D	E	A		R	O	R	E	M
	H	D	T	V	S	E	T		T	E	R	E	S	A
			A	E	O	N		J	O	A	D			
W	R	I	T	E	R		S	U	N	L	E	S	S	
Y	E	S	E	S		H	E	A	T		R	I	A	A
O	T	O	S		N	O	W	N	O	W		C	M	L
M	I	L		S	I	T	S			I	T	I	N	A
I	N	A	C	A	S	T		D	E	D	A	L	U	S
N	U	T	T	R	E	E		I	C	E	R	I	N	K
G	E	O	R	G	I	A		M	O	N	T	A	N	A

125

T	E	N	T	S		J	A	M	A		S	O	B	
S	P	O	O	K		A	L	A	S		A	L	E	K
P	E	T	R	I		S	U	D	S		F	A	T	E
S	E	V	E	N	C	O	M	E	E	L	E	V	E	N
			A	L	A	N			R	E	A			
N	A	N	T	E	S		P	E	T	E	R	S	O	N
A	P	E		S	H	A	R	E	S		E	A	S	E
C	R	A	P	S		L	O	O		T	A	B	L	E
R	O	T	A		B	O	X	C	A	R		L	E	D
E	N	O	R	M	I	T	Y		T	I	M	E	R	S
			A	I	G			A	H	S	O			
O	N	A	L	O	S	I	N	G	S	T	R	E	A	K
N	E	L	L		H	O	S	E		R	A	N	T	O
E	A	V	E		O	W	E	N		A	L	V	I	N
	P	A	L		T	A	C	T		M	E	S	T	A

126

A	C	E	D		A	R	E	N	A		T	O	B	Y
M	A	C	E		P	O	W	E	R		I	S	E	E
O	R	A	N	G	E	Z	E	U	S		M	T	N	S
C	O	R	T	E	X			R	O	G	E	R		
O	L	D	E	N		P	H	O	N	E	Z	A	C	H
			D	O	B	R	O			M	O	C	H	A
A	M	I		M	A	I	N	S	T		N	I	L	S
C	O	N	S	E	R	V	A	T	I	V	E	Z	O	O
E	T	C	H		B	Y	L	I	N	E		E	E	N
R	E	L	E	T			E	R	A	S	E			
B	L	U	E	Z	I	N	E	S		T	R	O	P	E
			S	T	E	N	O			W	E	E	Z	E	R
C	L	I	P		C	O	O	K	I	E	C	Z	A	R
F	A	V	A		U	S	A	I	N		T	I	C	O
O	X	E	N		R	E	S	T	S		S	E	E	R

127

C	I	A	O		C	A	L	C			I	C	B	M
A	M	F	M	R	A	D	I	O			M	E	R	E
H	A	A	G	E	N	D	A	Z	S		O	M	E	N
N	C	R		W	I	E	N	E	R		G	E	E	S
		H	I	D	D	E	N	A	G	E	N	D	A	
G	L	U	O	N					A	N	T	S		
R	E	S	I	D	E	N	T	A	L	I	E	N		
R	O	E		D	E	E	R	E		A	I	M		
	D	E	N	T	A	L	F	I	L	L	I	N	G	
	A	C	N	E				E	U	L	E	R		
G	R	A	N	D	O	P	E	N	I	N	G			
A	C	R	E		B	A	D	E	N	D		D	S	L
L	I	L	A		I	N	S	I	D	E	D	O	P	E
A	N	O	D		D	E	L	I	R	I	O	U	S	
S	G	T	S		A	L	L	A		E	R	R	S	

128

T	A	S	M	A	N			B	O	N	J	O	V	I
O	N	E	Y	E	A	R		A	N	T	I	W	A	R
S	A	N	G	R	I	A		S	E	E	G	E	R	S
I	D	S	A	Y	S	O		H	I	S	S			
R	E	E	L		H	U	M			T	A	K	E	S
	M	I	S	O		L	I	S	P		W	I	S	H
		A	Z	O		D	O	H	A		E	S	A	
	H	L	M	F	F	W	V	D	M	R	V			
X	O	O		A	I	R	E		S	E	E			
V	I	S	E		D	I	S	C		R	I	S	D	
I	L	E	F	T		T	A	C		N	E	A	L	
			F	I	S	T		S	A	L	E	R	N	O
C	L	E	A	N	E	R		E	R	O	D	E	N	T
S	I	N	C	E	R	E		D	O	M	I	N	O	S
I	Q	T	E	S	T	S		B	A	N	A	N	A

Using H-S (HISS), M-O (MISO), L-P (LISP), etc., 39-Across represents SPOT THE CODE.

129

C	O	L	A		N	O	M	E		S	P	R	A	I	N
A	M	A	S		O	M	A	N		L	E	A	D	T	O
T	A	X	I	S	T	A	N	D		A	R	T	O	I	S
T	H	E	F	I	R	S	T	L	E	T	T	E	R	S	
L	A	S		S	E	U	R	A	T			N	N	E	
E	N	T	S		M	A	T	H	I	S		I	T	S	
		T	M	I		S	E	I	S	M		N	S	A	
	O	F	E	A	C	H		C	L	U	E	G	O		
L	D	L		L	E	A	R	N		E	T	D			
Y	O	U		I	S	S	U	E	S		A	B	C	S	
E	R	R			I	N	T	H	A	T		A	R	C	
	F	R	O	M	A	T	O	Z	I	N	O	R	D	E	R
A	R	I	S	E	N		V	E	R	T	E	B	R	A	E
S	E	E	S	I	N		E	R	T	E		I	A	T	E
S	E	D	O	N	A		R	O	S	S		S	P	E	D

130

OIL	T	A	N	K	E	R		OIL	T	Y	C	O	O	N
C	A	B	O	O	S	E		P	I	E	H	O	L	E
A	C	A	D	I	A	N		A	L	P	I	N	E	S
N	O	T	O	N		E	R	I	E		M	A	S	T
		U	G	H		E	N	S	U	E				
OIL	R	U	B		E	T	A	T		F	I	S	H	OIL
P	E	N	T		S	O	L		P	O	N	I	E	S
U	S	H		OIL	S	P	I	L	L	S		L	E	K
M	E	A	G	R	E		T	A	I		M	A	L	I
P	E	T	R	I		O	I	S	E		A	S	S	N
		A	G	I	L	E		D	S	T				
U	L	A	N		S	I	S	I		H	I	L	T	S
M	O	L	O	T	O	V		M	A	I	L	O	U	T
P	R	A	L	I	N	E		A	I	R	D	A	T	E
S	E	S	A	M	E	OIL		C	L	E	A	N	U	P

131

L	E	A	N	T		S	W	A	M		I	H	O	P
E	N	D	O	W		H	O	Y	A		M	A	L	L
C	O	M	B	O	N	O	V	E	R		P	N	E	U
A	L	I		S	O	R	E		S	C	A	G	G	S
R	A	T	A	T	A	T		A	B	O	I	L		
	J	A	M	A	I	C	A	N	R	O	A	M		
S	O	L	A	R		X	E	R	S		O	L	A	
K	N	O	X		S	A	N	D	S		A	S	I	A
I	T	I		B	A	J	A		I	B	E	A	M	
D	O	N	T	P	L	A	Y	D	O	M	E			
	C	H	O	I	R		E	P	I	T	A	P	H	
B	A	L	E	E	N		L	E	I	S		B	E	E
A	V	O	W		G	N	O	M	E	S	K	U	L	L
B	E	T	H		E	Y	R	E		E	A	S	E	L
E	C	H	O		R	U	D	D		D	I	E	G	O

132

B	L	U	F	F	S		S	P	A	M	A	L	O	T
L	A	N	D	A	U		I	S	E	E	B	E	E	M
E	R	S	A	T	Z		M	A	R	S	B	A	R	S
N	A	H		S	Y	S			N	E	D			
D	I	O	R		Q	U	E	U	E	E	Y	D	I	E
E	N	R	O	L		B	A	L	D		S	O	S	A
R	E	N	O	I	R		S	E	I	S		G	M	T
		D	E	E	D	E	E	T	E	A				
H	A	S		N	E	U	F		H	A	V	A	N	A
A	D	A	M		S	P	U	D		L	I	L	A	C
Y	O	U	A	R	E	E	L	L	E		S	T	I	R
	S	R	O			I	L	L		E	V	O		
A	L	A	N	B	A	L	L		M	I	R	R	E	N
C	A	G	E	Y	B	E	E		S	L	E	E	T	Y
U	S	E	R	N	A	M	E		T	A	N	D	E	M

133

P	H	D	S	■	E	Z	R	A	■	I	N	E	P	T
E	E	R	O	■	■	S	O	A	R	■	S	E	X	E	S
K	N	O	W	A	T	O	Y	O	T	A	W	O	N	K
O	N	S	E	T	■	■	■	U	E	Y	S	■	■	
E	A	S	T	T	O	W	E	S	T	■	C	A	S	H
■	■	O	N	L	I	N	E	■	T	A	B	L	E	
A	I	R	■	■	L	L	D	■	S	A	S	H	E	S
S	P	O	T	P	A	L	E	L	A	P	T	O	P	S
P	A	T	O	I	S	■	A	S	I	■	R	T	E	
E	N	O	L	A	■	B	R	A	N	D	S	■		
R	A	R	E	■	W	E	S	T	T	O	E	A	S	T
■	■	R	O	O	F	■	■	U	N	I	T	E		
R	E	M	A	R	K	A	L	A	K	R	A	M	E	R
E	L	I	T	E	■	L	I	V	E	■	T	A	N	S
V	I	D	E	O	■	L	E	A	N	■	E	T	T	E

134

S	O	A	R	■	L	A	G	■	E	L	N	I	N	O
A	T	T	E	S	T	T	O	■	B	Y	E	N	O	W
C	O	N	C	E	R	T	O	■	B	R	U	R	O	N
S	H	O	U	R	■	A	S	K	■	I	T	E	R	S
■	■	■	L	I	C	■	E	R	I	C	A	■		
F	E	E	D	O	N	■	B	A	S	I	L	I	C	A
O	N	M	E	■	N	O	U	M	P	S	■	H	A	M
A	D	O	R	E	■	S	T	E	■	T	B	O	N	E
L	O	T	■	G	E	S	U	R	N	■	E	P	I	S
S	W	E	A	R	S	I	N	■	I	S	L	E	T	S
■	■	R	E	P	A	D	■	A	L	L	■			
C	H	A	O	S	■	N	H	L	■	O	C	T	A	D
N	E	B	U	S	E	■	E	A	R	M	U	R	V	E
B	A	L	L	E	R	■	I	M	N	O	F	O	O	L
C	R	E	A	S	E	■	T	E	A	■	F	I	N	E

135

H	T	T	P	■	T	E	T	R	A	■	B	R	A	S
A	R	E	A	■	E	X	E	C	S	■	H	A	L	T
J	O	E	S	I	X	P	A	C	K	■	A	B	B	A
J	U	N	T	A	■	■	R	O	S	I	N	B	A	G
■	■	■	M	U	D	S	L	I	N	G	I	N	G	
Y	A	M	S	■	L	O	U	A	N	N	■	■		
E	X	I	T	R	A	M	P	■	E	P	S	O	M	
G	E	N	U	I	N	E	■	T	I	E	I	N	T	O
G	L	I	N	T	■	B	O	N	D	G	I	R	L	
■	■	U	S	U	A	L	S	■	S	P	O	T		
J	A	V	A	A	P	P	L	E	T	S	■			
I	D	E	C	L	A	R	E	■	H	A	Z	E	S	
F	O	N	T	■	C	O	F	F	E	E	T	A	L	K
F	R	A	U	■	E	A	U	D	E	■	O	N	M	E
Y	E	L	P	■	D	R	L	A	O	■	M	E	O	W

136

S	P	O	R	T	S	■	B	O	I	L	U	P	■	
T	A	P	E	U	P	■	I	N	S	U	L	A	R	■
O	N	E	I	D	A	■	P	A	L	M	T	R	E	E
M	A	N	N	E	R	S	■	H	I	P	■	Q	T	S
A	C	A	I	■	■	C	L	O	P	■	Q	U	I	P
C	H	I	N	S	T	R	A	P	■	Q	U	E	R	Y
H	E	R	■	C	R	I	P	■	Q	U	O	T	E	S
■	■	■	P	R	O	P	■	Q	U	A	D	■		
B	A	D	R	A	P	■	Q	U	I	K	■	O	C	D
A	D	R	E	P	■	Q	U	I	T	E	S	U	R	E
B	O	O	P	■	Q	U	E	S	■	■	E	T	O	N
A	R	P	■	Q	U	I	■	P	S	A	N	D	Q	S
R	E	C	I	T	A	L	S	■	O	U	I	O	U	I
■	S	A	D	I	S	T	S	■	T	E	L	N	E	T
■	P	A	P	I	S	T	■	S	L	E	E	T	Y	

137

```
R O Y A L   A G E S   H A I R
A R E N A   S A M E   A R M A
B B G U N   A F A R   J E A N
B I G T E N   F L A P J A C K
I T S   A D E L P H I
    B I D E   H I S S A T
O R G A N I S M S   E G O
T H E A F R I C A N Q U E E N
I E R   S I G O U R N E Y
C O M B A T   E R I N
    A S H A N T I   B A L
A L A N K I N G   A I R A C E
J U N K   R O A M   S E N N A
A C T I   S U I T   O A T E S
R E I N   T K O S   F L U S H
```

138

```
J A S P E R   F G S   S T U D
O P I A T E   O A T   T U N A
G O R G O N Z O L A   E R I N
      E N D I T   R H E B O K
V E E R S   P R O V O L O N E
E X E S   O P U L E N T
R U N   G L O B E   C O R O T
S L I C E D   C H E E S E
A T E A T   A B O V O   C A L
      T O P L E S S   C U K E
L I M B U R G E R   L O R A X
I N C I T E   F I B E R
E N G R   M A S C A R P O N E
T E E D   E M U   R O S T E R
O R E S   D I P   B I E B E R
```

139

```
B A M A   F E D O R A   R A Y
O V I D   E D U C E S   A L A
W E D D I N G C H A P   T O R
S C I E N C E   E L I S I O N
    N A E   R E R O O F S
P A N D I S C U S S I O N
A L E   R I F T   N E S T S
T E A K   N O E L S   Y O R K
S C R A G   R I I S   U I E
    T H R O W I N T H E T O W
O O H L A L A   S A L
T H E O M E N   A B R A H A M
T A T   M O D T R A I N S E T
E R O   A L A R I C   D I O N
R A P   R E S E E K   S A N S
```

140

```
B A R B   S H A L T   S W A N
O D E R   S I L A S   A H S O
G O↑I N S M O K E   T O P↑
G R A T E S O N   T O I L
S E P T A   M E A S U R E D↑
      L T R   L E T I N O N
B R A E   A S T O   E C O L E
L U C   S I T↑F O R   T O R
I N U S E   E S T O   T E R P
P A T I N A S   H B O
S T A N D S↑T O   O P E R A
    B U S H   I T S A T R A P
(UP)D O S   C O M E↑S H O R T
H A V E   A L E R O   I D E E
W Y E S   N A X O S   S E E D
```

141

```
E T A I L   T E S H   N A T O
A E T N A   A N T E   A L I T
S L E E T   P T A S   F O N T
T E M P O R A R Y T A T T O O
    T Y E     I O T A
A L T   A N T E N N A   S T A
R I O T   T O V     R I T A S
T E N N E S S E E T I T A N S
S U E T S     N T H   S T Y E
Y T D   T E E T H E S   S A T
    S E T A     F T D
T E E T E R T O T T E R I N G
H T T P   A S T O   P O S I T
A T T A   D A R T   P I N T O
T A U T   E T A S   E T T E S
```

142

```
U P S   S T A S I S   E S P Y
Z O O   P I N A T A   D A R E
I N F I E L D S I N   G L E S
  D A N C E R     D R Y
    S T R E E T P I   A N O
A I R E R S   G A I T   D O R
S C O R E   N O L T E   D E A
S E C T   M E T E S   G A L T
E C K   B O A R S   F O Y L E
S A C   A N T I   T O S S E D
S P A   C E O P E R A S
    S K Y     T I M I N G
W E N T   B A R H O P P I N G
D A D A   A R M A D A   N A E
S T Y X   G I N N E D   E W E
```

143

```
W E E B   T B A R   E P S O M
U C L A   H O R A   M I N G O
S T E A M R O O M   I G O R S
S O M B R E R O   A L L W E T
    A S E   B R E A
S C R A P P A P E R   T V A D
T R E   E M I R S   L I E T O
R O L F E   R O T   O N R E D
I W I L L   W O O E R   S I G
P E T A   W A F F L E C O N E
    T H E Y   E L O
A B A S E D   L O V E R B O Y
B U X O M   F I V E I R O N S
B R E D A   A M I N   A D E E
A L L A N   D A D S   L E A R
```

144

```
R O S E   Z E L D A   E M T S
O R E M   E M A I L   P E S T
X S Q U A R E D P L U S T W O
Y O U   B O N E S   N O R A D
    E M B E D   L I N I N G
A N N O Y S   G U A C   C A Y
L O C O   F I S H E R
T W E N T Y O V E R F I V E X
    S H O R E S   G A T E
C A M   E D E N   J E E R E D
A R A B I A   M I L L I
T R I E S   S T O N E   A K A
N I N E M I N U S X C U B E D
I V E S   R I N S E   S L E D
P E R T   S P A Y S   B E N S
```

145

C	H	E	N		M	A	R	S		P	S	H	A	W
R	O	T	A		A	T	O	P		I	P	A	N	A
I	W	A	S		N	C	A	A		X	A	N	A	X
M	A	L	L	E	T	O	R	C	L	A	W			
E	R	I		Q	A	S		E	A	R	N	I	N	G
A	D	I	E	U		T	A	M	I		N	O	M	
		R	A	J		P	E	R	I	O	D	I	C	
W	R	I	G	L	E	Y	A	N	D	C	O	O	R	S
A	E	R	O	S	T	A	R		S	I	N			
I	N	A		S	R	T	A		C	A	B	I	N	
F	E	E	L	B	A	D		R	E	L		A	N	Y
	L	I	M	A	O	R	L	E	N	T	I	L		
M	Y	B	A	D		R	B	I	S		O	H	T	O
B	E	A	M	E		M	O	V	E		R	E	I	N
A	W	M	A	N		S	E	E	S		A	D	O	S

146

O	B	I		I	M	A	C	S		C	R	A	Z	E	D
P	A	C		C	A	[BFA]	R	E		D	E	N	I	R	O
T	H	E	H	O	B	B	I	T		S	L	A	[MBA]	N	G
	[MA]	I	N	E		E	A	P		A	R	L	E	S	
O	N	K	P		L	T	R		A	N	I	M	I	S	T
A	G	E	N	A		I	S	O	P	O	D		S	T	A
F	O	R	E	S	E	E		R	E	F		[BA]	T	O	R
			S	I	X	D	E	G	R	E	E	S			
S	E	T	S		C	I	R		B	E	A	S	T	I	E
C	[MD]	R		M	O	N	A	C	O		T	H	R	O	W
R	A	I	M	E	N	T		R	Y	E		O	U	S	E
A	S	T	E	R		O	V	O		N	E	R	D		
W	H	E	N	C	E		[JD]	S	A	L	I	N	G	E	R
L	E	S	S	E	R		A	S	L	A	N		E	P	I
S	S	T	A	R	S		Y	E	T	I	S		R	A	G

147

X	M	A	S		R	A	D	A	R	S		P	A	T
R	A	I	L		U	N	C	L	E	S		O	R	E
A	T	R	O	P	H	Y	C	A	S	E		R	T	E
Y	A	B	B	E	R		A	M	I		A	T	I	T
L	H	A	S	A		E	B	O	N	Y	F	I	S	H
A	A	S		L	A	V			E	L	A	T	E	
B	R	E	A		C	A	R	D	I	A	C			
	I	S	L	A	N	D	E	R	T	R	I	A	L	
		C	R	E	E	P	I	N		O	L	E	O	
A	L	L	O	T			F	O	G		E	A	R	
O	L	I	V	E	B	A	I	T		M	A	U	N	A
L	A	T	E		A	N	D		W	A	N	T	O	N
E	M	T		U	N	I	T	P	I	C	K	I	N	G
R	A	E		R	E	M	A	I	N		L	A	M	E
S	S	R		U	S	A	G	E	S		E	N	E	S

148

S	E	N	S	E		F	O	O	D		B	S	M	T
A	M	O	U	R		E	L	M	O		A	W	A	R
S	C	R	E	A	M	E	D	A	T		S	I	S	I
S	E	A	T		O	L	I	N		C	I	S	C	O
Y	E	S		L	O	S	E		A	R	C	S		
			N	E	T		C	L	O	B	B	E	R	
E	A	S	E	S		S	H	E	S	A	L	A	D	Y
K	N	O	W	S		H	U	R		T	A	N	I	A
C	O	N	E	S	T	O	G	A		I	C	K	E	S
O	N	A	D	A	R	E		D	A	K				
		T	I	L	E		S	P	I	N		E	S	C
R	A	I	T	T		W	E	E	P		E	X	P	O
O	M	N	I		T	R	O	L	L	E	Y	C	A	R
C	I	A	O		S	A	U	L		D	R	E	C	K
A	S	S	N		K	Y	L	E		S	E	L	E	S

149

```
L A P P   S O D A S   I N M Y
O D O R   T R O L L   C O D E
C A L I F O R N I A G I R L S
I M O V E R I T     T E C
    A D E N     H E L P M E
P L A T O S   W O E   E L A L
R A K E R   B O H R   D A R T
O V I   A M O R I S T   T K O
P I N S   A C R O   W A T E R
E S T A   N A Y   B O L E R O
R H O N D A     A R A B
    C O G   B R O C A D E S
L I T T L E S A I N T N I C K
A B O U   R A B A T   I A T E
R O O M   S T Y N E   A L O E
```

150

```
A M M O   L A B E L   B A S H
POOH     A B O V O   U L N A
S T R I P M I N E S   ZOOM
      G E T   R E G I F T S
K A S P A R O V   S U N
E R A S   F A L S E G O D S
R E L A T E   C E L S   N I E
M A T   EXCUSES       T A N
I C I   P O E M   P O M O N A
T H I S E N D U P   R U N T
      T E M   P A L M T R E E
A C H E S O N   P A R
BEEP       B A B Y D I A P E R
O L D E   I N U R E   PAGO
T O S S   L O G I N   T R O T
```

151

```
M E S S   S T A P L E   C P U
E X P O   T E R R O R   H A G
T H E B O U N C I N G B A L L
R O E   A N T O N   A R M Y
O R D E R S   C A P R A
S T Y X   T H E L E A D E R
    O S S I A   T A K E T O
O V A   T H A T C A R   S E Z
J A G U A R   E A R L Y
O N E S H E A R T   S O R T
    G E L D S   F O L L O W
Z E R O   K A R A T   D E I
I N O N E S F O O T S T E P S
N Y U   R O O K I E   A S E T
G A P   A P R I L S   I T R Y
```

152

```
S T U E R W I N   S E L E C T
E A S T E R L Y   I R O N E R
T R A C T I L E   D E N A L I
H E F   Y E N   S E M I T I C
    A P R E S S K I   E E K
W O L F E   V E R I T E
P T U I   A E S   C E N S E
M E R R Y P R A N K S T E R S
  A E S O P   M O S   R A S P
    T U R R E T   K E S E Y
I V A   R A I S A B L E
N O L I M I T   B L U   J F K
D I T T O S   T O O D L E O O
I L E A V E   A V O G A D R O
C A R T E D   R E M E D I A L
```

153

```
S P Y . . D A U B S . P E W S
A L E S . I T S O K . I H O P
N A T U R E V S N U R T U R E
K N I V E S . R E L O A D E D
. . S U D S . S K Y . . . . .
S H E . P O L E . S A V A G E
M A N V S W I L D . L A R A S
A S T I . N E V I S . T A M P
S T E V E . R E N T V S B U Y
H E R A L D . R A R A . S T S
. . F R Y . H A N D . . . . .
W O O K I E E S . T E R E S A
A L I E N V S P R E D A T O R
V E N N . I N C O G . B A U M
Y O K O . L O A M Y . . S P Y
```

154

```
. A R R E S T . A N I M A L .
B R E A D T H . R I B E Y E S
R E S T O R E . C H I A N T I
O C T . M I O . H I D . R S T
K I S S . A N S E L . W A L T
E B O A T . I E R . A R N I E
N O N U N I O N . A B I D E R
. . . . C O R N E R L O T . .
C O S E T S . C U L D E S A C
L U C R E . C A N . E I E I O
E T E S . B A S A L . N E R F
A L P . C E N . W I S . I M F
N O T T H A T . A L U M N A E
S O R I A N O . Y A C H T I E
. K E E P E R . S C H O O L .
```

155

```
Z E B U . A R Y A N S . M C A
I R A N . R E E D I T . I A N
G A R D E N G R O V E . D V D
. . E L O I . E R A S E R .
P U R R S . O C E A N S I D E
E M U S . I N O N . U Z I S
U P B E A T . R U M P . E N S
. . B A K E R S F I E L D .
O P E . A M I E . S A U C E S
F I R S . C T R S . N A S H
S A N T A R O S A . T E R S E
O N E D G E . M A R T . . .
R I C . I N N E R C I T I E S
T S K . L I E S O N . E T T A
S T S . E N C O D E . S T A X
```

156

```
S T A R F R U I T . W E B B S
E S P E R A N T O . A L E U T
D A I L Y M A I L . M I N D Y
E R N S . P B S . . P A S S
R S T . D E L I C O U N T E R
. . . T I D E . A R M . E L M
. F A A . B R A . R I I S
. D I L L Y D A L L Y I N G
T Y N E . E A R . A B S . .
A N A . L L D . A P R S . .
D O L L Y P A R T O N . S N L
. M E A T . A T L . B A I O
F I X I T . D U L Y N O T E D
I T A L O . I C E P A L A C E
R E M A N . T H E S T O N E S
```

157

P	E	A	C	E		B	O	I	S		E	B	A	Y
A	T	L	A	S		O	N	C	E		M	I	N	E
T	H	E	T	A		S	T	E	T		A	C	O	W
E	A	R	C	U	T	S	O	L	U	T	I	O	N	
	N	T	H		D	E	P		P	O	L	A		
		A	S	S	D	I	S	M	I	S	S	E	D	
A	M	O	L	E			C	P	A			T	Z	E
D	U	L	L	A	R	D		A	N	T	F	A	R	M
I	N	D			E	R	R			K	O	L	A	S
A	I	M	S	A	D	J	U	S	T	O	R			
		A	A	N	D		S	E	N		E	D	O	
	A	S	H	O	F	T	H	E	T	I	T	A	N	S
A	C	T	A		O	R	D	S		N	O	F	E	E
B	R	E	R		X	I	I	I		C	L	O	U	T
S	E	R	A		X	M	E	N		A	D	E	P	T

158

P	O	P	U	P		P	I	S	A		O	N	E	L
I	R	E	N	E		R	O	A	R		D	I	R	E
G	R	A	D	E	B	O	N	U	S		D	C	I	V
			R	A	F		S	E	M		E	T	E	
C	U	P	C	A	K	E		A	N	T	I	Q	U	E
S	T	O	O	G	E	S		G	I	N	S	U		
P	E	S	T	E	R	S		E	C	S	T	A	S	Y
A	R	I									L	I	E	
N	O	T	E	P	A	D		T	H	E	S	I	M	S
		I	R	A	T	E		R	O	P	E	T	O	W
S	A	V	A	N	T	S		A	N	O	D	Y	N	E
N	A	E		T	I	P		S	E	N				
A	R	E	A		M	A	T	H	S	Y	M	B	O	L
F	O	N	D		E	I	R	E		M	A	O	R	I
U	N	D	O		S	R	A	S		S	T	A	B	S

159

A	S	H		V	I	S	T	A	S		E	L	A	N
C	E	O		A	T	T	I	L	A		N	A	L	A
C	A	A	N		R	E	P	E	A	L		T	R	A	P
R	I	D	D	E	R		A	N	A	A	L	I	C	I	A
A	R	O	U	S	A	L		I	M	E	T			
		S	E	T	U	P	S		O	L	D	I	E	
O	B	I	T		I	L	A		S	N	E	E	Z	Y
S	A	A	B		D	O	U	B	L	E	A		S	A	A	R
H	E	I	D	E	N		L	E	G		P	I	K	E
A	D	D	E	R		H	O	A	R	S	E			
		N	E	M	O		N	E	O	N	A	T	E	
A	F	R	I	K	A	A	N	S		G	U	N	N	E	R
Q	U	I	Z		L	I	A	N	A	S		N	A	A	N
U	R	G	E		O	N	L	A	T	E		I	C	I
A	L	A	N		X	G	A	M	E	S		E	T	E

160

Y	A	W		I	N	N	A	T	E		B	A	S	K
A	L	I		P	E	O	R	I	A		A	N	T	I
D	I	D	Y	O	U	H	E	A	R	A	B	O	U	T
A	S	T	I		M	O	A		P	R	Y	N	N	E
	T	H	E	L	A	W	S	U	I	T	S			
		L	A	N			R	E	S	I	D	U	E	
M	A	N	D	M		A	T	I	C		T	E	S	T
A	G	O		B	E	T	W	E	E	N		M	E	T
R	U	T	H		V	I	A	L		E	R	O	D	E
S	E	V	E	N	A	M		I	R	A				
		H	A	N	E	S	A	N	D	B	V	D	
M	A	S	H	I	E		T	O	D		B	A	R	E
B	R	I	E	F	S	W	E	R	E	F	I	L	E	D
A	M	A	H		C	A	N	T	B	E		E	G	G
S	Y	M	S		E	R	S	A	T	Z		T	S	E

161

```
M A M A   S T A B   R A F T S
O P A L   T O R A   A L L A H
S P L I T A G U T   G L A R Y
H A W   A R A B I C   O R T S
I R A   B R E A K A S W E A T
N E R D         I N S U R E
G L E E M   P L A N A   P E R
    C U T A C H E C K
I C E   Z E L D A   K E A T S
P O L E A X         G L E E
C R A C K A S M I L E   A L P
R O T H   S O O N E R   M A T
E L I O T   B U S T A M O V E
S L O E S   A S T I   E D I T
S A N D P   D E R N   R E V S
```

162

```
R A C E D   F A T H O M   G D P
A P A C E   O N A U T O   L E A
D O T H E B R I G H T T H I N G
I S A O   I B M     I O N I A
O T C   B E A S T O F E D E N
A L O F T   S L U R P   D A D S
D E M O N S     L E E K
    B O U T O F A F R I C A
        T O I L   A D L I B S
C I T Y   O L A F I   D E R M A
H O W A R D S B E N D   P O T
A D A N O   S C I   D L V I
S I N G I N I N T H E B R A I N
E N G   D E C R E E   R A N E E
R E Y   S W E A R S   A T E S T
```

163

```
S P A S   B B C   [W/B]N E R
L A M P[B/W]  A R A B   B E D E
A L O R S   B A N A N A O I L
B E S E A T E D   C A R N E Y
    A L A S   S K I T
[B/W]A D D E R   V E I L   A L L
W I R E S   T E E N S   L E I
A M O R  [B/W]A N D[W/B]  F O A L
S E W   S M I T S   V I N N Y
H E N   P A L S   K A R E N[B/W]
    J U T S   D I N E
A S L A N T   B E A N T R E E
C L O C K E D I N   A R O M A
H U N K   R A T S  [B/W]A N T S
E G G[W/B]   B E E   P A S T
```

164

```
A G A P E   A D Z E   A G A S
S O L O S   D R E S S R A C K
S T O P P E D O N A P E N N Y
O T O   X I S   A W G E E
C A P T A I N S D I M E S
    A F T   A M S   I C I
H O O H A   V E R A   E G A D
I N C O R R E C T C H A N G E
L U C E   E R O S   A T S E A
L S U   O A S   S H E
    P U M P E R Q U A R T E R
A M A N A   O A F   I L E
P I N C H I N G N I C K E L S
A C C L A I M E D   E E R I E
R A Y E   N I T A   O N S E T
```

165

```
. P A L E A S A👻 . I N B I G
E A T I N G O U T . W H E N I
A D A P T E D T O . O L A F V
U S D A . . . W A N . N A E .
. . R U R . T N T . S I T U .
👻W R I T E R S . F R E E U P
O O O . A D E U X . A T B A T
F O G . H A U N T E D . A T H
A D E L A . P A R E D . B E E
C Y R A N O . M A R L E Y S👻
H A E C . A H I . Y E T . . .
A L B . U F O . . . R A U L .
N L E R S . L H A S A A P S O
C E R T S . Y E S I N D E E D
E N T E R . 👻B U S T E R S .
```

166

```
C A R L . S E M I . R A S P Y
O B O E . T R A C . I C H A T
T O D I V O R C E . G U A R D
S U E . O O O H . C A R R . .
. T O P U L L U P S T A K E S
. . A S S . A P O . S L O . .
A S A P . S A R A N . K E W .
S P L I T I N F I N I T I V E
S I L . R O U T S . O N E D .
E R I . I N F . A L F . . . .
T O G O F I F T Y F I F T Y .
. A R E A . H A G S . A I D .
A T T I C . T O S H A T T E R
S H O O T . A S I A . H A L E
L O R N A . B E R N . U S D A
```

167

```
L A V A . A B O D E . S M O G
A L E G . S A V O R . Q E I I
S I R E . C L A R A . U R N S
H A Y N E E D L E S T A C K .
. . D O N . M E A T . . . .
. C A N D Y K I D S T O R E .
I C E . S E E N . K E N Y A .
M A L L . D W E E B . R E A R
A S L O W . L E E S . U N S .
C H I N A B U L L S H O P . .
. G R A S . . T E N . . . .
. H A N D H E L L B A S K E T
J O K E . A D I E U . A N T E
E P I C . M U T E D . L E N A
M I N K . A P E R S . E X A M
```

168

```
G M A N . M S R P . S O H I O
R O L O . O T O E . O P A R T
O P E N T O A L L . F I R S T
W I N N I N G F O O T E D . .
D E C A F S . S D S . H O O .
I S O . F I N N I S H T A N K
M T N S . G I E . O A T E S .
. . I N N K E E P E R . . .
G U A N O . D N A . A I M S .
S I N N I N G S O N G . T A L
T E A . S U E . T O A S T Y .
. G U I N N E S S A G A I N .
T E R R E . I N A U D I B L E
C R A G S . A N T I . L E D S
U N M E T . L E S T . E T A S
```

169

```
I N U I T   I S T O   P S I S
K I N D A   N E I N   L E N A
E X C E L   W E A K L I N K S
    L A K E I N S P A N I S H
C I O   E S T       W Y L I E
A C T O R C H A N E Y   E N D
L A H R       D O S E D
F L E E S F R O M P R I S O N
      S T R A P     A H M E
T S P   P A S T U R E L A N D
A L O N E     S I X   G I S
C A P I T A L L E T T E R
O Y S T E R B E D   A B U T S
M E I R   G A I T   N A G A T
A R N O   O R S O   T Y S O N
```

170

```
B V D S   A M B L E   B O W L
A L A I   C A R O L   A C H E
B O T T L E N E C K   T H E E
A G A Z E   O A K   S M E A R
        G A R D E N P A R T Y
L A P T O P     I A N
O L E O   P R E A C H   P L O
B A R R E L O F M O N K E Y S
O N E   M A T S U I   A W O L
    E M U     S A Y S N O
B E L L Y D A N C E R
I R O N S   R E A   C H A R T
C O S I   B E E R C H A S E R
E D E N   U N D E R   L I N E
P E S O   N A S T Y   F A T E
```

171

```
F E N D S   P A D S   A C D C
L A U R A   A B U T   F A I R
O U T O F O R D E R   O N C E
    P E K O E   A E R A T E
A S E C   A L L M I X E D U P
W A L L E Y E   I N C   A M Y
K I L O S   U S E I T
  L E T T E R S O R T I N G
    H U M A N   E M I L Y
O P T   A P I   R O S E B U D
R E A R R A N G E D   L S T S
B O L E Y N   N A O M I
I R E S   A N A G R A M M E D
T I N T   D A T A   Z I P P O
S A T S   A S S N   E T H A N
```

172

```
S I N S   S U C H   A C H E D
A D A M   A S H E   M A I N E
C I A O   W H I R   E R G O T
R O C K T H E C A S B A H
E M P E R O R     I A M T O O
    Y E R   R O S E B O W L
S A C   A S K E W   A N N O
T I O   T E A L E A F   E E G
A M M O   H O N D O   D R Y
B E E R P O N G   O Y S
S E A L E D   A R E A R U G
    G A R D E N V A R I E T Y
S W A N K   B A R B   D Y E R
A R I D E   A N I L   N E R O
S Y N O D   Y A L E   O S O S
```

173

```
S R I S   B A B A   A H A B
C A S H   A L I A S   S O R E
A R E A   F O R T H E G O L D
R E E N A C T     E R A S E R
A L I G N   T P S   I R E N E
B Y T H E B O O K   E D G E S
    A N O   T E E     O S T
  W I T H T H E F L O W
U G H   R O O   G I L
P R O O F   T O T H E D O G S
C O S M O   E K E   G S U I T
L O N E R S   S P E C T R E
O V E R T H E T O P   O L L A
S E X T   I G O R S   R A I L
E S T A   N O G O   E W E S
```

174

```
A F T   G O A L   J E T L A G
P A H   U R D U   E L O I S E
L E E   M O O N E D S Q U A D
O R E S     A D I E U
M O N E Y W O R D     E C H O
B E D E V I L   Y A T   H U H
  Y O D E L   R A C I S M
  S T O N E A G E C O A C H
R E R U N S   A M A I N
A X E   E T S   I N S T A N T
D Y E S   L A R A M O N E S
  C L O U D     O G L E
G O N E I N R U M M Y   E S T
A T O N A L   L A T E   L O S
B O W E R Y   T R A P   O N E
```

175

```
B L A C K [JACK]   L U M B E R [JACK]
L O G I N S   B A R C O D E S
U N S T O P   A N N A L I S T
    E R R A T A   N O S I R
S H A D R A C H     S O D A
K A L   T E E T E R   N E W
A D M I T   D O T E R
  J A C K I N   T H E B O X
  H O S E D     F I R M A
A M F   S U D O K U   Z E N
P A L L   P I N G P O N G
P R E O P   D E N I R O
L I E S O V E R   O I L I E R
E A T E R I E S   N E E D L E
[JACK] H O R N E R   [JACK] F R O S T
```

176

```
K N E W   S A L S A   D A R
G O T H   A T E U P   A O K I
B R A I N W A V E S   F U E L
    L E S L E Y   C A B L E
L E T S R O L L   P A R L A Y
A B I T O F   P I N C E
T O M   F U L L C I R C L E
E L E N A   S A E   T Y R O S
R I S I N G S T A R   O T T
  S T A I R   O P T S T O
B B Q P I T   P A S S E S A S
L O U I S   C A R E E N
U S A C   Z E N E R C A R D S
T U R K   I N A N E   C I A O
O N E   G O M A D   E M M Y
```

177

```
P R A N C E    E V E N O N E
L E M O N Y    A V E M A R I A
A D O R E E    L A R A I D E R
I T E M T O R E C Y C L E
N A B S    P O X        S R T A
E P I    H E Y    M P H    L I T
R E C K O N    P A R O X Y S M
    G R E E N V I C E
B A R B A R I C    Z U R I C H
E W E    S S N    W E S    C O O
G L A D    C A F    S E R T
    C O M M E R C I A L C O W
G O T W O R S E    G U Y A N A
P R O S T A T E    H E L P E R
A B R E E Z E    T R Y S T S
```

178

```
M A N B A G    M E H    O R O S
A M A R N A    O B I    L A T H
R E P O T S    J O T    E Z R A
T R A D I T I O N A L I R A Q
    Y G O R    S A C
B E L    U N E V E N B A R Q S
R I O J A    A N A    C O U P
O E N O    P A N D G    I S E E
N I G H    H E Y    A D E L A
C O U N T Y F A Q I R    S L R
    M A S    U N O S
Q A T A R I C O M P U T E R S
T R O Y    Q E D    O S P R E Y
I N R E    U N D    R E A G A N
P O O R    E T S    T S T O P S
```

179

```
B A N A N A    H A T    T I E R
A V A L O N    O R R    A S T O
R E P E R T O I R E    C A R A
    A S S T    E N J O Y E D
E V A D E    T A S T E S
F O B    S A L T    T A L K S
F L U S    O W L    S E L E N A
E A S T    W A T C H    A G E D
C R E A M S    I O U    D R E D
T E R R E    M M D I    E L L
    B I G R E D    G E E S E
W E T O N E S    L O O P
A L M A    S U P E R S O N I C
L I A R    S L O    F E D O R A
L A N D    O U T    F E E D E R
```

180

```
S T E M    S A C S    E N C L S
T A M A    O S H A    K O R E A
R I C O    T H E B I G S E E P
A C E R B    R I N S E S
T H E I O N K I N G    S O L
A I D    Y E N    E A T D I R T
    S C R I M    H O D A D
C A S H O F T H E T I T A N S
A S Y E T    O N E N O
T I N S T A R    U R I    D S O
S A O    P U P F I C T I O N
    N I C E N E    E E N I E
W A Y N E S W O R D    N E R I
A R M E D    A N T E    O R E L
H E S S E    Y S E R    N O E L
```

181

```
D O D D   S K I T   D E U C E
A M I R   N E R O   I X N A Y
M E S A   O L A F   O C H R E
A R C T I C S Q U A R E
S T U   M O O     C A L V I N
K A S D A N   S E A M   A L Y
  T I M E S T R I A N G L E
A S H E   P O E     O U S T
B E R M U D A C I R C L E
E G O   P E R K   A D O N I S
L O W C A L   A M I   O C T
  S H A P E S H I F T E R
O L D I E   E X P O   A I D A
F I O N A   T E E M   V O I D
F L O Y D   A C N E   A N N A
```

182

```
C O H A B   H E R O   M A L T
P R A D A   A L A R   A G E E
L A M E D U C K P R E S E N T
    L A T K E S   M O N T H
S E W A N E E     A U N T I E
E L I   S P R E A D   S L R
R E S O W   A S I A N
  A C C E N T S H A P P E N
  T R I K E   O R D E R
J E B   C O S M O S   I R A
U N R I P E   I D T H E F T
I C O N S   K I L R O Y
C O N T I N E N T A L D I V E
E R T E   E R G O   I R W I N
S E E R   W R E N   C O O E D
```

183

```
E V A   A T I P   C R E D
N A S A   A L O H A   H E A D
G L I B   N A M E T H E O N E
E L M O N T E   A T O Z
L E O V I I   E R I E   T B A
S E V E N L E T T E R W O R D
    O O N A     A R I Z
  I N E N G L I S H T H A T
S P A R   L I A O
C A N N O T B E P U T D O W N
I D A   D O U R   N O E X I T
    S O D S   I T E M I Z E
I N S C R A B B L E   O D A S
N E A T   T O Y E D   S E R T
A Z O V   E Y E S     S D S
```

184

```
E G G S   E T S   G R O U N D
E A S Y   L E I   L O N D O N
G R A B   Y A K   O T T A W A
  A D S   H A W   A L A
D E C R I E D   D E E P L Y
U P R I V E R   H D L
C O A T I   O N E   E R E C T
A C T E D   P A R   C O P R A
T H E S E   O N E   T A C I T
    U R U   N O I S O M E
  S N A P A T   T R O T T E R
P A T   T S K   S N L
P I U S I I   U Z I   A M I E
A R R E S T   R O N   M I N D
Y O U A R E   T O O   B O D Y
```

185

```
J A L A P A   U S C G   A P E
A B A C U S   R I P A   B O X
B I Z E T S I G N A L   S O P
S T Y   T E H E E   P A O L O
    V I T O   W H A R F
A S W A N   P L A Y L I S Z T
D O I N G S   Y V E S   T O O
O O Z E   L O R E N   P E R K
P T A   S A K I   A M O E B A
T H R O W B A C H   A L L A Y
  D A I S Y   O P I E
B O O K S   B O R I S   H M S
E L F   H A Y D N G O S E E K
E G O   E L M O   G U I L T Y
P A Z   D E E R   Y I P P E E
```

186

```
A D I D A S       R C A S
N U M E R A L S   J U A R E Z
I M P E R I A L   U N B E N T
S P U M A N T E   G E L A T I
  E R E I   R E F S   E C O L
  R E D G R A V E   C O V E
    N O V E L S   A D E S
  B O N S A I   L E H R E R
L I D O   M A R A C A
E G O S   T E S T I N G S
S A M E   D A N L   R E N U
S P E R R Y   F E E L W A R M
O P T I O N   R E V I E W E R
F L E N S E   O P E N L A T E
  E R G S   N E S T E D
```

187

```
C B E R   B A B A S   P O X
H A R A   O X I D E   P O U R
E D I T   N O K I A   I O T A
E T C   S U N O N M O N D A Y
T H I G H S   S V E L T E
O R D E R   J O G   A R E E D
S O L E   D E T A I L
  W E D O N T H U R S D A Y
    L A T E N S   J E E P
A N T E D   A R T   F E R A L
S E A M E N   F E D O R A
S A T O N F R I D A Y   B L Y
I L E T   L A Z A R   B I O S
S O R E   E C O L E   A C N E
I N S   R E D I D   S S G T
```

188

```
P A W   L I M P   P A S S T O
I P O   L O C I   I C E P O P
E N T R A N C E   X E N O N S
R E A I M   A D M I R E R
S A N T A   R I L E   G T O S
    T S K T S K   B A S R A
Y E W S   A H H   B A L L O T
O X O   W H Y   O A T   A N O
G A R D E N   S N L   I W O N
A L K I E   O N E I L L
S T A S   A H A B   A G E N T
  H I S T O R Y   D W E E B
A T O N E R   F O R M U L A S
M I L T I E   E N Y A   E L P
A L I E N S   D E N G   R E S
S E C R E T
```

189

M	O	N	E	T		O	K	S			A	N	T	Z
A	R	E	N	A		V	I	C	I		L	O	W	E
S	C	A	D	S		E	L	A	N		I	R	I	S
C	A	T	A	S	T	R	O	P	H	E		A	R	T
		L	E	A	H		E	A	R	T	H	L	Y	
B	O	I	L		M	E	A	S	U	R	E			
A	R	R		T	E	R	P		L	A	T	K	E	S
N	E	A	T	H		E	A	R		T	E	N	T	H
C	O	Q	U	E	T		R	O	S	A		I	T	E
		S	W	E	P	T	U	P		E	T	A	L	
M	I	S	H	E	A	R		T	A	S	K			
A	L	A		B	R	O	K	E	N	H	E	A	R	T
Z	I	N	C		A	L	L	O		I	O	N	I	A
D	A	T	A		T	E	E	N		P	U	T	O	N
A	D	A	M			S	E	E		S	T	E	T	S

190

Y	I	P	S		A	B	C			C	R	U	M	B
O	N	E	O	C	L	O	C	K		Y	E	N	T	A
G	U	A	C	A	M	O	L	E		C	E	D	E	D
I	S	L	A	M	A	B	A	D		L	X	I	V	
	E	E	L	S		O	M	G		E	A	V	E	
			N	O	P	E	S		M	I	R	O		
T	I	M	E	W	A	S		S	O	L	I	D	E	R
A	R	O	M	A	S		3		H	O	N	E	S	T
D	E	B	O	R	A	H		B	O	W	E	D	T	O
S	N	I	T		L	U	M	E	T					
	E	L	I	S		B	E	N		S	H	A	G	
	C	E	C	E		C	L	E	O	P	A	T	R	A
S	A	B	O	T		A	L	A	B	A	S	T	E	R
O	R	A	N	T		P	O	T	E	N	T	I	A	L
S	A	Y	S	O			W	H	Y		O	C	T	O

191

O	P	T	S		O	S	I	E	R		M	E	S	A
H	A	R	I		B	A	L	S	A		O	P	E	N
M	R	I	G	G	I	N	S	A	N	D	M	I	S	S
S	C	E	N	E		G	A	U	D	Y		L	A	W
		S	A	R	A			I	N	C	O	M	E	
D	O	O	L	I	T	T	L	E		E	A	G	E	R
U	R	U		W	E	E	L	A	S	S				
E	A	T	S		A	R	T	I	S		E	W	E	R
		C	A	R	R	I	O	N		E	S	E		
E	N	D	O	R		A	T	T	E	M	P	T	T	O
D	I	A	T	O	M			R	O	E	S			
I	C	H		S	E	E	T	H		P	E	P	S	I
S	O	L	V	E	A	C	R	O	S	S	W	O	R	D
O	L	I	O		R	O	O	M	Y		E	T	T	E
N	E	A	L		A	L	T	E	R		E	S	A	S

192

A	D	M	I	T		R	A	W		H	O	Y	A	S
T	O	I	L	E		E	W	E		A	L	U	L	A
E	N	D	O	R		S	A	N	D	R	A	K	E	S
A	N	D	S		C	I	S	T	E	R	N	S		
M	I	L	E	H	I	G	H	S	T	A	D	I	U	M
S	E	E		I	N	N		O	O	H		T	R	I
			P	D	Q		L	U	X		J	U	G	S
T	O	Q	U	E		N	O	R		T	A	P	E	S
A	B	U	T		A	O	L		L	A	X			
L	O	A		R	P	M		V	O	X		S	A	T
C	E	N	T	E	R	I	C	E	C	I	R	C	L	E
		D	O	M	I	N	I	C	A		I	H	O	P
S	T	A	Y	A	L	E	R	T		B	O	O	N	E
A	I	R	E	D		E	C	O		A	D	O	Z	E
C	L	Y	D	E		S	E	R		R	E	L	O	S

193

I	S	L	A		B	U	S	M	A	P		S	I	R
A	T	E	U	P	A	S	T	O	R	M		A	W	E
M	E	N	T	A	L	N	O	T	E	S		M	I	G
S	A	T	O	R	I		L	E	T		C	O	L	A
	M	A	S	T		S	E	T	O	N	H	A	L	L
S	S	N		O	W	N		S	O	U	R			
T	H	E	O	N	S	E	T		T	O	P	I	C	
D	I	A	L		W	E	D	G	Y		N	E	N	A
S	P	R	E	E		S	T	E	N	O	P	A	D	
		O	A	K	S		O	S	U		P	T	S	
F	A	L	L	T	O	N	E	S		D	O	E	R	
R	U	D	E		R	A	E		T	I	A	R	A	S
I	D	O		T	U	R	N	T	O	S	T	O	N	E
Z	I	P		O	N	E	S	E	N	T	E	N	C	E
Z	O	A		E	A	S	Y	A	S		R	I	E	N

194

C	O	N	D	E	M	N		S	T	E	L	L	A	S
O	N	T	A	R	I	O		W	I	P	E	O	U	T
A	C	H	R	I	S	T	M	A	S	S	T	O	R	Y
L	E	S	T		S	A	I	T	H		M	M	I	X
			E	D	Y		S	H	A	D	E			
M	I	S	D	O		A	S	S		R	I	C	O	H
I	P	O		R	A	N	I		B	I	N	A	R	Y
C	A	N		M	I	A	S	M	A	L		P	I	E
A	N	N	E	A	L		S	I	L	L		R	O	N
H	A	Y	D	N		Q	I	X		E	D	I	N	A
			A	T	E	U	P		O	R	I			
S	A	K	S		M	O	P	U	P		S	H	I	A
T	R	A	N	S	I	T	I	O	N	P	O	I	N	T
A	U	R	E	O	L	E		M	I	D	W	E	S	T
G	N	A	R	L	E	D		O	N	A	N	D	O	N

195

A	H	E	M		I	Q	S		A	B	S	C	A	M
M	R	P	E	A	N	U	T		P	A	L	A	C	E
Y	E	A	R	N	F	O	R		I	N	A	R	U	T
			C	V	I		U	S	E	D		I	T	E
W	I	L	K	I	N	S	M	I	C	A	W	B	E	R
I	D	A		L	I	L		R	E	N	E			
T	A	L	C		T	O	P		N	A	A	C	P	
C	H	A	R	L	I	E	M	C	C	A	R	T	H	Y
H	O	W	I	E		S	H	H		S	L	O	G	
		E	A	S	E		A	O	L		A	R	M	
L	O	R	D	P	E	T	E	R	W	I	M	S	E	Y
A	P	A		F	L	E	A		L	E	A			
S	A	T	I	R	E		T	W	I	T	T	E	R	Y
T	R	I	T	O	N		M	O	N	O	C	L	E	S
S	T	O	O	G	E		E	W	E		H	I	L	L

196

R	E	D		C	R	E	M	A		A	S	I	A	N
A	X	E		H	I	M	O	M		S	A	N	T	A
M	O	R	S	E	C	O	D	E		A	S	H	O	T
A	T	I	M	E			E	L	E	P	H	A	N	T
D	I	V	A	S		D	L	I	X		A	L	I	I
A	C	E		Y	A	O		A	P	E		E	N	L
S	A	D	E		D	O	I		E	N	E	R	G	Y
						·	·	·	·					
J	E	T	S	K	I		O	L	E		H	A	S	T
A	Y	E		A	O	L		I	D	E		B	A	H
Z	E	A	L		N	A	S	A		S	T	A	I	R
Z	E	R	O	E	S	I	N		P	A	S	D	E	
A	X	O	N	S		C	A	R	P	A	T	H	I	A
G	A	S	E	S		A	R	Y	A	N		E	D	T
E	M	E	R	Y		L	E	E	Z	A		S	O	S

197

```
S O W   C H I     I A M B I C
T B A   D O C S   O M E R T A
R A T   X M E N I N B L A C K
A M E S   B A U M   L I T H E
P A R L O R X G A M E S
    P O R E     A S S A I L
D I R T Y   P R A Y   A N K A
U N O   X R A Y B A N   K E Y
E C O N   A L E C   A T L A S
S A F A R I     E P E E
    P A N D O R A S X B O X
E W O K S   E W E S   T I M E
X A X I S O F E V I L   T E N
E V E N L Y   D U N E   E G O
S E N S E S     E G G   R A N
```

198

```
T A C O   S T R A W     T O I
O N A N   V I O L A   E R I Q
G A M E H U N T E R   M E L T
  R E M Y   S E T P I E C E
S C R A P E D   S A N T A S
P H O N E L I N E   L E A N T
A Y N   M O O D   E N G S
  H E A D F I R S T
  A J A X   E A S Y   R U E
S T E N T   S T O N E C O L D
E R A G O N   N E T L O S S
L A N D L O C K   T A F T
D I N O   B A N D M A S T E R
O N E G   E N E M Y   S O R T
M S S   L E E Z A   A P S E
```

199

```
B A B A   B A N C   S C A B
A B O M B   E L B A   P A B A
G U M B O   A B C S   A B B R
S T A L B A N S   B Y R O A D
  E B B S   A B E T S
B A R R I O   A B H O R
A B E   N U B B Y   R I G B Y
N I B S   T A B O R   B O L O
S T A U B   R E B E C   B U B
  B O S S Y   B A B I E S
  B R U S H   B E B E
B E A R E R   B E L L L A B S
L A M B   U B E R   E L B O W
A L B A   B I E N   D E B R A
B E O N   S O B E   S A A B
```

In this crossword, every clue and every answer contains at least one letter B.

200

```
J A D A   S T A T S   A S I F
E B O L A   P A D R E   C H A I
F O O T B A L L D I A G R A M S
F O R E N S I C S   L O O K A T
  R E S T   J E T S
  I B E R T   P R O V O S T S
S N U G   S H A K E N   I T S
E N D O F A L O V E L E T T E R
L E G   A L I N E S   E L M S
R E S U L T E D   C U R E S
  A L E S   L I N T
A C U I T Y   P O I N C I A N A
H O L L Y W O O D S Q U A R E S
A N N E   A S L I P   T R I C K
B E A D   Y U L E S   Y A K S
```

201

```
B I N S   A V O N   U M B E R
I S E E   R A G U   S T I L E
B A R N A C L E C H E S T E D
S O F T C   E L O   I S M S
    C H O C   E R I N
  S C O T C H P I N N A C L E
W A R D   T E A   T I L E D
O S O   T O R N A D O   A G A
O H W O W   D O E   F R O M
F A N N I E M A N A C L E S
    E T T A   E L H I
M O A N   U R N   E E R I E
A D D A P I N C H O F S A L T
G I Z M O   E A S T   B R I C
S N E E R   R A T S   Y E A H
```

202

```
S L E E P   P O L S   O R G
P A C E R   A S T I   A N T E
A L O N E   T I D E   G I R O
M A L   S I R E   F A C E D
S S E   S S O R C A Y R E V E
    L E O N   H S I
R O T O R   S P O T   S L A G
M O R F S D A E R R E W S N A
S P I T   E I R E   M A D A M
    D E N   O M E N
T F E L O T T H G I R   N O B
A L L I N   O R C A   O R E
D O O R   T A M A   L O R N E
A J A R   S T E P   D A M O N
S O N   P O O H   S T A T E
```

203

```
M E G A   A P P   A D L I B S
A L I T   F E U   D E T O U R
R A zz M A T A zz   J A C U zz I
C I A   M A R L B O R O
O N R Y E   S E R I   L O F T
S E D E R S   I N G   G R E
    N I C K E D   E E R I E
  C A T C H I N G S O M E zz
J O L L A   S T E L M O
A S P   N I M   R E T A G S
zz T O P   N E W S   T E R R A
    I M I T A T O R   T I N
Q U I zz E D   F U Z Z Y W U zz Y
B A C A L L   E P I   A R L O
S W I zz L E   R E E   R O Y S
```

204

```
A M I D   A I D A   S E V E N
D A V E   B R E D   D E I C E
D R A M   C A P I T A L E L L
U L N A   S Q U E A K   W I L
C O H N   T U X   K E P I
T W O D A S H E S   P E R S E
S E E S T A R S   R I N S E S
    O K S   P U N
P S A L M S   P E N C A S E S
A C R E S   S L A S H M A R K
S R T A   G N U   A L O E
S I R   A R O M A S   T A S E
A P O S T R O P H E   O M I T
I T O U T   Z E S T   R I V E
C O M M A   E R O S   Y S E R
```

205

R	O	T	C		K	N	O	T		S	A	G	A	S
A	S	E	A		A	C	N	E		P	L	A	T	E
P	L	U	M	B	T	R	E	E		A	L	G	E	R
T	O	T	E	R	M			S	A	M	I	A	M	B
			L	O	A	F	S		S	S	N			
L	L	D		C	N	O	T	E	S		A	B	B	A
A	A	A		A	D	R	A	W		P	L	E	A	S
D	U	M	B	D	U	M	B	B	U	L	L	E	T	S
E	R	N	I	E		A	L	A	N	A		P	I	A
S	A	S	S		S	T	E	N	T	S		S	K	Y
		C	L	U		S	K	I	T	S				
B	E	Q	U	I	E	T			M	E	A	N	I	E
L	I	E	I	N		P	A	P	E	R	J	A	M	B
E	R	I	T	U		K	I	E	L		A	S	I	A
W	E	I	S	S		E	D	G	Y		K	A	T	Y

206

J	O	I	N	T		I	M	A	X			S	B	A
A	G	N	E	W		S	E	L	F		S	H	A	G
B	E	R	L	I	N	W	A	L	L		T	A	N	A
S	E	E		T	O	E			B	A	R	Q	S	
	S	T	R	A	D	I	V	A	R	I	U	S		
H	E	C	H	E		R	E	N	E	W		L	O	I
M	Y	H	E	R	O		A	N	G	L	E	E		
S	E	A	L		T	U	L	S	A		A	W	R	Y
	S	L	E	E	P	S		S	T	R	I	K	E	
A	C	E		B	R	U	T	E		I	T	S	O	N
R	O	S	T	R	O	P	O	V	I	C	H			
M	U	C	H	O				E	N	T		A	M	O
A	G	E	E		A	Z	E	R	B	A	I	J	A	N
D	A	N	E		L	A	S	S		C	R	A	Z	E
A	R	E		E	X	P	O		S	A	X	E	S	

207

M	A	L	A	Y		D	E	B		I	R	A	T	E
A	M	O	L	E		E	P	A		N	E	X	U	S
R	O	S	E	S		R	I	A		D	I	E	T	S
L	E	I	F	E	R	I	C	S	S	O	N			
I	B	N		S	I	D		I	N	E	R	T		
N	A	G	S		C	E	L	I	N	E	D	I	O	N
		H	A	H		O	N	E	S		B	T	U	
P	R	E	S	I	D	E	N	T	W	I	L	S	O	N
I	T	A		G	R	E	G		A	S	P			
P	E	R	I	H	E	L	I	O	N		D	R	A	W
	S	T	R	A	D		S	O	S		E	R	E	
	O	L	D	M	A	C	D	O	N	A	L	D		
G	A	U	N	T		O	V	A		L	A	D	E	D
A	P	N	E	A		O	E	R		I	L	E	N	E
S	T	A	R	R		S	R	S		D	A	R	E	D

208

	D	A	N	K		J	A	I	L		H	A	W	K
L	I	B	E	L		A	C	N	E		A	R	A	N
E	N	S	U	E		R	I	N	G	C	Y	C	L	E
V	E	E	R	E	D		D	E	A	R		A	K	A
I	O	N	A		R	I	S	E	T	O		D	U	D
N	U	C	L	E	I	C		D	O	W	S	E	R	S
E	T	E		S	V	E	N				U	S	E	
		O	P	E	R	A	G	O	E	R				
	S	U	M		G	E	N	X		T	O	W		
C	O	N	G	E	S	T		R	O	T	H	I	R	A
O	P	T		M	O	U	L	I	N		A	P	I	G
M	R	I		I	N	R	I		E	L	S	T	O	N
B	A	R	I	T	O	N	E	S		O	S	O	L	E
A	N	E	W		M	E	T	E		F	L	E	E	R
T	O	D	O		A	R	O	W		T	E	S	S	

209

```
R E A R M   B A B E   I L E S
A N G E R M A N A G E M E N T
R O A D T O S I N G A P O R E
E L I S   O R G   S T E N O S
R A N   L A H R   L E N
    B A A   T O P P S
A T E A M   A G A R   T I C
L A S T P I C T U R E S H O W
O N T H E W A T E R F R O N T
T K O   R O T H   A T R A S
    H E N C E   W B A
  A B O   H O C H   T O A
O L E O L E   P I A   L O C H
H O R T O N H E A R S A W H O
T H E C O L O R O F M O N E Y
O A T H   S E A S   U S E R S
```

210

```
M R S P O C K     S T A C Y
D E C O R O U S   M A C R A E
I W O U L D N T   U T U R N S
    R T E   G O D L Y   O T B
B E E S   I F I W E R E Y O U
A L P   B R U C E   R O O T
R E A M E R   S E R A I
B A D I D E A   B A C K O F F
    L E G G S   T O A M A N
E L B A   O H W O W   N U M
T H I N K A G A I N   M I N A
R A S   A C O R N   H O V
A S T E R N   D O N T D O I T
D A R E M E   S U B M E R S E
E N O L A   T A L L E S T
```

211

```
S O N A R   A T S E A   U S O
A T A R I   D U M P Y   T A R
F I R E A N D R A I N   O V A
E S C A L A T O R   S P A N
      C O W T I P P I N G
C A U S A L   R E L A T E
O R R I N   B E W A R E
D I N N E R E T I Q U E T T E
    A M I D S T   S N O O K
S T A T I C   L E S S E E
C H U R C H L A D Y
Y O G A   I R O N S I D E S
T R U   O P E N I N G B E L L
H A S   U S U A L   T E A S E
E X T   R I T Z Y   S T R A W
```

212

```
S S T   H A N   T H E F A R S
I L O V E L A   H I B A C H I
D E V I C E S   R E B A T E D
E W A L K S A L E     E O E
  S H E L   H E A V Y
      S E R T A   S T A T E S
S E C T   O H S   K E N O B I
I R R   H E X A G O N   G O D
D O O W O P   A P U   M A N E
E S W I P E   P A T T I
    T I R E S   I D D O
S K A   M O U N T A I N S
I N S P I R E   S A L I E R I
D E T E N T E   E M E R G E D
E W I N D E R   D E S   O D E
```

213

```
S I O N   V I L E   C A S C A
E N N E   C R U X   R U T H S
A S T A   H O N E   E N R O L
S H O P P I N G C E N T E R
T A P   E P I   U S N   A T E
A P O R T   C A T T A C K L E
R E F O R M   M O E   A Y E S
    B I T T E R E N D
A S T I   F O E   M Y R I A D
S H I N G U A R D   L E N T O
H O E   O J S   I D O   A L I
  W I C H I T A L I N E M A N
C I N C O   E L A N   G O N G
L E T E M   R O T E   G O T O
E R O D E   S T E R   S D A K
```

214

```
F E D S   A L F A S   J A M B
E P I C   N I O B E   O B O E
M A S O N D I X O N   B A S H
  S T A Y   A D O   C H A
W H I T E S T A R   O A K E N
O O P S   E N D A L L
M T A   D R N O   P A T I N A
B E T W E E N T H E L I N E S
S L E E V E   H E X A   T A K
    L O D G E R   T E T E
D W E L T   F R E E T H R O W
R O Z   E S O   R E A D
O W I E   P R O D U C T I O N
V E N I   A C T U P   I C E E
E D E N   R E S E T   S T O W
```

215

```
O C A L A   E R G S   T H E N
C I V I L   R I L E   E A S Y
H E A V Y M E T A L   A S A P
E R S E   E S T D   A P H I D
R A T C H E T   H I M O M
    H A K U N A M A T A T A
A R H A T   I N A T   R O M
S E A T   H A N D M   W K R P
C P U   B A N O   B O S O M
H O T E L M A N A G E R
  M N E M E   S M E L L E D
F J O R D   R O T A   D O N E
L E N O   H O R A C E M A N N
A D D L   U B E R   R A D I I
K I E L   M E M E   E P S O M
```

216

```
A M P   S L A W S   S H U N S
L E I   L A U R A   C O R E A
U T A   O P C I T   A N D O R
M A N   B O T T O M R O U N D
S L O P   F I E R I E R
    H E M   O R I G   H O T
O M I C R O N S   R O M A N A
M E N T A L   P A R T I E S
E N G I N E   D I A G R A M
N O E N D   B L A N C
    M O U E   E L B O W S
P I E C R U S T S   E L V I N
P O L E S I T T E R   O U Z O
P L A N   J E E R S   C L E O
S E N T   A R R E T   K E N T
```

217

```
A N G   I Z O D   O P P O S E
T O E   N O I R   D O E S O K
H D L   K O L A   E S T A T E
R E A L I T Y B I T E S
O A T E N       L O I T E R S
B L O O D B A N K   D O P E Y
      L O U   G O R I E R
  P A I N I N T H E N E C K
K I D N A P   R U R
P L A N T   B A T M O B I L E
H E R O I N E     R I G O R
    C O U N T D R A C U L A
L E G E N D   A D I N   E I S
A D O N A I   F A N G   S T E
T O O T L E   T Y K E   S A D
```

218

```
M A C   A C H   B R I D G E S
A S H   M O E   R E M O R S E
W H A T I S A   I S O L A T E
R E O R D E R   M T V   B A T
    E S T O P   E R A T O
G H O S T S F A V O R I T E
E E L S   S E R I O
E Y E   D E S S E R T   M I X
    G E N I E       M I N E
  B O O B E R R Y P I E A N D
F A N T A   S A U C Y
I N S   T R E   K L E E N E X
E D I T I O N   I S C R E A M
F I T I N T O   M E A   A V E
S T E N G E L   A S P   T E N
```

219

```
B O T H   F I T   N E V A D A
I N N O T I M E   U N I S E X
N E T P R O F S   C O S I N E
    O E R   T E L   T A T S
  T E N N E S S E E T A N S
P A L   T L C   L I E
A B E T   L A M   A S T R O
N O V I S O R S A L L O W E D
E R E C T   N C O   T O G O
    A I G   T W P   A I R
  L E A R N E R S P E R M S
B A R B   J O E   I R A
E U R O P E   C U T I T O U T
E R O D E S   U N C L E L E O
P A R E N T   R A H   R A Y S
```

220

```
● P U N C H   P E N D   A A A
C A S T L E   I G O R   C S I
A Y E S I R   N O M A T T E R
R E T   P O T ● S   P O S T ●
D R O P P E R S   F E R N
    D E S I   O R N A T E
R A D A R   P R O X Y   I R A
A M I S   L O O P ●   O V E R
T B A   S I D E A   K N E E ●
● I N O N E   Q U I Z
  A X O N   S U P R E M E S
P A R E R   N I E L S   R Y E
I R O N E D O N   A T T L E E
A M S   R I S K   N I N E ● S
F ● S   S P Y ●   D E T E S T
```

221

```
POPS  LEAST  SOLI
EVAN  AMNIO  TMEN
EECUMMINGS  REBS
PREFAB  HHMUNRO
  FUDGES  ONION
JJABRAMS  BBKING
LEROY  ACCTS
ONYX  STRAW  RAJA
  BISON  NIGER
LLBEAN  WWJACOBS
LEILA  PSEUDO
AAMILNE  MITTEN
MRIS  CCSABATHIA
ANNI  IAMSO  AARP
STIR  SNAPS  SWEE
```

222

```
ABBES  POLK  TSPS
MARCH  OLIO  WHET
ATARI  NYES  OOZY
NHZUHOZ  UOZHU
DEO  TWIG  VORTEX
ASSIZE  AGAR  ONE
  TURNTURNTURN
TAIS  OEN  ATYA
SNOISSIWNOOW
OKD  HORA  RUSTED
SHIRAZ  YANG  HMO
  ZOHZC  ZOHZOOZ
ERIC  LAST  TORTE
WINK  ELIE  TOPER
EDGY  DISC  OMERS
```

223

```
CRIB  ELPASO  ALA
AARE  LARDER  SIR
BROADSMILES  SOC
  ENDO  AXIS  TUNA
ABASED  BADOMEN
PIG  SECT  WALESA
UTES  SAAB  LEDS
  HAIRBRAID
SPAS  BLEW  OYEZ
UNUSED  EWOK  ESO
POPTART  LEGATO
SRTA  IRAE  NERO
ITE  HEARTHSTONE
DEN  OSCARS  UNIS
EDT  STYLET  PEAT
```

224

```
AJAX  MERIT  ASFAT
LUXE  IVANA  QUICK
EMIR  FEVER  AGGRO
XBOX  FRIZZ  BASED
  ONEG  AJAR
  SUSTAINS  IAM
JFK  AQUAS  BINGED
QUADRUPLEPANGRAM
ARMADA  TEACH  ADZ
  YAZ  WHOAWHOA
  ZEKE  TVPG
JELLS  YWCAS  CHEW
EQUIP  KOOKY  LARA
SUNNY  IRVIN  USMC
TIEGS  DEEMS  BESS
```

225

```
I N C H E D   B O W L   G T O
T A H I N I   U V E A   I R K
E N A C T S   C O L U M B I A
M C L   I C U S   C R A B B Y
S I L I C O N   C H E Z
    E L E V A T E   L E E Z A
S I N I S E   I C E S   N O L
W A G E   R U B E N   T T O P
A G E   P Y R E   D A R E T O
B O R G E   G R E E N E R
      I D L E   C A T S P A W
B A N Z A I   M O V E   R U E
A T L A N T I S   O N S I D E
N O R   T H O R   U N U S E D
E M B   S O U P   R A V E N S
```

226

```
D I O   S W I T   G O T O I T
A N G E L I N A   E T H Y N E
M A L C O L M X   T O R E A T
A N I T   L A C S     O Z M A
G E N O A   T O N A L   O O N
E R G   V E E   O N L Y Y O U
      K E R   S U C C E E D S
      G E N E R A T I O N Z
F E R G U S O N   E O S
T E A S E T S   S N L   S S R
M L S   Q U A I L   J E T T A
E S P O   S T I R   L R O N
A K I M B O   S P E C I A L K
D I N N E R   M U S C A T E L
E N G I N E   E P P S   O N E
```

227

```
W O O D Y   B E A   M A T C H
A S I R E C A L L   S T O L A
R A D I O D A Y S   R O M A S
      M I S S T E P   C S T
A L I C E   I O N   B A S E
R A M O N   M A N H A T T A N
A M A H   K A N   A W W
B A N A N A S   S L E E P E R
    B A T   A N O   L A L A
A N N I E H A L L   A V I O N
A O U T   I D I   Z E L I G
A N C   P E R G O L A
M O L T O   I N T E R I O R S
A N E A R   F E B R I L I T Y
P O I N T   T D S   A L L E N
```

228

```
F A R E A S T   S I T U A T E
A V I A T O R   O N E S P O T
D E G R A D E   B E N E A T H
E R A   L O S E S   U T E S
      A L I S T   S T P
S E W S   D O P E   A B C
P R O N O U N   N U M E R A L
E N T E N T E   E M P A T H Y
W E A R O U T   R E T R E A D
S S N   U R S A   P L I E
      E R N   S N A G S
S L A W   S A Y S O   B A H
L I B E R A L   A T L A R G E
A V E R A G E   S I G N I F Y
G E T S M A D   A R I S T A S
```

229

```
J A D E . O S H A . W A S N T
A P O P . R A T S . A L T A R
Y P S I L A N T I . R E A T A
. C A L Y P S O M U S I C .
A C T . I L O . V O T I V E
G O A W R Y . S L A V . S E R
A M M O . C O O L I O .
. A P O C A L Y P S E N O W
. F A M O U S . E N I D
A T V . L U T Z . K P D U T Y
S H A W L S . L A I . S H E
S E C R E T A G E N T S .
U S A I R . G Y P S Y M O T H
C E N T I . A R E A . O W I E
H A T E D . R O W S . G E N X
```

230

```
P L O D . S C A M S . P S A T
E L H I . H O V E L . O C T O
R A Y E . E M I L E . T R O Y
C N O T E . B L O W O P E N
H O U S E B O A T . L I E
. O L A V . T A L E N T S
B A W D . N E W . N A S D A Q
O S H A . D R A M A S . O S U
M C I . M A S C O T . S O S A
B I T T E N . O R O . P R O D
S I E R R A S . A L I I
. T I L . H O L Y C R O S S
. F R E E B I R D . H I M O M
Y E A S . A N G U S . T A R O
A M S O . S T A T E . O N E K
Z A H N . S O N Y A . F I R E
```

231

```
K I T H . F L E X . A T B A Y
A B R A . L A V E . S H U T E
N O I R . O D I N . S E R T A
J O C K F U L L O N U T S .
I K E . O N E S . A M A T O L
. T L C . W I E . O R A
J E E R L E A D E R . S P I T
A L L E Y . Q U E . S C E N T
M I T E . J U M P C H A N G E
U S O . M I A . H A M
P E N P A L . G L A D . S T P
. J E S T P R O T E C T O R
B R O N C . O O R T . A L P O
E T H N O . P U C E . P E A L
T E N E T . S T A R . O O Z E
```

232

```
A R I A . O R V A L . I N K Y
M A W R . N A I V E . N O N E
T H A T R E M A I N S S E E N
. N Y E T . E T O I L E S
O P T . B O R N W I L D .
N R A . A T E E . L U E L L A
B E L . W A S T . T R U E S
A M O . N O T T O B E . C S I
S I N G E . A L K Y . K I A
E X E R T S . E A R S . Y O N
. I T H A D Y O U . A N S
P A M E L A S . N E I L .
Y O U V E G O T K I D D I N G
R U N E . G R I T S . O V E R
O T I S . Y E A S T . L E E R
```

233

```
FAVOR  PALM   OTIS
READE  ASIA   OHNO
OILED  CHER   LEFT
GOODTIME  SNAFU
SUR  ANA   ABELARD
     FINN  LARAMIE
SMALLS  CERF  IAT
CADY   ONE   ALTE
ACA  BTEN   SPRYER
LAYDOWN  SURF
ARSENIO  PLO  FRO
 TWEEN  YOURHEAD
SHOR  KHAN  AERIE
PURE  LUNG  TEAMO
ARKS  EDGY  ALLIN
```

234

```
ITS  HOMER   ZEBRA
SET  OFAGE   OBOES
THEGHFROMENOUGH
HELLO   SILENT
MELISSA  TORYISM
IDAS  EGGS   QED
   TORAH  KAUAI
 THEOFROMWOMEN
SEENO   TRISH
ARR   FIEF  ENDS
PRELUDE  DETROIT
 WATERY  OSTEO
THETIFROMNATION
BAGEL  EDGES  CUE
SNORE  TAROT  ETD
```

235

```
POD  RENAME  BLAM
ACE  EMINOR  LAVE
BEN  PIÑACOLADAS
LASVEGAS  DAHLIA
ONEEAR  STEP  ELS
   SLAP  ASTA
APAT  TIKI  OMBRE
JALAPEÑOPEPPERS
ANGLO  ASEA  HASP
  STAT  ISTO
BAP  ISAO  THREAT
AMIGOS  MARIACHI
MAÑANASEÑOR  OYL
BIOL  DOGOOD  NED
ANNA  SPASMS  OSE
```

236

```
ASH  SLO   PIANO
CHAR  TERM  EMBER
OUSE  ATCO  CALEB
PLAN  TMAN  AGER
 STEVIE  ORNO
   WIN  ETAS  TER
JAPES  AVOW  ARNO
OPERA  TIN  GROOM
KIAS  OTAY  AMPLE
EAR  THAN  GEL
   FISC  OOLONG
 FORT  HERE  CORD
NONET  EMMA  KWAI
NOTRE  SPAS  SING
ELVER   TNT   NTS
```

237

```
A M E N D   B E A D S   G S T
R E N E E   U N M E T   Y E W
F L Y S P R Y L Y B Y   P R O
  T A T T O O     T E A S E S
    S H I F T S     S Y N E
C O S I     F R A I D Y C A T
H A Y N E S   A R T I E R
E R N   A L L W I S E   Y E A
  C A S U A L   A D A P T S
L O T T E R I E S     P T A S
E B R O   D R Y M O P
S T Y M I E     Z I P L O C
A A S   P Y G M Y R H Y T H M
G I T   O R A N G   I T H E E
E N S   S E P O Y   R O O F S
```

238

```
J I M J A M S     P A G E ANT S
A R R I V A L   M E D E V A C
C O M B A T ANT E R O T I C A
K N E E   H E S S E   M A I N
S S T   R I D E     S E N D S
    D O S   C H A T
G A L A S   F ANT A B U L O U S
I K E B A N A   M E F I R S T
ANT A G O N I Z E S   F O R A Y
    N L E R   T I N
I S S U E   S P O T   R I A
W H E N   W A T E R   P E N N
ANT A R C T I C   R E J E C T S
I N B U I L T   E R A S U R E
N E S T E D   C O N T R O L
```

239

```
S C U M   A T E A S E   P E Z
T U T U   S I N T A X   A L A
I R I S M U R D O C H   S A P
R E L E A S E S   R I V A L S
    E D U     L U B E
B R R   D A I S Y M I L L E R
R U E D   L O O S   T C E L L
I S N O T   D L I   A R N I E
A S T R A   I O N A   O T O S
R O S E K E N N E D Y   O T S
    M E M E     V A S
A S S I S I   O P E N C A S E
J O Y   F L O W E R G I R L S
A N N   O I L E R S   F L I T
X E S   R O A D I E   I O T A
```

240

```
T H A T S H O T     O D E T S
S I D E W I T H   I T A L I A
A D D R E S S E D T O K I L L
R E A M     M E S O   Z E E
    S P A C E B A L L A D S
B M I   E M U   G E O
R A D I O B R A V O   F A D S
U C O N N   I B O   E A T I T
T E L L   T O A D Y S T O R Y
    E R E   K T S   M E X
B E S T I N S H A D O W
Y M A   S O I E   A N T I
C O M M E R C I A L B R E A K
A R B O R S   S T A R D A T E
R Y A N S   T E X A S T E A
```

241

M	E	A	N		B	U	M	P	S		A	J	A	R
S	I	R	E		I	S	A	A	K		S	O	D	A
N	E	S	T		S	U	C	T	I	O	N	C	U	P
B	I	O		A	H	A			F	A	K	E	S	
C	O	N	T	R	O	L	G	R	O	U	P	S		
		I	M	P		L	E	A	S		T	H	E	
P	E	S	T	O		L	E	A	H		D	R	E	D
O	N	W	A	R	D	A	N	D	U	P	W	A	R	D
R	Y	A	N		A	I	D	S		R	E	P	A	Y
T	A	R		E	T	T	A		E	E	L			
	M	O	N	E	Y	S	U	P	P	L	I	E	S	
S	W	I	F	T			S	O	S		D	I	E	
W	O	N	T	O	N	S	O	U	P		T	A	D	A
A	R	T	E		S	P	A	R	E		A	H	E	M
P	E	O	N		C	A	R	P	E		G	O	R	Y

242

	P	E	R	S	O	N	A	L		C	O	S	T	
F	I	V	E	T	O	O	N	E		D	C	C	A	B
A	G	A	M	E	M	N	O	N		S	H	A	M	U
N	O	D	S			T	A	S		S	P	A	T	
C	U	E		S	L	E	E	P	O	N		U	R	N
Y	T	D		E	E	R		E	R	E		L	I	E
		O	P	T	I	C		E	R	R	A	N	T	
	C	U	T	S	C	O	R	N	E	R	S			
N	E	A	R	E	R		O	A	S	I	S			
E	M	U		T	O	M		Z	E	D		I	S	A
X	E	D		S	L	O	V	E	N	S		S	T	L
T	R	I	S		L	O	O			K	O	O	L	
T	A	L	L	S		L	I	M	E	J	E	L	L	O
O	L	L	A	S		A	L	E	X	A	N	D	E	R
	D	O	W	N		H	E	R	E	G	O	E	S	

Note: Each corner represents "nothing."

243

B	A	N	D	B		G	R	O	H		A	B	A	B
I	R	E	N	E		L	O	L	A		M	A	C	E
T	E	X	A	S	T	A	X	E	S		I	B	L	E
E	A	T		T	I	D	Y		P	O	N	Y	U	P
		G	I	F	T		A	U	T	O	S			
	D	I	A	L	F	O	R	F	L	O	R	I	D	A
H	O	T	E	L	S		U	R	L	S		T	R	U
U	R	S	A		A	N	O		I	T	I	N		
N	E	T		A	N	T	I		A	B	S	E	N	T
K	N	O	W	R	Y	E	N	E	W	Y	O	R	K	
	O	R	A	T	E		Z	A	H	N				
S	A	L	A	M	I		H	I	K	E		J	A	M
T	R	A	P		M	A	I	N	E	A	N	I	M	E
E	T	T	U		E	L	L	E		R	O	B	O	T
W	E	E	P		S	E	T	S		T	R	E	K	S

244

S	O	F	A	S		L	A	I	T		Q	U	I	Z
O	R	R	I	N		E	T	N	A		U	N	T	O
F	L	A	M	I	N	G	O	I	L		E	S	S	O
I	O	N		P	O	I	N	T	E		S	E	M	I
A	N	C	I	E	N	T		I	N	D	E	X	E	D
		I	N	R	E		T	A	T	E	R			
D	I	S	C	S		T	E	L	E	C	A	S	T	S
A	S	I	A		T	W	E	E	D		S	W	A	Y
T	H	I	R	D	H	A	N	D		H	E	E	D	S
		N	E	R	D	Y		P	O	R	E			
T	S	H	A	P	E	D		M	U	T	A	T	E	D
H	E	A	T		E	L	E	C	T	S		E	D	U
A	G	R	I		P	I	N	K	T	H	I	N	G	S
I	N	D	O		I	N	G	E		O	N	E	A	T
S	I	G	N		O	G	R	E		T	E	R	R	Y

245

B	A	T	E	S		E	N	O	S		C	A	R	B
O	Z	A	R	K		L	O	V	E		A	L	O	U
B	U	G	G	Y		I	D	E	E		G	I	S	T
B	R	U	S	H	Y	O	U	R	T	E	E	T	H	
Y	E	P		O	A	T	H		H	W	Y			
		A	O	L		D	R	E		B	E	A		
	P	I	C	K	U	P	Y	O	U	R	T	O	Y	S
C	O	L	T		O	A	R		R	A	C	K		
D	O	Y	O	U	R	H	O	M	E	W	O	R	K	
S	P	A		S	E	L		D	I	N				
		I	N	Q		J	A	Y	Z		A	I	R	
	B	E	C	A	U	S	E	I	S	A	I	D	S	O
W	E	R	E		I	T	A	L		R	O	W	E	L
H	A	I	R		T	Y	N	E		D	W	A	R	F
Y	U	K	S		E	X	E	D		S	A	R	E	E

246

S	P	A	C	E	A	G	E		C	A	R	D	E	D
W	A	L	L	Y	C	O	X		O	T	O	O	L	E
A	L	O	U	E	T	T	E		M	E	T	R	I	C
P	L	E	B	S		R	H	E	A		I	T	A	
S	I	R	S		B	A	T	E	S	M	O	T	E	L
O	A	T		H	A	V	E	A	T		R	O	S	S
U	T	E		U	S	E	D	T	O	B	E			
T	E	R	S	E				O	O	Z	E	S		
			E	S	T	R	A	G	O	N		O	V	O
P	S	S	T		W	I	N	E	R	Y		E	E	R
R	I	C	H	L	I	T	T	L	E		S	T	A	R
I	M	O		O	R	Z	O		C	I	R	R	I	
M	O	N	G	O	L		N	E	M	A	T	O	D	E
E	N	C	A	S	E		I	S	O	T	O	P	E	S
D	E	E	M	E	D		O	P	P	O	N	E	N	T

247

X	I	N	G		K	A	R	A	O	K	E	B	A	R
E	W	E	R		A	D	A	M	A	N	D	E	V	E
R	A	T	E		N	O	S	I	R	E	E	B	O	B
O	S	C	A	R	S		S	N	E	E		R	N	A
X	H	O	S	A		P	L	O	D		M	A	L	T
E	A	S	Y	R	I	D	E	R		L	E	V	E	E
D	D	T		E	T	A	S		P	O	S	E	A	S
		I	B	I	S		W	A	S	H				
A	C	T	S	I	N		B	R	I	E		S	A	O
C	A	R	E	T		L	O	A	N	S	H	A	R	K
C	L	U	E		S	O	A	P		I	O	W	A	S
L	O	S		G	A	R	S		S	T	I	T	C	H
A	R	T	O	O	D	E	T	O	O		S	O	H	O
I	I	M	A	G	I	N	E	S	O		T	I	N	O
M	E	E	T	H	E	A	D	O	N		S	T	E	T

248

S	P	I	T	B	A	L	L		A	B	O	M	B	
H	A	V	E	I	T	O	U	T		S	U	P	E	R
O	R	A	N	G	E	F	R	E	E	S	T	A	T	E
T	E	N	T	C	A	T	E	R	P	I	L	L	A	R
			A	I	M	S		R	O	S	E			
E	J	E	C	T	S		T	A	N	T	R	U	M	S
D	O	L	L	Y		P	E	P	Y	S		N	A	P
I	S	L	E		M	A	X	I	M		C	A	R	E
T	I	E		P	A	G	A	N		D	A	R	I	N
S	E	N	T	R	I	E	S		T	E	R	M	E	D
			R	O	T	A		C	H	E	T			
A	F	R	I	C	A	N	E	L	E	P	H	A	N	T
L	E	A	V	E	I	T	T	O	B	E	A	V	E	R
D	A	V	I	S		S	A	N	A	N	G	E	L	O
A	R	E	A	S		T	E	N	D	E	R	L	Y	

249

```
T W I T T E R ■ M A A N D P A
R O G A I N E ■ I N D O O R S
Y O U R E A B E T T E R M A N
S L A T ■ C O L T S ■ M I C E
T E N A ■ T O B E Y ■ A N T E
S N A R L ■ T O N ■ B R A I D
■ A N E W ■ S E A N C E
A S S U M E D ■ F A C E T E D
S W A N E E ■ Y U C K ■
S I N E S ■ M O R ■ S A L E M
E T T A ■ P A U L A ■ L E S T
N C A R ■ R U N O N ■ S A K S
T H A N I A M G U N G A D I N
T O N E T T E ■ G I A C O M O
O N A D A T E ■ H E R E N O W
```

250

```
■ G A M E C H A N G E R ■
■ B I T E T H E B U L L E T
C A S T I R O N S T O M A C H
O L E ■ N E W N E S S ■ D E I
O L L I E ■ L I N ■ S P I L T
K O L N ■ P I N T A ■ H E L M
S T E T T I N G ■ N E I S S E
■ E I N E ■ B I T S ■
I B A N E Z ■ S A M E H E R E
N I P S ■ A F I L E ■ E T A S
S O R E N ■ E L A ■ C R A S S
I L O ■ A D D E N D A ■ I T E
N A P O L E O N C O M P L E X
■ B O R D E R T E R R I E R ■
■ S A I D A P R A Y E R ■
```

251

```
S K I P A G R A D E ■ O R B S
U N D E R L I N E D ■ G O R P
P A L L I A T I V E ■ L A I R
S P E E D D E M O N ■ E D D A
■ T O A T ■ T E Y
T S P ■ S O F T I E ■ B O Z O
I M O U T ■ E O N ■ E R I N
P A S S A G E ■ N O F A U L T
P R I M ■ R A E ■ A V I L A
E T T A ■ R U M P L Y ■ N A N
C P I ■ D A L E ■
A H O Y ■ S E N A T E S E A T
N O N E ■ E V A N S V I L L E
O N A N ■ W I N T E R T I D E
E E L S ■ S E T S E Y E S O N
```

252

```
A C T C A S U A L ■ A H A L T
N O O F F E N S E ■ W I N E R
I M S O T I R E D ■ A G G I E
M I T ■ A J A X ■ S C H U S S
A C A B ■ I T U N E S P L U S
L A D E D ■ E A U X ■ R A R E
S L A T E ■ D L I T ■ O R E S
■ A S H ■ S P F ■
R A P T ■ U H O H ■ D I V A S
A C R E ■ M A N Y ■ A L I B I
T H I S S I D E U P ■ E V I L
T I N T E D ■ E N R Y ■ A G E
L E T I N ■ M A D E A P L A N
E V E N S ■ I C A L L E D I T
S E R G E ■ C H I L L P I L L
```

253

E	A	S	E	░	L	A	G	E	R	░	A	F	T	A
D	U	H	S	░	E	X	A	M	S	░	N	O	O	R
I	R	O	C	░	D	O	U	B	T	░	T	R	I	M
C	O	W	A	B	U	N	G	A	░	P	I	E	L	S
T	R	I	P	U	P	░	U	N	P	E	G	G	E	D
S	A	N	E	R	░	W	I	K	I	Q	U	O	T	E
░	░	░	S	L	A	I	N	░	Q	U	A	N	T	A
R	U	B	░	E	R	G	░	D	U	O	░	E	E	L
E	N	L	I	S	T	░	F	R	E	T	S	░	░	░
C	H	I	S	Q	U	A	R	E	░	W	I	C	C	A
R	E	S	O	U	R	C	E	░	C	A	L	L	O	W
E	A	T	M	E	░	T	E	X	A	R	K	A	N	A
A	T	E	E	░	I	N	B	E	D	░	H	U	C	K
T	E	R	R	░	N	O	I	R	E	░	A	D	U	E
E	D	Y	S	░	Q	W	E	S	T	░	T	E	R	N

254

E	P	I	T	A	P	H	░	J	E	W	E	L	E	R
T	H	R	I	L	L	A	░	U	N	I	T	I	V	E
H	I	A	L	E	A	H	░	S	T	R	O	B	E	S
E	L	I	░	R	N	A	░	T	O	E	░	E	L	O
L	I	S	P	░	C	H	E	F	░	D	A	R	I	A
S	P	E	A	R	░	A	N	O	N	░	R	A	N	K
░	░	░	R	A	Y	░	G	R	A	C	K	L	E	S
AN	TI	DIS	ES	TAB	LISH	MEN	TA	RI	AN	ISM	░	░	░	░
E	G	G	S	H	E	L	L	░	L	E	S	░	░	░
L	A	L	A	░	S	A	I	D	░	D	A	B	L	L
B	R	E	N	T	░	T	T	O	P	░	S	L	O	E
O	B	I	░	W	V	U	░	R	I	P	░	O	S	A
W	A	R	R	I	O	R	░	E	N	R	O	O	T	S
E	G	O	I	S	T	E	░	M	O	O	N	P	I	E
D	E	N	O	T	E	S	░	I	N	F	E	S	T	S

255

P	A	P	E	R	B	A	G	░	T	H	E	G	A	P
I	T	A	L	I	A	N	O	░	M	O	D	E	L	A
P	O	R	T	L	A	N	D	░	A	V	A	T	A	R
E	N	R	O	L	░	U	S	O	N	E	░	A	N	I
I	C	O	N	░	R	A	G	U	░	L	I	R	A	S
N	E	T	░	L	O	L	I	T	A	░	S	O	L	I
░	░	░	S	E	S	░	F	D	R	░	S	O	D	A
S	T	I	C	K	I	T	T	O	T	H	E	M	A	N
O	H	N	O	░	N	A	T	░	I	I	I	░	░	░
P	E	N	T	░	S	H	O	R	E	S	░	M	P	H
H	O	U	S	E	░	O	W	A	R	░	F	O	R	E
I	N	E	░	L	I	E	O	N	░	B	E	R	E	A
S	I	N	B	A	D	░	M	C	H	A	M	M	E	R
T	O	D	A	T	E	░	E	H	A	R	M	O	N	Y
S	N	O	P	E	S	░	N	O	N	S	E	N	S	E

256

P	A	N	A	R	A	B	░	J	A	M	T	A	R	T
A	R	C	S	I	N	E	░	A	M	A	S	S	E	S
N	E	W	A	G	E	R	░	M	A	K	E	S	D	O
J	A	Y	░	S	A	G	U	A	R	O	░	Y	I	N
A	M	E	R	░	R	E	T	I	E	░	D	R	A	G
B	A	T	H	S	░	N	I	C	░	L	E	I	L	A
I	P	H	O	N	E	░	L	A	T	E	P	A	S	S
░	░	░	M	O	M	S	░	N	A	I	L	░	░	░
J	I	M	B	R	O	W	N	░	I	C	E	S	A	W
I	S	O	U	T	░	E	C	O	░	A	T	A	R	I
L	A	N	S	░	L	A	I	C	S	░	E	L	O	I
L	I	A	░	B	A	R	S	T	O	W	░	S	U	M
I	D	C	A	R	D	S	░	O	L	O	R	O	S	O
O	N	A	D	I	E	T	░	P	O	K	E	D	A	T
N	O	N	Z	E	R	O	░	I	N	S	C	A	L	E

257

```
O P A L   H E L D   S H E A
R I P E   S E X P I S T O L S
I Z O D   B R A S S T A C K S
O Z S   H A R M   R I P K E N
N A T T E R   G U L L
  D R U M R O L L P L E A S E
B O O N   O P I A T E   N P R
R U P E E   P A D   R U N I N
U G H   C O U N T S   R O C S
T H E L O N G G O O D B Y E
    A T E N   I T S A G O
E P H R O N   P A S S   N I X
S E A A N E M O N E   A C R E
C R I M E S C E N E   R E L Y
E K G S   S Q M I   E S S E
```

258

```
B E D I S R E S P E C T F U L
A M A N C A L L E D H O R S E
R I N G A R O U N D A R O S Y
S T E R L I N G S I L V E R S
    E E N   E E K A
L A M S   T I E   D L I S T
A L A   T H A R   S U D O K U
Z I G   H I J A C K S   N I X
A B I D E D   Q U I T   I R E
R I C O H   N I B   A C T S
    R I F E   R R R
S C A R L E T T A N A G E R S
P O L I T I C A L A S Y L U M
A L O T O N O N E S P L A T E
D O E S N T M A K E S E N S E
```

259

```
P E D A L S   P O W E R P C
I R O N O N   P A R A S A I L
G I N K G O   O V A L T I N E
S E A L A B   L I N K E D T O
    T E N   H A N G E R S O N
S L E D   H I N G E D
H O L E C A R D   T O D A T E
O N L E A V E   B R U I S E R
P E O P L E   F L E T C H E R
    I N L O V E   T E S S
S H I P B O A R D   L A V
M I N O R I T E   M O T I F S
U P G R A D E S   A P O L L O
S P O T T E S T   M E R L I N
H O T S E A T   A S S E T S
```

260

```
S H A S T A   M G M G R A N D
L I Q U O R   A R O M A T I C
I G U E S S   J O B T I T L E
C H A D S   M O W S   S E L L
E C C E   S O R T   F I N A L
A H A   M U N C H K I N
B A D S A N T A   R E E C H O
L I E W I T H   L A S T L A P
E R S A T Z   P I N T S I Z E
    P A U L A N K A   P A N
T A M M I   O N U S   D O R M
I N R E   D O T S   L Y N D A
L I F E L I K E   P O S T I T
E M O T I C O N   A N O I N T
S E X S C E N E   R E N E G E
```

261

```
J E T S T R E A M ■ O H G O D
E L E P H A N T S ■ N O R S E
T A X R E T U R N ■ E R A S E
E M T ■ W I F I ■ S A S S E D
■ ■ G I N ■ A R M R E S T S
E M B A R G O ■ O A T H S ■ ■
R E E V E ■ W H O S H O T J R
S I D E ■ S L O T H ■ C A P O
T R A N S P I R E ■ S K I E S
■ ■ Z O N E S ■ R E V E N G E
G A Z P A C H O ■ N E Y ■ ■
O I L E R S ■ R O L L ■ T A T
A R I A L ■ T I K I T O R C H
P E N C E ■ M O R S E C O D E
E D G E D ■ I N A T R A N C E
```

262

```
C L E O ■ L I M B S ■ N T S B
A U D I ■ O N R Y E ■ O R E O
T A I L G A T E P A R T I E S
S U B S I D E ■ O N E A C R E
■ ■ L E G ■ R A P ■ M L K ■
A S E A ■ D E B U T ■ O O N A
T O U L O U S E L A U T R E C
L E N ■ A R T ■ A R M ■ T R A
A U D I T O R S R E P O R T S
W R E N ■ C A R D S ■ P E S T
■ ■ R E F ■ T I E ■ B E A ■
C O W R I T E ■ M O U N T E R
C H E R R Y C H A P S T I C K
C H A O ■ P A I N T ■ O N T O
L I R R ■ O P E D S ■ E G O S
```

263

```
S H I P B I S C U I T ■ F T C
A U T O A N T E N N A ■ L O O
S M A L L M I N D E D ■ O W N
H E L I C O P T E R ■ P A N E
■ ■ D O S E ■ S T R E T C H
■ S C E N T ■ B I G A P P L E
S T O N Y ■ S A R A H ■ L E A
T A R T ■ C A S E S ■ C A R D
E Y E ■ V A L I D ■ M O N K S
P A S T I L L E ■ V A L E S ■
S W A H I L I ■ B A R I ■ ■
O H M Y ■ R E M I N I S C E S
N I P ■ S O M E T I M E A G O
I L L ■ P L A T T S B U R G H
T E E ■ F L E A S H A M P O O
```

264

```
F O R T M C H E N R Y ■ D E C
I D A H O P O T A T O ■ E L L
N O T E L L M O T E L ■ C E O
A R F ■ D U E ■ S K U L K S
L O I S ■ S E W S ■ S P A T E
S U N N Y ■ C R A G ■ T I R O
■ S K O A L ■ I A M W O M A N
■ ■ W R I S T B A N D ■ ■
A N E C D O T E ■ N E A P S ■
P I E R ■ N A T O ■ T T O P S
P C L A B ■ N O H O ■ E R L E
L E S B O S ■ O L E ■ T I N
A O K ■ S O U T H A F R I C A
U N I ■ C A S E O F F I C E R
D E N ■ O R A L H I S T O R Y
```

265

```
A S P I R E S ■ C I T A D E L
T H E D E E P ■ A N A T O L E
H I T B E L O W T H E B E L T
E P E E S ■ O H S O ■ A S I S
A P R ■ E I N E ■ M O R A S S
R E C E S S ■ N O E L ■ D O E
T R O T ■ T A P E ■ A S O N E
■ T H E S W I N E F L U ■
D I T S Y ■ O G O D ■ A B E T
E G O ■ R E L S ■ G A G L A W
C O N G E R ■ F I E F ■ E T O
E T T U ■ A L L S ■ F I T O F
I C A N T S A Y A S I H A V E
T H I N K E R ■ A L R O K E R
S A L S O D A ■ C A M P E R S
```

266

```
B R A S S ■ D R A M A
R U S H I N G ■ F L E E R E D
I N H A L E R ■ L O N G B E D
E L G R E C O ■ A V A R I C E
F O R O N C E ■ B E R A T E D
W A N T O N S ■ S I D E S
Y A K ■ I T C H I E R
E N J O Y
K L I N G O N ■ P I G
F I E N D ■ E F F A C E R
P A N T H E R ■ E R R A T I C
O L D T I M E ■ T O R N A D O
R A R E B I T ■ T W O S T E P
C L E R I C S ■ I N T E A R S
H A D A T ■ S E N S E
```

267

```
A G L O W ■ A T I T A G A I N
N E I G H ■ C O M E S O N T O
A T S E A ■ R O L L E D O U T
C A T E R ■ O T O E ■ N I N O
O R E ■ F I N I S ■ D O N E N
N O N U ■ M Y R T L E ■ T S E
D O T S ■ A M E ■ I N S
A M O S ■ M S D O S ■ A J A R
■ R N A ■ T E T ■ A O N E
P I T ■ I N M O N O ■ B A N D
E N A C T ■ A T O N E ■ N O M
A T N O ■ P O H L ■ I M B U E
R O A D T O R I O ■ D I A N A
L I K E A K I N G ■ E R E C T
S T A R R Y S K Y ■ R A Z E S
```

268

```
E S C A P E ■ A D A M W E S T
L O A D E R ■ L I B E R A T E
L A P D O G ■ L A S S I T E R
A P R O N S ■ G L O S S I E S
■ S I N S ■ D O O L I T T L E
E T C ■ T O N G U E ■
M O O N B A S E ■ T U S S L E
U N R E E L S ■ P I R A T I C
S E N D A K ■ M R S S M I T H
■ R E D E E M ■ R I O
G U A R D D U T Y ■ B O R G
A N G E L I N E ■ R E P E A T
F L A M E N C O ■ U S E D T O
F I V E S T A R ■ S E R I E S
S T E T S O N S ■ S T A N D S
```

269

```
H O G A N   S T A S H A W A Y
E A R L S   T H E P I R A T E
I T A L Y   A I R E D A L E S
S E V E N T Y N I N E   M A W
T R E N C H C O A T   G A L E
S S N     R A U L   L U R I D
    D W E L T   P A R T V I
R E Q U I E M   M I S U S E D
E X U L T S   P I N T S
P O A C H   M A C E   G A P
R U D E   P O L A R B E A R S
O T B   G A T E W A Y C I T Y
O L I V E D R A B   N O T G O
F A K E S M I L E   O N E U P
S W E E T E N E R   W O R M S
```

270

```
R E A L E A S Y   T A R G E T
O X T O N G U E   O T E L L O
D I L A T E R S   R E N O I R
A L A M O D E S   T A T A M I
N E S S   C I N E M A T I C
  W H A R F   C O N
M C M A H O N   C A R A V A N
D E A L I N   D A R E T O
I N D I T E D M A R S R E D
  S E E   O B A M A
J O A N O F A R C   A N T S
A R M A D A I G N O R E I T
M I O T I C G R A P E A P E
I N V E S T H A V E A T I T
E G E S T S   T W I N S O N S
```

271

```
S E X C A P A D E   H I G H S
A C R O B A T I C   O R L O P
P L A Y A L O N G   S O A M I
P A T   B I N G   P E N M E N
H I E R   N A B O R S   R R S
O R D E R   L A L O   L O U T
  P E W   T E N T A C L E
A S C E T I C   S T A L K E R
S Q U A D C A R   O P A
H U L L   C L A N   S L O P S
T E T   T A I P E I   A D U E
R E U B E N   S S N S   D M V
A G R E E   I T S G O T I M E
Y E A R N   N A I L B I T E R
S E L M A   F R E E S T Y L E
```

272

```
N E E D T O K N O W B A S I S
E D U C A T I O N A L F I L M
A G R E E T O D I S A G R E E
T E A L   O S S O   S H O R E
  S I L T   K A N   T A C
  L S A T   T R S   N C A R
  P H D   O N E I O T A
I S A D O R A   L E T S S E E
S I S E N O R   L E A
O T I C   E T C   R I N G
  T R E   A R P   L A R D
R A W E R   G A I A   S E A M
C L E A R A N D P R E S E N T
P E R S O N A L E F F E C T S
T R E E L I N E D S T R E E T
```

273

J	A	B	B	A		K	I	T	K	A	T	B	A	R
C	R	O	O	N		I	N	A	G	R	O	O	V	E
C	R	O	C	K		D	V	D	B	U	R	N	E	R
H	O	K	K	A	I	D	O		M	E	A	D	E	
A	W	W		V	O	L	T	A		M	O	A		
S	K	O	P	J	E		V	I	T	A	M	I	N	D
E	E	R	I	E		S	E	Z	W	H	O			
Z	Y	M	U	R	G	Y		Z	O	O	C	R	E	W
		S	K	U	N	K	Y		O	H	A	R	E	
M	R	M	I	Y	A	G	I		S	T	A	D	I	A
O	E	O		M	E	N	L	O		I	C	K		
H	A	R	U	M		F	A	T	H	E	A	D	S	
A	G	I	T	A	T	I	O	N		O	N	T	A	P
W	A	T	E	R	H	O	L	E		A	D	E	N	O
K	N	A	P	S	A	C	K	S		R	E	S	E	T

274

F	I	S	H	E	R	M	A	N	S	W	H	A	R	F
A	L	T	E	R	N	A	T	E	R	O	U	T	E	S
C	L	A	S	S	A	C	T	I	O	N	S	U	I	T
E	G	G			R	E	G				N	C	O	
T	O	S	S	I	N	O	N	E	S	S	L	E	E	P
		I	L	L			A	P	E					
S	C	A	R	L	E	T	T	A	N	A	G	E	R	S
H	A	R	E	B	R	A	I	N	E	D	I	D	E	A
I	N	O	N	E	S	S	P	A	R	E	T	I	M	E
P	A	S			T	I	S				T	I	N	
S	L	E	E	P	L	E	S	S	N	I	G	H	T	S
		L	O	A			A	T	O					
A	S	B	U	S	Y	A	S	A	B	E	A	V	E	R
S	T	A	T	E	U	N	I	V	E	R	S	I	T	Y
U	N	D	E	R	P	A	R	I	S	S	K	I	E	S

275

L	A	B	A	M	B	A		H	U	M	P	D	A	Y
A	S	A	T	E	A	M		O	B	S	E	R	V	E
C	A	T	E	R	T	O		T	O	G	G	L	E	S
E	G	G		L	O	S	T	C	A	T		A	R	I
U	R	I	S		R	O	B	O	T		H	U	T	S
P	A	R	E	S		Z	A	C		A	G	R	E	E
S	Y	L	V	A	N		R	O	E	V	W	A	D	E
		E	L	E	V		A	R	I	E				
S	I	G	N	O	V	E	R		A	L	L	O	W	S
A	R	R	A	N		R	A	J		A	L	O	H	A
L	O	O	M		N	A	I	A	D		S	H	A	D
U	N	U		M	I	N	D	S	E	T		L	U	C
T	O	P	S	E	E	D		O	C	A	N	A	D	A
E	R	O	T	I	C	A		N	O	R	U	L	E	S
S	E	N	O	R	E	S		X	Y	P	L	A	N	E

276

S	T	R	I	P	D	O	W	N		P	S	S	S	T
T	H	E	R	O	O	K	I	E		O	N	A	I	R
R	I	S	K	P	R	O	N	E		T	A	L	L	Y
I	N	C		A	S	K	E	D		S	P	I	E	S
N	O	A	M			S	S	E		P	E	N	T	
G	U	L	P	I	N	G		A	L	D	E	N	T	E
S	T	E	G	N	E	R		P	I	R	A	T	E	D
			T	W	A		U	S	A					
H	E	I	N	O	U	S		S	H	I	N	D	I	G
E	L	F	O	W	L	S		H	A	N	S	O	L	O
S	L	O	T		M	F	G			W	I	L	T	
B	A	R	E	R		R	E	C	U	R		D	E	W
A	M	O	V	E		O	N	A	V	E	R	A	G	E
C	A	N	E	D		G	O	N	E	V	I	R	A	L
K	E	E	N	S		S	A	T	A	S	P	E	L	L

277

```
P A T T I   M E D   S T R A P
A L I E N A B D U C T I O N S
V O L K S W A G E N J E T T A
E T E   E A S E   N U D I S T
    S O C K   R O N D O
S C E N T E D   R E E N T E R
H A T E S   C L A W S   O T O
E S T S   F A I T S   D R A W
A T E   C U R S E   E E R I E
F E R R U L E   S E X C E L L
    A T L A S   R E I N
A W H I L E   P L U M   T A M
P A I D A S T E E P P R I C E
I N V E S T M E N T T E A M S
A G E R S   I D S   S O L E S
```

278

```
A G A T E   S N E E Z E A T
S A B E R   S T A N D I N G O
A M B L E   W O R D O R D E R
P E E L S   U P C S   C O N S
  S Y S T E M S   H O W T O
L E R O U X   T A G O N
A V O N   C R A W L S   B A M
M E A   B E A R O U T   O Y E
A N D   U P T I L T   I S E E
    O F T E N   E A T S A T
F L U F F   G A I N S A Y
R O L F   T E A L   V A N E S
O W N E D U P T O   I L O S T
S P A R E T I M E   L I V I D
T H E S A U C E   S E A R S
```

279

```
H E A D L A M P   P R E F E R
E N D E A V O R   L O C A L E
P O S I T I V E   A T O L L S
    M E D I T A T E   S E E
P O B O X   E E R O   S E N T
E V A S   S T E T   S I C
N I B   J O H N G R I S H A M
A N Y T I M E   A E R I A L S
L E G A L E A G L E S   R I D
  O U T   T A L K   E G G O
B A T S   G E N E   O V E N S
O R B   H E R G R A C E
S L A P O N   S I T U N D E R
S E C A N T   T E A L E O N I
A N K L E S   A S P I R E T O
```

280

```
L I T T E R S     P O R E S
O N E O V E R   S A F E L Y
V A R M I N T   S P U T N I K
E R R   C O A S T A L   O D E
T A I N T S   P O R K P I E S
A G E E S   J A C K L O R D
P E R U   B A C K L E S S
      T R A C K M E E T
    F R E C K L E D   B O O R
C L O C K S I N   D O N N E
P L A N K T O N   P I X E L S
I A N   L I N G E R S   T E E
G I N G E R S   B O O L E A N
G R E A S E   A T W O R S T
Y E L P S   N O N A M E S
```

281

```
P A G E R A N K █ C A B A N A
E M O T I C O N █ T N O T E S
R E D S T A T E █ S K O R T S
M X S █ A L B E E █ A B A T E
I C A N █ L A P A Z █ J I L T
T A R E S █ D A V Y J O N E S
M R M O T O █ D E N E B █
E D Y █ Y U M █ S G T █ T I S
█ A R S O N █ A L C O V E
J U M B O T R O N █ I N D E X
U N E S █ S A R A N █ N O G S
S C R O D █ L U G A R █ L O C
T O L L E D █ L A T E N I T E
G L O V E R █ E N T E R S I N
O A T E R S █ S O Y L A T T E
```

282

```
I P O D █ A D I A █ U S E M E
N A R R A T O R S █ P I X A R
M A C I N T O S H █ S T P A T
E R A █ T A D █ E P I T O M E
█ V O C A B █ U D E █
█ T H I N K D I F F E R E N T
T O A D Y █ G I F S █ L I V
A W L S █ S N I T S █ N I N A
L A V █ S H O D █ O O H E D
C R E A T I V E G E N I U S █
█ N E V █ A O L E R █
T R U D E A U █ W E S █ Z I P
R E M A P █ S T E V E J O B S
A P P L E █ N O S E C O N E S
P O S E D █ A T T N █ N E X T
```

283

```
B R A S S N A M E P L A T E S
A U T O M O B I L E T R U N K
T S A R A L E X A N D E R I I
I S L E █ V E N T █ S N A P
K O L N █ H I D D E N █ P C S
█ I G A █ L E O I █
O N C E █ F O N D █ I N K E D
K O O L A I D D R I N K E R S
S T A I N █ A M Y L █ P S A T
█ T A I L █ A E R █
S S R █ L U S T R E █ S A N K
A L A S █ M C C L █ O D A Y
L O C K S B E H I N D B A R S
M A K E S A N E N T R A N C E
A N S W E R E D T H E D O O R
```

284

```
I T A L I A █ A B E T █ N I B
C E S A R R O M E R O █ O F A
K R I S T E N W I I G █ S Y R
E R A S █ S T A G E A C T O R
S A N E R █ A Y E █ A A U
█ S A A R █ S H A L L W E
C P A █ B L I P █ I D I G I T
F A C E B O O K P R O F I L E
C R O N I N █ G E E R █ A L S
S T U N T E D █ T E E S █
█ I S U █ E M U █ D E B R A
M A T I N G C A L L █ A R A M
E L I █ A E O L I A N H A R P
E T C █ V A C L A V H A V E L
K O S █ E R T E █ A L G O R E
```

285

```
K N I C K K N A C K ▓ S M U G
V A M P I R E B A T ▓ T I N O
E S C A L A T O R S ▓ O N C E
T H O ▓ O U T R E ▓ F A I L S
C U L L ▓ T E T E ▓ E S S E N
H A D O N ▓ D E N S E ▓ T S U
▓ ▓ P O L ▓ D E A D M E A T
C H E E T O S ▓ D I S A R M S
Z A N Z I B A R ▓ L O G ▓
O R S ▓ C E L E B ▓ N I P A T
L A N C E ▓ E L I N ▓ C A L S
G N A R S ▓ S L O O P ▓ S T K
O G R E ▓ A M E N T O T H A T
S U E S ▓ S E N I O R I T I S
Z E S T ▓ K N O C K K N O C K
```

286

```
J A C K B L A C K ▓ E Q U U S
I N H E R I T O R ▓ S U P P E
G A R G A N T U A ▓ N E G R I
G T O ▓ S E A R A C E ▓ R I N
L O N G S ▓ G A L A ▓ E A V E
E M I L ▓ B I G S P E N D E R
S Y C A M O R E ▓ I C E R S
▓ Z E A L ▓ R O N A ▓
U P P E D ▓ F O R E S T E R
S H A R O N T A T E ▓ E E R O
T O N S ▓ B O S H ▓ A D A N A
I N T ▓ P A R T I A L ▓ L E D
N E L L Y ▓ P O R T L I E S T
O N E I L ▓ I N A M O R A T A
V O G U E ▓ D E S E R T F O X
```

287

```
L L E D ▓ E L A T E ▓ S H E
T H R R I F L E W I N C H E S
I N S I D E ▓ A S T R O ▓
C E ▓ P I R A C Y ▓ R A T R A
S ▓ N B A ▓ G Y M ▓ A S
▓ M A I D ▓ A M F M ▓ G P S
N E R T I A ▓ B E A K E R ▓ I
E L D E S T R O Y I N G A N G
S ▓ E M C E E D ▓ L E A D I N
S I N ▓ A X I S ▓ E D E N
I R ▓ P S T ▓ A N N ▓ F
E A R U P ▓ I N L A I D ▓ C L
▓ O R A L S ▓ T R I F L E
C H A R T E R I S L E S L I E
E E D ▓ E V A D E ▓ S U C C
```

288

```
S O C I A L D A R W I N I S M
A R U N F O R T H E M O N E Y
F O R G I V E M E F A T H E R
E Z R ▓ T E A S E T S ▓ E N O
R C A S ▓ B E A N
▓ O N E S T A R H O T E L S
▓ T A L E B E A R E R S
▓ G O R A N G E R S
▓ B R A I N T E A S E R
▓ T R A N S G E N D E R E D
B R A M ▓ K T E L
A A H ▓ A N T I G U N ▓ A C A
A C M E C O R P O R A T I O N
L E A S T R E S I S T A N C E
S Y S T E M S A N A L Y S T S
```

289

```
W I F I H O T S P O T █ P B S
A C T S O N E S A G E █ I R A
R O M A N C A N D L E █ G A L
N N E █ G U M █ █ E N D S I T
I C A N █ E U R O █ A I O L I
N U D E S █ P A G O █ R U L E
G R E W U P █ M R K O T T E R
█ B E E F J E R K Y █
S H O E T R E E █ A I R I E R
T Y R A █ E M T S █ E A R L Y
E D I T S █ A S C H █ T O N E
P R E S T O █ R O D █ N O B
H O N █ I L T R O V A T O R E
E X T █ P A R A D E R O U T E
N Y S █ E N E W S L E T T E R
```

290

```
B L A S T O F F █ F O R A G E
M O R T I M E R █ O D E L A Y
I N C A M E R A █ R E N A M E
N E A T E N █ G N U S █ C B S
O L D E R █ L I A M █ C A L L
R Y E S █ D E L I █ T H R E E
█ W E A S E L S O U T O F
D E F O R M S █ G A R M E N T
O N E M I N T J U L E P █
L A M E S █ H A N K █ C H U M
I M I N █ M A C S █ S H A P E
T O N █ R A N K █ S T A N D S
T R I J E T █ A S L O N G A S
L E S L I E █ S T A R G A T E
E D M O N D █ S U M M E R E D
```

291

```
A N A I S █ G A B █ A N N E S
B A L T I M O R E O R I O L E
O N F A M I L I A R T E R M S
W A R L O R D █ T B O L T █
█ E I N █ C H E █ O S H E A
A C D C █ F A I N T █ E V E N
N O H █ A I R S █ E L N I N O
G R I L L E D █ R A M S E S I
E N T A I L █ C O R N █ T I N
L E C T █ D E L A Y █ C N E T
A T H O L █ X E D █ S L A
█ C R E P E █ S A L A M I S
A N O T H E R F I N E M E S S
S E C U R I T Y D E P O S I T
P O K E S █ S I E █ T R E S S
```

292

```
M R I █ B B C █ S K A █ A S A
C O N T O U R █ U N K E M P T
M A F I O S I █ R E A R E R S
I D I O █ I M A G E █ A R I E
I T T █ N I C E █ D I N A
█ O S S █ E N T O M █ I C K
E S A I █ S A U N A █ C A L E
M I N T █ S L A G S █ A N E W
U N D O █ M I L E S █ T I R E
█ G S U █ E Z I N E █ E N S
C A T T █ N A T E S █ S P Y S
O P A █ █ T Y R █ █ A S P
L O R E L E I █ A L B E R T A
A R T D E C O █ L O A M I E R
S E S S I O N █ S C H I S M S
```

293

```
J S B A C H ■ A C T O F W A R
A L E G R E ■ L O I S L A N E
W I E N E R ■ V O N S Y D O W
S T R E A M L I N E ■ W I D E
■ ■ S T A I N S ■ B E S E T
I R A ■ O J O ■ D U I
C O N C R E T E J U N G L E
E T T U ■ S T E A K ■ H A V E
■ C A P I T A L B E L T W A Y
■ H A Y ■ B O A ■ N N E
A P R O N ■ B I A F R A
S H E L ■ L I P R E A D E R S
S A I D N O T O ■ A M A N A S
A S N E E D E D ■ R I N G I N
D E A R S I R S ■ L E A R N S
```

294

```
R I D G E ■ D I A N A R O S S
O N I O N ■ A N D I Q U O T E
S P E R O ■ S C H N I T Z E L
A R T E S ■ T H E E ■ E V E
P O P S ■ T A U R ■ S A S E S
A T L ■ S E R P E N T S ■
R E A R E N D ■ D A R T I N G
K S T A R S ■ S E I N E R
S T E I G E R ■ T H E R A G E
■ T I R E S O U T ■ B A A
L O T T O ■ S E G A ■ P I T T
O R O ■ S T A G ■ M A K I N
G O T I N L A T E ■ A L I V E
O N E F O O T E R ■ R E N E W
N O M Y S T E R Y ■ C R I S S
```

295

```
H A L L ■ A M E B A ■ T M A N
A M O I ■ P E A R L ■ S I N O
H A W A I I A N I S L A N D S
A T H I R S T ■ D O O R D I E
■ A S K ■ T A G ■ D I Y
I S N O ■ S H I E D ■ N O A H
M I G N O N E T T E S A U C E
A R I ■ Y E R ■ O L E ■ R N A
G E N T L E M A N F A R M E R
E D G E ■ R O B O T ■ E A D S
■ F A R ■ M E W ■ I N N
M O R T I S E ■ H A V A N A S
S P U R O F T H E M O M E N T
E R I E ■ P E A R Y ■ E R N E
C Y T E ■ D R I E S ■ D S O S
```

296

```
A P P O I N T S ■ P R E S S E D
S E L L S O U T ■ H O L Y W A R
I N A L L P R O B A B I L I T Y
S A N A A ■ N O I S E S ■ M O R
A L T S ■ P O L L E D ■ A S N O
I T I ■ E R N I E S ■ C R U E T
D Y N A M I T E S ■ A R L I S S
■ D O S I D O ■ A L I O T H
C E N T R E ■ A P P L E S E E D
A C E R S ■ C L A R O S ■ D A E
E L S A ■ M O A N E R ■ D I R S
S I M ■ N E A L E S ■ G O T T I
U N I V E R S A L S T U D I O S
R E N A U L T ■ E K I N G O U T
A D D R E S S ■ D I S S E N T S
```

297

J O G G E R		F E A S T S	
P A U L I N E		I G N O R E S
I N T E N D S		V A N P E L T
S E L E S	I C E D		O V E R
A D A	U P D O S		B R I N E
N O I R	R E N T A L		N I A
S E D I M E N T A R Y R O C K
P O S T E R I T Y
M A N E A T I N G S H A R K S
I D A	T O A T E E	N E L L
C R I B S	L E N N Y	P E I
M E R E	J A D E	E F R E M
A N O T H E R	R A T L I N E
C A B O O S E	A L I A S E S
L I N G U A	L A S T E X

298

S O U P B O N E	O S C A R S
A N N A R B O R	C H A L E T
Y E T T O S E E	T A P E T O
S T R O K E S	F A K E T A N
M O A N E R	A A V E R A G E
O T C	O V A T I O N	P S S
R E E	F E V E R	
E N D	F R E L E N G	I B F
R I S E N	N R A
A D S	B E R E T T A	F I N
G O E S O V E R	S W A R D S
A V E N G E D	T H E M A G I
T I N E A R	W H O D I D I T
E S T E R S	G E T A L I N E
S H O R T O	N E S T E G G S

299

S C A N	S C A M	S N A R E
O H B E	A R T Y	N I P A T
R E B S	M I L L I O N T H S
E A R T H S C I E N C E
S P E L U N K	S T O P H I M
V E R E E N	O N I O N Y
F B I	L A T E N	E N N I S
L O A F	D E V I L	S E G O
E N T O M	R E L E T	Y O N
E G E R I A	R E G R A B
R O D E N T S	D R A Y A G E
W O O K I E E P E D I A
R U M O R M I L L S	S G T S
A M O R E	M I T T	H E M E
D A N D D	S E A S	A R O D

300

P A J A M A P A N T S	H R H
A L U M I N U M O R E	O O O
B I K I N I M O D E L	L S U
A T E	I M P S	E L I D E S
M B A S	S T I P P L E
S T P A U L	P I A N O L E G
W H A T S	J O N G G	E A U
E E L S	B I L K S	W A V E
A R E	D I V E S	N O S E S
R E S T O R E D	M O L E S T
W C H A N D Y	C E R F
O R E O O S	S H A W	S L O
R U R	T E A C A N I S T E R
D I R	G E T A L I C K I N G
S T Y	O D A R K T H I R T Y

301

	G	R	I	E	R		P	L	A	N	B		
	B	R	O	D	I	E		O	O	L	A	L	A
D	I	A	M	O	N	D	J	I	M	B	R	A	D	Y
R	E	N	E			L	O	N			A	C	R	E
O	R	D		S	W	E	E	T	E	N		K	I	A
S	C	I		T	A	G	S	A	L	E		S	A	T
S	E	N	S	O	R	S		T	E	U	T	O	N	S
	Q	U	I	Z				C	R	U	X		
S	O	U	P	C	O	N		S	T	O	P	S	B	Y
P	S	I		A	N	I	S	T	O	N		C	E	E
I	M	S		L	E	A	P	E	R	S		A	N	N
R	O	I	S		G	A	P			S	N	I	T	
O	N	T	H	E	R	A	Z	O	R	S	E	D	G	E
	D	O	O	V	E	R		N	O	R	M	A	N	
	R	E	A	T	A		E	T	A	I	L		

302

	F	I	R	S	T	S		A	S	P	E	N	S	
M	I	N	N	E	H	AHA		C	H	A	M	O	I	S
O	L	D	S	T	E	R		H	A	D	M	O	R	E
O	L	E		S	E	A	T	E	R		A	N	G	E
S	E	E	T	O		A	D	I	N		T	A	R	
E	S	P	O	U	S	A	L		F	A	C	I	L	E
			S	T	I	L	L	S		Y	A	M	AHA	S
I	M	P	S		M	I	AHA	M	M		M	E	D	S
M	AHA	L	I	A		T	S	E	T	S	E			
P	R	A	N	K	S		S	E	A	P	O	R	T	S
R	A	Y		C	A	S	E			I	N	O	I	L
E	N	E	S		T	H	E	O	N	E		O	R	A
S	E	D	A	L	I	A		M	A	D	E	M	A	N
S	E	A	L	E	R	Y	AHA	M	O	M	E	N	T	
	S	T	A	G	E	S		S	E	N	T	R	A	

303

S	T	O	C	K	I	N	G	S	T	U	F	F	E	R
M	A	C	H	I	N	E	R	E	A	D	A	B	L	E
A	U	T	O	A	C	C	E	S	S	O	R	I	E	S
S	R	A	S		A	R	E	T	E	S		F	I	T
H	I	V	E	D		O	N	E	R		L	I	S	A
U	N	E		R	E	S	A	T		C	O	L	O	R
P	E	S	T	E	R	E	R		P	O	T	E	N	T
			H	A	R	D	C	L	A	M	S			
S	P	E	A	R	S		H	A	V	E	A	C	O	W
H	I	N	N	Y		B	I	Z	E	T		A	R	R
R	A	F	E		D	U	T	Y		O	M	E	G	A
I	N	A		C	U	T	E	S	Y		E	L	A	N
V	I	N	T	A	G	E	C	L	O	T	H	I	N	G
E	N	T	E	R	I	N	T	O	D	E	T	A	I	L
L	O	S	E	O	N	E	S	B	A	L	A	N	C	E

304

P	I	Z	Z	A	B	O	X		D	O	O	W	O	P
A	N	A	E	R	O	B	E		A	L	B	I	N	O
P	A	N	D	E	R	E	R		R	A	I	N	E	S
E	P	I		S	O	S	O	R	R	Y		D	S	T
R	E	E	L		E	S	A	I		C	C	U	P	
S	T	R	A	P	S		I	N	N		I	A	G	O
			B	A	S	E	S	T		J	A	V	A	N
P	A	T	E	N	T	S		E	T	A	G	E	R	E
A	M	U	L	E		S	E	D	O	N	A			
R	A	Z	E		M	A	P		G	E	T	S	E	T
A	R	I	D		O	Y	E	R			E	E	R	O
F	I	G		D	R	S	E	U	S	S		P	O	P
F	L	O	W	E	R		I	M	E	A	N	T	I	T
I	L	O	I	L	O		S	O	L	S	T	I	C	E
N	O	T	N	E	W		T	R	A	S	H	C	A	N

305

```
S T U F F S ■ A S P H O D E L
H E N R I K ■ M I L A N E S E
A R M A N I ■ O M A R E P P S
F R A U D ■ W E N C E S L A S
T I N ■ S E A B E E ■ T O N E
E E L ■ F E R A L ■ P E R O N
D R Y F A R M S ■ L A P E L S
■ ■ L U I S ■ P E R U ■ ■
P A R O L E ■ T R A I P S E S
A D E P T ■ S H I N S ■ A A H
S E T S ■ C L I E N T ■ L S U
S N O W B O A R D ■ R A I T T
F I R E A N T S ■ D O R E M I
O N T A R G E T ■ O U T R A N
R E S T E A S Y ■ S T E I N S
```

306

```
A S P I R E S ■ G A R O T T E
C U L T U R E V U L T U R E S
C R E A S E R E S I S T A N T
U R A L ■ M A S T S ■ E N Y A
S O S ■ H I P T O ■ K A S E M
A G E M A T E S ■ B I T M A P
L A T I M E S ■ M A D E I R A
■ T A X E S ■ P A R I N G S ■
T E K E L ■ W O N K S ■ R E O
A M E S ■ C A L L S ■ M A N N
B O A ■ L A L L Y ■ M A T T E
I T S A L U L U ■ W I R I E R
T H E R O S E T T A S T O N E
H E A R S A Y E V I D E N C E
A R T S A L E ■ S T O S S E L
```

307

```
J A V A M A N ■ A D O P T E R
A L I B A B A ■ L I N E O N E
C R O S S U P ■ A D D E N D A
C O L E T T E ■ S T I R S U P
U S E N E T ■ I N S U R E
S E N T R A S ■ S M E A R E R
E N T S ■ L A T H E ■ T E S S
■ ■ T E E ■ ■
D O O M ■ S I X A M ■ C A S K
U N L A D E N ■ F O R O N C E
R E D Y E D ■ R E L Y O N
A L S O R A N ■ P O W E R O N
N I T R I T E ■ A N I M A T E
T R E A D E D ■ P I R A T E D
E A R L E S S ■ S C E N E R Y
```

308

```
F I S T B U M P ■ S P R E A D
A T T H E Z O O ■ T U I L L E
R A R E B I R D ■ A S S I G N
O L A ■ E S P I A L S ■ N O N
■ I T T ■ H U N K Y D O R Y
D A T A ■ R E M Y ■ C O R E S
E N O R M O U S ■ J A R ■
S O N A T A S ■ P U T I T T O
■ N E D ■ S A D S T O R Y
A B C T V ■ W O R D ■ O K I E
Z E R O E D O U T ■ S Y M
T S E ■ R U N R I O T ■ O M S
E T C H E S ■ S C R A M J E T
C O H O S T ■ O L D S C O R E
S W E E T S ■ P E S K I E S T
```

309

F	A	B	E	R	G	E	E	G	G	■	A	S	H	E
I	N	A	D	I	L	E	M	M	A	■	P	T	A	S
L	O	W	S	P	I	R	I	T	S	■	R	O	T	S
E	N	L	■	O	N	I	T	■	S	P	I	R	E	A
■	■	E	S	T	E	■	P	T	O	L	E	M	Y	■
S	P	O	R	T	S	■	F	L	O	P	S	H	O	T
E	L	U	D	E	■	S	L	A	V	E	■	O	N	E
M	U	T	E	■	P	E	A	C	E	■	M	U	G	S
I	R	S	■	B	A	R	G	E	■	B	E	S	E	T
M	A	H	J	O	N	G	G	■	S	E	D	E	R	S
A	L	I	E	N	E	E	■	C	E	E	S	■	■	■
T	I	N	S	E	L	■	H	U	A	C	■	M	A	O
U	Z	I	S	■	■	S	C	O	R	C	H	M	A	R	K
R	E	N	I	■	■	A	G	L	I	O	E	O	L	I	O
E	D	G	E	■	■	W	I	D	O	W	S	P	E	A	K

310

O	P	T	I	C	A	L	■	U	N	Q	U	O	T	E
F	A	R	G	O	N	E	■	P	U	T	T	O	U	T
F	R	E	E	Z	I	N	G	D	R	I	Z	Z	L	E
B	A	S	T	E	S	■	R	A	S	P	■	I	S	R
A	S	P	I	N	■	T	O	T	E	■	J	E	A	N
S	K	A	T	■	T	R	U	E	■	V	E	R	N	E
E	I	S	■	H	U	A	C	■	Y	E	S	■	■	■
■	■	S	E	A	R	C	H	P	A	R	T	Y	■	■
■	■	D	I	N	■	O	R	L	Y	■	M	O	W	■
O	R	D	E	R	■	S	M	E	E	■	C	A	N	I
J	E	E	R	■	P	L	A	Y	■	C	A	S	E	D
I	S	H	■	A	U	E	R	■	N	O	N	U	S	E
B	C	O	M	P	L	E	X	V	I	T	A	M	I	N
W	A	R	M	E	S	T	■	I	N	A	D	A	Z	E
A	N	N	E	X	E	S	■	M	E	N	A	C	E	D

311

M	A	U	I	■	A	B	E	S	■	B	E	E	B	E
I	T	S	N	O	T	O	V	E	R	U	N	T	I	L
T	H	E	F	A	T	L	A	D	Y	S	I	N	G	S
T	O	N	U	S	■	S	C	A	N	■	D	A	D	A
■	L	O	S	E	■	T	U	N	E	D	■	■	■	■
■	■	■	E	S	T	E	E	S	■	R	I	O	T	S
I	S	A	W	■	O	R	E	■	B	A	N	D	B	S
A	T	S	I	G	N	S	■	D	R	Y	H	E	A	T
M	A	I	T	A	I	■	W	I	E	■	O	A	R	S
S	T	A	H	L	■	P	R	A	W	N	S	■	■	■
■	■	■	E	L	I	O	T	■	O	P	E	C	■	■
A	M	O	I	■	E	N	T	R	■	V	I	A	L	S
L	E	T	S	M	A	K	E	I	T	A	T	R	U	E
D	A	I	L	Y	D	O	U	B	L	E	A	L	E	X
A	T	S	E	A	■	S	P	E	C	■	L	E	S	T

312

M	I	S	O	■	O	C	A	T	■	Y	E	A	S
E	H	U	D	■	Z	E	B	R	A	■	A	X	L	E
G	O	G	O	D	A	N	C	E	R	■	K	I	T	E
S	P	A	R	E	R	S	■	S	C	H	O	L	A	R
■	■	R	E	E	K	O	F	■	H	O	V	E	R	S
O	C	C	A	M	S	R	A	Z	O	R	■	■	■	■
L	O	O	T	S	■	■	W	A	N	N	A	B	E	T
G	O	N	E	■	D	U	C	K	S	■	D	A	D	A
A	P	E	R	T	U	R	E	■	■	T	V	S	E	T
■	■	■	S	M	I	T	H	E	R	E	E	N	S	■
M	R	T	O	A	D	■	T	A	M	E	R	S	■	■
C	H	I	R	R	U	P	■	L	E	E	T	I	D	E
J	I	L	T	■	M	A	S	O	N	D	I	X	O	N
O	N	T	O	■	S	T	E	E	D	■	S	T	L	O
B	O	S	N	■	S	A	S	S	■	E	Y	E	S

313

```
I D I D W H A T ■ S P I G O T
S A M E H E R E ■ O O L A L A
O N A L E A S H ■ B L I N D S
B E G E T T E R ■ S K A G G S
A L I ■ ■ N A S ■ ■ ■ W O E
R A N T ■ S I N K E R B A L L
S W E A R T O ■ I D C A R D S
■ ■ ■ G E O ■ ■ A M T ■ ■ ■
S O S U E M E ■ U M P I R E S
E X O P L A N E T S ■ K A N T
M I D ■ ■ O N O ■ ■ I T O
I D A H O S ■ O P T I O N E D
N I C O L E ■ R I E S L I N G
A Z A R I A ■ M A N O L E T E
L E N N O N ■ E N S N A R E S
```

314

```
B A I T B U C K E T S ■ S A G
E L S I E T H E C O W ■ E L O
G L A M O U R P O S E ■ T I L
S O Y ■ W R I T ■ S E E O F F
■ ■ ■ R U N S ■ W E P T F O R
B A G E L S ■ W I S E A C R E
O N O F F ■ T A N I A ■ L E S
N E O S ■ S E V E N ■ S U M O
U S D ■ B I P E D ■ D E B A R
S T R O L L E R ■ D O E S N T
T H E D U K E ■ D I N K ■ ■
R E A D E R ■ W E A K ■ P F C
A S S ■ F O R A L L I C A R E
C I O ■ I B M T H I N K P A D
K A N ■ N E S T I N G S I T E
```

315

```
S H O W O F F S ■ C M A J O R
C A P I T A L Q ■ R E Z O N E
O H I T S Y O U ■ E X T E N D
R A N ■ E P I C S ■ E C O N
C H E C K ■ P S A T ■ C A T E
H A D O N ■ E H S ■ O S M I C
■ ■ ■ H O W D Y E D O ■ E C K
J A C O B I ■ ■ A M B L E S
A L O ■ B I G P O P P A ■ ■ ■
Z L O T Y ■ D E B ■ H A Y E K
Z A L E ■ B A R S ■ S L A M S
E L K E ■ O Y V E Y ■ K I T
D O I N G S ■ A Q U A F I N A
U N D I E S ■ D U L C I M E R
P E S E T A ■ E Y E E X A M S
```

316

```
T H E B A D S E E D ■ R I G G
V E L O C I P E D E ■ A C R O
S U E Z C R I S I S ■ N E E D
E R N ■ U K E ■ T I C K L E S
T E A K S ■ L O M ■ A S A N A
■ ■ ■ R E M S L E E P ■ N B C
■ F R O D O ■ D N A ■ O D E R
R A I N ■ P F L U G ■ B I L E
A C N E ■ U B I ■ E J E C T ■
M E G ■ U P I N A R M S ■ ■
S T A R R ■ A E C ■ S E A M Y
H O B O B A G ■ T H Y ■ W O O
O W E N ■ R E B O U N D G U Y
M E L D ■ U N S U N G H E R O
E L L O ■ M T S T H E L E N S
```

317

```
I T O   W E B B E R     J L O
N O P R O B L E M O     D I O R
H Y P E R B O L I C     N U V A
A B O V E   O L L A   A J E T
L O S S   D D A Y     I P O
E X E   S E M     D O C T O R
    A L L O S A U R U S E S
  C O G I T O E R G O S U M
B L U E M A N G R O U P
L I T R E S     O N T   P U N
A N O     D A W G   H O P E
M I F F   B A R K   P A R S E
E Q U I   U N R E Q U I T E D
M U S E   S T A Y U P L A T E
E E E     Y E S S E S   L S D
```

318

```
D I S C   F L A V O R F L A V
E L L A   I A M A M E R I C A
F L O R   S P I C E G I R L S
  S W E E T D E A L   T A U T
  M E L B A   S E A T
I R O N L U N G   T R A M P S
P A T   Y M C A S   S T R U T
A S I A   P E L E G   A S T O
S T O U T   S A N E R   P T L
S A N T A S   S T T E R E S A
    O P A H   I O N I A
N A O H   L A T E L U N C H
I N L A L A L A N D   S O A P
B A D R O M A N C E   E C H O
S T E P S I S T E R   S K A T
```

319

```
  R E D U C E S P E E D
  B A R I T O N E S A X E S
W I D E S A R G A S S O S E A
E R I C H   P A S T E D O W N
A N A T   T O G O   L U T E D
V E T S   A R E N T   S O L O
E Y E   G R A S P E D   S L R
    E M T   R A E
C D C   M A E W E S T   W E D
R E A M   C R E M E   B A N E
A R R A Y   A B I T   E L B A
I M P R E C I S E   M A K E R
G O O G L E D I R E C T O R Y
  T R I P L E T E A M I N G
  T E S T R E S U L T S
```

320

```
A S H L A R   W A T C H O U T
T H E O N E   A D R I E N N E
T A L O N S   I M I T A T E S
I L I K E I T L I K E T H A T
C A P S   D E E R E   P E T E
A L A   G E N R E   R U G E R
  A D D E N D S   D E M O N S
    R O C S   H A R P
S E C E D E   D A T A S E T
P U R S E   S E V E N   V A L
I R I S   B E B O P   G E N E
R A N C H O C U C A M O N G A
A S G O O D A S   L O U S E D
L I E A B E D S   M O D U L E
S A D T O S A Y   S N A P O N
```

321

A	L	P		A	S	S	T		A	M	E	L	I	A
N	E	H	E	M	I	A	H		B	O	X	I	N	G
A	G	I	T	A	T	O	R		B	O	P	P	E	R
			L	E	N	I		I	M	A	G	E		
S	O	I		A	N	G	L	O		S	R	T	A	S
E	P	P	S		S	O	L	O	N		T	H	R	O
N	A	P	P	Y		D	A	N	C	E		E	M	O
A	L	I	F	R	A	Z	I	E	R	F	I	G	H	T
T	I	N		S	P	I	N	Y		S	T	R	O	H
O	N	E	R		E	L	M	E	R		D	E	L	E
R	E	S	E	T		L	A	S	E	R		A	E	R
			T	I	T	A	N		P	A	S	T		
P	A	J	A	M	A		I	R	O	N	H	E	A	D
S	M	O	K	I	N		L	A	R	G	E	S	S	E
S	P	E	E	D	S		A	N	T	E		T	K	O

322

S	S	T	S		L	E	M	O	N	T	A	R	T	
P	E	E	P		C	A	L	I	F	O	R	N	I	A
R	A	N	I		A	D	U	L	T	S	O	N	L	Y
I	N	D	E	B	T	E	D		U	T	I	L		
G	O	O	G	L	E	S	E	A	R	C	H			
	C	L	E	A	R		R	A	H		G	M	T	
B	A	L	L	S		M	A	R	I	A		E	A	U
U	S	A		T	R	A	D	I	N	G		T	I	M
D	E	R		F	O	X	E	D		E	G	A	D	S
S	Y	S		U	N	I		A	N	A	R	M		
		P	R	I	M	A	L	S	C	R	E	A	M	
W	A	R	N		C	A	P	Y	B	A	R	A		
T	H	R	E	A	D	B	A	R	E		A	D	I	T
H	A	I	L	C	A	E	S	A	R		G	O	A	T
O	M	E	L	E	T	T	E	S		E	N	N	E	

323

S	T	E	E	R		C	A	N	A	A	N		
T	A	N	N	I	C		N	O	S	E	N	S	E
A	K	R	O	N	O	H		A	V	I	O	N	I	C
G	E	O	R	G	I	A		B	E	N	N	E	T	T
	A	L	M	O	N	D	J	O	Y		S	A	W	A
	L	E	F	T	J	A	B		P	I	L	E	R	
		F	O	I	L		W	A	G	E	R	S		
C	H	R	I	S	S	I	E	H	Y	N	D	E		
P	L	I	E	R	S		S	N	I	P				
H	O	R	S	E		A	C	U	T	E	S	T		
I	S	A	T		S	T	O	R	E	R	O	O	M	
L	E	G	R	O	O	M		E	N	V	I	O	U	S
I	S	A	I	D	N	O		D	E	I	G	N	T	O
P	E	N	N	I	E	S			D	E	N	I	E	D
S	T	A	G	E	S				W	E	E	D	S	

324

C	L	E	A	R	E	D	O	N	E	S	N	A	M	E	
H	O	S	T	I	L	E	T	A	K	E	O	V	E	R	
A	N	T	I	P	R	O	H	I	B	I	T	I	O	N	
R	E	S	T	S	O	N	O	N	E	S	O	A	R	S	
			S	A	Y	S		A	R	M					
	U	F	W						G	O	F	L	A	T	
	D	N	I	E	S	T	E	R			R	E	F	I	
G	R	A	N	D	T	O	T	A	L		I	T	O	R	
E	L	B	E		P	A	R	K	A	V	E	N	U	E	
S	A	L	S		T	E	E	N	I	D	O	L			
T	O	E	T	A	P				C	S	T				
			B	H	A		A	C	E	H					
O	C	T	O	B	E	R	S	U	R	P	R	I	S	E	
P	L	A	Y	E	D	F	A	V	O	R	I	T	E	S	
E	A	R	L	Y	R	E	T	I	R	E	M	E	N	T	
C	R	O	S	S	E	D	O	N	E	S	P	A	T	H	

325

```
B B Q C H I P S ■ S P L I F F
Y O U G O T I T ■ T O O F A R
J O E I S U Z U ■ D E V I C E
O Z S ■ ■ P A C T S ■ E D E N
V E T T E ■ R K O ■ F R I T Z
E S S E X ■ R U M O R ■ D I I
■ ■ ■ T H E O P E R A ■ I M E
W E T R A G ■ ■ C N O T E S ■
H M O ■ L A I D B A C K ■ ■ ■
A P O ■ E N S O R ■ I R I S H
C A K E D ■ S T E ■ S A N T O
K N O W ■ F O C A L ■ ■ J O N
J A V I E R ■ O K E Y D O K E
O D E N S E ■ M I N O R K E Y
B A R G E D ■ S N O O K E R S
```

326

```
B E A T S U P ■ ■ N E C T A R
O N T H E M A P ■ E T H A N E
V A R A N A S I ■ S T A I N S
A M E N D ■ S E P T U P L E T
R O U X ■ V I R U S ■ ■ F R Y
Y R S ■ B O O R S ■ S N A I L
■ ■ S E I N E S ■ P O N C E
B U T T E R F L Y K I S S E S
A N W A R ■ R E W I R E ■ ■ ■
R I O T S ■ U N I T E ■ G U S
B O P ■ ■ R I F L E ■ B A N E
A N E C D O T A L ■ G A M B A
D I N A R S ■ N O V E M B E R
O S C I N E ■ T W I N B I L L
S T E N O S ■ ■ S A T I A T E
```

327

```
I M K I D D I N G ■ I Q U I T
S A L T P E T E R ■ D U N N E
A N A S T A S I A ■ S I L V A
D U T Y ■ R O N D O ■ R E A P
O M S ■ S I N ■ ■ M I K A D O
R I C H I E ■ H E A V Y S E T
E T H A N ■ G E E N A ■ H R S
■ ■ J K R O W L I N G ■ ■
S E P ■ S I R E S ■ H U M I D
E X A M I N E D ■ N O T I M E
R U L I N G ■ W O E ■ S A C
I R A N ■ S A D A T ■ H U G O
A B Z U G ■ R O X Y M U S I C
L A Z E D ■ F R E E A G E N T
S N I T S ■ S Y N T H E S E S
```

328

```
W A L T Z I N G ■ A R C A D E
I D A R E N O T ■ F O L L O W
N O N O N O N O ■ F O O Z L E
O P A L I N E ■ V A S S A L S
S T I L T ■ U N I T E R ■ ■
■ ■ S H A T N E R E S Q U E
A D S ■ S T O I C ■ R E A R S
M O A S ■ M O C K S ■ T W A S
A D I O S ■ H O E R S ■ I L O
T O N Y A H A R D I N G ■ ■
■ ■ T A V E R N ■ A R A B S
T H E B A R D ■ J A I A L A I
H E L E N E ■ C U R L I E S T
A R M A N I ■ A N G E L P I E
N O O N A N ■ W O O D S H E D
```

329

R	E	S	O	D	S			B	E	D	A	Z	Z	L	E
E	X	O	C	E	T			I	D	A	R	E	Y	O	U
L	A	L	A	L	A			C	A	L	E	N	D	A	R
A	M	O			E	N	Z	Y	M	E	S		E	D	O
X	I	A	N		D	I	C	E	Y		C	C	U	P	
I	N	C	A	S		P	L	S		I	H	O	P	E	
N	E	T	S	C	A	P	E		I	D	A				
G	E	S	T	A	P	O		S	O	L	I	D	E	R	
			A	N	T		F	I	N	E	T	U	N	E	
H	T	E	S	T		B	L	T		D	E	N	E	B	
O	R	L	E		T	R	E	A	D		A	C	R	O	
B	O	I		T	H	E	A	T	R	E		E	G	O	
N	U	D	E	B	O	M	B		E	L	I	C	I	T	
O	P	E	N	A	R	E	A		A	B	L	A	Z	E	
B	E	S	T	R	O	N	G		R	A	S	P	E	D	

330

C	H	I	P	P	E	W	A		P	A	L	A	T	E
R	E	Q	U	I	R	E	S		O	B	E	R	O	N
I	S	U	P	P	O	S	E		O	R	A	T	E	S
S	T	O	P	S		E	X	T	R	A	F	I	N	E
C	O	T	Y		A	R	U	B	A		S	C	A	M
O	N	E	L	A	P		A	T	T	S		L	I	B
		O	T	O	O	L	E		T	C	E	L	L	
B	R	A	V	E	S	T		S	T	R	A	S	S	E
J	U	D	E	A		T	S	T	R	A	P			
T	S	A		T	R	O	I		O	W	E	S	T	O
H	T	M	L		E	I	L	A	T		C	H	O	W
O	B	S	E	S	S	I	V	E		B	O	R	O	N
M	E	A	N	T	O		E	S	C	A	R	O	L	E
A	L	L	I	E	D		R	O	D	L	A	V	E	R
S	T	E	N	T	S		S	P	I	E	L	E	R	S

331

G	A	P	I	N	G			C	L	A	R	A	B	O	W
O	N	E	P	E	R			N	O	S	E	D	I	V	E
O	T	T	A	W	A			T	A	K	E	S	T	E	A
D	I	S	S		D	I	O	D	E	S		E	R	R	
G	E	T	S		U	N	W	E	D		B	O	D	E	
A	T	O		B	A	K	E	D		M	A	N	O	R	
M	A	R	K	E	T	E	R		F	E	B				
E	M	E	R	G	E	D		P	L	A	Y	S	O	N	
			O	E	D		M	A	I	N	M	E	N	U	
F	A	I	N	T		R	I	V	E	T		A	B	C	
O	N	M	E		S	O	N	E	S		S	H	U	L	
R	A	P		I	N	C	U	R	S		C	O	T	E	
O	K	E	Y	D	O	K	E		O	P	O	R	T	O	
N	I	N	E	I	R	O	N		L	A	W	S	O	N	
E	N	D	T	O	E	N	D		O	L	S	E	N	S	

332

B	I	G	M	A	C			S	A	D	S	O	N	G	S
O	G	L	A	L	A			O	U	T	T	H	E	R	E
D	O	A	J	I	G			F	T	S	U	M	T	E	R
Y	T	D		T	E	N	T	O		N	I	T	T	I	
C	O	S	T		S	E	T	H	S		C	L	E	F	
A	R	O	A	R		L	O	A	T	H		E	L	S	
S	I	M	I	A	N		P	R	O	A	M				
T	O	E	L	O	O	P		P	O	L	E	M	I	C	
			S	U	M	A	C		D	O	S	I	D	O	
O	R	S		L	A	P	A	Z		S	A	L	E	M	
N	A	T	L		N	A	P	E	S		S	L	A	B	
S	C	R	A	M		B	I	D	E	T		P	L	O	
T	E	A	C	A	K	E	S		T	O	T	O	I	V	
A	M	N	E	S	I	A	C		B	R	O	N	Z	E	
R	E	D	S	C	A	R	E		Y	O	N	D	E	R	

333

S	U	R	F	E	R	G	I	R	L		O	C	T	S
O	R	E	O	C	O	O	K	I	E		H	O	W	E
S	A	F	E	T	Y	B	E	L	T		M	A	I	N
A	L	T			C	U	T	E	S	T		T	N	T
		C	R	E	S	T		D	A	S	H	E	R
S	L	A	S	H		T	E	X	A	R	K	A	N	A
T	O	L	T	E	C		S	I	N	G	I	N	G
E	V	E		O	A	R		I	C	E		G	I	N
	E	X	I	S	T	E	D		E	T	H	E	N	E
S	P	A	R	T	A	C	U	S		E	A	R	E	D
C	O	N	T	A	C		S	T	A	D	T
Y	T	D		T	O	M	T	O	M		R	E	F
T	I	E	R		M	Y	P	L	E	A	S	U	R	E
H	O	R	A		B	R	A	I	N	C	H	I	L	D
E	N	I	D		S	A	N	D	S	T	O	N	E	S

334

C	L	A	P	P	U	S	H	U	P	S		W	A	H
O	U	T	E	R	P	L	A	N	E	T		I	T	O
S	T	O	N	E	C	I	R	C	L	E		R	E	S
M	E	N	D	S		P	A	L	T	R	I	E	S	T
O	D	E	S		B	O	L	O		E	N	S	U	E
				S	A	N	D	A	L		A	P	P	L
P	R	A	Y	E	R		S	K	I	P	R	O	P	E
H	I	B	A	C	H	I		S	N	O	O	K	E	R
O	V	E	R	T	O	N	E		D	O	W	E	R	S
N	E	R	D		P	A	Y	P	A	L
E	R	R	E	D		P	E	A	S		B	O	B	S
T	R	A	D	E	L	A	W	S		C	A	R	O	L
I	A	N		M	I	N	I	S	T	O	R	A	G	E
C	F	C		O	P	I	N	I	O	N	A	T	E	D
S	T	Y		S	O	C	K	M	O	N	K	E	Y	S

335

S	T	O	P	S		F	O	T	O		N	O	L
T	A	N	Y	A		I	B	A	R		B	E	B	E
A	L	E	R	T		R	O	L	E		L	O	S	T
L	E	A	R	S		E	L	K	S		A	N	O	S
A	S	C	H		D	A	I	S		S	C	A	L	P
G	E	T	I	T	O	N		T	O	O	K	T	E	A
		C	H	E	T		O	U	T	E	A	T	S
S	T	O	V	E	S		S	T	Y	L	E	S
C	A	P	I	T	O	L		A	T	E	E
A	T	E	C	A	K	E		R	E	D	D	E	E	R
L	E	N	T	S		A	P	E	R		S	U	M	O
D	R	N	O		U	V	E	A		T	U	R	I	N
I	T	E	R		G	E	R	M		A	S	O	N	E
N	O	S	Y		L	I	M	A		L	A	P	E	L
G	T	S			I	N	S	P		E	N	E	M	Y

336

A	B	L	E		T	H	E	R	A	S	C	A	L	S
L	Y	E	S		H	A	D	A	S	H	O	T	A	T
A	G	T	S		I	R	A	N	C	O	N	T	R	A
N	O	H	O		S	A	M	T	H	E	S	H	A	M
A	N	A		I	R	E				E	M	P
R	E	V	E	R	S	E	S	I	D	E
K	E	E	N	A	N		C	A	L		I	F	S
I	R	I	D	I	U	M		E	D	I	T	O	U	T
N	A	T		S	T	A		B	O	N	N	E	R
			A	S	P	H	A	L	T	T	I	L	E
U	P	C			U	L	A		A	P	E
S	E	E	D	P	E	A	R	L	S		T	N	U	T
I	T	S	A	S	E	C	R	E	T		U	S	M	A
N	A	T	H	A	N	H	A	L	E		R	E	P	R
G	L	A	S	S	Y	E	Y	E	D		F	A	S	T

337

W	R	I	T	H	E	D				P	O	U	L	T	S
H	A	R	V	A	R	D			P	E	R	D	I	E	M
I	C	E	S	T	A	T	I	O	N	Z	E	B	R	A	
S	I	N	E	S			N	O	N	O		R	N	S	
K	N	I	T		M	A	D	L	Y		L	E	A	H	
S	E	C		T	U	B	E	S		B	E	T	T	E	
			B	O	S	O	X		B	O	A	T	E	R	
		M	A	R	K	O	F	Z	O	R	R	O			
G	R	I	T	T	Y		I	O	W	A	N				
R	E	L	E	E		A	N	N	E	X		P	H	D	
I	S	I	S		N	I	G	E	R		B	O	A	R	
P	E	T		D	I	K	E			C	L	I	N	E	
P	R	I	S	O	N	E	R	O	F	Z	E	N	D	A	
E	V	A	S	I	O	N		C	O	A	S	T	E	R	
R	E	S	E	T	S			T	E	R	S	E	L	Y	

338

A	R	F	A	R	F			F	A	S	T	D	R	A	W
W	E	L	T	E	R		I	D	L	E	R	I	C	H	
E	C	A	R	T	E		R	O	U	L	E	T	T	E	
		T	A	R	E		S	N	E	E		Z	O	E	
S	E	N	I	O	R	I	T	I	S		B	E	N	Z	
E	T	O	N		A	D	O	S		G	O	S	E	E	
P	C	T		P	N	I	N		S	E	Z				
T	H	E	B	I	G	G	E	S	T	L	O	S	E	R	
			A	T	E		T	E	E	D		A	L	E	
E	N	D	I	T		S	O	R	E		S	L	I	T	
J	A	I	L		B	O	B	B	L	E	H	E	A	D	
E	V	A		A	R	A	L		J	E	R	I			
C	A	L	A	M	A	R	I		A	N	I	T	A	S	
T	H	E	R	A	V	E	N		W	I	N	E	R	Y	
S	O	D	A	J	E	R	K		S	E	E	M	E	D	

339

A	T	W	O			S	H	E	A		T	B	A	R	
L	E	A	D		C	H	I	L	L		H	O	M	O	
T	E	L	E	P	H	O	N	I	C		E	L	M	S	
A	P	E		L	O	A	D		H	A	R	L	E	Y	
R	E	S	T	A	R	T		H	E	R	M	I	T		
S	E	A	I	C	E		L	U	M	M	O	X	E	S	
		M	E	S	S	I	L	Y		P	U	R	L		
F	R	E	E	D		T	E	C		G	Y	P	S	Y	
L	A	V	A		P	I	N	E	S	O	L				
U	T	E	N	S	I	L	S		Q	U	A	H	O	G	
	I	N	D	E	N	T		C	U	R	E	A	L	L	
B	O	O	T	E	D		G	O	A	D		N	E	A	
A	N	D	I		O	P	E	N	S	E	A	S	O	N	
L	A	D	D		W	E	N	C	H		G	O	L	D	
E	L	S	E		N	A	S	H		A	M	E	S		

340

L	J	U	B	L	J	A	N	A		P	A	B	L	O	
A	U	N	A	T	U	R	E	L		T	R	O	O	P	
B	R	I	M	S	T	O	N	E		A	L	I	C	E	
S	E	T	S		E	M	E	R	Y		E	L	A	N	
			A	S	A		T	A	S	S	E	L	S		
S	W	I	R	L		S	T	I	N	T		D	I	E	
P	A	M	E	L	A		I	N	K	S	P	O	T	S	
A	L	M	A		B	U	D	G	E		A	V	I	A	
C	L	A	R	I	S	S	A		E	S	T	E	E	M	
E	A	T		S	C	A	L	D		T	E	R	S	E	
S	W	E	A	R	A	T		A	O	L					
H	A	R	M		M	O	A	N	S		O	M	A	N	
I	L	I	A	D		D	R	Z	H	I	V	A	G	O	
P	L	A	Z	A		A	L	I	E	N	A	T	E	D	
S	A	L	E	M		Y	O	G	A	C	L	A	S	S	

341

```
N A R C S ■ S A L E S T A G S
A M O L E ■ P O O L T A B L E
P E C A N ■ A L L S E W N U P
I N K S T E R ■ ■ ■ S E T A
E R O S I V E ■ I N S ■ G A R
R A N A M O K ■ N E T ■ A M A
■ ■ ■ E N E ■ M O R I T A T
■ J O H N N Y ■ O N E N O T E
B O R A T E S ■ T A S E R E D
L E E R ■ ■ H T S ■ ■ ■
I T S A ■ B E M I R E D
P O T S ■ A S A R U L E
P R E S C H O O L ■ R E N E S
E R I E C A N A L ■ K N I C K
D E A D S P O T S ■ S E C T S
```

342

```
C T S ■ B E B E ■ N O T H I N
D E L I R I U M ■ O C E A N O
C L E M E N Z A ■ T H A N K S
■ L U C R E Z I A B O R G I A
E S T O S ■ E L L E ■ G E N L
S A H L ■ F R E E ■ G A R D E
P L E D ■ A B R A X A S ■
O L D ■ L I E ■ J O B ■ I B O
■ M I R A M A X ■ T M A X
T A M E D ■ T A C O ■ H E R E
O M A N ■ Z E I T ■ D R A I N
S O U T H E R N A C C E N T ■
S U N H A T ■ M E R C A T O R
E N D O R A ■ A S T A T I N E
S T Y L E S ■ N T S B ■ T E X
```

343

```
L A G ■ C A P P ■ C L O S E R
A L E H O U S E ■ R I P P L E
T I N A C T I N ■ E A S E L S
T A T T O O ■ C B E R ■ C S I
E S S E N ■ B I R D ■ S I B S
■ ■ U V U L A ■ M A M E T
■ M O T O R S C O O T E R S
■ P A R O L E H E A R I N G ■
W A L K I E T A L K I E S ■
E T A I L ■ T R E S S ■ ■
B R Y N ■ K E P T ■ S I M B A
C I A ■ R I S E ■ R E C A L L
A L L O U T ■ N E A T E N U P
M E A N I E ■ E G G T E E T H
S Y M O N S ■ R O S E ■ D O A
```

344

```
E C H O S O U N D E R ■ P B J
S H A R O N S T O N E ■ O R U
M A N B I T E S D O G ■ L I N
E K G ■ L I M B ■ L I B I D O
■ A S S U M E ■ M A N A T E E
■ ■ I R E ■ M E G A H I T S
M A D G E ■ R A H A L ■ C O Q
E L A N ■ N A T T Y ■ S A B U
A P T ■ T I B I A ■ G E L E E
T H E T E X A N ■ D O C ■
C A M E L O T ■ B E T T O R
A M Y T A N ■ Y E A H ■ L E M
S A M ■ V E N U S D E M I L O
E L O ■ I R A R O L L O V E R
S E M ■ V A N I T Y P L A T E
```

345

```
HMM   ARCH  GASCAP
EAU   RARA  ESPANA
NUS   CHURCHHYMNS
  RIOT  DIR   PAT
MICHAELCAINE
MTSINAI   GETAT
EAT  CELT  OUCH
NAUGHTYORNICE
INSO  OSLO   IRE
ADAGE   EASEDIN
  CHRISTMASEVE
AVA   OAK   LONI
SILENTNIGHT TEN
SCENEI  TREE  ARE
TICTAC  SEED  LAW
```

346

```
CBSNEWS  DECIMAL
RATATAT  EMANATE
ONADARE  LILLIAN
CATALINAISLAND
    NON   SOY
DAZING  DOIN  JAM
IVORY  ARNO  PURE
MONICAMOUNTAINS
LIES  DEMS  INCAS
YDS  RUSE  SNEEZY
    AOL   DOT
ANITARACETRACK
ANIMATE  TREACLE
DONATES  ENDPLAY
DNATEST  TOSSUPS
```

347

```
JALOPY   THEWIRE
JEANIE   TEENIDOL
ARISEN   IMSOGLAD
BOL  STOMP  SIDE
RNA  ABETS   NIS
AAA  ISLA  WIDGET
MULAN  AFLAME
STICKITTOTHEMAN
  TEPEES  ITALO
SSTARS  REAP  POW
TAU  ASTIR  QUA
ORRS  AITCH  UEY
PTBARNUM  HAVETO
BROMANCE  ERESTU
YESISEE  SEXTET
```

348

```
WITHERS  PFIZER
ONEOCAT  PERRINE
OFNOUSE  ORATORS
LOAD  TEFLON  NAT
ERNO  ALRITZ  IGO
NICOL  MIT  MSEC
STY  ADAGIO  OMSK
  ROUGHCAST
BALE  INTAKE  RAF
ENID  OWL  AIOLI
EGO  FILIAL  MMIX
FUN  EMIGRE  PUMA
ALIBABA  EPAULET
LAZARUS  NEPTUNE
ORELSE  ARRESTS
```

349

```
R A I S A   P E T T I S H
E S S E N E   G O N E I N T O
S T I P E S   A L L M E T A L
T U T T U T   S L I P P E R Y
A T T I R E   B U S L I N E
F E R M I S   A T T E N D S
F L U E S   O G E E
  Y E S M A N   R E E F E R
      T R A S   S O N E S
  I M P E T U S   T O O T L E
  N O R M A N S   Y T T R I A
A T R O P I N E   R E P A S T
C U I S I N E S   O R A C H E
E N T E R E R S   S I T T E R
R E A D E R S   C H E S S
```

350

```
C A D S   S H R O U D   P R Y
I B E T   C O A R S E   I O U
A S F A R A S I C A N T E L L
  E L A T E S     T H R E E
T A N K S   E R A S E R
I R S   H A S T E N   N E A R
D O E   E T C H E D   E D D A
B U L L S E Y E L A N T E R N
I S E E   A T T I L A   R I D
T E S T   S H I N E R   O A R
  S T R E E T   K E N N Y
M I N E O   A N G E L S
A M E R I C A N I N D I A N S
J U S   L U M I N A   T R A P
A S S   S E A C O W   E D G Y
```

351

```
U S M A R S H A L   S A F I N
P H O N E H O M E   P R O M O
C O U N T Y T A X   E G R E T
L O N E R   D I P L O M A T
O F T   O P T I C A L   U N O
S L I P   A R S O N   G L I B
E Y E S O R E   N A R R A T E
    A I D     T E A
S W A L L O W   H E L I P A D
H A R M   N A V E L   L O G E
O R S   P E L I C A N   K I T
T H E F O R C E   O D E T O
P E N I N   O F F I C E M A X
A R I S E   T O O K A V O T E
R O C K S   T R E E L I N E D
```

352

```
C I T E D   C O O L E D O F F
O N I C E   U R S A M I N O R
L A N Z A   R O C K O P E R A
G R E E N A L G A E   S L A T
A M A M E M B E R S   B I B B
T O R A   N A N S   C A N I O
E R S   W I R Y   N I C E T Y
  L A O S   B E A K
I N K E R S   A L T O   P Y E
C E N S E   C R A T   R E O S
E W E S   B A T C L E A N U P
S T A S   I L I K E D T H A T
H A D A B L A S T   U S O N E
O K I L L B I T E   C O L D S
W E N T T O S E A   E N D I T
```

353

```
S T A G E M O M ▮ ▮ A S P I C
P O T A T O R O T ▮ M E A R A
A R E T H A N O W ▮ B E S E T
S T A ▮ N O N O N O ▮ O M A
M E T U P ▮ T A W N Y ▮ D E W
▮ ▮ S U L ▮ N E W ▮ B O M B
▮ S T A M P E D E ▮ A A B B A
B E E R A N D S K I T T L E S
R E A M S ▮ H I S O R H E R ▮
A D R Y ▮ T A X ▮ N I E ▮ ▮
C M D ▮ M O R P H ▮ A S C A P
K O R ▮ I M R E A L ▮ A L A
I N O I L ▮ I N S O F A R A S
S E P T A ▮ S C O R E C A R D
H Y S O N ▮ ▮ E N D R H Y M E
```

354

```
W A T E R L I L I E S ▮ D O E
A B R A C A D A B R A ▮ O P S
T H E C A T S M E O W ▮ N A P
T O S H ▮ A S T I I I T A L Y
S R S ▮ C A Y ▮ ▮ C N O T E
▮ ▮ E R N ▮ B A A ▮ L E S H
S P E L U N K E R ▮ D E L C O
O O D L E S O F N O O D L E S
F R U I T ▮ F O O T L O O S E
A T C O ▮ S I G ▮ R E S ▮ ▮
▮ F A T H A ▮ P O D ▮ I V S
S O T T O V O C E ▮ R H E A
A L I ▮ G E N E R A T I O N X
M I O ▮ A M E R I C A N P I E
E O N ▮ N E D F L A N D E R S
```

355

```
L E A P T ▮ M O T T ▮ A P B S
A R N A Z ▮ O R E O ▮ M O O T
L I V I A ▮ P A N A T E L L A
A K I N T O ▮ T O D O L I S T
W A L T Z E S O F F W I T H ▮
▮ ▮ E I D E R ▮ I S A B E L
O Z A R K ▮ E S T S ▮ S U V A
H E N ▮ I A M ▮ E H S ▮ R I P
M T G S ▮ R E F S ▮ N O O K S
S A L A A M ▮ I S A A C ▮ ▮
▮ J I M M Y C R A C K C O R N
S O C I A B L E ▮ K E L S E Y
O N A S T R E A K ▮ P U L S E
B E N E ▮ A R N O ▮ I D I O T
A S S N ▮ T K T S ▮ T E N D S
```

356

```
Z I N F A N D E L ▮ A D O P T
I D A L U P I N O ▮ S E P O Y
P I N E T R E E S ▮ T W E R P
P O A C H ▮ S M A S H I N T O
O M S K ▮ K E Y L I M E S ▮
▮ ▮ E L A L ▮ T R A S H T V
F A N D O M ▮ H O N ▮ T O R E
R B I ▮ L I V E S O N ▮ P I N
O L E O ▮ K A Y ▮ S A M S O N
G E T R E A L ▮ N I N E ▮ ▮
▮ Z A N Z I B A R ▮ G U L P
R U S T L E D U P ▮ R A T I O
A S C I I ▮ A T O N E T I M E
H O H O S ▮ T Y L E N O L P M
S C E N T ▮ E L I O T N E S S
```

357

C	A	T	H	A	I	R	S		C	A	N	I	F	F
O	N	I	O	N	S	E	T		A	T	O	N	A	L
P	I	T	V	I	P	E	R		V	E	S	T	R	Y
S	T	E	E	L	Y	D	A	N		A	H	E	A	P
E	A	R	L				P	E	L	T		G	P	A
			T	A	C	O	M	A			F	R	A	S
	W	A	R	M	O	N	E	S	H	E	A	R	T	
	A	E	R	I	A	L	A	S	S	A	U	L	T	
D	I	A	M	O	N	D	F	I	E	L	D	S		
O	R	L	Y		D	O	E	S	N	T				
D	B	L		S	A	N	E			P	A	S	O	
G	O	D	E	L		E	D	M	C	M	A	H	O	N
I	R	O	N	I	C		B	L	O	O	P	E	R	S
E	N	I	G	M	A		A	L	A	C	A	R	T	E
R	E	T	S	Y	N		G	E	T	S	L	O	S	T

358

T	E	A	T	R	O	S		W	E	D	I	D	I	T
O	N	C	E	I	N	A	L	I	F	E	T	I	M	E
S	T	R	E	E	T	M	U	S	I	C	I	A	N	S
S	E	O	U	L		O	P	E	L	S		L	O	T
I	N	S	P		A	V	O	T	E		A	S	T	I
N	T	S		A	D	A	N	O		R	U	N	I	N
G	E	T	T	H	E	R	E		B	O	R	I	N	G
	C	H	A	M	P	S		B	R	Y	A	N	T	
G	O	E	S	A	T		L	O	O	K	S	E	E	S
O	R	B	E	D		S	A	Y	T	O		O	R	I
O	D	O	R		R	E	T	C	H		I	N	E	S
D	I	R		R	O	L	E	O		A	N	E	S	T
M	A	D	E	A	M	E	N	T	A	L	N	O	T	E
E	L	E	P	H	A	N	T	T	R	A	I	N	E	R
N	E	R	I	S	S	A		S	C	R	E	E	D	S

359

H	A	R	S	H					N	O	N	C	E	
A	R	E	T	E		P	R	E	R	E	C	O	R	D
B	A	G	E	L		R	U	S	T	E	A	T	E	N
I	M	I	M	P	R	E	S	S	E	D		U	V	A
B	E	S	T	W	I	S	H	E	S		C	P	A	S
		H	A	N	S	E	N		T	O	T	S		
	A	V	E	N	G	E	D		M	I	R	O	S	
	N	A	T	T	E	R		F	A	N	N	I	E	
	I	C	I	E	R		B	A	S	K	E	T	S	
	M	A	D	D		L	U	T	H	E	R			
B	A	N	E		M	O	T	H	E	R	S	D	A	Y
A	T	T		C	E	N	T	E	R	S	T	A	G	E
D	I	L	L	I	N	G	E	R		D	O	R	E	N
G	O	O	D	D	E	E	D	S		A	R	E	N	T
E	N	T	R	E					M	E	S	T	A	

360

G	E	O	M	E	T	R	I	C	S	E	R	I	E	S
A	C	T	I	V	E	I	N	T	E	R	E	S	T	S
T	H	E	D	E	S	C	E	N	T	O	F	M	A	N
S	T	A	I	N	L	E	S	S	S	T	E	E	L	S
				T	A	R			F	I	R			
R	A	J	A	H	S		L	A	R	C		O	W	S
O	Z	O	N	E		E	A	S	E		T	R	A	P
Y	O	U	K	N	O	W	T	H	E	D	R	I	L	L
A	L	L	A		P	O	K	Y		A	I	O	L	I
L	E	E		J	A	K	E		C	Y	G	N	E	T
			J	A	R			F	O	B				
E	S	S	E	N	T	I	A	L	O	R	G	A	N	S
T	E	L	L	S	I	T	L	I	K	E	I	T	I	S
R	E	A	L	E	S	T	A	T	E	A	G	E	N	T
E	D	M	O	N	T	O	N	E	S	K	I	M	O	S

361

```
ZORBA   ICC   CHAUD
AWILL   TRY   LASSO
RADIOJOURNALIST
FRESHVOCABULARY
    ASAS   INAS
OAS    OVO    OFME
SETADATE   ALLIED
CROSSWORDSOLVER
AERATE   BELPAESE
ROMP   CAN     GED
     COAL   URDU
MOBILELIBRARIES
OPENINGSENTENCE
STEIN   OTT   EWERS
TORTE   NSA   LUAUS
```

362

```
OFFICEBOY    TBARS
HARTCRANE    ELIEL
BROWNEYES    CARGO
AMWAY   SANA   CRIS
BENS      OSHKOSH
YRS   WAGS   SALUTE
    BASTE   AGATES
 JOETHEPLUMBER
RUPAUL   ISLAS
EDESSA   ATTN   HMS
RINSING     FOAL
ACLU   DICE   HILDA
TIARA   LADIESDAY
EATEN   DRIVETIME
SLEDS   SPEEDSTER
```

363

```
BIGMAC   MISSTEP
ADRATE   PARTTIME
NEARER   ONEARMED
KAZMATSUI   COBRA
ELIOT   KILO   DAIL
RIOT   SOLARCELLS
STS   FOAL   IOU
 YOURFLYISOPEN
    NET   FROS   PEI
ROADTORUIN   LIEN
ACME   NEIN   GELDS
STARA   USAINBOLT
HANDGUNS   BORGIA
ENDORSEE   AMOUNT
SEAGODS   RENEGE
```

364

```
  THEWHO   SCHWAB
 PEELOUT   PHRASE
SANSKRIT   ORELSE
CLOSERS   CRI   KEG
HERESY   CHESHIRE
ITS    FOE   TANTE
STAGEMANAGER
MEXICANSTANDOFF
 BOYMEETSGIRL
CRIBS   AND    LAU
HISSYFIT   HOOFIT
UPI   SIL   CABRIDE
ROTATE   CLUELESS
NUMBER   HANSOLO
STEAMY   INTEND
```

M	A	D	P	R	O	P	S	■	P	A	T	I	N	A
I	V	E	H	A	D	I	T	■	O	H	S	N	A	P
L	A	N	D	M	I	N	E	■	L	E	A	D	U	P
A	L	I	■	S	U	N	R	O	O	M	■	E	T	E
N	O	E	S	■	M	E	N	D	S	■	M	I	A	
O	N	D	V	D	■	D	U	O	■	T	B	A	L	L
■		E	R	A	■	M	R	P	E	A	N	U	T	
C	A	T	L	I	K	E	■	S	O	A	N	D	S	O
B	R	A	T	P	A	C	K	■	I	C	K	■	■	
A	R	I	E	S	■	L	E	S	■	H	E	S	S	E
T	E	L	■	P	A	T	E	N	■	R	U	I	N	
T	S	O	■	E	A	T	C	R	O	W	■	R	E	C
E	T	R	A	D	E	■	H	E	R	E	W	E	G	O
R	E	T	I	N	A	■	U	N	S	E	A	T	E	D
Y	E	O	M	A	N	■	P	E	E	P	H	O	L	E

The New York Times

Crossword Puzzles

The #1 Name in Crosswords

Available at your local bookstore or online at nytimes.com/nytstore

St. Martin's Griffin